European Family Therapy Association Series

Series Editors
Maria Borcsa, University of Applied Sciences, Nordhausen, Thüringen, Germany

Peter Stratton, Emeritus Professor of Family Therapy, Leeds Family Therapy and Research Centre, University of Leeds, Leeds, West Yorkshire, UK

This series offers contributions from the European Family Therapy Association's community of senior authors and experienced editors. It brings together state-of-the-art contributions on crucial issues in family therapy in Europe with a focus on systemic family therapy. The topics alternate between those that make research findings accessible and of immediate value to practitioners and those that cover clinical areas. This series is essential reading for family therapists, counselors, and social workers across the globe.

More information about this series at http://www.link.springer.com/series/13797

Mauro Mariotti • George Saba • Peter Stratton
Editors

Handbook of Systemic Approaches to Psychotherapy Manuals

Integrating Research, Practice, and Training

Editors
Mauro Mariotti
Iscra, Institute of Systemic and Relational
Psychotherapy
Modena, Italy

George Saba
Emeritus Professor of Family and
Community Medicine
University of California, San Francisco
San Francisco, CA, USA

Peter Stratton
Emeritus Professor of Family Therapy
Leeds Family Therapy and Research Centre
University of Leeds
Leeds, West Yorkshire, UK

ISSN 2569-877X   ISSN 2569-8796 (electronic)
European Family Therapy Association Series
ISBN 978-3-030-73642-2   ISBN 978-3-030-73640-8 (eBook)
https://doi.org/10.1007/978-3-030-73640-8

© Springer Nature Switzerland AG 2021, Corrected Publication 2022
This work is subject to copyright. All rights are reserved by the Publisher, whether the whole or part of the material is concerned, specifically the rights of translation, reprinting, reuse of illustrations, recitation, broadcasting, reproduction on microfilms or in any other physical way, and transmission or information storage and retrieval, electronic adaptation, computer software, or by similar or dissimilar methodology now known or hereafter developed.
The use of general descriptive names, registered names, trademarks, service marks, etc. in this publication does not imply, even in the absence of a specific statement, that such names are exempt from the relevant protective laws and regulations and therefore free for general use.
The publisher, the authors, and the editors are safe to assume that the advice and information in this book are believed to be true and accurate at the date of publication. Neither the publisher nor the authors or the editors give a warranty, expressed or implied, with respect to the material contained herein or for any errors or omissions that may have been made. The publisher remains neutral with regard to jurisdictional claims in published maps and institutional affiliations.

This Springer imprint is published by the registered company Springer Nature Switzerland AG
The registered company address is: Gewerbestrasse 11, 6330 Cham, Switzerland

Preface and Dedication

It has been a period of loss. The Covid 19 is still with us, and we hope that by the time you are reading this book, we will be free of this plague, and relationships will flourish again– not only virtually but also in one another's presence, allowing hugs, glances, kisses, short distances and all the beautifulness and wisdom coming from the complexity of analogic language.

During the preparation of this book we lost friends and here we want to remember particularly Rodolfo de Bernart and Mony El Kaim. Mony was the founder of EFTA, the European Family Therapy association and Rodolfo was the President until his death. A chapter is written in Rodolfo's honor in this book.

And we dedicate this book to Mony.

Hello dear friend. We remember you happy with us, during one of the many moments shared in 30 years of friendship. You will always be with us. I want to remember you with the words of many colleagues who have esteemed you and enjoyed your presence full of stimuli. Your work on mourning allows us to look at you with affection and still feel close and present to soothe the sense of loss that we experience year after year with what the life cycle offers us.

Mony Elkaim was an example in the 1970s as the leader of the European movement of Democratic Psychiatry and then the driving force behind the development of family therapy. Mony Elkaim was Honorary Professor and Lecturer in Family Therapy at the "Universitè Libre de Bruxelles" Founder of EFTA, President of the EAP European Association of Psychotherapy. He has written numerous books including in Italian "If you love me don't love me" and "How to survive your family. Mony Elkaim was born in Marrakech in Morocco in 1941. He left us on November 20, 2020 after a long illness against which he fought bravely without ever showing the suffering of him, defeated by a Covid that leaves no room for people with fragility. He was a neuropsychiatrist and a psychotherapist who has occupied central roles within various European, American and African institutions, born as he was from a noble Moroccan Jewish family.

There are many concepts and intervention strategies that he left us. For Mony, each of us has experienced in their lives the feeling of being trapped within their own family as a representation of it. "It is a complicated bond, like a braid full of knots, which forces them into a suffering for which they are themselves responsible". Mony taught that the psychotherapist shows that showing one's diversity does not necessarily mean becoming aggressive "In fact, the problem is not to know who is right or who is wrong, but rather to get out of this dynamic in which two people are convinced that each is the victim of the other." The psychotherapist helps the family as if they were on a boat in a watercourse. The family asks for help to open a sluice, the psychotherapist opens the sluice and immediately another one appears, until the family is able to open the other sluices on its own that arise in the stream, in the course of life.

In Mony Elkaim's therapeutic system the concept of the mourning ritual occupies an important space, remembering that the psychotherapist is placed in the place of the deceased, a situation defined as a "heavy third" by his most important colleague and director of the same center, Edith Goldbeter. It is always Mony Elkaim who defines "revolving doors" the impasses created by the same people. For Mony, each of us wears armor that can be replaced by a shield with which to protect oneself that we can always lower and place next to us. The concept of secrecy is of great importance to Mony. "This is the secret of the secret: it can be seen as a sort of witness, a vector, a transmitter, which is passed on from one generation to the next, a ghost ship carrying on board the hidden treasure of family rules". : "If we learn to be autonomous without blaming ourselves, we can help those around us discover that they too have a right to autonomy. And our independence will be more successful if we manage to create some form of alliance with those we separate from - because it is not at all necessary that the other is wrong for me to be right."

Finally, Mony Elkaim enhances the concept of self-reference and structural coupling by creating a unique bridge with the concept of "resonance", not only between systemic epistemology and family therapy, but also between the therapist and the members of a family system. Thanks to the concept of resonance, Anne Chouhy reminds us, the paradox of self-reference ceases to be a limitation to become a possibility.

If you love me, do not love me is the pivotal example of Mony's complex thought. He teaches us freedom and the human use of paradox, the importance of participating in relationships with totality and lightness. This is what remains of Mony, his smile, his mediatory ability, his elegance in connecting oppositions by making orchestral conversation. You will always be with us.

Acknowledgements

Mauro Mariotti says:
Thanks to Nico, my wife and essence of my life, to my marvellous daughter Ilaria with Antonio. Thanks to Enrico,the beloved son of Nico and his beautiful wife, Lisa and thanks to my incredibly lovable grandchildren Anna, Andrea, Agata. Thanks to my sister Olga, to his husband Vittorio and to my nephews Riccardo and Paolo. They showed care and love for me regardless of my relative presence. Unexpectedly they take care of me also in this period despite my odd attitude to use time for curious things, like editing this book and spending time for those things instead of being there where things really matter. But let's think and act positively. This book is a real contribution to our field because it clearly shows how the magic of the systemic world is only a creative expression of the scientific asset subsumed and staged by systemic therapists worldwide with convincing and replicable results

George Saba says:
I want to thank my wife, Teresa, an incredible systemic physician who has provided unfailing support, remarkable patience, wise counsel and constant love during this project and throughout my career. I also want to thank my son, Geo, for his inspiration to meet challenges with creativity, hope, collaboration and humility. In addition, I want to thank the individuals, couples, families who trusted me and our clinic when they came for help and for their contribution to our work. And of course, I greatly appreciate all that I have learned from the trainees and my colleagues who have shared, shaped and support our collaboration with these communities in our collective liberation.

Peter Stratton says:
My thanks go first and especially to my wife Helga Hanks, the most intrinsically systemic person I know and on whom I have relied totally during the long gestation of this Handbook for everything from unstinting loving support to more mundane aspects like communicating with authors and improving text. Both Helga and the rest of my families and friends have been remarkably tolerant of my unavailability as the book extended far beyond what we had anticipated and became a kind of

absorbing hobby. I owe all of them a great debt for the love and tolerance they have shown me.

We also want to recognize the extraordinary life circumstances that all of our authors have had to cope with while completing their chapters during a pandemic. The editors as well of course. There is perhaps a parallel with the very demanding situations of research, of therapeutic practice, and of training. Situations in which we can expect the unexpected and be required to cope with challenges which we do not readily understand and for which we have not prepared. But at least in each of these there is the potential for a systemic stance to enable us to respond productively and at least in the professional worlds of the authors in this book, a choice of manuals to provide a secure base from which to creatively tackle the challenges. We hope that the Handbook will fulfil that role for many readers in many different ways.

Contents

1 **Towards a Truly Systemic Account of the Current and Future of Manualisation** 1
  Mauro Mariotti, George Saba, and Peter Stratton

Part I Issues and Experiences in the Creation of Manuals

2 **Another Loop of the Spiral: A Re-examination of 18 Manualized Prescriptions from 1978** 15
  Carlos Sluzki

3 **Six Different Approaches to Manualisation from the Leeds Family Therapy and Research Centre** 39
  Peter Stratton and Helen Pote

4 **Co-creating 'Fluid Manuals' for Feedback-Informed Systemic Therapy and Collaborative Research** 63
  Robert van Hennik

5 **Manualizing Human Systems Therapy Towards a Few-Sessions Therapy** 81
  Nicholas Paritsis

6 **Manualizing the Therapeutic Process in Systemic Therapy: From the Construction of the Hypothesis to the Assessment of Change** 101
  Andrea Mosconi and Barbara Trotta

7 **Manualising the Exeter Model: Couple Therapy for Depression – A Behavioural-Systemic Approach** 123
  Janet Reibstein and Hannah Sherbersky

8   Systemic Approaches to Therapy Manuals: Family Situation
    Mapping and Systemic-Relational Assessment of Treatment
    for Families, Couples and Individuals........................ 141
    Francesco Colacicco

9   A Model of a Systemic Therapy Clinic 159
    Cigdem Alper

10 The Map of Competences in Systemic Therapy: Targeting
    Associated Abnormal Psychosocial Situations in Axis 5 177
    Lennart Lorås

Part II Research Issues in the Use and Evaluation of Manuals

11 An Integrative Approach to Systemic Therapy 193
    Alan Carr

12 Research and Manualisation at ISCRA Institute: The DAN Model:
    Digital, Analogic, Narrative 215
    Mauro Mariotti, Achille Langella, Nicoletta Scaltriti,
    and Greco Muratori

13 The Digital Analogic Narrative (DAN) Model in Practice:
    Transformations and Enhancement of Resilience in a Non-clinical
    Parental Couple. A Case Report 241
    S. Miazzi, M. Zagni, Greco Muratori, F. Bassoli,
    and Mauro Mariotti

14 Taking Care of Adoption (TCA): Development of a Treatment
    Manual for Adoptive Families 263
    Francesco Vadilonga, Barbara D'Avanzo, Gloriana Rangone,
    and Angelo Barbato

15 Manualized Family Therapy in a Controlled Study
    on Childhood Depression: Therapists' and Supervisors'
    Reflections on the Use of the Manual 281
    Valeria Pomini and Vlassis Tomaras

16 Working Alliance, Attachment, and Mentalization as Relational
    Indexes for a Systemic Manualization of Psychotherapy 299
    Franco Baldoni

17 A Manual Developed Through a Variety of Online Resources:
    The SCORE Index of Family Functioning and Change 317
    Peter Stratton

Part III Uses of Manuals in Clinical Practice

18 Intergenerational Couple Therapy 343
    Maurizio Andolfi and Anna Mascellani

19	From Treatment Models to Manuals: Maudsley Single- and Multi-Family Therapy for Adolescent Eating Disorders Julian Baudinet, Mima Simic, and Ivan Eisler	349
20	Suggestions for a Creative Manual: The "Intervention for Change" and the Therapeutic Relationship. The Floating Therapies and Working on the Self Lia Mastropaolo	373
21	"Triangular Mirroring" in Teaching, in the Clinic and in Research: A Procedure to Evaluate the Outcome of the First Session in Infant Systemic Psychotherapy Mariarosaria Menafro, Rossella Aurilio, Maura Ruggiero, and Ferdinando Ivano Ambra	391
22	The Treatment of Mutual Demonization in Post-separative Conflict Renzo Marinello and Davide Sacchelli	407
23	Basic Model of a Couple's Crisis: A Manual for Couples' Therapy Virginia Ioannidou and Christina Lagogianni	427
24	Marte Meo and Coordination Meetings: A Systemic, School-Based Intervention Ulf Axberg, Bill Pettit, and Ingegerd Wirtberg	447

Part IV Training as a Basis for Development of Manuals and a Context for Their Application

25	Image, Family, and Clinical Practice: Image and Family of Origin as Tools for Training the Family Therapist Rodolfo de Bernart and Mauro Mariotti	467
26	A Manualized Systemic Family Therapy Training Program Camillo Loriedo	479
27	Healing Relationships: A Manualized Curriculum for Systemic Primary Care Physicians George W. Saba	507
28	Changing the Trainees' Epistemology in Systemic Family Training: The Manual as a Secure Base Dubravka Trampuž and Maja Rus Makovec	527
29	Trainee-Focused Training: A Second-Order Approach in the Making of Therapists Elena Ceuca	543

30 **Family Therapy Training in the Greek Public Sector: The Manualization of an Experiential Learning Process Through Personal and Professional Development**................ 557
Katia Charalabaki, Kia Thanopoulou, and Athanasia Kati

31 **"From Mind to Culture": Developing a Treatment Plan Manual for the Enriched Systemic Psychotherapy Model *SANE-System Attachment Narrative Encephalon*®** 571
Athena Androutsopoulou, Tsabika Bafiti, and George Kalarritis

32 **Manualising – Personalising – Without Compromising (Either the Manual or the Systemic Approach) Except When** 593
John Burnham, Nicky Maund, Beki Brain, Ellen Twist, Shila Desai, and Rubina Singh

33 **Implications of the Handbook for the Future of Manualization of Systemic Therapies**...................................... 617
Peter Stratton, George Saba, and Mauro Mariotti

Correction to: Handbook of Systemic Approaches to Psychotherapy Manuals...................................... C1

Index.. 629

The original version of this book was revised. The correction is available at https://doi.org/10.1007/978-3-030-73640-8_34

About the Contributors

Cigdem Alper MA, MFT: psychotherapist, trainer and supervisor in the Couple and Family Therapy Training Program at the Institute of Intercourse Psychotherapies. She is also a founding member of the Couple and Family Therapies Association (CATED), Yasamca Psikoloji Merkezi, Izmir, Turkey

Ferdinando Ivano Ambra Psychologist, Psychotherapist, Dottorando in Scienze Motorie e Sportive Università degli Studi di Napoli Parthenope *Istituto di Terapia Relazionale, Scuola di Specializzazione in psicoterapia ad indirizzo sistemico-relazionale, Napoli – Caserta, Italy

Maurizio Andolfi MD, Professor of Psychology at La Sapienza (University of Rome), Director of the Accademia di Psicoterapia Familiare in Rome, Italy

Athena Androutsopoulou PhD, EuroPsy, ECP Clinical Psychologist, Psychotherapist, and Family Therapist in Private Practice. Founding Co-director of the Training & Research Institute for Systemic Psychotherapy "Logo Psychis", Athens, Greece

Rossella Aurilio Psychologist, Psychotherapist, Director of the TeR, President of S.I.P.P.R., Italy

Ulf Axberg Professor, VID Specialized University, Dept of Family Therapy and Systemic Practice, Oslo. Lic. Psychologist, Lic. Psychotherapist, Clinical Supervisor, Sweden

Tsabika Bafiti Psychologist and systemic therapist, Co-director of the Training & Research Institute for Systemic Psychotherapy "Logo Psychis"®- Training and Research Institute for Systemic Psychotherapy, Athens, Greece

Franco Baldoni Department of Psychology, University of Bologna, Italy

Angelo Barbato Psychiatrist and psychotherapist, Istituto di Ricerche Farmacologiche Mario Negri IRCCS, Milan, Italy

Fabio Bassoli MD, Psychiatrist, Co-Director and founder Iscra, Modena, Italy

Julian Baudinet Principal Clinical Psychologist, Maudsley Centre for Child and Adolescent Eating Disorders, South London and Maudsley NHS Foundation Trust, National and Specialist CAMHS, London, UK. Julian.Baudinet@slam.nhs.uk

Rodolfo de Bernart Founder and Director of the Florence Family Therapy Institute, Florence, Italy, and President of EFTA

Beki Brain Family & Systemic Psychotherapist, Inpatient CAMHS, Parkview Clinic, Birmingham Women's and Children's Hospital

John Burnham Consultant Family and Systemic Psychotherapist, Inpatient CAMHS, Parkview Clinic, Birmingham Women's and Children's Hospital

Alan Carr Professor of Clinical Psychology University College Dublin and Senior Systemic Psychotherapist at Clanwilliam Institute, Dublin, Ireland

Elena Ceuca MD, PsyD, systemic therapist, co- chair at Institute for Couple and Family, Independent Mental Health Care Professional, Iasi, Romania. ceucaelena-iasi@gmail.com

Katia Charalabaki Psychiatrist, Systemic Psychotherapist, ex Coordinating Director of Family Therapy Unit, Psychiatric Hospital of Attica, NHS,Athens, Greece. katiacharalabaki@hotmail.com

Francesco Colacicco Director of the Istituto Dedalus, post-graduate training school of specialization in psychotherapy recognized in Italy by the Ministry of Education, University and Research; and teacher within the Centro Studi di Terapia Familiare e Relazionale di Roma, Italy

Barbara D'Avanzo Istituto di Ricerche Farmacologiche Mario Negri IRCCS, Milan, IRIS School of Psychotherapy in Milan, Italy

Shila Desai Family and Systemic Psychotherapist, Head of Systemic Training, Clinical Supervisor, Birmingham Women's and Children's Hospital

Ivan Eisler Professor of Family Psychology and Family Therapy, Institute of Psychiatry, King's College London, London, United Kingdom. ivan.eisler@kcl.ac.uk

About the Contributors

Robert van Hennik Doctor. Systemic Therapist, Supervisor, Researcher. University of Bedfordshire, Ordiver, Centrum voor Gezinsbehandeling

Virginia Ioannidou Psychologist, Systemic therapist, supervisor & trainerAdministrator of the Institute of Systemic Therapy of Thessaloniki (ISTT)President of the Systemic Association of North Greece, Greece. ioannidou@istt.gr

George Kalarritis Psychologist and systemic therapist, Co-director of the Training & Research Institute for Systemic Psychotherapy "Logo Psychis"®- Training and Research Institute for Systemic Psychotherapy, Athens, Greece

Athanasia Kati Msc Psychologist, Systemic psychotherapist, trainer and supervisor, Family Therapy Unit, Psychiatric Hospital of Attica, NHS, Athens, Greece. athkati@gmail.com

Christina Lagogianni Psychologist Institute of Systemic Therapy Thessaloniki, Anatolia College, Pylaia, Thessaloniki Greece

Achille Langella psychologist, psychotherapist, theacher and researcher at Iscra Institute, Modena, Italy

Lennart Lorås Professor, Western Norway University of Applied Sciences, Bergen, Norway and VID Specialized University, Oslo, Norway

Camillo Loriedo MD, PhD, Professor of Psychiatry, University of Rome, Italy; Research and Training Director of the Istituto Italiano di Psicoterapia Relazionale; President Italian Society of Psychotherapy, Rome, Italy

Maja Rus Makovec Psychiatrist and systemic family therapist at University psychiatric hospital Ljubljana, Assoc. professor at Medical faculty University of Ljubljana, Center for Mental Health (CMZ) Slovenia. rusmakovec@gmail.com

Renzo Marinello Psychologist, systemic family psychotherapist at the Integrated Family Counseling Center, President of SIRTS, Milan, Italy

Mauro Mariotti MD, child psychiatrist, psychiatrist, Director, Iscra Institute, Modena, Italy

Anna Mascellani PhD, Psychologist and Psychotherapist, Vice Director and Professor of Accademia di Psicoterapia della Famiglia of Rome, Italy

Lia Mastropaolo Psychologist, systemic psychotherapist; Director of the Metalogo-Systemic Genoa School, Co-founder of the Genoese Center for Family Therapy. Genoa, Italy

Nicky Maund Lead Family & Systemic Psychotherapist, Inpatient CAMHS, Parkview Clinic, Birmingham Women's and Children's Hospital

Mariarosaria Menafro Psychologist, psychotherapist, family mediator, Mental Health Center, Member of SIPPR Research Commission; Founding Member and Teacher of ITeR. Naples, Italy

Samantha Miazzi PhD, Psychologist, Neuropsychologist, EMDR Therapist, Neurofeedback Trainer, Family Therapist.Founder and Scientific Director at The BrainLab Group – Clinical Neuroscience Lab, Verona, Italy, Research Team, Iscra, Modena, Italy

Andrea Mosconi Psychiatrist and faculty Centro Milanese di Terapia della Famiglia, co-founder and Direttore del Centro Padovano di Terapia della Famiglia, President of AIMS, Padua, Italy

Greco Muratori psychologist and researcher at Iscra Institute, Assistant Psychologist. Norfolk and Suffolk NHS, UK

Nicholas Paritsis Center for the Study of Human Systems Bettering and Therapy, Athens, Greece and Society for Therapy and Intervention on Individuals, Families and Larger Systems, Athens, Greece

Bill Pettit Consultant, Logos A. B., Lerdala, Sweden

Valeria Pomini PhD, Family & Couple Therapy Unit, 1st Department of Psychiatry, National and Kapodistrian University of Athens, Co-Chair of the Training Program in Systemic Family & Couple Therapy, University Mental Health, Neurosciences, and Precision Medicine Research Institute "Kostas Stefanis", Athens, Greece

Helen Pote Clinical Director & Deputy Programme Director, DClinPsy, Department of Psychology, Royal Holloway, University of London, UK

Gloriana Rangone Psychologist and Systemic Psychotherapist, trainer and supervisor, Co-director of IRIS School of Psychotherapy in Milan, Italy

Janet Reibstein Professor Emerita, University of Exeter, UK; Psychologist and systemic therapist, Child and Family Practice and London Intercultural Couples Centre, London

Maura Ruggiero Psychologist, Doctor of research in psychology, Department of Psychology, Dipartimento di Studi Umanistici Università degli Studi di Napoli Federico II, Naples Italy

George Saba PhD, Emeritus Professor of Family and Community Medicine, University of California, San Francisco, San Francisco, California, USA

Davide Sacchelli Psychologist and systemic psychotherapist, Milan Center for Family Therapy, Milan, Italy

Nicoletta Scaltriti psychologist, psychotherapist, teacher and researcher at Iscra institute, Modena, Italy

Hannah Sherbersky Co-director of Systemic Portfolio, Senior Lecturer and Systemic Psychotherapist. University of Exeter, Exeter, EX4 4QG UK

Mima Simic MD, MSc, MRCPsych, Joint Head of the Maudsley Centre for Child and Adolescent Eating Disorders and Consultant Child and Adolescent Psychiatrist at the South London and Maudsley NHS Foundation Trust, N&S CAMHS, London, UK. Mima.Simic@slam.nhs.uk

Rubina Singh Family & Systemic Psychotherapist, Lead for Family Therapy, Forward Thinking Birmingham, Birmingham Women's and Children's Hospital

Carlos Sluzki MD, Clinical Professor of Psychiatry, Department of Psychiatry and Behavioral Sciences, George Washington University School of Medicine School, Washington, DC; and Professor Emeritus, School of Conflict Analysis and Resolution, George Mason University, Arlington, VA

Peter Stratton PhD, Emeritus Professor of Family Therapy, Leeds Family Therapy and Research Centre, University of Leeds, Leeds, West Yorkshire, UK

Kia Thanopoulou MSc, Europsy, ECP Psychologist, Systemic psychotherapist, trainer and supervisor, Family Therapy Unit, Psychiatric Hospital of Attica, NHS, Athens, Greece. kthanopoulou@gmail.com

Vlassis Tomaras Ex Prof. of Psychiatry, Consultant of the Family & Couple Therapy Unit, 1st Department of Psychiatry, National and Kapodistrian University of Athens, Co-Chair of the Training Program in Systemic Family & Couple Therapy, University Mental Health, Neurosciences, and Precision Medicine Research Institute "Kostas Stefanis", Athens, Greece

Dubravka Trampuž MD, psychotherapist and systemic family therapist, Slovenia Institute of Family and Systemic Psychotherapy, Ljubljana, Slovenia. dubravka.tramp@siol.net

Barbara Trotta Psychologist Psychotherapist, Teacher of the Milanese Center of Family Therapy, Teacher of the Paduan Center of Family Therapy, Member of the SIPPR Research Commission

Ellen Twist Family & Systemic Psychotherapist, Inpatient CAMHS, Parkview Clinic, Birmingham Women's and Children's Hospital

Francesco Vadilonga Psychologist and Systemic Psychotherapist, trainer and supervisor. Director of Adolescence therapy center (CTA) and co-director of IRIS School of Psychotherapy, Milan, Italy

Ingegerd Wirtberg Associate Professor, Department of Clinical Psychology, Lund University, Lund. Primary School Teacher, Lic. Psychotherapist, Clinical Supervisor, Lic. Marte Meo Supervisor, Lund, Sweden

Michele Zagni Psychologist, Psychotherapist, Research Team Iscra, Modena, Italy

Chapter 1
Towards a Truly Systemic Account of the Current and Future of Manualisation

Mauro Mariotti, George Saba, and Peter Stratton

1.1 The Origins of the Handbook of Systemic Approaches to Manualisation

The editors of this handbook share a long-standing commitment to manualising effective practice in their therapies. We were aware of a wide range of strongly held views about therapy manuals in our field ranging from an enthusiastic welcoming of the opportunities they afford to a deep conviction that effective systemic therapy will be hindered rather than helped by attempting to follow any kind of manual. Within this context, we also knew that great progress had already been made not only in establishing and testing highly effective manuals but also in those that might be called a proto-manual, a partial manual, or a process relevant to manualisation. We felt there would be great value in compiling a survey of the current state of manualising in our field and that we could use a broad formulation as a basis for accepting articles. Manuals are receiving widespread attention which has been welcomed by

---

The original version of this chapter was revised. The correction to this chapter is available at https://doi.org/10.1007/978-3-030-73640-8_34

M. Mariotti (✉)
Iscra Institute, Modena, Italy
e-mail: dottmauromariotti@gmail.com

G. Saba
Emeritus Professor of Family and Community Medicine, University of California, San Francisco, San Francisco, California, USA
e-mail: George.Saba@ucsf.edu

P. Stratton
Emeritus Professor of Family Therapy, Leeds Family Therapy and Research Centre, University of Leeds, Leeds, West Yorkshire, UK
e-mail: p.m.stratton@ntlworld.com

© Springer Nature Switzerland AG 2021, Corrected Publication 2022
M. Mariotti et al. (eds.), *Handbook of Systemic Approaches to Psychotherapy Manuals*, European Family Therapy Association Series,
https://doi.org/10.1007/978-3-030-73640-8_1

some and lamented by others. Manuals are a marker of our field's development. They are to be used for different purposes. Manuals can be used in studies and also in evaluation of work, and in clinical teaching and training. They can also be used by clinicians in guiding, doing reviews of and in evaluating their own work. It might even have financial possibilities. Manuals are one of the tools and processes that exist at the research-practice intersection. As such, they can contribute to the lessening of the characteristics of the research-practice gap – one of which was the feeling that true clinical insight and relevance was being lost in the research arena. Good manuals will demonstrate that good science and good clinical thinking and work can inhabit the same space. However, little research exists on what makes a good manual and few guidelines exist for the development of manuals, hence this handbook.

Today, manuals are present in many different forms and support aspects of our daily lives. For example, repair manuals, cookery recipes, any number of official specifications of how to conduct government business, instructions for assembling, using and repairing objects in our homes, and prescriptive therapy manuals for use in RCTs. Taking a broad definition, any publicly available detailed specification of a process can be regarded as a manual. We have a contribution by Carlos Sluzki, whose publication of possibly the first systemic manual to be badged as such makes up Chap. 2. Taking a more focused definition, this handbook has included specifications that were developed specifically for systemic applications and also specifications that were developed interactively within a context of systemic therapy. In a few cases, these manuals have only been available within the context of the clinic in which they have originated, and we have included them here as part of the process of making the valuable work open to wider consideration and to encourage the authors to make them more widely available. At the other end of the spectrum, we have contributions from teams with multi-year experiences with the process of manualisation (the Maudsley Group, Burnham and colleagues), with well-developed specifications.

So we hope that the handbook provides practitioners with a valuable resource and an impetus to capitalise on their progress towards manualisation. We have attempted to operate a consistently systemic stance in all aspects of our work to present to the field the achievements and future potential of manualisation.

We started our survey of approaches to systemic manualisation with a statement of what we considered to be a manual, or an approach towards a manual that had not yet reached fruition – as a basis for accepting articles. The first letter we sent to all European Family Therapy Association (EFTA) members and to our friends around the globe summarises our initial thinking:

> We want the book, which will be number 6 in the EFTA Springer series, to break new ground. And to show different approaches in different nations. We have a concept of 'training as manual' and 'manuals as therapy'. Both distinguished from and in addition to manuals for use in research where they must make it possible to say in some detail exactly what therapy was provided. We will construct an imaginative definition of what forms manuals can take so that the book can be as creative and as inclusive as possible.
>
> A mission for the EFTA book of manuals is to create a flexible and diversified concept of what forms manuals can take and to offer varied examples from throughout Europe and beyond. One point for our proposal is that we do not know how many manuals there are that have been developed within European countries and are not widely known about. The book will truly represent EFTA while also being able to look further afield.
>
> We want to explore many possible forms that do the job of a manual:

1. We would include reports of current experiences with major manuals.
2. Formulations of innovative practice by their founders.
3. Specifications of training courses that are explicit enough to be more widely used. It might be that the epistemology of a course is close enough to that of practitioners in a different country that it would be worth their while to translate it and use it as a manual for their continuing professional development.
4. Training for different levels of practitioners (in the United Kingdom, we have a grade of 'Systemic practitioner' intended for professionals who will work systemically but within their core profession).
5. Formal documents prepared for FT organisations or for government provision that set out the basic requirements of qualified practice.

   But it will be important to be able to claim that the manuals have been tested in some way. No point having a superb manual for an approach that is later found to do more harm than good.

   We want to ensure we cover specific applications of specify SFCT (while avoiding being colonised by DSM).

This invitation generated a very enthusiastic response from across our field and many countries, which has resulted in the 33 chapters of this handbook.

1.2 A Brief History of Manuals Related to the Wide Field of Systemic Therapies and Interventions

In the second part of last century, systemic ideas spread throughout the world with a revolutionary strength. Systemics influenced all fields: from economy to philosophy; from literature to computer science; from robotics to psychotherapy; from micro particles to universe, to multiverse (El-Kaim, 2005). The notion of dissipative structures; the idea of order out of the chaos; the theory of catastrophe; the subsequent concept that change is discontinuous and that from state 1 to state 2 the system can change its structure and its organisation being completely different from state 1 but still function; the ideas of recursivity, of self-reflexivity, the web of life, the Gaia system and so on. The Macy conferences mixed ideas from every scientific approach not only accepting standard science but also introducing cybernetics as a way of thinking and acting. The systemic movement shook the world with an incredible strength creating new ways of acting and thinking that became the basis for a new conceptualisation of psychotherapy.

At the time, Freud's conceptualisation of the ego, superego and ID dominated psychotherapy. Analytic therapists sought to grasp the forces of energy, while systemic therapists shifted to focusing on information. For some, the promise of systemic ideas leads to beliefs that we no longer needed long therapies, long trainings or expensive treatment; rather the system needed to understand that to foster change, it needed information and then would be capable of changing itself. Simple, not costly, brief. As we later learned, treatment and training are much more than a set of ideas about how people and the world 'work'. When systemic ideas and ideals were introduced in the treatment and research spheres, there was trouble. People said, 'wait you can't reduce therapy to specific conceptualisations like that, you're "chopping the ecology" – dis-membering what has to be considered as a whole'. And of course, we all recall Bateson's strong aversion to and caution of the premature application of systemic ideas to psychotherapy. A good example of this could be found in a dissertation for the School of Education, University of Massachusetts (Blount, 2003) in which it is clearly represented how context, logical types and categories of learning, communication and the double bind do not necessarily pertain to the psychotherapeutic field but to the ecology of human beings and in nature.

Nonetheless, from the 1960s to the end of last century, there was an incredible flourishing of systemic therapies born under the aegis of[1] first and second cybernetics (first-order cybernetic) and second-order cybernetics, the last one founded over the concept of self-reflexivity that substitutes the observed system (first order) with the observing system. We can quote among many other authors and methods: the structural family therapy (Minuchin, 1974), the strategic therapy (Haley, 1963) and the epistemologically based systemic therapy – founders Luigi Boscolo and Gianfranco Cecchin (Hoffmann & Penn, 1987).

Emerging like separate branches from the same systemic roots, they were in time joined by additional approaches such as constructive, constructionistic and narrative. A range of new systemically oriented schools of therapy populated the psychotherapy map. The approaches were often named after one of their prominent developers, a philosophical basis, its similarity to a previous psychotherapy approach and/or the geographical location from which it arose. As proponents of models engaged in dialogue, hotly debated questions emerged: Does one need to swear fidelity to one approach? Could some previous ideas from reductionistic approaches (e.g. behaviour, psychoanalysis) be incorporated in a systemic approach? Is eclecticism the ideal way to take the best of different models? Then, the misnomer of the term 'family therapy' became increasingly problematic. It was always seen as privileging the social *context of the family*, while also acknowledging the interactions of the larger contexts, and also a *euphemism for the systemic idea*. As differentiation occurred over time, some shifted the name of the field from 'family therapy' to a more comprehensive term such as 'systemic therapy' or 'relational therapy' acknowledging the multiple interdependent contexts. This, of course, was vulnerable to blurring and confusion of the place of the family in the work. Some whose model originally was named strategic therapy would now call themselves systemic therapy, while others would maintain a view that that they were still practising strategic family therapy. Similarly, Minuchin while appreciating some of the ideas of the narrative approach challenged that narrative therapy did not maintain

---

[1] *First-order cybernetics is about how to know and manage and control a system and how a family system organizes itself to maintain homeostasis and balance. It is divided in two components: first cybernetics which studies the system in equilibrium and, after 1963, with Maryuama (1963), the second cybernetics begins the study of far from equilibrium systems and what happens when there is a deviation. For instance, what happens in a family who lives for years in a complex situation in which a symptom maintains an unstable equilibrium? Second-order cybernetics is about observing systems* (von Foerster, 2002; Sluzki, 1985).

the key focus on family relationships. Moreover, the stream of the various rivers of knowledge during the last 50 years has contributed to differences in Europe and the United States but also in Australia, New Zealand, Africa, Russia and lately the Middle East and China, which makes it impossible to recognise who specifically contributed to the single aspects of the systemic archipelago.

Within the field, attempts to clarify one's approach could often result in evangelisation claiming one approach being better than others, without much evidence, and conversation that was well termed as 'epistobabble' (Coyne & Liddle, 1992) and was about the necessity to convey the systemic intervention to identify the working elements and common factors that could lead the various rivers into a stream of sharable knowledge.

The points of agreement among many of the family therapies and the systemic therapies seemed to be avoiding linearity; avoiding the cause-effect principle; improving knowledge of the feedback; focusing on interactions, interconnections and the interdependence of relationships; and allowing the system freedom to find better organisation and structures through digital, analogic and narrative interventions (DAN Model presented in this volume, Chaps. 13 and 14).

Agreement about value and effectiveness of any one approach was less clear. Evidence began to emerge that family and couple therapies had systemic origins, among other origins and influences. Approaches such as constructive, constructionist and narrative lagged in offering evidence or a body of work on effectiveness or efficacy. In fact, many from those approaches have been critical of, or even opposed to, standard research values and methods.

We are promoting manualisation of various systemic approaches because as far as we know, they are not considered within those treatments that have an accepted empirical base; some examples are offered in the *Journal of Family Therapy* (2014) and in the ongoing reviews of CFT by Carr (2014a, 2014b).

During the last few decades, systemic therapy proved its efficacy, and the importance of the common factor (CF) (Sexton et al., 2004) approach emphasises that if therapy is to be successful, the common factors should be maximised as the therapist uses an empirically validated therapy model to conduct therapy. The basic tenet of the CF approach is that therapy will be successful to the extent it reflects those common factors. The therapist is attentive to client factors, is able to create a strong therapeutic relationship with the family or the individual, stimulates the family's expectations for therapy, and gives an acceptable rationale for the family's problem and uses credible interventions. She/he also applies the common factors that are unique to family therapy by thinking of the family and treating the family in systemic terms, involving more than the person who is symptomatic and forming balanced alliances with various family members. This approach offers hope for simplifying and unifying the field of therapy. It will also be important to examine any factors that differ and are important mechanisms of action.

While the systemic field explored such issues as common factors and how one can research the complexity of systemic work, other approaches of psychotherapy were actively responding to governmental and consumer policies that demanded the health and mental health field to move away from the gold standard being expert opinion to prove the efficacy of any approach through the paradigm of evidence-based medicine and evidence-based psychotherapy – (Goodheart, 2006). We can see in the monumental work done realising the PDM 2 (*Psychoanalytical Diagnostic Manual* (Williams & Lingiardi, 2006) promoted by the American Psychoanalytic Association, the international psychoanalytical association and other associations) and by the series of manualised cognitive-based therapies made to intervene on every diagnosis listed by DSM (Rosner, 2018).

Systemic therapists continued along their own path that reflected beliefs, attitudes and values – identity and mainly used their own tools in many different contexts. However, they neglected the official languages that policy makers were demanding of scientists. The departure of systemic therapy from the mainstream mental health field was actually a continuation of what family therapy had wanted to do all along – to be different, unique, with a certain exclusionary and narrow definition of what it means, in practical terms, to be systemic.

While this stance was acceptable for systemic family therapists and mental health systemic practitioners, it is less understandable for health managers, policy makers and consumers; their response is: 'We don't understand your epistobabble' (Lanski, 1987). Consequence is that systemic therapists need to use proven methods approved by scientific, political and consumerist society.

1.2.1 But Proved with What and in Which Way?

The measurement of efficacy in the policy and government domains was based on the *Diagnostic Statistic Manual* (DSM) based on diagnosis and on the disappearance of the symptom; and the symptom was read following mainly an individual and linear perspective. However, they sometimes have endorsed therapeutic approaches that are based on a paucity of research evidence, without addressing the validation of manualisation and using an overly simple view of outcome (Silverman, 1996). For example, depression has particular symptoms, so what intervention will decrease those symptoms at the least cost? For instance, a 2013 study (Hiltunen et al., 2013) in Sweden suggested that cognitive behavioural therapy (CBT) was an effective form of treatment. Though being effective does not mean being better than other therapies (Wampold, 2001). After this study, the Swedish government decided to invest 300 million Euros to train people to deliver CBT particularly for anxiety and depression. No funding was provided for training or treatment in other methods. But after a 5-year period, it was shown that the widespread adoption of the method had no effect whatsoever on the outcome of people disabled by depression and anxiety. After this, the Swedish government officially ended the CBT monopoly.

For us, pulled by the epistobabble, cybernetics, constructivism, narratives, but mainly from circular causality, it is hard to work just to solve the symptom if the symptom is understood as the best way to let this family survive in this particular period of their life cycle. We have to demonstrate that working on the relationships we also solve symptoms. Our manuals are complex and cannot be made by specific procedures but by specific indications of subsequent phases of a process that involves all the family and the contexts in which they live.

In the 1980s and 1990s, the field saw an explosion of research about systemic theory. Many papers published during those years tended to increase the awareness of systemic practitioners on mental health. Finding methods to enhance research was a pathway for survival of the field, such as developing qualitative and quantitative methodologies (Steinglass, 1995), recursive sequences (Breunlin & Schwartz, 1986) and narrative transformation (Sluzki, 1992). Yet we still find that realising these methodologies remains challenging and full of obstacles. It has taken considerable time to get to the bottom line of any treatment point of view, or indeed how our profession can offer help/services to the public.

While systemic therapy was at the top during the end of the past century, especially in Europe where the schools of systemic thinking were flourishing and psychoanalysis at bottom with only few students asking for this kind of knowledge, today we have a great enhancement of psychoanalysis and a wider use of cognitive methods.

1.2.2 The Lack of Research and Operalisation Helps Systemic Psychotherapy to Lose Relevance

This post-systemic revolution can be attributed to the scarce strength and relative failure of the systemic movement to produce research and manualisations but mostly to our lack of capacity to translate our languages in a manner understandable by clients and policy makers. We must continue to move beyond the dialogue of 'we must articulate what we do through research and manuals' vs. 'we are unique and any attempt at specification destroys the beauty and value of our work'. However, despite this backdrop of the 'either/or debate' done with good intentions and wonderful suggestions on both sides, the years from 2000 to now have shown a decrease of the impact of family therapy and systemic therapy in the United States and worldwide. A question arises: why are the systemic model and family therapy not a reference point for policy makers to introduce systemic practices in the fields of prevention, treatment and education?

One answer to this question is that we still need to conduct research that demonstrates the value and find meaningful and understandable ways to describe what we do in practice. In fact, a survey of articles claiming to be outcome studies in family therapy from 2000 to 2009 (Stratton et al., 2015) identified 225 studies in English. One hundred and fifty of the studies claimed to be RCTs, but in a rigorous analysis, the authors found that only 23 fully met their criteria for a rigorous RCT. Relatively few provided full descriptions of the therapy, or referred to a published manual. So although the great majority claimed the therapy was effective, the reader had no way of knowing what therapy it was that was found to be effective. This dearth of clearly articulated approaches has compromised our ability to provide the help we can to our communities and the development of our field in general.

1.2.3 Constraints and Resources: A Balance to Be Done with Positive Attitude

We believe that to address our challenges with systemic research and the dissemination of what we do to others requires a fundamental shift from basing research and hence manuals on procedures to being based on processes. Reductionistic evidence-based research is grounded in procedural thinking, and thus we believe it provides an extremely limited understanding of a system and the impact of any intervention. The need to think of processes as a way to respect, understand and learn within the systems we work in is the premise of this handbook on manualisation.

1.3 What Is a Process?

In simple terms, a process produces an output when activated, and a procedure is a way in which one works to produce an output. An output will only be produced if a procedure is placed in the hands of people having the competence, authority and resources to use it. A process includes everything that produces and influences the output which will include the people, the tools, the environment, the procedures and other resources needed for people to execute the activities required to produce the required process outputs. The results that an organisation achieves are the product of the interaction between its processes and not its procedures.

Table 1.1 illustrates the difference between procedures and processes.

Table 1.1 Procedures and processes

Procedures are driven by completion of the task	Processes are driven by achievement of a desired outcome
Procedures are implemented	Processes are operated
Procedure steps are completed by different people in different departments with different objectives	Process stages are completed by different people with the same objectives; departments do not matter
Procedures are discontinuous	Processes flow to conclusion
Procedures focus on satisfying the rules	Processes focus on satisfying the customer
Procedures define the sequence of steps to execute a task	Processes generate results through use of resources
Procedures are used by people to carry out a task	People work through a process to achieve an objective
Procedures are static until changed	Processes are dynamic they cause change
Procedures only cause people to take actions and decisions	Processes make things happen, regardless of people following procedures
Procedures prescribe actions to be taken	Processes function through the actions and decisions that are taken
Procedures identify the tasks to be carried out	People select the appropriate procedures to be followed at each stage of a process

To make a transition away from managing procedures towards process management, an organisation must answer whether it has:

- Clearly defined what its objectives are and how it will measure and review the success of achieving those objectives
- Evaluated the impact of those objectives on the interested parties, the stakeholders
- Designed the critical, end-to-end processes necessary to deliver the objectives
- Assessed and provided the resources, skills and competence to make the processes work

Those suggestions come from the International Organization for Standardization (2015), an independent non-governmental company whose aim is to improve quality and increase the capability of an enterprise to survive in the jungle of real life. They employ systemic concepts used by every business to achieve better results. These guidelines have relevance for our thinking of process-oriented research and manualisation.

Our research and manualisation, based on processes, should really abandon the idea that there are so many variables inside human behaviour that it is almost impossible to understand how the change inside the human system is certainly to be attributed to this particular element. Of course, we are not understanding all the factors by examining parts of a system. However, it does not mean we should leap to the other extreme, throwing up our hands and saying it is impossible to explore patterns, and still respect that they remain interconnected with other variables. We need to understand we are part of the investigation and remain humble in our conclusions that are always in the context of complexity, uncertainty and coevolution of systems in which we also exist.

We suggest that research only examine three, maximum four variables at a time. This allows for the investigation of patterns and of how variables within a system reflect mutuality in action. That means that the most important thing in a research study is the question you pose: if your question is about the symptom (for instance, the patient presents obsessive compulsive behaviours at the end of intervention?), you can verify the existence or not of the symptom. But you are unable to say anything about the family functioning or the presence of intergenerational barriers. The fact that the symptom disappears says nothing about family functioning and therefore nothing about whether the symptom will reappear.

We can say that the symptom is a procedural aspect of family process. If the family or the system works follows a particular process, then the procedures of how it behaves will foresee the symptom; if the system works in a different process, the procedures will not foresee the symptom. As a field, we know that a key focus is processes, and the procedures are one expression of these processes. Therefore, in this sense, systemic research is processual, not procedural. And if we look at the family processes, three variables are more than enough to increase deeply the self-knowledge of the system.

This is the specificity of the systemic research: we look for family system processes, not for procedures that are embedded inside the system. The mistake made by policy makers has been exactly this: to believe that the research, because made with statistical models, represents science and certainty. But instead, the procedural research speaks only about this particular symptom and does not tell anything about the processes which maintain the symptom.

So what exactly is a systemic research looking for and in which manner? We do not need different methods than those that reductionistic research uses, but since we have different lenses, we will ask different questions for example:

- If a family system is able to answer triadic questions future oriented, is it more protected than a system which can answer only to linear questions?
- If a family system presents triangulation and intergenerational alliances between family members, is it more exposed to illnesses or conflicts?
- If a family system is attuned with its life cycle, is it more protected from problems than one in which the son acts as grandfather and the father acts as an adolescent?

And finally:

- If we use a manualised intervention in which we expose the system to the best digital, analogic and narrative operationalised tools of the systemic repertoire, will this increase the family health more than another kind of intervention?
- If we use a manualised way to teach family therapy, will we develop a group of therapists who are more skilled than those trained in creative approaches which lack manualisation.

To develop meaningful and effective ways to help those who come to us for care, to further understand the complexity and engage in mutual interdependent learning of the systems in which we exist, to advance the scientific and creative dimensions of our field and to find the political, economic and cultural support necessary for us to survive, we propose that moving beyond a reductionistic view of manualisation to a systemic one will aid these interconnected efforts. This handbook serves as a way to take our pulse on manualisation in systemic practice, training and research with a goal of communicating how far we have come and understanding how far we yet must go.

1.4 A Map of the Book

We begin our journey in Part I with contributions related to *Issues and experiences in the creation of manuals*. Carlos Sluzki starts us off with a reflection on a chapter he wrote in 1977, since we believe it constitutes one of the first systemic attempts of manualisation. We have then asked a group of colleagues to discuss issues that they have faced in their creation of manuals. Represented is a wide range of reflections from those with decades of experience in the process of creating manuals for therapy, research and training and those that have recently begun the process of grappling with how to rigorously convey what they consider important in systemic therapy. We hope one can see how developing process oriented manuals can assume many forms, will depend on the geopolitical context in which they develop, will co-evolve both in real time and over time among all participants and will need to make decisions of the essential material to include.

Part II groups the chapters on *Research issues in the use and evaluation of manuals*. Experienced systemic researchers delve into multiple issues that arise in manual development: the interplay among a conceptual model and the evidence emerging from the manualised research, the combination of complementary systemic perspectives that are further refined and integrated through the process of manualisation, the use of manuals for understanding both families seeking care and those who are not, and reflections and dialogue from the users of the manual that then shapes the future iterations.

Part III explores the *Uses of manuals in clinical practice*. We begin with the most recent work by Maurizio Andolfi in which he describes his intergenerational approach to couples therapy. The additional chapters highlight the development, use and evaluation of manuals designed for particular clinical populations and settings. Included are a great variety of manuals for: therapy with families of infants, children and adolescents; with couples in crisis and in divorce, in the setting of the courts and the schools, and in the important work on eating disorders in single and multi-family therapy groups in the Maudsley model.

While manuals have had a longer history in research and in clinical care, the training context has received less attention. Our final section, Part IV, brings together a wide variety of reports of *Training as a basis for development of manuals and a context for their application*. By recognising the critical work that Rodolfo de Bernart contributed to balancing rigor and creativity through his unique manualised approach; while he had planned to write a chapter himself for this handbook, he unfortunately passed away before being able to do so. Thus, we offer a chapter that includes both excerpts from his work and our reflections on his contributions. Also included are training manuals that articulate the process and content of multi-year training programmes for both systemic therapists and systemic physicians, manualised approaches to orient therapists to key moments in the therapeutic process, such as the beginning sessions, a range of training manuals from the highly specific to general specifications and the isomorphic nature of training and therapy. We conclude this section with a fascinating dialogue among a team of systemic clinicians who have had the history of using eight different manuals in which they discuss their reflections on what it was like to learn and implement the manuals and more meta lessons they learned.

As we finalise this handbook, we realise how grateful we are to its many authors for widening our concepts of manualisation and awareness of the enormous number of therapists who are just getting on with it rather than arguing about whether we should do it or not. We especially appreciate the enormous efforts they each made to deliver such high-quality work during the difficult circumstances of the Covid pandemic. We thank all our authors and offer the book in the hope that it will have similar value for everyone who reads it.

In our final chapter, we present our reflections on the current state of manualisations of systemic therapies as evidenced by our colleagues and try to envisage what the future might hold.

References

Blount, F. A. (2003). Gregory Bateson on deuterolearning and double bind: A brief conceptual story. *Journal of the History of the Behavioral Sciences, 39*, 269–278.
Breunlin, D., & Schwartz, R. (1986). Sequences: Toward a common denominator of family therapy. *Family Process, 25*(1), 67–87. https://doi.org/10.1111/j.1545-5300.1986.00067.x
Carr, A. (2014a). The evidence base for family therapy and systemic interventions for child-focused problems. *Journal of Family Therapy, 36*, 107–157. https://doi.org/10.1111/1467-6427.12032
Carr, A. (2014b). The evidence base for couple therapy, family therapy and systemic interventions for adult-focused problems. *Journal of Family Therapy, 36*, 158–194. https://doi.org/10.1111/1467-6427.12033
Coyne, J. C., & Liddle, H. A. (1992). The future of systems therapy: Shedding myths and facing opportunities. *Psychotherapy: Theory, Research, Practice, Training, 29*(1), 44–50. https://doi.org/10.1037/0033-3204.29.1.44
El-Kaim, M. (2005). Observing systems and psychotherapy: What I owe to Heinz von Foerster. *Kibernetes, 34*, 471–484.
Goodheart, C. (2006). *Evidence based psychotherapy*. APA.
Haley, J. (1963). *Strategies of psychotherapy*. MW Books.
Hiltunen, A. J., Kocis, E., & Walqvist, R. (2013). Effectiveness of cognitive behavioral therapy: An evaluation of therapies provided by trainees at a university psychotherapy training center. *Psych Journal, 2*(2), 101–112.
Hoffmann, L., & Penn, P. (1987). *Milan systemic family therapy*. Basic Books.
International Organization for Standardization. (2015). *ISO9001:2015*. Geneva, Switzerland. *Journal of Family Therapy* 2014 36 (2)
Lanski, L. (1987). Cybernetico-epistobabble, the emperor's new clothes and other sacred cows. *Journal of Family Therapy, 9*(3), 207–215. https://doi.org/10.1046/j..1987.00276.x
Maruyama, M. (1963). The second cybernetics: Deviation-amplifying mutual causal processes. *American Scientist, 51*(2), 164–179.
Minuchin, S. (1974). *Families and family therapy*. Harvard University Press.
Rosner, R. (2018). Manualizing psychotherapy: Aaron T. Beck and the origins of cognitive therapy of depression. *European Journal of Psychotherapy and Counselling, 20*(1), 1–23. https://doi.org/10.1080/13642537.2017.1421984
Sexton, T. L., Ridley, C. R., & Kleiner, A. J. (2004). Beyond common factors: Multilevel-process models of therapeutic change in marriage and family therapy. *Journal of Marital and Family Therapy, 30*, 131–149.
Silverman, W. H. (1996). Cookbooks, manuals, and paint-by-numbers: Psychotherapy in the 90's. *Psychotherapy, 33*(2), 207–215.
Sluzki, C. (1985). Minimal map of cybernetics. *Networker*, May/June, 26.
Sluzki, C. E. (1992). Transformations: A blueprint for narrative changes in therapy. *Family Process, 31*(3), 217–230. https://doi.org/10.1111/j.1545-5300.1992.00217.x
Steinglass, P. (1995). The clinical power of research. *Family Process, 34*(2), 125–253.
Stratton, P., Silver, E., Nascimento, N., McDonnell, L., Powell, G., & Nowotny, E. (2015). Couples and family therapy in the previous decade – What does the evidence tell us? *Contemporary Family Therapy, 27*, 1–12. https://doi.org/10.1007/s10591-014-9314-6
von Forester, H. (2002). *Understanding, a volume of von Foerster's papers*. Springer.
Wampold, B. E. (2001). *The great psychotherapy debate: Model, methods, and findings*. Lawrence Erlbaum.
Williams, N. M., & Lingiardi, V. (2006) *Psychodynamic diagnostic manual*. PDM1.

Part I
Issues and Experiences in the Creation of Manuals

Chapter 2
Another Loop of the Spiral: A Re-examination of 18 Manualized Prescriptions from 1978

Carlos Sluzki

2.1 Editors' Prologue

We asked Carlos Sluzki to revisit his chapter on couples (1977), since we believe it constitutes one of the first systemic attempts of manualization. Our handbook, collecting so many manuals from so many countries, confirms the economic efficacy and validity of the systemic model for the health of the human being. Throughout his career, Carlos Sluzki has fostered the evolution of the systemic field through work in such varied areas as follows:

- The double bind as universal pathogenic situation
- The interface between family and genomics
- Difficult babies, difficult parents: toward a model based on a reciprocal fit
- The pathway between conflict and reconciliation: coexistence as an evolutionary process
- Transformations: a blueprint for narrative changes in therapy
- The better formed story
- The impact of the social network on the health of the individual and the impact of health of the individual on the social network
- Process, structure, and world views: toward an integrated view of systemic models in family therapy
- The impact of authoritarian regimes on families … and on the therapist

---

C. Sluzki (✉)
Department of Psychiatry and Behavioral Sciences, George Washington University School of Medicine School, Washington, DC, USA

Carter Center for Peace and Conflict Resolution, George Mason University, Arlington, VA, USA
e-mail: csluzki@gmu.edu

© Springer Nature Switzerland AG 2021
M. Mariotti et al. (eds.), *Handbook of Systemic Approaches to Psychotherapy Manuals*, European Family Therapy Association Series,
https://doi.org/10.1007/978-3-030-73640-8_2

In his publications on these topics, Carlos has provided instructions for the reader about how to approach the described problem and useful tools to better operate with families and individuals from a consistent epistemological systemic base. Systemic Manualization has Carlos Sluzki as a mentor, and we encourage the reader to take advantage of his thinking among his many publications and books like:

- *The Presence of the Absent: Therapy with Families and Their Ghosts* (2012) (in Spanish). Also (in French) Paris, DeBoeck 2016, and in English, Routledge, 2015.
- *Shame and Humiliation: A Dialogue between Psychoanalytic and Systemic Approaches* (2011). Sao Paulo, Zagodoni Editora (in Portuguese) and Karnak, London, 2013 [English].
- *Double-Bind: The Foundation of the Communication Approach to the Family* (1976). New York, Grune & Stratton (and in Italian: Roma, Astrolabio, 1979) [English].

This is a metachapter, not a chapter, not a prologue to the handbook, in which the legacy of Carlos Sluzki offers to us a way to reflect over the meaning of the word manualization. In fact, in his wide scientific activity, Sluzki never thought to formalize a manual, but in many fields, he offered specific steps, practical, theoretical, and epistemological, which have allowed a formal progress of our discipline, giving the possibility to the readers and to the practitioners a better understanding of the basics of the systemics and the correct way to apply them. The 18 systemic practices constitute a guideline for a therapist to travel the path of the therapy with precise indications, to avoid traps, and to take clients by the hands toward the capacity to solve relational problems autonomously. This chapter ends with a broad, rich guideline or spelling out of the core set of epistemological transformations that were being heralded at the dawn of the systemic era, and that we wish to include here to make it book end this chapter: They are the qualitative shift:

- From individual to larger systems as a unit of analysis
- From intrapersonal to interpersonal-in-context processes
- From objectivism to constructionism
- From interpretations to questions, relabeling, and reframing
- From assumptions about intentions to the observation of effects
- From a focus on origins to a focus on present self-perpetuating loops
- From linear causality to cybernetic complexity

The Editors
And now Carlos Sluzki

2.2 18 Systemic Practices in Couples Therapy: An Early Attempt Toward a Systemic Manualization

SLUZKI'S PROLOGUE 2020

In 1977, more than 40 years ago, I became a member of an interdisciplinary team that developed and then implemented the curriculum of an innovative Family Practice Residency Program at San Francisco General Hospital/ University of California San Francisco Medical School, where physicians were trained to provide medical services within bio-psycho-social, multicultural, progressive, family-oriented approach.

By that same time, I had also reconnected with the Mental Research Institute in Palo Alto –of which had been appointed Research Associate after a three-month fellowship in1965 – where I was, in fact, newly named Director of Training.

Both responsibilities entailed musing on how to train health care professionals to think systemically and to translate those thoughts and models into action in our training programs, courses, clinical externships, conferences, and practicums. Reasonably, during that period I wrote several articles that reflect my pondering whether the via regia toward acquiring a systemic perspective view should transit from theory to practice or from practice to theory (Sluzki, 1973, 1975, 1981, 1983, 1984; Gerber & Sluzki, 1978).

While immersed in those dilemmas, I was invited to represent the systemic voice for a symposium on marriage and marital therapy convened at Brown University at Providence, Rhode Island, where they included key presenters to discuss and perhaps contrast views on marital therapy from psychoanalytic, behavioral and systemic perspectives. Those presentations appeared in a book published the following year (Paolino & McCrady, 1978).

For my 1977 presentation, I decided to <u>deconstruct</u> systemic practices into discrete components – not assuming that that <u>was</u> systemic practice but only that those were visible enactments of what systemic practitioners would (or could) do at different moments. My expectation was that, <u>if behaving that way</u>, systemic phenomena would become evident for the therapists and a systemic epistemology would, in the long run, permeate their practice. It was, in fact, an early attempt at <u>manualizing systemic practice</u> –while that label didn't yet exist in our vocabulary.

> *Re-reading that chapter forty years later, I find it a bit naïve, disorganized, and conceptually fuzzy, but imaginative and filed with still recognizable components of my current practice. Its main fuzziness derives from using the label "systemic" in a loose sense: some of its prescriptions are rooted in communication theory, some in basic cybernetics, some are derivations of MRI's early Brief Therapy Center interactional practices (Watzlawick et al., 1974), and others show inklings of more advanced systemic/narrative ideas, models, and language.*
>
> *The skeleton of that 1978 chapter is retained in the text that follows, as my intention is to revisit this early experiment in manualization rather than revising it critically. It should be note, however, that all the clinical examples of the original article have been omitted (to comply with the editors' specification of words-per-pages-per-chapter of this volume) and a couple of footnotes have been added. Because of the year of its original publication, most bibliographical references, while adequate, are extremely dated. Nonetheless, this chapter has the merit of constituting, as far as I know, the first effort at manualization in the field of family therapy.*

2.3 Introduction

The problems posed by any attempt at discussing the treatment of human systems are complex and exceedingly difficult to solve, for, viewed from any angle, therapy, like art, is unteachable. **Only repertoires of forms can be transmitted**, together with a certain intellectual grounding for them. This chapter aims at proposing some of those forms and sketching some of their conceptual roots.

Systemic couple (and family) therapy constitutes not just a treatment method. It is a whole new way of conceptualizing human problems, understanding behavior, and conceiving the development of symptoms and their resolution. The qualitative shift in the conceptual framework that characterizes the systemic approach to the couple requires that one utilize as primary data or basic unit of analysis the interactions between individuals, rather than the characteristics of each given individual. Even when, for one reason or another, attention is centered on one person, his/her behavior is analyzed in terms of its power to affect and shape, and be influenced and shaped by, the behavior of other members of the system, and the impact of the variables of the eco-system of which they are a part, and vice versa. This approach is based on a cybernetic epistemology concerned with the notions of communication processes, organization of complex systems, language, and reality construction, that is, with an ecosystemic epistemology, as defined by Auerswald (1968, 1971). Further, in what follows, process, structures, and worldviews (reality constructed and grounded in narratives) are utilized as intertwined lenses for the observation, conceptualization, and participation in the process of therapeutic change; rather than either-or, the capacity to incursion in one or another, and to harmonize these levels of analysis of interpersonal processes, only enriches the language and the practice of systemic therapy (see Sluzki, 1983).

When observing couples' interactions, **a system-oriented therapist will take into consideration effects, rather than intentions**. The impact of behaviors upon behaviors, the way interpersonal sequences are organized, will be carefully noted, while, on the contrary, inferences about the motivations of the participants will be avoided. Even further, issues about motivation or intention (ultimately, "mind-reading") will be irrelevant to the understanding of interpersonal processes. This choice should not be understood as the blunt denial of the existential experiences of motivation, intentions, emotions, or human volition in general. It only happens that those inferences do not add any relevant information for purposes of conceptualizing and treating couple distress when operating from a systems perspective.

As happens with the applications of any model, the utilization of a systems vantage point for the understanding and modification of the way couples interact necessarily requires focusing on specific behaviors and interpersonal processes at the expense of others – selectively observing events, filtering in those observables that are relevant to the model. This is true even within the systems model. From Don D. Jackson's then-revolutionary "The Question of Family Homeostasis" (1957) on, many authors have developed rich, internally consistent, intellectually attractive models of therapy for couples and families coherent with a systemic framework, while utilizing remarkably different conceptual tools and therapeutic strategies. Compare, for instance, among the pioneers, Haley (1963, 1977), Hoffman (1971), Bowen (1972), Minuchin (1974), Watzlawick et al. (1967, 1974), and Kantor and Lehr (1975): All of them are sound examples of a systemic vantage point; each of them is original and distinct. In this regard, see also Sluzki (1983).

This chapter deals, therefore, with gross simplifications of extraordinarily complex interactional processes of social systems (as couples and, even more, couples-in-context are) with an evolving ecology and history of their own and immersed in multiple, extensive, continuously changing, overlapping social organizations. However, such simplification must not be considered a fallacy of the model: **its power as a scientific device rests in its capacity to simplify while adding to the ability of the therapist to intervene successfully in introducing change**.

2.4 The Need of Manualization

To teach therapists to "think systems" has been my main activity during recent years. In doing so, I initially followed a classic training format that went from theory to technique. That is, I started by speaking about general principles and progressively specified their concrete application of those principles. But that tack did not prove to be the best choice, for what I considered fascinating general principles seemed to be more relevant to the teacher than to the students. The latter, sometimes unmoved by general principles, were consistently attracted, however, by the pragmatics of their concrete applications. That observation stimulated me to make a 180° turn in my training strategy and start with the concrete and specific, deferring to later stages the gradual introduction of theory.

This approach – from technique to theory – is followed in this chapter, which consists of a series of "naked" prescriptions about concrete, specific therapeutic interventions that can be carried out by the therapist whenever a member of a couple, or both members of it, display certain types of behaviors during the consultation. Each prescription is formulated and grounded separately.

2.5 The Root of a Manual

The overall series, far from being an exhaustive list, constitutes an open-ended attempt to conceptualize treatment principles. However, if you, the reader, follow these prescriptions even loosely, they may lead your work with couples to rather unusual and quite fascinating places, displaying in front of you the power of systemic interventions. Perhaps, they may even stimulate you, the reader, to create systemic interventions and even a systems model of your own for the treatment of couples, which would be indeed the best possible way to learn.

Let us, then, end this prologue and begin with the instructions.

2.6 18 Instructions

> **#1. If A (a member of the couple AB) uses <u>the first-person plural</u> while expressing opinions, judgments, or values, tell A to shift to first-person singular.**

It may be convenient to establish and maintain a set of communicational premises aimed at neutralizing problematic practices of the couple about spokesmanship and roles, as reflected in their linguistic style. One of those regularities may relate to the use of the first-person plural for referents other than facts or events. It constitutes a particular case of what will be later discussed as "mind-reading."

The case is particularly blatant in couples where one spouse is labeled as "patient" and the other as "informer" or "helper." The latter will frequently use the first-person plural, a use that proposes, reminds, or explores a collective agreement on that role. To question it, to tell that person in one or another way, **"Speak for yourself," challenges what may have been a stable interactional pattern of the couple.**

> **#2. If B speaks in <u>impersonal terms</u> about personal matters (such as value judgments and opinions), tell B to make a personal statement.**

This proposition establishes the basis for a cardinal premise, namely, that **value judgments as well as emotions emanate from self** and not (only) from external consensus or situations per se. Values are opinions, not immutable facts. The reification of values automatically externalizes them and transforms them into stone-carved truth. Demystifying value judgments is a necessary step toward changing them or, at least, toward introducing the possibility that alternative values or meanings can be equally legitimate, regardless of how compatible they may be with the holder or with the mainstream of the culture. Even further, "I" statements materialize the speaker as an agent, that is, as a person responsible for his/her actions.

The establishment of this premise may also facilitate a step toward a first agreement: that **they can disagree in terms of values or opinions.** This entails a radically different starting point than the description than self is right and the other is wrong, or, in its variations, that one is sane and the other crazy, or one is good and the other evil.

To mind-read is to assume that one can know what is in the mind of the other – thoughts, feelings, intentions, or motivations, without the need for verification. Mind-reading can be a powerful interactional tool with devastating consequences: If a spouse knows what his/her mate thinks or feels better than he/she does, then no argument is going to convince the spouse of the contrary.

"Mind-reading" is a frequent intervention of parents with children and of brainwashers with victims. The difference between a benign anticipation and a paralyzing disqualification may be assessed by the context and function of the mind-reading statement or by the recipient's response – sometimes a baffled or hurt facial expression will do. There is no way out of this bind within the system: It locks and perpetuates roles and rules about who is sick or evil and who is healthy or right, in sum, who is in charge. This polarization frequently requires outside intervention to be untangled – shadows of the "double-bind" model (Bateson et al., 1956, Sluzki & Ransom, 1976).

> **#3. If A makes an unsupported reference to B's subjective state ("mind-reading"), then ask A what it is that A perceives that makes him/her say that, differentiating perceptions from inferences.**

The systematic demystifying of mind-reading statements not infrequently attains by itself a remarkable change in the couple's patterns of interactions. More frequently, it merely shatters assumptions previously taken for granted by the couple and contributes to the establishment of the general rule that each one will be considered an expert about him/herself and not about the partner.

> **#4. If A speaks to you about B (rather than to B), then: (a) keep looking at A rather than at B while A speaks; and (b) instruct A to talk to, not about B; or (c) ask A how him/herself feels about it; or (d) address a comment about A to B.**

It may be obvious but crucial to point out that, while the study of couple conflicts require an analysis of a dyadic system (in context), the study of the treatment of marital disorders implies the examination of triadic systems (in context), encompassing the couple and the therapist.

One unavoidable characteristic of human triads is their tendency to establish coalitions, that is, relationships of inclusion and exclusion between two members versus the third party for their mutual benefit (Caplow, 1968). A considerable amount has been written about coalitions, from the first inquiries about the nature of interaction in triads published at the turn of the twentieth century by one of the founders of modern sociology, Georg Simmel (e.g., 1902), to Haley's (1963) insightful observations and prescriptions about coalitions in family therapy, to Caplow's (1968) elegant book on inclusions and exclusions, to the author's article on coalitions (Sluzki, 1975).

The process of coalition seeking and coalition negotiation, which generally runs rampant at the beginning of any couple's treatment, requires careful monitoring and laborious calibration if the therapist wishes to establish instrumental ground rules that will frame and guide a useful course of treatment. One of these implicit rules is that "the therapist is going to establish only shifting, instrumental coalitions without binding himself/herself to stable, aprioristic ones or following the culturally established patterns of negotiation" (Sluzki, 1975, p. 71).

This prescription is formulated in four parts, each of which discussed separately.

> **(4a) If A speaks to you about B (rather than to B), keep looking at A (rather than at B) while A speaks.**

The process of establishing and enforcing rules about relationships happens only occasionally through verbal exchanges. The bulk of these transactions occurs mainly implicitly, through the myriad exchanges of information that take place both through the nuances of the linguistic and nonlinguistic components of speech and through nonverbal processes. What would the therapist imply is she or he would look at B's reaction while A talks about B? Probably, the equivalent to "What do you have to say in your defense?" In turn, when maintaining eye contact with A, the therapist signals that A is speaking about A's views (of B's views), not about B, in sum, that A is talking about A.

> (4b) If A speaks to you about B (rather than addressing to B), then tell A to talk to B.

When the speaker defines the therapist as the recipient of the complaint about his or her mate, it favors a defensive statement or a counter-complaint by the mate. It also conveys a request that the therapist does something about it. On the other hand, when one member of the couple speaks to one the other, the weight of the responsibility for the change is transferred back onto them. At the same time, the therapist has further defined the nature of his/her relationship with the couple, namely, that she/he will not be the middle person or take sides or pass judgment.

The "speak to, not about" instruction is sometimes a powerful trigger to enact the drama of the conflict in the session, for it allows direct access to the couple's process under duress.

> (4c) If A speaks to you about B (rather than to B), then ask A how he/she feels about it.

This intervention is a less instructive version of "Speak to, not about," while redirecting the flow of interaction.

This question also "humanizes" A and allows to relabel emotions toward less toxic ones (such as, for instance, from "furious" to "frustrated"). It increases the probabilities of exploring some conflicts in terms of, for example, "expectations" and "wishes" (impossible when the frame is one of "fury") and creates more workable alternatives.

At the same time, while focusing on A, the therapist will keep in mind the vicissitudes of the whole coalitionary field as the conversation evolves, being careful to avoid generating in B a sense of exclusion and in A one of privilege, or a sense of excessive protection of B by the way he/she manages the interaction. The desired effect of multipartiality (of not taking undue sides in a dispute, while guided by clear ethic principles) is achieved in the long run, as in different moments of the session the therapist will engage in a strategic alliance with one or the other member of the couple.

> (4d) If A speaks to you about B (rather than to B), then address a comment to B about A.

This type of intervention is especially pertinent when couples complain of "difficulties in communication" due to intense anger or cutoff, a situation that requires some defusing before attempting other means of facilitating direct interaction between them. In those circumstances, these "aside comments" constitute a very powerful move aimed at maintaining equidistance in stormy waters.

The enactment of the next two recommendations may overlap.

> **#5. If A is defined as an "identified patient" (B becoming implicitly or explicitly defined as "the sane helper" or a sacrificed secondary victim), then reduce physical distance with A or mirror A's body position.**

It is assumed in our culture, and in most cultures, that symptoms and sickness are not voluntary acts, and, in turn, caretaking of the sick is an act of social responsibility, with a varied degree of voluntarism. However, when diseases or disabilities become severe, long-lasting, or cyclic, alternative relational designs appear in couples and in larger social systems, contingent on many variables: prior reciprocal loyalties, ledgers of emotional debts and social responsibility ("in sickness and in health"), degree of support from the social network, socioeconomic strain, cultural norms, etc.

One or another of this panoply of scenarios and role distributions has the risk of becoming rigidly entrenched in a couple as a pattern in their reciprocal relations as well as in relationships within their close social networks, reducing more flexible reciprocal interactions. The roles of "identified patient" and of "helper," as well as other complementarities, are configurations of roles/counter-roles that contribute to trapping the couple into rigid patterns and relational suffering. At the same time, externalizing responsibility and evoking sympathy in third parties assure a modicum of community support. In fact, labeling any incompetence on inability as a permanent trait – a "handicapped person" vs. "a person with a handicap" – risks blocking rehabilitation and reducing self-sufficiency while fixing the role of the helper as a prisoner in that role. Along the same vein, a few years later, I heard Mara Selvini-Palazzoli during presentations and discussions admonish not to label a patient as "schizophrenic" but instead as "a person with schizophrenic behavior."

When a couple displays a narrative that defines their reciprocal relationship as sick/healthy, crazy/sane, or deviant/normal during a consultation, the therapist may shake such a culturally enforced view by not accept a priori.

These configurations allow the therapist to predict that the couple is proposing a definition of the therapeutic relationship, which will involve a coalition between the therapist and the "healthy" spouse against the identified patient.

Therefore, to signal a lack of agreement with their proposition about their definition of the relationship, the therapist may display body signals indicating willingness to coalesce with the other one via mirroring body postures. The two behaviors contained in this instruction signal that intention. The reader who wants to explore further the communicational function of the behaviors included in this prescription, as well as expand this repertoire with other equally expressive displays, may consult the work by Albert Scheflen (1974, 1976), especially his insightful observations on territoriality and the interpersonal patterns of body behavior, including the message values of body distance, body mirroring, leg crossing, and multiple other postures and gestures.

Once that is clear, the therapist will be able to navigate the coalitionary oscillation that characterizes the dynamics in couple therapy. The discussion of this theme will be continued in the next section.

> **#6. If A and B agree in defining A as identified patient and B as a sacrificial victim, then find a way of destabilizing their story and equalize or reverse their roles/labels.**

Some consultations confront us with couples where the pattern of victimization is patent (actual physical, emotional, legal, and economic power of one and extreme lack of abilities or access to resources of the other). However, many interpersonal perpetrator-victim sequences appear hammered down by contrasting – and sometimes concurrent – punctuation in the sequence of events, namely, decisions by one or both participants about who is the cause of problems and who suffers from their consequences. The notion of "punctuations," as well as procedural matters dealing with this prescription, will be discussed in #7, in part an application of this prescription. A prime example of this "impotence to change from within" is the vicious cycles that plague the "conversational games" without end of the protagonic couple of Edward Albee's extraordinary 1962 theater play (or its 1966 film adaptation) "Who's Afraid of Virginia Woolf" – as well as the penetrating analysis of those patterns provided in Watzlawick et al. (1967).

> **#7. If A and B describe a sequence of events that leads to conflict or the emergence of symptoms, then search for events or steps that preceded it. If they cannot specify it, state nonetheless your belief in their existence. If detected and accepted by both as possible, then repeat the cycle, that is, search for a still previous step, or at least assert its existence.**

Except for spousal abuse and legal submission, sexual abuse and violence of children, abuse of elderly, slavery, cults, and political prisoners, there is no a totally passive victim-like position within interpersonal systems. The emphasis is in the word "total," as most societies contain norms that empower men more than women, majorities more than minorities, and able-bodies more than handicapped, to mention just a few.

All members are contributing parties to the interactional sequences, the behavior of each being induced by, and, in turn, influencing the others. Even the nascent dyad parent-newborn can be analyzed with that optic, as exemplified by a somewhat disturbing article I wrote years after this chapter was originally published (Sluzki, 2009).

For strategic purposes (in the real-politiks sense of the term), each actor will tend to favor narratives that locates him or her in the position of victim while placing the other in the position of perpetrator. Occasionally, however, one of them may yield to the description of the other and accept the role of perpetrator… to become the ultimate victim, who admits the role of perpetrator, purges some guilty, and cleans his/her slate. However, those varied narratives derive from the magic of punctuation (when/why/who started the sequence) that supports the narrative that, in turn, contains the moral corollary: who is to blame. Is it that he nags because she withdraws or that she withdraws because he annoys?

Even though some behaviors may be defined as stimuli, some as responses, and some as reinforcement (a reinforcement or calibration of the stimulus in the light of the response), each communicational act can be considered "simultaneously a stimulus, a response, and a reinforcement, according to how we slide our identification up and down the series" (Bateson, 1969, p. 176). The beginning of a sequence (the "punctuation" of when/who/why a pattern started) may remain ill-defined but is frequently associated to an event or context marker ("It started after a minor car accident"; "Since he had that affair") or an ideological anchor ("We belong to different cultures"; "She comes from a rigid, moralistic family").

The tenacity against a change of contextualized conflict narratives, be they interpersonal, cultural, national, and other foundational histories, is a testimony of the strength of their ideological underpinning. The destabilization of those stories – and therefore the proposal of alternative punctuation of events, when successful, may debunk many family myths and other covert agreements and leads toward a dramatic restructuring of the rules of relationships.

#8. If A complains about a symptom centered on self, then find a way of complimenting A for what A may be doing for B.

This prescription, a spinoff of #6, is part of a series of recommendations centered in core destabilizing interventions in therapy, namely, positive connotation, relabeling, symptoms prescriptions, and other paradoxical interventions. This set of interventions, with the addition of circular questions, is lodged at the core of systemic practices. The reader interested in pursuing these themes beyond the limits of these short comments should consult, to start with, the pioneering works by Haley (1963, 1973, 1977), Watzlawick et al. (1974), and Selvini Palazzoli et al. (1975).

To start with, it affirms two "rules of the game" of the therapy: the therapist is going to apply a dialectic logic instead of the traditional causal one utilized in regular conversations, and the core task of the therapists is not one of stamping-off (suppressing) the symptom. There are several messages embedded in this specific seemingly paradoxical prescription:

A is defined as having potential control over his/her symptom.

The connotation of the symptom is changed from negative to positive, as it is defined as having some far-from-obvious positive relational value, accomplishing a useful function for the other member of the couple.

It hints a shared responsibility of A and B over the symptom.

The therapist may have done a first step toward destabilizing the couple's sick-healthy pattern sustained by their original narrative.

> **#9. If the symptom-bearer member A reports a decrease in the intensity of symptoms since the last consultation, then express vague worries and recommend a slight relapse, even soliciting the aid of B to achieve it, or express concerns that B may develop in turn some symptoms.**

The system comprised of a symptomatic individual and his/her mate (plus, of course, their context) may define the symptom as devoid of context, as "just happening." The interactional therapist describes it otherwise: Symptoms accomplish functions within the system; that is, they are part of the relational sequences within a complex interpersonal system. How to proceed with the process of change entailed in therapy without transforming the session into an arena for the confrontation of views, a struggle between the patterns of a stable system – the couple-in-context – and the challenging destabilization triggered by a new one – the couple plus the therapist?

Discussions about intentionality, sterile and unfair as they are, will be activated if the therapist appears explicitly advocating the dissolution of rigid patters (the hopeless "Stop it!" or "Be different!").

Order (*morphostasis*, the processes aimed at the retention of pattern) and change (*morphogenesis*, the process of generating new adaptive or exploratory relational ways of being) are complementary tendencies in interpersonal and all complex systems (Speer, 1970). They maintain a delicate balance through subtle homeodynamic processes. When any living system deviates toward one of the poles – toward rigidity or chaos–, processes are activated that pull the system in the opposite direction, keeping the system within an unstable equilibrium between poles. The triumph of morphostasis is total rigidity and, in the long run, the death of the system. The triumph of morphogenesis is, in turn, chaos or complete reconfiguration and, equally, the end of that system. The balance between both tendencies – stability and change – is crucial for the evolutionary capability of any system, couples (in context) included.

Therefore, to favor change both in excessively rigid or near-chaotic systems, the therapist will have to calibrate the tension between those tendencies in his/her actions, preserving stability while freeing the system from restrictive rules that prevent the members from working out changes.

An expansion of intervention #9 is the "prescription of the system," that is, a recommendation NOT to change the problem, symptom, or conflict maintaining pattern that triggered the consultation, arguing the serious risks entailed in a change in family dynamics. Prescription of symptoms or of its interpersonal pattern of maintenance (the "keep on doing what you do") is a potent example of the effect of the "be spontaneous" paradox: whatever behavior and sequence that was enacted "in automatic pilot" is disjointed by becoming the explicit focus of attention or enactment (Selvini Palazzoli et al., 1975; Watzlawick et al., 1974) This comment also applies to the prescriptions #10–#13.

> **#10. If A has a symptom that fluctuates within the day or the week, then instruct A (not privately, but during the couple's consultation) to select times in which the symptom improves to tell B that it is worse.**

Through prescribing the symptom to a symptomatic member in the presence of the mate, the therapist aims at shattering the very collective patterns tied to the symptom. That effect occurs through three processes.

(a) When the patient is told "exaggerate or fake the symptom," the other member of the dyad is implicitly being told that, in the future, symptomatic behavior to which he/she may be exposed to and reacting may be false, therefore inhibiting "spontaneous" responses that, in turn, may have reinforced and perpetuated the pattern of which the symptom is a part.

(b) It subtly increases the consensus about the patient's potential ownership over the symptom: if the subject can produce (or fake) a symptom, he/she may also be able to control.

(c) It sabotages the patterns of symptom maintenance, which is based on the assumption of its spontaneity.

> **#11. Whenever making a prescription of a given behavior or a symptom, the more basic the implied change, the more trivial (the less "magic") it should be made to appear: involve both members in the prescription and admonish that, despite it sounding trivial, they will find it challenging to comply.**

As it has become clear by now, the maintenance and exacerbation of chronic conflicts, problems or symptoms tend to be part of a feedback loop that includes those very behaviors of other members aimed at resolving the difficulty; thus, the assertion: the attempted solution becomes part of the problem (cf. Haley, 1963, 1973; Hoffman, 1971; Watzlawick et al., 1974; Wender, 1968). By recommending symptomatic or problematic behaviors, the complaint becomes the compliance, and the very act that was used previously as a marker of roles becomes now the result of a prescription made by the therapist. The system is robbed of a basic rule.

The reason behind the recommendation to prescribe behaviors to both members must be quite apparent by now: to further establish their joint participation in both the problem and its resolution.

> **#12. If the couple reports having complied with a task or prescription, then express some surprise, praise them, and predict amiably that it may not last, or that they will find it challenging to retain the task or that they will fail next time.**

The more challenging the change implied by the prescription, the less it should be touted. Otherwise, the investment of the therapist in the specific change becomes itself a relational marker, and the couple may utilize alternative outcomes to the prescription to reward or punish the therapist, or each other. For the same reason, the therapist may express his/her doubts about the stability of any success, which precludes any improvement or relapse made "for him/her" (as the triadic couple-therapist system is filled with potential paradoxes of its own). Further, relapses may even be encouraged, a strategy that, as already discussed regarding prescription #10, conveys the notion that the symptomatic or problematic behavior is under the control of the actor, rather than an allegedly random process. Once this is established, one of the interactional values of a symptom is debilitated, and with it, its conjoint pattern of maintenance.

The surprise-mild praise-doubts response by the therapist (its rationale already discussed earlier) can also be displayed if the couple has NOT followed the recommendation, be it of a symptom prescription or some other pattern-challenging behavior. This postponement can be defined as a sensitive (while perhaps unconscious) perception by the couple that they were not yet ready for change, or that that was not the proper moment, given some intercurrent problematic event that the couple is confronting, or that they were doing the preliminary steps by thinking of doing what the therapist had suggested. [11] A sweet example that appears in a remarkable book on brief therapy (Furman & Ahola, 1992) refers to a period in which one of the authors had volunteered to coach his 6-year-old son's school soccer team. During the first game that he witnessed in his new role, he noted that, whenever any kid was in possession of the ball, all the team would run forward but would seldom if ever pass the ball – not surprising, given the the maturity required to aprehend the complex notions of team play, including passes and support of teammates' moves. As a result of his observation, he dedicated the team's next training session to highlight the importance of team play, followed by a practice of passes. However, at the next game, his squad repeated its prior performance: when in possession of the ball, all the kids would run forward in parallel, so to speak, with the kid in possession of the ball just kicking forward rather than passing it back and forth. After the game, he convened the team and congratulated them for their progress, stating that he had noted that, at different moments, many of them had been thinking of passing the ball. The kids received those praises with joy and pride, and several of them agreed that that had been the case. In subsequent games, some inklings of passes started to emerge.

This stance binds the couple in a positive experience of joint creation (or of non-creation!), a move forward in the therapeutic process, and a progressive destabilization of narratives and of patterns of interaction…although what they have done, or failed to do, is superficially identical to what brought them to the consultation.

> **#13. If A (or B, or both) expresses or attributes to the other feelings that have negative connotations in our/their culture, implying that to have those feelings is to be mad or bad or sick, then attempt to relabel or reframe those feeling into one with a positive connotation.**

This recommendation should have been perhaps located as number one, as this intervention constitutes a central piece toward the destabilization of patterns (and, shifting optics, the destabilization of narratives), a central piece in the process of therapeutic change. However, its location in this sequence signals that relabeling and reframing are core strategic choices around which the therapist must respond to a critical epistemological and pragmatic question: "Why have I selected this versus that relabel or reframe?" "What did I attempt at disturb, and what did I hope to achieve with it?"

To reframe is to change the frame of reference against which a given event is considered or judged, thus shifting the meaning and value judgment attributed to the event (without a change in the event itself). A panic attack in a person that mobilized the spouse and perhaps their extended family may be defined as "a cry for help while hiding the request," as "a volcano of emotions kept encased even without the individual's awareness until exploding," as "an unconscious effort to change a pattern of who takes care of whom," "to self-denounce crippling mythology of strength," as "a metaphoric portray of things to come relationally," as "unspoken worries about one or the other's health," as "a blessing in disguise," as an escalation, as a white flag of surrender, and so on, all that without changing the description of the clinical manifestation of the panic attack.

When a patient, who seeks consultation due to vomiting that seems to be triggered by stressful events, is told, "Good, you should not stop vomiting until those things that bother you (or your spouse) change. How wise of your body to devise such a clever way of forcing some changes in this unpleasant situation, a load for both of you!" The complaint (vomiting) is not at all changed. Still, the frame (from something that "just happens" to something that is somehow purposeful) and its value from negative (as an annoying symptom) to positive (a behavior leading to change) are both changed.

In turn, to <u>relabel</u> is to change the name of the behavior with a label that will change the frame of reference evoked by that word. A complaint of overarching pessimism, crying, and emotional distress can be labeled as "depression," which evokes a medical frame of disease and may be met with medications, or as "sadness" or "distress," which evokes a potentially universal experience that invites the question "What about?" The act of relabeling someone's "anger" as hurt, or someone's "depression" as sadness, or someone's symptom as an act of kindness and goodwill toward others may exert a dramatic, exorcizing effect on the system.

Reality depends on our beliefs. There are no labels that are intrinsically more "correct" than others. At most, some are more consensual than others. Therefore, different observers may, in turn, provide different meanings to the same given act or circumstance. Far from an a-moral "anything goes," those choices, as so many other interventions in the construction of alternative narratives in the process of therapy, are guided not only by pragmatic principles but also by both aesthetic and ethic ones. A discussion of this core constitutive guideline in the field of therapy may be found in Sluzki (1992).

With the attribution of meaning comes the adjudication of a given value within different "scales" evoked by that meaning, such as goodness-badness, sanity-madness, and health-sickness. And those values, when rigidly attached to members of a family system, pin them down to fixed roles, as they consolidate interactional roles within the family, facilitating a self-fulfilling prophecy.

It is essential to point out here that to relabel a problem, or a symptom does NOT mean to minimize it, an issue discussed in depth by Haley (1977) and so many after him. Even more, there are specific cases in which the interpersonal impact or value of a symptom may be challenged through paying attention to it beyond what was expected by the participants, to the point of generating in the symptomatic subject a corrective reduction of its relational weight. An alternative could be to focus our attention and concern in the minor distress of a nonsymptomatic member to generate a symmetrizing load between both members.

This prescription on "crazy talk" is an illustration of the principle that, when symptomatic behaviors are deprived of their interactional power, they tend to reduce their value as a message or their presence as fulcrum of interactions, and therefore their display. Through dealing with "crazy" behavior as if it were mere "misbehavior," the therapist de facto relabels that action with a nonpathological tag. At the same time, he/she will provide the other, nonsymptomatic members with a model of how to handle some symptomatic behavior.

> **#15. If you detect a central family myth or guiding narrative, then do not question it frontally. Explore its origins and ethics, and tests its counter-stories without directly challenging it. Even when members of the couple themselves suggest that the myth may not reflect their reality, thread it cautiously.**

> **#14. If A talks "crazy" amid an interaction between you and B, then tell A not to interrupt or distract and follow your interaction with B.**

As was discussed in detail already by Jackson (1965a, b) early in the development of the field of family therapy, relationships between family members are guided by typical repetitive patterns of interaction, redundancies that we, as observers, call family rules. These rules –from the most nourishing and growth-promoting practices to the vilest and most oppressive – constitute core governing principles that assure coherence and predictability, a recognizable "familiarity." When prompted, family members can articulate some of those regularities, described as normative beliefs, family histories and family myths, or just described as "our family way of functioning." In most cases, these interactive regularities tend to be enacted without any mindful awareness – except when those patterns are violated for one reason or another, generating distress, escalations, conflicts, or corrective actions.

Family myths are a particular case of the narratives that sustain guiding family rules, frequently across generations. Ferreira (1966, p. 86) defined them as "well-systematized beliefs shared by all family members, about their mutual role in the family, and the nature of their relationship, even though some of those beliefs may defy existing evidence." Once established, family myths tend to remain as a valued ordering force in the relationship. In the same way as direct questioning of the validity or values of a myth (consequently, of core values of the family) may constitute a violation that risks shunning of family members, a direct challenge of it may threaten the continuity of therapy.

Prescription #15 further stresses the notion, proposed in #11, that the therapist should work along with the family system rather than challenging core relational rules and beliefs frontally. This "working along" constitute a central component of therapy: the development of a respectful, collaborative relationship with all family members that will permit us eventually to challenge them.

That is what in the jargon of therapy is called "joining." Throughout the interview, the therapist probes different interactional patterns and the values they represent and may choose to challenge some of them gently. This process will prove to be more feasible with regularities that are not crucial to the maintenance of core (morphostatic) patterns, sometimes explicitly mythical, sometimes not. Far from being myth-bashers, we way unveil and, if possible, help the couple/family to make explicit the function/values/ patterns/beliefs that myths support for the system, question and, whenever feasible, reduce the hidden nature of their power, making them explicit, even naming them or inviting the patients to do. If shattered in the course of therapy, create, if possible, a respectful ritual around their demise and, if not, let it fade away into oblivion. The therapeutic goal is to help the patients to destabilize or even denounce the patterns the myth commanded or the problematic values it enforces, and to free themselves from their potential oppression.

> **#16. If you find yourself not understanding what is going on with the couple, then cease paying attention to content, and observe verbal patterns, sequences, gestures, and postures, or observe your own emotions, attitudes, or postures.**

This and the subsequent prescriptions are variations of the dictum "If you don't like what you are getting, change your behavior." They aim specifically at dealing with the not infrequent situation of the therapist finding him/herself unable to understand what is going on in the session or failing to detect meaningful regularities, to understand quid pro quos, and to devise effective interventions or other such problems. These difficulties are frequently the result of ourselves.

 I. Being mesmerized by the aesthetics or the dramatic nature of the couple's narrative, losing the relative distance necessary to notice interactive patterns or narrative constraints. Hence, the wise advice that I heard on several occasions from Gianfranco Cecchin: "Don't fall in love with the story."

 II. Becoming captured ideologically by the constrictions of the consulting system – such as having taken sides in a dispute, defining who is right and who is wrong, or empathizing with the one identified as a victim –, and therefore having lost perspective or grasp of the multilayered complexity of conflicts.

 III. Resonating with the presenting problem or its interpersonal dynamics because of its structural or content similarity with the therapist's own current conflicts/traps, and hence replicating in the session relational blind spots.

This prescription gently reminds the therapist of his/her fallible humanity, and of ways of luring him/herself out of those morasses by shifting the focus of attention to other equally rich sources of information – refocusing from process to content or from an emphasis on the content of their story to attention on extraverbal clues. If this method doesn't work for you, try #17 or even better #18.

Until now, this chapter has dealt with observable behaviors rather than with narratives of historical reconstructions. Consultations frequently include (o even focuses on the) exploration of the problems' or conflicts' history, or of the couple's or couple members' history. Family history is a theme than many couples and families gravitate toward, and both patients and therapists like to make is a focus. That thematic choice is not trivial: many process or event in a couple's history has repercussion on, or are engrained in, their present relationship, evoking or invoking robust markers and enhancing vicious or virtuous cycles – conflicts or resilience – in their current life. Focusing almost exclusively on the personal and familial history, and actively intervening in family-of-origin relations, reconstructions, and management, has been the choice of therapists within the Bowen (1972) tradition. Many others, as is the case of the author of this chapter, will enter historical explorations

> **#17. If the actual observation of the couple's interactive process fails to provide you with a meaningful entry toward a process of destabilization of their problematic predicament, switch to the exploration of the couple's history.**

to learn about cultures and myths and gain additional common language and common metaphors with the couple, or when "family of origin" is brought forth by the couple as an explicit source of conflicts, or, as is the case of this prescription, when failing to develop a workable therapeutic fulcrum based on narrative/interactional observables.

The change of focus of this prescription rescues the historical process as a source of information for the development of the therapeutic relationship as well as of therapeutic strategies. Its value rests not solely on providing clues toward the reconstruction of the couple's evolvement of norms, agreements, and myths; it may also prove to be a useful way of working through lagging, long-term misunderstandings, and conflicts. Also, that process of historical information gathering can be a fertile terrain to further observing the couple in action, allowing to detect specific styles evoked by the discussion of different periods in the history of the couple. Finally, the developmental perspective is crucial to study how the couple has dealt with previous "passages" (first encounter, commitments, parenting, moves, separations, etc.) to learn about their strengths and possible pitfalls. In fact, the mere act of sharing with a couple – when it fits – the hypothesis that the development of the present marital conflict or symptom is part of a transition crisis in their own family's life cycle (highlighting actual resilience resources mobilized in the past) often has a powerful soothing effect, as they begin to view their situation less as an arbitrary, whimsical, or quirky event, and more as an explainable and temporary problem within a steady trajectory. The discussion of prior or new effective ways of counterbalancing whatever predictable problem will strengthen their resilience.

This final prescription derives from two observations. One is that on many occasions, the couple may not be the critical unit of analysis, as it may not include all of the participants in the minimal meaningful system. It is not an infrequent observation that, when treatment of a couple fails to show progress, a qualitative leap takes place when the couple offspring, or one of their parents, or a sister, or any other relative, or even a close friend is invited into a session as "visitor" or "consultant." The effect is sometimes the unveiling of issues that were up-to-then mystified or simply not detected by the therapist or brought forth by the couple, thus expanding the narrative, showing other sides of conflicts, or triggering confrontations that appeared dormant until then.

An equivalent enriching experience is provided by introducing a co-therapist (even for one session): it will expand our views, re-align the coalitionary field, enhance the texture of the collective narrative, and, overall, enrich the experience for all the participants. In fact, this practice should be considered by all therapists,

> **#18. If you find yourself unable to generate meaningful change, increase the number of participants in the session (invite offspring, parents, friends, co-therapists, or supervisors into the session/treatment).**

novices, and experts, whether stuck in a treatment process or not, both as a learning experience and as an experience of humility. A more frequent and equally valuable resource is a consultation, supervision, or, as many do, a stable cross-supervision with a colleague friend, which adds joy to the process of being a therapist.

2.7 Conclusion

As happens in any manual, to state that a therapeutic activity consists in a combination of these prescriptions plus any other behavior by the therapist plus other specific systemic and contextual variables is obviously and irritatingly unsatisfactory: maybe, it is useful to master this repertoire of prescriptions to be an accomplished therapist, but that does not tell us anything about joining, timing, and the multiple other *sui generis* enactments, resonances, and other variables that constitute the art of therapy and that make a therapist a therapist.

Considering another, more general, level of abstraction, this chapter portrays a major epistemological shift in the behavioral sciences. This qualitative jump results from the incorporation of the systemic vantage point. It affects the unit of analysis, the process being observed, the type of goals and the variety of means, and the logic being utilized.

This epistemological revolution is characterized by a shift from:

> **Individual to larger systems as a unit of analysis**
>
> **Intrapersonal to interpersonal-in-context processes**
>
> **From interpretations to questions, relabeling, and reframing**
>
> **From Objectivism to constructionism**
>
> **Assumptions about intentions to the observation of effects**
>
> **A focus on origins to a focus on present self-perpetuating loops**
>
> **Linear causality to cybernetic complexity**

References

Auerswald, E. H. (1968). Interdisciplinary versus ecological approach. *Family Process, 7*(2), 202–215.
Auerswald, E. H. (1971). Families, change, and the ecological perspective. *Family Process, 10*(3), 263–280.
Bateson, G., Jackson, D. D., Haley, J., & Weakland, J. H. (1956). Toward a theory of Schizophrenia. *Behavioral Science, 1*(4):251–264, and in Bateson, G. (1972). *Steps to an ecology of mind.* New York: Chandler (translation in multiple languages).
Bateson, G. (1969). Exchange of information about patterns of human behavior. In W. S. Field & W. Abbot (Eds.), *Information storage and neural control.* Springfield, IL: Charles C Thomas, and in Bateson, G. (1972). *Steps to an ecology of mind.* New York: Chandler.
Bowen, M. (1972). Family psychotherapy. *American Journal of Orthopsychiatry, 31,* 40–60.
Caplow, T. (1968). *Two against one; coalition in triads.* Prentice-Hall.
Ferreira, A. (1966). *Family myths.* Psychiatric Research Report 20. American Psychiatric Association. In P. Watzlawick & J. H. Weakland, (Eds.) (1977). *The interactional view.* New York: Norton.
Furman, B., & Ahola, T. (1992). *Solution talk: Hosting therapeutic conversations.* Norton.
Gerber, W., & Sluzki, C. E. (1978). The doctor-family relationship. In R. B. Taylor (Ed.), *Family medicine, principles and practice.* Springer.
Haley, J. (1963). *Strategies of psychotherapy.* Grune & Stratton.
Haley, J. (1973). *Uncommon therapy: The psychiatric techniques of Milton H. Erickson, M.D.* Norton.
Haley, J. (1977). *Problem solving therapy.* Jossey-Bass.
Hoffman, L. (1971). Deviation-amplifying processes in natural groups. In J. Haley (Ed.), *Changing families.* Grune & Stratton.
Jackson, D. D. (1957): The question of family homeostasis. *Psychiatric Quarterly Supplement, 31*(1), 79–90. Also, in: D. D. Jackson (Ed.), *Communication, family, and marriage.* Palo Alto: Science and Behavior, 1968.
Jackson, D. D. (1965a). Family rules- Marital quid pro quo. *Archives of General Psychiatry, 12,* 589–594.
Jackson, D. D. (1965b). The study of the family. *Family Process, 4,* 1–20. Also in: P. Watzlawick & J. H. Weakland (Eds.), *The interactional view.* New York: Norton, 1977.
Kantor, D., & Lehr, W. A. (1975). *Inside the family.* Jossey-Bass.
Minuchin, S. (1974). *Families and family therapy.* Harvard University Press.
Paolino, T. J. & McCrady, B. S. (Eds.). (1978). *Marriage and marital therapy: Psychoanalytic, behavioral, and systems theory perspectives.* New York: Brunner/Mazel; and translated into Italian in *Terapia Familiare, 6*(57–80), 1979; into Finnish in *Perheterapia, 1*(2), 18–23, 1985 and *2*(1):6–12, 1986; and into Spanish, as a "classic", in Mosaico #61, July 2015.
Scheflen, A. E. (1974). *How behavior means.* Aronson.
Scheflen, A. E., & with Ashcraft, N. (1976). *Human territories: How we behave in space-time.* Prentice-Hall.
Selvini Palazzoli, M., Boscolo, L., Cecchin, G., & Prata, G. (1975). *Paradosso e Controparadosso.* Milano: Feltrinelli (Translation in multiple languages).
Simmel, G. (1902). The number of members as determining the sociological form of the group. *American Journal of Sociology, 8*(1), 1–16, 158–196.
Sluzki, C. E. (1973). On training to 'think interactionally'. *Social Science and Medicine, 8,* 483–485.
Sluzki, C. E. (1975). The coalitionary process in initiating family therapy. *Family Process, 14*(1), 67–77. and (in Italian) in V. Cigoli (Ed.). *Interazione Familiare ed Intervento Psicoterapico.* Milano: Franco Angeli, 1977.
Sluzki, C. E., & Ransom, D. (Eds.). (1976). *Double-bind: The foundation of the interactional approach to the family.* New York: Grune & Stratton; and (in Italian): Roma: Astrolabio, 1979.

Sluzki, C. E. (1981). Process of symptom production and patterns of symptom maintenance. *Journal of Marital and Family Therapy, 7*(3), 273–280; (in Italian), Terapia Familiare, *10*, 1981; (in Spanish) Terapia Familiar, *6*(12), 139–156, 1983.

Sluzki, C. E. (1983). Process, structure and world views: Toward an integrated view of systemic models in family therapy. *Family Process, 22*, 469–476. (in Italian) as a chapter in C. Cipolli & A. Silvestri, (Eds.), *Communicazione e Sistemi: Un Approccio Interdisciplinare all'Interazione Umana.* Milano: Franco Angeli, 1985.

Sluzki, C. E. (1984). The patient-provider-translator triad: A note for providers. *Family Systems Medicine, 2*(4), 397–404.

Sluzki, C. E. (1992). The 'better-formed' story (in Italian). In G. Cecchin & M. Mariotti, (Eds.), *L'Adolescente e i suoi Sistemi.* Rome: Kappa (pp. 37–47). Expaded in Sluzki, C. E. (2006). Victimizacion, recuperacion, y las historias con 'mejor forma' (in Spanish). *Sistemas Familiares, 22*(1–2), 5–20.

Sluzki, C. E. (2009). *Difficult babies, difficult parents: Toward a model based on a reciprocal fit* (in French) in Cahiers critiques de therapie familale et de pratiques de reseaux, *43*, 151–167; and (in Spanish) in *Redes, 22*, 11–27. An earlier version (in Italian) in *Maieutica, 25/26,* 9–18, 2006.

Speer, D. C. (1970). Family systems: Morphostasis and morphogenesis, or "is homeostasis enough?". *Family Process, 9*(3), 259–278.

Watzlawick, P., Beavin, J., & Jackson, D. D. (1967). *Pragmatics of human communication.* New York: Norton (Translation into multiple languages).

Watzlawick, P., Weakland, J. H., & Fisch, R. (1974). *Change: Principles of problem formation and problem resolution.* New York: Norton (Translation into multiple languages).

Wender, P. H. (1968). Vicious and virtuous circles: The role of deviation-amplifying feedback in the origin and perpetuation of behavior. *Psychiatry, 31*, 317–324.

Chapter 3
Six Different Approaches to Manualisation from the Leeds Family Therapy and Research Centre

Peter Stratton and Helen Pote

In the mid-1990s, the effectiveness of family therapy was being questioned in the UK. A culture of evidence-based practice was requiring psychological interventions to demonstrate how effective they were in achieving positive mental health outcomes for individuals. Systemic family therapy (SFT) was widely used within the health service and previous research broadly supported family work. A small body of research from the British context supported systemic interventions (Lask & Matthews, 1979, Leff et al., 1985, Carr, 1991) but most of the evidence came from North America (Brent et al., 1997; Russell et al., 1987, Simpson, 1991). The quality of the research evidence was poor with few studies providing detailed accounts of the systemic therapeutic process employed (Stratton et al., 2015). Therapists and researchers alike remained unclear as to what constituted effective family therapy.

At the same time, cognitive-behaviour therapy (CBT) was stridently fulfilling the evidenced-based agenda, conducting multiple randomised controlled trials which asserted its efficacy. These trials defined outcomes in non-systemic ways, considering therapy success primarily in terms of individual diagnostic status or changes in individual symptomology post treatment. The improvements in family functioning overall and improvements in family communication patterns which were central to a systemic approach were largely ignored, including that symptom disappearance is not a sign of better communication inside the system but sometimes a way to avoid conflicts.

The original version of this chapter was revised. The correction to this chapter is available at
https://doi.org/10.1007/978-3-030-73640-8_34

P. Stratton (✉)
Emeritus Professor of Family Therapy, Leeds Family Therapy and Research Centre,
University of Leeds, Leeds, West Yorkshire, UK
e-mail: p.m.stratton@ntlworld.com

H. Pote
Department of Psychology, Royal Holloway, University of London, London, UK

© Springer Nature Switzerland AG 2021, Corrected Publication 2022
M. Mariotti et al. (eds.), *Handbook of Systemic Approaches to Psychotherapy Manuals*, European Family Therapy Association Series,
https://doi.org/10.1007/978-3-030-73640-8_3

Some systemic therapists were opposed to engaging in trials with such narrow definitions of therapeutic outcomes particularly as these were based on positivist quantitative research approaches that ignored qualitative and social constructionist perspectives in understanding the effectiveness of therapy. However, as the commissioning of services became driven by evidence, it was clear that participation in systemic outcome research was essential and there was hope that participation in trial design would broaden outcome criteria to be more systemic in nature.

The Leeds Family Therapy & Research Centre (LFTRC) has a tradition of combining research with practice and then rigorously formulating its processes to make them available to other users in published documents. The result has been a series of six manuals created for different purposes, with correspondingly different formats. They reflect both our wish to undergo the discipline of rigorously specifying therapeutic procedures for training and also to provide a sound basis for research into families and family therapy. Five of these products are presented in this chapter to help us expand the concept of what we can include as a manual and to show how different types of manuals can helpfully advance systemic practice and research. Chronologically, we first present the *Leeds Attributional Coding System Manual* (Stratton et al., 1988a, b); second an attempt to create a parallel version for analysing attachment processes in therapy sessions (Stratton et al., 1998); third a manual for independent practitioners and trainers *Family Therapy: Training and Practice (1990)* which was published as a book so that it would be widely available; fourth, a detailed presentation of the research processes that created the *Leeds Systemic Therapy Manual* (Pote et al., 2000), and an account of how it has been used. *The LSFT Manual* which includes an *Adherence Protocol* is a "classic" therapy manual created in order to conduct RCTs in which the form of therapy needs to be clearly specified, but which we also find has been used extensively by systemic therapists and trainers, and fifth, from projects outside of LFTRC but involving the authors of this chapter, we offer a comprehensive account of systemic therapist competences which was itself created through a detailed analysis of systemic therapy manuals (Stratton et al., 2011). Our final example is the SCORE Index of Family Functioning which takes a different form, in that its manual has been developed progressively through a variety of Web resources. This has been a complex process and is described in detail in Chap. 17. An overview of each of the six manuals is provided in Table 3.1.

We conclude by drawing together what we have learned about effective uses of manuals from these varied experiences.

3.1 The Leeds Attributional Coding System Manual

From its start in 1979, LFTRC included a weekly research team meeting aiming to find new ways of understanding family interactions. These meetings were not exclusive to the research team but included invited family therapists and others working with families so that we could work with a better understanding of family diversity. Our first attempt was to identify and tabulate all of those phenomena that we could recognise as occurring during family therapy sessions, and which related to our current theoretical interests. "It rapidly became apparent that a therapy session was too

Table 3.1 Overview of each of the six LFTRC Manuals

Manual	Published	Focus
Leeds Attributional Coding System Manual	1988	Enabling therapists and researchers to distil out the causal beliefs and expectations of self and family members. Identify patterns related to particular relationships
Analysing attachment processes	1998	Coding indicators of attachment processes as they occur during therapy
Family Therapy: training and Practice	1990	A sequential training text usable for courses and for independent, preferably group, self-training
Leeds Systemic Family Therapy Manual and Adherence Protocol	2000	A complete manual of systemic family therapy derived through rigorous research of a well-specified training
Mapping systemic therapist competences	2010	A comprehensive mapping of the 254 identifiable competences of trained systemic family therapists
SCORE. See Chap. 17	Ongoing	A distributed manual for using the SCORE measure for both outcomes and interactively as part of the therapy. Building progressively through various Web media

rich in material to be digested all in one go. We therefore adopted a strategy of taking theoretical perspectives singly, and working them to the limit of what they could tell us in relation to the pattern of interactions in a session ....The first theoretical perspective to be adopted was that of attributional theory. There were three main reasons for this choice. The first was that perceptions of cause appear to be a significant factor in cognitive, social, and affective functioning from birth and throughout the life span. Secondly, we were struck by the often strong beliefs expressed by individuals in therapy, and by the extent to which agreement and disagreement about the causes of events was an issue within families. Thirdly, attributional theory appeared to offer a well formulated set of concepts which identified, and potentially allowed the measurement of, the significant components of causal beliefs" (Stratton et al., 1986, p. 6).

The research team took existing ways of analysing causal attributions and refined them to be applicable to those made by families during therapy. Although the significance of attributions had been recognised for some time in social psychology (e.g. Nisbett & Valins, 1970), we found there was at the time no coherent system of analysing those offered spontaneously, as they were in SFT sessions. As the potential of coding of attributions made during therapy emerged, we decided to work towards specifying the whole process in a manual so that it could be used by other therapist-researchers.

3.1.1 The Process

We assembled a research team of family therapists and clinical psychologists and met weekly over nearly 2 years to develop reliable coding of spontaneous attributions (Stratton, P.M., Heard, D.H., Hanks, H.G., Munton, A.G., Brewin, C.R. and Davidson, C.) Our initial procedures were recognised by Martin Seligman and Judy

Dunn who were organising a workshop of attribution researchers at Kiawah Island, USA in 1982 and invited Peter Stratton to present our coding system. This was the start of a fruitful period of application of attribution theory in psychology with major contributions such as Seligman's work on depression (Peterson & Seligman, 1984), attributions of spouse behaviour in distressed and non-distressed couples (Fincham et al., 1987) and expressed emotion in relatives of patients with schizophrenia (Brewin et al., 1991).

The weekly research meetings in which we had intensively discussed ways of specifying a reliable and valid way of analysing attributions allowed us to publish our first analysis of attributions during a systemic family therapy (Stratton et al., 1986) which was the first to apply attributional analysis to a substantial body of natural discourse. Publishing the findings made it essential to also make the complete manual available, and the *Leeds Attributional Coding System Manual* (LACS Manual) was published in 1988. The manual (Stratton et al., 1988a, b) provides the rationale for analysing attributions in psychotherapy, detailed instructions on identifying spoken attributions in transcripts and an extensive coding of each attribution according to dimensions labelled *Stable, Global, Internal to the person, Personal to that person and Controllable.* Taking as an example three attributions by a mother whose partner was convicted of abusing their daughters, for which he was sentenced to three 5-year jail terms. In the session she made 97 attributions related to the abuse, which she consistently denied. Our convention is to present the cause in the first line and the outcome in the second, and three characteristic causal statements were:

because he (father) got convicted on technicalities
　he still denies it (CSA)
Because she's got the hatred
　D (victim, 18 years old) can say the very angry things
because its only them (girls) that know what's happened
　none of us (family) know

These examples perhaps give an indication of why we concluded that extracting attributional statements from everything that was said during a session helped us to see patterns that could otherwise have got lost in the detail or be difficult to understand during the session. Patterns also emerged from analysing the frequencies with which the dimensions were used. In this example, mother's attributions allocated causal responsibility to the victims in 61% of her statements but to herself on only 26% and to the abuser even less at 14% (Silvester et al., 1995).

Circularity was achieved by applying the coding to the speaker and others such as family members that the attribution was made about. The manual concluded with substantial sample data from therapy sessions and analyses of reliability and validity of the method. LFTRC initially focussed its research using the manual to understand processes in families in which child abuse had occurred (Stratton and Swaffer, 1988; Silvester et al., 1995; Stratton, 2003a, b). An extension was to set up a research company, The Psychology Business Ltd., which used the LACS Manual to train a large team of researchers who undertook projects for some 20 of the UK's largest companies. The methodology became a fully integrated qualitative-quantitative research method which has been applied to a wide range of issues, many of them reported in Munton et al. (1999). The availability of the manual also enabled a large number of students from trainees on SFT MSc courses and PhDs to conduct successful research projects.

3.2 An Attempt to Manualise the Recognition of Attachment Processes in Family Discourse

One outcome of our experience with the LACS was the discovery that family members expressed attributional beliefs at about two per minute during a 1 h therapy session. We then found that just reading through the list of over 100 extracted attributions gave great insight into how the family members construed each other's behaviours and how they anticipated that they would behave in future. Our experience has been that sharing the emerging patterns with the family could often be helpful in enabling them to achieve changes and resolution of misunderstanding and conflict. By this stage in the development of LFTRC we had developed a strong basis in attachment theory and particularly with Dorothy Heard joining the team from having worked in the Tavistock Institute with John Bowlby. We were also fortunate to participate in seminars organised by John Byng-Hall. During this phase Pat Crittenden (1995) provided training for some of the team in her method of detecting attachment patterns. So we took the extracted lists of attributions during family sessions and developed a system to identify and classify every kind of indication of an attachment process within the spoken attributions. In this case we moved directly to try to construct a manual for identifying attachment references through the process of jointly working through each family's attributions. In some sense the project was too successful in that we created a classification under ten headings with up to ten aspects of attachment in each. When we presented the work in the Byng-Hall seminars, John Bowlby suggested we should restrict our analyses to the categories to do with proximity, but by this stage we had already created a comprehensive account of the categories. We wrote a paper to report the method (Stratton et al., 1998) but found that the work to agree definitions and procedures for all of the categories was far beyond what we could manage. Our decision was that without manualising the decision processes so that they would be examinable by other therapists and researchers, we were not justified in claiming usability of the method and the paper was not published.

One conclusion from this experience is that a decision to create a manual should, at an early stage, estimate the amount of work required, double that estimate because it will be over-optimistic and decide whether it is practicable. Comparing the experiences with the attribution and the attachment manuals, it appears that a process of developing an effective system, testing that it works and then proceeding to formulating it into a manual that others could use, may be more functional than setting out to create a manual as the core of the project as we attempted with the attachment coding. In fact, the LFTRC systemic family therapy manual (reported in detail below) followed this process in that it started from the well-developed and established systemic family therapy that the training clinic had developed and then researched those processes to specify them in a manual.

Before turning to the Leeds Systemic Therapy Manual, we want to describe two more projects that are relevant to manualisation, and which might be instructive about significant aspects of the enterprise of creating a manual.

3.3 Family Therapy: Training and Practice

By the time that LFTRC had been in operation for 10 years, we had developed a coherent approach to systemic therapy through strong links with the Milan group, especially Gianfranco Cecchin and Luigi Boscolo, and KCC (Kensington Consultation Centre) in London especially with Peter and Susan Lang and John Burnham. By this stage although LFTRC had not yet set up a qualifying training, it had been running trainings in systemic practice for professionals such as psychotherapists, psychologists, social workers, care home staff, paediatricians and speech therapists. At the same time LFTRC was operating as a free clinic providing services to the National Health Service and other sources of referrals, with a prime objective of developing our skills for effective family therapy through mutual team supervision. This background led us to write our training manual (Stratton et al., 1990)[1] as part of the philosophy of making our achievements available while exposing them for critical consideration by others.

Our experience with the LACS Manual (above) was that publishers would not consider publishing a manual and so we offered *Family Therapy: Training and Practice* in the guise of a book. It was written, as are many therapy manuals, as an analysis and report of their practice by a team of therapists. As is often the case, it was a team with good grounds from their experiences as therapists and as trainers to believe their approaches were effective and worth making known. LFTRC had been set up in the Psychology Department of Leeds University in 1979, and all three authors also had a broad base in adult education and a particular focus on active autonomous learning (Stratton, 2005). A further source of background came from the work of Helga Hanks and Peter Stratton as external examiners for several UK courses through which we learned about the approaches to training in these institutions.

The book is structured in two sections. In the first section, we present the basic concepts, techniques and core skills in systemic family therapy, with examples and extensive use of exercises to illustrate and facilitate the introduction and use of theoretical ideas, and to provide a solid base of technique. In the second section, we

---

[1] In addition to the authors of the book, other members of LFTRC made major contributions to the training programme around which this book evolved, especially: Dick Agass, Dorothy Heard and Gill Tagg.

apply these concepts and skills to specialist issues. Here, as our main focus, we took child abuse, because of its centrality, and challenge, to much of the practice of social welfare and health agencies (Hanks et al., 1988; Preston-Shoot & Hanks, 1998). Other chapters were directed to taking systemics beyond the clinic for example to working in the home, with parents whose children had been hospitalised and to staff in residential settings; and to "close encounters in and between professional systems". The book differs from a classic manual in that although it was principle driven, it is less prescriptive and certainly not specifying proscribed practices.

Most relevant for this Handbook are perhaps the suggestions we made for users in different contexts. These suggestions are hopefully still useful for consideration when using any therapy manual. We first advised that the book had been written as a progression so that it would be unlikely to be useful to search for specific techniques out of context, but we also advised that it should not be followed rigidly. For example, we proposed that anyone using the book as the basis for a structured course is advised to start with the discussion in the final chapter of how the training can be evaluated so that these methods can "be built into their plans from the start".

A major feature of the book was that drawing on concepts of active autonomous learning (Kolb, 1983), all major items were accompanied by an exercise. These were clearly marked in the text with an instruction to stop reading at that point in order to undertake the exercise, with an accompanying message that subsequent text would be of limited value if the reader did not bring the experience of doing the exercise "We do not expect that simply reading the book will be very useful". (p. 5). Also, because we wrote the book to be useful both in training and by qualified practitioners, we included the caution: "if you are using the book outside of a structured training environment, we would urge you to take seriously the comments made about the importance of supervision in Chapter 8" (p. 5).

The introduction listed six contexts in which the book could be used, and offered recommendations about how to get the most benefit from it in each context. The core recommendations are summarised here because they encapsulate the ideas we had at that time of how to use systemic therapy manuals.

1. By an individual who has some training in systemic family therapy and who wants to refresh and extend their skills and understanding. Many of the exercises can be done by one person and some of the others will have figured in a similar form in other training. There are however several reasons why individual practice cannot be fully satisfactory, and if you are in this position, we would urge you to seek out a partner.
2. By two people who have some training, perhaps who work together, and who want to develop their abilities. Most of the exercises can be done in some form by two people, and the training will be particularly useful if the two can work as a team as they start to implement the ideas in their practice.
3. By (short, focused) training courses. This is likely to be the most common use, ... the advantage that the book offers to experienced systemic trainers is that it provides a coherent progression in which all of the exercises needed for the development of the trainee's skills are integrated. Many of the exercises can be undertaken during the periods between training sessions so that the contact time can be used most productively. ... the material of Section 1 can be covered to the extent that a trainee with a good basic training in therapeutic skills, and experience of working with families, could take it away and develop it in a supportive setting, after such a course.

4. By experienced trainers who may wish to use the material selectively to incorporate into their courses.
5. By mutual training groups. We believe that a group of practitioners who work together to consult to families, could use the book for mutual training. In saying this we must hasten to point out that we have no experience of such usage, but the origins of the LFTRC and of many other family therapy institutions that became established before there was any formal training available, suggest that a mutual training model can be very effective.
6. As a reference. The book is not intended to work as a source of reference when you first acquire it. The various sections are too interdependent, and one of our more important objectives is to build up a systemic understanding and competence in a coherent incremental way. The result is that looking up a topic in isolation is likely to be unrewarding. However, once you have worked through the book, each of the topics should have acquired a rich meaning, and it will then be possible to use it for repeated reference as you progressively acquire experience. (Stratton et al., 1990, pp. 5–6)

The approach of this manual, using concepts of active autonomous learning, was developed into the form of a learning spiral by Stratton (2005) and has continued to be developed. Its most recent manifestation being a chapter (with extensive exercises for the reader) in this case combined with current thinking about the development of the self of the therapist anew in each encounter (Stratton & Hanks, 2016). As part of a guide to systemic supervision (Vetere & Stratton, 2016), the chapter title offers "processes of learning that enable the practitioner to create a self that is equipped for higher levels of professional mastery".

3.4 The Leeds Systemic Family Therapy Manual (LSFT Manual)

3.4.1 Creation of the LFTRC Manual

Why Was a Comprehensive Systemic Therapy Manual Needed in the UK?

Existing outcome trials had taken manuals as a core design feature, to detail the content and process of the therapeutic intervention in order to ensure treatment fidelity and consistency in the models being compared. Progression to more specific efficacy research, investigating which components of family therapy are effective for which circumstances, was hindered by the lack of specificity in defining interventions. This decreased the utility of research in informing service planning and clinical work. Many CBT manuals already existed, and these focussed on specific psychiatric disorders such as depression or anxiety. The ethos of some family therapy schools questioned the prescriptive nature of manuals, so a manual for SFT was treated with caution and scepticism. Systemic therapists were wary of manuals which embraced intrapersonal psychiatric definitions of mental health problems and called for some definition of the content or process of therapy which was by its nature more systemic, interpersonal, creative and transdiagnostic. Such a manual required sufficient standardisation of procedure for the therapy to be accurately described and replicated. As family therapy encompassed a wide range of therapies, there was an urgent need to specify more clearly the key components of SFT in the UK. For example, Shadish et al. (1993) classified the 71 family therapy studies in one meta-analysis into 22 different theoretical models and still had 7 studies left over that they were unable to classify.

For manuals to be successfully used in outcome research, they require a comprehensive adherence protocol. This measures the ability of the therapist to comply with the prescriptions of the manual and ensures the standardisation of treatment so essential in forming specific conclusions about the effectiveness of therapy. Previous attempts at adherence measures in family therapy had been basic, and often reliant on self-report measures by therapists (Hogue et al., 1996). It was important that any SFT manual in the UK had an adherence protocol which could be reliably applied using observational methods.

In 1997 the Leeds Family Therapy Centre (LFTRC) in the UK set out to develop a systemic family therapy manual and accompanying adherence protocol. The project was funded by a Medical Research Council Grant employing Helen Pote for a year to research the training clinic's best practice and create and test the manual. The aim was to develop a manual which was prescriptive enough for therapeutic outcome research whilst also being palatable to systemic therapists. It was to capture the essence of their work, without ignoring the richness and diversity of their ideas and practices. The full manual can be accessed at: https://www.researchgate.net/publication/338389429_Leeds_Systemic_Family_Therapy_Manual.

Research Process

The first step to creating a manual was to obtain a detailed account of representative good practice. To do this the therapeutic practice of the Leeds Family Therapy Research Centre (LFTRC) was tabulated and observed. LFTRC used a form of systemic family therapy which has grown out of the Milan school (Boscolo et al., 1987) and which is representative of practice in many parts of the world. The Centre had been chosen as being illustrative of current practice in the UK, and this assumption was tested through consultation at each stage of the research process with five major family therapy centres around the UK.

In approaching the task, we had three principles in mind:

(a) The manual should be both a research and practice tool, grounded in current systemic practice through the UK.
(b) The manual should have an interpersonal focus in describing the intervention and not be constrained by individual, intrapersonal definitions of mental health problems.
(c) The manual should be developed using a research process which was systemically informed. Using qualitative process research with opportunities for systemic practitioners to contribute to its development and reflect on its utility.

The research itself was systemically informed by the process-outcome research methods described by Sprenkle and Moon (1996). We followed a six-step mixed-method design to develop the manual.

1. *Therapist interviews*: Following a literature review of current process and outcome literature, semi-structured interviews were conducted with five senior therapists at LFTRC, using the Brief Structured Recall method (BSR, Elliott & Shapiro, 1988). A total of ten BSR interviews across different stages of therapy (beginning, middle and end) were completed and analysed in two ways:

   - Quantitatively: Ratings of therapist intentions were summarised using descriptive statistics.
   - Qualitatively: Free text responses were analysed using Grounded Theory (Strauss & Corbin, 1990) to describe therapist activity divided into approach, method, technique (See Burnham et al., Chap. 32 in this volume) and family events which triggered these activities.

The information generated by the interviews was grouped in five key areas: 1. therapist intentions; 2. systemic guiding principles; 3. systemic methods and techniques; 4. indirect work; 5. proscribed practice.

The ten theoretical concepts which therapists identified as systemic guiding principles informing their work were critical to the development of the manual. They steered therapists to the overall stance of the manual before specific techniques were detailed. The principles were:

- Keeping a *systems focus*
- Attending to *circularity* in the form of repetitive patterns of behaviour that develop within systems
- Considering new *connections and patterns* between beliefs and behaviours within systems
- Concentrating on *narratives and language*, constructed by, around, and between individuals and the system itself which construct the reality of their everyday lives
- *Constructivism*, understanding that people form autonomous meaning systems and will interpret and make sense of information from this frame of reference
- *Social constructionism*, utilising the idea that meaning is created in the social interactions that take place between people and is thus context dependent and constantly changing
- Attention to *cultural context*, the cultural meanings and narratives within which people live their lives, including issues of race, gender, disability and class etc.
- *Co-constructed practice*, the therapist should take a reflexive stance in relation to the power differentials that exist within the therapeutic relationship, and within the family relationships, appreciating that in therapy reality is co-constructed between the therapist (and team) and the client
- *Self-reflexivity*, the therapist should be alert to their own constructions, functioning and prejudices and apply systemic thinking to themselves

- *Strengths and solutions*, taking a non-pathologising, positive view of the family system, and the current difficulties they are struggling with

2. *Observational rating of therapy sessions*: Analysis of the BSR data was used to develop a therapy observational rating system, with categories to rate therapists' intentions, methods and techniques. This was applied to video material of family therapy session to check whether therapists were actually doing what they had identified as important at different stages of therapy. The ratings also aimed to tabulate family behaviours which triggered therapists' behaviours.

Fifteen-minute therapy segments were rated from 15 randomly selected LFTRC family therapy sessions (5 each from beginning, middle and end sessions). The referred client in these sessions was between 10 and 20 years old. The rating scale had reasonable reliability; inter-rater reliability for therapist intentions and techniques was 0.75 with variability across first, middle and end sessions (range across sessions 0.40–0.90) (Pote et al., 2003).

Overall, therapists were very sensitive to their activities in therapy, as observed by an "independent" researcher. Therapy goals and therapist interventions were consistent between therapist descriptions and observational ratings. The findings from the video observations illustrated how therapists achieve different goals by using different types of interventions. More complex goals were associated with circular questioning, and statements were used to clearly distinguish team and therapists' ideas. The analysis also highlighted how therapists' interventions changed across the course of therapy. These differences were sufficiently clear to give a basis for structuring the prescriptions in the manual in terms of opening, mid-therapy and ending sessions.

3. *Consultation with family centres*: Five family therapy centres in the UK were consulted to gather feedback and check the representativeness of the LFTRC specification. Data from these focus group consultations were analysed quantitatively and qualitatively using transcripts of the meetings (Grounded Theory – Strauss & Corbin 1990). The data from the focus groups was synthesised with the LFTRC specification to form a draft manual of systemic family therapy practice for the UK.
4. *Use of manual in practice:* Three family therapists were trained to deliver therapy using the draft manual. Questionnaires were used to obtain feedback on the utility of the manual in practice. Aspects of practice used by therapists but not covered by the Manual were added to form the final manual.
5. *Development of an adherence measure*: A measure of adherence to protocol was developed using the video recorded sessions from the therapist using the manual in practice (total sessions = 5).

The findings from these observations were interesting. The observational ratings also added other specific details at a much more micro-analytic level. It allowed me (HP) to take a meta stance and consider the patterns which were apparent across therapists' practice. Using a "pick-and-mix" metaphor, to look overall at the bag, and the commonalities between the sweets. Observations from this process highlighted practices such as therapist's gradually increasing focus on family solutions and successes, across the process of therapy. It also found an increasing use of circularity in therapist's language and questioning, once they had connected with the family, and gained initial descriptions of the family's concerns.

3.5 Outline of the LFTRC Manual

As differences had been shown to exist temporally between initial, middle and end sessions of therapy, the manual was structured in this manner. The manual structure is shown in Table 3.2.

Therapist goals were identified across the course of therapy alongside interventions to achieve these goals (see Table 3.3).

Table 3.2 Overall structure of the manual

Section	Description
1. Introduction	An introduction to the scope of the manual as a tool for outcome research, and guidelines on how to follow and use the manual
2. Guiding principles	An outline of the theoretical principles which should be informing therapists
3. Outline of therapeutic change	A hypothesised model of change, which was drawn from LFTRC practice
4. Outline of therapist interventions	A summary of the central interventions therapists should use across the course of therapy, for example linear and circular questioning
5. Therapeutic setting	Information for therapists and therapy teams about the methods they should use to organise the work with families, for example the use of screens and videos
6. Initial session guidelines	Specific outline of therapy goals for initial sessions and the interventions appropriate in achieving these, for example gathering family information through the use of linear questions
7. Middle session guidelines	Specific outline of therapy goals for middle sessions and the interventions appropriate in achieving these, for example, working towards change at the level of behaviours and beliefs through reframing
8. End session guidelines	Specific outline of therapy goals for end sessions and the interventions appropriate in achieving these, for example, collaborative ending decision using linear and circular questions
9. Indirect work	Outline of the areas of indirect systemic work that will be helpful in supporting the direct work with the family
10. Proscribed practices	Information regarding elements of practice that should not be common in systemic work
11. Samples of correspondence	Examples of letters to families and professionals that should be used by therapists in following the manual

Table 3.3 Therapist goals for each stage of the therapy

	Beginning	Middle	End
Goals	Eliciting family information Hearing the family's view of the difficulties Exploration of beliefs	Eliciting family information Hearing the family's views about the difficulties Continuing to explore beliefs Eliciting information about the wider system Eliciting information about family patterns of decision making and interaction Reframing difficulties	Exploring beliefs Successes and solutions
Central intervention	Linear questions	Circular questions Linear questions Statements	Circular questions Linear questions Statements

3.6 Impact of the LSFT Manual

The manual has been used and adapted for four main purposes: as a research tool in RCTs; as a teaching tool for systemic training; to support the practice of qualified therapists; and in the development of competence frameworks.

3.6.1 Research Using the LSFT Manual

Several international research groups have used and adapted the LSFT Manual to describe the standardised delivery of practice in research trials to evaluate the efficacy of family therapy. For example, Lock et al. (2012) undertook an RCT of treatment for adolescent eating disorders which compared the Maudsley-originated Family-Based Treatment (FBT) manual with Systemic Family Therapy (SyFT) based on the Leeds manual. They found no statistically significant differences between treatment groups for eating disorder symptoms or comorbid psychiatric disorders at the end of treatment (EOT) and follow-up. Remission rates and indicators of psychological health were similar across interventions, but FBT did perform better than SFT on some outcomes, such as leading to significantly faster weight gain early in treatment and significantly fewer days in the hospital. However, an exploratory moderator analysis found that SyFT led to greater weight gain than did FBT for participants with more severe obsessive-compulsive symptoms (Agras et al., 2014). This study also reported improvements in a variety of indicators of psychological health, but these were not statistically tested and: "there was no evidence that these changes were greater in FBT than comparison treatments [e.g., Adolescent Focused Therapy and Systemic Family Therapy". Therefore, both interventions had their strengths and were offering similar success for adolescents struggling with eating disorders and their families.

Another major RCT comparing manualised systemic family therapy with treatment as usual for adolescents who self-harm, used an adapted version of the LSFT Manual to suit the specific issues of this population. The result was the Self Harm in Adolescence Treatment manual (SHIFT, Boston et al., 2009), along with an adherence manual based on this version of the Manual (Masterson et al., 2016). This substantial project has generated a significant body of data and a correspondingly large number of publications which continue at the time of writing. The main findings were that the manualised systemic therapy did not produce a significant improvement in self-harming compared with good quality treatment as usual but had other therapeutic effects such as an improvement in family relationships. The main report is by Cottrell et al. (2018). A helpful comparison of the LFTRC and the SHIFT manuals is used by Davies (2019) for a general critique of manualisation of systemic practice.

Clinical research centres internationally have also adapted the LSFT manual, utilising the basic manual structure and the rigorous process research methodology developed at Leeds to map their own systemic practice in the form of a manual. For example, Carrot, Godart and colleagues at the Institut Mutualiste Montsouris, Paris, adapted the LSFT Manual to reflect their practice with adolescents with eating disorders. This forms part of an ongoing international trial regarding the efficacy of different family interventions with this client group (Carrot et al., 2017).

In the years since it was published, the LSFT Manual has been used as a starting point for other researchers to develop their own manuals.

Liu and Miller (2013) developed their manual for systemic family therapy in China from the LSFT Manual and the London depression manual (Jones & Asen, 2000). In distinguishing between the ways the two manuals were developed, the first by researching actual practice, and the second through a standard process of experts reporting their best practice, they also caution on using these UK-based manuals in other cultures, reminding us of the importance of context in the application of manuals:

> Jones and Asen (2000) produced a manual for systemic therapy of couples struggling with depression. However, their manual was compiled based on their subjective clinical experience and not on empirical analysis of daily therapy practice. Through analysing representative systemic practice in the UK, Pote et al. (2003) manualised systemic family therapy into a structural and flexible procedure. Nevertheless, all the therapists and cases in their study came from Great Britain and generalisation of their conclusion to other cultures should be cautioned (Liu & Miller, 2013, p. 449).

3.6.2 Uses of the LSFT Manual in Training

Within the UK the authors and the broader team at Leeds have used the manual widely for Masters and Doctoral level training for both family therapists and other psychological practitioners using systemic models, such as clinical psychologists. Feedback from this work has been extremely positive, with training programmes evidencing an increase in systemic competences following use of the manual as a training tool. The international reach of the LSFT manual as a training tool was significantly enhanced by two published translations. We, and many users, are enormously grateful to Ismael Otero who made a Spanish version available in 2004, and Guido Rocca who provided an Italian version in 2019.

The Spanish version by Ismael Otero C[2] has been available since 2004 and has so far been downloaded 36,000 times. It is unlikely that anything like this number originated in Chile, and we know that the manual has been uploaded to websites and blogs in Ecuador, Peru and Mexico but we suspect it has been downloaded throughout the Spanish-speaking world. For example, a therapist in Valencia, Spain reported: "I use your wonderful Manual (Spanish version) all the time, for teaching and supervision."

Taking Chile as an example of how usage of the manual will be influenced by the national context, Ismael Otero reports that "students are using it at the start of clinical practice – using the manual gives students a degree of security to know what they are doing. Because they can start practicing once qualified from the (five year) undergraduate degree, where the training is entirely theoretical, the Manual shows them how to plan treatment, what techniques to use. … The Leeds manual was and still is useful not only on professional training postgraduate (cohorts 30) but UG (cohorts 60)". Also, the national child protection service in Chile (SENAME, 2019) has an official protocol on how to proceed in the therapy room that is based on the Leeds Manual. However, the manual has not been used in research because of the lack of financial support for psychotherapy research in the health system in Chile.

Guido Rocca and Jessica Lampis (personal communication, 2020)[3] offer the following perspective from experiences of using their translation in Italy:

> We think this manual has important implications for the clinical practice and training of systemic psychotherapists in the Italian context.

---

[2] Equipo de Psicología Sistémica Constructivista EPSIC, Departamento de Psicología, Universidad de Chile.

[3] Jessica Lampis* is a research fellow and lecturer in Dynamic Psychology at the Department of Pedagogy, Psychology, Philosophy, University of Cagliari, Italy – jlampis@unica.it

Guido Rocca* is Clinical Psychologist and Psychotherapist at Italian NHS – Cagliari, Italy – guidorocca@gmail.com

*Responsible for scientific research by IEFCOSTRE (European Institute of Systemic Counseling and Relational Therapy – Cagliari, Italy) – cagliari@iefcostre.org

The Italian version of the Leeds Systemic Family Therapy Manual can be downloaded from the website www.iefcostre.it

1. Primarily, it precisely defines a theoretical and clinical intervention model that can permit clinicians to clearly focus the specificities of the systemic approach and setting, allowing them to distinguish it from other forms of psychotherapy. It can also allow comparison between systemic clinicians of different cultural and theoretical backgrounds (structural, strategical, analogical etc.), favouring the sharing and synthesis of what is truly systemic and also offering the possibility to enhance and promote the cultural and methodological specificities of different systemic training institutes.
2. Furthermore, it can be used in systemic psychotherapy training to define (in a non-dogmatic way) the general and specific skills of systemic therapists. It would be important that the acquisition of these skills be included as a training objective in the official training programmes of the institutes and be monitored during the training.
3. Finally, it can represent a theoretical and practical basis for projecting randomised controlled trial (RCT) studies and, more generally, for planning research into evaluating the outcome of systemic treatments and the therapeutic alliance.

They also reflect on some issues related to departures from specific aspects of the manual in order to adapt it to some of the theoretical and clinical specificities of their institute:

1. In our clinical model, the trigenerational perspective and the principles of developmental theory and life span theory represent a basis for a theoretical and precise clinical intervention model (e.g. the genogram is a specific technique for working with families and not simply a reconstruction of the family history carried out by the team during the pre- and post-session). In this model, symptoms acquire fullness of meaning when the significant connections between emotions, thoughts and events are reconstructed in individual and family history.
2. Furthermore, we pay close attention to family myths, representations and symbolic dimensions underlying the behaviours and beliefs in the family. These dimensions are explored, in the therapeutic setting, through a series of techniques that use analogical/non-verbal language (e.g. family sculptures) (Personal communication to PS, 2020).

3.7 Reflections on the Development of an SFT Manual in the UK

We were aware that manuals are often criticised for the lack of grounding in real clinical practice, and represent unrealistic ideals of therapeutic practice. Throughout the process of developing the LSFT manual, we therefore drew on actual therapy encounters. The data collected which formed the basis of the manual, and examples used in the manual, were all taken from the clinical material of practising family therapists. By developing the manual directly from the successful work of therapists in practice, it is more likely to reflect actual therapy than an unrecognisable form of treatment. This makes the manual grounded and meaningful, whilst still achieving the rigour required for adherence protocols.

The process of developing a manual through a reflective research process was invaluable. The varied practice of the research team and the family therapy centres we consulted enabled contrast in descriptions of therapy which allowed us to achieve greater richness and clarity in the final manual produced. In many ways the research network approach mirrored many of the reflective assets systemic family therapy teams provide for therapists.

During the construction of the manual, many questions were raised by systemic therapists and researchers about the feasibility of a manual for SFT which could meet the prescriptive requirements of a manual without being reductionist and restrictive to the variety and creativity characteristic of systemic models.

Social constructionist approaches provided a strong challenge in developing a manual. Defining each therapeutic conversation as unique, created by the current thoughts, feelings and contexts of therapist and family, somewhat contradicts a manualised approach. We risked creating a modernist document in a therapeutic world, which was increasingly being influenced by post-modern ideas. However, from the interviews and observations, we conducted of therapy both cross-sectionally, across different therapists/families, and longitudinally, with the same therapists/families over time, we did find some common repeating patterns. It was these common patterns that we felt could helpfully contribute to a manual, and form a prescriptive base, from which therapists could develop their own creative, unique components with each family.

Another dilemma was whether a manual should attempt to encompass the broad range of theoretical models and techniques under the umbrella of systemic family therapy. Complete inclusivity of approaches was impossible, and we pragmatically confined the descriptions of practice to those that were most represented within the clinics at the Leeds Family Therapy and Research Centre. Thus, the systemic practice described was more reliant on Post-Milan and Narrative models, and is focussed on therapeutic work with families across the lifespan, rather than organisational, couple or individual consultations. This led to varied responses from other family therapy centres about whether the manual characterised their practice. Though most recognised the practice in the manual, we met with a few therapists who were practising in a manner quite distinct from the practice described in Leeds. Their practice was drawing on many more structural concepts than the practice we had described. Although they welcomed some of the generic systemic ideas in the manual, they felt it was not capturing some important elements of their practice. This begs the question of whether systemic manuals have to be school specific? In many ways we felt that they did not, there were common ideas shared across many schools, and we were able to develop a more generic model of change which excluded rather fewer systemic therapy orientations than we first thought.

Another tension was needing the manual to be specific enough to ensure coherent replicative practice for research trials but not so prescriptive that it was not useful to practitioners. Silverman (1996) was pessimistic about manuals being little more than "cookbooks", feeling they focus on techniques at the expense of therapist variables to deliver a form of treatment that does not reflect the actual process of therapy. In the Brief Structured Recall analysis, therapists identified a number of goals or intentions that they were trying to achieve through the course of therapy. These varied across the course of therapy and were used to form a task analysis model, similar to those prescribed in other models of therapy, such as cognitive behavioural work. However, in this manual, to move away from a sole focus on techniques, we have enriched the manual by discussion of theoretical principles and models of change, we outlined broad and flexible goals and developed any techniques described through the use of multiple clinical examples.

3.8 Using Manuals to Specify the Competences of Systemic Therapists

An application of the LSFT manual was its contribution to a UK Government initiative to delineate a full specification of competent psychotherapy practice. The Leeds Systemic Family Therapy Manual played a significant role in the enterprise that included the authors of this chapter to create a comprehensive specification of the competences of systemic psychotherapies. This project serves as an example of using manuals to generate a mapping of the competences used by therapists in successful practice, and an exploration of potential relationships of manuals and specifications of competences.

The project was run by Steve Pilling and Anthony Roth of University College London and four major forms of therapy were selected: CBT, psychoanalytic/psychodynamic, systemic and humanistic. The systemic arm was run by an Expert Reference Group (ERG) chaired by Peter Stratton. The procedure was to identify all published manuals that had been the basis for research that had found the specified methods to be effective, the rationale being that this ensured that the manuals reported competences of proven effectiveness. They should be active ingredients for success within therapeutic interventions while linking process to outcome. While this did not guarantee that all of the contents of each manual contributed to the effectiveness, it did give reassurance about the overall approach. Two researchers, Emma Silver and Natasha Nascimento, analysed the selected manuals to generate a comprehensive list of the competences from each manual, and the ERG synthesised the growing list to create a map of the *competences required to deliver effective Systemic Therapies* (Pilling et al., 2010). The map is available at:

> https://www.ucl.ac.uk/pals/research/cehp/research-groups/core/competence-frameworks/Systemic_Therapy.

The map of systemic competences is interactive and provides two layers of specificity, with the first layer providing an overview of competences and additional detail and definition, then providing through hyperlinks, more detail for each competence.

To explore the map, click on the "map of systemic competences" (not the title but the map itself). This provides the full interactive map in which, if you click on any entry, it opens up much more detail about that topic. The map mainly functions as an overview – it is not the full list of competences. From the map itself – placing the cursor over any of the boxes in the map links you to the competences. To see the full list of competences in each domain, click on the header (e.g. if you want to see all

Table 3.4 Example of a "metacompetence" *ability to hold a non-pathologising view of the system*

An ability to take a non-pathologising, positive view of the system including the ability:
To recognise and work with the strengths of the clients(s)
To work with the client(s) to generate potential solutions
An ability to balance an externalising, non-blaming stance with one which helps clients to take responsibility for their actions, where this is appropriate
An ability for the therapist to maintain a stance of curiosity when working with colleagues and with clients and to convey this stance to clients
An ability to convey this stance to clients through the experience of the methods employed in systemic therapy

the competences for generic therapeutic competences, click on the box with this label). To give an indication of the level of specificity, Table 3.4 provides the detail of an ability to hold a non-pathologising view of the system from the domain of the "metacompetences". To see all the competences associated with a specific activity, click on the relevant box. To see the competence lists independently of the map (arranged by domain), click on the relevant link:

- Generic Therapeutic Competences
- Basic Systemic Competences
- Specific Systemic Techniques
- Problem Specific Competences/Specific Adaptations
- Metacompetences

A current example of a use of the Map is the work of Butler et al. (2020) which drew on it when creating a Systemic Family Practice-Systemic Competency Scale, now called the Systemic Practice Scale (SPS). The authors make a strong case, ethically as well as politically, not just to specify but to go on to measure therapeutic competences:

> Ensuring that practitioners are competent in the therapies they deliver is important for training, therapeutic outcomes and ethical practice. …. Initial reliability assessment of the SPS with twenty-eight supervisors of systemic practice evaluating students' competence using an online recording of a family therapy session is detailed. The SPS was found to be a reliable measure of systemic competence across training settings. (Butler et al., 2020, p. 79)

3.9 Conclusion: Indications for Systemic Approaches to Manualisation from the LFTRC Experiences

We all use manuals in everyday life and others that are specific to our work. Examples might include cookery recipes; instruction manuals for assembling and using a new product; child care manuals; car and other repair manuals; Health and Safety procedures etc. This chapter demonstrates that a research-oriented training clinic may develop a similar range of products that fulfil the purposes of a manual. A relevant factor for LFTRC may have been that its research positioning naturally creates an orientation to making its outputs public as this is a fundamental criterion for research activities, and a positive attitude to manualisation stems naturally from this (Stratton, 2013).

In this chapter, we have described the rationale, processes in creating and final form of five of the different kinds of manual emanating from LFTRC. The sixth, for the SCORE Index of Family Functioning, being somewhat different, is described separately in Chap. 17. As an orientation to the progression, the manuals are listed in Table 3.1.

As the work on these manuals proceeded, it became clear that most manuals are written to be used in research by therapists who are already well versed in the fundamentals of the therapy, and therefore, these very basic aspects are not spelled out in the manuals. However, in the Handbook, many manuals are reported that are closely tied to training, and in these cases, it is appropriate to include this more basic material. For example, the Leeds Systemic Family Therapy Manual Section 3.9 does provide guidance for making appointments, setting up the first session, taking notes etc.

We have also learned that making a manual public exposes the work to scrutiny and to generating surprising and informative feedback from people who have used it. Both responses can be used to improve the manual. We have also found that by making a manual freely available (so long as its origin is recognised), it can come to be used more widely than the clinic that produced it. Users have been within our own country and internationally, and in some cases translated versions are made. This recognition has been one of the motivations for this Handbook which has aimed to make more widely known the manuals and proto-manuals that we know are widespread especially in training contexts.

A full specification of a qualifying training can function as a manual. It should be progressively adapted through experience of trainees and developments in the field, as described in several chapters of this Handbook. But it can be argued that it is an aspiration, and it progressively builds to the complete requirement. The LSFT manual started from the actual functioning of a clinic that itself had undergone the development engendered by establishing a qualifying training, including meeting the criteria of the validating bodies (AFT and UKCP). It then took the empirical step of researching and analysing in detail the actual therapeutic processes of the clinic and formulating these as a manual that could be disseminated to the whole field. But at a much less formal level, we believe that many training clinics could easily consolidate their practice training into a document that therapists who have qualified from that course could use to maintain the quality of their practice in their future careers.

We hope that by presenting these varied examples of the manualisation of the work of LFTRC, we may encourage other systemic practitioners to recognise that they have already generated valuable material that could be articulated and made more widely available.

Acknowledgements We would like to extend our thanks to all the therapists who have contributed to the thoughts and ideas contained in the manual. Particularly to the research team at Leeds Family Therapy and Research Centre: Peter Stratton, David Cottrell, Paula Boston, Helga Hanks and David Shapiro.

References

Agras, W. S., Lock, J., Brandt, H., Bryson, S., Dodge, E., Halmi, K., et al. (2014). Comparison of 2 family therapies for adolescent anorexia nervosa: A randomized parallel trial. *JAMA Psychiatry, 71*(11), 1279–1286. https://doi.org/10.1001/jamapsychiatry.2014.1025

Bosocolo, L., Cecchin, G., Hoffamn, L., & Penn, P. (1987). *Milan systemic therapy: Conversations in theory and practice*. Basic Books.

Boston, P., Eisler, I., & Cottrell, D. (2009). *Systemic family therapy manual for adolescent self-harm*. Leeds University.

Brent, D. A., Holder, D., Kolko, D., Birmaher, B., Baugher, M., Roth, C., & Johnson, B. (1997). A clinical psychotherapy trial for adolescent depression comparing cognitive, family, and supportive treatments. *Archives of General Psychiatry, 54*, 877–885.

Butler, C., Sheils, E., Lask, J., Joscelyne, T., Pote, H., & Crossley, J. (2020). Measuring competence in systemic practice: Development of the 'systemic family practice – Systemic competency scale' (SPS). *Journal of Family Therapy, 42*, 79–99. https://doi.org/10.1111/1467-6427.12251

Brewin, C., MacCarthy, B., Duda, K., & Vaughn, C. E. (1991). Attribution and expressed emotion in the relatives of patients with schizophrenia. *Journal of Abnormal Psychology, 100*(4), 546–554.

Carr, A. (1991). Milan systemic family therapy; a review of ten empirical investigations. *Journal of Family Therapy, 13*, 237–263.

Carrot, B., Godart, N., Kaganski, I., Jeremic, Z., Duclos, J., Carletti, E., Radon, L., Van Effenterre, A., Gueguen, J., & Pote, H. (2017). *Development of a family therapy manual*. In European Council on eating disorders conference, Lilnius, Lithuania.

Cottrell, D. J., Wright-Hughes, A., Collinson, M., Boston, P., Eisler, I., Fortune, S., Graham, E. H., Green, J., House, A. O., Kerfoot, M., Owens, D. W., Saloniki, E. C., Simic, M., Lambert, F., Rothwell, J., Tubeuf, S., & Farrin, A. J. (2018). Effectiveness of systemic family therapy versus treatment as usual for young people after self-harm: A pragmatic, phase 3, multicentre, randomised controlled trial. *Lancet Psychiatry, 5*, 203–216. https://doi.org/10.1016/S2215-0366(18)30058-0

Crittenden, P. M. (1995). Attachment and psychopathology. In S. Goldberg, R. Muir, & J. Kerr (Eds.), *Attachment theory: Social, developmental, and clinical perspectives*. The Analytic Press.

Davies, B. (2019). Critique of manualized therapies: Systemic family therapy manual for adolescent self-harm. *Systemic Practice and Action Research, 32*(4), 403–409.

Elliott, R., & Shapiro, D. A. (1988). Brief structured recall: A more efficient method for studying significant therapy events. *British Journal of Medical Psychology, 61*, 141–153.

Fincham, F. D., Beach, S., & Nelson, G. (1987). Attribution processes in distressed and non-distressed couples: 3. Causal and responsibility attributions of spouse behavior. *Cognitive Therapy and Research, 11*, 71–86.

Hanks, H. G. I., Hobbs, C. J., & Wynne, J. (1988). Early signs and recognition of sexual abuse in the pre school child. In K. Browne, C. Davies, & P. M. Stratton (Eds.), *Early prediction and prevention of child abuse and neglect* (pp. 139–160). Wiley.

Hogue, A., Liddle, H. A., & Rowe, C. (1996). Treatment adherence process research in family therapy: A rationale and some practical guidelines. *Psychotherapy: Theory, Research, Practice, Training, 33*, 332–345.

Jones, E., & Asen, E. (2000). *Systemic couples therapy for depression*. London, UK: Karnac.

Lask, B., & Matthew, D. (1979). Childhood asthma: A controlled trial of family psychotherapy. *Archives of Disease in Childhood, 54*, 116–119.

Leff, J., Kuipers, L., Berkowitz, R., & Sturgeon, D. (1985). A controlled trial of social intervention in the families of schizophrenic patients: Two year followup. *British Journal of Psychiatry, 146*, 594–600.

Liu, L., & Miller, J. K. (2013). Miller systemic family psychotherapy in China: A qualitative analysis of therapy process. *Psychology and Psychotherapy: Theory, Research and Practice, 86*, 447–465.

Lock, J., Brandt, H., Woodside, B., Agras, S., Halmi, K., Johnson, C., Kaye, W., & Wilfley, D. (2012). From the research in anorexia nervosa (RIAN) group. Challenges in conducting a multi-site randomized clinical trial comparing treatments for adolescent anorexia nervosa. *The International Journal of Eating Disorders, 45*(2), 202–213. https://doi.org/10.1002/eat.20923

Kolb, D. (1983). *Experiential learning: Experience as the source of learning and development.* Prentice Hall.

Masterson, C., Barker, C., Jackson, D., & Boston, P. (2016). Constructing a SHIFT adherence measure (SAM): The development of a family therapy integrity measure for the SHIFT trial. *Journal of Family Therapy, 38*, 274–290.

Munton, A., Silvester, J., Stratton, P., & Hanks, H. (1999). *Attributions in action.* Wiley.

Nisbett, R. E., & Valins, R. S. (1970) Perceiving the causes of ones own behavior. In E. E. Jones, et al (Eds.), *Attribution: Perceiving the causes of behavior.*

Peterson, C., & Seligman, M. E. P. (1984). Causal explanations as a risk factor for depression: Theory and evidence. *Psychological Review, 91*, 347–374.

Pilling, S., Roth, A. D., & Stratton, P. (2010) *The competences required to deliver effective systemic therapies.* http://www.ucl.ac.uk/clinical-psychology/CORE/systemic_framework.htm

Pote, H., Stratton, P., Cottrell, D., Shapiro, D., & Boston, P. (2003). Systemic family therapy can be manualised: Research process and findings. *Journal of Family Therapy, 25*, 236–262.

Pote, H., Stratton, P., Cottrell, D., Boston, P., Shapiro, D., & Hanks, H. (2000). *The Leeds systemic family therapy manual*, Leeds, LFTRC. https://www.researchgate.net/publication/338389429_Leeds_Systemic_Family_Therapy_Manual.

Preston-Shoot, M., & Hanks, H. G. I. (1998). Social work practice with sexually abused children and foster parents. *PRACTICE Journal for Social Workers, 4*, 373–387.

Russell, G. F. M., Szmukler, G. I., Dare, C., & Eisler, I. (1987). An evaluation of family therapy in anorexia nervosa and bulimia nervosa. *Archives of General Psychiatry, 44*, 1047–1056.

SENAME Servicio Nacional de Menores, dependant of the Justice and Human Rights Ministery. (2019). Accessed at https://www.sename.cl/web/wp-content/uploads/2019/05/08-protocolo-sala-terapia.pdf

Shadish, W. R., Montgomery, L. M., Wilson, P., Wilson, M. R., Bright, I., & Okwumabua, T. (1993). Effects of family and marital psychotherapies: A meta-analysis. *Journal of Consulting and Clinical Psychology, 61*, 992–1002.

Silvester, J., Bentovim, A., Stratton, P., & Hanks, H. (1995). Using spoken attributions to classify abusive families. *Child Abuse and Neglect, 19*, 1221–1232.

Simpson, L. (1991). The comparative efficacy of Milan therapy for disturbed children and their families. *Journal of Family Therapy, 13*, 267–284.

Silverman, W. (1996). Cookbooks, manuals and paint by numbers: Psychotherapy in the 90s. *Psychotherapy, 33*, 207–215.

Sprenkle, D. H., & Moon, S. M. (1996). *Research methods in family therapy.* The Guilford Press.

Stratton, P. M., Heard, D. H., Hanks, H. G., Munton, A. G., Brewin, C. R., & Davidson, C. (1986). Coding causal beliefs in natural discourse. *British Journal of Social Psychology, 25*, 299–313.

Stratton, Hanks, & Heard. (1998). A *Methodology to study family attachments communicated through causal attributional statements.* Leeds Family Therapy and Research Centre, Dept of Psychology, University of Leeds.

Stratton, P., Munton, A.G., Hanks, H., Heard, D. H. & Davidson, C. (1988a) *Leeds Attributional Coding System (LACS) Manual* (133 pp.) LFTRC, Leeds.

Stratton, P., Munton, A. G., Hanks, H., Heard, D. H., & Davidson, C. (1988b). *Leeds Attributional Coding System (LACS) Manual* (133 pp.). LFTRC, Leeds.

Stratton, P., Preston-Shoot, M. & Hanks, H. (1990) *Family therapy: Training & practice* (156 pp). Birmingham: Venture Press.

Stratton, P. M., & Swaffer, R. (1988) Maternal causal beliefs for abused and handicapped children. *Journal of Reproductive and Infant Psychology, 6*, 201–216.

Stratton, P., Silver, E., Nascimento, N., McDonnell, L., Powell, G., & Nowotny, E. (2015). Couples and family therapy in the previous decade – What does the evidence tell us? *Contemporary Family Therapy, 27*, 1–12. https://doi.org/10.1007/s10591-014-9314-6

Stratton, P. (2003a). Causal attributions during therapy I: Responsibility and blame. *Journal of Family Therapy, 25*, 134–158.

Stratton, P. (2003b). Causal attributions during therapy II: Reconstituted families and parental blaming. *Journal of Family Therapy, 25*, 159–178.

Stratton, P. (2013). Manuals: A secure base for playful therapy? *Human Systems: The Journal of Therapy, Consultation and Training, 24*, 176–187.

Stratton, P., Reibstein, J., Lask, J., Singh, R., & Asen, E. (2011). Competences and occupational standards for systemic family and couples therapy. *Journal of Family Therapy, 33*, 123–143.

Stratton, P., & Hanks, H. (2016). Personal and professional development as processes of learning that enable the practitioner to create a self that is equipped for higher levels of professional mastery. In A. Vetere & P. Stratton (Eds.), *Interacting selves* (pp. 7–32). Brunner-Routledge.

Stratton, P. (2005). A model to coordinate understanding of active autonomous learning. *Journal of Family Therapy, 27*(3), 217–236.

Strauss, A., & Corbin, J. (1990). *Basics of qualitative research: Grounded theory procedures and techniques*. Sage.

Vetere, A., & Stratton, P. (Eds.). (2016). *Interacting selves: Systemic solutions for personal and professional development in counselling and psychotherapy*. Brunner-Routledge.

Chapter 4
Co-creating 'Fluid Manuals' for Feedback-Informed Systemic Therapy and Collaborative Research

Robert van Hennik

4.1 Introduction

In this chapter I present a research-based account of designing and practising manualised systemic family therapy and doing practice-based, collaborative work.

Some time ago my colleague Bruno Hillewaere and I were asked to start providing standardised, evidence-based systemic therapy. In reviewing the range of standardised approaches that were available at the time, we decided we could not commit to a single model or treatment manual. Our experience suggested to us that in times when therapy derives its legitimacy from control, standardised protocols and benchmarking, little attention is paid to the therapist's improvisations, and those small, unpredictable and non-replicable differences can make the difference for family members. Accordingly, we decided to develop, describe and research our own family therapy practice that was full of improvisations in response to the exchanges that take place, from one moment to the next, in the context of family therapy.

We co-created our 'fluid manual' FITS (Feedback-Informed Therapy within Systems) as a Practice Based Evidence Based Practice (van Hennik & Hillewaere, 2017). Practice Based Evidence Based Practice implies that no therapy is provided without measuring its effects and no research is done outside of the practice itself. The therapist is both practitioner and researcher and involves clients as co-researchers. The therapist and clients examine the effects of their collaboration. The output of research is input for therapy in the 'collaborative learning community' constituted together.

R. van Hennik (✉)
University of Bedfordshire, Luton, UK

Centrum voor Gezinsbehandeling, Dordrecht, The Netherlands
e-mail: rovhennik@icloud.com

In this chapter I illustrate the creative process of co-creating 'fluid manuals' for feedback-informed systemic therapy and collaborative research. I will describe a process of co-creating 'fluid manuals', substantiated by collaborative practice-based research in three steps: (1) Co-creating a collaborative learning community, (2) co-creating a 'fluid manual', with agreed-upon steps in a road map and (3) doing collaborative research, learning how to learn, and making a difference that matters. I show how therapists can produce Practice Based Evidence Based Practice through collaborative and practice-based research. In a way I manualise how to develop 'fluid manuals' for therapy and research. I hope to inspire systemic practitioners to manualise and research their own practices and develop effective Practice Based Evidence Based Practices.

4.2 'Fluid Manual' as a Navigation Tool in Complex Systems

The social worlds we operate in are complex and I believe they cannot be described in terms of a single organisational principle. Social systems are non-linear complex systems, 'unities of differences' (Guattari, 1996). Small changes may have dramatic effects and generate a great deal of complex behaviour, because they are amplified repeatedly by self-reinforcing feedback (Capra & Luisi, 2014). This means that control and structure are counter-productive and have a paradoxical effect: the more we seek to control a symptom, the more the symptom ends up controlling us. Transformation in complex non-linear systems cannot be predicted or controlled by plan or through instruction. Only difference can trigger a response (Bateson, 1979). It is hardly possible to create models that mirror the complexity of social life, models that we can use for prediction, control and solving problems in complex non-linear systems.

A living system needs both sufficient order and sufficient disorder in order to remain an identifiable and flexible entity, interconnected and open to change. A living system unifies unrelated parts, without totalizing them. Guattari (1996) speaks of the *chaosmos*. Living systems are autopoietic, self-organising or self-learning systems. Systems conserve and develop manners of living, make and break patterned habits, through generations and within bio-cultural contexts that permit their existence (Maturana & Verden-Zoller, 2008). They do so through feedback mechanisms. Feedback is classified as positive or negative on the basis of its effect on the system, not on its content. The effect of negative feedback is to maintain structural constancy (morphostatic), while positive feedback produces a deviation in the variability of response-abilities, structural change, through intra-action (morphogenic).

The systemic therapist has to improvise and respond in a 'fitting' manners to particular circumstances (Shotter, 2007). As these circumstances evolve spontaneously, one can never know what they will be, or when – or how – they might arise (Andersen, 1991). The question for systemic therapists is how to navigate complexity, to open up space for change and produce reliable information about the process that will correspond to the demands and expectations of clients, families, social networks and organisations.

Navigating complexity means anticipating and (feedback-informed) learning how to respond when something unexpected takes place in order to maintain balance or transform in preferable ways. Navigating is a constant remapping, a finding of new coordinates (Braidotti, 2011). The co-creation of 'fluid manuals' as a temporary result in a process of becoming (Evans, 2008) can help to navigate complexity and balance structure with spontaneity in a way that allows for a methodical exploration of uncertain processes and outcomes.

4.3 Co-creating 'Fluid Manuals' for Feedback-Informed Systemic Therapy and Collaborative Research

I set out to create accountability for unplanned organic processes as the main focus of our practice by co-creating a fluid manual and conducting multi-method research. Together with Hillewaere we (2017) co-created a 'fluid manual' of FITS (Feedback Informed Therapy within Systems). The therapist uses a manual and a time frame on the one hand and co-creates an appropriate configuration of theory and procedure in dialogue with family members on the other. Co-creating a manual is not an obvious move, and it might even be considered controversial from a social constructionist perspective. Tilsen and McNamee (2015) question the use of manuals: 'EBP often relies on manualised approaches, thus silencing creativity in the therapeutic practice, marginalizing relational inclinations, restricting therapists' capacity to respond to clients' unique circumstances' (Tilsen & McNamee, 2015: 125). They argue: 'When we view therapy as social construction, we are not particularly interested in predetermining what sort of interactions will produce transformation' (Tilsen & McNamee, 2015: 127). In our search (developing FITS) we were interested in learning what kind of interactions produce transformation, but in the local sense. What works for this particular therapist and these particular family members in their particular collaboration setting?

Therapists improvise, but they do so on the basis of knowledge, skills and values. The organisational adviser and former jazz musician Frank Barrett (2012) links the art of improvisation to training in skills and learning standards, as applies in the world of jazz. He quotes the jazz legend Charles Mingus: 'you can't improvise on nothing; you got to improvise on something' (Barrett, 2012: 67). We improvise in therapy, based on our knowledge and skills, clustered in a coherent and flexible narrative, our 'fluid' manual.

'Manualising' refers to a process of describing, re-describing and adapting a 'fluid' manual as a result of learning by feedback. It enables us to present FITS as a coherent and flexible narrative, open to exploration, critique and development. We do not desire to generalise knowledge or to establish a uniform approach. Rather, we constitute a 'learning community' and set out to learn how therapists and family members learn together. I present a 'fluid' manual in which actors form a multi-actor collaborative learning community, in which they learn how they learn how to improve collaboration and encourage developments.

Collaborative learning is established in a process of co-creating fluid manuals for feedback-informed systemic practices and collaborative inquiry. I describe a process of co-creating 'manuals', substantiated by collaborative practice-based research in three steps. I now consider these three steps in turn.

4.3.1 Co-creating a Collaborative Learning Community

In 'collaborative learning communities' (Anderson, 2014), the therapist and family members and other participants learn, through feedback, how to become an effective team and to collaborate in ways that will benefit all the members as well as the group as a whole. Collaborative learning means mutual reflective learning. Participants (actors in the network) become partners in dialogue who work, create and learn together. They appreciate and value each other's expertise, truth, knowledge and experience as equals. They share in participation, accountability and responsibility (Anderson, 2014).

Co-creating a collaborative community can be done answering three questions (Fig. 4.1).

- Multi-actor-network: Who takes part in a multi-actor-network? Who participates in unproductive patterns, offers support and/or can participate in more productive (preferred) patterns? Do they want to join and contribute in the collaborative learning community we are making?
- Patterns/response abilities: What and how are we (therapist/researcher, client, family, participant in the multi-actor network) making together? How do we (as a collaborative team) evaluate the quality of our collaboration, in unproductive or productive patterns, co-creating a better social world (Pearce, 2007).
- Context/response-space: In what context do we operate? How are we shaped by cultural norms, do we question assumptions, relate to a frame of reference, co-create a shared response-space for learning?

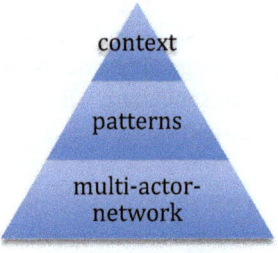

Fig. 4.1 Co-creating a collaborative learning community

4.3.2 Co-creating a 'Fluid Manual', with Agreed-upon Steps in a Road Map

A manual provides a culturally acceptable rationale for change and is in line with the idea of 'allegiance': a shared theory of change and agreed directions in therapy (Duncan et al., 2004) promote commitment towards collaboration. Therapists and clients together negotiate a collective frame of reference that permits them to undergo family therapy, to challenge dominant ideas, to break repetitive patterns and to do something unusual towards seeking beneficial change.

I introduce a roadmap (Fig. 4.2) based on Jan Olthof's therapeutic framework (2017), in which participants in the collaborative learning community discuss and agree upon the steps they make. This roadmap offers structure for co-creating a 'fluid manual'.

Step 1. 'Connection goes before correction'. The systemic therapist/ researcher who joins with the family, the actor-network, becomes accepted as such (Minuchin, 1974). The therapist connects through joining, accepting and accommodating with family members/participants, and connects to their views on the problem, asking about worries, wishes and values. The therapist/researcher summarises storylines and then asks participants to agree upon becoming a team with a motive for collaboration, development and learning.

Step 2. Therapist, family members and other participants explore the context of their resilience, worries and wishes. The main questions here are: What are (good) reasons why we act as we act; what sustains unproductive patterns and problem-saturated narratives; what are the intended and unintended, often unforeseen consequences of our interactions? Systemic therapists use their 'systemic/family therapy' theories, skills and experience, answering these questions,

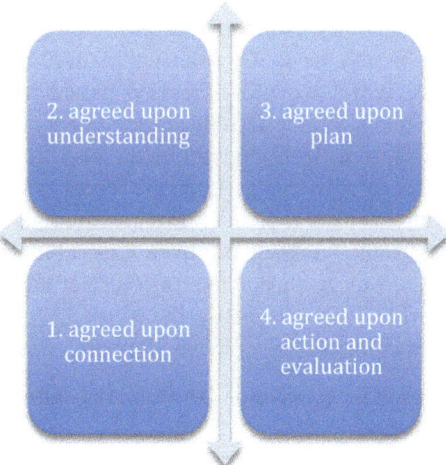

Fig. 4.2 Co-creating a roadmap

inquiring cultural frames, intergenerational transmission, transition, family structure, circular patterns, emotional life, beliefs and narratives. The therapist/researcher summarises co-created storylines and then asks participants to agree upon a shared understanding of what is happening.

Step 3. Therapist, family members and other participants make a plan with everyone having their contribution. We use William Madsen's (2009) Collaborative Helping Map in this stage. We ask about an organizing vision: Where do we want to get headed in our life, in harmony to what is precious for us, to our values? We ask about obstacles: What gets in the way? We ask about supports: What helps us to get there? We make a plan: What needs to happen? All activities to take place must be agreed upon within this plan, the contract we make.

Step 4. This step is about action, reflection and finding ways to go on. How do we make a difference and a connection, do we create productive patterns and preferred narratives? Systemic therapists use their 'systemic/family therapy' theories, skills and experience from different perspectives like dynamic, structural, strategic, attachment based, narrative and dialogic systemic/family therapy. The systemic therapist/researcher organises structural feedback in order to evaluate collaboration, developments and learning. The main question here is: How do we collaborate more effectively as a team to create productive patterns and preferred narratives and to achieve negotiated goals?

4.4 Collaborative Research: Learning How to Learn, Making a Difference That Matters

Collaborative learning entails asking the question: 'How do we learn how we learn?' The systemic therapist/researcher, family members and participants explore how they initiate, sustain and transform patterns of communication within contexts of meaning (Oliver, 2014) and they examine how they learn through collaboration.

In our collaborative inquiry we use Coordinated Management of Meaning (Barge & Pearce, 2004; Pearce, 2007) to explore the ways in which patterns evolve within different layers of meaning. Pearce introduced the concept of 'logical forces' or 'perceived oughtness' (Pearce, 1989) to explore the ways in which patterns evolve within different layers of meaning. Logical forces shape our interactions. C.M.M. helps to identify 'critical moments' that can become 'turning points' when we manage our meanings that make up our lives. Critical moments are moments in which: 'if we act wisely, we can change the trajectory of the conversation and thus create a different "afterlife"' (Pearce, 2007: 3).

Pearce distinguishes prefigurative, contextual, implicative and practical forces.

(a) Prefigurative forces: The connection between one 'turning' antecedent action and a subsequent action.
(b) Contextual forces: The connection between the contextual frame of reference (episode, relationship, self, culture) and a subsequent action.

(c) Implicative forces: The connection between action and a possible contextual reframing.
(d) Practical forces: The connection between an action and a subsequent 'turning' action.

Prefigurative and contextual forces describe interactions in which persons act *because of* pre-existing stories, meanings or actions.

Implicative and practical forces describe interactions in which persons act *in order to bring about* something in the future (Pearce et al., 2011).

We systemically learn when we improvise, reflect and accept relational responsibility for the effects of our actions. I distinguish between a high or low level of reflexivity in the pattern that is produced by therapist and family members.

- 'High level of reflexivity' exists when the contextual and prefigurative forces are relatively weak, while practical and implicative forces are strong. A high level of reflexivity provides opportunities for change, for making a difference.
- 'Low level of reflexivity' exists when contextual and prefigurative forces are relatively strong and practical and implicative forces are weak. A low level of reflexivity limits the opportunities for change, for making a difference.

I set out to identify the kind of learning that is being produced by therapist and family members. In this collaborative inquiry we distinguish zeroth-, first- and second-order learning, and third-order learning, or learning how to learn (Fig. 4.3) (based on Bateson's levels of learning 1972).

– Zeroth-order learning occurs when we sustain repetitive patterns without reflecting on the 'why' or 'how' of this interaction.
– First-order learning is learning by instruction, through adapting to external norms or expert knowledge.
– Second-order learning is learning through reflexivity, triggering structural changes within the system that open up new possibilities to connect. The 'knower' is not seen as separate from his or her knowledge. Knowledge is defined as knowing how to go on.

Fig. 4.3 Levels of learning

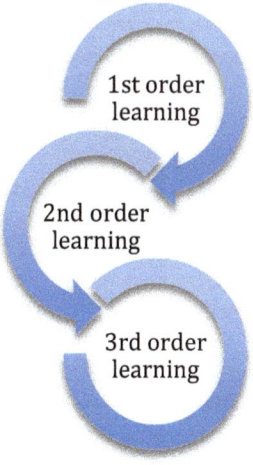

- Co-constructing frames of reference that fit makes it possible to explore different ways of living together and to expand the response space.
- Third-order learning means learning how to learn. Visser (2007) describes third-order learning and refers to Bateson's (1972) concept of deutero-learning (creative, implicit, unconscious anticipations) and meta-learning or planned learning (collaborative practice-based research).

4.5 A Case: Working with 'Fluid Manuals' for Feedback-Informed Systemic Therapy and Collaborative Research

I will illustrate working with 'fluid manuals' for feedback-informed systemic therapy and collaborative research with a case about Myrna and her mother Angelique.[1]

Myrna (15 years) was hospitalised and joined an inpatient therapeutic program for adolescents. Myrna lived alone with her mother Angelique and had never met her father. Myrna suffered from many inexplicable somatic symptoms. She had no contact with peers and didn't go to school for the last four years. Before, she attended many different schools for short periods of time. According to mother Myrna gets very sick at schools. She believed Myrna is not completely incarnated in her physical body. 'Her soul lives in between heaven and earth. Myrna is spiritually wiser and develops much faster than her peers', according to mother. 'She just doesn't fit in a school system' and 'we have to trust that she finds her own way herself'. Angelique was held responsible for Myrna's school absence. Under pressure of Child Protection mother gave approval for the inpatient therapeutic treatment.

When I met Angelique, she made clear she didn't believe this treatment would work. But against all odds Myrna revived, enjoyed company with peers and she did very well in the therapeutic program. When I told mother this in a family therapy session, she turned to me and said: 'Robert, you disappoint me, can't you see she is playing a game, this is exactly what is making her sick'. Myrna protested and told her mother that she liked being at the program. Angelique froze. She said: 'well let them take care of you, then. I stop being a mother to you'. After this session Myrna expressed anger to her mother who kept distance from her. The treatment-team felt an enormous pity for Myrna and team members got in conflict with mother. Myrna reacted depressed; she harmed herself and expressed suicidal tendencies. One week later she wanted to leave the program. Myrna said: 'Only my mother understands me, she can even accept my dead wish'. The team wanted to ask Child Protection to place Myrna in custody, while mother was making an official complaint against our institution to get her back home. I organised a meeting between mother, Myrna, the team and me (as systemic therapist). We used the 'fluid manual', trying to become a 'collaborative learning community.

---

[1] Names and details have been changed to preserve the anonymity of the family.

4.5.1 Co-creating a Collaborative Community

Becoming a 'collaborative learning community' means that all participants reflect on their contribution to change, to different patterns, co-creating narratives, within different frameworks of meaning. The participants learn how they have learned in ways they can transfer to other domains in their lives. Therapy is successful when families expand their response-abilities and response space through spontaneous interaction and reflexive dialogue.

We organised a meeting with Myrna, her mother, team members and the systemic therapist. We asked ourselves how we could become a more effective team. Together we draw the quality of the different relations in the network in 4 stages (Fig. 4.4). The first drawing refers to our collaboration at the beginning of the treatment. The second drawing refers to the phase when Myrna experienced connection with the

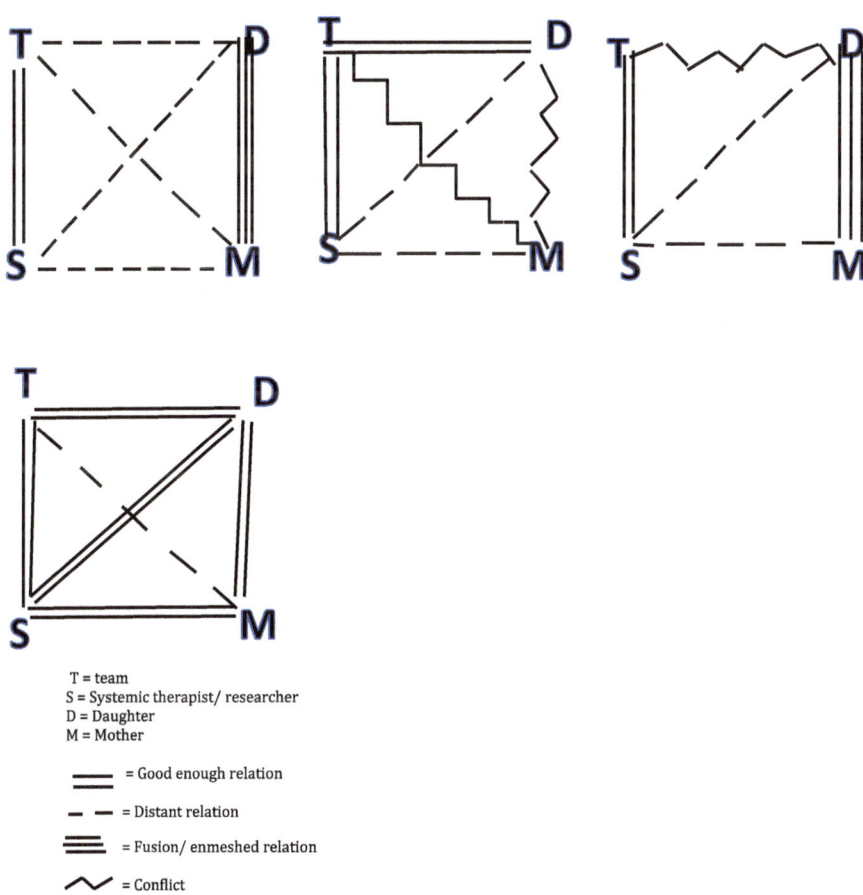

T = team
S = Systemic therapist/ researcher
D = Daughter
M = Mother

═══ = Good enough relation
— — = Distant relation
≡≡≡ = Fusion/ enmeshed relation
∿ = Conflict

Fig. 4.4 Maps of structure

team/program and conflict with her mother. The third drawing illustrated the current situation at that time. All participants agreed that the fourth one represents a preferred effective collaboration in the (near) future. We discussed how to achieve this.

4.5.2 Co-creating a 'Fluid Manual', with Agreed-upon Steps in a Road Map

We have developed this roadmap (Table 4.1) to discuss and agree upon the steps we make. Inspired by Rober (2014), I believe that it is better to focus on *worries* rather than *problems*. When family members talk about their worries, they express the ways in which they relate to others: 'I am worried about you or about what is happening to us'. Family members often have different worries and often wish for different things. It is important to co-create a context for differences, dissent, while at the same time seeking to arrive at a consensus about shared wishes for change. For example: 'Everybody seems to want the current situation to be different'. Therapist,

Table 4.1 Roadmap with agreed-upon steps

Yes response	2. Making meaning
	How to understand why and what is happening, that goes against intentions, values, preferences.
	    Timelines (horizontal/vertical).
	    Structure.
	    Patterns.
	    Emotional life.
	    Narratives (dominant, subordinate).
		Yes response

1. Making a connection Problem-free talk Worries Wishes Values		**3. Making a plan** How do we (multi-actor-network) cooperate as a collaborative team in order to achieve preferred goals and live in harmony with values?
Yes response A fit and a difference within the community	**4. Making a difference that matters** How do we make a difference and a connection, productive patterns and preferred narratives? Evaluation of collaboration (in the multi-actor-network), the developments and learning.	Yes response

family members and participants explore the context of their resilience, worries and wishes. I interview family members and invite family members to interview each other. I ask circular questions, make lifelines, drawings, genograms and so on. Within this framework we co-create a shared understanding about what is happening and what to do.

We (mother, Myrna, team members, systemic therapist) looked to the roadmap/ the framework (Table 4.1) and concluded there is no agreed-upon motive for change, no agreed-upon understanding about what is happening and no agreed-upon plan about what to do. 'No wonder therapy is failing', we concluded. 'We have to discuss step 1, 2 and 3 again before we can decide what to do next'. All participants in the network meeting expressed their worries about our collaboration as a team and Myrna her development. All participants wanted the current situation to be different.

Team, mother and Myrna didn't share the same understanding about what was happening. The team spoke about a 'symbiotic' relationship between mother and daughter. Inexplicable somatic symptoms helped to maintain homeostasis, a structural constancy; it helped to avoid individuation and separation. Mother spoke about how Myrna didn't fit in societal structures because of her 'high sensitivity' and 'spiritual wisdom'. Myrna agreed with what her mother said. Mother concluded: 'Myrna develops faster than children of her age' and 'we have to trust that she finds her own way herself'.

Afterwards the team members were divided about what to do. Some team members wanted to activate a procedure to get Myrna in Custody. Other team members were afraid further escalation would confirm mother and daughter in their conviction about not fitting in. Some other team members were afraid that Myrna, locked in our conflict, could possibly see suicide as the only way out. In an intervision group we used the 'fluid manual' for orientation and to think about meaning and a way out of the escalating pattern everyone could agree on. We wanted to step out of an unproductive escalating pattern and we asked ourselves these questions: (1) what invitation do we feel, (2) what pattern do we sustain if we act according that invitation, (3) how can we make a difference without losing the connection? We decided to write Myrna and mother a letter, to communicate our dilemma, to look for shared understanding of what happens and to search for a possible way out everyone could agree on.

Myrna and Angela, prepared to argue and fight, responded surprised when we read them our letter. We gave words to the different voices in the team, expressed our worries and shared two different interpretations about what was going on. We explained the escalating pattern and our thoughts about outplacement and custody. We introduced a second explanation and wrote: 'Maybe we shouldn't be that concerned about Myrna'. We repeated the words of mother. 'Myrna develops faster than peers'. We witnessed her separating and reconnecting with her mother. This is what adolescents do. She showed her anger and resistance. Maybe we witnessed her puberty passing and she is ready for a new stage in life? Angelique often said to us: 'we have to trust that she finds her own way herself'. Myrna can't find her own way if mother and the treatment team put pressure on her. We decided to let go for now, to give Myrna space to think and decide whether she wants to continue the treatment program. We suggest a two-week break and we are curious about Myrna's decision. Two weeks later Myrna read a letter back to us. She didn't want to return to the inpatient program but wanted to join the after-care therapy group so she could stay connected with the some of the peers she had met. Mother looked proud of her daughter. I met Angelique a couple of times alone. We drew a genogram and she told me about a lot of violence in her family of origin.

4.5.3 Collaborative Practice-based Research: Creating a Culture of Feedback

Doing collaborative practice-based research I use standardised Routine (self-report) Outcome Measurement (ROM), Client Directed Outcome Interview, ORS & SRS (Miller & Duncan, 2000) and a Family Goals Rating List (Van Hennik & Hillewaere, 2017). I use quantitative outcomes as conversational tools evaluating collaboration, developments and learning in FITS. The qualitative research includes an analysis of 'critical moments' in the transcripts of evaluations in FITS. I examine patterns within frames of reference and try to ascertain how we can collaboratively learn how to learn.

In FITS the therapist takes responsibility for creating a culture of feedback using two scales: the outcome rating scale (ORS) to measure the affected dimensions of a family member's life and the session rating scale (SRS) to measure the quality of the therapeutic alliance (Miller & Duncan, 2000). Exchanges based on the ORS and SRS make it possible for clients to tell us what is not working well, when we are not being helpful and when we need to make changes in order to keep the dialogue going in a meaningful way (Bargmann & Robinson, 2012).

Figures 4.5 and 4.6 *show ORS-scores and SRS-scores of Myrna and her mother Angelique.*

I use the ORS (Outcome Rating Scale, Miller & Duncan, 2000) and the SRS (Session Rating Scale, Miller & Duncan, 2000) in the systemic therapy sessions. We evaluated collaboration, developments and learning in session 3, 7 and 10. During session 7 mother decided to withdraw. During session 9 we read Myrna and mother the letter we wrote.

I audiotape sessions in which the collaborative learning community evaluate their collaboration, developments and learning. I study patterns within layers of context in an intervision group. I inquire how logical forces shape our actions and

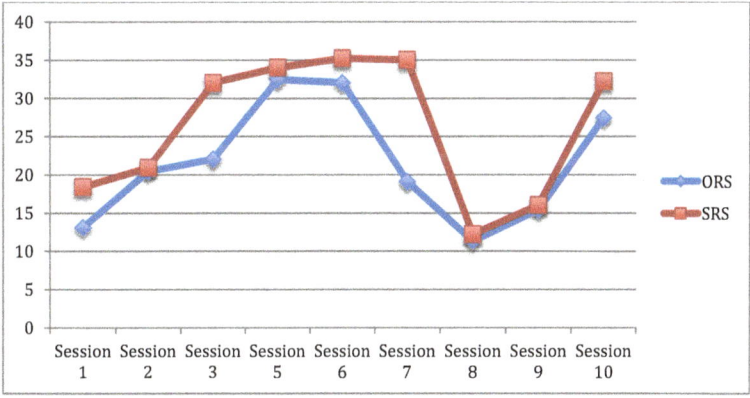

Fig. 4.5 CDOI Myrna

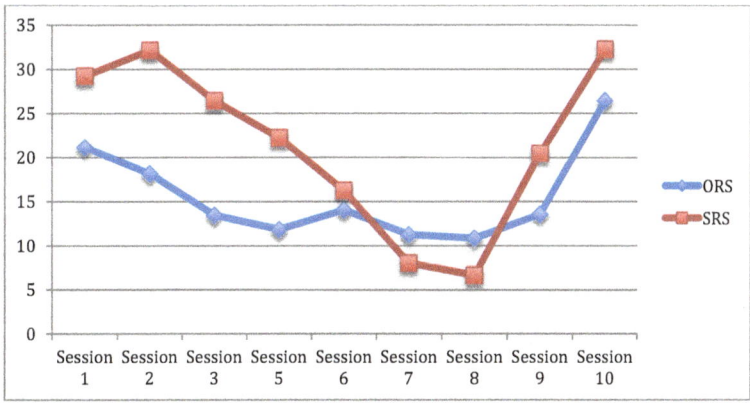

Fig. 4.6 CDOI mother

meanings (Pearce, 2007). I distinguish between a high or low level of reflexivity in the pattern that is produced by therapist, family members and other participants. I bring back my reflections in conversation with the collaborative learning community in order to learn how we learn.

   The team almost got stuck in an unproductive and escalating pattern. In our intervision group we were able to ask ourselves the questions: What am I being invited or encouraged to do? What pattern would I be sustaining if I accept this invitation? How can I make a difference without losing the connection? We responded in an unexpected way reading our letter, with shared understandings and *a way out without loss of face. I consider this to be a high level of reflexivity, opening up space for something new. I consider this as 'second-order learning', we took a risk and the outcome was unpredictable. Later I discussed the transition with Angelique. We talked about control as a symptom of distrust. Only when we started to trust her, she was able to start to trust us (a little bit). I consider this conversation as an example of third-order learning.*

4.6 Manualisation Producing Practice Based Evidence Based Practice

Practice Based Evidence Based practice implies that no therapy is provided without measuring its effects and no research is done outside of the practice itself. The therapist and family members examine the effects of their cooperation in collaborative research. The output of research is input for therapy and for the reconstruction of the fluid manual. The outcomes of research serve as the input for collaborative learning in the system that the therapist and family members co-create together.

In the process of producing Practice Based Evidence Based Practice the practitioner/ researcher seeks to balance structure with spontaneity in a way that allows for a methodical exploration of uncertain processes and outcomes. Therapist/ researchers can produce Practice Based Evidence Based Practice in a process that I describe in five domains (Fig. 4.7) (1) Manualisation: Therapists/researchers can develop their own personalised 'fluid' manual. We (Van Hennik & Hillewaere, 2017) co-created a 'fluid' manual of Feedback-Informed Systemic Therapy. (2) Coordinated improvisation: Therapists improvise in unpredictable situations within (professional) frames of reference. We coordinate our improvisations when we are able to reflect on the connections and frameworks we devise together. (3) Systemic feedback: We organise structured feedback, discuss developments and collaboration, and learn how to improve collaboration. (4) Collaborative learning, which is central to this approach, is enhanced in the process of improvisation, feedback, and research. By using feedback and collaborative inquiry, we learn how we can learn together. (5) Multi-method research: Using quantitative and qualitative data, participants explore the way they navigate in complex systems on the basis of their improvisations and collaborative learning in Feedback-Informed Systemic Therapy.

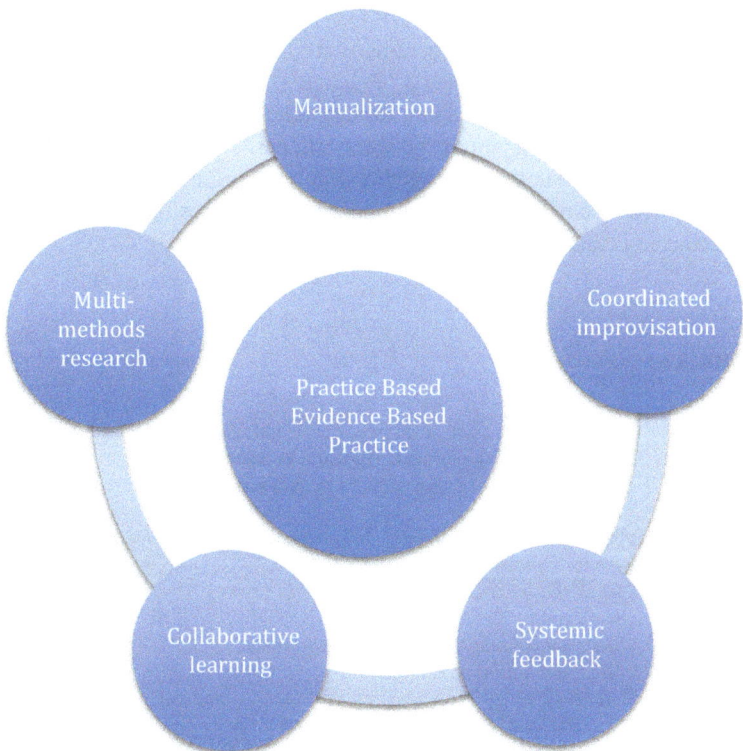

Fig. 4.7 Practice Based Evidence Based Practice

4.7 Conclusion

In this chapter I have written about the process of co-creating a 'fluid manual' for feedback-informed systemic therapy and collaborative research. Therapist, clients and other participants form a collaborative learning community. Participants learn in a spontaneous interplay (deutero learning) and by structured analysis, reflection and co-construction (meta-learning) to expand and conserve response-abilities and response-space, thereby finding multiple ways to approach living together. A 'fluid' manual is a temporary result in the process of collaborative learning. Therapists co-construct a manual in conversation with participants in the collaborative learning community and in harmony with their knowledge, values and experiences. Therapists navigate, remap and find new coordinates, taking accountability for results producing Practice Based Evidence Based Evidence.

No one really knows if an Evidence-Based Protocol (proven evident in different situated contexts) works for this therapist with this family in their unpredictable circumstances and complex contexts. Practice Based Evidence Based Practice enables therapist, clients and managers to make adjustments based on outcomes and meaning-making in conversations between all participants in the collaborative learning community we constitute together. I hope to inspire systemic practitioners to manualise and research their own practices and develop effective Practice Based Evidence Based Practices.

References

Andersen, T. (1991). *The reflecting team, dialogues about dialogues about dialogues*. Norton.
Anderson, H. (2014). Collaborative-dialogue research as everyday practice. In G. Simon & A. Chard (Eds.), *Systemic inquiry, innovations in reflexive practice research* (pp. 60–73). Everything is Connected Press.
Bargmann, S., & Robinson, B. (2012) *Manual 2: Feedback-informed clinical work*: The basics. International Centre for Clinical Excellence.
Barrett, F. (2012). *Yes to the mess: Surprising leadership lessons from jazz*. Harvard Business Review Press.
Bateson, G. (1972). *Steps to an ecology of mind*. Jason Aronson.
Bateson, G. (1979). *Mind and nature*. E.P. Dutton.
Braidotti, R. (2011). *Nomadic theory. The portable Braidotti*. Columbia University Press.
Capra, F., & Luisi, P. L. (2014). *The systems view on life: A unifying vision*. University Press.
Duncan, B., Miller, S., & Sparks, J. (2004). *The heroic client: Principles of client-directed, outcome informed therapy*. Jossey-Bass.
Evans, F. (2008). *The multi voiced body*. Columbia University Press.
Guattari, F. (1996). *Soft subversions*. Semiotext(e).
Madsen, W. C. (2009). Collaborative helping: A practice framework for family-centered services. *Family Process, 48*, 103–116.
Maturana, H., & Verden-Zoller, G. (2008). *The origin of humanness in the biology of love*. Imprint Academic.
Miller, S., & Duncan, B. (2000). *The outcome rating scale*. Author.
Minuchin, S. (1974). *Families and family therapy*. Harvard University Press.
Oliver, C. (2014). Coordinating logics of meaning and action. In S. W. Little John & S. McNamee (Eds.), *The coordinated management of meaning. A Festschrift in Honour of W. Barnett Pearce* (pp. 271–289). Fairleigh Dickinson University Press.
Olthof, J. (2017). *Handbook of narrative therapy*. Karnac.
Pearce, W. B. (2007). *Making social worlds. A communication perspective*. Blackwell Publishing.
Pearce, W. B., Sostrin, J., & Pearce, K. (2011). CMM solutions. Field Guide for Consultants. You Get What You. Make Publishing
Rober, P. (2014). *Gezinstherapie in de praktijk*. Acco.
Shotter, J. (2007). Not to forget Tom Andersen's way of being Tom Andersen: The importance of what 'just happens' to us. *Human Systems, 18*, 15–34.

Tilsen, J., & McNamee, S. (2015). Feedback informed treatment: Evidence-based practice meets social construction. *Family Process, 54*, 124–137.

Van Hennik, R., & Hillewaere, B. (2017). Practice based evidence based practice. Navigating based on coordinated improvisation, collaborative learning and multi-methods research in feedback informed systemic therapy. *Journal of Family Therapy, 39*(3), 288–309.

Visser, M. (2007). Deutero-learning in organizations: A review and reformulation. *The Academy of Management Review, 32*, 659–667.

Chapter 5
Manualizing Human Systems Therapy Towards a Few-Sessions Therapy

Nicholas Paritsis

5.1 Introduction

5.1.1 Manualized Family Therapies

Manualization is extensively used in cognitive behavioral therapy which has made this therapy easier to run, possibly because the principles used are well defined and largely based on scientific grounds. Systemic approaches have the benefit of using systemic principles that are also scientifically valid so they offer a similar benefit. However, family therapies do not just use well-accepted systemic principles but also other principles that are part of their theory but which are not well documented scientifically. Furthermore, systemic principles used in various family therapies are not always the same. We believe that this is also reflected in the work of discussion and formation of manualization of family systems therapy (Pote et al., 2003).

In this context Human Systems Therapy (HST) uses: (a) some core General Systems principles and a model of human systems intelligence based on core systemic and cybernetic principles, (b) the process of the unconscious in the context of scientific work and its proven paleologic thinking and its logic (Freud, 1898; Von Domarus, 1944; Arieti, 1978), (c) an epistemology integrating first- and second-order cybernetics which are considered as both valid, and (d) the use of a large number (over 40) of additional to the existing technics in other schools of therapy. In this way, many of the principles of HST (Paritsis, 2006, 2010, 2020) have scientific validation, and it is expected to be well manualized.

N. Paritsis (✉)
Center for the Study of Human Systems Bettering and Therapy, Athens, Greece

Society for Therapy and Intervention on Individuals, Families and Larger Systems, Athens, Greece
e-mail: nparitsis@gmail.com

5.2 The Issue of Time and Effectiveness

Manualization is useful as it is expected to reduce the time spent in therapy and induce its effectiveness. In addition, a practical guide for conducting the therapy is more useful for less-experienced therapists. In particular, as soon as the manualization of HST was introduced for conducting therapy by third- and fourth-year trainees in systems therapy, it became obvious how important manualization is. Furthermore, the time spent in therapy was reduced and its effectiveness was increased (see trials by the end of the chapter).

Difficult cases usually need more time which is where manualization becomes less useful. The above is partly overcome when circularity is introduced in manualized process.

For this reason, manualization of HST introduced also a circular process so that in difficult cases the same procedure may be repeated until the therapy ends successfully. This will also be analyzed in describing manualization further.

5.3 An Outline of the Development and Present State of Human Systems Therapy

5.3.1 Some Steps of the Development of Human Systems Therapy

Human Systems Therapy was developed gradually. The main steps can be considered as follows:

(a) The author (1959) suggested that the basic motivation for humans is the need for interactions that lead to satisfaction and to development. Development in turn leads to bettering of interactions that further lead to development in a circular way. This idea came during reading and thinking about the various theories of basic motivation within the schools of psychoanalysis. The circular process was in the way of thinking of the author in general.

(b) Suggesting that a client having headaches was to follow a particular way of behavior to overcome her problem (1970), against the generally different way that the client used. This without telling to the client that his general strategy is wrong nor that the therapist's suggestion is related to treatment. This very effective technique immediately causing therapeutic change has been explained recently possibly as a kind of therapeutic paradox. This proved to be an important therapeutic technique.

(c) The use and test of the previous and some other new techniques (1978) were applied to change human relations through individual intervention, at the Maudsley Hospital, Institute of Psychiatry, London, England.

(d) The intervention (1982) in a Residential House as a system aiming to reduce aggression of teenage residents against the stuff. This succeeded mainly by changing the hierarchical structure of the whole system (see a sort outline by the end of this chapter). The success of intervention led to the invitation by Mony Elkaim to the author to join the European Family Therapy Network (later EFTA) as a founding member (1987).
(e) Interventions in schizophrenics (1986–1998) on the two levels, that of the individual and that of the family level (see a sort outline by the end of this chapter). This was facilitated by a big research program sponsored by the European Community (1997–2000). During this project Harlene Anderson and Lynne Hoffman gave the name "General Systems Therapy" to the present method.
(f) The application of the already developed HST and testing and improving it, in the therapy of patients at the Psychiatric Department (1993–2008) of the General Hospital School of Medicine, University of Crete. This led to forming and testing specific hypotheses for specific major psychiatric disorders. Besides, new techniques of HST were tested, with a number of them being paradoxical (the intervention on hashish users presented by the end of this chapter was realized at that time).
(g) Teaching Systems Therapy as a founding member of the Teaching Institutes Chamber of the EFTA and discussing new ideas with students.
(h) Full-time research, teaching, and offering therapy at the Society of Therapy and Intervention on Individuals, Families and Larger Systems (2005–2014). This gave the opportunity to develop and test many new techniques and improve the details of the theory.
(i) The realization that human systems are not simply living systems (2015) but constitute additional characteristics such as culture, language, consciousness (and the unconscious). Use the paleologic of the unconscious (Freud, 1898) for constructing many new therapeutic techniques that led to therapy that could be completed in a few sessions. We started to think about the need of a "Human Systems Theory" as a necessary part of systems thinking and sciences.
(j) Start of manualization (see the last examples of therapy at the end of this chapter).

By looking at the above sequence of events, the process by which HST was developed is related to events that could not have happened. The foundation on the basis of basic motivation had a circular process and had a developmental aspect, a systemic thinking from the beginning.

It is also interesting that in the second step, a technique developed, as a simple idea by the author, turned to be a basic very effective one, with general applicability therapeutic paradox. Namely, the presentation by the therapist of a particular simple solution to a particular problem, which is contradicted by the general disadaptive and/or ineffective strategy of human interactions used by the client related to his personality. This contradiction between the particular and the general (two levels of logical types) forms a therapeutic paradox on the level of the unconscious, since paleologic cannot discriminate the difference between logical types.

Later on, after the founder of HST studied systems and cybernetics (PhD), the application of relevant principles on systems therapy was open. Besides, his work (as a Director at the Department of Social Psychiatry at Research Institute and then as Head of the Department of Psychiatry and Behavioral Science at University) offered the liberty and facilitated the use of resources for developing a psychotherapeutic method.

5.3.2 Basic Principles of Human Systems Therapy

A Definition of the Open System

The definition of the open system, namely of the living system, in the context of HST, favors multilevel intervention. This definition is extended to three levels. The first level is based on the classic definition of a system comprising the members and their relations. The second level is the emergent properties of the system which derive from the members, their properties and their relations. The emergent properties also influence in a circular way the members, their properties and their relations. The third level is the context or the direct environment that exercises an influence on the system. Again, this environment is influenced by the system and its emergent properties and also influences the living system.

We have in the definition of the open system three levels influencing each other. It clearly shows the need for multilevel intervention. Interactions are close to the multiplication mathematically, and the intervention in more than one level offers a multiplicative rather than additive result producing higher effectiveness in therapy.

Epistemology of Human Systems: Use of First- and Second-Order Cybernetics

Each of the different views and theories on epistemology used in family therapy refers to a certain level of description, such as biological (e.g. Maturana & Varela, 1984), social (e. g. Berger & Luckmann, 1966; Gergen, 1982), or sociocultural (Foucault, 2006). In fact, different levels of human systems organization have different ways of perceiving reality while the various epistemological approaches have differences also because of the level of analysis of living systems organization.

In HST there are three levels, biological, social, and scientific, which are different with different functions, perception and description of reality, consequences, and implications.

On the biological level, reality is perceived (by each of the species) in the same way. All the people would agree that a woman on TV is blonde or has blue eyes. However, on the social level, the woman on TV may speak about political issues, some people could understand it differently and they may disagree on whether she is a good politician and they are going to vote her. Furthermore, almost everyone would agree on the way that science analyzes how her brain works in order to perceive and see.

HST accepts that (a) on the biological level human systems have one valid description and perception of reality (first-order cybernetics), (b) on social issues different human systems may have different descriptions of the situation (second-order cybernetics) with a different degree of truth (or degree of doubt or belief) and (c) scientific issues are considered basically to be valid (the therapist knows better than the client when it comes to some issues).

The practical implication of this position is the advantage that we can use both first- and second-order cybernetic techniques in HST.

An Outline of Human Systems Intelligence

Psychology examines and analyses the main parts separately and does not pay attention to the relation of the parts, as the systems approach does. Let us understand the relations of psychological functional parts in order to make a whole. By considering the relations of psychological functional parts, we can better understand and influence them through psychotherapy. We can view three main functional subparts: (a) one that offers the contact of the environmental matter-energy external world with the information processing systems of an internal world (b) the part of a control system that realizes the achievement of goals of human systems, and (c) the part of having a model of the world that assists and helps the achievement of the control system for understanding, planning, and controlling.

Interaction with the Environment Subsystem

This part includes the senses that perceive a small part and aspect of the external world, relevant to our goals as living systems. According to living system theory, the interaction with the environment subsystem include the senses that translate matter-energy to information and the muscles and other organs that transform information to matter energy (Miller, 1978).

The Control Subsystem

From a cybernetics point of view, it is impossible to achieve a goal without a control system (Wiener, 1948). The controller, the part that has and exercises the control, basically consists of four main parts. The subsystem of carrying the goals, the subsystem that perceives the part to be controlled, the subsystem that compares the two, and the subsystem that acts in order to exercise control (Wiener, 1948). In organisms that are simpler than man the controller is simple. Human systems have cognitive, emotional, or complex communication functions. Thus, in human systems there are three main control subsystems: (a) one for motivation and emotions, (b) one for cognitive functions, and (c) one for human communication (Paritsis, 2006).

The Modelling Subsystem

In human systems this part of a model of the world is important for helping and assisting the control system (Conant & Ashby, 1970). It is the most developed subsystem in human intelligent systems and includes all types of learning including education, human knowledge and language description, logic, complex skills, and models of social roles.

This part includes the parts where psychotherapy is modifying. Psychotherapy changes the model of the world. By taking into account psychology, artificial intelligence and artificial life, and the different types of main schools of psychotherapy we can consider in the model three main interacting aspects of the model of the world: the (a) language description, (b) cognitive/emotional and verbal structures, and (c) interactional schemata. Cognitive/emotional structures are a network where cognition and affect interact and are integrated. This interaction is tested empirically.

Interactional schemata are internal representations of human social interactions, relations, and roles. The concept of schemata in general and of scripts in cognitive science is similar but not the same as interactional schemata For example, schemata and scripts are also used for representation of knowledge, as cognitive schemas are. The role of interactional schemata is important in that it is possible to change human relations by influencing interactional schemata and change interactional schemata by influencing human relations.

Some Other Important Components and Functions

Freud suggested that the unconscious is using paleologic thinking (Freud, 1898). Paleologic thinking cannot discriminate among levels of generality namely between the general and the particular, the parts from the whole, or the levels between logical types of Russell (1903). On the basis of paleologic, Freud arrived at the interpretation of dreams. In dreams objects and/or subjects can be represented by their parts.

Aggression is not considered to be a need; however, it developed when there is dissatisfaction, pain, and harm. In other words when the opposite of satisfaction or/ and development occur. There is a general important implication in that aggression is not continuously produced in the human systems but only when they are damaged or suffer usually from an external agent. Hence there is no need for aggression to be continuously expressed in order to be ceased. On the contrary, a continuous satisfaction of aggression in the long run will increase more and more needing more and more satisfaction according to the interaction theory of motivation.

Increase of Order and Variety

Order is used by systems and cybernetics as the opposite of entropy. Increase of order is related to development (Miller, 1978) and evolution (Prigogine & Stanger, 1986). Besides, variety is related to development and evolution (Miller, 1978; Ashby, 1952). In diseases, mental disorders, in all dysfunctions, in all psychological problems, and in couple problems the appropriate and existing order and variety are destroyed or reduced. Hence in psychotherapy there is the goal to increase appropriate order and variety of actions and family organization.

5.4 Steps and Content of Manualization

5.4.1 History and Experiences of Manualization. Its Importance for Creating Effective Therapists

The History of Main Steps Contributing to Manualization

The first step (1998) was when the HST had to be taught to the first students to fulfil the requirements of the project by the European Community for preparing schizophrenics and persons that left high school in order for both to find jobs. We had to select the important points in therapy.

The second step (2005) was after the first trials of using HST (Aivalioti et al., 2009; Lambraki et al., 2014). To our surprise we realized that its effectiveness was exceptionally high after 8 sessions of intervention (reduction of delusions and hallucinations by 39%). We had to find out and select which parts out of the whole method were the points that made the most difference. Professor Julian Leff of the Institute of Psychiatry encouraged the author (in 2005) to develop and apply HST to schizophrenia.

The third step (2012) was when we decided to increase the time of teaching HST to students of the 4-years program in systems therapy besides the other schools of family therapy, because of its higher effectiveness in a short time.

The fourth step was when the third- and fourth-year students participating in therapy under supervision had to be effective in short time as much as possible for the students to see the results of therapy within one academic year.

The fifth step was a possible explanation of therapeutic paradoxes and other techniques through the paleologic of the unconscious. A relevant explanation to Milton Erickson's "unconscious suggestions." This, facilitated the finding of many new techniques for use and led to a few-sessions therapy.

The sixth and last step put together all the previous considerations in order to teach the students during their training how to conduct therapy under supervision and implementation of the manualization in their therapeutic activity.

Manualization was a process that came out by an external observer of the process of therapy. It is not easy to conduct a therapy and at the same time observe the therapy. The process was that the trainees in systems therapy observe another trainee conducting a therapy to repeat it. In this way, the observer can see what is more and less effective.

The teaching of HST together with the main methods of family therapy was included in the curriculum of the 4 -years program (the program now has more than 100 students in various groups). HST was also applied in the third and fourth year of practical application of systemic therapy trainees who needed as much as possible a method of family and systemic therapy in order trained in system therapy to be able to cover the requests the clients in a small number of sessions. As HST was further developed, the trainees became more and more capable, the teaching program improved and the final examination included requiring the students to be able to cover the clients' requests within 10 sessions or near to that number. Then when the trainees of the third and fourth year conducted therapy under simultaneous supervision, the need for manualization became more important. The trainees were encouraged to strictly follow the guidelines and steps of manualization. The further development of HST and its application in research trials led to a less than 10 sessions therapy (except for cases with psychoses) being the required limit for trainees' final exams.

Manualization improved together with the effectiveness of HST. Now all trainees during their education have to strictly follow the manualization that is going to be described in detail, independent of what mixture of family therapy they use. This led the trainees closer to the number of sessions for therapy in average in final exam becoming usually 6–8. This surprised us.

5.5 Steps of Manualization

5.5.1 The First Step Is Joining

This is the step where we meet the clients. The therapist welcomes the client(s) and introduces her or himself. Then the therapist asks general questions about the family that are present like their names, where they live, or their professions and for each one the therapist has to find and make positive comments to the client.

In fact, the therapist is good to use the technique of over-positive description of HST. According to this technique the therapist describes the characteristics of the client system (person, couple, family) as positive as possible (a little more than in reality) to the extent that the therapist can justify his or her description. This technique is used extensively and easily by the therapists since in all cases this can have positive results.

Over-positive description is different from the "emphasizing the positive" in multisystemic therapy (Henggeler, 1999) that emphasizes the positive as it is, while over-positive description presents the positive more that it is. Over-positive description also differs from Positive Connotation which is a therapeutic paradox and present a negative act of the family as positive on the basis of positive results or intentions.

The over-positive description contributes to improve relationships, and it is very useful for joining. We have to give the impression to the client system that we have an overall positive impression of them for both cognitively, ethically, and emotionally and that they are accepted as they are and possibly admired and understood.

We also try to be as pleasant as possible taking under consideration the severity and the unpleasant situation.

It is also useful to avoid any negative connotation. Reframing is also useful if it can be used. We present the characteristics of the identified patient as normal as possible. This needs some talent since there must be balance between accepting a problem which is negative enough for therapy and at the same time reducing the negative aspects of it.

We avoid to tell a diagnosis and instead describe the symptoms and complaints in their better version.

We go to the next step when we see that the client system has positive regard for the therapists, look friendly, and have positive feelings.

5.5.2 The Second Step Is the Identification of the Goals of Therapy

In order to save time, we have to take initiatives gently. We have to stop the client systems from starting to tell their story and their interpretation of the situation. Part of the problem is their view of the problem.

According to cybernetics the success of a goal rests upon the clarification and the precision of description of the goal or goals. Thus, the more precise and detailed description of the goals of therapy, the faster and more secure the success. We can make a catalog of what the client system likes to change. It is not necessary to be pathological. This is also useful later when we ask to be informed about the degree of improvement and record the date of their response. Furthermore, we keep track of the appearance of the symptoms and complains together with the events and the dates related to their appearance.

Another issue is the conflicting goals in the client system. In some cases, different members of the family have different goals of therapy. This is allowed if they are not conflicting. The therapist then has to try to make the members agree on common goals. If a goal of therapy conflicts with the values of the therapist then this also has to be discussed and the system under therapy and the therapist have to come to an agreement.

5.5.3 The Third Step Is the Categorization and the Formation of Hypotheses

Categorization

Before treatment there must be a diagnosis in medicine and according to diagnosis, treatment follows. In family therapy and systemic therapy it is not as simple as that.

For some different categories of identified patients and/or different schools of family therapy there are specific definable types of families related to the problems of the identified patient.

Furthermore, there are family studies researches, possibly independent from a specific school family therapy, that refer to specific individual psychiatric, psychological, and psychosomatic problems. Even more, there are theories about the causes related to the intrapsychic, relational, family, and the wider social environment.

HST also utilizes studies and theories regarding psychological studies on psychiatric and psychosomatic disorders.

A Hypothesis That Cannot Be Falsified Is Useless to the Therapy

There is a modification of the Popperian (e.g. Popper, 1959) principle for science (a hypothesis which cannot be falsified is useless to the science) a similar view on hypotheses and interpretations have the Milano school (Selvini Palazzoli et al., 1978). In HST before making the core of intervention, a cause or causes have to be found. Hypotheses first have to be tested and only if they are confirmed we move into the next step which is to use the various techniques. In fact, we make hypotheses that can be tested while if they are specified in such a way that they cannot be validated they will be not used for the therapy. Exceptionally a hypothesis can be tested indirectly, by using it in therapy and see the results. This is also used in medicine by exceptionally using a treatment in order to reject or confirm a diagnosis.

In the context of HST and for each category of psychiatric disorders, major psychosomatic disorders, couple therapy and major family problems such as different violence situations, there are specific hypotheses. Most of these hypotheses are already existing in different psychotherapeutic schools and a few are based on observations while using HST. These selected hypotheses are somehow confirmed over the many years use of HST but they are not published all together.

According to HST the therapist should never communicate to the client the hypothesis which is related with the problem they have or its reason. Besides, we avoid communicating the diagnoses. If we are asked about that we repeat the complaints. One important reason for doing so is the probability of resistance to therapy in many ways.

5.5.4 The Fourth Step Is the Intervention

Elaboration of Genogram on a Laptop

This is provisional and has the advantage of having a genogram where the properties and the relations of the members of the genogram are described in detail. In the classical genogram there are only a few details about the members, like the age and the name of the people involved. In the elaborative genogram on a laptop the genogram is in a general structure, the same as the usual but with the important addition that for members as well as their relations the properties are described in detail using word boxes.

Multilevel Intervention

Change in HST can be achieved in many ways which influence one another. The intervention in more than one level results rather in a multiplicative effect than an additive one. Since, mathematically, interactions are represented not as additive but as multiplicative (like in epidemiology for representing interacting factors). The different areas and levels of organization in intervention through HST are going to be presented.

Intrapsychic Intervention

Working with one person in HST can also be a relational intervention through the individual by an intervention in zeugmas or by discussing his or her relations with the individuals. A relevant method is used in systemic therapy with individuals (Boscolo & Bertrando, 1996).

The theoretical base that allows and enables us to achieve intrapsychic relations through an intervention in a third person is the part of human intelligence (and human systems intelligence in general) of the model of the world. By changing the internal representations and the model of the relations and interactions, we change the interaction and relations in the external world. A change in a given zeugma through therapeutic intervention, for example, achieves three things at the same time:

- the direct change of the individual behavior,
- the change of the specific relations and roles, e.g. with another person or persons related to that zeugma, and
- the change of the behavior of another person, or human system in general, which is (are) related with that person involved in the therapy.

At the same time is possible to influence the above by intervening in the individual by changing dissadaptive values and principles.

Intervention in the Relationships of the Person with the Core Problem

These relationships can be changed either directly by the presence of both human systems involved in that relation or by influencing the relevant zeugma through intervention in one of the individuals.

Intervention in Couples

The intervention in couples changes the relations of the people involved, the behavior of each one of them, and the global properties of couples.

Family Intervention

The intervention in the family is usually used in family therapy for an identified patient who is a member of the family. The intervention in the whole family or subsystems of the family, is necessary when the intervention with the person who has the problem is not enough for solving the individual problem. And when the problem is relational by its nature (e.g. violence), and/or it is a global problem of the family. This is so since the levels (individuals, relational, subsystems of the family, family, school, and organizations) interact with one another and the intervention on the one influence the behavior of the other.

Use of Appropriate Techniques

There are: (a) 17 general techniques used in all cases, (b) 6 techniques for schizophrenia, (c) 6 techniques for couple therapy, (d) 3 techniques for depression, (e) 2 techniques for suicide attempts, (f) 3 techniques for critical comments, (g) 2 techniques for aggression, (j) 2 techniques for bipolar and borderline personality disorders, and (k) 1 technique for hysteric personality and neuroses.

Most techniques of HST can be applied to more than one level of human systems organization (personal, relational, family, and larger systems). Furthermore, some are for individuals, some are for relations, and some for any larger level. We are going to present two techniques that are for general use (not for specific type of problem). General technics influence all cases, no matter what the type of the problem is or the level of systems organization is.

Two Examples of Techniques for General Use

The most commonly used technique is the *over-positive description*. This is not just to emphasize the positive attributes (e.g. Henggeler, 1999). It is to describe all characteristics of the client or of the client system more positive than they are, to the extent that the therapist can support its description using certain arguments. For example, a woman rather ordinary is described as effective, an effective woman as powerful, and a powerful woman as high achieving. A person with IQ of 70 is described as clever, a person with IQ 100 as very clever, a very clever person as genius. This technique is useful for anxiety because the client feels more secure, stronger, and more able to face the difficulties. In depression it is useful in that there is a core difficulty in the feeling of incapability, with low esteem. In the case of schizophrenia, the feelings of security are of paramount importance for the patients. In general, over-positive description is useful for all cases.

Another technique for any use is "*therapeutic alchemy.*" Its name comes from alchemists that changed the low value metals into gold or silver. This technique is based on the Ancient Greek saying "there is no bad without good." According to this technique when the therapist is faced with a property or symptom of the client system that has to be changed, the therapist finds a good component or a positive part or an aspect of the issue that is going to be changed. As a result, the client's system abandons this characteristic in a very simple and easy way. For example, a schizophrenic patient has bodily sexual hallucinations with a well-known man. Then the therapist congratulates the schizophrenic patient for the well-known man's preference for him. Then the hallucination stops and disappears. This technique is more general than the well-known *positive connotation* (Selvini Palazzoli et al., 1978) *and reframing* (Minuchin, 1974). "Over-positive Description" is a therapeutic paradox that finds a positive issue (part) within an overall negative characteristic (whole) or symptom under treatment.

5.5.5 The Fifth Step Is Monitoring the Degree of the Achievement

After having an intervention, the next step is monitoring the results. This is actually a separate step starting just after the intervention. The usual question is after seeing the goals and sub-goals of therapy to ask how much we have succeeded in achieving our goals. We usually ask about the percentage of the progress for each of the goals and the sub-goals. This is important in order to indirectly see if the hypotheses were correct or if there must be complementary ones. Also, in some cases where there are not relevant hypotheses that can be confirmed or rejected or by nature these hypotheses cannot be falsified then we consider if they can be indirectly tested by trying to achieve therapy on the basis of this hypotheses and if there is progress and reduction of the complains then we can accept that this hypothesis was correct. The monitoring of success in Brief therapy (DeShazer, 1985), the progress from 1 to 10 can be used also for monitoring the progress of therapy.

Besides that, it is good to use a more reliable standardized questionnaire for individuals and for family. This monitoring during the therapy is useful for the same reasons described above plus for us to have an overall view of the progress. In the case of psychotic patients, we use other relevant tests.

5.5.6 The Sixth Step Is a Circular Process if There Are Difficulties in Therapy

If there are difficulties in therapy, for example, if it lasts more than 10 sessions or there is no progress regarding the goals of therapy, in the monitoring of progress, then we start to examine the therapy from the beginning.

The difficulty may be due to partial joining. The client may not have accepted, admire, or believe that the therapist is a good one. The client, for various reasons, may be not ready to tell the whole truth and only the truth. These difficulties must be overcome otherwise it may be better to stop the therapy, or suggest another therapist. A relevant discussion may bring to light an important reason or issue and thus help the problem to be resolved.

The difficulty may be due to the incomplete specification of the goal or goals of therapy. It may well be that there are other additional goals or problems to be resolved that the client believed as no important. The therapist then if he or she thinks that the problem and reason for therapy is incomplete then must ask additional questions concerning the details of the problem for solution.

The most common reason of difficulties in therapy is the use for treatment of a wrong hypothesis. Sometimes because there is no way for us to test a hypothesis, it is possible for the therapist to accept a hypothesis without confirming and then even after years of therapy and by a person with ability in techniques, he or she cannot solve the problem and succeed in therapy. Revising, verifying, and thinking of a new hypothesis is a very good strategy for overcoming a difficulty in therapy. We must always remember "a hypothesis which cannot be falsified or verified is dangerous in therapy."

Sometimes, the techniques are not enough and the therapist must employ additional ones.

Presentation of Manualization in Details
For the presentation of the manual together with the 43 techniques of HST there is an upcoming book (Paritsis, 2020) including them together with recent theoretical advances of HST. In this book there is a chapter on Manualization describing in many details the stages and content of manualization. Another chapter is devoted to the techniques of HST in detail.

In this book there is also a proposal for interpretation of therapeutic paradoxes and many other techniques of family therapy as well as techniques from other psychotherapies using the paleologic of the unconscious.

In order to see whether and to which extent HST and its manualization works successfully, we present some trials realized for this purpose. If for the readers the relevant literature is not easily accessible, they can write to the author of this chapter (nparitsis@gmail.com).

5.6 Some Research Trials Before and After Manualization Using Human Systems Therapy

There are some research trials in general prior to manualization using Human Systems Therapy. For all of the following trials, the therapeutic outcomes have been more effective compared to the other psychotherapeutic trials on the same subject until now. This can be checked also by the reader. This effectiveness of HST also surprised us, because in the literature there were some other methods presented as the most effective for each category of problems.

5.6.1 Intervention in an Institution for the Reduction of Aggression in Their Residence

(Paritsis et al., 1987; Paritsis, 2006)

In a residential house for young girls, their caregivers expressed high aggression (even hitting). Instead of intervening on the individual level of aggressive girls there was an intervention in the institution as a whole, in particular in various groups of the residents and workers of the residential house. After 21 sessions within 2 weeks there was a reduction in aggressiveness ($p = 0.036$), an increase in popularity of staff among the residents ($p = 0.0067$), and an increase in the girls asking for help ($p = 0.027$). Besides, there was not any more hitting at the residential house.

5.6.2 Increased Discharge of Chronic Schizophrenics from a Psychiatric Hospital

(Paritsis, 1989; 2006)

In this work, the discharge of schizophrenics was compared between two wards at a psychiatric hospital. Those patients had 17 average years of hospitalization and 53 years of age on average. In both wards there were 20 beds for hospitalized patients. In the experimental group (ward) HST (General Systems Therapy 1989) was applied till that time developed in both the families and the patients. In the control group and ward the functioning and the treatment were as usual. Within 4 years of intervention in the control group there were 49 overall discharges, while in the experimental group there were 173 discharges ($P < 0.05$), that is, 353% more discharges at the experimental group.

5.6.3 Reduction of Psychotic Symptoms in Schizophrenics

(Aivalioti et al., 2009)

The sample comprised 15 young (about 26 years old on average) nonhospitalized schizophrenic patients. Seven in the experimental group and eight in the control group. They did not differ significantly in age, sex, years of illness, and total score of their psychopathology. For etiology biological, family, and psychological factors were considered (e.g. Paritsis, 1994). After 8 therapeutic sessions using HST the psychotic symptoms were reduced by 39% at a statistically significant level ($p = 0,04$). Therapy was on the schizophrenics and on their families with the presence of schizophrenics.

5.6.4 Elimination of Hashish Use in Adolescents

(Lambraki et al., 2014)

A group of 15 adolescents from a technical school who were approximately 17 years old and used hashish were divided into two groups. One control group with 7 adolescents and one experimental with 8 adolescents. The etiology of abuse in general is considered to be low satisfaction of human interactions (Paritsis & Stewart, 1979). The intervention was through group therapy following HST. After 8 sessions all users stopped using hashish ($p = 0,008$), while at the same time only some pupils stopped using hashish ($p = 0,62$). At the same time family satisfaction was increased only in the experimental group ($p = 0,04$).

Some Recent Research Trials After Manualization
We are going to present some results from 2016, a time when the students and staff of our institute clearly used the steps and content of manualization.

5.6.5 Reduction of Symptomatology in Cases by the Students in Their Final Examination

(Aliki et al., 2016)

In order for our students to receive the diploma in systems therapy they have to conduct therapy, within 10 sessions, if possible, in order to cover the aims of the client system. Seven of these students had 7 cases during the early summer of 2016. The results after 4 sessions of therapy are presented in Fig. 5.1, and they are based on GHQ 28 items (Goldberg, 1978).

There was a statistically significant difference of $p = 0,018$, with 74% overall reduction of psychopathology within that time.

Therapy continued for the 10 session maximum and achieved a total GHQ less than 5 (without psychopathology).

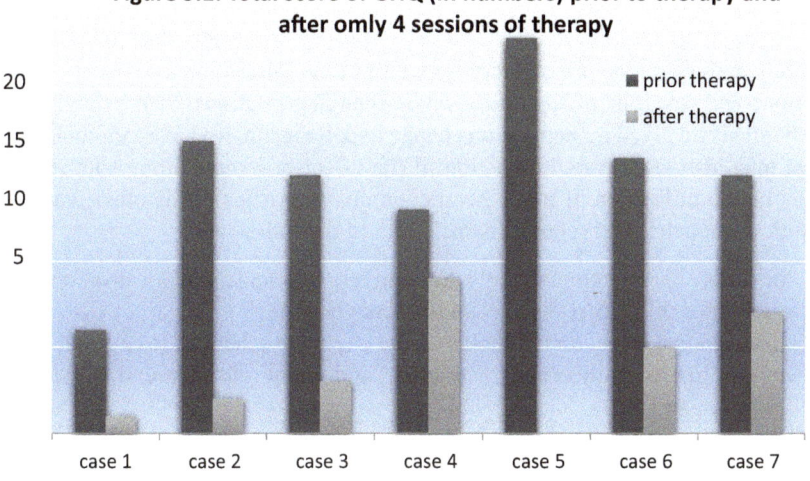

Fig. 5.1 Total score of GHQ (in numbers) prior to therapy and after only 4 sessions of therapy

5.6.6 Reduction of Symptomatology in Psychiatric Cases After 4 Sessions

(Lambraki & Paritsis, 2019)

A similar work was carried out by a senior teaching staff with measures after 4 sessions on nonpsychotic psychiatric cases. The degree of psychopathology was estimated by GHQ 28 items (Goldberg, 1978) and family functioning by SCORE (Stratton et al. 2014). The results after only 4 sessions show a statistically significant difference ($p < 0,001$) on both the GHQ and SCORE. At the same time, 77.8% of the cases became nonpsychiatric cases (score less than 5 which is the cut off point for psychiatric cases), which are basically treated.

5.7 Discussion

As we see from the history of HST and then from the results of trials, this method of systemic therapy is at the same time effective and short. This was always a surprise to the author without it being adequately explained, and thus remains a question. Only, perhaps, an external observer of the method can give a reason. One reason and possibly the most significant can be its multilevel nature. No other method is multilevel to such an extent. Multilevel intervention offers for mathematical and logical reasons a multiplicative effect in interventions on more than one level.

Another multilevel intervention is that of Liddle (2010) that also for drug abuse and is the most successful.

Relevant to multilevel intervention is the fact that individual intervention is largely applied on the internal representations (e.g. interactional schemata) of interactions and relations of the client. After changing relations, then behavior of the individuals involved in the relation change two. So again, we have a circular process that may also lead to multiplication of the effect of intervention. Another reason may be the utilization of main therapeutic characteristics of the other main therapeutic approaches and schools, namely that of the following:

- the family and systemic therapy utilizing relations and circular causation, and the techniques of the first- and second-order cybernetics,
- the Cognitive Behavioral Therapy, using cognitive schemata (as a result of learning) as its core theoretical structure and point of intervention, similar to zeugmas, and
- the psychoanalysis having as its core characteristic and place of intervention the unconscious and its paleologic.

Manualization improved the effectiveness of HST and possibly contributed to the effectiveness of the approach and leading to a few-sessions type of therapy.

HST always has success regarding the time used and effectiveness. However, manualization and the clear content of steps possibly contributed to the reduction of time spent and to the effectiveness of HST in our view.

Analyzing each step leads the therapist to follow what is important and necessary in order for them to achieve better results. In this way if a therapist does not achieve good joining this will certainly affect the degree of success of therapy. In particular, a detailed description of the goals of therapy also contributes to a shorter and better outcome. Furthermore, without confirming a valid hypothesis, the time spent in therapy and the success of it are in doubt, and it is like shooting in the dark to achieve the goal. After confirming a hypothesis, the time spent for discussing without using techniques or other means of therapy is a waste. Thus, through manualization the main points and ways for an effective therapy are emphasized as well. This applies in general and for sure to HST. We have to agree that the lack of a clear answer of how and why such effectiveness is realized by HST is a disadvantage.

Research on specific categories of problems is important for further testing and developing HST. Especially, psychoses and psychosomatics are possible targets for future research.

References

Aivalioti, H., Trikas, P., Chrisos, P., Papageorgiou, P., Katahanakis, K., & Paritsis, N. (2009). Reduction of psychotic symptoms in people with schizophrenia, using Human Systems Therapy, a randomized controlled trial. *Human Systems: The Journal of Therapy, Consultation & Training, 20*(1), 81–98.

Aliki, A., Anastasia, A., Kalliontzaki, I., Liakou, E., Pitsikakis, A., Pitsikakis, K., Savvaki, C., & Koutsou, A. (2016). *Effectiveness of intervention of senior students of a 4year training program in systemic therapy that emphasizes Human Systems Therapy*. Conference of the European Family therapy Association, October 2016, Athens Greece.

Anifandaki A., Kalliontzaki, I., Liakou, E., Pitsikakis, Pitsikakis, A., Savvaki, C.,& Koutsou A. (2016). *Effectiveness of intervention of senior students of a 4-year training program in systems therapy that emphasizes Human Systems Therapy, Book of abstracts*. Conference of European Family Therapy Association, 28 Sept-1 Oct. 2016, Athens Greece.

Arieti S. (1978). On schizophrenia, phobias, depression, psychotherapy and further shores of psychiatry. *Selected papers of Silvano Ariety* Brunner/Mazel, New York.

Ashby, R. (1952). *An introduction to Cybernetics*. Chapman and Hall, London.

Berger, P. L., & Luckmann, T. (1966). *The social construction of reality: A treatise in the sociology of knowledge*. Anchor Books.

Boscolo, L., & Bertrando, P. (1996). *Systemic therapy with individuals*. Guilford Press, New York.

Conant, R., & Ashby, R. (1970). Every good regulator of a system must be a model of that system. *International Journal of Systems Science, 1*, 89–97.

DeShazer, S. (1985). *Keys to solution in brief therapy*. W. W. Norton.

Foucault, M. (2006). *The history of madness*. Routledge.

Freud, S. (1898, released 1900). *The interpretation of dreams. 1910 The interpretation of dreams the illustrated edition 2010* (pp. 9–68). Sterling Press.

Gergen, K. (1982). *Towards transformation in social knowledge*. Springer.

Goldberg, D. (1978). *Manual of the general health questionnaire*. NFER-Nelson.

Henggeler, S. (1999). Multisystemic therapy: An overview of clinical procedures, outcomes, and policy implications. *Child Psychology & Psychiatry Review, 4*(1), 2–10.

Lambraki M. and N. Paritsis (2019) Four-sessions intervention outcome, International Conference of European Family Therapy Association, Napoli Italy, October 2019.

Lambraki, M., Kilaidakis, S., & Paritsis, N. (2014). Human Systems Therapy for adolescent cannabis use. In C. Soldatos, P. Ruiz, & D. D. M. Riba (Eds.), *Pluralism in psychiatry: Diversity and convergence* (Medimond International Proceedings) (pp. 161–164).

Liddle, H. (2010). Multidimensional family therapy: A science-based treatment system. *Australian and New Zealand Journal of Family Therapy, 31*(2), 133–148.

Maturana, H., & Varela, F. (1984). *The tree of knowledge: The biological roots of human understanding*. Shamhala Books.

Miller, J. (1978). *Living systems*. Chapman and Hall.

Minuchin, S. (1974). *Families and family therapy*. Harvard University Press.

Paritsis, N. (1989). Towards a general systems therapy of human behavior, In Ledington R. (Ed.) *Proceedings of the 33rd Annual meeting of the International Society for the Systems Science*. Edinburgh, Scotland UK, 225–260.

Paritsis, N. (1994). The identity of schizophrenia: A multilevel systems approach. *World Futures, 42*, 107–118.

Paritsis, N. (2006). *Human systems evolution and therapy, systemic psychiatry* (Vol. II). BETA Medical Publishers.

Paritsis, N. (2010). Human systems therapy. *Systems Research, 26*, 1–13.

Paritsis, N. (2020). *A new human systems therapy, systemic psychiatry* (Vol. III). BETA Medical Publishers.

Paritsis, N., & Stewart, D. (1979). An interaction theory of motivation and purpose in natural intelligent systems. In R. Ericson (Ed.) *Improving the human condition: Quality and stability in social systems*. Society for General Systems Research (pp. 866–874).

Paritsis, N., Lampidi, A., & Todoulou, M. (1987). *A systemic multilevel intervention model: Application and evaluation*. Abstracts, International Congress of Family Therapy, The patterns which connect, Prague, Czechoslovakia, p. 205.

Popper, K. (1959). *The logic of scientific discovery*. Basic Books.

Pote, H., Stratton, P., Cottrell, D., Shapiro, D., & Boston, P. (2003). Systemic Family Therapy can be manualised: Research process and findings. *Journal of Family Therapy, 25*, 236–262.

Prigogine I. and Stengers I. (1986). *Order out of chaos*, Fontana paperbacks, London.

Russell, B. (1903). *The principles of mathematics*. Cambridge University Press.

Savvaki, and Koutsou A. (2016). Efectiveness of intervention of senior students of a 4-year training program in systems therapy that emphasizes Human Systems Therapy, Book of abstracts, Conference of European Family Therapy Association, 28 Sept-1 Oct. 2016, Athens Greece.

Selvini, P. M., Boscolo, L., Ceccin, G., & Prata, G. (1978). *Paradox and counter paradox*. Iason Aronson.

Stratton, P., Lask, J., Bland, J., Nowotny, E., Evans, C., Singh, R., Janes, E., & Peppiatt, A. (2014). Detecting therapeutic improvement early in therapy: Validation of the SCORE-15 index of family functioning and change. *Journal of Family Therapy, 36*(1), 3–19.

Von Domarus, E. (1944). The specific laws of logic in schizophrenia. In A. Kasinin (Ed.), *Language and thought in schizophrenia* (pp. 104–115). Norton.

Wiener, N. (1948). *Cybernetics: Or control and communication in the animal and the machine*. The MIT Press.

Chapter 6
Manualizing the Therapeutic Process in Systemic Therapy: From the Construction of the Hypothesis to the Assessment of Change

Andrea Mosconi and Barbara Trotta

6.1 Introduction: Why Resume the Effort of Manualizing the Hypothesis and the Therapeutic Process Today?

For therapists who refer to the Milan approach, the **hypothesis** of starting to manualize systemic family therapy sessions is already mentioned in the work: "Hypothesising, Circularity and Neutrality." Selvini Palazzoli et al. (1980) placed themselves in such a perspective explicitly declaring that they wanted to set their work "on research for describable and transmissible methods that erode space into stereotypes such as: nose, sixth sense, etc." and concluded with the famous question: "May family therapy produce change only through the negentropic effect of our current method of conducting the session, regardless of a final intervention?". With this statement they shifted their interest from the final intervention, which had characterized the 1970s to 1980s, to the construction of the entire session, that is to say on the construction of an identifiable and repeatable therapeutic process (Mosconi et al., 1999) and therefore to its possible manualization. Throughout the article there are well-detailed indications and procedures regarding each of the three fundamental directives for conducting the session. With particular regard to the hypothesizing process, the foundation of all therapeutic work, its ability to have a "negentropic effect," is entrusted to precise characteristics. The abovementioned directives are considered essential for introducing new information, capable of reorganizing semantics and relationships in the client system or in the client's system(s).[1] We there-

---

[1] We will frequently use the word "client" in the text. We specify that for "client," we mean both the individual person and the family that, considered as a system, we consider a single client. Therefore, all the actions referred to the "client," if referred to the family system, must be applied to each component of the system.

A. Mosconi (✉) · B. Trotta
The Padua Centre of Family Therapy, Padua, Italy
e-mail: mosconia1@gmail.com; info@cptf.org

fore find it useful to highlight them for the purposes of the current discussion. In our opinion, they can be grouped into two categories: (1) the functional value of the hypothesis and (2) its structural characteristics:

1. General functional value and cognitive and conversational functions of the **hypothesis**:

    (a) *The* **hypothesis**, *in itself, is neither true nor false, but only more or less useful*, and, due to its guiding function, it occupies a central place in the investigation work.
    (b) Through such **hypothesis** the therapist *establishes the starting point of his investigation*, carried out with suitable methods for verifying the validity of the hypothesis itself, *that is its usefulness and shareability*.
    (c) The function of the **hypothesis** in conducting the family session is to *guarantee the therapist's activity*. This activity consists in *tracing (give a meaning to) relational patterns*.
    (d) The therapist's **hypothesis** *introduces*, instead, *the powerful input of the unexpected* in the family and therefore *acts in the direction of information*.

2. Structural characteristics of the **hypothesis**: the fundamental requirement rightly pointed out by the authors is that the hypotheses formulated are not "whatever hypotheses" but must be "systemic hypotheses"[2] (2) and therefore:

    (a) *Include all the family members* and provide a supposition regarding the *overall relational functioning*.
    (b) *Describe the relationships*.
    (c) *Not attribute faults but positively connote different behaviors*, linking them to one another to show reciprocity.
    (d) *Include the symptomatic behavior highlighting its positivity* in order to maintain the system's overall balance.

In the years following these statements, however, the "Milan team" will split about the "truth" or "usefulness" of the **hypothesis**, and the restructuring qualities of the hypothesis will be developed differently. In the Nuovo Centro per lo Studio della Famiglia (founded by Palazzoli Selvini and Prata), the clinical activity will highlight the qualities that underline the "validity of the hypotheses" (1.b), therefore its "investigative function." On the other hand, in the Centro Milanese di Terapia della Famiglia (founded by Boscolo and Cecchin), what will be kept in mind and developed are the more specifically cognitive qualities, which "trace (give a meaning to) relational patterns" (1.c); this is what we could call its "narrative function." This different use of the hypothesis will mark a clear dividing line between

---

[2] We write here for the first time the wording "systemic hypothesis" with capital letters as initials to indicate that, while remaining faithful to therapeutic work as a hypothesis process, the goal of our path is then the co-construction with the client (s) of a "systemic hypothesis" which has all the requirements described above and, moreover, is well done. We will use this term several times during our work.

family-oriented therapists and therapeutic relationship-oriented therapists. For the former the hypotheses will be part of the knowledge of the family, and for the latter they will become part of the construction of the therapeutic relationship. The ideas developed by second-order cybernetics that will start the constructivist trend in systemic therapy will contribute to widen this gap. The basic affirmation was then, as Maturana and Varela (1980) point out, that living is knowing and knowing is not explaining but generating descriptions within one's organizational closure and sharing them with other systems through language. The therapist was therefore considered, eminently, an organizationally closed observer who was only able to generate descriptions to share with the patient in the therapeutic conversation, a constructor of new interactive realities (Cecchin, 1987). However, as highlighted in a previous work (Mosconi et al., 1999), to which we refer the reader, the effect of this conceptual passage from hypothesis to description made the hypotheses' construction process much more generic. It was mainly aimed at producing different descriptions among which the client system would choose the most suitable one. The call to therapists during this period was frequent and determined. "Do not have an idea of what the family should be like" (Telfener, 1986), and later Boscolo et al. (1987) recommended to "change interpretations," and Cecchin (1987) added the invitation "to get engaged to the hypothesis." This amplification of the descriptions sometimes came to jeopardize the "systemic" characteristics, so well specified in the famous article, of the hypotheses themselves. The critics from some authors were precise (Minuchin, 1999). Therefore, in the wake of the scientific debate regarding these ideas, the desire to clarify certain aspects seemed to manifest again. Thus, a line of research on family psychotherapy and on the hypothesizing process as "conversation" and/or "narration" developed. The desire was, precisely, to reduce what ended up seeming an excessive generality. New attempts appeared to manualize it: trace its criteria, the linguistic structures that can be used, and the application methods. Among the authors who have worked in this direction, we find Watzlawick (1978), Bandler and Grinder (1975a, 1975b), Andersen (1987), Tomm (1987a, 1987b, 1988), Viaro and Leonardi (1990), Boscolo et al. (1992), Sluzki (1992), White (1992), and Mosconi et al. (1996, 1999), to name just a few. This debate became part of the wider chapter of research on the process in family psychotherapy that developed in the same years (Pinsof, 1995). However, in our opinion, there are still large areas to be clarified. In addition, over time, the need to verify the efficacy of therapies became increasingly present; today this is an indispensable requirement for the validation of any method.

In the team of the Centro Padovano di Terapia della Famiglia, these premises stimulated and supported the discussion on the methods of construction of the hypotheses and, more generally, of the therapeutic process and, therefore, on their manualization. All the work that we will explain below derives from it. This resulted in the possibility to structure clinical research projects and to give a strong boost to the teaching of which it has become the soul and internal structure. Students learn to conduct sessions by following the different steps that we will describe below. Research and teaching have thus mutually enhanced one another in a harmonious circuit.

6.2 Methodology

Our manualization is articulated on some specific points:

1. Phases of the therapeutic process
2. Methods of co-construction of the systemic hypothesis, their pace in the therapeutic process, and the construction of a relational folder suitable for detecting useful information
3. Use of the "systemic quadrilateral" in order to construct a plausible and complete systemic hypothesis
4. Coding of the interventions and their pace in the therapeutic process
5. Evaluation of the intervention's efficacy

In this work we will try to give a very brief description. We refer the readers to the cited bibliography to investigate further.

6.2.1 Phases of the Therapeutic Process

Already in previous works, one of the authors (Mosconi, 1992, 1993; Mosconi et al., 1996) had made the hypothesis that in the general construction of the therapeutic process of a systemic therapy, some fairly constant "phases" can be schematically identified. These "phases" could be independent from the therapist's specific style. This hypothesis was derived from the observation and codification of conduction styles of different therapists. Furthermore, each of them is characterized by specific "objectives," actions, and sub-objectives. Their definition, confirmed by clinical practice, guided us in describing all the further steps of our manualization. It allows to:

1. Frame and articulate all the subsequent actions in recognizable sequences.
2. Make clear that the progression given to the whole process aims at facilitating the client in following the succession of the topics treated according to the principle of "pacing-leading" (Bandler & Grinder, 1975a).

We therefore distinguish three phases and five objectives, each characterized by specific actions. Figure 6.1 presents the overview of the whole process.

Now let us move on to a more specific description:

1. Contact Phase

Objective A: Seek for connection with the client. It is the moment in which the therapist asks the client to explain their request for help and expose, more or less freely, the facts.

T: "Why are you here?" / C: "Well doctor this is the reason …".

At this stage the therapist is in a listening position.

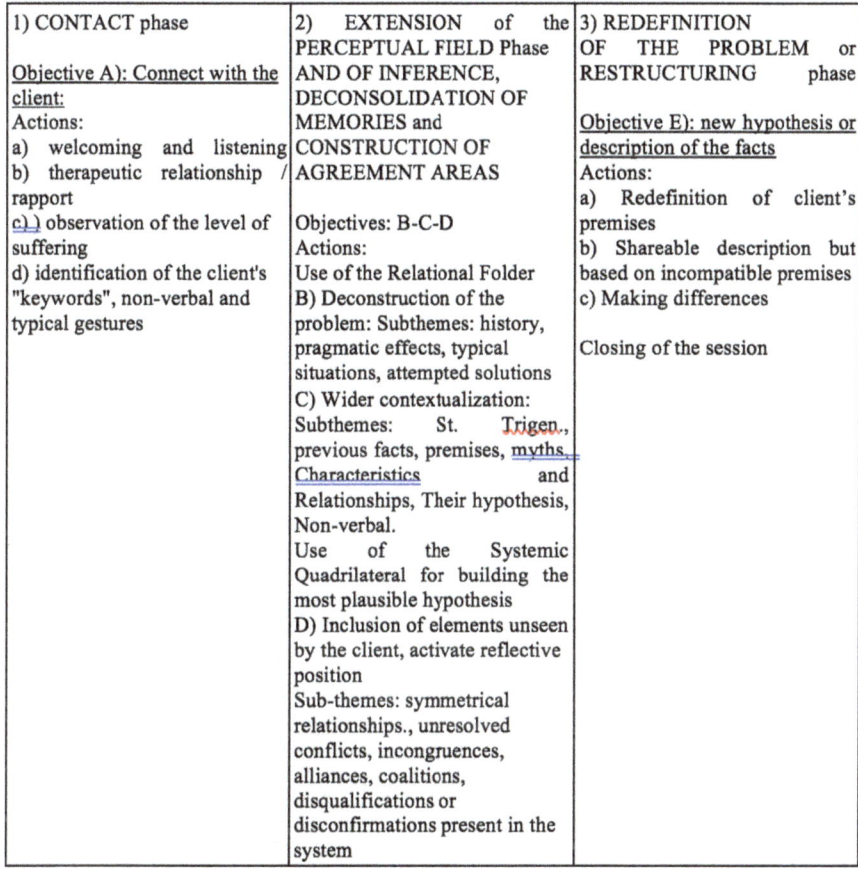

Fig. 6.1 Phases of the therapeutic process

Actions and sub-objectives:

1. Welcoming the client, making him feel comfortable
2. Construction of the therapeutic relationship through listening and through a responsive attention or "rapport" (Erickson & Rossi, 1979)
3. Assessment of the client's level of suffering
4. Observation of the keywords through which the problem is described and non-verbal and typical gestures that associate with the description

It is, therefore, a fundamental phase to begin that work of co-construction of the relationship that will lead to the choice of what we call the "gateway" to the problem.

2. *Phase of Expansion of the Observation and Inference Field, Deconsolidation of Memories, and Construction of Agreement Areas*

We want to underline that this expansion is fundamental for retrieving parts of history erased by the client(s) in the traumatic path full of unresolved conflicts that led to the problem's birth. Extending attention to this aspect acquires even greater importance today, in light of the recent theories that consider de-consolidation and reconsolidation of traumatic memories (Ecker et al., 2012) and the adaptive processing of traumas (Shapiro, 1995) as bases for the solution of problems.

It is characterized by Objectives B, C, and D.

T: "Help me understand better." / C: "I'll explain …".

Objective B: Guide the client towards expanding the problem's description. The therapist stimulates the client to specify the nature of the problem, suggesting him to talk about a whole series of information in order to co-construct a more exhaustive and detailed description. The expansions obtained will begin to widen the client's observation and inference field in the direction of the construction of the systemic hypothesis related to the problem.

Typical actions and sub-objectives:

1. Increase the welcoming and the rapport.
2. Historicize and contextualize the problem to start a deconstruction and depatologization.
3. Identify the pragmatic effects on the relations between the client and his system and between the system's components.
4. Identify the way in which the client(s) defines himself/themselves in the relationship regarding the problem. In the case of a system, it is necessary to identify all the members' positions.
5. Identify the problem's typical worsening and improving situations.
6. Identify the effects on the system of the attempted solutions.
7. Increase the observation of the client: language, keywords, and nonverbal and typical gestures.

Objective C: To further expand the client's observation field. It is the moment in which the therapist, starting from the facts exposed, stimulates the client to deconstruct and decode going backwards the process of coordination and calibration (Bateson, 1979) done to arrive to the problem. This, in fact, has become a fundamental part of the tautology that encloses it.

Actions and sub-objectives:

1. Deconstruct the problem through a wider contextualization.
2. Identify behaviors, relational sequences, facts, semantic premises, and family myths that built it.
3. Contextualize and connect them with the system's history.
4. Build in this way a systemic hypothesis of the problem intended as a shared description, thus activating the areas of agreement.

Objective D: Orient the client towards a specific focus of his observation and inference field on aspects not seen by him in order to prepare the restructuring. It is the moment in which the therapist invites the client to consider and focus on new, and/or previously unseen and unexpected, issues.

Actions and sub-objectives:

1. Focus, test, and make clearer elements which are new and useful to build the next restructuring: unseen aspects of the family game, pragmatic effects of the symptom, situations in which the client/s have shown skills and resources, etc.
2. Observe if these elements can be shared with the client.
3. Allow the client to recall and recover facts and emotions underlying the problem's birth or that preceded it.
4. Recall and begin to make clear for the client the sets of relational situations, thoughts, emotions, ideas of self, and marks of the facts that justify the "symptom's choice."
5. Activate in the client a thinking position concerning these elements.

The construction of these steps is, as previously mentioned, progressively oriented to allow the final passage of restructuring.

3. Phase of Problem Redefinition or Restructuring

Objective E: Propose a new hypothesis or description of the facts to the client. This new description is obviously closely connected with the systemic hypothesis constructed. It is the moment of "restructuring" that is of the difference useful for "making a difference" (Bateson, 1979).

Actions and sub-objectives:

1. Redefine the client's premises.
2. Enhance the client's issues that were unseen or unexpected but that emerged in Objective D.
3. Hand back to the client a description of the facts that is shareable as it is based on what they said but because it is based on the elements that had remained unseen before, based on premises that are incompatible with those from which he had started before.
4. Therefore, put the client in the position of having to get rid of one of the two premises.

For a process of internal mental economy, the system (individual or family) will find itself in the need to produce a new type of description and/or tautology in order to make the new elements emerged compatible.

This moment may be summarized in the following sentence:

T: "Here is my idea of why you are here." / C: "But, really, doctor …. (and, if all goes well) Ah! I had never thought about that."

The closing of the session comes next.

6.2.2 Methods of Co-Construction of the Systemic Hypothesis, Their Pacing in the Therapeutic Process, and the Construction of a Relational Folder Suitable for Retrieving Useful Information

It is very important for us to emphasize that the work of co-construction of the systemic hypothesis does not aim at a "true" hypothesis but rather a "more plausible and complete" one. Over time, some fundamental themes that must be dealt with during the session have been identified. There are three objectives:

1. Have, in an orderly manner, a sufficient amount of information to connect.
2. Allow that expansion of the client's observation and inference field, which has been mentioned above (Phase 2).
3. Identify and strategically decide the order to be used in dealing with them in the easiest way for the client, as mentioned, according to the principle of "pacing-leading" (Bandler & Grinder, 1975a, 1975b).

For this reason they have acquired the name of "pillars of the hypothesis" (Gonzo et al., 1999; Mosconi & Tirelli, 1997). Their dissertation and the achievement of the objectives mentioned above required the construction of a relational folder (hereinafter RF). The first version of it was developed by the SIPPR Research Commission a few years ago (Aurilio, 1996; Viaro, 1996). This first example was followed by extensive work by Gonzo et al. (1999) that included the application of specific RFs as an "interview intervention" in a series of different problematic situations.

The RF has become a consolidated procedure in our clinical practice. It is a tool that allows us to guide the therapeutic activity described above by providing for each pillar a list of previously well-formed questions. Not being able, due to the brevity of this chapter, to thoroughly expose the complete protocol, we will briefly describe the themes that constitute it by showing their connection with the "pillars of the hypothesis," the associated reflection themes, and Phase 2 of the therapeutic process.

1. **System composition or characters and interpreters.** It is usually the first theme dealt with and often humorously announced with the words "first the characters and performers and then the story," in order to lighten the passage of expansion to the system which may be difficult to understand for those who came to therapy only focused on the problem. It is often reconstructed by simultaneously drawing the trigenerational genogram.
    Topics considered in the RF:
    1. Data identifying the case and trigenerational composition of the system
    2. Personal data of each (e.g., name, age, job)

Often, already at this stage, it is possible to start having important information about the position that the various components occupy in the system or about some myths and family premises.

This topic already implicitly introduces the systemic vision of the problems with which we will work on during the sessions.

2. **History of the problem and of its pragmatic effects on the system.** This theme introduces in a decisive way the whole deconstruction of the problem and the deconsolidation of the traumatic memories: Objective B.

   Topics planned in the RF:
   (a) History of the problem: beginning, diagnosis (problem defined by the sender, initial diagnostic classification, final diagnosis), immediately preceding or coinciding circumstances, worsening, improvements, related "critical situations" that worsen or improve it
   (b) Problem's pragmatic effects (effects on the designated patient, on family members, including extended families and other potentially significant persons, what is the main aspect of the problem in the system's life, who suffers the most, if there are relatives or acquaintances who attend less or more frequently the house since the problem arose)
   (c) Attempted solutions

What comes next are "pillars" number 3 and 4 that are a structuring part of Objective C. They must be treated in a way that is considered easier for the client and for the conversation's fluency: either in sequence as shown below (3 and 4), in an inverted order (4 and 3), or combined in parallel (3 together with 4). We will describe them below:

3. **Trigenerational history of the system.** The theme of the third pillar describes itself.

   Themes planned in the RF:

   a) Dates of all the important events in the family's trigenerational history following the life cycle evolution. Sub-themes: extended family history also of the parents of the couple of the system in therapy, couple's prematrimonial history; period of marriage prior to the birth of children; birth and raising of children; adolescence of children; autonomy of children; and old age of grandparents. Identifying what has been the main problem for each sub-theme
   b) Traumatic events or changes in the system's composition, paying specific attention to the time preceding the birth of the problem

4. **Characters and relationships.** This theme is dealt with by asking the clients to qualify each of these aspects with three adjectives. The discussion of this pillar implies the systematic use of triadic or circular questions (Selvini Palazzoli et al., 1980).

   Planned sub-themes in the RF:

   a) Personal characteristics of each member of the trigenerational and relationships between them all, dyad by dyad
   b) Why are there conflicts
   c) Relationships with the families of origin
   d) Synthetic definition of the family

5. **Clients' hypotheses on the problem.** This theme is part of the analysis of the family's request. It addresses how people explain their discomfort and what ideas about the origin of the suffering they start therapy with.
    Themes planned in the RF:
    a) What hypothesis does each one have about how the problem was born?
    b) Why and since when each member has formulated that hypothesis?
    c) Which solutions each member thinks are best?

    The topic can be treated in two moments depending on the goals that may be achieved. If treated after theme 2 and before themes 3 and 4, it allows to better identify the availability to therapy of the system's different members: point (c) discussed above. If treated as theme 5, it can be useful to see if the discussion of themes 3 and 4 has already favored some elaboration of a relational hypothesis in the system.

6. **Nonverbal: this theme is transversal to the whole therapy.**
    Themes planned in the RF:
    a) It has no specific location because it regards the observation of how the various nonverbal behavior's comment on the statements made. It is recorded in the session's diary.

The discussion of all these issues, as mentioned above, marks Phase 2 of the therapeutic process, for the achievement of Objectives B, C, and D.

To achieve this goal and, therefore, formulate a possible systemic hypothesis of the problem, which is "plausible" and "complete," the information taken from the interview done with the relational folder is reordered with the guidance of the "systemic quadrilateral" (Mosconi, 2008; Mosconi et al., 2013).

6.2.3 Use of the "Systemic Quadrilateral" for the Construction of a Complete and Well-Done Systemic Hypothesis

We have already focused on this construct in previous publications, to which we refer for brevity reasons. In this text we will only describe some important aspects:

The systemic quadrilateral consists of four observational levels: (a) narration (the problem experienced), (b) person (the intrapsychical conflict), (c) communication (communicative incongruence), and (d) relationships (relational conflict). The left side of the quadrilateral allows us to think about individual dimensions and, the right side, about relational ones. Furthermore, the upper part describes the problem's visible dimension which we will call phenomenological-descriptive, while the lower part, the problem's unseen dimension or the one concerning deep dynamics which we will call the generator processes. In this way the quadrilateral can be represented as follows (Fig. 6.2).

Therefore, we have four descriptive levels available:

6 Manualizing the Therapeutic Process in Systemic Therapy...   111

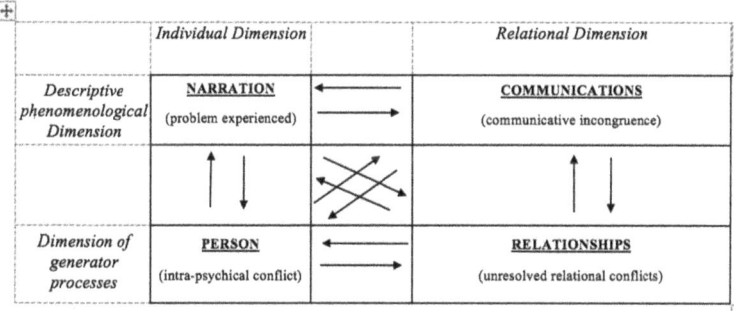

Fig. 6.2 The systemic quadrilateral

1. Individual phenomenological (narration of the problem: the problem experienced)
2. Individual generator (person: individual functioning and the intrapsychic conflict experienced)
3. Relational phenomenology (communication: the system's communication methods)
4. Relational generator (relationships: the system's history and developments and the unresolved conflicts)

What is important for the purpose of manualizing therapy is that at each level, we propose to the therapist some things to observe and some questions to answer which allow one to build the **hypothesis** progressively. All of this is part of the questionnaire called progressive questions for the construction of the hypothesis (PQCH) (Mosconi et al., 2013) which is further updated here:

1. *Individual Phenomenological (Narration of the Problem: The Problem Experienced):* it specifies the descriptive level that characterizes everything that emerges from the problem's description and all the various themes proposed during the session. An attentive and curious listening ability and the observations made at this level contribute to building Phase 1 and to support the therapeutic relationship.

    Pay attention to these aspects:

    a) Thoughts
    b) Words
    c) Actions
    d) Emotions

    Questions to answer: there are no specific questions. They will be proposed in the following polarities.

2. *Individual Generator (Person: Individual Functioning and the Intrapsychic Conflict experienced):* it describes the narration's cognitive qualities, the moods and managing of emotions, and the attitude in relationships of each and summarizes all the observations that can be made individually. The information for this polarity come from the observation of the participants and from the answers given to the session's various topics.

Pay attention to these aspects:
a) How each one defines the problem
b) Significant verbal patterns: semantics and keywords through which each expresses himself/herself and defines the relationship with others
c) Significant nonverbal patterns that comment on the narrations and define the relationship with others
d) Coherence of the descriptions
e) Congruence between verbal and nonverbal
f) Integration in emotion management

Questions to answer:
a) What idea does each one have of him/herself and of relationships with the world?
b) With which premises does each one evaluate him/herself?
c) What are the keywords of each one?
d) How much and in which area does the designated patient invalidate his/her self: self-worth, responsibility, competence, safety, etc.?
e) How compromised are the cognitive abilities (presence of dissociation) of the patient or of others?
f) Level of suffering of each.
g) From whom did each and specifically the designated patient expect the greatest confirmations?
h) Definition of each one's relationship with therapy.

Polarities (3) and (4) are the most important because they are relational. The information to answer the questions asked in these polarities is provided by the discussion of the "pillars of the hypothesis."

3. *Relational Phenomenological (Communication: the System's Communication Methods):* it describes the feedback circuits between the system's components translating them, according to the axioms of communication (Watzlawick et al., 1967), into relational rules and critical functions of the system: how does the system work in the *hic et nunc*?

Pay attention to these aspects:

a) Composition of the trigenerational system.
b) Stability or instability of relationships in the various systems.
c) How the problem is described by each one.
d) How the designated patient describes himself and his system.
e) How the system describes itself and the designated patient.
f) Significant verbal and nonverbal patterns of each (see above).
g) What behaviors build the problem and follow its manifestation.
h) Which aspects and behaviors does the therapist consider most relevant.
i) Redundancy.
j) Who is the most in agreement with whom and in what situations?
k) Who prevails over whom and in which situations?
l) Clarity and congruence of messages with particular reference to permissions and prohibitions.

m) Family myths and significant semantic premises of the system.
n) Pragmatic effects of the problem on the system.
o) Attempted solutions.
p) Symmetries or complementarities between the different hypotheses on the origin of the problem.
q) Distance of their hypotheses from a relational hypothesis.
   Questions to answer:

a) What is the "prevailing relational pattern" (PRP) of each one, in his system, in the social context? (Mosconi, 2014).
b) What does he/she do to look this way?
c) What do others do to allow him/her?
d) Which are the critical situations in which mostly emerge: conflict, abandonment, falling in love, etc., and with whom?
e) Which relationships involve acceptance, refusal, confirmation, disqualification, or disconfirmation?
f) Which relationships involve symmetry or complementarity?
g) How do borders (external, internal), hierarchies, alliances, and rules (permissions and prohibitions) work in the system?
h) What are the main inconsistencies in defining the mutual relationship?
i) Which inconsistencies reinforce the problem most?
j) Which relational rules can be hypothesized by the problem's pragmatic effects?
k) What are the effects of the solutions attempted on the relationships between the system's components, and what relational rules can be derived?
l) What solutions should not be tried again?
m) What willingness does each one have to accept a systemic therapy?

4. *Relational Generator (Relationships: The System's History and Developments and the Unresolved Conflicts):* it describes specifically which unresolved conflicts, occurring over time, can justify the inconsistencies observed: how did they get to work this way?
   Pay attention to these aspects:
   a) Differences in social variables and personal data between the components of the trigenerational system: gender, age, professions, generational order, etc.
   b) Evolution of the life cycle of the various system components
   c) Verbal and nonverbal comments on the various topics that make it possible to glimpse relational rules
   d) Problem's start date, worsening, improvements, and coinciding situations
   e) "Chronograms" or "parallel chronologies" useful for identifying the coincidence or succession between facts that permit to infer the rules of the family game
   f) Adjectives given to all the trigenerational system's components and to the relationships between them
   g) For the parents: what things did they like or dislike about the partner

h) For sons and daughters: adjectives given to sons and daughters and to the relationship between them
i) Critical events that characterized the system's life
j) Premises and family myths and consequent facts
k) Unresolved conflicts
l) Facts that favored them
m) What function has each one taken on in such situations
n) How this function can be correlated with the PRP of each
o) What the patient (s) does with his problem
p) What each one does or has done in response to the problem

Questions to answer:
a) Which "critical situations" seem to coincide with the beginning of the problem and then make it worsen or get better?
b) What is the function occupied by parents in their families of origin?
c) What is the PRP with which they left the families?
d) What is the couple's quid pro quo?
e) How did the relationship and the worsening events develop?
f) What is the position occupied by the children in the relationship with the parents?
g) How and where did everyone learn a certain idea of themselves and a certain way of defining themselves in relationships?
h) What relational history justifies what has been observed?
i) When and how did the patient "decide" to develop the symptomatic behavior?
j) Which conflict is most connected to the birth and maintenance of the problem?
k) How is having a designated patient useful for the system?

This work of connection is all done by the therapist in Phase 2 in order to reach Objective C. The construction of a possible hypothesis will be the basis for focusing on the unseen and unexpected aspects that are part of Objective D and that will be useful to stimulate the hypothesis as a plausible one.

Phase 3 with Objective E will come next: redefinition of the problem. For the rules to construct this redefinition, we refer to the rules that define the general characteristics of the construction of the systemic hypothesis. They have, as mentioned, an intrinsic power to redefine the problem.

6.2.4 Coding and Timing of Interventions in the Therapeutic Process

Each phase of the therapeutic process establishes the prevalence of certain conversational strategies that can be codified with a specifically designed intervention sheet (Mosconi et al., 1996). It is used at the end of each session and has proven to be useful both for research and teaching purposes (Fig. 6.3).

FAMILY_____   Session n°

	During the session	After the session
A) INTERVENTIONS ON THE CONVERSATION'S STRUCTURE		
A1 Allocation of speaking time		
A2 Thematic sequences strategy		
A3 Reconstruction of family history		
A4 Specification questions		
A5 Question for differences		
A6 Comparison of viewpoints		
A7 Circular (or triadic) questions		
A8 Summaries		
B) REFRAME INTERVENTIONS		
B1 Hypothesizing questions		
B2 restructuring summaries		
B3 restructuring hypothesis		
B4 restructuring metaphors and/or similarities		
B5 Positive connotation		
C) PRESCRIBING INTERVENTIONS		
C1 Paradoxical prescriptions		
C3 Restructuring prescriptions		
C4 Generational split		
D) INTERVENTIONS ON THE FAMILY/PATIENT RELATIONSHIP		
D1 judgment suspension		
D2 therapeutic impotence		
D3 Challenge the system		
D4 Splitting between therapists		
D5 Multiple hypotheses and/or Reflecting Team		

Fig. 6.3 Intervention codification worksheet

6.2.5 Efficacy Assessment

The evaluation of the intervention's efficacy is analyzed through a worksheet that we developed (Mosconi et al., 2019) (Fig. 6.4).

The worksheet, in addition to assessing the interventions' efficacy, allows us to have some indication on the progress of the entire therapeutic process and was built according to the following subdivision:

a) System's identification code, year in which the system first came to the center.
b) Number of sessions done.
c) In the "diagnosis" section, we indicate the system involved in the therapy, the main problem as it was brought by the system, and diagnosis reported by the system either made by a specialist or proposed during the therapeutic process. psychological tools eventually used for making the diagnosis;

SYSTEM CODE		YEAR	
NUMBER OF SESSIONS (total)			
NUMBER OF VIDEO RECORDED SESSIONS (dvd/ videotape)			
DIAGNOSIS			
System involved	☐ Family ☐ Couple ☐ Individual person ☐ Interchange (family / couple /individual		
Main problem (brief description as narrated by the patient/s)			
Diagnosis (DSM V)			
Psychological Tools (tests used and results)			
TECHNIQUES USED			
Assignments / Prescriptions			
Use of systemic tools (Genogram, FACES, joint drawing, score 15 etc)			
Impact and/or experiential techniques (sculptures, chair exercises, coat of arms, use of materials, etc)			
Integrative techniques (EMDR, hypnosis, Sensory Motor, etc)			
OUTCOME			
	☐ Positive ☐ Negative ☐ Therapist's interruption ☐ Client's interruption ☐ Client's drop out		
THERAPEUTIC PROCESS			
Highlight moments (mark the session/s number in which the positive change starts or in which negative change occurs)			
Therapeutic Relationship			
Audio quality			

Fig. 6.4 Therapy cataloging worksheet

d) "Used techniques" section. The information are taken from the intervention worksheet shown above. We point out the use of impact and experiential techniques or integrative techniques, i.e., those techniques that come from approaches that differ from the systemic perspective and that are proposed by the therapist starting from the hypothesis on the specific clinical case (Mosconi et al., 2019).

e) The outcomes are divided into positive and negative, if there has been an interruption by the therapist or by the patient and dropouts. For the evaluation of positive and negative outcomes, we accept the classic systemic conception of change thought in two levels:

- Change 1: reduction or containment of the problem
- Change 2: modification of the relational rules of the single person and of the relational games of the family system (Watzlawick et al., 1974)

Specifically, in order to observe changes, we have identified **eight indicators of change in systemic therapy**: four individual and four family indicators that document the coevolution of individual and system change (Mosconi, 2016). These parameters are consistent with the polarities of the quadrilateral and therefore take into account both the individual dimension and the relational dimension, the four descriptive levels mentioned above. We plan to use some tests for the coding of each of them. We summarize them in Fig. 6.5.

The choice was to use the same four parameters for the family and for the system in order to simplify the evaluation of the coevolution. All these deductions can be made using as tests: SCL 90 (Derogatis et al., 1973), ACL (Gough et al., 1978), SCORE 15 (Stratton et al., 2010), Faces IV (Visani et al., 2014), and the WHODAS 2.0 Scale of DSM V (Ustun et al., 2010).

Therefore, the outcome will be considered positive if the four parameters for the individual system and those for the family system are met. For research purposes during data processing, we unify the interruption of the therapy decided by the therapist and/or the patient, as agreed positive outcomes, agreed negative outcomes, and not agreed (Vanetti, Vanetti, 2009).

Figure 6.5: 8 Parameters that indicate change

CHANGE MARKERS	INDIVIDUAL	FAMILY
1. the symptom and/or the problem (Individual and Relational phenomenological descriptive Dimension)	Symptom's and/or problem's regression (DSM diagnosis, use of therapies, patient's narration, SCL 90)	Recognition of the problem's and of the associate behaviour's remission in the system. (narration of the system's members, SCL 90 triadic use, SCORE 15, FACES IV)
2. other symptoms and/or problems (Individual and Relational Generator Processes Dimension)	Non-emergence of other problems (DSM diagnosis, use of therapies, patient's narration, SCL 90 triadic use)	Non-emergence of other patients in the system (narration of system's members, SCL 90 triadic use, DSM diagnosis)
3. Life Cycle (Phenomenological Descriptive and Individual end Relational Generator Processes Dimension)	Restart making personal life choices (narration, WHODAS 2.0)	The system restarts making life choices (narration, WHODAS 2.0)
4. Idea of Self and of relationships with others life cycle (Phenomenological Descriptive and Individual end Relational Generator Processes Dimension)	Change in the idea of Self and in the personal relationships with the family and with the world (restoration of the idea of self and of the relationship with others) (narration, ACL, SCORE 15, FACES IV)	Change in the ideas about the designated patient and about the family (narration of the system's components, ACL triadic use, SCORE 15, FACES IV)

Fig. 6.5 8 Parameters that indicate change

Among the agreements:

- Agreed Positive: it includes cases in which therapy ended with an agreement between therapist and client system and ended with a positive outcome; there was therefore a change improvement.
- Agreed Negative: it includes cases in which therapy ended with an agreement between therapist and client but without having led to a change; it is therefore identified as a negative outcome.

Interruptions, regardless of whether proposed by the therapist or the client, are defined as agreed because there is in any case an agreement between the parties. For example, among the negative agreements also fall those cases in which another type of therapy is considered more useful either because the family does not seem predisposed to change or the client finds no reason and/or useful to continue therapy.

Between the not agreed are the cases that we can define as:

- Dropouts, the cases where the system decides not to show up on the set date and therefore to interrupt therapy without a prior agreement with the therapist

The outcomes are further analyzed according to the SCORE 15 "scale for the therapist" (Stratton et al., 2010) to have a measurement of the improvement/worsening of the system, once the treatment has been completed (Trotta et al., Trotta et al., 2019):

a) "Therapeutic process" section: it is where the therapy's highlight moments are marked, that is, when the client reports a change (in terms of improvement or worsening) and aspects of the therapeutic relationship. The criteria identified by Softa are used for the therapeutic relationship (Friedlander et al., 2006):

1. **Involvement in the therapeutic process:** how much the client considers the treatment meaningful and how much he feels that the objectives and tasks of the therapy can be negotiated.
2. **Emotional connection:** how much the client feels that the relationship with the therapist rests on affiliation, trust, care, and interest and feels that the therapist takes care of him.
3. **Safety in the therapeutic system:** how much the client feels comfortable and considers therapy a place where he can afford to take risks.
4. **Sense of a shared purpose within the family:** family members feel supportive and feel a sense of unity in relation to therapy.

This means that when an explicit sharing of goals, a meaningful emotional bond is built between therapist and patient, the therapeutic context is experienced as safe, and there is a clear definition of tasks with a sense of shared purpose, we can talk about a good therapeutic alliance. It is then useful for us to understand in terms of research how much this procedural aspect affects the results. Therefore, for the evaluation of the efficacy of therapies, we verify the impact of the constitutive dimensions of the therapeutic alliance exposed above, correlating the results of the SCORE 15 scale for the therapist with those of the Softa-s version for the therapist.

The tools we use to evaluate the results of our interventions and for the entire therapeutic process are:

- Therapeutic Process: Schedule of Therapy Cataloguing (SCT)
- Individual Functioning: ACL, SLC 90, and Whodas 2.0
- Family Functioning: SCORE 15, Faces IV, and Whodas 2.0 applied to all family members
- Therapeutic Alliance: SCORE 15 scale for the therapist results compared with those of Softa-s version for the Therapist.

6.3 Conclusion

In conclusion, the importance to manualize the therapeutic process responds to the need for providing clear references for the therapist in training, during his practice, and in supervision in order to keep his activity within precise guidelines that distinguish him from an improvised practice but with the awareness that in each phase the therapist will be able to provide his personal variation for preserving the relationship with the client.

References

Andersen, T. (1987). The reflecting team: Dialogue and meta-dialogue in clinical work. *Family Process, 26*, 415–428.

Aurilio, R. (1996). Alla ricerca del tesoro perduto. La cartella relazionale che non c'è: la cartella relazionale. In C. Loriedo, D. Solfaroli, L. Camillocci, L. Mercuri, & M. Micheli (Eds.), *Etica, Ricerca e Didattica in Psicoterapia Relazionale* (pp. 169–178). Milano.

Bandler, R., & Grinder, J. (1975a). *The structure of magic I: A book about language and therapy.* Science & Behavior Books. ISBN 0831400447.

Bandler, R., & Grinder, J. (1975b). *Patterns of the hypnotic techniques of Milton H. Erikson. M.D* (Vol. I). Meta Publications.

Bateson, G. (1979). *Mind and nature a necessary unity.* Dutton.

Boscolo, L., Bertrando, P., Fiocco, P. M., Palvarini, M., & Pereira, J. (1992). Linguaggio e cambiamento: l'uso di parole chiave in terapia. *Terapia Familiare, 37*, 41–52.

Boscolo, L., Cecchin, G., Hoffman, L., & Penn, P. (1987). Milan systemic family therapy: Conversations in theory and practice. Basic Books.

Cecchin, G. F. (1987). Hypothesizing, circularity and neutrality revisited: An invitation to curiosity. *Family Process, 26*, 405–414.

Derogatis, L., Lipman, R., & Covi, L. (1973). SCL-90: An outpatient psychiatric rating scale – Preliminary report. *Psychopharmacology Bulletin, 9*, 13.

Ecker, B., Ticic, R., & Hulley, L. (2012). *Unlocking the emotional brain: Eliminating symptoms at their roots using memory reconsolidation.* Routledge/Taylor & Francis Group.

Erickson, M. H., & Rossi, E. L. (1979). *Hypnotherapy: An exploratory casework.* Irvington Publishers.

Friedlander, M. L., Escudero, V., & Heatherington, L. (2006). *Therapeutic alliances in couple and family therapy: An empirically informed guide to practice.* American Psychological Association. https://doi.org/10.1037/11410-000

Gonzo, M., Mosconi, A., & Tirelli, M. (1999). *L'intervista nei Servizi Socio-Sanitari: uno strumento conoscitivo e d'intervento per gli operatori*. Raffaello Cortina.

Gough, H. G., Lazzari, R., Fioravanti, M., & Stracca, M. (1978). An adjective check list scale to predict military leadership. *Journal of Cross-Cultural Psychology, 9*, 381.

Maturana, H. R., & Varela, F. J. (1980). *Autopoiesis and cognition: The realization of the living*. Reidel Publishing Company.

Minuchin, S. (1999). Dov'è la famiglia nella terapia familiare narrativa? *Terapia Familiare, 60*, 3–20.

Mosconi, A. (1992). Livelli e strategie della conservazione terapeutica: Alcune considerazioni generali. *Psichiatria Generale e dell'Età Evolutiva, 1*, 183–197.

Mosconi, A. (1993). Alcuni spunti per un dibattito sui livelli e le strategie della conversazione terapeutica. *Psicobiettivo, 2*, 53–60.

Mosconi, A. (2008). Terapia relazionale-sistemica con l'individuo: il quadrilatero sistemico come riferimento per una costruzione di ipotesi ben formata e l'integrazione di differenti ottiche di lavoro, ovvero, "fai una buona ipotesi e poi fai quello che vuoi". *Connessioni, 20*, 55–82.

Mosconi, A. (2016). A systemic approach to psychological work with families. *Interdisciplinary Journal of Family Studies, XXI*(2), 60–78.

Mosconi, A., & Tirelli, M. (1997). Dalla "scheda telefonica" alla "cartella dati": uno strumento per il primo approccio e la catamnesi in terapia familiare. L'esperienza nel servizio di Terapia Familiare Dell ULSS 16 di Padova. *Ecologia della mente, 1*, 77–101.

Mosconi, A., Castellani, A., De Maria, L., Gonzo, M., Sorgato, R., Tirelli, M., Tomas, M., & Zago, E. (1996). Come costruisci la tua conversazione terapeutica? Breve glossario degli interventi in terapia sistemica e alcune considerazioni sulla possibilità di utilizzo. *Terapia Familiare, 50*, 25–41.

Mosconi, A., Gonzo, M., Sorgato, R., Tirelli, M., & Tomas, M. (1999). Ipotesi diagnostiche e relazione terapeutica: ricorsività e coerenza nel "Milan Model". *Connessioni, 5*, 67–96.

Mosconi, A., Tirelli, M., & Neglia, V. (2013). Il Quadrilatero Sistemico: Una Storia Per Narrare Altre Storie: Il caso di una supervisione sistemica in un Day Hospital Territoriale. *Terapia Familiare, 101*, 67–92.

Mosconi, A., Bozzetto, I., Carmignani, M., & Ferluga, V. (2019). Ipotesi sistemica e "tecniche di impatto": un'integrazione possibile. In P. Barbetta & U. Telfener (Eds.), *Complessità e psicoterapia* (pp. 251–272). Raffaello Cortina.

Pinsof, W. (1995). La ricerca processuale in Terapia della Famiglia. In A. S. Gurman & D. P. KnisKern (Eds.), *Manuale di Terapia della Famiglia* (pp. 682–706). Torino.

Selvini Palazzoli, M., Boscolo, L., Cecchin, G. F., & Prata, G. (1980). Hypothesizing – circularity – neutrality: Three guidelines for the conductor of the session. *Family Process, 19*, 3–10.

Shapiro, F. (1995). *Eye movement desensitization and reprocessing. Basic principles, protocols*. Guilford Press.

Sluzki, C. (1992). La trasformazione terapeutica delle trame narrative. *Terapia Familiare, 36*, 237–257.

Stratton, P., Bland, J., Janes, E., & Lask, J. (2010). Developing a practicable outcome measure for systemic family therapy: The SCORE. *Journal of Family Therapy, 32*, 232–258.

Telfener, U. (1986). *La terapia sistemica*. Ed. Astrolabio.

Tomm, K. (1987a). Interventive interviewing: Part I. Strategizing as a fourth guideline for the therapist. *Family Process, 26*(1), 3–13. https://doi.org/10.1111/j.1545-5300.1987.00003.x

Tomm, K. (1987b). Interventive interviewing: Part II. Reflexive questioning as a means to enable self-healing. *Family Process, 26*(2), 167–183. https://doi.org/10.1111/j.1545-5300.1987.00167.x

Tomm, K. (1988). Interventive interviewing: Part III. Intending to ask lineal, circular, strategic, or reflexive questions? *Family Process, 27*(1), 1–15. https://doi.org/10.1111/j.1545-5300.1988.00001.x

Ustun, T. B., Kostanjesek, N., Chatterji, S., & Rehm, J. (2010). *Measuring health and disability: manual for WHO Disability Assessment Schedule (WHODAS 2.0)*. World Health Organization.

Viaro, M., & Leonardi, P. (1990). *Conversazione e terapia*. Raffaello Cortina.

Viaro, M. (1996). Perché proporre una cartella relazionale? In C. Loriedo, D. Solfaroli, L. Camillocci, L. Mercuri, & M. Micheli (Eds.), *Etica, Ricerca e Didattica in Psicoterapia Relazionale* (pp. 269–288). Franco Angeli.

Visani, E., Di Nuovo, S., & Loriedo, C. (2014). *Il FACES IV. Il modello circonflesso di Olson nella clinica e nella ricerca*. Raffaello Cortina.

Watzlawick, P., Beavin, J. H., & Jackson, D. D. (1967). *Pragmatics of human communication: A study of interactional patterns, pathologies, and paradoxes*. W.W. Norton & Co., Inc..

Watzlawick, P., Weakland, J. H., & Fisch, R. (1974). Change: Principles of problem formation and problem resolution. W. W. Norton.

Watzlawick, P. (1978). *The language of change*. Basic Books, Inc..

White, M. (1992). *La Terapia come narrazione*. Astrolabio.

Online Document, & Mosconi, A. (2014). Identità ed Identità Sistemica. In A. Mosconi, M. Pezzolo, & G. Racerro (Eds.), *Identità Sistemiche*. UltimaBooks. http://www.ultimabooks.it/identita-sistemiche.pdf. Accessed 2014

Online Document, Mosconi, A., Trotta, B., Racerro, G. & Minorello, M. (2019). *Catalogazione e valutazione delle terapie: proposta di un metodo* Relazione alla giornata di studio dal titolo "Metodologia, processi e valutazione: percorsi nella ricerca sistemica" organizzato dalla SIPPR. http://www.cptf.it/web/biblioteca/elenco-testi.pdf. Accessed 2020.

Online Document, Trotta, B., Racerro, G., Mosconi, A., Spitaleri, M., & Dalla Pozza L. (2019). *Valutazione degli esiti attraverso l'analisi degli aspetti processuali in un campione di disturbi depressivi*. http://www.cptf.it/web/biblioteca/elenco-testi.pdf. Accessed 2020.

Online Document, Vanetti, S. (2009). *La psicoterapia di coppia: evidenze empiriche sul processo di cura*, Università di Bergamo. https://aisberg.unibg.it/retrieve/handle/10446/88/1165/TESI_Susanna%20Vanetti.pdf. Accessed 2009.

Chapter 7
Manualising the Exeter Model: Couple Therapy for Depression – A Behavioural-Systemic Approach

Janet Reibstein and Hannah Sherbersky

7.1 Introduction

This chapter will describe the context that formerly hampered and then permitted the development of a manual for the treatment of depression that uses an innovative, third-wave form of behavioural-systemic couple therapy called the Exeter Model.

Manualisation of attempts to define therapy's often inchoate processes can make transparent its elements in action, as well as render it more accountable. Research can then examine empirical, identifiable evidence for and elements of effectiveness. For training, manualisation can clarify, through specification, the elements needed to develop as therapists. As a necessarily partial attempt at specification, given the elusiveness of process, manualisation should be ongoing: a 'practice-based evidence' approach, with feedback modifying definitions. As discussion and controversy still surround psychotherapy research, the potential requirement and notion of manualising psychotherapy can often make therapists feel uncomfortable (Mansfield & Addis, 2001). We can ask whether or how empiricism could be useful in establishing the benefits of social constructivism but can concede that, while there are worthy areas of debate, to make systemic practice credible, we must try to establish its empirical validity.

Pinning down the process into definable, observable components is a pathway to establishing such credibility. Manuals can support research to operationalise therapy constructs, ensure that therapy is delivered as intended and provide a protocol for

---

J. Reibstein (✉)
Child and Family Practice and London Intercultural Couples Centre, London, UK

University of Exeter, Exeter, UK
e-mail: janetreibstein@me.com; J.Reibstein@exeter.ac.uk

H. Sherbersky
University of Exeter, Exeter, UK
e-mail: H.Sherbersky@exeter.ac.uk

treatment (Williams et al., 2014). This chapter details how the ability to specify has afforded CBT and behavioural therapies pride of place 'politically' (i.e. deployment of resources commissioning these therapies), and within universities (i.e. support for them in research), while lacking such precision, systemic therapies have lagged behind.

The Exeter Model for couple therapy is an attempt, through manualising, to operationalise a new method of systemic practice, defined through 'validated' interventions. Its development is a story of a shift in a 'political' context, and then in the university one can open opportunities for a shift in resources and credibility in best therapy practice, training and research. We define the political context in this case as the choices a society makes around what kinds of therapy, training and research to fund. The university context, in which those funded training and research programmes are housed, consequently will shift. The story of the Exeter Model manual reflects how changes in both of these contexts provided an opportunity for its development, within a university training and research setting, alongside older and more routinely funded therapy modalities. Within that setting and beyond, the model and its manual have continued to evolve. Its continuing evolution, through feedback from its use in clinics and trainings, has resulted in a unique systemic-behavioural central intervention, the 'Exeter Model circularity', and an additional form, the Intercultural Exeter Model. These additions and refinements show how a manual can continually develop responsively.

7.2 Background and Rationale

A solid research evidence base, both for medical and psychological therapies, forms a dominant facet of the politics of resource deployment. The National Health Service, the UK's main health provider, keeps a tight watch on expenditure. Inevitably, a requirement for an evidence base for treatments follows. As major health expenditure on depression increased in the UK dramatically, attention is focused on its 'best practice' treatment. This need – for fast, effective action toward a growing national problem – changed the context, on both levels, politically and in the university, and fostered the emergence of a systemic treatment. That is, the key to this shift, we shall see, was an expansion of criteria for 'evidence'. This expansion was demonstrated by the creation of commissioned groups of depression treatment experts, including psychotherapists, to supply their own current evidence for 'best practice'. Before this, the climate was more hostile. A by-product of the need for an evidence base is the salience in the UK of NICE – the National Institute of Health and Clinical Excellence. The best available scientific evidence for treatments is collated by experts in their respective fields with consequent NICE recommendations. The 'best available' equates to 'gold standard' treatments. Gold standard means randomly controlled research trials establishing effectiveness, an inarguably crucial standard for strictly medical interventions. All depression treatments assessed by NICE were held to this gold standard for recommended practice.

Applying the gold standard to psychotherapy (in this case for depression) is problematic and has consequences for the systemic world. Conducting RCTs can take years, involving getting research funding and organising proper control conditions (e.g. ensuring matching the variables of interest, control conditions can be both tricky and cumbersome). And maybe the most difficult and often elusive task is to clearly define the variables to show that they, and not something else, are the reasons for a treatment's effectiveness.

Partly for this reason, the gold standard studies cited by NICE within (couples) psychotherapy for depression have been on behavioural therapy and research conducted roughly within 1960–1990. It is much easier to pinpoint and therefore define a finite set of behaviours (e.g. to use a statement that starts with 'I feel' rather than 'you always do' or say) than to define an amorphous or abstract intervention (e.g., to attempt to 'explore attachment narratives'). Looking at discrete behaviours is easier than examining the context in which they occur. How do we define the relevant aspects of a family or couple's context? Where do we stop – at the level of the household, of the neighbourhood, of the family heritage? And what are the best ways to define these? If we have a control condition to ensure we are solely investigating the influence of our systemic treatment, how will we set up the right controls? Inevitably, this fits within a wider political argument about what constitutes evidence, who defines it and its limitations. If, further, we consider psychotherapy to be an art *and* science, the research needs to be also grounded in real-life clinical practice rather than only easily defined variables (Larner, 2004).

So behavioural therapies have primarily gained funding. They continue to form NICE recommendations, reifying the process: the type of research that is condoned and conducted is likely to continue being funded. CBT (cognitive behavioural therapy) – the inheritor of BT (behavioural therapy) – is more likely to be funded both as a therapy provision and the therapy of choice for clinical researchers than others. Others are less likely to be either funded or commissioned. The more validated the treatment, the more likely its progenitors will be commissioned. From this, university priorities arise, and most psychotherapy research is done within universities. Specifically, in the field of couple therapy, the results of RCTs showed behavioural couple therapy establishing effectiveness in treating depression.

Such was the climate discouraging research funding for systemic practice and, in consequence, for practitioners to pin down precisely and replicably the therapy experience. Finally, then, there was not a climate within a systemic practice that fostered manualising what we do.

Relevant, though, to the creation of the Exeter Model manual, merging as it does behavioural and systemic practice and ideas, was a gradual evolution occurring in another context: that of psychotherapy theory and practice. Particularly over the past decade, we have seen the emergence of what has been described as 'third-wave' psychotherapies (Prochaska & Norcross, 2013). 'Third-wave' refers to the fact that some therapy models have begun to converge over interventions and ideas about what is important in what produces change. The 'third wave' is a push towards the integration of practice. The notion of 'third wave' in behavioural psychotherapeutic development encouraged the confluence of themes such as empathy, collaboration and the therapeutic alliance and encouraged practitioners to 'notice convergence rather than divergence in their practices' (Reibstein & Sherbersky, 2012).

7.3 Developing a Clinic

In 2008, a new initiative was developed in England, Improving Access to Psychological Therapies (IAPT). This was a National Health Service initiative that aimed to provide more psychotherapy to the general population. It was originally developed and proposed by the Labour Party, the government at that time, and was based on the new therapy guidelines from NICE, as promoted by the clinical psychologist David Clark. Starting in 2004, NICE had systematically reviewed the effectiveness of various interventions for depression and anxiety disorders, which led to a series of clinical guidelines (Clark, 2018). The new IAPT service attempted to standardise care and reduce inequalities in access to services. In 2009 NICE recommended, among other treatments for depression, 'behavioural couple therapy', referred to here also as couple therapy for depression (CTfD), which was then offered as a treatment within IAPT services. NICE, in 2009, using a stepped-care model, recommended CTfD for persistent subthreshold depressive symptoms or mild to moderate depression with inadequate response to initial interventions and moderate and severe depression. The treatment is described as a high-intensity psychological intervention recommended for people who have a regular partner and where the relationship may contribute to the development or maintenance of depression or where involving the partner is considered to be of potential therapeutic benefit. The guidelines recommend that behavioural couple therapy for depression should normally be based on behavioural principles and an adequate course of therapy should be 15 to 20 sessions over 5 to 6 months. Here is the introductory statement by NICE in its guidelines: self-evidently, but not identified as, a systemic one:

> A time-limited, psychological intervention derived from a model of the interactional processes in relationships where the intervention aims to help participants understand the effects of their interactions on each other as factors in the development and/or maintenance of symptoms and problems. The aim is to change the nature of the interactions so that they may develop more supportive and less conflictual relationships.

What followed was a list of behaviourally based separate interventions culled from six gold standard behavioural couple treatment studies, such as 'making I statements' or 'homework tasks'. The wind of change – a change in the contexts – arose from the governmental pressure to provide treatments widely within its NHS services. The lag-time between execution and publication of therapy research and practice resulted in the available gold-standard evidence being dated. Thus, the evidence criteria needed changing. Involving standards set by experts meant adding a 'practice-based evidence' model. New agreed-on practices and standards had evolved using such measures as face validity of effectiveness, especially for some less precisely defined interventions (e.g. 'creating a safe space' and 'exploring family script issues'); anecdotal evidence from client feedback; consensually validated observations from qualified observers; and audits of various outcome variables. Expert reference groups (ERGs) across myriad therapeutic modalities (the first of these were convened around CBT, then around systemic and psychodynamic, while others followed, including an ERG around couple therapy). These ERGs comprised nominated experts in each modality that had been convened to define the best current practice. The first author (JR) was a member of the ERG on systemic practice, and advisor to the ERG on couple therapy (to ensure that there be a systemic input and oversight).

7.3.1 Progression Toward the Exeter Model: Development Within a University

Universities followed suit. In the midst of this change, at the University of Exeter, where the authors were based, the senior management team energetically prioritised scientific innovation. The clinical psychology group responded by establishing a clinic operationalising NICE-recommended behavioural therapies for depression in new, researchable methodologies. For the systemic approach, a manual was requisite but, crucially, now feasible, with the liberalisation of research standards and the push toward clinical innovation. Moreover, NICE recommendations were clearly systemic. JR, as an advisor to the couple therapy ERG and member of the systemic ERG, was positioned with readily defined *systemic* interventions (which she helped to edit) validated either as NICE 'behavioural', with additions derived within the couples' ERG. A manual, with those at its core, ensued. HS joined, to help refine and explicate these defined interventions, through illustrative clinical examples. Together the authors wrote a manual dividing intervention into 'systemic-*behavioural*', that is, those focusing mainly on changing behaviours within interactions. Setting 'homework' tasks was an example. ('Behavioural' were largely from within those 'gold standard' NICE ones). The rest were labelled 'systemic-*empathic*'. These, such as 'attachment narratives' or 'scripts', are interventions aiming to foster empathic connections and understandings.

An important piece of research supported the value of these 'empathic' interventions, underscoring why a good practice should avoid a too-narrow evidence base. Jacobson and Christensen's (1998) research revealed the short-term effectiveness of simple behavioural couple therapy (the therapy interventions forming much of the 'gold standard' ones), wearing off after about 6 months. Though themselves early advocates for such treatment, they posited that it lacked the glue that emotional connection might give, terming its missing elements 'acceptance' and 'tolerance'. In brief, people needed to place learned behavioural changes within reciprocal understandings of respective partner's needs and feelings, thus forging an empathic connection. Jacobson and Christensen added 'acceptance' and 'tolerance' interventions and found that treatment effects were longer lasting. Many of the systemic interventions published by the ERG were aimed at helping clients develop such understanding and empathy: those we labelled 'systemic-empathic', including such as 'making links between vulnerabilities', 'attachment narratives', or 'scripts'.

It should be noted that the initiative of this new training clinic was one of the first steps in a larger change within the university to support innovative and researchable therapies. A new department within the clinical group that, itself, sat within the school of psychology emerged. This new department became CEDAR (Clinical Education Development and Research), now one of the largest providers of training in evidence-based psychological therapies, including systemic ones, within the UK. Programmes within its training portfolios are competency-based and delivered according to the latest evidence-informed clinical pedagogic approaches (CEDAR, 2020).

7.4 The Model in Action

As a result, we based our manualised treatment in the 'AccEPT clinic (Accessing Evidenced Based Psychological Therapies)', which was sited at the university. Funded by NHS referrals from GP practices for 'depressed patients', it offered 'innovative, researchable' *behavioural* therapy. Apart from JR and HS, clinical researchers on the faculty were behaviourally based and trained. At its inception, until ours was introduced, the treatments had been individual and CBT-based. Ours uniquely treated couples and took external referrals from GP practices as well as internal referrals from colleagues within the clinic. In 2011 the Exeter Model treatment was launched within the University of Exeter AccEPT clinic, with JR and HS running and supervising it.

Manualisation was central both to establishing credibility, next to the other behaviourally based treatments, and to evidence a pathway for potential research projects. As part of the MSc in systemic psychotherapy and the doctorate in clinical psychology, student trainees had the opportunity to use the clinic for their research projects, with the manual used for much of the research. That these interventions formed what we categorised as 'behavioural' in our model and that they were evidence-based was self-evident, for the ERG, by definition, gave it that imprimatur. The manual made explicit that they were situated *explicitly* (as opposed to the implicit NICE declaration) within a systemic framework.

The manual helped establish the validity and potential effectiveness of a new treatment modality that put these interventions in such a frame together – one that is both behavioural and systemic. The innovative aspect was, indeed, that it was a *systemic* behavioural intervention. As it evolved, its particularly innovative feature was its combination of these two aspects within its central intervention: the Exeter Model circularity, described later in the chapter. Research aimed to indicate which parts of the process, as defined by the interventions, were operating when, how and to what effect. But its purpose also was to train clinicians in systemic work and to focus their thinking on when, how and to what effect they were using their therapeutic interventions. Training would become more effective: we could teach students about effective practices that, by being specified, could be observed largely through the use of their own taped sessions and by watching sessions of their fellow trainees in observation rooms with trainers. Through defining interventions, supervision standards were clearer. Manualising thus made for a clearer, more responsible and accountable training toward effective practice.

These interventions, all within a broad behavioural couples frame, were expanded beyond *behavioural* as now formulated by NICE: each intervention, separately and together, could be used to try to disrupt the patterns of interactions that maintain the symptoms of depression. The manual fits the interventions within a systemic frame and shows how they can be used in this context. The most important framer is that the interactions and patterns of the couple are the primary focus of the investigation. From these flow questions, deploying the defined interventions to explore these, about how they have come to be, why, what keeps them in place, and how they might be changed. These are all to be used within a view that is systemic.

However, in keeping with a systemic tradition of being open to change and to contextual factors, that it is *behavioural*-systemic is important. The manual reflects this melding of behavioural thinking with systemic. Its interventions would be familiar to a systemically trained practitioner. Its behavioural elements, but not its nonbehavioural ones necessarily, would be familiar to a CBT practitioner. However, putting these together in a logically coherent way remained a challenge and one that begged to be made rather than have an approach that was simply a collection of parts. The systemic perspective gave the interventions a frame in which to place them so they were not simply a collection, so the manual begins with the systemic frame. However, the model's systemic circularity now included aspects of a CBT circularity. Both types of therapy – that is, CBT and systemic – employ feedback loops within their practice.

The CBT loop shows how an individual's thoughts feedback into their feelings and, in turn, their behaviour, in turn, to their thoughts, etc., reinforcing each of these as the loop is created. The Exeter Model takes this a step further, making it interactive by charting a usual systemic circularity but breaking it down into showing how each individual's thoughts, feelings and behaviours are both influenced by and influence the other person's. Both types of therapy employ feedback loops within their practice. Breaking down the systemic circularity, then, clearly and specifically into how each individual's thoughts, feelings and behaviours as they are formed in response to the other person's thoughts, feelings and behaviours, as they play out in a feedback loop, adds an interactive aspect to the CBT feedback. At the same time, it underscores and gives a methodology for specifying precisely how a systemic feedback loop can play out within a dyad.

A profound truism established within the (largely behaviourally based) research of Gottman (1994) became a pivotal feature of the Exeter Model. In his research Gottman, notably one of the foremost researchers of early behavioural couple research endorsed by the NICE findings noted minute-to-minute interactions, over long chunks of time periods. (His data derived from having installed cameras to record behaviour in his 'love lab' house in which couples resided for weekends). Attending to these data, he could ascertain that couples' satisfying versus unsatisfying, as well as stable versus unstable, relationships could be identified by how each member responded, behaviourally, to the other. That could be either in a positive or negative direction, in a build-up over time, of moment-to-moment interactions. (Gottman et al., 1998) Yet these are hardly noticeable by people, even though these together form the sum total of their feelings about each other, about themselves in relation to the other and about the relationship, in general. How good the relationship is lies in these minute behavioural interchanges.

Thus, a conclusion is that the power to change the quality of the interaction – and relieve distress – can lie in changing these minute interactions. Interventions focus on the feedback loop of such interactions that have maintained the symptom causing malfunctioning within the couple. In the case of depression, this can be either wittingly or unwittingly so. For instance, in the case of very loving or caring couples, their interactions may have yielded a sense of helplessness or a sense of uselessness or guilt in the depressed partner that have 'helped' the depression to survive. That build-up of minute behavioural interactions in a feedback cycle is key to keeping the depression (or any problematic situation) going. So, as in the NICE recommendations, interrupting that usual pattern of interactions with new behaviours can be the key to stopping it, forming the basis of couple therapy treatment. We are talking here about feedback loops. However, this time, if we follow in Gottman's footsteps, these are loops built-up of tiny interactions, with the key to change lying in painstakingly translating meaning and understanding these processes. This would give us avenues for also understanding where to intervene to change patterns.

Systemic practice, indeed, focuses on feedback loops of interactions – how one person does something that produces a response in the other and then a response in return, etc. But more often than not such loops are explored in large swoops – one person *does* X, another *does* Y in response and so on. *Doing* is behavioural, yet emotional states and cognitive processes become conflated in this practice, remaining unexplored, perhaps becoming only assumed. For example, Sam gets angry and leaves. This leads to partner, Alex, feeling bad and withdrawing. That then leads to Sam closing further down and feeling depressed. That, in turn, leads to Alex feeling useless and accusing Sam of being cruel, and that, in its turn, leads to Sam being aggressive, feeling guilty and more depressed. These are thoughts, feelings and behaviours conflated, and the sequence is unclear. So, how is this couple able to pin down – in a potentially helpful way – *exactly* how, when and why to change this cycle? How can the couple understand how and why they are interacting the way they do? If they understood – if they could develop more acceptance and tolerance through it – they could modify their interactional patterns better.

Moreover, the accuracy of the responses that the couple report remains unexplored. That is, the individuals each do not know whether he or she has understood and is giving the appropriate response. Has his or her response accurately reflected what the other person's behaviour actually meant? Has the individual partner understood why the other partner behaved the way he or she did or felt the way he or she seemed to feel, even accurately labelled that feeling or understood what the thoughts were that lay behind the behaviour expressed? Or did the individual's response spring out of assumptions, which may or may not have been accurate? By precisely examining, as the interactions unfold, what are the thoughts and feelings, respectively, behind each bit of the interactional sequence new meanings are elucidated, and understandings are reached. Working with couples in an academic clinic, training trainees in systemic circularities in the traditional systemic way, the contextual frame within our university clinic of working *behaviourally* inclined us to experiment with adding in CBT methodology. Using a manual, as we have noted, predisposes the practitioner to analyse the therapy process painstakingly. The Exeter Model systemic-behavioural circularity breaks down and refines the former circularity to support tracking a circularity in a more granular sequential way.

CBT also looks at feedback loops, but these loops are individual and internal. A particular thought can, indeed, bring on a behaviour, which can, in turn, bring on a feeling or a thought or a behaviour, all in response to each other, reinforcing each other. Or this can occur in any order. Each of these, of course, reinforces the other in a feedback loop.

The Exeter Model has put these together, in a uniquely combined circularity or feedback loop. In our circularity CBT's loop has brought in the level of thoughts, feelings and behaviour that systemic has not in its general practice deconstructed clearly. And systemic has brought in to CBT the dimension of input from and response to the other (the interactional aspect) and its reinforcing power. The circularity itself also draws on a theoretical model of human behaviour from a postmodernist position, CMM (Pearce, 2007) or the coordinated management of meaning. As in CMM the Exeter Model circularity asks the couple to nominate a characteristic episode in which the symptom that brought them into therapy (e.g. depression) is being maintained or highlighted for them. Tracking the thoughts, feelings and behaviours over the course of the episode becomes the specimen example through which to investigate their maintenance patterns of interactions.

The interventions then probe for the meanings and explanations for those meanings that each person gives to their thoughts, feelings and behaviours in their responses to each other over the cycle. These will, as in CMM, draw on the history of their own interactions, on their family scripts and on cultural and historical contexts. Indeed, it is entirely possible to read Gottman's findings on couple satisfaction and endurance – the balance of positive having to outweigh the negative – in terms of *meanings* each member of the couple gives to the responses given to them, that is, whether they are positive or negative ones, by the other. A balance of mostly negative responses builds to a narrative of a negative relationship, fuelled by resentment and negative attributions of motives that help give a cohesive negative form to that narrative. A balance of mostly positive ones over time builds to a cohesively positive narrative, in which positive attributions are given (he or she is 'tired' rather than he or she is 'selfish', for instance, if something goes awry between them).

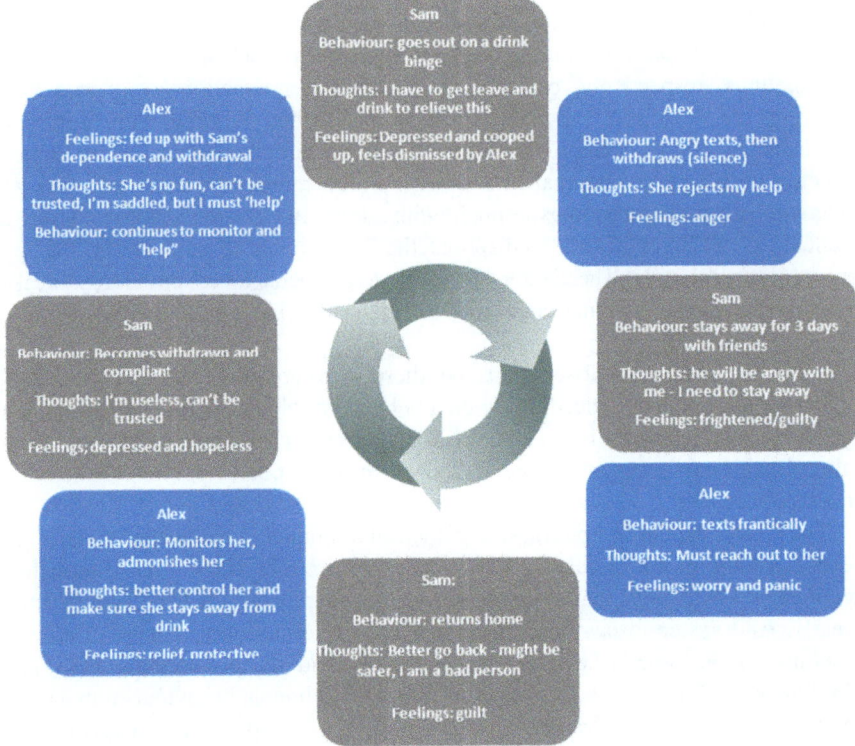

Fig. 7.1 Exeter Model circularity – Alex and Sam

Tracking a circularity, then, starts with the couple naming a prototypical episode. This is then charted, moment to moment: it links, in a feedback loop of responses, each member's *behaviour* that is observed by the other, in response to each other, on and on, until what is shown is that those behaviours are maintaining the behaviour that is the symptom of the presenting problem at the top of the cycle. (See Fig. 7.1). Then it goes back over the cycle which has described the observable behaviours and asks each couple member to describe what their *thoughts and feelings* were at each of those points. It tracks, that is, the *non-observables*.

The first part of the tracking cycle describes how the first one's *behaviour* (the *observable* or audible behaviour, itself, only) brings a reaction from the second partner (this can include silence or apparent non-reaction – for those are observable). It is the *observable* – what is observed or heard or not by the other that is important, for that is what has been responded to. It asks what is the reaction (i.e. observed behaviour) to that first person's observed behaviour by that second person and so on, until you see how the observed symptoms under investigation (depression, in our clinic) are being maintained. This is the first go-round in the circle: tracking the couple's *behavioural* interactional cycle.

Then, in this cycle the therapist goes back and tracks the *non-observables* in the cycle. The therapist asks each partner, as she goes through the cycle of behaviours, to add in the thoughts and feelings at each of these behaviour points in the sequence of the cycle. What were they thinking in response to the other person's behaviour, and what were their feelings in response to that other person's behaviour? They will have been making some inchoate sense of what had motivated, in terms of the other person's thoughts and feelings and the partner's observed behaviour; so what had been their own thinking and feeling that lay behind their own response (their own observed behaviour) to it? This all too often is a revelation. All too frequently partners had each thought the other meant by his or her behaviour was not at all what the other had thought or felt. Or sometimes it was a bit different or had a different but crucial emphasis that was different from what had been thought or assumed. The differences, large or small, could be both surprising and enlightening.

Thus, if these tacit moments are made explicit, it could change the other's assumptions and the attributions given, often erroneously, to the meanings of the observed behaviour. Guesswork about the partner's thoughts, and feelings – the reason why they might have behaved toward you the way they did – is adjusted to something more truthful about the partner. Not only would they learn what their partner actually thought and felt. They might realise their own attributions about their partner were askew. They might realise that they, each respectively, can learn better ways to communicate, what they think, feel and want from their partners. Through this process of better understanding, each might be able to adjust better to the other. The circularity opens opportunities for the couple to reflect on themselves and each other, to learn about each other and to gain the empathic understanding that taking away incorrect, often undermining assumptions can block. Achieving increased understanding is part of the process. The Exeter Model helps behavioural change as well as to extend understanding through others of the manualised set of interventions.

Together with new information and empathic understanding, other interventions in the manual guide change, such as trying out new forms of communication and behaviours. The interventions, used in conjunction with the central intervention, the Exeter Model circularity, open pathways to constructive relating and understanding. The couple, through guided work with the interventions, is freed up to make different choices of behaviour – and particularly at paradigmatic moments like the episode deconstructed in the model's circularity should they arise again between them.

Describing the *couple's maintenance cycle*, itself, can bring about and disrupt through the revelations about meanings it evokes. It can form the basis, through pointing to a point in the cycle and asking the couple how, with new insights and understandings of it, they might do something different. The circularity also acts as a basis for opening windows into other important potentially therapeutic experiences because, as you question why a person thinks or feels or chooses to behave the way they did at a given point you can bring in an intervention that opens up even more depth of understanding.

For instance, in order to investigate why someone might assume that their partner 'must' be feeling in a certain way for them to behave in the way observed, questions could be asked not only about the history of the couple's interactions but also about their family scripts (Byng-Hall, 1985) about such incidents or behaviours. Each point in the cycle represents a point at which questions arise about how they could change their thinking (and feeling) and then their behaviour to each other, disrupting the cycle, changing it for the better. This means not only increasing understandings, empathic connections and new behaviour repertoires but, in the end, creating new circularities that do not maintain the symptom (depression, in this case, but also any other, in theory, being treated), and therefore, treating the reason for coming into therapy in the first place.

7.5 The Model in Clinical Use

Over the years since 2011, more than 300 clinicians have been trained in the Exeter Model, predominantly from a family therapy, CBT or couple counselling backgrounds. Trainees on the doctorate in clinical psychology and the MSc family therapy students at the University of Exeter continue to receive an abridged version of this training. There has been enormous enthusiasm for the model, with trainees describing the rigour that the manual affords as being supportive in both their learning and clinical application. IAPT continues to recognise two forms of couple therapy, supporting training courses in each. One closely follows the traditional behavioural couple therapy model, and the other is a broader, integrative approach which, like the Exeter Model, has more of a systemic focus (Clark, 2018).

To date the manual has been the fulcrum of intensive training weeks in the practice of the Exeter Model, along with films of the use of the model from our clinic sessions. Trainees then have follow-up supervision sessions conducted by clinicians who have completed the training plus supervision and undergone a further supervisor training. Thus, the use of the manual has been closely watched, and reports have been positive: it is an easy and clear guide to practice. However, a forthcoming book on the extension of the Exeter Model, *The Intercultural Exeter Model*, contains and describes elements of the original model (with the additional intercultural ones a well), with clinical examples of it in use (Reibstein & Singh, 2020). This presents an opportunity to investigate the use of the manualised model outside of the training.

To date there has been no large-scale study of the Exeter Model. But anecdotal reports from its usage in its various settings as well as findings from small-scale student research projects indicate symptom reduction (in particular, using the Beck Depression Inventory in clinics addressing depression); clients' high satisfaction levels; and some insight into the usage of particular sorts of interventions in high- vs low-conflict couples. For instance, there is some indication that those entering treatment with high conflict seem to respond to the behavioural interventions initially, for instance, and then can make better use of the more empathic ones (Theodosius, 2014).

In recent years, behavioural couple therapy or CTfD achieved the highest recovery rates for both depression and anxiety out of all 'high-intensity' therapies (NHS Digital, 2017). However, there continue to be challenges in the UK about the availability of behavioural couple therapy. Although currently IAPT treats over 560,000 patients per year in the UK (Clark, 2018), a recent report, compiled following a Freedom of Information request, showed that only 0.62% of all sessions delivered at the high-intensity level in IAPT services were couple therapy for depression appointments (TCCR, 2013). This equates to just one in every 161 sessions offered. There continues to be a need for better-informed commissioning and training within services. The individual and CBT-orientated therapies still predominate in these services, and manualising and researching systemic approaches urgently needs to continue.

7.6 Future Developments

As we trained more and more clinicians across the UK within the model, taking it out of its base in Exeter with its fairly homogeneous ethnic and racial client base, people working in more varied contexts brought in a new direction into which the model and manual could evolve. One trainee, Dr. Reenee Singh, joined in modifying the model. The original manual did not include interventions that attended explicitly to the contribution of cultural inputs; with the rise both in incidence across the UK, and of consciousness about them, of intercultural families and couples, this seemed a serious omission. The strict adherence, within the AccEPT clinic, for an agreed-upon evidence base meant that the two most widely used interventions that focused on cultural inputs – the culturegram and the cultural genogram – were not part of the original manual or an additional incarnation of the Exeter Model. However, the Intercultural Exeter Model (IEM) has felt it important that these two interventions now form part of the additional, IEM, manual. The manual for the IEM also expands on the definitions of many of the original interventions. They explicitly now ask questions that pertain to the clients' respective cultural histories, practices, beliefs and ideas. An example of this is a same-sex couple Helen and Rebecca. Helen is a British Protestant, and Rebecca Israeli-Jewish. Their cultural genogram, which highlighted cultural ideas around pride or shame around expressiveness and around sexual preference, is shown in Fig. 7.2.

Figure 2. Cultural Genogram

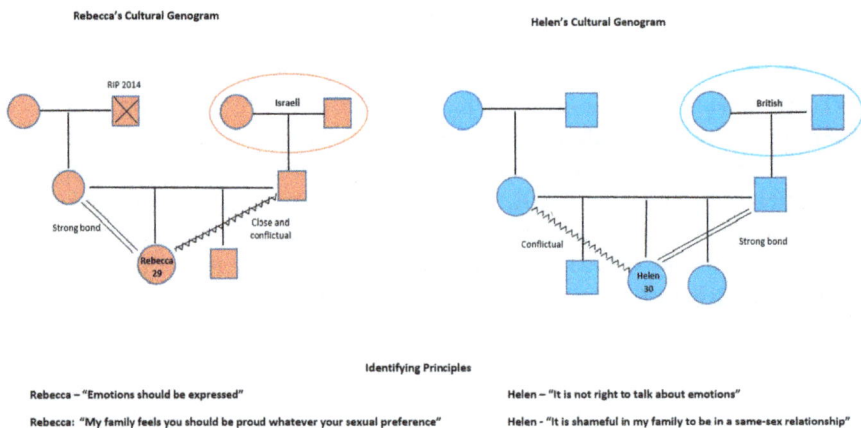

Fig. 7.2 Cultural genogram

7.6.1 Cultural Genogram

The couple began by choosing colours to represent their identities. Helen chose blue, and Rebecca chose red. A three-generational family map represented both sides of the family, and as it was constructed, the therapist asked questions to identify principles within these generations around issues of pride and shame (Hardy & Laszloffy, 1995) because these were ones that kept arising for this couple over their sexuality, as well as over how expressive they should be. Thus, in Rebecca's family, being emotionally expressive was both a core part of their identity and one of pride. But Helen's family disdained expressivity and prided themselves on their reserve. Equally, for Rebecca's family, being open and inclusive about different sexual preferences was a point of pride, while Helen's family was against same-sex relationships as a religious principle.

Differences in beliefs and practices around expressiveness were a particular problem for this couple, as was being open about their sexuality, particularly with their families. With the help of the IEM model through, in part, the cultural genogram, Rebecca and Helen identified where these different styles came from. The therapist could then intervene, using different interventions to help them think and behave differently. For example, instead of shouting, Rebecca was coached to explain how she felt to Helen, Helen was helped to listen, and they had other choices than for her to leave the room and both to be left feeling abandoned. Similarly, they were each coached to listen more empathically to the other about their respective family's abilities to adjust to their relationship, so that Rebecca could be more patient with Helen and Helen could be more open to thinking together with Rebecca about how to sensitise her family best to their relationship and to communicate to them her pride, rather than shame, about it.

The cultural genogram also opened them up to using another systemic intervention, Interviewing the Internalised Other (Tomm, 1998), specifically with sensitivity to their cultural differences around being open with their families about their sexuality. For instance, here is an excerpt from the 'interview' with Rebecca as Helen:

Rebecca (as Helen): I'm 30.

Therapist: How about your parents, Helen? Are they in London, like you and Rebecca?

Rebecca (as Helen): No, no. They live in Derbyshire in a small village. They're Sue and Jimmy.

Therapist: Okay. That's interesting. So, Helen, your brother is named for your father, is that right?

Rebecca (as Helen): Yeah. James Jr. But he's never called Jimmy. But, yeah, that's important. My dad is, well, he's sort of like a dictator in the family.

Therapist: But, Helen, Rebecca has said that he is different with you. That you are – she said – his 'angel'. Is she right? Do you feel like you are his 'angel'?

Rebecca (as Helen): Yeah. She's right. He is different with me. He's a lot gentler.

Therapist: So is that comfortable being his angel?

Rebecca (as Helen): Well, sometimes. But sometimes it isn't.

Therapist: Can you say which times it isn't?

Rebecca (as Helen): When I know that he wouldn't approve of things that his 'angel' shouldn't be doing?

Therapist: Can you give me an example?

Rebecca (as Helen): Well, obviously, he wouldn't approve of me being in a same-sex relationship! His religion just doesn't allow that!!

Therapist: And you know that for sure?

Rebecca (as Helen): Oh, yes! He's like, he's like, well anything that's not just like the 'normal', and what he understands is like, well, the enemy, the worst to him. And that's what that village, and certainly my family, is like: it's not 'normal' to be like me and Rebecca!!

Therapist: So, Helen, that must make you feel terrible. What a bind! When he does that what happens inside to you?

Rebecca (as Helen): I just hurt so badly. I just feel so terrible. And I know that just going silent is terrible. I know that… But I just wouldn't not be his 'angel'; I'd actually be his devil. I mean I really would.

And then, this excerpt, from Helen, as Rebecca:

Therapist: So, Rebecca, tell me, you're the only one of the children in your family that's not living in Israel, am I right?

Helen (as Rebecca): Yeah, I'm the only one; they're all back in Tel Aviv with my parents, the rest of them.

Therapist: And am I right that they all have partners, too? I think you told me that your brother is living with his girlfriend and their two kids and your sister has a boyfriend and they live near your parents?

Helen (as Rebecca): Yeah, that's right, but I think I also told you that my sister also once had a girlfriend. She's older than me; she sort of paved the way!

Therapist: Can you tell me more about that, like about how your family was about that then?

Helen (as Rebecca): Oh, they were absolutely fine. My parents are – they're like sort of anything's fine as long as you're happy and anyway, finding out about yourself is what they think is just one of the most important things in life, you know, and they always have said that. And, as you know, being 'expressive' as we've called it when we did that cultural genogram, they definitely express this all, and let us know! And they'd have let us know if they weren't cool with it!! My mother's a doctor, my father's an academic. They're cool with it – why should they care where your genitals go, is what they say, as long as you're okay with it and the other person is, and happy!

Therapist: So, Rebecca, have you ever thought about what it would be like for you if your family were different from that?

Helen (as Rebecca): I am just so grateful to my family for allowing me to be me, and expressing that, and I know it must be really horrible not to be happy to love and to be able to show that, and I know I am privileged to have come from that, even with all their mishagosh that might come from being so expressive all the time (by the way, 'mishagosh' is 'craziness' to you non-Jewish guys)!

The illumination of these cultural differences and practices through foregrounding them throughout the therapy, inflecting the interventions with cultural questions, can unlock the couple's empathic understanding of each other. Making the unconscious (the unspoken and often unwitting cultural beliefs) conscious, as the Freudian saw goes, can free them to make more fruitful and constructive choices about how to interact. Then a new, productive circularity can be introduced.

The Exeter Model continues to be taught to both trainees and external clinicians at the University of Exeter. The changing political landscape, developments in IAPT and increasing demands on services all continue to influence the model. In this way the manualisation process remains evolving as 'practice-based evidence'.

References

Byng-Hall, J. (1985). The family script: a useful bridge between theory and practice. *Journal of Family Therapy, 7*(3), 301–305.

Carr, A. (2018). Couple therapy, family therapy and systemic interventions for adult focused problems: The current evidence base. *Journal of Family Therapy*.

CEDAR. (2020). Clinical education development and research. Retrieved on 23rd May 2020 from https://cedar.exeter.ac.uk/

Clark, D. M. (2018). Realizing the mass public benefit of evidence-based psychological therapies: The IAPT program. *Annual Review of Clinical Psychology, 14*, 159–183.

Gottman, J. (1994). *Why marriages succeed or fail: What you can learn from the breakthrough research to make your marriage last*. New York: Simon & Schuster.

Gottman, J. M., Coan, J., Carrere, S., & Swanson, C. (1998). Predicting marital happiness and stability from newlywed interactions. *Journal of Marriage and the Family, 60*(1), 5.

Jacobson, N. S., & Christensen, A. (1998). *Acceptance and change in couples therapy: A therapists' guide to transforming relationships*. Norton.

Hardy, K., & Laszloffy, T. A. (1995). The cultural genogram: Key to training culturally competent family therapists. *Journal of Marital and Family Therapy, 21*(3), 227–237.

Larner, G. (2004). Family therapy and the politics of evidence. *Journal of Family Therapy, 26*, 17–39.

Mansfield, A., & Addis, M. (2001). Manual-based treatment part 2: The advantages of manual-based practice in psychotherapy. *Evidence Based Mental Health, 4*, 100–101.

NHS Digital. (2017). Retrieved from https://digital.nhs.uk/data-andinformation/publications/statistical/psychological-therapies-annual-reports-on-theuseof-iapt-services/annual-report-2016-17

Pearce, W. B. (2007). *Making social worlds: A communications perspective*. Blackwell Publishing.

Prochaska, J., & Norcross, J. (2013). *Systems of psychotherapy: A transtheoretical analysis* (8th ed.). Cengage Learning.

Reibstein, J., & Sherbersky, H. (2012). Behavioural and empathic elements of systemic couple therapy: The Exeter Model and a case study of depression. *Journal of Family Therapy, 34*(3), 271–283.

Reibstein, J., & Singh, R. (2020). *The Intercultural Exeter Model: Making connections for a divided world through systemic-behavioural therapy*. J. Wiley and Sons.

Tavistock Centre for Couples Relations. (2013). *A drop in the ocean: couple therapy for depression in IAPT.* Report from an investigation into the availability of couple therapy for depression in Improving Access to Psychological Therapies (IAPT) services. Retrieved from http://tavistockrelationships.org/images/uploads/Couple_therapy_for_depression_in_IAPT_-_TCCR_report.pdf

Theodosius, M. (2014). *A study of high-conflict vs low-conflict couples treated using the Exeter Model: Systemic-behavioural vs systemic-empathic interventions over the course of therapy*. Unpublished Masters project submitted for completion of MSc in Psychological Therapies, University of Exeter.

Tomm, K. (1998). A question of perspective. *Journal of Marital and Family Therapy, 24*(4), 409–413.

Williams, L., Patterson, J., & Edwards, T. (2014). *Clinician's' guide to research methods in family therapy*. The Guilford Press.

Chapter 8
Systemic Approaches to Therapy Manuals: Family Situation Mapping and Systemic-Relational Assessment of Treatment for Families, Couples and Individuals

Francesco Colacicco

8.1 Introduction

La Mappa del Terapeuta (The Therapist's Map), published in 2013 by Scione Editore (Rome), is a psychotherapy manual which can be adopted across different clinical contexts (psychotherapy centers and services) and for therapist training. This book is widely used by the *Istituto Dedalus* and other schools belonging to the *Centro Studi di Terapia Familiare e Relazionale di Roma* (Family and Relational Therapy Study Center in Rome) where it is adopted by trainee therapists specializing in family and relational psychotherapy when working under indirect supervision.

The manual provides a model for the assessment of therapy work with families, couples, and individuals, for data collection to facilitate therapists in collecting and organizing patient information which can be added to the patients' medical record. These forms enable the therapist to define the context for treatment and to follow its progress over time; they also enable the institution within which the therapist works to collect patient data and to assess interventions through a follow-up. Furthermore, the use of this manual can allow therapists, and the structures they work in, to conduct research projects and assess the effectiveness of the services provided.

Director of the *Istituto Dedalus*, post-graduate training school of specialization in psychotherapy recognized in Italy by the Ministry of Education, University and Research; and teacher within the *Centro Studi di Terapia Familiare e Relazionale di Roma*

F. Colacicco (✉)
Istituto Dedalus - Centro Studi di Terapia Familiare e Relazionale, Rome, Italy
e-mail: f.colacicco53@gmail.com

8.2 The Manual

"Many clinicians, psychotherapists and researchers have observed identical psychological phenomena; they labelled them in different ways, used them to construct a theory, and then added the fateful 'therefore' which led to the construction of an interpretative model of facts and - at times - to a psychotherapeutic approach. The consequences of this were a poor integration of ideas and a lot of confusion" (Cancrini & Harrison, 1983, *La trappola della follia*, pp. 121, La Nuova Italia Scientifica, Roma).

Many efforts at integrating and synthesizing different approaches have crashed against the barrier set by observer encoding and assessment. Much in the same way in which the psychoanalyst – fascinated by the complexity of his patient's inner world – could not see the system of family relationships in which the patient was immersed, so the family therapist, in turn, fascinated by family games, by the family dance, overlooked the fact that the family script is written by both subjective and group "internal parts," by the copy processes used and the attachment styles learned through the construction of bonds. There have been several developments in this field, and we are beginning to see some initial integrations and synthesis of approaches. Given that the object is determined by the interested observer's chosen focus and the background is therefore the context – or the frame – in which the object is inserted, we must be aware that the key or lens through which we "read" a situation will establish relationships and highlight some aspects instead of others. A therapeutic skill lies "in this reorganization, correlation, reformulation of data experience," and it does not thrive within a rigid therapeutic *schema*. The therapist's behavior should reflect the belief that it is possible – as it is in the classic illustration referred to by Gestalt therapists – to see both the young woman and the old woman, shifting focus between the inside figure and the outside figure. He should seek the double image of the self that the image always provides, a different organization of the relationship between the figure and its background.

Hence the idea led to this book, a psychotherapy manual. I collected from my working and teaching experiences and all my papers and notes to build a *map*, which is – naturally – a partial and approximated map to aid the therapist. It is a map which I offer to my students and which I keep on the desk during case supervisions. As family therapists know too well, the map itself does not represent the territory but rather a guide to cross it, to help, at every turn, identify the destinations to be reached and which path to follow. It can help the therapist have a firm grasp on the helm when the waters are stormy and to look for the right landing places. It is a guide to the construction of therapy, to the therapy process: it can help formulate hypotheses, define objectives, and gather results. I have used it, found it useful, and wanted to share it through *La Mappa del Terapeuta*.

8.2.1 Part One

The manual is divided into three parts. The first part focuses on *psychotherapy* and *psychopathology*.

I begin by emphasizing the importance of how psychopathological processes can inform psychotherapeutic treatment, underscoring that disorder assessment should not be based solely on the observation of symptomatic behaviors but must also take into account the type of personality structures encountered and the level acquired by the patient's defensive organizations and the subject's interaction both with his or her family and environment.

Family therapists know that a family does not become dysfunctional within a single generation (Bowen & Kerr, 1990); therefore – from the very first diagnosis – the clinician's attention should not focus exclusively on the presence of mental disorders. The great diversity of clinical cases is determined by many factors: by age and stage of the life cycle; by the effects of combined subjective needs; by defense mechanisms; by physical limits and possibilities; by the environment's reaction; and by the structural characteristics of personality disorders, not intended as a specific form of characteropathy but as a group of homogeneous character and personality disorders as seen from the perspective of cognitive and defensive structures.

Therefore patient care should not provide symptom-focused therapy (centered exclusively on symptom remission) but should focus on the symptom's function (on the function of disorders and problematic behaviors), looking for connections between a subject's personal and family history and the initial onset and further development of mental and behavioral disorders. The therapist must *plan* the intervention, putting together information regarding the patient's life cycle phase and the *subjective emergency* experienced by the patient. To this purpose, the ability to recognize the psychopathological processes acted by the patient is vital.

Furthermore, it is a known fact that countertransference is a common element shared by different forms of psychotherapeutic intervention: similar mechanisms are also activated when therapists work with a group rather than with a single patient. As it is true that the family will represent its myth to the therapist, it is also true that therapists will do the same, representing their own family myth: therapy is a setting in which two family myths meet and interlace. Family therapists can, therefore, use their perception of themselves as an object of transference to understand what is happening during family therapy, being however well aware of the complexity of the situation and of the developing emotional reactions towards the different parts and not just towards the family system as a whole. One of the risks when working with families is that the family could become enmeshed into the therapist's psychological economy and he or she could become dependent on it. To counteract the therapist's tendency towards fusion, it is advisable to structure the setting by providing a co-therapist, when possible, and a supervisor, always.

The first part of the manual devotes special attention to personality disorders. The diagnosis of borderline personality disorder has changed over time according to the different clinical paradigms that have dominated psychiatry, from the psychoanalytic paradigm to the medical and pharmacological one to the dominant one today which is that of specificity and specialization, both in terms of etiology and treatment.

Situations of distress generated by borderline functioning are far more common than those caused by neuroses and psychoses, and the various authors who have explored this topic over the years can be divided into two groups: those who emphasize "conflict" and those who focus on a "deficit," not considering that the different assessments were probably related to studies targeting different populations. From the etiological point of view, it is self-evident that factors of pathology are related to intrapsychic, environmental, and relational aspects as well as to the interaction of these aspects.

Patients who are diagnosed with BPD according to a language shared by psychiatrists, psychologists, and psychotherapists (in other words shared by those healthcare providers who are faced with the challenge of working with unmanageable patients) actually belong to three different categories: while only some of them manifest psychotic structures, others display an overlap between compulsive and self-aggressive behaviors and deeper mood disorders without however meeting the criteria for a psychotic description; in other words they only send signals of psychiatric distress (these situations will revert to normality if treated appropriately and promptly). Lorna Smith Benjamin authored a priceless contribution to the study of personality disorders and their treatment, and we refer extensively to her approach in this manual (Benjamin, 1996, 2003, 2018).

Patients with personality disorders are highly treatment-resistant and tend to react more to their internalized key figures than to the people they interact with in the here and now. Therapy success is therefore possible if and when the patient is freed from the expectations and hopes linked to these internalizations. We must keep in mind that even when treating adult patients, those patients are, ultimately, the injured children who still cry inside them, and it is these injured children that we must reach out to through our therapeutic work (Cancrini, 2012, 2017).

8.2.2 Part Two

The second part of the Manual focuses on *the growth of children*.

After summarizing the transformations undergone by the family system and after having defined its new functions, we identify the main family styles and risk factors as these are characteristic of multiproblematic families. Subsequently the close link between early experiences and some emotional and relational disorders during adulthood is highlighted. These disorders seem to be modeled through childhood experiences and – in turn – influence the articulation of subsequent experiences. This has been confirmed not only via the extensive research on the subject but also by clinical observation which highlights the frequency with which early negative experiences are associated to specific psychological problems in adolescence and adulthood.

Because of environmental and family continuity across the years, early childhood experiences and later events in adulthood are rarely independent of each other. For example, children raised in a high-conflict family environment, who – for extensive periods of time – are neglected or subjected to/witnesses of physical or sexual abuse, almost inevitably acquire behavioral patterns which are then exported to other environments (such as school). Thus their own behavior generates situations in which contexts external to the family – contexts which could potentially be beneficial to the subject and somewhat compensate the negative experience – cannot fully yield the benefits and compensatory values which they could provide. The idea that negative experiences have a lasting effect is linked to experiential continuity, i.e., the fact that other educational contexts or other relational resources end up being characterized by the persistence of the negative experiences. We can state that negative experiences and losses that occur during childhood do not necessarily determine the development of a personality disorder if these experiences are followed by authentic positive experiences.

This section of the manual ends with a focus on the challenges couples face when carrying out their own developmental tasks and the impact that these have on their children.

Families have changed over the years, and they must face many different distressing and difficult situations not to mention many developmental and critical steps (Scabini, 1995). Therapy should be progressively aimed at working on the difficulties in the relationships between the adult pair and between adults and their children; it should focus on preventing situations of distress and on supporting families as they face contingent difficulties. The issue at hand often requires activating parenting skills; building a place where family members can be heard; eliciting their requests for help; accepting the explicit requests made by members in distress; and recognizing forms of hidden distress which have not been voiced or defined yet. Systemic therapists often work with families which have a transitory structure: the definition of the system to be treated in these situations is not simple, it is never initially predetermined, but it develops during treatment. At times the difficulty and the impossibility of working with the entire family system lead to working with single individuals.

Often the couple represents the "thread" which therapy must "pull to loosen the tangle of family suffering." The transformation of the family system (Colacicco, 2003; Malagoli Togliatti & Rocchietta Tofani, 1987; Scabini, 1995), the dissolution of a typical family organization into different family realities, the constitution of multiple family groups, the revealing of new family situations, and the to-and-fro motions which different families build around the couple make this the hub around which the network of bonds – the web of relationships which we are a part of – revolve, enveloping itself on it. We have observed the increasing frequency of family therapists who, after having screened the entire family system, attempt to work directly with the marital couple, as well as psychodynamic therapists who – following an individual case assessment – recommend couples therapy. Whether psychotherapy begins with the family or whether it is centered initially on the individual, it seems to naturally lead to working with the couple.

8.2.3 Part Three

The third part of the manual, based on the concepts described above, focuses on *therapy with the individual, with couples, and with families*. In this third part, I refer to some case studies to exemplify the technical aspects of recommended therapist interventions.

Today it is a well-established fact that systemic-relational interventions are no longer aimed solely at the traditional family but can be adopted when working with families, couples, and individuals. As far as individual treatment is concerned, it must be stated that – despite the fact that family therapy was originally conceived in opposition to individual therapy – currently this controversy seems to have been largely overcome. While a few years ago family therapy was recommended by systemic therapists as the *panacea* for all ills, so much so that patients were almost automatically referred to family treatment, the current trend has changed; today the patient is assessed on several comparable parameters (age, personal traits, age at onset of symptoms, chronicity, configuration of the family system, life cycle phase, etc.) before defining a specific referral.

On the other hand, individual therapy is perfectly compatible within the systemic-relational model (Boscolo & Bertrando, 1996; Canevaro et al., 2008; Colacicco, 2001, 2007, 2017; Loriedo et al., 1989; Selvini Palazzoli & Viaro, 1989), even from a theoretical standpoint, given that treatment focuses on the interactions between systems, even if they are very specific systems such as the individual subject. Today individual treatment falls within the area of intervention of the systemic-relational therapist. It is for these reasons that I believe it is more accurate to talk about *an interpersonal and relational approach* (Colacicco, 2017) rather than of "family therapy" given that the latter term can be reductive and partial.

Moreover, since in our society the subsystem that performs parental functions is usually the marital couple, it follows that the characteristics of the parental role and the type and quality of family life will be determined by the childhood experiences of the parents and by the marital relationship that is structured by the couple.

Given that perception and social learning which occur during childhood are encoded in a person's memory and are subsequently "copied" into their adult relationships and given that adult behavior is determined as much by destructive as it is by constructive experiences, the potentially beneficial impact of therapy is self-evident because of the enormous potential of psychotherapeutic work contained here.

On these grounds it is increasingly clear that therapy must work with *the family inside the patients' mind* and must work more with the representation of the family in the head rather than the real present-day family. In fact, especially when working with adult patients, inviting the family to participate in therapy can be counterproductive[1], and more often than not, based on our clinical experience, it is not possible to arrange family meetings.[2] So, with increasing frequency, family therapists find

---

[1] The young adult in the organization phase, with neurotic area disorders, can be treated individually or in pairs, if his ability to build bonds outside the family allows him to carry out a job that looks forward instead of a job aimed backwards, towards the family of origin. The situation is different when the disorder occurs in other phases of the family life cycle, when the symptoms are at the service of family homeostasis. In all these cases, the first choice intervention is with the family (Cancrini L. & La Rosa C. 1991, *Il vaso di pandora*, pp. 132–133, Carocci editore, Roma).

[2] The delimitation of the system to be treated is particularly difficult with multiproblematic families. In these situations, the therapist is immediately confronted with the difficulty of summoning the whole family, for his tendency to come or not to come to therapy for instrumental and functional reasons with internal logic. Hence the inopportunity is to often convene the entire family and

themselves alone in the room with their patient, and which task is more congenial than working with the family in the patients' mind? In this setting family therapists can do their best work knowing well which techniques can be used to help the patient rebuild his or her story, knowing the how-to and where to go.

The systemic approach can be effectively applied and integrated with Lorna Smith Benjamin's *Interpersonal Reconstructive Therapy*. The latter approach is now an integral part of our training, and it is extensively and successfully implemented in the individual treatment of our patients (Colacicco, 2014). We often refer to this approach in our manual, and to exemplify its use, we have included in the manual the script of a role-play session conducted by Dr. Benjamin with a trainee therapist and the script of a session I held with another trainee therapist in which I used the *diagram of well-being*.[3]

Regarding couple therapy, the clinical experience shared by several couples' therapists leads us to assert that there is usually a unique pattern which characterizes the couple's relational system: the psychic root of the original and spontaneous attraction which originally bound the partners (Caillé, 1990; Caillé & Rey, 1998, 2005; Elkaim, 1992). Couple's relationships cannot be understood only in terms of *the object relation* of a *single subject*; rather it presupposes the organization of reciprocal attractions which originate the birth of an "us". Unconscious collusion is a general phenomenon, present in all couples and found at all unconscious libidinal levels. It is the product of the combination between the shared general problem and the two different, complementary and opposite ways of dealing with it.

Our interest in this aspect is not merely diagnostic since it also holds important indications for treatment: identifying a problem in one of the two partners allows us to infer its presence in the other partner as well, even if it is expressed in opposite and complementary ways. It is on this core theme that therapy interventions should focus on the psychic interlacing which the couple weaves around the theme it has "chosen," on the study of the couple's affective dynamics, and on the use that the two partners make of the mutual bond.

This part of the manual summarizes the main technical aspects of couple's interventions, illustrating different case studies and the related therapy processes. There are extensive references to the contributions made by the most important couple therapists.

---

to choose to see individual members individually (Cancrini L. 1994, *W Palermo viva. Storia di un progetto per la prevenzione delle tossicodipendenze*, pp. 112–113, la Nuova Italia Scientifica, Roma).

[3] This diagram is a new and useful technique which can help the systemic-relational therapist on many levels: it enables the patient to narrate his or her personal, marital, or family history, highlighting the dysfunctional aspects, while using an alternative channel to that of the spoken word, with all the pros that can be derived from using an analogue technique. This allows patients to activate new learning processes, become aware of new questions and emotions which they experience in other contexts or which could be highlighted if freed from the rigidity of their scripts, rigidity which does not belong to a "linear" dimension but rather to a dimension which is "relational and circular."

Chapter 9 of the manual focuses on the systemic assessment and setting of therapy work with families and presents a map of family situations. This section is the core of the manual.

In 2005 a team working at the *Unità Operativa Dipartimentale di Psicoterapia della Sapienza, Università di Roma* (Department of Psychotherapy of *La Sapienza* University of Rome) began a research project on the assessment of psychotherapeutic treatment of families, couples, and individuals.

The research team devised a data collection form, in the form of a questionnaire, which was submitted to therapists to collect data on their work, analyzing individual case studies and keeping in mind that – when organizing their intervention – the systemic-relational therapists always collect data regarding which life cycle phase which the family is currently going through. For the systemic-relational assessment of family situations, a series of tables have been developed by matching life cycle phase, the specificities of the situation and the subjective emergencies, modifying and integrating the tables created by Luigi Cancrini (Cancrini, 1987; Cancrini & La Rosa, 1991), from which I drew the inspiration.

While this map covers all the main transitions of life, it does not claim to describe the entire "territory" of the different life situations. It does aim at providing the therapist with a possible pathway within which to move to be able to explore it.

For the systemic and relational assessment of family situations, a series of tables have been developed, combining the phases of the life cycle, the specificities of the situation treated, and the subjective emergencies raised by patients. The phases of the life cycle have been summarized as follows: young adult without ties in the organization phase; adult/young adult without ties and/or with unstructured emotional ties; emerging couple, couple with no children, with young children, with preteen and teen children, and with adult children; retirement; and old age. For each phase there is a corresponding table (which is in turn correlated with all the others) that cross-references the data of the different specific situations with those of the subjective emergencies raised, at the various levels (individual, family, couple, parenting, children, the elderly).

Following is an extract of our *map*, specifically the tables relating to the *launching* phase (children leaving home) and regarding the situations generated during this phase: the symptomatic emergencies generated by children leaving home (Table 8.1) and the parents' problems in releasing the children (Table 8.2).

The sample on which, in 2006, the final version of the data collection form[4] for the assessment of treatment with families, couples, and individuals was defined consisted of families, couples, and individuals which were being treated in three different structures: a public one, *Unità Operativa Dipartimentale di Psicoterapia* (a local public health service where patients pay a minimal for treatment); a private one, the *Istituto Dedalus* which is a psychotherapy specialization school where patients are seen in private practice; and a third institute, the *Centro di Terapia*

---

[4] The first version of the form was conceived and tested in 2004 at the Unità Operativa Dipartimentale di Psicoterapia of the "La Sapienza" University in Rome.

Table 8.1 Analysis of possible combinations between life cycle phase, situation experienced, and subjective emergencies caused by children leaving home

Life cycle phase	Situation	Subjective emergency
Adult children: Children are adults and begin to detach (leaving-home phase). The system accepts the increasing number of in-and-out movements. Newfound interest in the marital subsystem, development of equal relationships between parents and adult children, redefinition of relationships to include grandchildren and in-laws	**If solved,** the actual focus shifts towards growth-related goals and further differentiation. If the *individuation process is so uncertain that it entirely prevents leaving home or only allows an attempt to do so while never fulfilling this step:* **1. Leaving home is impossible**: children who have manifested difficulties during the identification phase begin to shutdown any chance they might have of leaving home, long before the moment in which this would normally take place. **2. Leaving home is unacceptable**: the family cannot cope with the emotional emancipation of a child. *The leaving-home phase may also be:* **3. Difficult or problematic**: the child has effectively left the house but faces challenges in reconciling the demands of the family with those of external reality; however, the actual focus is still towards growth objectives and further differentiation. **4. Apparent**: leaving home can be incomplete and partial with unexpected returns and severe personal limitations. **5. Compromised**: leaving home can only happen if the child takes on a family-mandated project	**Child level:** **Personality disorder**[a]: intense unstable personal relationships, self-destructiveness, chronic dysphoria (anger or boredom), transient episodes with psychotic manifestations or cognitive impairment, impulsiveness, identity disorders, poor social adaptation, constant strained efforts to avoid abandonment (real or imaginary), although these patients are not psychotic they display psychotic mechanisms. 1. Functions occasionally 2. "Low threshold" functioning (subject is easily triggered) 3. Pervasive functioning (almost constant and without context distinctions) *If leaving home is impossible there can also be:* **4. "Developmental" forms of dissociative syndrome**: "true" schizophrenia according to authors who defend the need to distinguish between two types of dissociative disease. *If release is unacceptable:* **5. Psychotic breakdown in the form of psychosis or "acute schizophrenia"** (delusional *bouffée*, aigue of French psychiatrists). **6. Depressive breakdown or manic episode**, compensation, and chronicization of the same through **drug addiction.** **7. Severe psychosomatic disorders and psychogenic eating disorders**

[a]Different personality disorders can coexist within the same subject. According to Kernberg there is a borderline organization of basic personalities which can be found in different syndromes and in normal people when these are experiencing high stress levels. According to some clinical studies, this disorder can last a few years (five or so); then it calms down for a period and can return at a later age, when the children leave the home

Table 8.2 Analysis of possible correspondences between life cycle phase, situation experienced, and subjective emergencies raised by parents with children

Situation	Subjective and interpersonal emergencies	
If the *individuation process is so uncertain as to allow only an attempt to leave home, or prevents it entirely:* **1. Leaving home is impossible**: children who have manifested difficulties during the identification phase begin to shutdown any chance they might have of leaving home, long before the moment in which this would normally take place. **2. Leaving home is unacceptable**: the family cannot cope with the emotional emancipation of a child. *The leaving-home phase may also be:* **3. Difficult or problematic**: the child has effectively left the house but faces challenges in reconciling the demands of the family with those of external reality; however, the actual focus is still towards growth objectives and further differentiation. **4. Apparent**: leaving home can be incomplete and partial with unexpected returns and severe personal limitations. **5. Compromised**: leaving home can only happen if the child takes on a family-mandated project	**Parent experiences:** 1. Free-floating anxiety or related to specific situations, which can evolve into a current neurosis. 2. Reconversion hysteria or anguish. 3. Simple forms of *vaginismus, impotentia consundi, eiaculatio praecox.* 4. Different psychosomatic disorders. 5. Trauma-induced depression (neurosis) (possibly alcoholism or type A drug addiction, trauma-induced anorexia). *If parents cannot go through the leaving-home phase:* 6. Psychotic breakdown if leaving has not occurred. *or* 7. Depressive (or manic) crisis if the leaving phase is incomplete. 8. Possibly alcoholism or type B and C substance addiction, transitional anorexia and/or bulimia. **Personality disorder**: intense and unstable personal relationships, self-destructiveness, chronic dysphoria (anger or boredom), fleeting episodes of psychotic displays or cognitive impairment, impulsiveness, identity disorders, poor social functioning, constant efforts to avoid abandonment (real or imaginary), although these patients are not psychotic, they exhibit psychotic mechanisms. 9. Occasional functionality 10. "Low threshold" functionality (is easily triggered) 11. Pervasive functionality (almost constant and without context distinctions)	**Couple experiences:** 1. Conflict in the couple: brief and violent fights or continuous and explicit contrasts, with or without threats of separation. 2. Behaviors which signal a break in the marital pair or in the workplace: crisis of the couple with conspicuous betrayals and/or separations or divorces. 3. Different problems and difficulties in the area of sexuality, including recidivous or previously emerged issues. 4. Modulation of marital conflict through the involvement of children (triangulations) 5. Sudden professional crisis at work or search for new working conditions

Familiare of Lecce, which is subsidized by the local health authorities and therefore provides free treatment. Analyzing the data collected over a period of 3 years and relating to 150 case studies, we were able to reconstruct the main intervention models used by family therapist in these structures. This allowed me to summarize, in the manual, which systems the therapist intervenes on and how, who is called in for the sessions, and which interventions are made.

A) When

> *Children are small* and must be accepted as new members of the system, when the parental subsystem is formed, the marital subsystem is re-established, relations with the trigenerational family are reformulated, and the roles of parents and grandparents are re-negotiated.
>
> *And the children present that series of disorders which are typical of early detection*, problems in school, psychosomatic, and eating disorders or disorders of a psychotic type which are identified in secondary detection.
>
> *The family therapist's goal is to recreate conditions that foster the child's growth.* He or she immediately calls in the sub-system in which the difficulty arose and works on the situation. Interventions are rapid and symptom-focused. The therapist seeks to leverage the awareness of the child's caregivers so that the child is not left behind, to encourage the development of socialization initiatives and to create a feeling of "team" collaboration among the adults. Parental competence is never questioned.

B) When

> *Children are teenagers*, some have left school, others work, and others still don't; boundaries must become more flexible to allow for the independence of the children (relationships between parents and children shift and adjust to allow the adolescent to enter and exit the system); interests and relationships are newly discussed within the marital subsystem.
>
> *And children display disruptive behaviors which create a break* from family and or school, difficult social relations, psychosomatic problems, eating disorders, or drug problems.
>
> *The therapist initially carries out separate interviews with the parents and with the adolescent* and later builds a more flexible setting (sessions with the parents, the adolescent, the whole family); the therapist focuses on the system of alliances, trying to avoid falling into the trap of expressing compassion or solidarity for the younger patient or siding with the parents and assuming "normalizing" positions.

C) When

> *Children are adults and detach*, the family system must accept an increasing number of movements in and out of the family; new interests are discovered within the marital subsystem, and new peer relations are established between parents and adult children. Relationships are redefined to include new partners, in-laws, and grandchildren.
>
> And *the young adults express personality disorders, dissociative syndromes, severe psychosomatic disorders, depressive or psychotic breaks, or substance abuse.*
>
> *Therapist intervention is focused on involving the entire family*, enrolling parental collaboration during crisis interventions; interventions are characterized by a strong insistence. The therapist must think in systemic terms and

make use of a syntaxis of the second type[5] implementing counter-paradoxical interventions.

In the second part of the chapter, the data collection form for the assessment of family, couples, and individual treatment is presented.

It is divided into six sections:

- The first section collects data regarding therapy setting (treatment procedure, referral, patient request, patient/couple/family socioeconomic data).
- The data collected in the second section concerns the assessment of psychopathology in all symptom-presenting subjects (using the DSM as a reference).
- The third section structures therapy intervention based on the systemic-relational assessment (connecting phase of the life cycle, type of situation, and subjective emergency). This assessment also aims at answering questions such as "When did the patients seek treatment" and "When did the problems first arise."
- The fourth section collects data regarding the implemented intervention. The focus here is on the treated system, on previous therapies, and on other structures or institutes involved. Data is collected regarding past hospitalizations, suicide attempts, prescribed medications, and the "incurred cost" which all this had on the subjects' lives before therapy. Lastly the focus shifts onto the therapist, requesting him or her to define the adopted treatment rationale and specifying which treatment approach was implemented, which goals were defined and which techniques were used to pursue them. Subsequently different aspects of the described therapy are analyzed including setting, history of previous treatments, and liaison with other structures involved in the treatment process and treatment effects. Treatment is described using a range of intervention characteristics describing the therapist's approach, his or her rationale, techniques, and tools adopted. These categories refer to a treatment plan designed for couples, families, and all those individuals who agree that all human systems can be effectively treated using the systemic-relational approach.
- The fifth section of data collected helps the therapist analyze his/her countertransference ((Cancrini, 1997, 1999; Colacicco, 2001; Eiguer, 1983; Fissi, 1986; Fruggeri, 1992; Nicolò, 1983; Shapiro, 1983) following three different paths. Because there is always a specific connection between impasse in treatment and

---

[5] In his book *Psicoterapia, grammatica e sintassi*, Luigi Cancrini analyzes the basic common rules of different therapy approaches and develops a two-level analysis: syntax – which concerns intervention guidelines and objectives – and grammar, which instead concerns the practical ways in which sessions are managed. Drawing on this analogy between therapy and language, Cancrini proposes a verbal scheme of therapy construction shared by all psychotherapists, identifying two possible outcomes of the therapy process: after having understood and expressed the significance of the symptoms, the reasons of all parties involved and having sympathized with the (designated) patient, the therapist can then choose to push the patient (or family) to change or to respect the deep motivations of the symptom (either because they are important or because they are too strong). Assuming this second position (syntax of the second type), the therapist applies a new logic and assumes a new position (no longer pushing the patient to change as is usually expected in treatment), implementing indirect and counter-paradoxical interventions (Cancrini L. 1987).

the therapist's countertransferral fixation (especially when the therapist works alone), we decided to analyze this aspect as well when assessing treatment. This is also why we ask therapists to compile a specifically designed table for all those situations in which they felt strongly emotionally involved.
- The last section collects data regarding follow-up sessions. The forms here are different for the different systems treated (family, couple, individual). Data on "incurred costs" is once again collected, this time posttreatment.

This form is part of the patients' case formulation and is necessary to collect and systematically organize the data collected by the therapist. It helps the therapist to both structure the therapy interventions and monitor their progress. This data collection form also enables the structure within which the therapist works to collect data on its users and to assess therapist interventions.

Two chapters follow, 10 and 11: *The territory, notes from my travels* and *Effectiveness of psychotherapy*.

In the former I illustrate some case studies to convey the sense of what happens inside the therapy setting, without the expectation of "showing exactly how it is done," rather to sketch out a rudimentary map of the territory. These are therapy narratives, reconstructions of therapeutic processes which tie the therapist and his/her patients, and in which the topics chosen only function as an example. Substance abuse, mental health problems, mothers with difficult children, anorexia, separated couples under court supervision, children's requests for help, etc. are all problems which patients bring into the therapy room: different situations which present a variety of different symptoms and which relate to different phases of the life cycle.

In the final chapter, I tried to underscore the importance of assessing therapeutic work. Therapy effectiveness is an extremely relevant and current topic. We are constantly pressured by the national health service to provide evidence of the effectiveness and cost of our work, pressured to measure and assess the quality of our work, yet it is only recently that therapists have begun to consider how to effectively measure the impact of their interventions through research studies (Colacicco, 2005). In this concluding chapter of the manual, I summarize the main criteria used to assess therapy effectiveness, referring to other authors who have extensively researched the subject, and I quote a few studies specifically designed to assess the long-term effectiveness of therapy on family systems.

8.3 Dissemination and Study of the Manual

In writing this manual, I made a conscious effort of integration and synthesis in an attempt to overcome that "observer assessment encoding" barrier which hinders our work as systemic therapists. It has been an effort aimed mostly at "searching for a different organization of the relationship between the figure and its background."

Since its publication, this manual and its data collection form have been widely adopted. One of the most convincing examples of its utility is provided by a research conducted by the *Centro Psicoterapeutico Familiare per le Dipendenze della ASL di Lecce* (Family Psychotherapeutic Center for Addictions, national health services, of Lecce) and by the Istituto Dedalus. A total of 136 case studies were analyzed, all treated by a team of 6 expert therapists who worked in pairs. Therapies were designed for single individuals, couples, and families; the patient sample mostly reported anxiety disorders or mood disorders (depression). Almost all cases presented a diagnosis on Axis I paired with a personality disorder on Axis II. Subjective emergencies and the subsequent request for treatment were experienced mostly by young adults with no significant pair-bond, either still in the organizing phase or with very weak emotional ties.

A large part of the case studies experienced distress during the family life phase with adolescent and preadolescent children. Treatments prescribed in these cases were mostly structural and involved families, couples, and single individuals, outlining a different profile for each system that was being analyzed.

The report's conclusions read "… the results suggest that the team working at the *Centro Psicoterapeutico Familiare per le Dipendenze* is capable of welcoming and responding promptly to a variety of situations of distress, providing focused and functional interventions. The *Centro* provides good quality psychotherapeutic treatment to the territory. Specifically, the results yielded by the follow-up show an improvement in patient psychological well-being which seems to have a significant effect even on the "incurred costs." Intercepting suffering and distress and providing structured interventions seem first and foremost to prevent a degeneration of the situation and to significantly and effectively help families, couples, and individuals to overcome specific problems related to their phase of the life cycle. Furthermore providing therapy treatment seems to have been beneficial to the general community,[6] lightening the load shouldered by other public services and reducing the number of absences from work.

Lastly, these research results suggest the efficacy of a multilevel assessment which enables therapists to go beyond the standard diagnosis, favoring the structuring and development of a therapy process. Further work is necessary to refine and gain mastery of these research tools in order to allow therapists to better their understanding of clinical situations and work towards the constant improvement of their clinical practice (Colacicco et al., 2014).

---

[6]The usefulness and effectiveness of psychotherapeutic interventions with the observed patients emerge from the follow-up forms. The results recorded by the data collection form were submitted to the institutes' administration for the assessment and planning of services for the local territory.

8.4 Conclusions

La Mappa del Terapeuta is a manual through which I have tried to summarize, with clarity and simplicity, the experience I have gained during my last 40 years, experimenting myself and everything that I have learned working with individuals, couples, and families.

"In the footsteps of Milton Erickson and his monumental work (Haley, 1985). Within a training path based on systemic work with families and which then came to consider the possibility, in some situations, of a work centered on the person" (Cancrini, 2013, *Presentazione*, in Colacicco F., *La mappa del terapeuta*, Scione Editore, pp. 9, Roma). Other systemic therapists (Boscolo & Bertrando, 1996) have faced the issue of varying their methods of intervention when deciding to work alone with a patient. In the manual I express my thoughts on this point, I illustrate my approach, and I give some indications of intervention, trying to integrate the *systemic* with the *relational* and the *interpersonal*. It is a book that aims to train students who are starting with the difficult work of the psychotherapist.

The history of psychotherapy is made up of conceptual and personal quarrels, which have given rise to an incredible number of schisms and schools. The attempt to fly a little higher, above sectarianism and mutual disqualifications, in search of what should be saved as useful for the work we have all chosen to do, has always been for me, as for Luigi Cancrini and many other psychotherapists of the Center for Family and Relational Therapy Studies, the founding element of a serious training of students, trying to offer them a wide repertoire of information and experiences that allow them to use an intelligent, reasonable, and especially useful eclecticism (for them and their patients), making them capable of modulating their interventions according to settings variation, and teaching them to work with individuals, couples, and families.

Acknowledgements There are many people I would like to thank for the work which has led to the creation and implementation of this data collection form, first and foremost my students and colleagues (Fulvia Adragna, Gabriella Maria Bianco, Federico Bussoletti, Serena Cesi, Claudia Colamedici, Patrizia Costante, Silvia Curiale, Tania Di Giuseppe, Angela Falvo, Giusy Granata, Dora Monaco, Teresa Pomponi, Anna Rosa Prete, Adriana Romano, Sandra Stefanelli, Alessia Supino, and Claudio Tramentozzi, Rosangela Vaglio). Special thanks go to Francesca Martini, who worked by my side in both developing the form and coordinating the entire research project.

References

Benjamin, L. S. (1996). *Interpersonal diagnosis and treatment of personality disorders*. The Guilford Press.
Benjamin, L. S. (2003). *Interpersonal reconstructive therapy*. The Guilford Press.
Benjamin, L. S. (2018). *Interpersonal reconstructive therapy for anger, anxiety, and depression. It's about broken hearts, not broken brains*. American Psychological Association, Washington.

Boscolo, L., & Bertrando, P. (1996). *Terapia sistemica individuale*. Cortina Editore.
Bowen, M., & Kerr, M. E. (1990). *La valutazione della famiglia*. Astrolabio.
Caillé, P. (1990). *Il rapporto famiglia terapeuta. Lettura sistemica di una interazione*. La Nuova Italia Scientifica.
Caillé, P., & Rey, Y. (1998). *C'era una volta. Il metodo narrative in terapia sistemica*. Franco Angeli.
Caillé, P., & Rey, Y. (2005). *Gli oggetti fluttuanti. Metodi di interviste sistemiche*. Armando Editore.
Caillé, P. (2015). Viaggio nella sistemica. In *Il terapeuta, le domande di aiuto, la formazione*. Alpes.
Cancrini, L. (1987). *Psicoterapia, grammatica e sintassi*. La Nuova Italia Scientifica.
Cancrini, L., & La Rosa, C. (1991). *Il vaso di pandora*. Carocci editore.
Cancrini, L. (1997). *Lezioni di psicopatologia*. Bollati Boringhieri.
Cancrini, L. (1999). *La luna nel pozzo. Famiglie, comunità terapeutiche, controtransfert e decorso della schizofrenia*. Cortina Editore.
Cancrini, L. (2012). *La cura delle infanzie infelici. Viaggio nell'origine dell'oceano borderline*. Raffaello Cortina Editore.
Cancrini, L. (2017). *Asccoltare i bambini. Psicoterapia delle infanzie negate*. Raffaello Cortina Editore.
Cancrini, M. G., & Harrison, L. (1983). *La trappola della follia*. La Nuova Italia Scientifica.
Canevaro, A., Selvini, M., Lifranchi, F., Peveri, L. (2008). *Terapia familiar sistemica col coinvolgimento dei familiari significativi*, Psicobiettivo, 1/2008, anno XXVIII, (pp. 143–166), Franco Angeli.
Colacicco, F. (2001). *Oltre il muro delle resistenze: importanza dei processi psicopatologici nell'informare il trattamento psicoterapico*, Ecologia dellamente, N.24, 2/2001. Il Pensiero Scientifico Editore.
Colacicco, F. (2003). *Alla ricerca dell'intreccio psichico della coppia*, Ecologia della mente, 1/2003. Il Pensiero Scientifico Editore.
Colacicco, F. (2005). *In tema dell'efficacia delle psicoterapie, con particolare riguardo alla terapia familiare e al suo insegnamento*, Ecologia della mente, 1/2005. Il Pensiero Scientifico Editore.
Colacicco, F. (2007). *La ruota che stride. Meccanismi di difesa e trattamento psicoterapeutico*, Ecologia della mente, 2/2006. Ecologia della mente.
Colacicco, F., Martini, F., Bianco, G. M., Prete, A. R., Romano, A., Vaglio, R. (2014). *La valutazione del trattamento psicoterapico con le famiglie, le coppie, gli individui*, Ecologia della mente, Vol. 37/2014. Il PensieroScientifico Editore.
Colacicco, F. (2013). *La mappa del terapeuta*. Scione Editore.
Colacicco, F. (2014). *Ogni psicopatologia è un dono d'amore*. Scione Editore.
Colacicco, F. (2017). *Il giocatore di scacchi. Una metafora per le relazioni interpersonali*. Alpes.
Eiguer, A. (1983). *La terapia familiare come processo transferenziale: Transfert, contro- transfert e neuropsicosi da transfert*, Terapia FAmiliare, 14, (pp. 65–86), I.T.R.
Elkaim, M. (1992). *Se mi ami non amarmi*. Bollati Boringhieri.
Fissi, S. (1986). *Legittimità e delimitazione del concetto di controtransfert in terapia familiare*, in Terapia Familiare, (p. 21), I.T.R.
Fruggeri, L. (1992). *Le emozioni del terapista*, Psicobiettivo, 3, (pp. 23–34), Franco Angeli.
Haley, J. (1985). *Conversation with Milton H. Erickson, M.D.* (Vol. I, II, III). Triangle Press/ W.W. Norton & Co..
Loriedo, C., Angiolari, C., & De Francisci, A. (1989). *La terapia individuale sistemica*, Terapia Familiare, 31, (pp. 13–25), I.T.F.
Malagoli Togliatti, M., & Rocchietta Tofani, L. (1987). *Famiglie multiproblematiche. Dall'analisi all'intervento su un sistema complesso*. La Nuova Italia Scientifica.
Nicolò, A. M. (1983). *Sull'uso del contro-transfert in terapia familiare: spunti per una discussione*. Terapia Familiare, 13, (pp. 97–100), I.T.F.

Scabini, E. (1995). *Psicologia sociale della famiglia. Sviluppo dei legami e trasformazioni sociali.* Bollati Boringhieri.

Selvini Palazzoli, M. & Viaro, M. (1989). *Il processo anoressico nella famiglia: un modello a sei stadi a guida del trattamento individuale*, Terapia Familiare, 30, (pp. 5–19), I.T.F.

Shapiro, R. J. (1983). *Il controtransfert in terapia familiare*, Terapia Familiare, 13, (pp. 91–96), I.T.F.

Chapter 9
A Model of a Systemic Therapy Clinic

Cigdem Alper

9.1 Introduction

This chapter is about the development of a theoretical model for a systemic therapy clinic that integrates training, practice and research in a newly opened centre in Urla-Izmir, Turkey.

This is an attempt to combine the expertise and accumulated knowledge of experienced therapists to specify an optimal physical and interactional environment for systemic therapy. This part of the project has not been completely realised at this stage. A progress report and what might be achievable in future is included at the end of this chapter. This chapter focuses on the first of three stages. The development of a manual is the primary objective of the project, which will be created based on the completed part of the project. The manual will provide an example of challenges, opportunities and step-by-step guidance for practitioners who are interested in transforming private practices into a systemic clinic working in collaboration with others.

The context of the systemic clinic and the current state in Turkey is described in the following paragraphs. This is followed by an illustration of the beginning of a systemic clinic idea. The latter section focuses on how these ideas are embodied in a building with consideration to the specific needs of the professionals and clients. The paragraph to follow focuses on the steps of creating a learning environment to provide opportunities for exchanging information and intellectual discussion as well as to allow space for interpersonal and personal development. The subsequent paragraph explains cultivation of the professional relationships among therapists and supervisees, which include working together to solve fundamental problems of a systemic clinic (e.g. receiving information from clients, the privacy issues,

---

C. Alper (✉)
Yasamca Psikoloji Merkezi, Izmir, Turkey
e-mail: cigdem@alper.com

referrals). The sections that follow are an overview of the second and third manuals, which include practising systemic family therapy, training students, assessment strategies, supervision, research and an outline of the manual. The final part of this chapter covers a progress report regarding the first manual, discussion and conclusion sections.

9.2 The Context

Certified by the Republic of Turkey Ministry of Family, Labour and Social Services, "Yaşamca Family Counselling Centre" was opened in October 2019 in Urla-Izmir, Turkey. The identity of the Couples and Family Therapy in Turkey is still in its infancy and there is an increasing need for a structure to ensure the well-being of clients, therapists, students and the public (Kafescioglu & Akyil, 2018; Roberts et al., 2014).

Currently in Turkey, the main requisite to obtain the title of family counsellor is to hold an undergraduate degree from a four-year mental health-related undergraduate programme such as social services, sociology, psychology, psychological counselling, nursing and child development. Students must then complete a certificate programme in family counselling training to obtain a minimum of 300 theoretical hours and 150 supervised applied hours. Minimum supervision is 30 hours. Currently, there is no licensing process in place for any of the mental health fields in Turkey, including Couple and Family Therapy (Kafescioglu & Akyil, 2018).

We have seen a growing interest in Couples and Family Therapy (CFT) over the last decade. However, a recent study found that 20% of the therapists worked with couples and families without any specialised training in CFT and 34% of the participants worked unsupervised (Akyıl et al., 2015). None of the current undergraduate psychology programmes in Turkey offer comprehensive and systematic CFT training (Kafescioglu & Akyil, 2018). Limited information about the training and practices of Systemic Family Therapy calls for new mental health institutions that focus on qualified, accessible and economically viable supervision and training options and solutions in Turkey (Eraslan et al., 2012; Cosan, 2015).

This project is an attempt to meet the need and fill a gap by establishing a Systemic Therapy Clinic. Many senior psychotherapists provide services to families in private practices, usually in isolation and without any peer support or referral system, while many junior therapists require supervised experiences. Senior therapists and new graduates can become interdependent to solve problems and succeed in challenges much more effectively than working alone. Turkey is a collectivistic country based on cultural values of commitment to groups and family.

Ultimately our goal is to help families, improve communication and create a better functioning home environment. A self-learning team is needed to achieve this goal. Such a team must inform themselves in the systemic approach, do research considering cultural factors, improve treatment methods and communicate acquired experience to students. Our hope is that the knowledge acquired in this project might help multi-disciplinary groups to establish interdependent clinical practices where they can evolve into a systemic approach.

9.3 The Beginning

Every practitioner at Yaşamca has more than 10 years of experience working in private practice settings, therapeutically assessing and working with families and individuals, providing supervision, consultation and training to other professionals, consulting and liaising with other disciplines. Research suggests that Turkish clinicians are younger (25–30 year olds vs. 47–52 year olds) and less experienced (5 years vs. 13–15 years) compared to their counterparts in the United States (Akyıl et al., 2015). This is true to an extent because family therapy was only permitted in Turkey after a legislation that passed in 2007. There are family therapists, teachers and supervisors working at the clinic. Many integrate multiple theories, practices and skills acquired independently over the years in private practices and various appointments including hospital and military positions. Specialised in play therapy, some of us work with children and their families while others focus on couples and family relationships employing solution-oriented, strategic and brief therapy sessions. The clinic currently provides strength-based, systemic treatment for children, adolescents, adults and families experiencing behavioural or relational challenges (Jones-Smith, 2014; Sharry, 2004; de Shazer et al., 2007; Berg, 1994).

However, at times systemic therapy feels isolated in a field dominated by medical, psychodynamic and cognitive behavioural therapy models. One of the issues is the shortage of colleagues and experienced supervisors who are trained in the systemic approach to get the guidance needed to build on this profession. Another one is the shortage of financial means to attend international conferences, conventions or courses regularly that would expand awareness. Furthermore, the lack of access to research papers or the instruments to devise a research project prevents developing a mindset for research in the practice.

The possibility to learn, share, explore, practice, teach and grow together is an exciting prospect. Thus, the idea of establishing a systemic clinic emerged from these needs to develop a sustainable environment where therapists connect, collaborate, learn and transform together with practitioners, students, clients and the community.

9.3.1 The Building

The project started in October 2018 when we aggregated the means to construct a building designed specifically for this purpose. Therapists in private practice in Turkey usually rent a room or an apartment to provide their services. With the exception of hospitals and schools, it is not common to have a space built in consideration of a group of therapists/students/clients working together.

The idea that settings can influence treatment and outcome (Gross et al., 1998) is not new, but little research has focused on the healing potential related to the design of the counselling space (Pressly & Heesacker, 2001). An early study by Mintz (1956) found that participants in an "ugly room" were more likely to complain of monotony, fatigue and headache and showed irritability and hostility. People are found to be more forthcoming and extensive in their self-disclosure in a warm and intimate room (Chaikin et al., 1976, p. 479).

Dellinger (2010) proposed that counselling rooms can be organised to ensure a positive effect on the healing process. Interviews with therapists revealed 12 issues of importance in the design of counselling settings: location, image, degree of visibility, the proximity of restroom, privacy, easy-to-read clocks, entrance and exits, furniture, lighting, views, plants and artwork (Anthony & Watkins, 2002).

Considering the physical, mental and professional needs, the building in this project is designed to meet the needs of practitioners, students and clients. The following points are implemented to provide a psychotherapeutic environment:

- Easy access to the building and available parking space
- Comfortable seating, carpets, soft colours, natural lighting, artwork, plants
- A reception area
- Large windows and vistas of nature
- Two play therapy rooms and two adjacent family rooms
- A spacious room to teach and do activities
- A workspace for interns to study and converse
- A test room to conduct assessments
- Rooms for couples and family therapy
- A multi-purpose garden to relax, socialise, connect with nature
- A terrace to relax and have some alone time

9.4 A Learning Hub

Since February 2019, local, national and international colleagues who might be interested in working towards creating a learning hub have been contacted. A programme featuring reasonably priced courses, workshops and seminars are designed to provide support to various groups by local, national and international psychotherapists.

- The "Meeting Professionals" are periodic programmes where the team meet monthly to listen to one of the seniors or a visiting professional. The idea is to provide a space to learn from other experts and to develop a referral system by getting to know them. These low-budget gatherings consist of small groups of 10–15 people. It is convenient in terms of price and time while providing a chance for everyone to learn from each other, discuss and practice skills.

9 A Model of a Systemic Therapy Clinic

- The "Meeting Parents" are periodic programmes where group discussions are provided to families on various topics. Parents are supported via skill-building, psycho-education, and self-care interventions to manage their own emotional or developmental challenges and to build-on parenting abilities and improve problem-solving techniques.
- An online support group for women will be established to discuss sexuality and an LGBTI support group. Both these groups will remain anonymous and will be led by a senior therapist experienced in group therapy.
- There will be a support programme for couples where they can learn about relationship dynamics, practice problem-solving skills and learn from other people's experiences.
- A support group for divorced people will be provided to help them navigate through difficult times with the support of others.
- "Play-Assistant" is an introductory programme in which interns take part in play and leisure activities with children in their home. They also care for and supervise the children. By Play Assistant Introduction Programme interns gain both practical and theoretical experience and those who complete the programme receive referrals from senior play therapists.
- A series of activities for seniors will be provided to practice various skills and improve cognitive, mental and physical abilities. These activities can vary from Neuro-Dramatic Play® to geriatric support groups to art therapy sessions.
- Long-term certificate training programmes "Integrative Play Therapy with children, families and groups" will be provided to the members.

9.4.1 Collaborative Relationships among Professionals

Regular meetings are scheduled for day-to-day activities, case management, supervisions, consultation, and peer support.

1. Senior therapists have daily discussions to assess intake results and to use the information to determine a family's needs. Assessment is an integral part of determining the most effective way to work with a specific family. Through these meetings, the family is referred to as the most suitable professional.
2. Daily meetings with clinic members such as therapists, interns, administrative assistant and other staff continue to discuss general issues about the management of the clinic such as accounting, cleaning, maintenance, purchasing, calendar, client requirements, legal responsibilities.
3. Senior therapists meet weekly for an hour-long peer support session.
4. Senor therapists meet with interns in individual and group supervision sessions.
5. A family therapist from Germany who is trained in the Gestalt discipline pays a consultation visit biannually in exploring group dynamics to understand power dynamics and cultural issues in relationships.
6. Free seminars and workshops will be provided to local universities, schools, hospitals to develop collaborative relationships with medical practitioners, teachers and lawyers who are unfamiliar with the systemic approach.

9.4.2 Practice

The team focuses on ideas such as accountability and transparency in psychotherapy, involving clients as co-researchers to promote improvisation, collaboration and feedback (van Hennik & Hillewaere, 2017). The challenge will be to have everyone learn to be truly collaborative and not just co-operating and being collegial. Gilbert (2016) states that collaboration is different from just sharing and reflecting, and it goes beyond work being done together. It is a case of creating a place where people produce an output in response to a common goal which is greater than what any of the individuals could have produced working alone (Kayser, 2014; Fullan & Quinn, 2016, p. 48).

9.4.3 Training Students

A therapist must first establish a rapport, formulate the case, agree on treatment goals and build a working alliance in any therapy method. Our primary objective is to set a standard for competent delivery of any family therapy techniques. Training will combine theory, practice, supervision and consultation to facilitate students' development as a systemic family therapist. In addition to theoretical training, role-play and observation of therapy will be incorporated to enhance learning.

Scientific thinking is one of the essential skills that needs to be developed at the clinic and among students. It means engaging in the process of inquiry and assessment that results in case formulation. Interventions are then selected in light of the relevant literature and in consultation with the clients about their needs and preferences.

There might be barriers in developing a scientific approach such as inadequate research evaluation skills, lack of training in research methods and limited professional supervision (Aarons et al., 2009; Chan et al., 2010; Karekla et al., 2004). To overcome some of these problems, senior therapists will be modelling appropriate research attitudes and behaviour, and positively reinforce students' research activities and get the assistance of well-trained supervisors from universities.

The training will be comprised of clinical activities and skills that are necessary for effective systemic family therapy through teaching below concepts (Stratton et al., 2011).

1. Systems focus
2. Connections and patterns
3. Circularity
4. Social constructionism
5. Strengths and solutions
6. Cultural context
7. Co-constructed practice.
8. Reflexivity

9. Narratives and language
10. Power
11. Constructivism

Team members will be taught systemic therapy as suggested by Gail Simon (2014, p. 8), "Systemic inquiry can be understood as technique, as a method, as ethical, reflexive and collaborative ways of being with people, as reflexive inner and outer dialogue, as reflexive writing in training contexts". Team members they will be encouraged to study the questions that accumulated over the years, such as practical interventive questions (Tomm, 1987a, b, c), future-oriented questions (Penn, 1985), brief solution focused (de Shazer, 1985, 1988), self-reflexivity and relational reflexivity (Burnham, 1993, 2005), dominant narratives and their influence (White, 1988, White & Epston, 1990), power in therapeutic relationships (Combs & Freedman, 1990; Flaskas et al., 2007; O'Hanlon & Bertolino, 1998; Cooperrider & Srivastva, 1987), culture-sensitive questions (Burnham & Harris, 1996; Simon, 1998), professional relationships (Leppington, 1991; Burnham, 1999; Simon, 2012), shared process of reflection (Andersen, 1987) and ethical consideration (Leppington, 1991).

9.4.4 Assessment Strategy

The team will be using the Feedback Informed Supervision model (Bargmann, 2017). Following this model, a culture of feedback will be established in supervision and observing outcome data on a continuous basis. The outcome feedback will be integrated into supervision. Supervisees will provide ongoing feedback to a clinical supervisor about their progress, alliance and their needs. This will give a stronger voice to the supervisee during the supervision session. Students will also be assessed for completion of a learning portfolio, which contains a clinical log, reflective diary and self-assessments in systemic learning and a case study. The supervisor will assess their reflective learning capacity and evidence of being an active learner.

9.4.5 Supervision

The supervisor and trainee will be engaged in an active, collaborative, evidence-based endeavour involving careful assessment, consultation with the scientific literature, hypothesis formulation about interventions and systematic evaluation of their impact for cases.

The ability to understand and evaluate published research results, as well as to accurately assess the experiences of clients, is an essential part of supervision. Supervisors will model these thinking skills such as scientific-mindedness, critical thinking, integrative capacity and relational skills and expect the same from trainees. For example, students could be assigned to assess the empirical database for some aspect of the problem situation. The relevant material can be reviewed to find specific interventions of relevance. Then the underlying logic for treatment would be taken into consideration.

9.5 Research

The research process will have many different parts with various stages of data collection and analysis. The research design will include data collection at different times, using various procedures, both observational and self-report measurements, and multi-informants such as the perspective of the therapist, the clients, the family and the external observers.

The team will explore several effectiveness and efficacy groups of research and create a better-suited combination of methods for our programme. The models are below:

1. Feedback-informed treatment (FIT) is a pan-theoretical approach involving the routine and formal administration of empirically validated outcome and alliance measures to monitor client progress and the therapeutic alliance in real time (Prescott et al., 2017). FIT as Practice-Based Evidence-Based Practice (van Hennik & Hillewaere, 2017) uses a fluid manual, multi-methods research and collaborative inquiry. The outcomes of research are the inputs for collaborative learning in the system that the therapist and family members co-create together.
2. Process research investigates what occurs within a therapy session and strives to explain, how and why change occurs in the process of therapy (e.g. Pinsof & Wynne, 2000).

The team will use a multi-method design and combine quantitative and qualitative methods to understand both the process of change and interventions evaluation (Gambrel & Butler, 2013). The range of assessments will be evaluated to assess various aspects of family functioning, family adaptability, family strengths, the emotional context and therapeutic alliance.

(a) The Systemic Clinical Outcome and Routine Evaluation-15 (SCORE-15), which is a proven measure of family functioning (Carr & Stratton, 2017), consists of a group of self-reported measures of family processes (Stratton et al., 2010) and records perceptions of the family from each member over the age of 11. The Score is translated into several languages, including Turkish. SCORE will be carried out at the start of the first, sixth and last sessions.
(b) The Turkish version of the Family Adaptability and Cohesion Scale IV (FACES IV) Questionnaire Package, is used to evaluate the family cohesion, family adaptability, family communication, family satisfaction and the family functioning as a whole in Turkish culture (Türkdoğan et al., 2018). The results will

help the clinician in the formation of a treatment plan. It will be administered at the start of the first, middle and last session.

9.6 The Manual

The research at the clinic involves observing and analysing the delivered therapeutic interventions, and assessing whether we can produce a manual from these data.

The key stages in the research process of the Systemic Clinic Model are:

1. Initiating the project, forming the collaborative professional relationships
2. Alliance, creating a culture of feedback
3. Observing and gathering information, reflecting, planning and acting
4. Evaluating effectiveness
5. Creating programme formats and content and writing an initial manual
6. Revising the programme and manual
7. Trial of the manual in practice and clarify the final manual and a preliminary adherence protocol

9.6.1 Progress Report

The team has focused on the first three stages of the Systemic Clinic Model Manual. These are:

1. Initiating the project and establishing collaborative relationships
2. Creating a culture of feedback
3. Observing and gathering information, reflecting, planning and acting

9.6.2 Initiating the Project and Establishing Collaborative Relationships

The team is working on developing the internship programme admitting new applicants every 3 months. Accepted undergraduate psychologists are expected to complete a one-month internship at the clinic. This is an observation period to see if the intern is suitable to be part of the team. The succeeding interns are then admitted to a three-month-long internship. This is a trial period to see if they find a place in the organisation. Interns are expected to become more involved by joining regular meetings, participating in ongoing projects, focusing on learning psychotherapy and counselling techniques that they find interesting. Hence, interns participate in the ongoing learning process. The team encourage members to become skilled at subjects complementary to other projects in the clinic. If interns remain consistent about their interest and improve their knowledge at the end of 3 months, the team shall grant a one-year-long internship. In this phase, they are expected to participate in meetings, provide support in preparing activities or doing research with seniors. They can also bring new solutions to problems such as "organising the nursing room" or "free seminars in the local library", and seek cooperation from other members regarding assistance, training, reference, supervision or financial support.

Furthermore, interns are strongly encouraged to continue their graduate training and complete family counselling courses as well as to learn other models such as Somatic Therapy, CBT, Schema Therapy or Eye Movement Desensitization and Reprocess (EMDR), in line with their interests. This will help the team to have a diverse background and ability to draw from various experiences.

Meetings are an essential part of developing collaborative relationships. Senior therapists and interns meet once a week to discuss the internship programme, intake process, research methods and relationship dynamics. Additionally, smaller groups gather for supervisions and various projects such as "Play Assistant Programme", "Neuro-Dramatic Play® Group", "Child Abuse Prevention Group".

The team has been working on the intake process for several months. A questionnaire form has been developed and interns practise answering calls with a role-playing session. An online platform to collect information securely for research has also been created. The intake methods are routinely updated according to feedback received from interns and clients. Interns formulate new methods for collecting, recording and transferring information and working on how to get feedback from our clients in terms of acquiring and providing information, the appointment procedure and accuracy of the referrals.

Furthermore, the team is working on many other issues such as forms, advertisement material, brochures, general information on family therapy, ethical standards, referral system, book references, rules and boundaries with clients and such.

The team has continued working on the collaborative professional relationships and completed several programmes for both professionals and the general public. Currently, the team is utilising its available skills and resources to develop collaborative relationships:

1. The first meeting by an international visitor presented in October 2019 by Virginia Blue. She was a guest speaker from California who gave a seminar on MRI Family Therapy. Three seniors and four students attended this programme. A translator was provided.
2. The first local "Meeting with professionals" programme took place in December 2019. A professor from the Psychology Department at Izmir Economy University lectured on the topic of "Acceptance and Commitment Therapy". Eighteen senior and junior psychology professionals attended.
3. A senior therapist contacted an international trainer called Dr. Ariel Shlomo and began training with him. Together they prepared a long-term certificate programme on "Integrative Play Therapy". Dr. Ariel visited the clinic for the first Integrative Play Therapy training module in January 2020. Three seniors and six juniors attended.

4. A senior therapist created The Child and Family Clinical Observation programme as a preparation course for interns and organised internal and external experienced therapists to present various topics at the clinic. Completed in December 2019, this programme consisted of 10 h of theoretical training, 14 h of counselling skills training, 10 h of clinical observation and 10 h of case consultation.
5. Two senior therapists developed The Play Assistant Introduction programme for interns. The interns have been attending clients under supervision as Play Assistant since October 2019. They are visiting pre-school children who need more playtime at home. This programme has been functional in terms of modelling parents to play with their children and also providing extra needed help and space for single parents.
6. The team applied to the Association for Play Therapy to become an approved provider for Izmir, Turkey. The application was rejected. The team is processing this outcome to learn and re-apply again in 6 months.
7. Conversations with local business managers, schools and individuals suggest that families need help in guiding adolescents into adulthood. A senior therapist planned a three-week psycho-education programme in April 2020. Also, a support group will be formed, which will give families a space to meet regularly and share their experience of raising adolescents.
8. The first "Meeting Parents" programme was organised in January 2020. A senior therapist trained in the "Triple P" programme presented this well-structured course material to 16 parents over 3 weeks. Each week consisted of 2 h of group discussions on various topics. Parents are supported via skill-building, psycho-education and self-care interventions to manage their own emotional or developmental challenges and to build-on parenting abilities and improve problem-solving techniques.
9. The seniors programme is still work in progress at this time.
10. One of the long-term interns recently received a graduate degree in Clinical Psychology and became the first junior at the clinic. She is currently handling low-budget cases under supervision.
11. Four of the juniors are getting training on Neuro-Dramatic Play® therapy.
12. The online support groups of female sexuality and LGBTI group were announced. There was a lot of interest but few applied. This programme is postponed due to lack of applications.
13. Support programme for couples and divorced people are announced, but many couples refused to share their intimate problems in groups. These programmes have been postponed until better conditions are prepared for the locals.
14. The consistency of the number of interns is accomplished. Three interns have completed two terms at the clinic and chose to continue elsewhere. They became part of the clinic's referral system and members in contact for training programmes. Six interns decided to continue at the end of 6 months. A waiting list for new applicants has been developed and three new interns have been accepted into the programme.

15. The team is currently studying to learn the Feedback Informed Treatment (FIT) method. FIT can be administered on tablets and smartphones; however, it needs to be purchased. The team is considering using the paper version at this time.
16. The team has planned to start Foundation Level Family and Systemic discussion group in June 2020. The aim is to provide a refresher course and a way to establish a useful language. Training is reserved for the core members of the clinic, which includes four seniors and four juniors who are willing to practise systemic therapy and develop a collaborative relationship. The course will consist of weekly 2 h of systemic seminars, discussion groups and skill practising workshops and reading materials.

In sum, the team is still in the process of developing the first manual of The Relationship Building. The first manual will provide experiences acquired in developing the following associations:

- "Collaborative relationship" among therapists
- "Collaborative relationship" between therapists and staff
- "Collaborative relationship" between teachers/supervisors and students/supervisees

9.6.3 Financial Resources

This project has been financed by private sources. The building is owned by a family member and rented for a very low fee for a limited time. All team members work as independent contractors and a 40% commission is left to finance the expenses. Also, most team members provide low fee or free trainings and supervision to students. Many senior and junior therapists also provide low fee therapy sessions and trainings to clients. The team is looking for ways to fund research projects, trainings, supervisions, low fee therapies, books and materials.

9.7 Discussion

This chapter deals with issues and experiences in the development of systemic manuals. In general, manuals can offer many potential roles such as being a link between clinical practice and research, setting standards for training and evaluation of therapists or providing an overall structure for the treatment and many more (see Castonguay et al., 1999; Crits-Christoph et al., 1991; Rounsaville et al., 1988). However, they may not reflect the working practices of clinicians of great diversity regarding experience, discipline and clinical expertise (Addis et al., 1999). Many therapists draw from a range of models which can have limited applicability to the wide range of populations and problems (Abrahamson, 1999; Henry, 1998; Norcross, 1999). Even the best manual is not likely to be adopted by clinicians unless it is feasible, cost-effective or acceptable to the clinical community (Fishbein, 1995; Fonagy, 1999) or it may be misused within a practice (Couturier & Kimber, 2015).

Research shows that ensuring the fidelity of the model is a core principle of moving intervention research into practice (Robbins et al., 2011; Schoenwald et al., 2004). Working in teams is a viable solution to ensure shared goals, clearly defined roles, shared knowledge and skills, effective, timely communication, mutual respect, an optimistic, can-do attitude (Mitchell, 2012). Family therapy teams and uses of the team in interventions with family systems are nothing new (e.g. Cade, 1980; Ferrier, 1981; Papp, 1980; Selvini Palazzoli et al., 1975, 1977, 1978). In The Dialogical Therapist (Bertrando 2008, p. 62), Paolo Bertrando 2008 suggests that the trainee in systemic therapy learns in a team and through a team, and develops a systemic sensitivity. The team concept is paramount to the development of systemic work, and Szapocznik et al. (2015), in their Brief Strategic Family Therapy model, used systems orientation to conceptualise parallel systemic processes across the multiple systems that influence therapists' ability to help families. On the other hand, the concept of systemic teamwork as it relates to client-counsellor collaboration has never been explicitly defined.

In this manual, we focused our attention on the functioning of the team itself. This process includes developing the ability to carry out essential tasks for the growth and well-being of its members. Any team that works together over time will develop its own implicit rules of functioning. Observing these implicit rules of functioning in its development offers the team a good sense of its own pattern, which will help the members to develop an understanding of systemic concepts. Also, the study of our own teamwork aims to identify aspects of team's processing that is useful to establish a format for collaborative relationships that would be both efficient and effective.

Teamwork is fostered by developing open communication, clear expectations, limits and boundaries. Building a supportive environment of trust and respect is vital. This is achieved by solving the clinic's problems by allowing members to participate in the decision-making process. This involves listening and thinking, considering options, respecting other people's opinions, finding constructive solutions and working towards compromises. The team strives to develop a collaborative relationship to create a feeling of connection.

Multi-orientation clinical practices such as ours might be a way to facilitate the use of systemic family therapy techniques where the exchange of ideas, collaboration on case formulations and treatment suggestions and discussion of relevant research findings are encouraged.

In this first manual, private practices will find some ideas of how to combine resources, how to become aware of their system, their unique skills and how to create collaborative relationships. Readers who need more in-depth exploration on developing a manual and adherence protocol for systemic family therapy can look at Leeds Systemic Family Therapy Manual (LSFTM) (Pote et al., 2013 and Chap. 3).

9.8 Conclusion

At this point in the evolving study of the team process, we have concentrated our study on the development of collaborative relationships. There are several other avenues and one will be to obtain a better understanding of the environmental and relational processes that take place behind the therapy room. For example, starting from client's first call, scheduling the first appointment, the atmosphere in the waiting room, the mood around temperature/lighting/furniture, last-minute cancellations, rules, rights and boundaries. By discussing these issues, the team develops problem-solving skills, collaborative relationships and common language.

The next manual will focus on practising systemic therapy as a team, and the third manual will be about gathering and analysing data. There is no doubt that revisions will be necessary over time. We are looking forward to the prospect that this book will create exciting discussions about future developments about systemic therapy training, competencies and occupational standards all around the world. So, we would like to state that "training and practice manuals might be more effective if we have a better understanding of team functionality", and manuals can incorporate the functioning of the team itself.

Acknowledgements I wish to thank my loving husband Okan Alper who provides unending inspiration, guidance and support. This work would not have been possible without his emotional and financial endorsement. A very special thanks to my family and friends for their invaluable advice and feedback on this project and for always being so supportive of my work. I am especially indebted to my colleagues Seniha Naşit Gürçağ and Hatice Çelik who actively worked with me to make this project possible with their patience, perseverance, motivation and hard work. My deep appreciation goes out to the cooperation and support provided by the Yasamca team members. Their outstanding work has made an invaluable contribution. I am grateful to all of those with whom I have had the pleasure to work with during this project.

I would like to extend my gratitude to the editors of EFTA-Springer Book Series, Peter Stratton, George W. Saba and Mauro Mariotti, for helping me to conceptualise a vague idea into a clearly defined programme. I would not be able to do it without their encouragement, support and guidance.

References

Aarons, G. A., Wells, R. S., Zagursky, K., Fettes, D. L., & Palinkas, L. A. (2009). Implementing evidence-based practice in community mental health agencies: A multiple stakeholder analysis. *American Journal of Public Health, 99*(11), 2087–2095.

Abrahamson, D. J. (1999). Outcomes, guidelines, and manuals: On leading horses to water. *Clinical Psychology: Science and Practice, 6*(4), 467–471. https://doi.org/10.1093/clipsy/6.4.467

Addis, M. E., Wade, W. A., & Hatgis, C. (1999). Barriers to dissemination of evidence-based practices: Addressing practitioners' concerns about manual-based psychotherapies. *Clinical Psychology: Science and Practice, 6*(4), 430–441. https://doi.org/10.1093/clipsy/6.4.430

Akyıl, Y., Üstünel, A. Ö., Alkan, S., & Aydın, H. (2015). Türkiye'de çift ve ailelerle çalışan uzmanlar: Demografik özellikler, eğitim ve klinik uygulamalar. *Psikoloji Çalışmaları Dergisi, 35*, 57–84.

Andersen, T. (1987). The reflective team: Dialogue and meta-dialogue in clinical work. *Family Process, 26*, 415–427.

Anthony, K. H., & Watkins, N. J. (2002). Exploring pathology: Relationships between clinical and environmental psychology. In R. Bechtel & A. Churchman (Eds.), *Handbook of environmental psychology*. Wiley.

Bargmann, S. (2017). Achieving excellence through feedback-informed supervision. In D. S. Prescott, C. L. Maeschalck, & S. D. Miller (Eds.), *Feedback-informed treatment in clinical practice: Reaching for excellence* (pp. 79–100). American Psychological Association. https://doi.org/10.1037/0000039-005

Berg, I. K. (1994). *Family based services: A solution-focused approach*. Norton.

Bertrando, P. (2008). *The Dialogical Therapist: Dialogue in Systemic Practice (The Systemic Thinking and Practice Series)* (p. 59). Karnac Books. Kindle Edition.

Burnham, J. (1993). Systemic supervision: The evolution of reflexivity in the context of the supervisory relationship. *Human Systems Journal of Systemic Consultation and Management, 4*(3–4), 349–381.

Burnham, J. (2005). Relational reflexivity: A tool for socially constructing therapeutic relationships. In C. Flaskas et al. (Eds.), *The space between: Experience, context and process in the therapeutic relationship*. Karnac.

Burnham, J. (1999). Approach, method, technique: Making distinctions and creating connections. *Human Systems: Journal of Systemic Consultation and Management, 3*(1), 3–26.

Burnham, J., & Harris, Q. (1996). Emerging ethnicity: A tale of three cultures. In K. N. Dwivedi (Ed.), *Meeting the needs of ethnic minority children. A handbook for professionals*. Jessica Kingsley Publishers.

Cade, B. (1980). Resolving therapeutic deadlocks using a contrived team conflict. *International Journal of Family Therapy, 2*, 253–262.

Carr, A., & Stratton, P. (2017). The score family assessment questionnaire: A decade of progress. *Family Process, 56*, 285–301. https://doi.org/10.1111/famp.12280

Castonguay, L. G., Schut, A. J., Constantino, M. J., & Halperin, G. S. (1999). Assessing the role of treatment manuals: Have they become necessary but non-sufficient ingredients of change? *Clinical Psychology: Science and Practice, 6*, 449–455.

Chaikin, A. L., Derlega, V. J., & Miller, S. J. (1976). Effects of room environment and self-disclosure in a counseling analogue. *Journal of Counseling Psychology, 23*, 479–481.

Chan, F., Bezyak, J., Ramirez, M. R., Chiu, C., Sung, C., & Fujikawa, M. (2010). Concepts, challenges, barriers, and opportunities related to evidenced-based practice in rehabilitation counseling. *Rehabilitation Education, 24*(3/4), 179–190.

Combs, G., & Freedman, J. (1990). *Symbol, story, and ceremony: Using metaphor in individual and family therapy*. W.W. Norton.

Cooperrider, D. L., & Srivastva, S. (1987). Appreciative inquiry in organizational life. In W. Pasmore & R. Woodman (Eds.), *Research in organization change and development* (Vol. 1, pp. 129–169). JAI Press.

Cosan, D. (2015). The perception of psychohterapy in Turkey. *European Journal of Social & Behaviroural Sciences, 13*(2). https://www.futureacademy.org.uk/files/menu_items/other/13vol165.pdf

Couturier, J. L., & Kimber, M. S. (2015). Dissemination and implementation of manualized family-based treatment: A systematic review. *Eating Disorder, 23*(4), 281–290. https://doi.org/10.1080/10640266.2015.1042312

Crits-Christoph, P., Baranackie, K., Kurcias, J. S., Beck, A., Carroll, K., Perry, K., Luborsky, L., McLellan, A., Woody, G., Thompson, L., Gallagher, D., & Zitrin, C. (1991). Meta-analysis of therapist effects in psychotherapy outcome studies. *Psychotherapy Research, 1*, 81–91.

de Shazer, S. (1985). *Keys to solution in brief therapy*. W.W. Norton.

de Shazer, S. (1988). *Clues: Investigating solutions in brief therapy*. W.W. Norton.

de Shazer, S., Dolan, Y. with Korman, H, Trepper, T., McCollum, E., Berg, I. K., & Steve. (2007). *More than miracles: The state of the art of solution-focused brief therapy* (p. 101). Routledge. isbn:978-0-7890-3397-0.

Dellinger, B. (2010). Healing environments. In C. McCullough (Ed.), *Evidence-based design for healthcare facilities*. Indianapolis, IN.

Eraslan, D., Camoglu, D., Harunzade, Y., Ergun, B., & Dokur, M. (2012). Interpersonal communication in and through family: Structure and therapy in Turkey. *International Review of Psychiatry, 24*, 128–133. https://doi.org/10.3109/09540261.2012.657162

Ferrier, M. J. (1981). Lying: A family perspective. *Journal of Strategic & Systemic Therapy, 1*, 10–19.

Fishbein, M. (1995). Developing effective behavioral change interventions: Some lessons learned from behavioral research. In T. E. Backer, S. L. David, & G. Soucy (Eds.), Reviewing the behavioral science knowledge base on technology transfer (NIDA Research Monograph Series Number 155). Rockville, MD: NIDA.

Flaskas, C., McCarthy, I., & Sheehan, J. (Eds.). (2007). *Hope and despair in narrative and family therapy: Adversity, forgiveness and reconciliation*. Routledge.

Fonagy, P. (1999). Achieving evidence-based psychotherapy practice: A psychodynamic perspective on the general acceptance of treatment manuals. *Clinical Psychology: Science and Practice, 6*, 442–444.

Fullan, M., & Quinn, J. (2016). *Coherence: The right drivers in action for schools, districts, and systems*. Corwin.

Gambrel, L. E., & Butler, V. I. J. L. (2013). Mixed methods research in marriage and family therapy: A content analysis. *Journal of Marital and Family Therapy, 39*(2), 163–181. https://doi.org/10.1111/j.1752-0606.2011.00260.x

Gilbert, J. (2016). *Leading in collaborative complex education systems*. Education Council NZ [Web log post]. Retrieved 6 January 2021. Accessed at: file:///C:/Users/gsaba/Downloads/Michele%20Whiting%20-%20leadership%20for%20complexity%20-%20sabbatical%20report%202017.pdf.

Gross, R., Sasson, Y., Zarhy, M., & Zohar, J. (1998). Healing environment in psychiatric hospital design. *General Hospital Psychiatry, 20*, 108–114.

Henry, W. P. (1998). Science, politics, and the politics of science: The use and misuse of emğirically validated treatment research. *Psychotherapy Research, 8*, 126–140.

Jones-Smith, E. (2014). Chapter 1: Strengths-based therapy: Connecting theory, practice and skills. Sage.

Kafescioglu, N., & Akyil, Y. (2018). Couple and family therapy training in the context of Turkey. https://doi.org/10.1007/978-3-319-71395-3_9.

Karekla, M., Lundgren, J. D., & Forsyth, J. P. (2004). A survey of graduate training in empirically supported and manualized treatments: A preliminary report. *Cognitive and Behavioral Practice, 11*, 230–242.

Kayser, T. (2014, April 18). *True collaboration is a partnership: Six ingredients for making it so* [Web log post]. Retrieved from https://www.linkedin.com/pulse/20140418191855-78767208-true-collaboration-isa-partnership-six-ingredients-for-making-it-so

Leppington, R. (1991). From constructivism to social constructionism and doing critical therapy. *Human Systems: Journal of Systemic Consultation and Management, 2*(2), 217–31.

Mintz, N. L. (1956). Effects of esthetic surroundings: II. Prolonged and repeated experience in a "beautiful" and an "ugly" room. *Journal of Psychology, 41*, 459–466.

Mitchell, G. (2012). Revisiting truth or triviality: The external validity of research in the psychological laboratory. *Perspectives on Psychological Science, 7*, 109–117.

Norcross, J. C. (1999). Collegially validated limitations of empirically validated treatments. *Clinical Psychology: Science and Practice, 6*, 472–476.

O'Hanlon, B., & Bertolino, B. (1998). *Even from a broken web: Brief, respectful solution-oriented therapy for sexual abuse and trauma*. Wiley.

Papp, P. (1980). The Greek chorus and other techniques of family therapy. *Family Process, 19*, 45–57.

Penn, P. (1985). Feed forward: Future questions, future maps. *Family Process, 24*(3), 299–310.
Pinsof, W. M., & Wynne, L. C. (2000). Toward progress research: Closing the gap between family therapy practice and research. *Journal of Marital and Family Therapy, 26*(1), 1–8. https://doi.org/10.1111/j.1752-0606.2000.tb00270.x
Pote, H., Stratton, P, Cottrell, D., Shapiro, D. & Boston, P. (2013). *Final LFTRC manual*. https://www.researchgate.net/publication/338389429_Leeds_Systemic_Family_Therapy_Manual
Prescott, D. S., Maeschalck, C. L., & Miller, S. D. (Eds.). (2017). *Feedback-informed treatment in clinical practice: Reaching for excellence*. American Psychological Association. https://doi.org/10.1037/0000039-000
Pressly, P. K., & Heesacker, M. (2001). The physical environment and counseling: A review of theory and research. *Journal of Counseling and Development, 79*(2), 148–160.
Robbins, M. S., Feaster, D. J., Horigian, V. E., Puccinelli, M. J., Henderson, C., & Szapocznik, J. (2011). Therapist adherence in brief strategic family therapy for adolescent drug abusers. *Journal of Consulting and Clinical Psychology., 79*, 43–53.
Roberts, J., Abu-Baker, K., Fernandez, C. D., Garcia, N. C., Fredman, G., Kamya, H., & Vega, R. Z. (2014). Up close: Family therapy challenges and innovations around the world. *Family Process, 53*, 544–576. https://doi.org/10.1111/famp.12093
Rounsaville, B. J., O'Malley, S., Foley, S., & Weissman, M. M. (1988). Role of manual-guided training in the conduct and efficacy of interpersonal psychotherapy for depression. *Journal of Consulting and Clinical Psychology, 56*(5), 681–688. https://doi.org/10.1037/0022-006X.56.5.681
Schoenwald, S. K., Sheidow, A. J., & Letourneau, E. J. (2004). Toward effective quality assurance in evidence-based practice: Links between expert consultation, therapist fidelity, and child outcomes. *Journal of Clinical Child and Adolescent Psychology, 33*(1), 94–104. https://doi.org/10.1207/S15374424JCCP3301_10
Selvini Palazzoli, M., Boscolo, L., Cecchin, G., Prata, G. (1975). Paradox and Counterparadox. A new model in the therapy of the family in schizophrenic transaction. : Jason Aronson 1978.
Selvini Palazzoli, M., Boscolo, L., Cecchin, G. F., & Prata, G. (1977). Family rituals: A powerful tool in family therapy. *Family Process, 16*(4), 445–453. https://doi.org/10.1111/j.1545-5300.1977.00445.x
Selvini-Palazzoli, M., Boscolo, L., Cecchin, G., & Prata, G. (1978). *Paradox and Counterparadox*. Aronson.
Sharry, J. (2004). *Counselling children, adolescents and families: A strength-based approach*. Sage.
Simon, G. (1998). Incitement to riot? Individual identity and group membership: Some reflections on the politics of a post-modernist therapy. *Human Systems Journal of Systemic Consultation and Management, 9*(1), 33–50.
Simon, G. (2012). Praction research: A model of systemic inquiry. *Human Systems Journal of Systemic Consultation and Management, 23*(1), 103–124. https://docs.google.com/file/d/0B5TWuGoJVPe_UDNYdGJ5NXl1dGs/edit?pli=1
Simon, G. (2014). Systemic inquiry as a form of qualitative inquiry. In G. Simon & A. Chard (Eds.), *Systemic inquiry. Innovations in reflexive practice research* (pp. 3–29). Everything is Connected Press.
Stratton, P., Bland, J., Janes, E., & Lask, J. (2010). Developing an indicator of family function and a practicable outcome measure for systemic family and couple therapy: The SCORE. *Journal of Family Therapy, 32*, 232–258. https://doi.org/10.1111/j.1467-6427.2010.00507.x
Stratton, P., Reibstein, J., Lask, J., Singh, R., & Asen, E. (2011). Competences and occupational standards for systemic family and couples therapy. *Journal of Family Therapy, 33*, 123–143. https://doi.org/10.1111/j.1467-6427.2011.00544.x
Szapocznik, J., Duff, J. H., Schwartz, S. J., Muir, J. A., & Brown, C. H. (2015). Brief strategic family therapy treatment for behavior problem youth: Theory, intervention, research, and implementation. In *Handbook of family therapy* (pp. 286–304). Taylor and Francis. https://doi.org/10.4324/9780203123584.

Tomm, K. (1987a). Interventive interviewing: Part I. strategizing as fourth guideline for the therapist. *Family Process, 26*, 3–13.

Tomm, K. (1987b). Interventive interviewing: Part II. Reflexive questioning as a means to enable self healing. *Family Process, 26*, 153–183.

Tomm, K. (1987c). Interventive interviewing: Part III. Intending to ask lineal, circular, reflexive or strategic questions? *Family Process, 27*, 1–15.

Türkdoğan, T., Duru, E., & Balkıs, M. (2018). Turkish adaptation of the family adaptability and cohesion scale IV. *International Journal of Assessment Tools in Education, 5*(4), 631–644.

van Hennik, R., & Hillewaere, B. (2017). Practice based evidence based practice. Navigating based on coordinated improvisation, collaborative learning and multi-methods research in feedback informed systemic therapy. *Journal of Family Therapy, 39*(3), 288–309.

White, M. (1988). The process of questioning: A therapy of literary merit? *Dulwich Centre Newsletter*, Winter, pp. 8–14.

White, M., & Epston, D. (1990). *Narrative means to therapeutic ends*. Norton.

Chapter 10
The Map of Competences in Systemic Therapy: Targeting Associated Abnormal Psychosocial Situations in Axis 5

Lennart Lorås

10.1 Background

Throughout most of its history, systemic therapy has involved many facets without attempting to identify a unifying description. However, the need for a unifying description has become especially apparent, as child and adolescent mental health is increasingly becoming subject to political debate and an increasing degree of control from policymakers. Neoliberalist ideas can generally be described as a broad-based political and intellectual movement to advance the market as the most efficient mechanism for organizing virtually all aspects of human/social life, with the consequence that the patient is considered a consumer (Esposito & Perez, 2014). This movement has led to a steady increase in the focus on diagnosis and problem-specific therapeutic approaches (Brinkmann & Petersen, 2015), which is a focus that seems to lead to the fact that systemic therapy has drifted away from the field of mental health (Bertrando, 2009).

Systemic therapy's lack of precise definitions opens the door for creativity, flexibility and being "where the client is". Nevertheless, poor specifications of systemic interventions make it easy to become lost in the multitude of definitions of what constitutes the assessed systemic family therapy intervention, if the intervention is defined at all (Asen, 2002). Therefore, a certain number of therapeutic guidelines and requirements for documentation and administration are both necessary and appropriate (Lorås, 2016a).

Historically, systemic therapists' resistance to competences and manuals has been significant (Sundelin, 2013). Some of the criticism against manuals and "collections" of competences has been their tendency to privilege the more easily specified and measurable aspects (i.e. whether circular questions were used) and their

---

L. Lorås (✉)
Western Norway University of Applied Sciences, Bergen, Norway
e-mail: Lennart.Loras@hvl.no

lower level of reliance on therapy process research from clinical contexts (Pote et al., 2003). The main goal of such manuals/competences also seems to be to reduce the amount of therapist variance. Therefore, the use of manuals and competences has been criticized for oversimplifying "everyday practice", restricting creativity and provoking resistance from therapists (Silverman, 1996). On the other hand, quality assurance in mental health has increased the requirements for standardized procedures. A considerable amount of research also documents the efficacy of these methods of treatment for a variety of disorders (i.e. anxiety, depression) (Manassis, 2009). Based on my research, I consider the degree of "instructive interactions" to be that which decides the extent to which the *map of competences* maintains the central epistemological tenets of systemic therapy within systemic and social constructionism (Lorås, 2016a, b, c).

The identified competences in this research target the psychosocial difficulties that are categorized as associated abnormal psychosocial situations in the multiaxial classification of child and adolescent psychiatric disorders/Axis 5 (ICD-10) (WHO, 1996).

10.1.1 Axis 5, Associated Abnormal Psychosocial Situations

Axis 5 is a tool for the coding of seriously abnormal aspects of a child's psychosocial situation regarding the child's developmental level, previous experiences and the relevant socio-cultural conditions (Norwegian Directorate of Health, 2008). Axis 5 is divided into nine main categories with relevant subcategories. It is unavoidable that the nine categories (with subcategories) that comprise the axis do not cover all the different variations in the psychosocial conditions that can be relevant in each individual case (Norwegian Directorate of Health, 2008). Therefore, Axis 5 is limited to covering the categories in which the available documentation indicates the direction of the potential cause of a significant psychiatric risk factor for a significant number of children. Several categories are likely to be relevant/overlap with one another in relation to the same situation in individual cases. For example, a psychologically ill parent can also be connected to disharmony in the family (Norwegian Directorate of Health, 2008). The nine categories are (1) abnormal intrafamilial relationships; (2) mental disorder, deviance or handicap in the child's primary support group; (3) inadequate or distorted interfamilial communication; (4) abnormal qualities of upbringing; (5) abnormal immediate environment; (6) acute life events; (7) societal stressors; (8) chronic interpersonal stress associated with school/work; and (9) stressful events/situations that result from the child's own disorder/disability.

10.2 Context for the Research

This chapter is based on the authors' doctoral research, which was conducted at Tavistock Clinic in conjunction with East London University in the period 2012–2016 (Lorås, 2016a). The overarching aim of the research project was to identify a comprehensive and detailed outline of the systemic therapist competences in Norwegian child and adolescent mental health services that target the psychosocial difficulties that are categorized as associated abnormal psychosocial situations in the multiaxial classification of child and adolescent psychiatric disorders/Axis 5 (ICD-10). The project is based on 12 qualitative in-depth interviews with six experienced systemic family therapists, fieldwork observations of the therapists (participants) in practice and an analysis of the Norwegian Directorate of Health's guidelines for child and adolescent mental health outpatient clinics. The participants were recruited through recommendations by my research supervisors and by searching for systemic therapists who have made important contributions to the research topic. All participants had more than 15 years of clinical experience, either as systemic therapists or as therapists in mental health, if not both. They are therefore to be considered as experienced therapists (Rønnestad & Orlinsky, 2006). Thus, they were representing the history of common systemic practice in Norway. Although gender is not the subject of this research, I ensured that both men and women were represented.

All data were analyzed using grounded theory (Charmaz, 2014). Detailed information on the research project is available (Lorås, 2016a, 2018).

In the beginning of this research project, I thought of the concept of competences as a collection of session-specific and clearly defined systemic elements. Thus, I learned quite early in the research process that the systemic therapist I was interviewing and observing was much more epistemologically or philosophically driven (even if they rarely used the word epistemology) than they were emphasizing a competence-based therapy. I was therefore led to the exploration of several epistemological positions to identify the epistemological basis of my participants' descriptions and practices.

10.3 The Map of Competences as a Framework for Flexible Systemic Therapy

Although there are some clear similarities between competences and manuals, the differences are significant. Manuals tend to be written for use by trained therapists (or those in training) and often omit some basic skills based on the assumption that they are knowledge that therapists should already have. *Competences,* on the other hand, refer to the documentation and description of specific skills that are expected to be mastered by systemic therapists (Northey, 2011).

Following systemic ideas, the map of competences does not have a pre-defined beginning and end. However, I will argue that some of the competences are more likely to be used in specific phases of the therapeutic process (i.e. described in the initial, middle and ending sessions). The identified competences overlap significantly with earlier systemic research (Tomm & Wright, 1979; Pote et al., 2000; Stratton et al., 2009, 2011). The map of competences therefore supports and adds validity to their work. However, the map of competences differs from earlier research by emphasizing a multi-epistemological stance, targeting the difficulties categorized as associated abnormal psychosocial situations (Axis 5) and situating competences within the context of child and adolescent mental health care (Lorås, 2016a, 2018).

In this chapter, the identified overarching categories are named competences. The subcategories are named skills and micro-skills. The term "skills" and micro-skills refers to the overarching competences operationalized into detailed and practice-oriented descriptions. The map consists of five overarching competences. All therapists are obligated to adhere to the legal requirements of the context that they employ. This means that competences described in the map of competences (Fig. 10.1) cannot be adhered to without considering how they could fulfil the legal requirements.

1. The first overarching theme is *the therapists' stance*. This theme is based on how the systemic therapists position themselves within epistemology and their views of the families in therapy. The therapist's epistemological stance is based on primarily systemic and social constructionism. However, the complexity of human difficulties makes it occasionally necessary to be irreverent towards these ideas. The therapists therefore take up normative positions or relate to so-called normative knowledge at certain times in therapy, if it is considered appropriate by both the therapist and the family. The systemic therapy approach is therefore multi-epistemological, consisting of systemic, social constructivism, constructivism and critical realism.

   The systemic therapists view families as experts in their own lives. The therapist's role is to help the families address their own difficulties and be loyal to their experience of the situation. Instead of giving advice, the therapist asks for the family's own perspectives (without taking an expert role in the family). Thus, the participants argue that the solution(s) to the families' difficulties is to be found in their history of previous attempts to find solutions. Although the families' own knowledge is preferred in therapy, there are situations in which families ask for expert knowledge and specialist competence.

   The systemic therapist aims for transparency in all stages of therapy. Being transparent is important to ensure that there is no hidden agenda of the therapist and that the parents/family has a freedom of choice regarding the agenda for the therapy. Additionally, being transparent involves sharing potential concerns. In such cases, the therapist has the main responsibility of arranging conversations regarding the concerns so that the people who are concerned do not feel reduced. Provided that the therapist is consistent and transparent regarding his/her assessment (including reports of concerns), even serious concerns will not necessarily damage the therapeutic alliance. Transparency also involves expressing concerns in the cases in which treatment does not lead to the desired achievement of the goal of the therapy. In this case, it is crucial that the therapist shares his/her possible thoughts and ideas about what is required to reach the goals of the therapy and the possibility of change, for example, that specific person should participate in the treatment course. However, the final decision lies with the family.

LEGALLY REQUIREMENTS	SYSTEMIC COMPETENCES	SKILLS AND MICRO-SKILLS
↕	The therapists' stance	**Multi-epistemological** - Systemic and social constructionist basis - Multi-epistemological, when appropriate **Therapist's view of the family** - "Not-knowing" - Transparent
	Ethical and contextual awareness	**Ethical considerations** - The assessment of contraindication - Being both a therapist and a social controller - Consideration of contraindication - Normative judgement - Avoiding shame and guilt **Contextual considerations** - Generating context relevant solutions - Information about context as crucial for understanding the family's difficulties
	Session-specific features	**Initial sessions** - The becoming acquainted phase - Creating a safe place to talk - Shared decisions on the therapeutic process - Tailored and collaborative therapy - Discussing the structure of the therapy process - Evaluating **Middle sessions** - The working phase - Activation and working flexibly with the family system - Using the systemic "toolbox" - Evaluating **Ending sessions** - Reviewing the achievement of therapy goals - Negotiating the ending - Evaluating -
	The systemic "toolbox"	**Language practices** - Positive connotation and reframing - Solution and strength focused **Narrative practices** - Exploring the narratives - Creating unique stories - Externalizing **Reflecting practices** - Facilitating listening positions - The use of a co-therapists to generate new ideas and opportunities - Challenge and support - Explore differences - The use of micro-hypotheses **Emotional expressions** - Identifying emotionally important topics - Being emotional aware
	Child-oriented therapy	- Considering the child's developmental stage - Organizing to hear the child's expressions - Using creative techniques

Fig. 10.1 The map of competences

2. The second identified competence in the map of competences is *ethical and contextual awareness*. Ethical and contextual awareness is central at all times in the therapy process and must be continuously considered by the therapist. In particular, this theme refers to their double role as both a therapist and a social controller (Lorås, 2016a). This is closely connected to the concept of power. The therapist should be considered the family's ally. However, the therapist (in this research) is legally bound by the Norwegian Directorate of Health's (2008) demands to notify Child Protection Services when required. Therefore, the role as a systemic therapist consists of the constant consideration of whether the therapy may be contraindicated or if the need for urgent (and perhaps normative) interventions is covered. Contraindication concerns the consideration of any factors that weigh against an intervention or treatment (amv.legehandboka.no). The participants also emphasize an ethical understanding of the clients' behaviour as always being guided by good intentions. Although the clients' verbal responses and actions can seem inconvenient, they are considered an unfortunate result of basic good intentions (Lorås, 2016a).

   A focus on the client's context is considered crucial. As there are significant differences between the therapy room and the family's everyday life, all solutions need to be context-relevant and transferable to their everyday contexts. Optimally, it is desirable to include observation and participation in contexts in which the difficulties are and are not experienced. A thorough focus on context allows the understanding that the family's difficulties can be at the mercy of the chaos in which they live and that even a small change of context can change the difficulties and ensure that their difficulties are viewed in a new way.

3. The third overarching theme is *session-specific features*. This section presents a small selection of the therapeutic elements that seem to be session-specific and could be expected to be used at certain times during therapy.

   The initial sessions are considered as the becoming acquainted phase. This phase is often achieved by the use of genograms and asking questions relating to who was most interested in attending therapy and so forth. It is of great importance to create a therapy context that is considered a safe place to talk. If people are offered conversations when they feel unsafe or afraid, they often respond in more defensive ways than in a changed modality. People who experience themselves as insecure or attacked do not have good opportunities to listen and actually hear what other people are saying, even when they are arranged in a listening position. It is important that clients must be asked regularly about what is necessary for them to feel safe in the course of therapy. Through secure frameworks that make listening positions and reflections possible, one can thus come to a position of working with issues that the clients were not initially in a position to manage on their own. In the initial phase, the therapists always discuss their clients' needs, potential previous experiences with what was useful/not useful in therapy and how they together can tailor a therapy that is especially adapted to their needs. It is important in this phase to invite all family members to share in the exploration of what the aim of the therapy should be. It is considered the therapist's responsibility to ensure that an appropriate structure of the therapy sessions is being introduced and discussed in the initial sessions. The therapists should structure the conversations to ensure that the family does not get stuck in old and stalled communication patterns with little potential for change. An overarching aim of delivering a structured therapeutic approach is to ensure that all people who are present in therapy are given the opportunity to be heard. *The middle sessions* are to be considered as the working phase where many of the therapeutic competences are put into action (see theme no. 4: the systemic "toolbox"). In this phase, the therapist is actively working together with the family to gain a broader knowledge of their struggles, working on generating solutions to their difficulties (based on their previous experiences) and generally activating all family members in their joint battle against their struggles. The *ending sessions* are about reviewing the initial goals of the therapy, discussing how new solutions could be used in a broad range of different situations to develop a significant "toolbox" for future challenges and negotiating the end of the therapy.

In all phases of therapy (initial, middle and ending), feedback and evaluation from the client(s) are considered crucial. Client feedback is necessary to ensure that the course of the therapy is experienced as relevant with a basis in the clients' described goals. These goals are based on the original referral if it is consistent with the wishes of the family. If not, new goals are made based on the family's described needs and wishes. Therefore, feedback from the clients is gathered at the end of each session.

4. *The fourth theme, the systemic "toolbox",* consists of the participants' descriptions of different therapeutic practices used during all phases of the therapy process, such as language practices, narrative practices, solution- and strength-focused practices, and reflecting practices, as well as being aware of the emotional expressions and the use of hypotheses. *Language practices* concern meaning as constructed in social interactions and negotiated through language. The use of disease language in mental health is considered potentially inappropriate with regard to creating an unnecessary distance between the therapist and the family. Therapists use positive connotations, which are concerned with how the therapists position themselves regarding their understanding of humans and their difficulties, for example, by reframing the words being used by the clients. Reframing can be accomplished through parallel listening for descriptions that can be positively reinforced. The use of positive connotation is helpful to avoid a non-pathologizing view of the family and to avoid shame and guilt. Referrals are often characterized by problem descriptions and are less directed towards clients' resources, what they have achieved and what is important to them as a family. It is therefore important to facilitate dialogues that focus on solutions and strengths that can be expected to have the best potential for change. This is closely connected to the focus of unique outcomes and the preferred stories known from narrative practice.

The narrative practice skill consists of the exploration of narratives as a way of creating preferable unique stories in which the family's problem is not dominant and externalizing is used. Although it is not a goal to change anyone's history, it is a goal to find ways for a person to live with their history. A tool often used in narrative practices is that of externalizing. Externalizing involves a more specific way to externalize how a therapist systematically interviews individuals to locate the consequences of the problem before the family members are then invited to name the problem.

The reflecting practice skill is concerned with different ways of facilitating appropriate ways of talking and listening to each other. It is particularly necessary to strictly structure the listening position when families or parents are in high-conflict situations. To expand and nuance the family's actions and reflections, it is often an advantage to work with a co-therapist. Working with a co-therapist can also give clients opportunities that could otherwise be difficult to address with only one therapist, for example, if there is a wish to divide up the conversations (e.g. siblings, parents). In high-conflict conversations, the therapists need to be clear regarding who should speak, as well as when this person is expected to be in a listening position. In these cases, it is not required that people in high-conflict situations should talk to one another, but it is expected, at a minimum, that they should be able to speak with the therapist while the other listens. It is the therapists' responsibility to account for potentially negative outcomes that the clients' choices could have so that the family members can make nuanced and reflective choices. The therapists therefore offer themselves as discussion partners who not only confirm the person's experiences but also challenge his/her thoughts and perspectives so that several sides of the same situation are revealed. The therapists should attempt to be nuanced and reflective in regard to acknowledging other family members' diverging views of the same phenomenon. In this way, the therapists should continuously explore the differences and disagreements within the family. If the differences are considered irreconcilable or very divergent, it is a goal to challenge the family members through dialogue to find ways to acknowledge and live with these differences even though they disagree. For example, questions such as the following can be used: "*If you, despite your disagreement with your father, were to try to see something positive in what he has said, what would that be*"? In this manner, differences and disagreements are facilitated so that they can be explained and understood although they cannot be shared. The multi-epistemological systemic therapists present their thoughts and ideas concerning the nature of the problem in the form of undetailed micro-hypotheses that the family is asked to take a position on. In this way, the therapist avoids becoming enchanted with his/her own constructions and blind to other possible understandings. The hypotheses are presented as thoughts, not as well-founded facts, which, again, can contribute to the clients' ability to refute the hypotheses without feeling that they are rejecting the therapist's contribution.

As part of the therapeutic process, the therapist is expected to be aware of the client's nonverbal communication. A continuous focus on the clients' emotional expressions is important because this focus is a potential way of identifying topics that are important for the client to discuss. Therapists are considered an important emotional confirmer; however, therapists should be conscious that their emotionality is not the focus. Thus, emotional expressions should not be viewed as noise but as important information. Regardless, the extent and degree to which a therapist comments on emotional expressions are considered dependent on the therapist's knowledge of the client(s) and their assessment of the client(s) as being able to tolerate the focus being on them.

5. Theme five is *child-oriented therapy*. Children's and adolescents' expressions go beyond the use of words. Organizing to hear the child's expressions is therefore a fundamental premise of delivering systemic family therapy. However, being child-centred also involves considerations of the child's developmental stage. This is closely connected to the need for somewhat normative judgements (a multi-epistemological stance) at certain times in therapy. Children are often outstanding at seeing and sensing signals, and they have a tendency to know far more than what their parents believe they know. Thus, therapists must be attentive to the fact that the child can find it difficult to put their thoughts, feelings and experiences into words, often because of their loyalty to his/her parents. Children's stories can be harrowing, and in many cases, it is difficult for parents to hear their children discussing them. The therapists therefore need to be attentive to how this discussion affects the parents.

It is crucial to capture the child's interest and give them the opportunity to participate in their own terms so that the therapeutic process does not become too boring. Some examples include using creative techniques, such as Post-it Notes, puppet theatre or play as the starting point for the conversations and the use of metaphors/externalizing language and drawings. Most of these approaches are self-explanatory. Nevertheless, I will briefly describe two of these methods. (1) Post-it Notes: On these notes, each person writes down three things that he/she wants more of in the family and three things that he/she wants less of. In this way, the therapist(s) can quickly become acquainted with the family, and the family members can become acquainted with one another's points of view. After this exercise, all the points are written down on a board, which creates a starting point for the coming dialogue. To ensure the parents' participation, one of the parents, for example, can be responsible for writing the points on the board. Another possibility is to open up for the children's creativity, by having them write the points. This method also gives children ownership of their own statements. By actively using the board, information can emerge concerning sibling dynamics with regard to seeing who writes first, whether someone is excluded, and so forth. Thus, writing positive responses to different family members, drawings, puppet theatre, and play can be used as the starting point for conversations, etc. (2) The use of metaphorical and/or externalizing language regarding difficult topics can make it easier and safer for children to discuss topics because this approach does not linguistically identify problems with any particular family member and can contribute to creating distance between them and the problem. Through the use of animal names, for example, it can be easier for children to name difficulties that they otherwise do not have the language to describe. A similar approach is drawing a cartoon series in which the next frame remains open (where what one wants to occur will be drawn). The frame can remain open until the next conversation, in which the child is then asked to draw how things have gone since the last time. To the extent that this new drawing is consistent with the child/family's previous wishes, the process can create a starting point for conversation.

10.4 Discussion

The discussion is divided into two parts: (1) *a multi-epistemological systemic approach* and (2) *using the map of competences*.

10.4.1 A Multi-Epistemological Systemic Approach

Systemic and social constructionist ideas are still the most relevant theoretical perspective for systemic therapists. However, the participants in this research also expressed a general scepticism towards all stringent theories that attempt to embrace human complexity because of the danger of promoting reductionist thinking where everything can be reduced to only linguistic meanings and possible simplicity. Based on this research, the participants' epistemological stance was identified as being multifaceted and consisting of social constructionism, critical realism and constructivism. Thus, the continuum was named multi-epistemological systemic therapy.

I will argue that it is important to include both constructivism and critical realism in a future systemic portfolio. By this, I mean that to acknowledge only a social constructionist stance as the foundation for systemic therapy is insufficient regarding the complexity in child and adolescent mental health care. For example, although systemic therapists cannot define what the correct family interactions are, they can instead say that family violence is wrong and illegal (Lorås, 2016a, c). The social constructionist idea that everything can be re-constructed is not actually useful when working with vulnerable children and adolescents living under adverse conditions (Lorås & Sundelin, 2018).

According to the findings, the participants argued that they occasionally take up normative positions or relate to so-called normative knowledge, such as developmental psychology and that which gives children and young people healthy opportunities for their development, which is inconsistent with a strong social constructionist stance. From this perspective, even a relational diagnosis is considered as normative knowledge because it somewhat defines unhealthy family interactions (e.g. abnormal intrafamilial relationships, abnormal qualities of upbringing).

I claim that it is time to discuss whether constructivism, with its extended focus on other significant aspects of life, such as the internal, cognitive processes of individuals, should be included and acknowledged as part of the epistemological basis of systemic therapy instead of only as the idea of systemic and social constructionist epistemological purity (Lorås & Sundelin, 2018). Knowledge about internal, cognitive processes is also described as one of the therapists' expected competences in the Norwegian Directorate of Health's (2008) guidelines (i.e. basic knowledge about normal development and abnormal development), and it is described by the participants as one of the areas that must be considered, especially regarding the client's development.

All of the participants noted that they had experience with individual clients who wanted diagnostic assessments. Therefore, the participants were not critical of relating to biology or diagnostic assessments per se (repeatedly referring to Maturana). These research participants also described repeated examples in which clients had experienced receiving a diagnosis as a valuable contribution in regard to removing shame and guilt (i.e. in the case of mental retardation) (Rimehaug & Helmersberg, 1995). In this manner, the actual result of receiving a diagnosis can have the paradoxical effect of removing guilt and shame and creating a distance between the individual and the problem, which is the same result that one attempts to achieve through externalizing conversations with narrative therapy (White, 2007). Simultaneously, in contemporary society, a diagnosis can grant rights (e.g. assistant teachers, access to treatment) (Sundet, 2015).

Critical realist ideas became apparent through the participants when they discussed therapeutic autonomy and professional judgement, in addition to an expressed desire for delimited interventions. The participants defended this desire with the idea that, provided that the descriptions of the competences are not exaggeratedly stringent, they could be helpful in ensuring that the therapist did not wander off into a confusing and complex landscape. Therefore, I add a critical realist element to systemic therapy theory and practice. In critical realism, there is a belief that all scientific work must be based on informed opinions about what actually exists within the current area of study and the basic properties of this form of existence (Davidsen, 2004), although it is never possible to predict the outcome of interventions. The critical realist directs our attention towards understandings and explorations of the tendencies identified (e.g. the identified competences in my study). Therefore, critical realism is polemical regarding positivism and shares with positivism the positive concern with developing knowledge (Pocock, 2015). It stands in contrast to social constructionism, which embraces relativism and scepticism in the attempt to delegitimize knowledge claims by exposing them as symptoms of underlying discursive power relations (Pocock, 2015).

10.4.2 Using the Map of Competences

As a teacher and clinical supervisor of hundreds of family therapy students, my experience is that many students view systemic therapy's theoretical background as vague. I intend the map of competences to be a contribution of making this somewhat complicated and unclear landscape easier to grasp.

The map of competences is a useful pedagogic tool to ensure that therapists in training are prepared to work with families (under live supervision) but can also be a contribution to safeguard that clients receive adequate treatment (Figley & Nelson, 1989). The need for supervision (among others) is to ensure that the trainees (or others) do not use the map of competences as a blueprint for how therapy should be conducted, with the therapist deciding on behalf of the client's which intervention is best suited to their problem (McLeod & Sundet, 2015).

The map of competences consists of the fundamental elements of systemic therapy, without neglecting the therapist's own professional judgements. The map of competences is intended to be used as a tool for delivering consistent practice, consistent with Wampold and Imel's (2015) research. The map of competences can therefore be a valuable contribution to both educational institutions, supervisors and students by offering a more unified version of systemic therapy, while simultaneously adhering to the therapists' need for flexibility (Lorås, 2016a, b, c). This outline is called a map of competence, instead of a manual. This is because a map, following systemic ideas, doesn't have a pre-defined beginning and an end. However, I consider that both the map of competences and the Leeds manual can inform each other. The Leeds manual is more descriptive and theoretical driven, based on the fundamental ideas of systemic practice. By drawing on both, the therapists will base their practice on systemic ideas, adapted to the context of child and adolescent mental health, targeting associated abnormal psychosocial situations in Axis 5.

The level of detailed descriptions of systemic competences provides the possibility for the supervisor to explore the supervisee's use of specific systemic competences (i.e. the use of positive connotation, exploration of differences, etc.). In this way, one can work with systemic competences at a more specific level of detail, if desired, than the more traditional way of considering systemic therapy in more general terms allows.

The map of competences is to be considered as a tool and a framework to assist and guide the process of becoming an expert and having theoretical and practical knowledge about systemic therapy. However, the term "expert" has a somewhat negatively connotation in the field of systemic therapy (Anderson, 2005). Nevertheless, Anderson (2005) argue that the not-knowing position also not consider that the therapist is ignorant to their knowledge but emphasizes a therapist who is humble about what he/she knows. Therefore, the therapist's contributions are presented in a manner that conveys a tentative posture and portrays respect and openness to the client (Anderson, 2005) but still consists of some specific techniques (i.e. the use of hypotheses, creating unique stories, etc.). As emphasized by Andersen (2005), the use of the term "expert" in this research means that the therapist is expected to have expert knowledge of the theoretical and practical elements of systemic therapy but is humble about his/her own knowledge.

10.5 Limitations of the Research

Although I conducted 12 interviews with six experienced systemic therapists, my research is based on the practice of a relatively small number of practitioners. By extending the number of participants and their different child and adolescent mental health care contexts, this could have nuanced the analysis and perhaps produced greater variation in the data. However, I consider the idea of saturation in qualitative research functions more as a goal than a reality. The families that were observed during my fieldwork observations can hardly be categorized as a homogeneous group, although they fulfilled the criteria of multiaxial diagnosis/axis 5. Accordingly, it can be questioned whether the identified systemic therapy competences tend to favour the associated abnormal psychosocial situations instead of child and adolescent difficulties in general. The fieldwork observations were limited to 68 h of clinical practice with each of the six participant therapists. If the hours of fieldwork observations were extended and/ or were conducted to include observations before the first interview, then the data material could have been even more comprehensive and a thicker descriptive account considering the aim of this research.

10.6 Concluding Comments

The participants in my study praised the flexibility of systemic therapy but also desired clearer guidelines regarding which systemic competences they were expected to deliver so that they would not become lost in the complexity of the work (Lorås, 2018). Therefore, a certain degree of therapeutic guidelines and requirements for documentation and administration are viewed as necessary and appropriate to ensure that people receive good therapeutic services and to ensure the protection of their rights (Rimehaug & Helmersberg, 1995). Thus, this research offers a framework (the map of competences) for delivering flexible yet specialized systemic therapy in the context of child and adolescent mental health care, targeting associated abnormal psychosocial situations/Axis 5 (Lorås, 2018).

References

Anderson, H. (2005). Myths about "not-knowing". *Family Process, 44*(4), 497–504. https://doi.org/10.1111/j.1545-5300.2005.00074.x
Asen, E. (2002). Outcome research in family therapy. *Advances in Psychiatric Treatment, 8*(3), 230–238.
Bertrando, P. (2009). Surviving in psychiatry as a systemic family therapist. *Australian and New Zealand Journal of Family Therapy, 3*(30), 160–172. https://doi.org/10.1375/anft.30.3.160
Brinkmann, S., & Petersen, A. (2015). *Diagnoser: perpektiver, kritik og discussion* [Diagnosis: Perspectives, critique and discussion]. Aarhus: Forlaget Klim.
Charmaz, K. (2014). Constructing Grounded Theory (2nd ed.). Sage Publishing.
Davidsen, B. I. (2004). 'Kritisk realisme og økonomisk-vitenskapelig arbeid' [Critical realism and financial and scientific work]. *Norsk Økonomisk Tidsskrift, 118*, 62–76.
Esposito, L., & Perez, F. M. (2014). Neoliberalism and the commodification of mental health. *Human & Society, 38*(4), 414–442.
Figley, C. E., & Nelson, T. S. (1989). Basic family therapy skills, conceptualization and initial findings. *Journal of Marital and Family Therapy, 15*(4), 349–365.
Lorås, L. (2016a). *The map of competences in systemic therapy. A qualitative study of the systemic competences in child and adolescent mental health that target ICD 10 Axis 5 associated abnormal psychosocial situations.* Doctorate thesis of Systemic Psychotherapy awarded by the University of East London in conjunction with the Tavistock Clinic.

Lorås, L. (2016b). Systemisk familieterapi og helsedirektoratets krav innen barne og ungdomspsykiatrien i Norge [Systemic family therapy and the Norwegian child and adolescent mental health demands]. *Fokus På Familien, 02*(2), 93–112.

Lorås, L. (2016c). Paolo Bertrando: "To some extent" an interview with the Italian systemic family therapist. *Fokus På Familien, 2*(1), 8–26. https://doi.org/10.18261/issn.08077487-2016-01-03

Lorås, L. (2018). Systemic family therapy competences in child and adolescent mental health care. *Contemporary Family Therapy, 40*(1), 1–9. https://doi.org/10.1007/s10591-017-9440-z

Lorås, L., & Sundelin, J. (2018). The multi-epistemological systemic therapists. *Australian and New Zealand Journal of Family Therapy, 39*(4), 408–420. https://doi.org/10.1002/anzf.1335

Manassis, K. (2009). *Cognitive behavioural therapy with children: A guide for the community practitioner*. Routledge.

McLeod, J., & Sundet, R. (2015). Integrative and eclectic approach and pluralism. In M. Cooper & W. Dryden (Eds.), *The handbook of pluralistic counselling and psychotherapy* (pp. 158–170). Sage.

Northey, W. F. (2011). Competency, common ground, and challenges: Response to the development of systemic therapy competencies for the UK. *Journal of Family Therapy, 33*(2), 144–152.

Norwegian Directorate of Health. (2008). *Psychological health care for children and adolescents – Guide for outpatient clinics*. The Norwegian Health Directorate.

Pocock, D. (2015). A philosophy of practice for systemic psychotherapy: The case for critical realism. *Journal of Family Therapy, 37*, 167–183.

Pote, H., Stratton, P., Cottrell, D., Boston, P., Shapiro, D., & Hanks, H. (2000). *The Leeds systemic family therapy manual*. Leeds Family Therapy Research Centre.

Pote, H., Stratton, P., Cottrell, D., Shapiro, D., & Boston, P. (2003). Systemic family therapy can be manualized: Research process and findings. *Journal of Family Therapy, 25*(3), 236–262.

Rimehaug, T., & Helmersberg, I. (1995). Barnepsykiatrisk utredning: Fra produkt til prosess. Veien mot rollen som med-ekspert [Child psychiatric diagnostic assessment: From product to process]. *Fokus På Familien, 23*(2), 145–156.

Rønnestad, M. H., & Orlinsky, D. E. (2006). 'Terapeutisk arbeid og profesjonell utvikling: En internasjonal studie' [Therapist practice and development: An international study]. *Tidsskrift for Norsk Psykologforening, 11*(1), 6–24.

Silverman, W. H. (1996). Cookbooks, manuals, and paint-by-numbers: Psychotherapy in the 90's'. *Psychotherapy, 33*(2), 207–215.

Stratton, P., Pote, H., Cottrell, D., Boston, P., Shapiro, D., & Hanks, H. (2009). *Systemic family therapy manual therapist adherence protocol training edition*. University of Leeds.

Stratton, P., Reibstein, J., Lask, J., Singh, R., & Asen, E. (2011). Competences and occupational standards for systemic family and couples' therapy'. *Journal of Family Therapy, 33*(2), 123–143.

Sundet, R. (2015). Kunnskap i evidensens tid [Knowledge, in the time of evidence]. *Fokus På Familien, 43*(1), 6–24.

Sundelin, J. (2013). Karta eller tvångstrøja? En klinikers møte med 4 familjeterapeutiska manualer' [Map or straightjacket? A clinicians meeting with 4 family therapy manuals]. *Fokus På Familien, 41*(3), 216–235.

Tomm, K. M., & Wright, L. M. (1979). Training in family therapy: Perceptual, conceptual and executive skills. *Family Process, 18*(3), 227–250.

Wampold, B., & Imel, Z. E. (2015). *The great psychotherapy debate. The evidence for what makes psychotherapy work*. Taylor & Francis.

White, M. (2007). *Maps of narrative practice*. W.W. Norton.

World Health Organization. (1996). *Multiaxial classification of child and adolescent psychiatric disorders. The ICD-10 classification of mental and behavioral disorders in children and adolescents*. Cambridge University Press.

Part II
Research Issues in the Use and Evaluation of Manuals

1.1 Introduction

Over the long history of manualization of systemic therapies, some major therapeutic approaches have undergone substantial and systematic research development. The well-researched and well-established approaches include Multidimensional Family Therapy (Liddle & Rigter, 2013, Liddle, 2016), Brief Strategic Family Therapy (Szapocznik & Williams, 2000), Functional Family Therapy (Sexton, 2019), and Multisystemic Therapy (Henggeler & Schaefer, 2016). They have particularly concentrated on adolescence and drug use, possibly because the kind of substantial research funding needed is more available for issues of major societal concern. A different approach was taken by conducting an RCT in which the systemic therapy was provided by two highly experienced therapists, and at the conclusion of the trial, their approach was written up as a manual (Jones & Asen, 2000).

In this second part of the handbook, we include chapters that highlight some of the research issues that emerge in the use and evaluation of manuals. This selection is not to undermine the many other chapters in the handbook that include reporting the research that has underpinned their processes of manualization.

As a summary for this section, Liddle and Rigter (2013) state: "Overall, comprehensive, multifaceted, multi-target treatments show feasibility and promise in clinical outcomes. Likewise, implementation research promises to unlock some of the mysteries in understanding the systemic influences on the growth and change in services in regular care settings" (Liddle & Rigter, 2013, p 203). We hope that the chapters in this section and throughout the handbook serve as examples of the importance of rigorous and creative research of therapeutic approaches and on the process of manualization itself to further the development of the systemic therapy field..

Henggeler, S. W. and Schaeffer, C. M. (2016), Multisystemic Therapy: Clinical Overview, Outcomes, and Implementation Research. *Fam. Proc.* Early view: 2 JUL 2016 I DOI: 10.1111/famp.12232. doi:10.1111/famp.12232

Jones, E., & Asen, E. (2000). *Systemic couple therapy and depression*. London & New York: Karnac Books.

Liddle, H. A. (2016) Multidimensional Family Therapy: Evidence Base for Transdiagnostic Treatment Outcomes, Change Mechanisms and Implementation in Community Settings. *Family Process. Early View*. doi:10.1111/famp.12243

Liddle, H., Rigter, H. (2013). How developmental research and contextual theory drive clinical work with adolescents with addiction. *Harvard Review of Psychiatry, 21*(4), 200-204. doi: 10.1097/HRP.0b013e31829aaa6b

Szapocznik, J., & Williams, R. A. (2000). Brief Strategic Family Therapy: twenty-five years of interplay among theory, research and practice in adolescent behavior problems and drug abuse. *Clinical child and family psychology review, 3*(2), 117–134. https://doi.org/10.1023/a:1009512719808

Sexton, T. L. (2019). *Functional family therapy: An evidence-based, family-focused, and systemic approach for working with adolescents and their families*. In B. H. Fiese, M. Celano, K. Deater-Deckard, E. N. Jouriles, & M. A. Whisman (Eds.), *APA handbooks in psychology®. APA handbook of contemporary family psychology: Family therapy and training* (p. 171–188). American Psychological Association. https://doi.org/10.1037/0000101-011

The Editors

Chapter 11
An Integrative Approach to Systemic Therapy

Alan Carr

11.1 Integrative Systemic Three-Column Framework

The variety of traditions, schools and models of systemic therapy may be classified in terms of their central focus of therapeutic concern, and in particular with respect to their emphasis on

1. Repetitive problem-maintaining behaviour patterns (and associated feelings);
2. Constraining narratives and belief systems which subserve these behaviour patterns; and
3. Historical, contextual and constitutional factors which predispose families to adopt particular narratives and belief systems and engage in particular problem-maintaining behaviour patterns.

In the same vein, hypotheses and formulations about families' problems and strengths may be conceptualized within these three domains. Also, interventions may be classified with respect to the specific domains they target. Our integrative model of systemic therapy is based on these insights. The model evolved in routine clinical practice in Canada, the UK and Ireland starting in the 1980s. It was informed by the clinical and theoretical couple (Gurman, 2008; Gurman et al., 2015; Gurman & Jacobson, 2002; Jacobson & Gurman, 1986, 1995), family therapy literature (Gurman & Kniskern, 1981, 1991; Sexton et al., 2003; Sexton & Lebow, 2016) and empirical research on the effectiveness of systemic interventions which we periodically reviewed (Carr, 2000a, 2000b, 2009a, 2009b, 2014a, 2014b, 2016, 2018,

---

A. Carr (✉)
Clinical Psychology University College Dublin, Dublin, Ireland

Systemic Psychotherapist at Clanwilliam Institute, Dublin, Ireland
e-mail: alan.carr@ucd.ie

2019). The treatment manual detailing this approach has evolved through four iterations (Carr, 1995a, 2000c, 2006, 2012). There is also a truncated version of the manual specifically adapted for use with families with adult-focused problems (Carr & McNulty, 2006, 2016). If you want to use the model in routine practice, the most up-to-date version for both child and adult-focused problems is Carr (2012), and for adult-focused problems is Carr and McNulty (2016). Carr (2012) is the most comprehensive sources. This third edition of *Family Therapy: Concepts Process and Practice* contains an overview of key ideas and practices from many schools of family therapy; a summary of the evidence-base for systemic therapy; a detailed description of our integrative, systemic three-column model; guidance on how to the model in routine clinical practice; and training exercises that may be used to learn how to use this approach to systemic therapy. Throughout the remainder of this chapter, this source will be referred to as 'the manual'.

In addition to the manual, we have published brief descriptions of the model (Carr, 1994a, 1997a, 1997b, 1997c, 1999, 2005, 2017) and a series of papers describing aspects of this approach to systemic therapy including engagement (Carr, 1990a), formulation (Carr, 1990b), goal setting (Carr, 1993), giving directives (Carr, 1990c), involving children in family therapy (Carr, 1994b; Carr, 2002), working with countertransference (Carr, 1989) and resistance (Carr, 1995b), managing disengagement (Carr, 1996) and training (Carr, 2007). What follows is a brief description of key elements of the model.

11.1.1 Problem Formulation

In routine practice, for any problem, an initial hypothesis and later formulation may be constructed in which the behaviour pattern (and feelings) which maintain the problem are specified, the constraining narratives and beliefs which underpin family members' roles in this pattern are outlined, and the broader contextual factors that predispose family members to have these beliefs and behaviour patterns are given. For example, in the case presented in the second half of this chapter, our initial hypothesis was that the family got involved in regular conflictual patterns of interaction (and negative feelings) in which the children's expression of their needs, the fathers' anger control problems and the mother's panic attacks might have played a part. Our second hypothesis was that the narratives and beliefs which underpinned their roles in these interaction patterns involved the father having views about being entitled to certain things from the mother (in their marital relationship), and the mother believing that she was either in danger or powerless. Our third hypothesis was that these beliefs and behaviour patterns (and associated feelings) had their roots in adverse family-of-origin experiences. These hypotheses were checked out during the assessment interviews and led to the development of the three-column

11 An Integrative Approach to Systemic Therapy

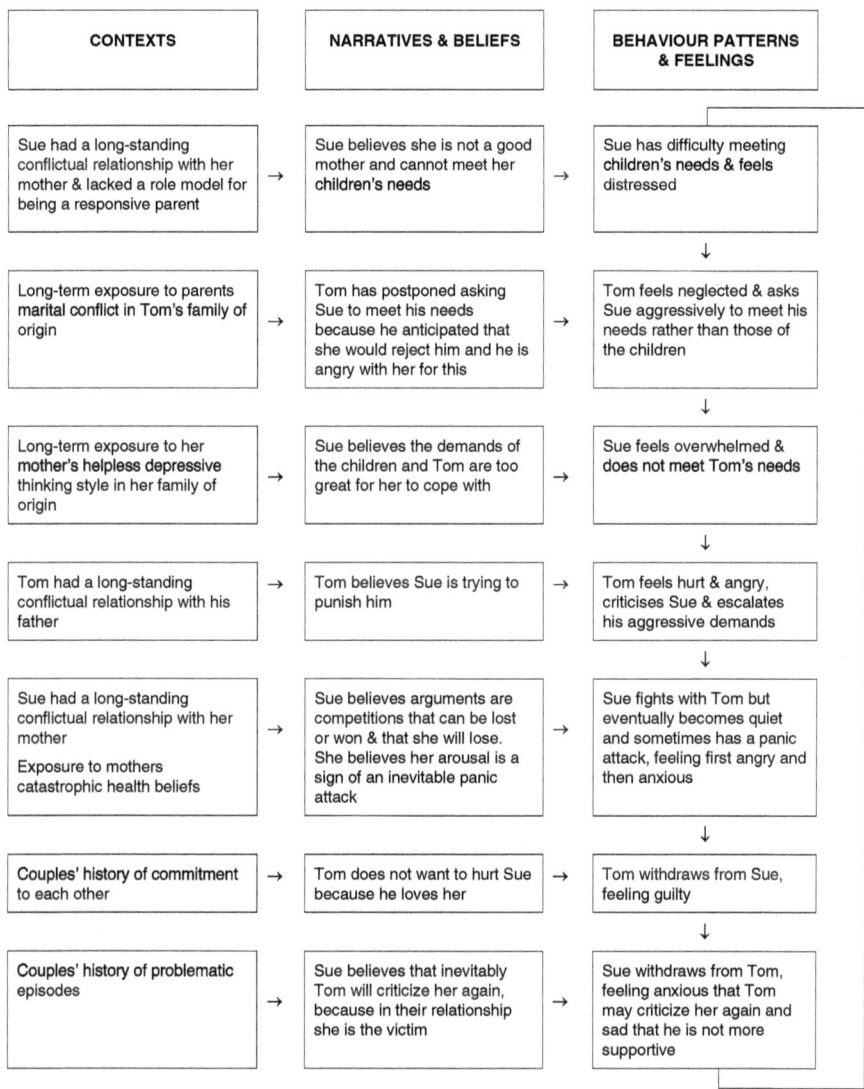

Fig. 11.1 Three-column formulation of Tom and Sue's problematic episodes

problem formulation presented in Fig. 11.1. This specific formulation drew on the general problem formulation model in Table 11.1. A review of the literature on which this model is based, and the types of questions to ask when co-constructing formulations with families is detailed in the manual.

Table 11.1 Problem formulation

Contexts	Narratives and beliefs	Behaviour patterns

Constitutional
• Genetic vulnerabilities
• Debilitating somatic states
• Early illness or injury
• Learning difficulty
• Difficult temperament
Contextual
• Current life-cycle transitions
• Home-work role strain
• Lack of social support
• Recent loss experiences
• Recent bereavement
• Parental separation
• Recent illness or injury
• Unemployment
• Moving house or school
• Changing jobs
• Recent bullying
• Recent child abuse
• Poverty
• Secret romantic affairs
• Constraining cultural norms and values
Historical
• Major family of origin stresses
  1. Bereavements
  2. Separations
  3. Child abuse
  4. Social disadvantage
  5. Institutional upbringing
• Family of origin parent-child problems
  1. Insecure attachment
  2. Authoritarian parenting
  3. Permissive parenting
  4. Neglectful parenting
  5. Inconsistent parental discipline
  6. Lack of stimulation
  7. Scapegoating
  8. Triangulation
• Family of origin parental problems
  1. Parental psychological problems
  2. Parental drug or alcohol abuse
  3. Parental criminality
  4. Marital discord or violence
  5. Family disorganization
	• Denial of the problem
	• Rejection of a systemic framing of the problem in favour of an individualistic framing
	• Constraining narratives about personal competence to solve the problem
	• Constraining narratives about problems and solutions relevant to the presenting problem
	• Constraining narratives about the negative consequences of change and the negative events that may be avoided by maintaining the status quo
	• Constraining narratives about marital, parental and other family relationships (e.g. differences are battles which can be won or lost)
	• Constraining attributional style (internal, global, stable, intentional attributions for problem behaviours)
	• Constraining cognitive distortions
	  1. Maximizing negatives
	  2. Minimizing positives
	• Constraining defence mechanisms
	  1. Denial
	  2. Passive aggression
	  3. Rationalization
	  4. Reaction formation
	  5. Displacement
	  6. Splitting
	  7. Projection
		• The symptom or problem behaviour
		• The sequence of events that typically precede and follow an episode of the symptoms or problem behaviour
		• The feelings and emotions that accompany these behaviours, particularly positive feelings or payoffs
		• Patterns involving ineffective attempted solutions
		• Patterns involving confused communication
		• Patterns involving high rates of negative exchanges and low rates of positive exchanges
		• Patterns involving expression of negative emotions due to fears of attachment needs being unmet
		• Symmetrical and complementary behaviour patterns
		• Enmeshed and disengaged behaviour patterns
		• Rigid and chaotic behaviour patterns
		• Coercive interaction patterns
		• Patterns involving inadvertent reinforcement
		• Patterns involving lack of marital intimacy
		• Patterns involving a significant marital power imbalance
		• Authoritarian, permissive, neglectful, punitive and inconsistent parenting patterns
		• Patterns involving triangulation of children
		• Patterns including lack of co-ordination among involved professionals and family members

11.1.2 Exception Formulation

Exceptions are formulated by identifying interaction patterns within which the problem might be expected to occur, but does not; empowering narratives and beliefs which inform family members' roles within these exceptional interaction patterns; and broader contextual factors that underpin these competency-oriented narratives and beliefs that provide a foundation for exceptional behaviour (and positive feelings). For example, in the case study presented in the second half of this chapter, our first hypothesis was that occasionally the mother and father became involved in co-operative, rather than conflictual, patterns of interaction (with associated positive feelings). Our second hypothesis was that the narratives which underpinned their roles in these interaction patterns involved the couple's commitment to their marriage and to raising their children together. Our third hypothesis was that these narratives and behaviour patterns had their roots in positive family-of-origin experiences and positive experiences within the family of procreation. These hypotheses were checked out during the assessment interviews and led to the development of the three-column exception formulation in Fig. 11.2. This specific formulation drew on the general exception formulation model in Table 11.2. A review of the literature relevant to exceptions, and the types of questions to ask when co-constructing exception formulations with families are detailed in the manual.

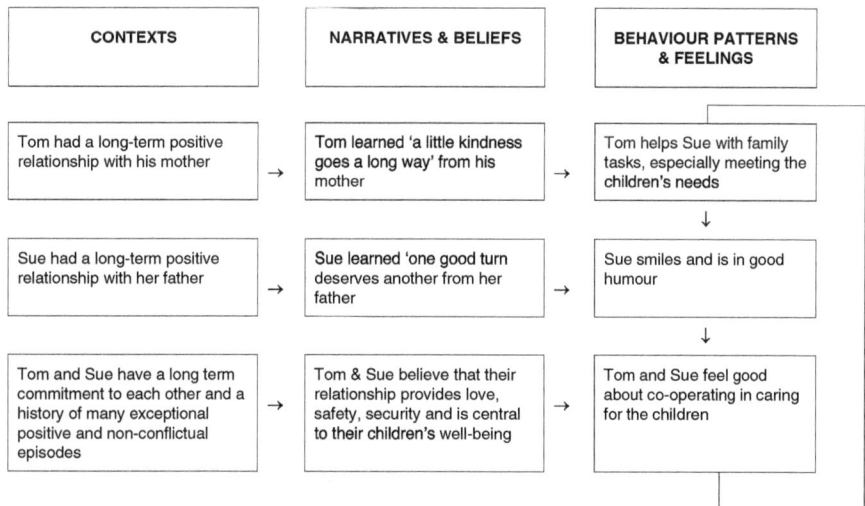

Fig. 11.2 Three-column formulation of Tom and Sue's exceptional episodes

Table 11.2 Exception formulation

Contexts	Narratives and beliefs	Behaviour patterns
Constitutional • Physical health • High IQ • Specific talents • Creativity • Wisdom • Easy temperament • Positive personality traits (stability, extraversion, openness to experience, agreeableness and conscientiousness) **Contextual** • Good social support network • Low family stress • Balanced home and work roles • Moderate or high SES • Positive work environment • Positive preschool or educational placement • Empowering cultural norms and values **Historical** • Positive family of origin experiences • Positive family of origin parent-child relationships • Secure attachment • Authoritative parenting • Clear communication • Flexible family organization • Good parental adjustment • Parents had good marital relationship • Successful experiences of coping with problems	• Acceptance of the problem • Acceptance of a systemic framing of the problem • Commitment to resolving the problem • Empowering narratives about personal competence to solve the problem (self-efficacy) • Empowering narratives about problems and solutions relevant to the presenting problem • Narratives in which the advantages of problem resolution outweigh the negative consequences of change and the negative events that may be avoided by maintaining the status quo • Empowering narratives about marital, parental and other family relationships particularly those which privilege loyalty • Positive or benign narratives about the characteristics or intentions of partners and other network members • Optimistic attributional style (internal, global, stable, intentional attributions for productive behaviour and situational attributions for problem behaviour) • Healthy defence mechanisms 1. Self-observation 2. Humour 3. Self-assertion 4. Sublimation	• The sequence of events that occurs in those exceptional circumstances where the problem or symptom was expected to occur but does not occur • The feelings and emotions that accompany these behaviours, particularly positive feelings or payoffs • Patterns involving effective solutions and good problem-solving skills • Patterns involving clear communication • Patterns involving high rates of positive exchanges and low rates of negative exchanges • Patterns involving clear expression of attachment needs • Emotionally supportive (rather than enmeshed or disengaged) behaviour patterns • Flexible behaviour (not rigid or chaotic) patterns • Patterns supporting marital intimacy • Patterns supporting marital power sharing • Patterns involving consistent, authoritative, co-operative co-parenting • Patterns including good co-ordination among involved professionals and family members

11.1.3 Interventions

In light of formulations of families' problems and exceptions, a range of interventions which address interaction patterns, narratives and broader contextual factors may be considered. Those which fit best for clients and for which there is the best

11 An Integrative Approach to Systemic Therapy

evidence of effectiveness may be selected. Some interventions aim primarily to disrupt problem-maintaining interaction patterns. In the case example presented later in the chapter, the self-regulation work we did with the father, the graded challenges work we did with the mother, and the parenting skills training we did with the couple fall into this broad category. Other interventions aim to help couples evolve more liberating personal and family narratives. Some such interventions will be mentioned in the case example. These include reframing the family's difficulties in interactional rather than individualistic terms, externalizing the problem, pinpointing strengths and building on exceptions. A third group of interventions aim to modify the negative impact of broader contextual factors, or draw on positive historical, contextual or constitutional resources and factors that may promote problem-resolution. In the case example presented later in the chapter, building support is an intervention that falls into this category. A three-column framework within which to conceptualize a wide range of couple and family therapy interventions is given in Table 11.3. A review of the literature on interventions is contained in the manual.

11.1.4 Therapy Stages

In our integrative approach, the overall strategy is to work collaboratively with families to formulate their problems and exceptional episodes where their problems were expected to occur but did not, using the three-column models outlined above. Once this has been achieved, treatment goals are set, and a therapy plan developed which aims to increase the occurrence of exceptions, disrupt problematic behaviour patterns, transform problematic personal and family narratives, address problem-maintaining contextual factors, and draw on historical, contextual and personal resources.

However, systemic therapy is not that straight forward. Sometimes clients have difficulty engaging in therapy. It is therefore critical to establish who is the primary customer for therapy, and invite them to encourage other members of the family to attend the first session. In the case example presented later in this chapter, the parents probably would not have attended therapy at all, without us identifying the referring social worker as the customer and inviting them to bring the family to the first meeting. Furthermore, many families show marked improvement following assessment only. That is, once they develop a shared three-column systemic understanding of their difficulties and exceptional situations where their problems were expected to occur but did, they spontaneously avoid problematic interactions and engage in exceptional non-problematic interactions instead. Finally, some families come to therapy with one problem, such as parenting difficulties and when this is resolved, request therapy for adult-focused concerns. To address these various challenges, the process of therapy is conceptualized as a developmental stage-wise process.

The framework set out in Fig. 11.3 outlines the stages of therapy from the initial receiving of a referral letter to the point where the case is closed. The first stage is

Table 11.3 Intervention

Contexts	Narratives & beliefs	Behaviour patterns
Addressing constitutional factors • Psychoeducation about condition • Facilitate adherence to medication regime • Refer for medical consultation • Arrange placement appropriate for person with constitutional vulnerability (e.g. intellectual disability) **Addressing contextual issues** • Network meetings • Child-protection interagency meetings • Home-school liaison meetings • Advocacy • Changing roles • Building support • Rituals for mourning losses • Exploring secrets **Addressing family of origin issues** • Facilitate exploration of transgenerational patterns, scripts myths and relationship habits • Facilitate re-experiencing, expressing and integrating emotions from family of origin experiences which underpin destructive relationship habits • Coach clients to reconnect with cut-off parental figures	**Reframing problems** • Frame problems in interactional terms • Frame problems in solvable terms • Frame intentions in positive terms **Pinpointing strengths** • Find unnamed obvious strengths • Attribute them to clients as defining characteristics **Relabelling** • Find negatively labelled behaviours • Relable them in positive non-blaming terms **Presenting multiple perspectives** • Split messages • Reflecting team practice **Externalizing problems and building on exceptions** • Separate the problem from the person • Identify and amplify exceptions including pre-therapy improvements • Involve network members • Link the current life exceptions to the past and future • Build a new positive narrative based on the series of exceptions **Addressing ambivalence** • Explore ambivalent narratives about the pros and cons of change and maintaining the status quo • Explore narratives about catastrophes associates with change • Explore narratives about powerlessness and change	**Creating a therapeutic context** • Contract • Lay ground rules • Facilitate turn taking • Manage time and space **Changing behaviour patterns in sessions** • Facilitate enactment • Coach new behaviours • Unbalance system • Mark boundaries **Facilitating expression of unmet attachment needs** • Distinguish primary (vulnerable/adaptive) emotions from secondary (hard/maladaptive) emotions • Facilitate intense expression and reception of primary emotions and attachment needs **Changing rates of positive and negative behaviour in couples** • Facilitate behaviour exchange • Build acceptance **Changing rates of positive and negative behaviour in parent-child interactions** • Schedule special time • Introduce reward systems • Coach behaviour control skills **Problem-solving and communication skills training** • Communication skills training • Problem-solving skills training **Tasks to change behaviour patterns between sessions** • Symptom monitoring • Restraint • Managing graded challenges • Practicing symptoms • Self-regulation

11 An Integrative Approach to Systemic Therapy

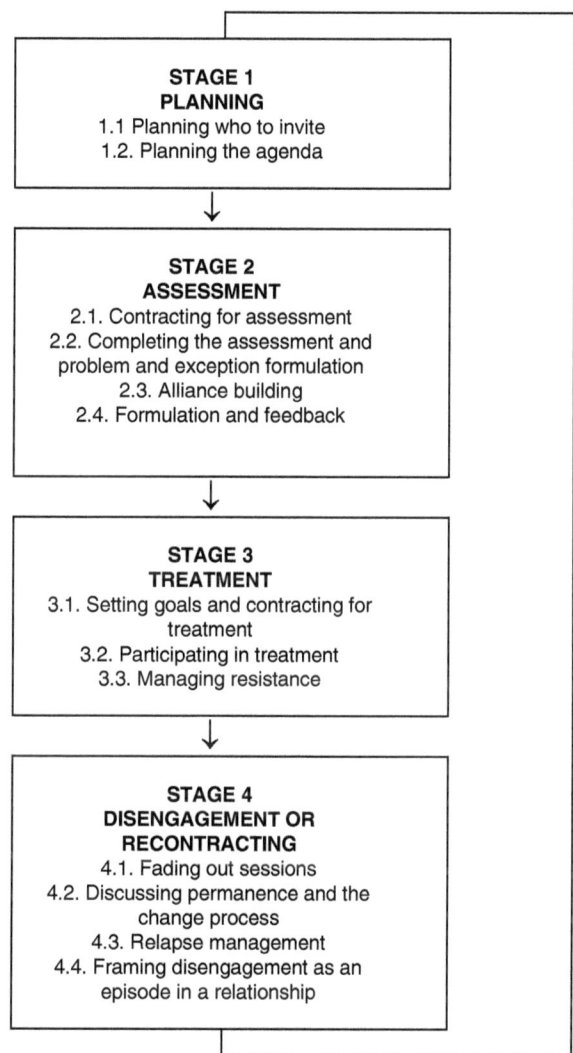

Fig. 11.3 Therapy stages

concerned with planning, the second with engagement and assessment, the third with treatment and the fourth with disengagement or recontracting for further intervention. At each stage, key tasks must be completed before progression to the next stage occurs. Failure to complete the tasks of a given stage in sequence or skipping a stage may jeopardize the consultation process. For example, attempting to conduct an assessment without first contracting for assessment may lead to co-operation difficulties if the couple find the assessment procedures arduous or threatening. Failure to complete the assessment before treatment compromises decision making about goal setting and selecting specific therapy strategies. Therapy is a recursive process insofar as it is possible to move from the final stage of one episode to the first stage of the next. In the remainder of the chapter, the use of the model in routine clinical practice is illustrated with a case study.

11.2 Case Example

Tom and Sue, a white, working class couple in their mid-20s, were referred by a social worker for therapy at a psychology clinic in a UK market town. In the referral letter, the social worker indicated that the couple had multiple problems. Tom had an explosive temper, which was frightening for Sue and her two children. Sue, who had a history of panic attacks, had developed a constricted lifestyle because of fears of having panic attacks outside the home. The couple argued constantly. Although no violence had occurred, the potential for violence led to the referral. The case was referred to social services by a health visitor who became concerned for the welfare of the couple's children, Maeve (4 years) and Mike (1 year), when conducting a routine developmental assessment with Mike around the time of his first birthday. The social worker met with a frosty reception when she visited the couple at their home. They initially insisted that everything was OK and that no family evaluation and support was required. The social worker explained that she had a statutory obligation to evaluate the capacity of parents to provide a safe home environment for the children. In the conversation that followed, the social worker concluded that the couple frequently argued about how best to care for the children. These arguments often escalated towards violence and rarely led to shared decisions. The social worker, therefore, referred the couple for systemic therapy to address the conflict between them, since this was interfering with their capacity to co-operatively meet their children's needs.

11.2.1 Assessment Contracting

From the referral letter, it was apparent that the social worker was the main customer, and the couple were probably ambivalent about attending therapy. Therefore, invitations to the first session were sent to the referring social worker and the couple, with a request that the social worker arrange transportation for the couple to attend the clinic. In the intake meeting, the couple expressed their ambivalence about attending therapy, but the social worker pointed out that if the couple decided not to attend therapy, then their children's names would be placed on an at-risk register held at her department. In light of this information, the couple agreed to attend two sessions during which an assessment would be conducted. If that indicated that they were suitable for therapy a further contract for 10 sessions of therapy would be offered.

11.2.2 Problem Formulation

In developing a problem formulation, diagrammed in Fig. 11.1, we asked Tom and Sue to describe conflictual episodes, detailing how they began, what happened during them, how they concluded and how the next episode started. We asked them about their behaviour, feelings, beliefs and family-of-origin experiences where they

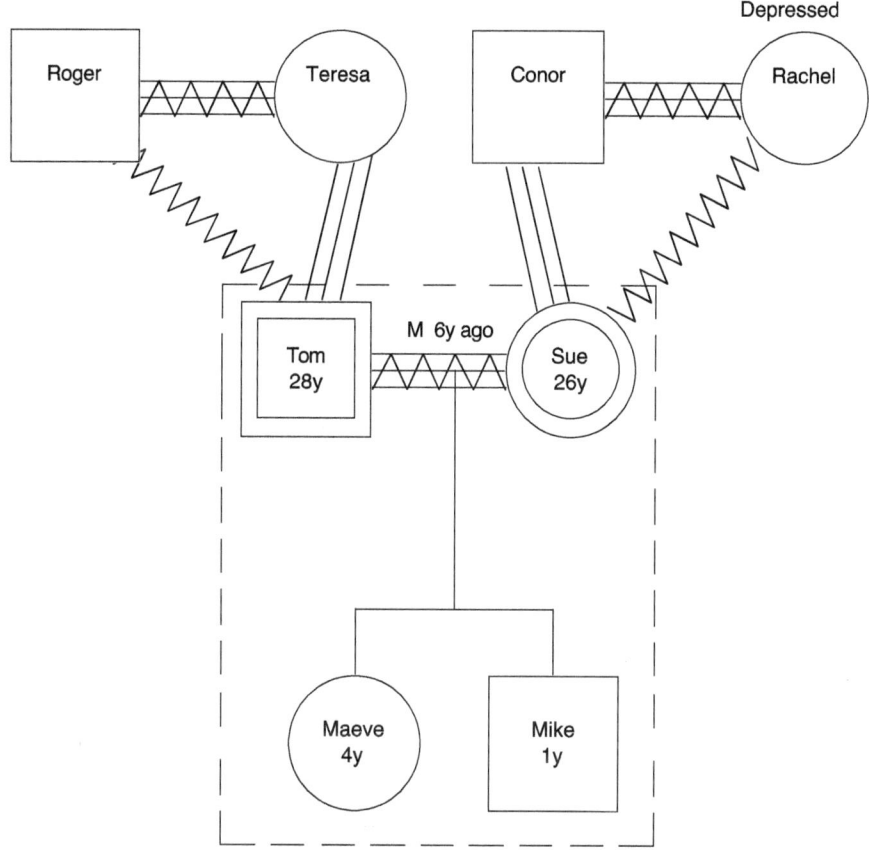

Fig. 11.4 Tom and Sue's genogram

may have learned to respond to each other in the ways that they did during these episodes. A genogram, given in Fig. 11.4, was drawn to clarify family-of-origin relationships. We also observed the family during enactments in which we invited the parents to reach an agreement on how best to schedule regular periods of positive family interaction. The children were present in one of these enactments.

It became clear that Tom's aggression was commonly expressed when Sue had difficulty being attuned to her children's needs and responsive to these in an effective way. Underlying this, Sue had a belief that she was not a good mother and could not meet her children's needs. This belief had its roots in her family-of-origin experiences. She had a longstanding conflictual relationship with her mother, who did not meet her needs responsively, and so lacked a role model for being a responsive parent.

Tom's demands that Sue meet his needs, rather than those of the children, were expressed aggressively, because typically he was angry for having postponed asking Sue to prioritize his needs over those of the children, believing that Sue would inevitably reject or neglect him. These beliefs had their roots in Tom's family-of-origin experiences where his parents had a stormy conflictual relationship.

Sue's difficulty in meeting Tom's needs arose from a feeling of being overwhelmed, by the demands of the children and of Tom. She believed that the demands of the children and Tom were more than she could cope with. This belief in her helplessness arose in part from having grown up in a family where her mother suffered from depression, and frequently expressed beliefs about her own helplessness.

In response to Sue not meeting his needs, Tom, feeling hurt and angry, criticized Sue and escalated his aggressive demands. He behaved as he did during problematic episodes because he believed that Sue was being purposefully uncooperative to punish him, and that it was unfair that she didn't cherish him, because he was devoted to her. Another aspect of his personal narrative was the belief that others, including Sue, were trying to take advantage of him. He had learned this when he was young by observing his father. Tom had a conflictual relationship with his father, who treated his mother as Tom treated Sue.

During conflictual episodes, Sue would initially fight back against Tom's escalating demands, feeling both angry and anxious. Eventually, she would withdraw into anxious silence or, following stressful exchanges, have a panic attack. Sue believed that arguments between couples were competitive exchanges that were won or lost. She believed that she could never beat Tom in an argument and this is why she gave in to him each time, a process that reinforced her beliefs in her own lack of power to influence Tom. Also, when she became distressed she believed that her increased physiological arousal was a sign that she was about to have a heart attack, a belief that often preceded her panic attacks. Sue had learned this way of thinking as a child from her mother who often expressed these types of catastrophic views.

Conflictual episodes would typically conclude with both Tom and Sue withdrawing from each other. Tom would feel hurt and angry at Sue. He would also feel guilty for feeling angry because he did not want to hurt the Sue, whom he loved. Sue would feel anxious that Tom might criticize her again, because in their relationship she saw herself as a helpless victim. She also felt sad to lose support from Tom, whom she loved. The couple would then not be on speaking terms for a few days. Gradually they would have increasingly more contact until the next conflictual episode occurred.

11.2.3 Exception Formulation

In contrast to the problem formulation, a three-column formulation of exceptional episodes in which the problem was expected to occur but did not is given in Fig. 11.2. This formulation of exceptional episodes was based on interviews and observations of family interaction mentioned in the previous section. During exceptional episodes, Tom helped rather than criticized Sue when she was having difficulty with the children. In response, she smiled at him and good feelings between them followed. Tom had learned from his mother that 'a little kindness goes a long way' and it was this story that underpinned his generous behaviour. Tom's mother was well disposed towards the children. Both she and her husband valued them highly, since they were their first grandchildren. Sue had learned that 'one good turn deserves another' from her dad with whom she had a good relationship and this story underpinned her good feelings when Tom was kind to her. Both Sue's father and mother valued the children highly, since they were their first grandchildren.

11.2.4   Treatment Contracting

On the basis of the assessment and the problem and exception formulations, the couple were offered and accepted a contract for 10 sessions of therapy. Their acceptance of the therapy contract was partially due to the strong therapeutic alliance that developed during the assessment sessions. In the treatment manual it is noted that all other features of this approach to systemic practice should always be subordinated to efforts to build a strong working alliance, since without it, research consistently shows that clients drop out of assessment and therapy or fail to make progress. The overall goals for therapy agreed between the couple, the referring social worker and the therapist were to help the couple reduce the level of conflict in their home and increase the safety of the children's parenting environment. The children attended five of the 10 sessions.

11.2.5   Therapy

The following interventions were used in 10 sessions of therapy:

Interactional reframing
Externalizing the problem
Pinpointing strengths
Building on exceptions
Tom's challenge: Self-regulation
Sue's challenge: Being courageous
Managing resistance
Parenting
Building support
Disengagement
Relapse management

The interventions were implemented (broadly speaking) in the order listed, although the therapy was by no means as neat and packaged as it appears in the following description. The selection and implementation of the interventions were informed by the problem and exception formulations in Figs. 11.1 and 11.2, the treatment manual, and also the therapist's creativity, flexibility and clinical judgement in matching interventions to clients' needs.

Interactional Reframing

In the early sessions of therapy, the problem formulation was revisited repeatedly. The couple's difficulties were reframed as an interactional problem rather than as a reflection of personal psychological or moral deficits. There was a gradual moving away from the dominant narrative that each of them suffered from individual psychological problems. This narrative, couched in deficit discourse entailed the view that the main problem was either Sue's 'bad nerves' or Tom's 'short fuse'. As therapy progressed the couple came to understand the family's difficulties as the problematic interaction pattern described in Fig. 11.1, in which a central concern was how to co-operatively respond to the children's needs.

Externalizing the Problem

In the early sessions of therapy, the couple's difficulties were externalized and framed as peripheral to the core of their essentially positive relationship. They were invited to name their problem in a metaphorical way, and in response they began to talk about their problematic episodes, mapped out in Fig. 11.1, as 'the North Wind that blew through their house'. They began to monitor the occurrence of problematic episodes and to withdraw from these if they spotted themselves contributing to them. They referred to this as 'closing the shutters to keep the North Wind out of their house'.

Pinpointing Strengths

Reframing the problem in interactional rather than individual terms, externalizing the problem, naming it in a metaphorical way, and adopting joint ways of combating the problem offered many opportunities to highlight Tom and Sue's personal strengths (e.g., thoughtfulness, courage, persistence) and strengths that characterized their family relationships (e.g., loyalty, warmth, sensitivity, steadfastness). Through naming these strengths, Tom and Sue began to develop a more optimistic narrative about their relationship, and a more positive view of themselves as parents.

Building on Exceptions

The therapy also involved revisiting the exception formulation in Fig. 11.2. The couple were repeatedly invited over the course of therapy to remember and recount, in emotive detail, many exceptional episodes in which the problem might be expected to occur, but did not. Invitations to give accounts of such episodes initially focused on the pattern of interaction, then the underlying personal narratives, and then finally the constitutional, historical and contextual factors that underpinned the positive personal narratives. The similarities between these exceptional positive episodes and other similar past episodes were explored. The couple were also invited to consider what the occurrence of these episodes said about them as a family and how they expected such episodes to recur in the future. Through this process, the couple developed a narrative about their relationship and their family marked by kindness, concern, sensitivity, warmth, closeness, understanding, compassion and many other positive qualities, which they recognized, had always been there and would probably persist into the future. In this way, an optimistic narrative about their family was developed.

Tom's Challenge: Self-regulation

A third aspect of the therapy focused on helping Tom to define himself as a man who was engaged in learning to identify and express his attachment needs in a direct way. He came to talk about himself as a man who was learning to sooth his own sense of panic or anger when he feared his attachment needs would not be met by Sue immediately. In developing this new narrative about the sort of man he was, Tom gradually gave up the story that Sue was to blame for his aggression. He adopted a more optimistic narrative about himself as a man in charge of his own feelings and responsible for his own behaviour. Some skills training was offered to Tom to help him identify and state his needs, and to monitor and contain rising frustration if his needs were not met.

Sue's Challenge: Being Courageous

A further aspect of the therapy focused on helping Sue to define herself as a courageous woman who was learning to accept that a racing pulse and sweaty palms were signals to relax, not panic. To help her revise her personal narrative, Sue was invited to set herself challenges in which she made her pulse race and her palms sweat, and then deal with these challenges by using relaxation skills and support from her partner. She and Tom planned and completed a series of graded challenges. Earlier challenges involved containing and soothing Sue's increased physiological arousal in the therapy sessions. In later challenges, the couple travelled away from the house for gradually increasing distances, until eventually they both went on a date in the city. This was a major achievement for the couple. It consolidated Sue's optimistic story about herself as a courageous woman who was increasingly ready to take on greater challenges in her life.

Managing Resistance

Progress in therapy was intertwined with periods of slow movement, and ambivalence about change. Managing resistance was the main therapeutic activity during these periods. Indeed, as part of the contracting process, we explained to Tom and

Sue that ambivalence about change and resistance to it were an inevitable part of therapy and to be welcomed, since they are an indicator that the therapy is working and change is really happening. Resistance showed itself in many ways. Below, two examples will be mentioned.

While Tom was moving towards defining himself as a man who was engaged in learning to identify and express his attachment needs in a direct way rather than blame Sue for his aggression, progress was not straightforward. He would occasionally doubt that the benefits of defining himself in this new way outweighed the costs of giving up the view that Sue, and not he, was responsible for his aggressive and violent outbursts. When this occurred, we invited Tom to address his personal dilemma about the costs of maintaining the status quo and the costs of changing his situation. He came to see that if he maintained the status quo he could preserve a story about himself as a good man provoked to violence by Sue, but he would have to give up any hope of a truly intimate and loving relationship with her and the two children. This, we suggested was because Sue could not be fully intimate with a man who attacked and blamed her for things that she had not done.

Similarly, progress was far from straightforward when Sue was learning to define herself as a courageous woman. She would occasionally doubt that the benefits of defining herself in this new way outweighed the costs of giving up the view that she was a helpless victim who could justifiably remain cocooned at home forever. When this occurred, we invited Sue to address her personal dilemma about the costs of maintaining the status quo and the costs of changing her situation. She came to see that if she maintained the status quo she could avoid the terror of facing her fear, but she would have to give up any hope of defining herself as a powerful woman in her own right, a competent role model for her daughter, and an equal partner for Tom.

For both Tom and Sue, the theme of abandonment underpinned the catastrophic narrative that fuelled their ambivalence about change. Tom's personal narrative was that if he accepted full responsibility for his anger and violence, then this meant that he was not a good man, and so Sue would have to leave him. Sue's personal story was that as long as she was a helpless terrified victim, Tom would remain to protect her, but if she showed signs of sustained courage and strength, he would leave her to fend for herself. To address these catastrophic narratives, Sue and Tom were invited to explore alternative more optimistic narratives of the future in which Tom could allow himself to be forgiven and accepted by Sue and Sue could allow herself to be on an equal footing with Tom (rather than in a one-down position). The pessimistic narrative of abandonment and the related ambivalence about change receded over the course of therapy as Tom and Sue's more optimistic story about their lives came to the fore.

Parentings

Therapy also focused on inviting the couple to explore their story about themselves as good-enough parents. Parenting issues were addressed in all sessions, but were the central focus of four sessions in particular. Invitations were offered to them to describe ways in which they successfully met their children's needs for safety, security, nurturance, control, intellectual stimulation and age-appropriate responsibilities. Through describing many examples of good-enough parenting and enacting these within conjoint family sessions, Tom and Sue developed a story about themselves as competent, but not perfect parents. This optimistic parenting narrative, led them to ask us for expert advice on parenting skills so that they could improve the way they managed the challenges of child-rearing. It was into this context that behavioural parenting skills training was offered. This covered all the usual skills to enhance parent-child interactions, increase positive behaviours and extinguish aggressive and destructive behaviours. The couple incorporated these skills into their own parenting styles and into their own story about themselves as good-enough parents. This skills training involved direct coaching during conjoint family sessions. During these sessions Maeve (aged 4) began to describe herself as more 'grown up', as viewing her father as a 'gentle daddy' rather than a 'cross daddy' and her mother as 'more fun'.

Building Support

The couple were invited in the middle and later stages of therapy to strengthen their ties with their families of origin. This was not an easy invitation for the couple to accept. Over the years both couples had become increasingly distant from their parents because in each of their families they felt triangulated. This is illustrated in the genogram in Fig. 11.4. During her teens, Sue had gradually become a confidant for her father and was estranged from her depressed mother. Tom, in contrast, had become a confidant for his mother and had frequent conflicts with his father. In both Tom and Sue's families of origin their parents were locked into rigid, close, conflictual patterns of marital interaction. Despite all this, as Tom and Sue's narrative about their own relationship became more hopeful, they became more understanding of their parents' difficulties and were prepared to visit their families of origin more frequently. They let their parents know that they had come through difficult times, but were now hopeful that there were better times ahead, and that they were strong enough to build a good family. This admission of vulnerability and declaration of hope strengthened ties between Tom and Sue and their families of origin. Also, the grandparents, Roger and Teresa, and Conor and Rachel, welcomed the opportunity to spend time with their grandchildren, Maeve and Mike. This created a context within which they could be more supportive of Tom and Sue.

Disengagement

The first 6 sessions were held at weekly or fortnightly intervals. As the family began to make progress, the final 4 sessions were spaced at three to five weekly intervals. Much of the therapy in the last three sessions focused on helping the couple make sense of the change process, develop relapse management plans and understand the process of disengagement as the conclusion of an episode in an ongoing relationship with the clinic rather than the end of the therapeutic relationship. Tom and Sue were invited to forecast the types of stressful situations in which relapses might occur, their probable negative reactions to relapses, and the ways in which they could use the strengths they had discovered in therapy to deal with these relapses.

After 10 sessions a review conducted with the referring social worker indicated that the family was doing much better. The social services department decided that frequent monitoring of the family was no longer necessary. At the review, the following specific treatment gains were noted. In the social worker's view, the conflict between the couple no longer placed the children at risk. The frequency of episodes of conflict between Sue and Tom had reduced from five to one per week and the couple was confident that these arguments would never become violent. Both children were healthy, well-adjusted and were being well cared for. There were marked improvements in Tom's anger management and Sue's panic disorder with agoraphobia. The couple said their marital satisfaction improved. Supportive links with each of their families of origin were strengthened. In short, the therapy goals had been attained.

Relapse Management

A relapse occurred a couple of years later at a time when Sue began working outside the home for the first time since the birth of the first child. After two sessions in which the couple explored ways that they could use their strengths to jointly manage the new challenges in their lives, the frequency of the couple's unproductive arguments reduced again.

Therapist Dilemmas

There were three dilemmas central to the therapists' experience in this case. First, there was the issue of customerhood. Clearly, the main customer initially was the referring social worker, not the family. We addressed this issue by conducting a careful network analysis and inviting the social worker to bring the family to the contracting session and explain the implications of accepting or rejecting an offer of therapy. Second, in this case, there was a statutory requirement to monitor the risk that the parents posed to the children's welfare, and the conflicting requirement for the parents to engage in a trusting therapeutic relationship to reduce this risk. We addressed this dilemma by agreeing that the referring social worker would adopt the statutory risk-monitoring role, and the therapist would adopt an exclusively therapeutic role. A third issue, in this case, was making space for both the narratives of the children and those of the parents. The needs and welfare of the children Maeve and Mike, both of whom were under 5 years were paramount in this case. But the parents, Tom and Sue, were also 'needy clients' with limited personal coping resources. Throughout the therapy, we were mindful of balancing the needs of the children and the needs of the parents. This was challenging because Tom and Sue's stories were well articulated, but specific steps had to be taken to make the implicit narratives of Maeve and Mike more salient. We did this during the assessment sessions through facilitating enactments and commenting on episodes in which the parents made good-enough or ineffective attempts to be attuned to the children's needs and co-operatively meet these. Throughout the ten sessions of therapy, parenting issues were addressed, and parent training was a central focus of 4 sessions. Our approach to parent training involved helping Tom and Sue become attuned to the needs of Maeve and Mike, and in doing so to be able to listen to their implicit or unarticulated narratives. In this sense, Maeve and Mike's narratives were central to the success of this episode of therapy. The therapy as a whole was very demanding and the management of the dilemmas mentioned in this section was addressed in peer supervision, with reference to the manual.

11.3 Summary

In the integrative model of systemic therapy summarized in this chapter and detailed in the treatment manual, therapy is conceptualized as a developmental and recursive process involving the stages of planning, assessment, treatment and disengagement or recontracting, as shown in Fig. 11.3. Specific tasks must be completed at each stage before progressing to the next. For any problem, an initial hypothesis and later formulation may be constructed, informed by Table 11.1 and illustrated by the example in Fig. 11.1. In the initial hypothesis and later problem-formulation the behaviour pattern (and related feelings) which maintains the problem are specified; the constraining narratives and beliefs which underpin the family members' roles in this pattern are outlined; and the broader contextual factors that predispose family members to become involved in these narratives and behaviour patterns are given. In addition, a similar three-column formulation may be constructed to explain exceptional episodes in which problems might be expected to occur but did not happen. This is informed by Table 11.2 and illustrated by the example in Fig. 11.2. These three-column formulation models provide a template for guiding the assessment of problems and strengths and for planning systemic therapy. Therapeutic interventions, listed in Table 11.3, may be classified in terms of the specific domains they target within three-column problem and exception formulations, with some interventions targeting behaviour change, some targeting narratives and beliefs, and others focusing on contextual risk and protective factors. In any specific case, the selection and implementation of interventions are informed by problem and exception formulations for that case. However, therapists must also exercise considerable creativity, flexibility and clinical judgement in matching interventions to clients' needs in any particular case.

References

Carr, A. (1989). Countertransference to families where child abuse has occurred. *Journal of Family Therapy, 11*(1), 87–97. https://doi.org/10.1046/j.1989.00335.x

Carr, A. (1990a). Failure in family therapy: A catalogue of engagement mistakes. *Journal of Family Therapy, 12*(4), 371–386. https://doi.org/10.1046/j.1990.00403.x

Carr, A. (1990b). A formulation model for use in family therapy. *Australian and New Zealand Journal of Family Therapy, 11*(2), 85–92. https://doi.org/10.1002/j.1467-8438.1990.tb00798.x

Carr, A. (1990c). Giving directives effectively: The implications of research on compliance with doctor's orders for family therapy. *Human Systems: Journal of Systemic Consultation and Management, 1*, 115–127.

Carr, A. (1993). Systemic consultation and goal setting. *Human Systems: The Journal of Systemic Consultation and Management, 4*, 49–59.

Carr, A. (1994a). Positive practice: A structured integrative approach to family therapy. *Journal of the Irish Association of Counselling and Therapy, 1*(31), 48–61.

Carr, A. (1994b). Involving children in family therapy and systemic consultation. *Journal of Family Psychotherapy, 5*(1), 41–59. https://doi.org/10.1300/j085V05N01_03

Carr, A. (1995a). *Positive practice: A step-by-step approach to family therapy*. Harwood.

Carr, A. (1995b). Resistance, dilemmas and crises in family therapy: A framework for positive practice. *Journal of Family Psychotherapy, 6*(4), 29–42. https://doi.org/10.1300/j085V06N04_03

Carr, A. (1996). A structured approach to disengagement in family therapy with child-focused problems. *Contemporary Family Therapy: An International Journal, 18*(4), 471–487. https://doi.org/10.1007/BF02195711

Carr, A. (1997a). Positive practice in family therapy. *Journal of Marital and Family Therapy, 23*(3), 271–293. https://doi.org/10.1111/j.1752-0606.1997.tb01036.x

Carr, A. (1997b). Development of positive practice. *Feedback, 7*(2), 23–29.

Carr, A. (1997c). Three stages in the development of an integrative approach to working with families. *Éisteacht: Journal of the Irish Association of Counselling and Therapy, 1*(40), 9–15.

Carr, A. (1999). Positief behandelen in gezinstherapie. *Gezins Therapie, 10*(1), 30–60.

Carr, A. (2000a). Evidence-based practice in family therapy and systemic consultation. II. adult-focused problems. *Journal of Family Therapy, 22*(3), 273–295. https://doi.org/10.1111/1467-6427.00152

Carr, A. (2000b). Evidence-based practice in family therapy and systemic consultation: I: Child-focused problems. *Journal of Family Therapy, 22*(1), 29–60. https://doi.org/10.1111/1467-6427.00137

Carr, A. (2000c). *Family therapy: Concepts, process and practice*. Wiley.

Carr, A. (2002). Compendium of practices for including children in family sessions. In L. D. Miller (Ed.), *Integrating school and family counselling: Practical solutions* (pp. 73–87). American Counselling Association.

Carr, A. (2005). Narratives of hope. In A. Vetere, E. Dowling, & E. (Eds.), *Narrative therapies with children and their families: A practitioner's guide to concepts and approaches* (pp. 268–282). Routledge.

Carr, A. (2006). *Family therapy: Concepts, process and practice* (2nd ed.). Wiley.

Carr, A. (2007). Family therapy training on a clinical psychology programme. *Journal of Family Therapy, 29*(4), 326–329. https://doi.org/10.1111/j.1467-6427.2007.00394.x

Carr, A. (2009a). The effectiveness of family therapy and systemic interventions for child-focused problems. *Journal of Family Therapy, 31*(1), 3–45. https://doi.org/10.1111/j.1467-6427.2008.00451.x

Carr, A. (2009b). The effectiveness of family therapy and systemic interventions for adult-focused problems. *Journal of Family Therapy, 31*(1), 46–74. https://doi.org/10.1111/j.1467-6427.2008.00452.x

Carr, A. (2012). *Family therapy: Concepts, process and practice* (3rd ed.). Wiley.

Carr, A. (2014a). The evidence base for family therapy and systemic interventions for child-focused problems. *Journal of Family Therapy, 36*(2), 107–157. https://doi.org/10.1111/1467-6427.12032

Carr, A. (2014b). The evidence base for couple therapy, family therapy and systemic interventions for adult-focused problems. *Journal of Family Therapy, 36*(2), 158–194. https://doi.org/10.1111/1467-6427.12033

Carr, A. (2016). How and why do family and systemic therapies work? Keynote address to AAFT, Melbourne, 2015. *Australian and New Zealand Journal of Family Therapy, 37*(1), 37–55. https://doi.org/10.1002/anzf.1135

Carr, A. (2017). Narratives of hope. In A. Vetere & E. Dowling (Eds.), *Narrative therapies with children and their families: A practitioners guide to concepts and approaches* (2nd ed., pp. 289–312). Routledge.

Carr, A. (2018). Couple therapy, family therapy and systemic interventions for adult-focused problems: The current evidence base. *Journal of Family Therapy*. https://doi.org/10.1111/1467-6427.12225

Carr, A. (2019). Family therapy and systemic interventions for child-focused problems: The current evidence base. *Journal of Family Therapy, 41*(2), 153–213. https://doi.org/10.1111/1467-6427.12226

Carr, A., & McNulty, M. (2006). Chapter 5. Systemic couples therapy. In A. Carr & M. McNulty (Eds.), *Handbook of adult clinical psychology: An evidence based practice approach* (pp. 157–219). Brunner-Routledge.

Carr, A., & McNulty, M. (2016). Chapter 6. Systemic couple therapy. In A. Carr & M. McNulty (Eds.), *Handbook of adult clinical psychology: An evidence based practice approach* (2nd ed., pp. 161–205). Routledge.

Gurman, A. (Ed.). (2008). *Clinical handbook of couple therapy* (4th ed.). Guilford.

Gurman, A., & Jacobson, N. (Eds.). (2002). *Clinical handbook of couple therapy* (3rd ed.). Guilford.

Gurman, A., & Kniskern, D. (Eds.). (1981). *Handbook of family therapy*. Brunner/Mazel.

Gurman, A., & Kniskern, D. (Eds.). (1991). *Handbook of family therapy* (Vol. II). Brunner Mazel.

Gurman, A., Lebow, J., & Snyder, D. (Eds.). (2015). *Clinical handbook of couple therapy* (5th ed.). Guilford.

Jacobson, N., & Gurman, A. (Eds.). (1986). *Clinical handbook of marital therapy*. Guilford.

Jacobson, N., & Gurman, A. (Eds.). (1995). *Clinical handbook of couple therapy* (2nd ed.). Guilford.

Sexton, T., & Lebow, J. (Eds.). (2016). *Handbook of family therapy* (4th ed.). Brunner-Routledge.

Sexton, T., Weeks, G., & Robbins, M. (Eds.). (2003). *Handbook of family therapy* (3rd ed.). Brunner-Routledge.

Alan Carr, PhD. Professor of Clinical Psychology and Founding Director of the Doctoral Programme in Clinical Psychology at University College Dublin. Couple and family therapist at Clanwilliam Institute, Dublin. He has practiced in Canada, the UK and Ireland. He has written over 20 books and 500 papers and presentations in the fields of clinical psychology, family therapy and positive psychology. His work has been translated into a number of languages including Portuguese, Polish, Korean and Chinese. E. alan.carr@ucd.ie

Chapter 12
Research and Manualisation at ISCRA Institute: The DAN Model: Digital, Analogic, Narrative

Mauro Mariotti, Achille Langella, Nicoletta Scaltriti, and Greco Muratori

12.1 Introduction

Manualization is a way to organize and share meaningful data with methods that have been proved to work. We think of manualization as one of most interesting experiences students should encounter in their training to become psychotherapists. The Iscra Institute began its activity in the field of systemic psychotherapy in 1981, stemming from the Milan School of Boscolo and Cecchin. Up to this date, we have trained more than 1000 psychotherapists, wrote and edited different books as the 'Manual of Systemic and Relational Therapy' (Bassoli et al., 2004), conducted research in the field with our students and prepared a manualization with the use of the best instruments we found or invented during our experience. We called it 'DAN: Digital, Analogical and Narrative Model'. Many tools were invented and experienced in different contexts: The relational style profile (RSP) (Mariotti & Langella, 2011), the tridimensional genogram and the better formed tale (BFT).

RSP: We were struggling with the fact that the triadic questions were sometimes difficult to understand by less reflexive people, but at the same time equally important to use with them. The idea was to split the triadic question in couples of dyads and then let the computer put them together again forming triplets. The RSP follows

---

The original version of this chapter was revised. The correction to this chapter is available at https://doi.org/10.1007/978-3-030-73640-8_34

M. Mariotti (✉) · A. Langella · N. Scaltriti
Iscra Institute of Psychotherapy, Modena and Cesena, Italy
e-mail: dottmauromariotti@gmail.com

G. Muratori
Iscra Institute of Psychotherapy, Modena and Cesena, Italy
Norfolk and Suffolk NHS, Norwich, UK

© Springer Nature Switzerland AG 2021, Corrected Publication 2022
M. Mariotti et al. (eds.), *Handbook of Systemic Approaches to Psychotherapy Manuals*, European Family Therapy Association Series,
https://doi.org/10.1007/978-3-030-73640-8_12

this principle. It is an open door to reflexivity and a way to allow the couple to understand the main family systemic principles.[1]

Tridimensional Genogram: Born simply from playing with wooden blocks, it allows people to clearly represent relationships in their family with an extraordinary and immediate power.

BFT: The better formed tale derives from the better formed story of Carlos Sluzki (1982). We prepared a manualized instrument made by 16 cards with titles and images on them. We ask the family members to co-create a tale with us. Different series of images were selected for the use with children and adults.

Finally, we worked to imagine how to combine the best of these instruments (in our book 'Quaderni di Maieutica', we collected many different tools) in a manualized therapy. We did it under the direction of Mauro Mariotti with the help of Fabio Bassoli, who shaped *the house drawing draft* for the manual, with Achille Langella and Nicoletta Scaltriti whose brilliant brain realized the computerization of the RSPc and the specification of the manual, with Valeria Campanella the first person who loved the RSP more than 10 years ago and with Greco Muratori who helped us with his constant presence during the period he worked with us.

12.2 Research and Manualization at Iscra

National and international associations constantly underline the importance of research in psychotherapy, but only a few among the psychotherapy schools, and even less systemic schools, decided to address this matter systematically. For about 20 years, Iscra has been committed to research, being one of the first schools in Italy to have a whole module dedicated to the topic. Iscra believes that this is the best way to sensitize new therapists on this subject and help them better perform in their role.

In the beginning, Iscra focused on developing new instruments, such as the relational style profile (RSP) and on evaluating the effectiveness of classical systemic tools through microanalysis-based research. Iscra also took part in a research project on the effectiveness of psychotherapy through mentalization processes (Allen et al., 2010) lead by Prof. Franco Baldoni.

Since 2017, the school chose to switch from the study of singular tools to the study of therapeutic processes as a whole. The main purpose of this study is to define the processes that lead the therapist to choose a particular tool in a specific moment and context of the therapeutic process.

A further aim of this study is to evaluate how these choices influence the effectiveness of therapy. Dr. Langella and Dr. Scaltriti, who were first involved in the RSP research as Iscra trainees, became at this point again part of the Iscra research group with the school directors, Dr. Mariotti and Dr. Bassoli.

The group first studied previous research and the available documentation, including videotapes, to build the theoretical structure and to frame the needed recommendations to the therapeutic process.

---

[1] The computer processes the data and in half an hour provides a lot of processual information that the couple is not aware of, promoting deutero-learning.

We defined *a manualized model focus not on procedures but on the processes* of evaluation, elaboration and practice that guide the practitioner's work. We laid the groundwork for this research discussing the base concepts of systemic therapy, such as system, information, relation, coupling, circularity. Our goal was to find a working tool, a definition of therapeutic change through a systemic point of view, useful in guiding the research development.

Change happens when the therapeutic process influences how a system obtains pieces of information about itself and its environment, how it elaborates this information and how much it is aware of how it utilizes and expresses this, conscious of the action's circularity. We inferred that communication is essential to the wellness and richness of the relationship. The working hypothesis was:

> The quality of communication depends on the couple's skill in digital, analogical and narrative aspects of communication: this skill enhances the couple's resources to face life events, both predictable and unpredictable.

Clinical practice has shown us how important the practitioner's freedom and style are to the therapeutic relationship. Using the tools the school had already researched (Bassoli et al., 2004), we defined a base format useful to enhance both the couple's communication and relational processes; the format was respectful of the practitioner's style. This format is not based on a formal, procedural protocol. It is grounded in the communication processes seen by observing the couple's relationship using our tools, based on second-order cybernetics.

The research group involved students in this project in an action research way, engaging them in executing the format and in many discussions and reflexive sessions.

12.3 Format and Principles

We verified our premise through the format we developed and tested in 2018: a further elaboration based on previous format and on research and experiments done with specific tools, like the *RSP*, the *tridimensional genogram* and the better formed tale. These experiments began in 1990. In 2000, the development of a therapy protocol began. This was manualized in seven sessions plus a follow-up: the DAN model.

As previously stated, the idea of manualizing a systemic therapy is born from the necessity to combine the complexity of such an approach with the social research field, aiming to bring together the basics of systemic theory using *digital, analogical* and *narrative* (DAN) tools.

12.3.1 Axioms and Hypotheses

We started from five axioms:

1. The family is one of the main matrices of meaning.
2. The minimum unit of analysis is the triadic relation (Bowen, 1976; Kerr & Bowen, 1988).

3. The minimum family unit has at least three generations.
4. Human systems tend to homeostasis and the process of balancing between morphogenesis and morphostasis is the most difficult task for a family (Bateson, 1977); tuning the individuals inside a family to accept the variation of the life-cycle is essential in reducing symptoms that are often expression of a homeostatic strength aimed to save the system from change (Boscolo et al., 1983).
5. Focusing interventions on parents and grandparents of a toddler will have many different results: the family as a whole learns better forms of communication that will be useful also for the other life cycles they are living or will live (in a family with a new born there might also be an older great grandparent).

The hypotheses:

- Coupling and reflexivity will be two significant predictors of a couple's functioning.
- The use of systemic tools will ease the expression of the relational aspects of couples.
- The analysis of a couple's coupling will highlight the relational style internalized by individuals and will increase reflexivity.
- A good level of knowledge shared through the genogram stories and house drawing will determine a good level of relational harmony.
- The narrative use of the BFT and the coat of arms, also called heraldic shield (description at p. 20), will introduce transformative elements within the narrated story.
- The assignment of homework will ease the emergence of strengths and weaknesses within the family system, increasing the couple's reflexivity in a final analysis.

12.4 DAN Synopsis

The DAN is a manualized therapeutic intervention dedicated to couples. We initially worked with 'peri-matrimonial' couples (generally stable couples, with no children or with children up to 3 years of age). The choice of this range is to obtain a homogeneous sample, which will also be easier for trainees to acquire. Working with such couples, the main objective is prevention.

- The intervention's aim is to make couples gain a series of skills, which are hypothesized to represent protective factors to individuals' and couples' psychological well-being.

We work on a conceptual continuum that ranges from a digital level (more rational and guided), a narrative one (in which the couple has more freedom to express itself and can make the most of its creativity) to an analogical one (see Table 12.1 below). Each 'level' is paired with a specific clinical tool used in each session and with specific homework assigned to the couple.

The reasoning behind this therapeutic intervention is the hypothesis that the couple that experiences these situations and abilities in a safe environment will then be able to make use of them to maintain a significant level of well-being whenever its homeostatic structure may be jeopardized.

Table 12.1 Overview of the DAN tools

	Tool	Skills gained	Homework
Digital	RSP	Ability to observe oneself and the other Ability to understand one's own behaviour and that of the other, as a function of the couple system Ability to recognize personal habits, their underlying rules and roles deriving from these	Role reversal (the aim is to provoke a system disturbance, to make the couple aware of its flexibility)
Analogical	Three-dimensional genogram Home draft	Ability to provide a meaning to events that take place throughout time Ability to communicate one's personal and couple experiences with the other, identifying how these may affect the couple itself Ability to link space, time and emotions	Each couple member must bring an object with personal emotional value and a letter in which they explain its meaning The letter will be read and discussed in the following session (shifting from the 'representation' to the 'narration' of what emerged from the tridimensional genogram) Videotaping of a normative family meal (lunch or dinner), lasting approximately 15 min. The video is brought to the following therapy session, where the therapist will make comments on the triadic interactions and on the reflexivity taking place in it
Narrative	Better formed story	Ability to talk within the couple, to listen to each other and to build a shared product (a story) from this	Better formed story

12.4.1 Session Structure

The different meetings take place over 16 weeks (see Table 12.2) or in 20 weeks, if a follow-up after 2 months is included.

This structure concerns the therapeutic intervention in question. To evaluate the outcomes, we opted for the SCORE-15 index of family functioning and change (Stratton et al., 2010, 2014). We adapted it to the needs of our research. Working with non-pathological families, we avoided the use of pathological terms. The SCORE had been administered three times, the third time being the one with best results.

12.5 The DAN Manual in Practice

The original way to apply the DAN will be described here.

The research group – formed of students from the four academic years of the Iscra Institute – autonomously worked on finding families with small children and

Table 12.2 The 2018 DAN structure

Weeks after beginning therapy	Session	Content	Homework
0	1	Intervention is described, the therapeutic relationship is formed; administration of the SCORE	
1	2	Administration of individual RSP; clinical discussion	
2	3	RSP feedback	Role reversal
3			
4 (1 month of therapy)	4	Homework is returned; administration of the three-dimensional genogram; house drawing	Object and letter
5			
6	5	Homework is returned; SCORE	Family meal video
7			
8 (2 months of therapy)	6	Homework is returned and discussed	
9			
10	7	Better formed story	Story formation
11			
12			
13			
14 (3 months of therapy)	8	Dismissal ritual (coat of arms)	
15			
16	9	Follow-up and SCORE administration	

conducted the manualized therapies. This pilot study included about 30 families. At present, we have a contract with family paediatricians who refer families to our institute.

The project consists of seven sessions, plus one follow-up:

First session: The couple is informed of the ethical considerations connected to the themes. Subsequently, the SCORE outcome measure (Stratton et al., 2010) is administered. The therapist listens to the family.

Second session (1 week after): Administration of the tridimensional genogram to the couple.

Third session (1 week after the second one): The relational style profile couple interviews are administered individually.

Fourth session (takes place 1 week after the third): Feedback regarding the relational style. The SCORE is administered once again. The couple is given homework assignments, which are mainly based on inverting the roles that emerged from the RSPc.

Fifth session (2 weeks after the fourth one): The couple reports their homework's outcomes. The therapist provides feedback. They then go on to focus on the problems and on how to solve these.

Sixth session (2 weeks after the fifth one): The better formed tale (BFT) is administered to the couple and carried out together with the therapist. At the end of the session, the couple is assigned to perform a BFT at home.

Seventh session (takes 1 month after the sixth one): A dismissal ritual is performed with the making of the coat of arms by the couple.

Eighth session: Two months after the seventh session, a follow-up meeting with the family takes place, and the SCORE is administered once again.

12.6 Tools

12.6.1 The Digital Section: The RSPc

The RSPc is a structured interview that was developed because of the desire to replicate essential elements of the systemic therapeutic conversation in a proceduralized way (Mariotti & Langella, 2011).

The interview has three different sections: a brief introduction outlining the interview's objectives and the basic information regarding the subject and the couple; a part on 'generative forces' – that is, how each subject differentiated themselves from their own parental figures; in the third section – which concerns the couple's relationship – reflexive questions are overlapped in a 'dichotomy-environment matrix structure' (Mariotti & Langella, 2011) using triadic questions.

Data Interpretation

From the second part, relating to generative forces, four categories are obtained: *fusional/dependent, similar/differentiated, mediatory/aversive and mixed*. They describe the type of relation from the couple member and his or her parent.

Through the elaboration of the third part relating to the 'performative styles', an analysis of the dichotomies combined to the significant life contexts is obtained, allowing for a descriptive in-depth analysis of significant semantic value, visually identifying how a dichotomy may become harmful or may favour resilience. For instance: 'Is an order/chaos dichotomy good or bad regarding family or regarding friendship'?

The cross-comparison of the answers that each participant has provided to the triplet of questions provides information regarding similarities between the two participants, their abilities to recognize each other and their reflexivity – that is to say, whether each one is aware of how their partner would like them to be and to what degree such awareness is present.

Fig. 12.1 An example of a completed tridimensional genogram

More specifically, the processual aspects relating to the life phase in which the couple finds itself at present are observed in the first subtest; the process relating to the individual style – acquired within the family system – should emerge from the second subtest; the variability introduced by the structural coupling with the partner, should emerge from the third subtest.

12.6.2 The Analogical Section: The Tridimensional Genogram

The Tridimensional Genogram represents an original form of the use of the genogram, using coloured wooden blocks (see Fig. 12.1), with a particular focus on the relational distance between significant people and generational boundaries.

The parental couple is asked to represent, each in their own area of the table, their own past, including their family of origin and, if present, any significant people known outside of the family context. Subsequently, working together, they represent their present time and hypothesized future.

The tridimensional genogram therefore becomes a powerful tool, because:

- The use of wooden blocks makes administration as simple as it is informative.
- The choice of shapes, colours and distances provides information on the level of openness of the individual.

- It becomes a tool for the meta-communication of meanings.
- The operating styles emerge from the intertwining of three factors:
  - The form assumed by the interactive behaviours implemented by the family members.
  - The type of rules that inform family action.
  - The way in which each family builds reality.

Therefore, the subject of study becomes the vision of the world shared in the family how this determines its functioning.

12.6.3 The Narrative Section: The Better Formed Tale

The therapist and the clients sit around a table.

The therapist shows the couple the cards with different pictures on them and the writings representing the stimulus words, and they introduce the 'task': 'Today we are playing a game with images. Out of the cards I have shown you, you must choose the one that strikes you the most, and on this card, we will write a story together that must have some reference to your own story/that must be metaphorically connected to your story…'.

As the couple chooses, the therapist takes note of comments and considerations.

The therapist asks one or the other: 'What is it that hit you about the card you have chosen?'; they listen to the answer and take note of it.

The therapist continues by saying: 'You have chosen this card, which we will now use as a starting point for the construction of the story. Each of us, in turns, will add a piece of the story, taking as a starting point one of the images of the card. I'll start by considering the title…' The therapist could also start with a standard sentence, such as: 'Once upon a time, there was a couple who…' and then refer to the title.

The therapist begins the story and then passes the card, and the word, to one of the two couple members, inviting them to continue. Once they have finished, the therapist asks them to pass the card to their partner, who must pass it to the therapist once again, when they have finished their story.

The therapist co-constructs the story, in turns, with the couple. When it is the therapist's turn (on the third and the sixth image), they must tell the story from the beginning, to consolidate it. Furthermore, the therapist adds a transformative element, a positive change aimed at emphasizing the couple's resources.

Finally, the therapist provides a summary of the performed task, in which the issues addressed and the transformative potential are reviewed, including the couple in this final activity.

The therapist asks the couple to repeat the same exercise at home with their children.

When administering the BFT, the therapist must keep in mind the following points:

The therapist introduces elements metaphorically linked to the history and the problem narrated by the family, then adds elements of reality. In this regard, it is interesting to note whether the couple reacts by remaining on the fantasy level, or by passing to the realm of reality. The therapist must provide a positive connotation of the various cardinal elements of the couple's 'real' story, reinforcing positive relationships and emphasizing good intentions. The BFT that is assigned to do at home is a training for what they will do at home with their children. The cards we give to them for use at home are children adapted and the task is to perform a game to co-construct a better formed tale.

12.7 The Final Version of the DAN Model

The 2018 format is a prevention process carried out by the two psychologists and aimed at couples with young children. We presumed that better communication and relational skills within the couple result in better parenting skills. Eighteen families with at least one child over 3 years of age were the sample for this part of the project. We required that neither the families nor the individuals within the sample were taking part in another form of psychological therapy, so that the sample was a non-clinical one. We set up the format trying to balance the processual input we developed with the uniqueness of the systemic-relational setting, which mandates the therapists the freedom to relate to the system in attendance.

The format consists of seven sessions plus one follow-up session.

At this point in the project, the format dictates that the system works primarily on a digital level, then on an analogical one and last on a narrative level. This sequence is not mandatory but it follows an inner logic. The digital tools allow the couple members to get to know each other better with low emotional impact.

The homework between different sessions introduces emotions in the system. With each session, the focus switches from how the couple is to the way the couple interacts. Narrative tools in the last two sessions represent a natural way to conclude the intervention. They enhance the wrap-up and the closure of the format. At the same time, they increase the ability to connect the dots in our lives and add meaning and value. The time frame between sessions is initially short, providing frequent sessions to improve attention and compliance. The subsequent sessions become less frequent to give the couple enough time to do the homework, process the contents and let them set in.

We scheduled lectures about each tool and continuous supervision during the training year. Trainees' feedback allowed us to refine the format and tools to enhance the project's outcomes. The 2018 format was structured as follows (Table 12.3), which was then developed in the current structure (Table 2):

Table 12.3 The 2018 DAN structure

	Content	Homework
After…	Practice explain, history collection, genogram	
1 week	RSP and SCORE	Photograph choice
1 week	RSP and photograph choice discussion	Role reversal
2 weeks	Role reversal discussion, 3D genogram	Object and letter
2 weeks	3D genogram discussion, systemic house drawing, SCORE	
2 weeks	Better formed tale	Tales
2 weeks	Coat of arms	Coat of arms
1 month	Follow-up and SCORE	

12.8 Tools

12.8.1 Genogram

Thinking about systemic psychology, one of the first tools that surely come to mind is the genogram. This tool, introduced by Bowen (1976), has become irreplaceable not only for systemic therapies but also for most family therapy due to its ability to promote questions and reflections resulting from the redundancies and/or oppositions between the history of individuals and generations.

Starting from the classical structure of the genogram, various authors have made changes that in some cases transform the genogram and allow for a collection of different data from the initial purpose.

What most instruments derived from the original genogram have in common is the use of conventional symbols that allow us to represent, typically on paper, the relations of kinship and the relational quality, often accompanied by information on residence, on employment. Another common type of information is when the events occur over time.

Within the process, the genogram is used as an 'opening' tool with a double goal: on the one hand, it allows for the gathering of significant information in little time and allows the system to start making the first hypotheses; on the other, it is a way to test the couple's ability to shift their focus from a contingent problem to its course and timing.

Use in Practice

For its administration, at least one A4 plain sheet is required and one or more pens.

We recommend filling out the genogram so that it is also visible to the couple and describing the signs so that it can still interact and participate in the completion of the genogram.

In filling it out, we use the 'classic' rules, and therefore, the genogram must contain information about four generations, starting from the grandparents of the couple to their children. It will also contain the date of birth, death, marriages, separations as well as information on the level of education, occupation, residence and any specifics that may emerge from the discussion during its administration.

Obviously, the main focus is on the couple and its main relationships. The further away we get, the less relevant the data will be.

Purpose

The administration of the genogram has, as we have already said, first of all a strategic aim: to help the couple focus on the objective, the context, their own individual and relational history and how this influences their relationships, primarily with their children.

Another task of the genogram is to guide, allowing to collect objective information that will be the stepping stone for the subsequent instruments. We expect that the 'actors' that emerge from the genogram are the same ones that will be represented in the following exercises; the presence or lack of key actors can help therapists recognize possible points of friction in the couple's history.

12.8.2 RSP, Photograph Choice and Role Reversal

Among the instruments developed by the school, probably the one on which more research has been carried out is the RSP. This is a clinical tool that allows to obtain from the interviewee a wide range of information starting from some questions on the representations of themselves and the emotionally significant subjects which constitute the internalized generative figures[2] who act in the construction and maintenance of relationships.

This information is generally accumulated by people, but not operationalized, not mentalized. The RSP, in contrast, intends to help couples and therapists build a graph of the relational correlations of individuals with their family of origin and partner. This graph gives the couple the possibility to see how they work in the differentiation process from their family of origin; it shows in which areas there is complementarity and in which symmetricity, in order to identify potential origins for some points of strength or fragility of the couple in their ability to face the inner and relational world, giving a measure of the validity of the coupling.

---

[2] With 'internalized generative figures', we refer not only to the maternal and paternal figures, but also to the set of indications and expectations that parents transmit to the child. For simplicity, in RSP we refer to these as parental ideal.

In about an hour of administration and half an hour of data interpretation by the therapist, the RSP makes it possible to obtain a large amount of information for the results discussion, but also as a starting point in subsequent sessions.

The interview is divided into two sections, called *generative* and *performative*.

In the first section, the relationship between the individual, his parents and the perceived parenting ideal is investigated, asking where they are placed on a series of dichotomous continuums, simply called dichotomies.

In the second one, the individual is asked to indicate the position of the self, of the partner and of their ideal partner perceived in a matrix that includes the dichotomies and the relational object.[3]

Dichotomies and the Relational Object

The dichotomies used in the interview were initially chosen empirically. Therefore, the first data collected with the RSP were subjected to statistical analysis to select the meaningful and non-overlapping dichotomies.

The current dichotomies, which refer to the most significant categories in the field of mental health, are:

- *Optimism/Pessimism* concerns the field of constraints and possibilities, the attitude that each of us has towards everyday challenges. Optimistic people are more confident, they tend to recognize the available resources more easily, to see the glass half full; pessimistic people tend to see it half empty, they recognize the limits more, towards which they pay more attention.

- It pushes the individual to define him or herself and to define the other in the perspective of freedom and constriction, of self-esteem and the other. Those who are more optimistic in intimacy are more confident and hopeful. Those who are more pessimistic see more clearly the problems and difficulties with which the couple clashes.

- *Order/Chaos* investigates how people manage their activities and relationships. Ordered people tend to a stable, predictable organization and favour situations in which they perceive greater security; chaotic people maintain a freer, unpredictable organization and are more open to experimentation. This dichotomy concerns the subject's field of orientation between the need for information repetitiveness to maintain the homeostasis of an ordered system and the generation of new information through the continuous opening of new processes.

- *Body/Mind* investigates the style of reaction to individuals' life events; in its place between the two soma/psyche extremes on the somatopsychic equilibrium, the individual is his or her elective modality of response to stimuli. Those who place themselves towards the pole of the body tend to act in a more instinctive,

---

[3] Relational objects: we refer to those concentric relational spaces in which the various relational figures of reference are orbiting. The focus in the RSP is placed in particular on those relational objects most involved in the couple's life.

impulsive and emotional way; those who place themselves towards the pole of the mind tend to react to life events in a more thoughtful, rational and reflective way.
- *Male/Female* regards stereotypes on gender identity. It leads to reflect on the imaginary components of the self's identity: aggressiveness, audacity, assertiveness, resourcefulness, action and exploration as masculine stereotypical components and the ability to wait, care, listen sensitively as female stereotypes. For example, 'male' individuals tend to be proactive and guiding, 'female' ones tend to comply and be guided.

Subsequently, the dichotomies are crossed with the following relational objects to give greater scope to the current ones and to gather more information.

- *Intimacy*: This refers to the relationship life between partners. The field of intimacy includes not only the physical/sexual relationship but also the aspects of trust, esteem and sharing that allows partners to express their values and feelings, mutually accept their limitations and support the potential of the other, sharing their fragility and forgiving each other's mistakes.
- *Affectivity*: This refers to the set of the most significant family and friendship relationships for the couple, the inner circle of relationships.
- *Daily Life*: This indicates the scope of tasks related to everyday life and daily commitments.
- *Career*: That is to say, the field of personal, work and economic realization.

Use in Practice

The therapist and co-therapist administer the RSP to the members of the couple separately according to the indications of the relative sheets (question sheet and answer sheet), then gather the couple and inform them that the results will be discussed in the following session. More specifically, they explain that the RSP aims to identify the personal characteristics of how relationships are constructed and it allows hypothesizing about how a couple 'performs'. The 'answer sheet' is given and the therapist asks questions related to the 'generative forces', concerning how the individual differentiated from his or her parental figures. The therapist then asks questions related to 'performative forces', concerning the individual's perceptions about his or her current relationship and how it is co-influenced with their main areas of life. At the end of the administration, the couple is reunited and the therapist provides instructions for the first home task, the 'photographs choice': he or she asks each member to individually imagine the suggestions resulting from the RSP and to individually choose five photos that recall those characteristics. The first three photos must have something to do with a personal memory, dating back to before the couple was formed or referring to an event in which the other member of the couple is peripheral; the other two instead must relate to situations in which the couple is the protagonist.

In the following session, the third, the RSP output is discussed and the contents are compared with those that the individuals bring through the images they have chosen.

For the discussion on the RSP results, the therapist follows this scheme:

- She or he firstly discusses the generative profile of both members individually, then evaluating how the emerged profiles interact.
- She or he shows the graph of the 'generative position' and explains the hypothesis that the more two people are illustrated as close to each other, the more they are supposed to have similar ways of approaching relationships.
- She or he explains the results of the performative indexes to the couple, focusing on the positive and growth aspects.

During the discussion, the therapist asks if the couple recognize themselves in the description, individually and as a couple and if they found the photos reflect some of these aspects or not.

Then, the therapist proposes the second home task, the 'role reversal', starting from what emerges from the discussion and the data from the scoring. For the role reversal, each couple member is asked to behave oppositely to their usual mode in a specific situation, generally, one that is routine and/or emotionally meaningful.

Purpose

The RSP and its related homework form the core of the digital part of the format, as it is expected that they will allow us to gather an initial series of information useful to create a basis for the conversation that will be useful both during the return and in the subsequent sessions.

The homework aims to help the couple recognize the importance of balancing individual descriptions. The *photograph choice*, in particular, allows them to recognize how much of the story that they tell of themselves, brought into the session through the pictures and corresponds or not to the concise description the partner has of them. On the other hand, the *role reversal* highlights how the couple is capable of breaking their behavioural patterns, what emotions and resistances 'putting oneself into the other's shoes' produces, to help the couple recognize how their individual roles operate to help or hold the couple in a routine that is evermore the same, until it became a source of conflict.

12.8.3 Tridimensional Genogram and Object and Letter

The *tridimensional genogram* constitutes a significant variation of the classic *genogram*, the attention is no longer on the genealogy but on the composition of the individual's social network and how this was constructed and deconstructed over time in the interaction with that of their partner. The tridimensional genogram allows people to immediately represent the emotional/supportive aspects of their significant relationships and, in the same way, leads them to think about the importance that relationships have in the construction of their world.

The depth of the representation is made possible by the variety of ways, colours, shapes, distances that individuals have at their disposal to represent something as complicated as being in a relationship. The possibility to use shapes, colours and construction to communicate allows people to freely choose to use the channels that feel more similar, with a more or less accurate description.

If the RSP provides a comparison between the individual generative relational nuclear models and the most important performative relationship, the tridimensional genogram inserts the dimension of time into the discussion, connecting the couple to construct three distinct representations:

- The Past Genogram: The therapist asks both individuals to describe their relationships before the composition of the couple, through the pieces of coloured wood in place.
- The Present Genogram: The two previous constructions collide into a single one, highlighting how the 'relational we' of the couple and providing information on how the couple manages the current relational network.
- The Future Genogram: This brings the couple to tell each other and the therapists their expectations regarding the future of the relational network and the family configuration.

The related exercise, Object and Letter, is a simple exercise that fits into the category of 'classic' homework and is designed to bring up emotions linked to the founding elements of the couple's relationship.

Use in Practice

The therapists prepared the desk placing the box with the pieces in the middle, in order to divide the 'building space' of each couple member. The therapist asks the couple to think back at the time just before the formation of their couple and to represent their families and their supportive friendship network through the pieces contained in the box.

Once the couple has completed the construction, they are asked, in turn, to indicate which piece represents the self and what the other pieces represent.

After the individuals have described their genograms, the therapist asks separately if this representation reflects how much they knew about the other; they then ask the other partner if he or she thinks we should add, remove or move a single piece, to better reflect how he or she understands the other's relational network in the past.

The box containing the pieces is moved, to remove the separation between the two genograms, but leaving the pieces in the box available for use. The therapist explains that the compositions on the desk represent the network of relationships from which their couple was born and that he or she would like them to illustrate how this has changed, through a portrayal of their current network.

The therapist starts this part of the exercise asking if they think that the pieces that represent them should be closer, as they are now a couple and invites them to move the various pieces according to their current perception.

The therapist explains that, if the people of the past are still present, the same or different pieces can be used and that they can use the pieces in the box to eventually add other people.

When the couple finishes this part, the therapist asks them to indicate which characters from the past genogram are still present and which characters have been added. Then he or she asks both couple members to describe them. The therapist asks them individually if this representation reflects what their family network and important friendships are today and asks if, in retrospect, they would like to add, remove or move a single piece. As for the future genogram, the therapist asks how they expect their network will change 3 years from now and to represents this by modifying the present genogram. When the couple completes the construction, the therapist invites them to indicate which people have changed and for what reason; they are then asked to describe the new people. The therapist asks the members of the couple if some pieces have changed position. After the two have described the genogram, the therapist asks them, individually, if this representation reflects their expectations and he or she asks if they would like to add, remove or move a single piece.

Once the tridimensional genogram has been discussed, the delivery will be explained by the subject and letter task.

The therapist asks each member of the couple to identify an object (a song or a photo of the object if this cannot be brought into the session) that for the individual refers to the couple – something related to the beginning or to a milestone in their story as a couple. Subsequently, they are asked to write a letter to the partner in which they explain why they chose that particular object. The letter and the object must be kept hidden from the partner until the following session, in which the two members will show the object and read the letter in front of the therapist. The therapist and co-therapist pay particular attention to the emotions that the exercise arouses.

The therapist asks to show the object and to read the letter, then he or she proceeds with some questions on how they each think their content is taken by the other. After the reading, the therapist asks the members if they are surprised by the choice of the object and the meaning (as well as the importance it has for the other).

The therapists summarize the homework, bringing the focus on the similarities/differences in choosing and telling an important event of their life as a couple and about the ability/difficulty to recognize the event as important for the other.

Purpose

During the session, the therapists gather information both from the structure and composition of the genogram and from the emotions aroused by the exercise.

In particular, their attention is focused on the movement 'in time' of the pieces deemed as significant and on 'plausible' changes that do not occur.

As a guide for reading the tool, we recommend using the following questions as a pattern:

- Which channels (shapes, colours, relative positions) did the individuals and the couple use during the construction of the tridimensional genogram? Did they use a single or multiple channels?
- Do the representations have congruence between what is expressed verbally and how much is represented?
- Do the members of the couple have a common way of representing and verbalizing relationships?
- Are the parts built by one member of the couple understandable to the other?
- Does the representation of the present appear to be balanced between the two or does the part built by one appear more important than the other?
- Does the representation of the future appear realistic?

From these considerations, details emerge on what we have defined as four 'dimensions', elements emerging from the exercise that reflect the internal representations of the couple:

- *Richness*: This refers to the ability to use what the couple has at their disposal (colour, shapes, distances) to communicate something of their relational network. The hypothesis is that descriptive richness influences the ability to externalize the qualities of relationships.
- *Harmony*: The couple's ability to find an agreement on the rules for the composition of the genogram. The hypothesis is that a couple with harmony can negotiate on relationships while maintaining a low level of conflict.
- *Equilibrium*: This indicates whether the representations are built up equally by the members of the couple or if one prevails over the other. The hypothesis is that a couple with a good balance has harmonically integrated relational networks.
- *Knowledge*: The degree of knowledge that one has of the relationship network of the other. The hypothesis is that good knowledge indicates the ability to recognize the nuance of the partner's social network.

The role of the 'Object and Letter' homework, as mentioned above, is to shift the attention of the system towards those memories that constitute the 'history' of the couple. In our clinical experience, as we expected, the elements that emerge from the task are always very emotionally rich and powerful generators of stories and memories, often bringing the couple to remember a problem-free time. This shifts the attention from the details of the story to the emotions of the time, allowing a comparison with the current ones, particularly when the couple is in a non-fluid relational situation.

12.8.4 Systemic House Drawing

While the tridimensional genogram widens the field analysis to the extended relational network of the couple, the systemic house drawing (Bassoli, 2008) focuses on the central core of those who live in the house, who share the most important and private physical spaces.

The systemic house drawing offers the opportunity to visualize the dynamics of balance and relational boundaries in a quick and easily shared way. The house is, in most cases, the place where the family eats, sleeps, lives and consequently reflects its affinities and differences.

The work is guided by some questions that focus on these issues: where the house is, who lives in the places and when, how and why certain spaces and not others, if there is a difference in experiencing the house among the members.

This analogical mode of analysing family balances allows the couple to communicate information more quickly, in a way that they are not necessarily aware of; it allows the therapists to gather important knowledge on the relational dynamics within the family.

As with the tridimensional genogram, chronological work is also done with the systemic house drawing, gathering information on the home that the two individuals recognize as originating, the 'house of the past', on the 'house of the present' and on the 'house of the future', which investigates not realistic expectations, as in the tridimensional genogram, but wishes, hopes or disillusions about the future composition of the nuclear relational network.

Use in Practice

The therapists ask the couple to draw a few maps. It is not important that the drawing respects all the proportions, as questions will be asked about the people who are in the various houses and their relationships.

The therapist hands over two sheets to the couple and three pens or pencils of different colours.

The therapist explains that he or she wants a diagram of their main parental house, the one to which they are more connected, remembering that they can draw it without worrying about respect for the square footage or the precise shape.

When this task is complete, the therapist asks the couple (if they have not already) to describe the various places in the house, paying attention to the description strategy.[4]

The therapists ask, specifically, to indicate who 'inhabits' the rooms most of the time (e.g. favourite rooms to do what).

---

[4] With description strategy, we refer to how the couple describes the house (from which room they start, what the logic of adding the rooms is and if they are characterized with objects). We are also interested in whether this strategy arises from the couple or from a single member.

The therapist asks each member which, in their opinion, is a characteristic that struck them – then or today – of the other's home or of how the rooms were used in her main parental house.

A new sheet of the same size as the previous ones is given to the couple; the therapist explains that they want to see their present home that they would like a drawing done by both members of the couple, without worrying too much about respecting the square footage or the shape.

The therapist asks each member how much the present house is different from their past home. If it is possible to find signs of the peculiar characteristics of the parental house, what inheritance has been transmitted.

The therapist asks (if they have not already done so) to describe the various places in the house, paying attention again to the description strategy.

He or she asks to indicate who 'occupies' the rooms most of the time (e.g. preferred rooms to do what).

If applicable, the therapist asks the couple why some rooms have been excluded from the description.

The therapists give one last sheet and ask the couple to draw their home as they would like it to be in the future, in 3 years. It is specified that this is an imagination exercise that they can decide to move where they want, add or remove rooms, modify existing ones without worrying about 'reality'.

The therapists observe the way the couple regulates themselves in drawing the house.

The therapist asks the couple to describe the various places in the house, who and when they occupy the various rooms, noting the strategy of describing the various rooms.

If it has not been made clear, the therapist asks what are the main differences between this house and the present one.

Then the therapists, working together with the couple to bring into the spotlight the discrepancies and redundancies between how the various houses are experienced and inhabited, ask whether there are connections or not with the family structure described in the tridimensional genogram.

Purpose

The goal of the systemic house drawing is to focus on the pragmatic and emotional aspects in the organization of everyday life, through the metaphorical use of the house drawing.

For example, it might be less emotionally stressful for a wife to reveal that her husband 'lives' between the couch and the bed rather than declaring that his work does not allow him to be part of the family's everyday routine.

12.8.5 Better Formed Tale and Fables

The better formed tale is a narrative tool that allows the couple to experience their ability to use metaphors to emphasize the cornerstones of their history, to try to read them from a different angle and reconstruct them in a coherent narrative form that can be shared in the couple and with the whole family.

The instrument is composed of two sets of 15 boards, one developed for adults and the other for children; both series include tables composed of five pictures and one sentence.

Each card is built to stimulate different considerations: in the adult set, images and phrases refer to the phases of the life cycle and the formation of couples; the children's one concerns the challenges that a child has to face in their growth (Fig. 12.2).

The session is done using the 15 adult cards.

The therapist starts the session by distributing the boards on the surface and explaining that they will be asked to construct a story that tells, through images, an aspect of their being parents and/or a couple; they are then asked to choose a table that will be the basis of the story.

The therapist starts the story using the sentence and then explains that, in turn, everyone will use one of the five images as a stimulus to add a part of the story until all the pictures have been used.

WHO COULD HAVE GUESSED IT?

Chi lo avrebbe mai detto?

Fig. 12.2 Use in practice

When the table returns to the therapist, they use the third image to introduce a better formed element[5] as a contribution to the story.

After the fifth image is used, the therapists:

- If they believe that the contribution given by the member of the couple who uses the last image has concluded the story, they ask the other member of the couple what they think of the conclusion and if they would have chosen a different one; they then ask the other why they chose that ending.
- If they believe that the story looks unfinished, they propose a different ending, more related to the elements of the better formed story, asking the couple if they accept this closure or would prefer a different one. They accept the couple's proposal.

After the discussion, the therapist explains that, as a homework task for the next session, the same exercise should be performed with their children. The children's tables are then given to the couple, explaining that they will decide together whether to be satisfied with the conclusion of the story or to propose another.

Purpose

The better formed tale constitutes a metaphoric activity that allows the couple and the therapist to tell the story of the family, experiencing – through the therapist's interventions during the exercise or later in the discussion – the transformative effect of paying attention to performative rather than destructive aspects; the same story acquires new nuances. For example, the focus may be placed on the absence of a husband to work on his career or to support the family, which keeps him away from home.

12.8.6 Coat of Arms

The 'Coat of Arms' (also referred to as 'heraldic shield') is a narrative tool that stimulates in the couple a vision of their problems to create a frame that helps them observe their situation in a broader temporal field, inserting the current situation in the flow of their own story.

---

[5] With "better formed element," we refer to the indications of C. Sluzki (2012) for a better formed story that must include a temporal dimension that presents evolutions, change, progress and hope in balance between stability and change; depicts the participants in a favorable manner, competent and with constructive intentions; creates connections between individuals and their context; it possesses ethical/moral values such as respect, self-interest and mutual support.

This is the last tool of the itinerary and as such has the task of summarizing and closing the process, helping the couple to internalize the contents that were discovered and processed during the journey.

Use in Practice

The therapist reminds how, during the practice, the attention has shifted to various moments in their history, from when they were still part of their parental families to the present, but also to what they expect to happen soon, up to 3 years from now.

The couple receives the sheet for the coat of arms and a set of coloured pencils or markers. The therapist explains that every ancient family possessed a Coat of Arms, which represented, through metaphors, the history and goals that the family handed down between generations.

The couple then builds their coat of arms, deciding first of all how to complete the shield, closing the upper part, obtaining space for the motto and then dividing it into four sections. The co-therapist takes note of the decision strategy.

At this point, it is explained that the four sections must be filled each with a drawing made by both members of the couple. One section will have to contain a drawing that represents the past, one drawing for the present, another one representing what they would like from the future, and in the last what they expect from the future. The co-therapist notes the order in which the boxes are filled. Once this is done, the couple must identify a short motto that summarizes the meaning of their shield and write it down. At this point, if they have not yet done so, the therapist asks to explain what each section of the shield represents and the meaning of the motto. Once the exercise is completed, the therapists work with the couple on linking what emerges from the coat of arms to what emerged in the previous sessions, focusing on the differences in the level of representations, emotions and narratives. If it has not yet been explained, the therapists speak about the meaning of the exercises and their order, and in particular, it is revealed that this exercise wants to be a moment of closure of a process, but that it must not be forgotten, just like the ancient coat of arms, as it can be a point of reference in the difficulties. However, it is explained that the coat of arms are a family thing and they are a couple, so the last homework is to replicate the exercise with their children.

Purpose

As said above, the coat of arms has the task of closing the process and at the same time building a memory of this; what the couple will do with the heraldic shield is not important, it could be one of the topics of follow-up. The coat of arms leads the couple to re-compose and re-narrate its history through metaphors, to identify moments seen to be meaningful. This work of building up metaphors from their stories leads the couple to re-use all the abilities tested during the journey, in a 'summary with activities'.

12.9 The Iscra Training and the DAN Manualization

The research and teaching activity on the topic was divided into two stages. Following the manualization required from Italian laws[6] to the Institutes of Psychotherapy, we manualized the training asking students to follow the prescribed rules about when, where and how to perform the programme. A specific part was to experiment the DAN model allowing students to work directly with families using the manual.

During the first part of the lessons, we focus on providing colleagues with the theoretical information and, above all, the practice in using the instruments according to the preventive protocol that we developed. This first phase has been made not only more complex but also more fruitful, by the fact that the protocol was not yet completely defined and has undergone rearrangements following discussions with colleagues in class and first experiments of the complete process carried out by the research team and by students.

Already at this stage, we used focus groups dedicated to the various tools and their use in practice, as the correspondence among theory and application; this revealed very quickly several blind spots that helped us correct some imperfections. The direct comparison between the therapists who developed the protocol, the expert in the clinical and theoretical field, and the students in training, has allowed to quickly highlight shortcomings related to personal style, simplifying and redistributing some details of the process to make it more efficient.

During the second part, the teaching was instead almost entirely discussion, working in groups on the cues, stimuli and critical points identified by the students. This helped them to feel 'able' not only with the tools, but also with the reasoning behind the choice of one action or another in the session.

The collection of student feedback allowed us to highlight a trend: students who were more ahead in their training or who participated more often in discussions in the second part were also those who gave more articulated feedback and worked more according to the theoretical reference model.

Another significant element is that a more structured process eases the approach with the first family they meet as trainees of a psychotherapy school.

Following these initial findings, the project continued and the teaching was even more discursive and concentrated on focus groups dedicated both to the difficulties concerned the application of the protocol and to building a reflection on the opportunity to shift the attention to the communicative processes in a therapeutic process.

---

[6] XIII Legislatura Decreto 11 dicembre 1998, n.509, Gazzetta Ufficiale 15 febbraio 1999 n.37.

12.10 Conclusions

The work done by the students allowed us to formulate hypotheses on the model.

Two fairly important elements have emerged: the level of general satisfaction is good, with positive evidence both during the journey and in the evaluation forms delivered at the end. From the evaluation forms of the therapist, it also emerges that, during the journey, the couples have recognized not only that this guided them to see their history and current situation according to a different point of view, but that this also offers them a way to find new solutions to problems that they did not think they could ever face.

The general success of our processes and the ideas that emerged during the focus group with our colleagues, pushed us to start with DAN processes with more problematic couples, changing the process focus from preventive to therapeutic. We invented a path to follow all together, teacher and students to discover new territories with the certainty that our students will develop curiosity, rigor and imagination, that is what we believe they mostly deserve in their path to become skilled family therapists.

References

Allen, J. G., Fonagy, P., & Bateman, A. W. (2010). *Mentalizing in clinical practice*. American Psychiatric Publishing, Inc.

Bassoli, F. (2008). Psicoterapia senza aggettivi: nuovi paradigmi della complessità. Il disegno sistemico come forma di narrazione. *Maieutica*, 27-28-29-30.

Bassoli, F., Mariotti, M., & Frison, R. (2004). *Manuale di Psicoterapia Sistemica e Relazionale*. Roma.

Bateson, G. (1977). *Steps to an ecology of mind*. Jason Aronson Inc. Publishers.

Boscolo, L., Caillé, P., Cecchin, G., Hoffman, L., Keeney, B., Malagoli Togliatti, M., Selvini Palazzoli, M., & Telfner, U. (1983). *La Terapia Sistemica: Nuove tendenze in terapia della famiglia*. Astrolabio.

Bowen, M. (1976). Theory in the practice of psychotherapy. In P.J. Guerin Jr ed.) Family Therapy: Theory and practice (pp 42–90). New York: Gardner Press.

Kerr, M., & Bowen, M. (1988). *Family evaluation: An approach based on Bowen theory*. Norton.

Mariotti, M., & Langella, A. (2011). Stili Relazionali- Relational Style Profile (RSP). Una conversazione proceduralizzata: dall'intervista circolare al profilo di stile relazionale. In P. Chianura, L. Chianura, E. Fuxa, & S. Mazzoni (Eds.), *Manuale clinico di terapia familiare vol. 3: Metodi e strumenti per la valutazione dei processi relazionali*. Franco Angeli.

Sluzki, C. (1982). The 'better-formed' story. Chapter in. In G. Cecchin & M. Mariotti (Eds.), *L'Adolescente e i suoi Sistemi* (p. 1992). Kappa.

Stratton, P., Bland, J., Janes, E., & Lask, J. (2010). Developing a practicable outcome measure for systemic family therapy: The SCORE. *Journal of Family Therapy, 32*, 232–258.

Stratton, P., Lask, J., Bland, J., Nowotny, E., Evans, C., Singh, R., Janes, E., & Peppiatt, A. (2014). Validation of the SCORE-15 Index of Family Functioning and Change in detecting therapeutic improvement early in therapy. *Journal of Family Therapy, 36*, 3–19. https://doi.org/10.1111/1467-6427.12022

Chapter 13
The Digital Analogic Narrative (DAN) Model in Practice: Transformations and Enhancement of Resilience in a Non-clinical Parental Couple. A Case Report

S. Miazzi, M. Zagni, Greco Muratori, F. Bassoli, and Mauro Mariotti

13.1 Introduction

DAN (Digital, Analogical, Narrative) model is now ready for an official manualization, following the RCT (randomized clinical trial) rules aiming to a better diffusion on large scale. We agreed with paediatricians to involve families on a large scale, to increase their resilience and we are experimenting with the DAN as treatment pathway, not only as preventive method. This research project is coherent with the systemic principles and respectful of complexity and relationality. Using analogical, digital and narrative techniques and tools, the DAN model does not force therapists to close themselves in a procedural cage of rigid respect for protocol. Even if we think back to the path taken with other couples in 2017, there is a clear impression that the DAN prevention model does change the way the system acquires information about itself, about the way it processes this information and improves its ability to use it more consciously.

S. Miazzi (✉)
The BrainLab Group – Clinical Neuroscience Lab, Verona, Italy

Research Team, Modena, Italy
e-mail: s.miazzi@thebrainlabgroup.it

M. Zagni
Research Team, Modena, Italy

G. Muratori
Iscra Institute, Modena, Italy

Norfolk and Suffolk NHS, Norwich, UK

F. Bassoli · M. Mariotti
Iscra Institute, Modena, Italy
e-mail: info@iscra.it; dottmauromariotti@gmail.com

The couples we followed in these 2 years showed changes as individuals and as a couple, they showed signs of morphogenesis through new pregnancies, requests for personal paths, redefinitions of themselves within and outside the couple.

Consistently with the intentions of the research group, it is desirable that such a valuable manualized path can be used on a large scale in different contexts of prevention such as premarital courses, prevention of eating disorders, parenting pathways and in any setting in the presence of a conflict in the couple, between children and parents or within the extended family. In the present time, we are experimenting it with Covid-affected families.

13.2 The Case

The case relates to the research work carried out in 2018–2019 at the Istituto di Psicoterapia Sistemica e Relazionale di Modena (ISCRA), in the context of the manualization of the DAN model. The couple was monitored during a period whereby the protocol was close to its final structure; thus, the reader might find some differences compared to the research model previously presented in this book.

13.3 Couple Description

The case concerns a married couple (Alberto, 45 years, and Rita, 43) with children (Anna (11), Giorgio (7) and Sara (5)). Names and identifying details have been changed.

Anna attends the fifth year of primary school; she is described as the one who carries the 'burden' of being the firstborn. Giorgio attends the second year of primary school; he is described as highly active (maybe hyperactive). Sara is defined as the strongest and most determined amongst the three and she is described as like her maternal grandmother (of whom she bears the name) in character and physiognomy.

According to the couple's view, Sara arrived by her decision (unlike the other two children who were programmed) and continues to have an extraordinarily strong and determined character.

Alberto is a freelance architect engineer who works in his own firm with other associates. His family of origin is deeply religious, and still he often frequents the religious environment. Since his family was living in the outskirts, Alberto attended a religious boarding middle school in another town and used to come home only during weekends. His brother Giuseppe is a philosopher and theology graduate and is committed to various religious associations, as well as his sister.

Rita, after various experiences in different companies as a commercial employee, is now taking care of their own guesthouse, started in Alberto's parental house, where they also live. She works as a freelance consultant, too. Rita's family of origin has gone through a lot of life events.

The couple immediately conveys the impression of being quite heterogeneous. Rita is extrovert, more practical and ironic, but at the same time willing to leave the scene to her husband. Alberto instead is calmer and mild-mannered, apparently more interested in psychology. He often has the leading role in the expressions and manifestation of the couple.

They show a high tendency to social desirability.

What we feel during the therapeutic session is that Rita seems to passively accept all the definitions of the couple proposed by her husband, as if he had the role of 'exclusive expert of happy families' to rely on. A co-definition seems to be missing. We shall see, further, a change in this aspect.

All the tools described in this chapter are explained in detail in the preceding chapter.

13.4 First Session: Presentation of the Programme, Gathering of Relational History, Genogram, Score 15

The session started with the bureaucratic compilation of privacy documents, following Italian laws, with assurances about anonymity in case of publication of the case study.

We also investigated the reasons why the couple applied for this research and their expectations. Concerning the research process, Rita participates with confidence, though upon Alberto's request. Alberto, as a matter of fact, defines himself as the one who pays more attention in the psychological aspects. Rita instead defines herself as more pragmatic and practical. Both wish to acquire more instruments and relational skills in the interest of their family wellness.

13.4.1 Genogram

After informing the participants about the purposes of the research, we started gathering their relational history and drafted their trigenerational genogram. Alberto and Rita married in 2003. Both families of origin are quite numerous, and it was not possible, for reasons of time, to investigate all the family connections. The impression, however, is of a couple with a deep desire to talk about themselves and their history.

Rita was the one who did the speaking most of the time, with frequent attempts by Alberto to take part in the narration of the events and to focus the attention on aspects related to his professional history.

What characterizes the formation of the couple is a series of clumsy attempts to develop mutual harmony, in which Rita seems to engage with ambivalent attitude towards the relationship. Alberto interprets the events in a 'serious relationship' perspective, while Rita remains on a 'seeing him' perspective, without too much involvement. Their relationship continues between ups and downs, being a 'on-again and off-again couple' for a period of almost 2 years (1995–1997), during which Alberto already had a clear idea in wanting to settle down definitively with her, while Rita felt that she still had a way to go before thinking about a stable relationship and has no intention of seeing Alberto as a possible fiancée. In fact, Rita, in 1999, after her father's death and after Alberto's graduation, went to London to work and learn English.

After returning from her working experience in England in 2001, her relationship with Alberto resumed, facing a phase of 'adjustment'. In 2003, Alberto asked Rita to marry him, and from this moment on Rita started to feel more engaged in the relationship.

After their marriage, they faced a series of negative life events (accidents, losses, economic hardships) and normative events (childbirth, handling of old parents, relocation) that were experienced differently by the couple: Alberto was more inclined in accepting the events as they come. Rita instead was more combative but, all in all, more able to give them a meaning.

13.4.2 Score-15

We administered the SCORE-15, explaining to the couple that the purpose of this instrument is to obtain a self-assessment of the quality of their family life.

It seemed appropriate to us to give some indications about the terminology used in the second part of this questionnaire where words like 'problem', 'gravity of the problem' and 'therapy' are used, giving a more suitable connotation to the context, that is, thinking in terms of goals and expectations in relation to the path undertaken.

The two SCORE results are quite similar, tending towards the positive side of the continuum 'Best Family Functioning'. The continuum goes from a minimum of 15 (best functioning) to a maximum of 75 (worst functioning). Alberto scored 27 out of 75 (10 in the Strengths and Adaptability subscale, 7 in the Overwhelmed by Difficulties subscale, 10 in the Disrupted Communication subscale). Rita scored 33 out of 75 (13 in the Strengths and Adaptability subscale, 11 in the Overwhelmed by Difficulties subscale, 9 in the Disrupted Communication subscale).

Alberto describes his family as: 'willing to be together, sharing love and happiness with all the problems that life and relationships bring'. Rita instead describes it as: 'happy, dynamic, generous and noisy'.

We verbally reworded some of the questions presented by the Score to make them more appropriate to the context. The question 'The main problem is?' was rephrased by us as 'The main motivation for participation in the research is?': Alberto answered, 'Quality of the relationship'. Rita replied, 'I accepted my husband's proposal to get involved'.

The question on 'Severity' was verbally rephrased into 'How much is the need to work on the quality of the relationship?': Alberto indicated a score of 5, while Rita a score of 2.

The next question 'How are you managing as a family?' was reworded as 'How much is the family working on it?': Alberto answered with a rating of 6 (in the second half of the continuum that tends to negative side); Rita answered with a rating of 0 (particularly good), quite distant from Alberto's point of view.

Compared to the expectations on the 'Therapy', connoted by us as 'Research', both spouses responded with a score of 2 (this continuum has positive values on the left, in contrast with the previous ones), suggesting an attitude of confidence in the path they were starting.

13.5 Second Session: Relational Style Profile, Drawing of the House (Past and Present)

We started this second session by asking the couple if the previous session had somehow brought up some thoughts, they had the desire to share with us.

Rita tells us that analysing their life cycle led her to become aware that while her husband Alberto had a Family without any major negative events and without a so-called 'black sheep', her experience is to have already had many negative events which have left a mark on her. On the other hand, the acquisition of this awareness leads her to hope (expressing an analogical language that conveys bitterness and hope at the same time) that more positive things await her in the future.

13.6 Relational Style Profile

We introduced the Relational Style Profile. We explained the purposes of this instrument, which both spouses welcomed with curiosity and participation. For the administration of this tool, we used two different rooms: Rita with Dr. Miazzi in one room, Alberto with Dr. Zagni in the other one.

Rita was involved and very careful in providing the answers required, and Alberto also participated with great conviction, punctually expressing his thoughts, and sometimes his own misgivings.

Both were ultimately quick to provide the answers, but without lacking engagement and participation, instead generously sharing some of their considerations. For example, Rita, in thinking about the answers to be given in the context of the relational object 'Affective Relationships' and precisely in the dichotomy Order and Chaos, defined Alberto as 'Albipedia' to indicate his inclination towards structured and competent modalities.

Alberto showed a lot of interest in understanding the relationship between the first and the second part of the test, so we again explained that what was investigated in the first part of the test (the generative elements) represents the characterizing aspects of primary and family relationships, thus the models that influence our future relational models, while in the second part of the test, we investigate the quality and current functioning of the couple.

At the end, both expressed curiosity about the construction and the mechanisms of the test. We welcomed their curiosity by postponing the feedback of the results to the next session.

13.6.1 Drawing of the House

We then introduced the Systemic Drawing of the House. In accordance with the administration instructions, we prepared two A3 sheets with three pencils of different colour for each member of the couple and explained to them that this activity is aimed at collecting information about the houses of their lives, starting with how the houses of their families of origin looked like, choosing according to the period that had greater affective meaning to them. We also specified that the respect of square footage and form was not a fundamental component.

13.6.2 House of the Past

Rita chooses the house where she lived before marrying (2002–2003).

As to the drawing style, she uses one only colour for the drawing and adds another colour to point out orthographically some details regarding the past use of some rooms, that now are empty (former grandfather's room, former sibling's room).

She traces the plan of the house and then gradually adds details, as if the memories were flowing little by little while her mind moves on the different rooms. She begins by describing two empty rooms, 'Room 1' and 'Room 2' and she explains that the first one belonged to the grandfather (who died later), and the other belonged to the male siblings. One of the two empty rooms contained what Rita calls the 'remains' of her brother Marco, that is, some furniture and personal items that her brother used to carry and to remove during his sporadic and unexpected presences in the house. The two empty rooms are next to the bathroom and are separated from other two rooms (hers and her mother's) by means of a connecting room. She tells that over time the occupants of the bedrooms changed and remembers when she slept near the parents' room and was forced to hear everything that happened there at night. There is a kitchen, with an exit to the outside, in which Rita's mother used to spend most of her time, and a living room, where the family was not used to spend time together until Alberto's arrival in Rita's life. It is very striking that Rita chose the house in the period before the wedding, when her father had already died, and her brothers had already left the house. Was it possible that Alberto's arrival might have brought the warmth that had previously been lacking?

The use of spaces in the house seems rather fragmented: Rita reports that there were basically neither moments nor spaces for 'staying together as a family' within the house. She was almost always withdrawn in her room, while her mother used to stay in the kitchen for the housekeeping, or to sit in the outside watching the life of the village. To further demonstrate the lack of moments of relaxation and 'physical closeness', Rita tells us that in their house, they did not have a sofa. Her mother used to watch television on a chair taken from the kitchen and Rita would eventually sit in the living room in an armchair. The sofa was purchased only after Rita had started her relationship with Alberto, so that the couple could stay at home watching television or spend time together. The impression is that of a bare, impersonal house, almost like an uninhabited house where the inhabitants could not create moments of intimacy and sharing, and which lacks a 'homely' component. When we asked Alberto to enrich the information provided by Rita, we were all incredibly surprised to learn that, in the period covered by the representation, in the same house lived also a sister, Alessia, detail that was completely missed by Rita.

Alberto represents the house of when he was a boy (1988). He makes the whole drawing with the same colour. The only two details of different colours were then inserted by Rita. His house is on two floors, with a living room dominated by a large sofa, in clear contrast with Rita's house. He says that the house was very much lived-in, and that often in the common areas (kitchen and living room), they found themselves together in carrying out the typical activities of the different members of the family. On the first floor, there were the bedrooms: he used to sleep with his brother, while his sister had a room by herself. The bedrooms were on the same floor as the kitchen and living room. On the ground floor, there was a laboratory where the father did a second job as a craftsman and a tavern where the boys had parties. There was a large garden, where Alberto remembers with pleasure to have spent a lot of time. When ask to comment on Alberto's house, Rita notes out loud the great differences between the two houses and the relational meanings that emerge and how, in particular, her home-family comes out heavily defeated by a hypothetical comparison with Alberto's house. She enriches the information reminding Alberto of the presence in the garden of a corner with a statue of the Virgin Mary, consistently with the religious values of the family, and a place where Alberto's father used to relax in his free time.

Rita represents the home of a moment in life characterized by what may seem to be the pinnacle of the fragmentation of her family, which contrasts with the style of Alberto's family, more characterized by the sharing of spaces and the warmth of the family. This moment, chosen by Rita, which may appear to be the one of the greatest solitudes in the house, is also the one in which Alberto arrives.

Present House

Today the couple lives in Alberto's family house, the same one he chose to draw as the house of the past.

The house was completely renovated and fully modified. The new structure was studied considering Rita's needs, who had expressed very clearly the desire to have a house with a direct connection to the outside, on the ground floor.

Now on the ground floor, there is a small independent apartment for Alberto's parents (no longer self-sufficient), but also the living area with kitchen, bathroom and living room. Rita points out the presence of the sofa ('inevitable for Alberto's family').

The spaces on the ground floor are lived in by all the members of the family, but Rita complains that in the living area, she would like to have more space to optimize her work (e.g. more space for ironing). The children do their homework and play in the kitchen or in their bedrooms, and in the evening, Alberto reads them a story.

Upstairs there are the children bedrooms on one side and the parental room with walk-in closet on the other. A door divides the private area from the rent rooms. There is also a small attic area that is currently used as a closet.

The interaction between the two spouses during the task was collaborative. They used a much greater richness of colours than the drawings of their respective houses of origin. Observing them, we noticed almost an automatism in the exchange of colours with each other. The part of the drawing of the house of the future was postponed to the next session for issues related to the lack of time.

13.7 Third Session: Drawing of the House (Future), Feedback of the RSP, Homework (Role Exchange)

We asked the spouses if the previous session had generated any suggestions: this question served as a stimulus for Rita to begin to talk about the relationship with her sister Alessia, which has always been conflictual.

We then asked to proceed with the Drawing of the House of the Future, as they imagine it and as they would like it to be in 3 years' time. The couple seemed to be rather satisfied with the house as it is now. Most of the time was marked by a continuous flow of thoughts between the two concerning the arrangement of functional and aesthetic details rather than expansions or major changes. The exercise proved to be an opportunity to take some time to discuss things that are normally hard to discuss, and there were times when one was amazed at the needs and desires of the other.

Concerning the interaction between the couple during the task, Alberto immediately took control of the sheet, leaving no room for Rita to participate graphically. Rita, in an absolutely spontaneous way, created her own workspace using a smaller sheet on which she gradually represented details and clarifications with respect to what was said and designed by Alberto, as in respect to his position as an expert, but without giving up her contribution. This exercise highlighted the tendency of the couple to maintain a situation of asymmetry in which Alberto stands in an 'up' position and Rita tries to adapt and somehow to find some kind of comfort zone, in the 'down' position.

13.7.1 RSP Feedback

Alberto and Rita achieved surprisingly similar results, both in terms of generative and performative indices.

In the field of generative forces, the couple appeared to have a *'symbiotic'* style of differentiation with the parental figures, with an openness to change that can be defined as *'rigid'*. This could indicate a poor ability of both to build their own personality independently from the parents' one, in the face of an equally poor ability to build and determine themselves freely from parental expectations.

The way of defining oneself with respect to the parents, therefore of entering structural coupling with them, results in both spouses as *'fusional'*. This means that the profiles of the subject, of the parents and of the ideal child for the parents practically coincide.

This might indicate a mimesis between the attitude of the subject and those of the parental figures, with the difficulty of distinguishing between these and the Self and to define oneself with respect to the parents. In this case, the greatest danger for the current relationship might be that the parental figures, real and internal, continue to have authority over the choices of the subject, polluting the serenity and the self-generative autonomy of the couple. This could be considered as a problematic profile, particularly in the case of Alberto, whose parents are still alive. In the case of Rita instead, the parental dyad being deceased, the presence of contingent influences will be less likely; anyway, the influence of the internal parental figures remains strong for both.

The excessive level of similarity with the self-referred parental ideal could indicate some problems of self-esteem and of positive self-awareness. Further similarities within the generative forces are the alliance with the same-sex parental figure, and the mediatory function between the parents.

In the field of performative forces, the couple appears to have an identical Similarity index, with the dichotomy 'Body/Mind' in lowest resemblance. The Recognition Index is also very high (= *predictable*), with the lowest recognition in the dichotomy Order/Chaos.

What do these figures tell us, which reveal in both spouses a strong adherence to generative forces and a high degree of similarity and recognition? A certain degree of similarity between the two spouses indicates a good structural coupling and a good level of recognition between the two facilitates the process of understanding the other. It also further facilitates the process of coupling and maintaining low levels of conflict. But, on the other hand, we are in the presence of a potential risk factor, because a too fast or excessive coupling could cause difficulties for the couple in unusual or unexpected situations. Moreover, if on the one hand similar generative forces indicate similar ways of approaching the relationship, in this case we are in the presence of extremely converging data. This could constitute a sort of relational rigidity, a potential enemy in moments of transition or redefinition of the relationship.

These potential risk factors could also be supported by a further criticality, that is, the degree of Plasticity, which results as *'fragile'*. Couple Plasticity refers to the awareness about the aspects of one's own way of being that the other would like to change.

A *fragile* plasticity reveals a low degree of reflexivity, both self-referred and referred to the relationship, showing that the ability to adopt the point of view of others is not well developed. It also evaluates the ability of the couple to accept a certain degree of difference of each other. Both have a similar couple plasticity, particularly fragile in the dichotomies Body/Mind and Optimism/Pessimism.

We gave to the spouses a positive reading of the results of the test, highlighting that as individuals they have many aspects of similarity in the acceptance of values, education, and parental ideals, to which they decided to adhere in large part. And it was something that they also recognized in the other. Making a transition from the education received by their parents and to the couple relationship they have built – strong of the models they carry inside – they chose a person with whom they share much from this point of view. If a person shares the values of his family, adheres to them, continues to respect them and feels them as their own, they will hardly choose someone different in this aspect, someone who wants to move away completely from the family models, rejecting them.

We also informed the spouses that the area of criticality that emerged is related to possible situations that require a change, both for normative and non-normative events. Their being so similar, and with a low couple plasticity, could eventually become an obstacle in case of a potential perturbation of the system. Both spouses accepted and acknowledged the potential criticality that emerged and thanked us for the cue offered.

13.7.2 Homework: Role Reversal

We asked the spouses to use one of the dichotomies in which their degree of plasticity was low (Body/Mind), to perform the exercise of *reversing roles at home*.

Rita, being the most instinctive, messy and creative one, will have to try to be more reflective, calm and organized. Alberto, on the contrary, will have to abandon his characteristics of rationality, rigor and organization in favour of a greater space for instinct, emotionality, creativity.

13.8 Fourth Session: Homework Feedback, 3D Genogram

13.8.1 Homework Feedback

The session started by asking the spouses to tell us their experience in the role reversal task. Alberto took the floor, as usual, to tell us that they took the task in a profoundly serious and structured manner, starting with the analysis of their differences and discussing about the aspects on which they could test themselves. They decided to focus on the differences they have in their relationship with each of their three children. After this analysis, they decided that Rita should try to be softer, let it run and joke a little more with Anna. Alberto should be a bit more persistent and meticulous.

Later, Alberto explains that they decided to give more emphasis to the positive aspects of their parental approaches and therefore to convert his being 'insistent and meticulous' in a dimension of a more significant presence and involvement, rather than being stressful and pedantic.

Rita admits she has not succeeded as she would have liked, in being softer with Anna and that, despite her attempts, her daughter did not notice anything. Alberto blames her for not having done enough and brings an opposite impression: Anna probably did not understand that there was an attempt to reverse the roles, but still noted some changes. In his opinion, Anna seemed to be chattier; she 'responded' to the relationship in a more positive way; with him, she behaved differently.

This comment by Alberto gave rise to a confrontation between the spouses, who discovered to have a diametrically opposite view of Anna and her character.

As for the other two children, both agree they had more difficulties and less results, although they reported 'critical' episodes solved positively, thanks to the partial change of perspective.

Reflecting with the couple about this experience, what emerged was the importance and the difficulty of being able to put oneself in the other's shoes, particularly in terms of feedback, retroactions and associated emotions. It allows to reflect on what everyone brings into the relationship with their children and what the efforts of the other are.

After discussing together, the meaning of the construct of mentalization, we gave a positive connotation to their task at home: Although they may have the impression of not having done well as they would have liked, they actually performed the task by finding their own way, and at least they tried. They made a great effort of understanding 'what the other would do, how the other would react in this situation'.

13.8.2 3D Genogram

We introduced the 3D genogram. After bringing the tray with the wooden pieces to the desk, we explained that these materials would serve to represent their nets of relationships visibly and immediately.

13.8.3 3D Genograms of the Past

We started with the two genograms of the past, referring to the families of origin and when they were not yet a couple.

Rita chooses the period after the baccalaureate exam. Her genogram is quite essential: she represents only the family and some friends. Rita puts herself in a position halfway between her parents and friends and represents her siblings very far from the rest of the family, as to indicate 'family sections'; we also notice that she does not enrich the genogram with descriptive or emotional information. The genogram is as essential and bare as the representation of the house of the past.

Alberto represents his being in relationship in a very particular way: On the one hand, he expresses with a certain richness his relational network using colours to group and distinguish the different categories, appropriately modulating the degrees of closeness and using various forms; on the other hand, the content, and the meaning of the relationships themselves impressed us a lot, because he represents them in 'groups' and does not indicate the individual people.

Only upon Rita's request, he completes the genogram by specifying the identity of the people who were part of it.

Both spouses tell us that the representation of the two genograms reflects what they knew about the other, and both still give suggestions and indications to make the genogram of the other more precise from their point of view. The two genograms appeared to be quite different, with Alberto's genogram much richer in relationships.

13.8.4 3D Genogram of the Present

The couple represented the genogram of the present with an excellent harmony; in fact, they managed rather quickly to negotiate adjustments and small shifts. Rita's parents are not there anymore and there have been changes in her social network, now richer than in the past.

Alberto's social network has remained almost unchanged, except for the inclusion of some social groups in addition to those of work and church (scouts, professional order, meditation group, soccer). Each spouse represented and described their network of relationships in their part of workspace, but both contributed to the overall improvement and completion of the representation.

In the genogram of the present, we noticed what we called an 'illustrious absence': Rita and Alberto completely forgot to represent their children! We delicately brought this information to the couple's attention, and together we asked ourselves about such a 'forgetfulness', which expresses a discrepancy that is far too evident from the values professed by the couple. In any case, we tried to define what had happened in a not too negative way, pointing out how they were perhaps thinking as they would see themselves if there were no children.

13.8.5 3D Genogram of the Future

We then proposed to represent the genogram of the future, explaining that we would like to know how they expect their relational network to change in next 3 years.

Alberto, in his representation, brings his group of friends closer because in the future, he expects and hopes there will be greater closeness. Rita also brings some of her work colleagues closer, because she would like to feel them as friends in the future. Alberto's parents may not be there anymore.

When asked how they see each other's future views, Rita asks Alberto about his desire to make closer friends. In Alberto's perspective, as the children grow up, it seems natural to look a little outwards; when the children are still young, all the attentions are on the children, thus having a more family-oriented view.

At the end of the task, my colleague and I took a few minutes to agree on a feedback about the work done.

When we got back, the spouses themselves insisted in clarifying about the non-representation of the children within the Genogram of the present, so we asked them what explanation they would give themselves. Alberto's take on this was that being young children, they are still somehow 'internalized', although he realizes that they should be represented for what they are, that is, as individuals. Rita, in a much more sincere way, imagines that the two of them, despite the precious and indispensable presence of their children, still feel very much like a couple, as if their transition to the parental status is not yet complete.

Rita also takes the opportunity to tell us that she reflected a lot about her forgetfulness to include her sister Alessia in the Drawing of the House. She explains that at that time their relationship was very conflictual, unlike today, and perhaps 'erasing' the sister in that context was like 'erasing' the conflicts of the time.

On our part, the feedback we brought to them was of an excellent ability to represent their way of being in relationship through this tool, with a unique harmony and balance in finding an agreement on the rules of composition and a good mutual understanding of their networks of relationships.

We decided not to dwell further on the information that emerged during the genograms, so that the spouses could reflect, individually and as a couple, on what had appeared, because this could be a beneficial opportunity for them to learn by difference.

13.8.6 Homework: Object and Letter

This task stimulates the couple to retrace the emotionally significant parts of the formation of their relationship. It is an exercise of communication with a high emotional content, centred on the phase of composition of the couple.

We asked the spouses to choose an object (an object, a song, a photo), or something related to the very first or pivotal moments in their story, and then to write a letter to the partner in which they explain the reasons behind the choice of that object. Finally, we asked them to keep the object and letter secret. In the next session, they will show the object and read the letter in front of the therapists. Rita and Alberto welcomed our proposal with curiosity and joy.

13.9 Fifth Session: Restitution of the Homework, Score 15

13.9.1 Restitution of the Homework

This session began asking Rita and Alberto to express their emotions about the exercise, the selection and collection of this object and the writing of the letter.

As an object, Rita chose the letter that Alberto wrote to her when they started their relationship. This letter at the time scared her away, but later it became the foundation of their relationship, because it made her understand Alberto's seriousness, depth and love for her. Both were moved. In the end, Rita also told us about the importance to her of the positive opinion that her father (who died soon after) had of Alberto ('he has a child's face, but you can see that he has his head on his shoulders').

Alberto chose a photo taken on Rita's birthday in 1995. They were in the same group of friends but were not yet engaged. He chose it because, 'now like then', he feels a spark that makes him want to 'insist, insist, insist', as he did at that time, to continue to be with her.

Both wrote a love letter, which retraced and actualized the old feelings, emotions and intentions and were moved by each other's words.

Both the objects referred to the initial moments of their relationship, even earlier. These were founding moments, perceived as particularly meaningful, which they firmly wish to keep alive. This task had a compelling impact on the emotional level: Rita and Alberto reconfirmed their mutual feelings, the desire to be together as a couple but also to engage in the role of parents. Rita told that these tasks, like the genogram and the life cycle, were essential to stop and think about their stages, their choices and, in her case, to see that all the choices made so far have proven to be good.

13.10 Score-15

The session then continued with the second administration of the Score-15 (Stratton et al., 2010). The total scores of family's functioning improved (compared to the first measurement).

13.11 Sixth Session: Better Formed Tale

This session began with Rita confessing to us that she feels the need to make a personal journey, to 'untie some knots'. She feels that retracing the moments of her life and having the chance to look at it from a more distant perspective helped her to understand that working on the path that has made her the woman of today could help her to improve some aspects of her present and future life. These moments of re-reading have opened new windows, new reflections and the need to take time to work on new levels of her being. We accepted the request, explaining that there would undoubtedly be the possibility, ideally once the research is over.

We then moved on to the activity to be carried out in this session: The Better Formed Tale (Sluzki, 1982). This exercise is designed to stimulate the couple to a view of their issues in a narrative context, allowing the creation of a framework in which the issue can be observed in a more detached way, with the possibility to create a solution and prefigure the effects of the change. The choice of the tables to be proposed is designed to stimulate a discussion on the parenting function.

We introduced the BFT explaining that we would like to build together a story that tells, through images, an aspect of their being parents and couple. Alberto and Rita selected the table 'Journey' among the 14 available, by process of elimination. During the creation of the story, we felt a difficulty by the spouses in detaching themselves from the real data in favour of a more 'meta' dimension.

At the end, the colleague and I positively connoted the clue elements of the story, focusing on their strong desire to be good parents, while remaining firm in their identity as a couple. The tale abided on a level rather close to reality, although characterized by metaphors. In the spouses' story, we see traces of many parental functions that the couple has in their educational model and that represented the cornerstone of the story itself: the protective function, which includes the behaviours of proactive response to the needs of the child; the affective function, that is, the ability of parents to share positive emotions with their children, assisting them in building a stable and safe emotional world; the significant function, that is, the intention to create a framework that can give meaning to the events that the child has to deal with. Also, the projective function, in which the parent manages to balance the desires and expectations towards the child with their real skills and inclinations, accompanying them in their autonomy and development. But, in our opinion, this couple has a high strength in the triadic function, because they show an excellent ability to build a parental alliance that allows the child to acquire a sense of stability, completeness and belonging.

At the end, we gave Rita and Alberto the tables designed to build the Better Formed Tale at home with the children, with the indication to co-construct a story with the whole family.

13.12 Seventh Session: Ritual of Discharge with the Heraldic Shield, Restitution of the Better Formed Tale Done at Home

Unfortunately, in the days after the last session, the family was not able to carry out the task at home, so we agreed that they will bring it at the follow-up session.

We summarized the general sense of the past sessions, explaining that in this journey, we worked together to experiment with different ways of recalling and thinking about situations, people, relationships and their founding values. We also explained that the purpose of today's exercise, the 'Coat of Arms', is to try to 'put into practice' what emerged so far. Each ancient family had a heraldic coat of arms, which represented the history and objectives that the family passed down from generation to generation. We asked them to create their heraldic shield, which sums up the essence of their family.

We delivered the sheet and a set of coloured pencils and markers, asking both members of the couple to decide how to complete the shield by closing the top, make room for the motto and then divide it into four sections. We explained that the four sections must be filled each with a drawing made by both members of the couple: In the various sections, they will represent the past, the present, the desired future and the expected future.

Here too, we decided to loosen the links of the research design, based on the knowledge, we have acquired on the characteristics of this couple: We decided to let them work in our absence, in order to leave the maximum freedom of interaction between the two, and then review the video recording to evaluate the interactivity of the spouses without external interference. This modality allowed us to confirm the pattern of interaction that had already emerged during the sessions: Alberto tends to guide the decisions of the couple and to take control of the situations. What impressed us was Rita's change: At the beginning of the path, Rita accepted entirely the definition of their positions. In this session, we noticed that now she still follows Alberto's modalities, but no longer without showing her opposition and highlighting her point of view, in a more assertive modality.

In this task, two different approaches emerged: Alberto was more creative, regardless of our indications, Rita was more respectful of the rules we provided. The result was a heraldic shield mostly done by Alberto, who decided that the imagined and the desired future in his opinion coincide, so he did not keep them separate, despite our precise indication. Even the various periods were not kept separate but drawn together with a deliberate continuity. In the bottom, they drew roots that develop from a rock symbolizing the past and their resilience at the same time. They wanted to represent that from unforeseen and adverse events, there is still the possibility to come out stronger and more united. There are two trees, representing Rita and Alberto as a couple, grown from the same ground, and sharing a lot but, as Alberto suggests, at the same time well individuated. *The description does not mention the children, again!* At this point, we asked where they were, and Alberto indicated them in the many small fruits on the trees. The stars high up in the sky express a happy and prosperous future. The motto recalls the union that gives strength to all the family members, and that allows them to face difficulties and be resilient.

Rita continued to send out signs throughout the description of the drawing, indicating that we were watching at 'Alberto's heraldic shield'. We asked her to show what she had of herself in this drawing. She shares a role in the part of the past, represented by the roots in the difficult terrain, and the motto. Having gone through many difficult moments is, in fact, an information that Rita has provided several times during the various sessions: 'despite all the difficulties encountered we are still here, we are strong, we push forward'.

After a few days, we received an email with the Better Formed Tale created with the children. Unfortunately, we did not have the opportunity to make a return to the couple.

13.13 Eight Session: Follow-Up, Score-15

This time Alberto was able to respect the deliveries and, despite having directed the works, he managed to leave space for the children to express themselves according to their possibilities, allowing them to leave space to simplicity and spontaneity using stamps and drawing of everyday objects, and in the identification of a more immediate motto, appropriate to the language of the children.

The impression is that Alberto has developed a higher reflectivity about the needs of space and expression of the other.

The children introduced the concept of trigenerationality, which was missing in the previous heraldic shield: in the tree that symbolizes the past, the hearts represent the whole family with grandparents and uncles. The children's sensitivity to the importance of the trigenerational is expressed also in the quadrant of the future, where they represented Alberto and Rita as grandparents who take care of their future grandchildren. The ideal future was taken up by Alberto, who suggested the idea of love that unites them in the future.

The values indicated in the top of the drawing were spontaneously developed by Anna, the eldest daughter; each of these qualities is personified in each family member: Rita is peace (red), Anna is happiness (pink), Alberto is solidarity (green), Giorgio is union (light blue), Sara is love (yellow) and their cats are happiness (grey).

13.13.1 Score 15

We then administered for the last time the Score-15. The perceived family functioning has further improved, and the values expressed by the spouses now are much more similar. Alberto's initial general score of 27 has now decreased to 24, and Rita's scores from 33 to 25.

13.14 General Thoughts on the Discharge Session

This was as a meta-communication session, in which we revisited the meaning of the results of the various instruments and of the impact they had on the couple.

Alberto and Rita told us that the comment of a friend on their way of relating with their children rekindled in them the memory of when, both in the 3D Genogram and the heraldic shield in session, the children were little or not represented at all. Their friend noticed that Alberto and Rita are not the type of parents who are overwhelming or excessively stressful towards their children, which Alberto immediately connected to having 'ignored' the children on the occasions described above. Rita told us that, in this period, they reflected on the path taken and particularly on the meaning of this specific aspect, of which they were totally unaware, which Rita defines as 'couple selfishness'. Rita was darker than usual, sometimes crying. She told us that in the last period, she reflected a lot and that now she is living a particular moment. As she said before, she feels the need to work on herself and on some aspects of her life, her self-esteem and her tendency to exclude herself from the family's activities. This attitude was put in relationship with Alberto's being too centralist, and we pointed out that these two modes are complementary. Together we reflected on the possibility for the couple to try to 'fill in' the relational spaces in a more balanced way.

She feels she has a deep need to work on it. She is also looking for a better balance in his relationship with his children and with Alberto. This impressed us a lot because the results of the RSP interview focused on the excessive level of similarity with the self-referred parental ideal, which might indicate some problems of self-esteem and positive self-knowledge.

The spouses then spontaneously went on to talk about trigenerational influences, making considerations about how their family histories are different.

To conclude the session and the journey, we made a brief restitution saying that the fact that something moved in them was one of our objectives: the research hypothesis is that the exposure to the three-level communicative approach (analogical, digital, and narrative) allows highlighting and reflecting on some aspects of our ways of relating to others as individuals, in the couple and the family. One of the goals is to help improving awareness and developing strengths, but also to highlight areas where there is room for improvement or enhancement.

We also wanted to share with the spouses that relationships often need to be redefined and that these are continuous redefinitions, which we can define as necessary and inevitable 'upgrades'. These upgrades can be better tackled with a new level of awareness of the relational mechanisms, that in our opinion, they succeeded in achieving.

This is also a part of the prevention we set ourselves with the manualization of the DAN model: to avoid being faced with moments of tension or with strong and unexpected crisis that can catch a couple unprepared, bringing out criticalities that – if not addressed in time – could undermine the family stability and reduce its ability to deal with problematic events. What Alberto and Rita during the session called 'a huge advantage'.

13.15 Therapists' Reflections

13.15.1 *Couples in the Mirror: Therapists and Spouses*

Manualization is one of the fundamental aspects of empirical research in psychotherapy (Dazzi, 2006), that is, that area aimed at providing information on the ability of a specific type of treatment to induce improvements in the general functioning of the patient, while making it clear and usable to anyone. Manualization consists in specifying the principles of a psychotherapeutic treatment so that what is done can be verified and reproduced.

We know that the systemic-relational model, characterized in the principles and in the techniques by the attention to the complexity of human functioning (Mariotti et al., 2004), is even more difficult to reconcile with the strict and linear criteria of scientific research.

What we tried to do in this process was to maintain consistency with the systemic principles, remaining within the framework of the research design and following its guidelines as faithfully as possible. We tried to pursue the objective of the research, providing a consultancy programme centred on increasing the awareness of the dynamics that take place within the relationships, according to the indications of the protocol, while trying to be sufficiently flexible within each session and in the administration of each instrument. At the same time, we did our best to give the necessary space to the couple to communicate their feelings and let it express at its best.

It is a shared opinion that therapeutic efficacy is not based exclusively on the therapist's mere technical competence – in this case, the administration of specific instruments – but that it is also necessary to consider the active participation of the patient, achieved with the construction of the therapeutic alliance, as proposed by Peter Stratton's team (Pote et al., 2003) for the standardization of the therapeutic process in the controlled research on the results.

From our point of view, this experience was very enriching. It allowed us to experiment with the use of systemic instruments in a semistructured way – within a grid with flexible meshes – that gave us the space to accommodate our style and the style of the spouses, allowing a structural coupling between the couple of therapists and the parental couple in the right times and in the right ways. A sort of synergic dance between the 'observant' therapeutic system and the 'observed' couple, to the extent of making this distinction meaningless in favour of the creation of a unique and non-repeatable system.

Systemic family therapy does not follow a sequence of rigid and pre-established interventions. However, the therapist must be familiar with the guiding principles that influence all the aspects of research and therapy without forgetting *his own* guiding principles (Mariotti et al., 2004). This is what we kept in mind throughout the research, modulating from time to time, from session to session, the degree of adherence to the protocol and its guidelines with the flexibility necessary for respecting the systemic essence and for being able to be tuned to each single, unique and unrepeatable moment of interaction.

Always remaining within the framework of the research, from the first session, we tried to establish a good relationship with the couple. In this context, perhaps it might be inappropriate to use the term 'therapeutic alliance'. What we focused on, instead, was the quality of the relationship, sharing with the couple the research's objectives from the very beginning. We did our best to always remain open to all kinds of questions, leaving wide room for debate, openness and acceptance of the moments in which the spouses detached themselves from the 'track', in order to let them confront each other, even expanding their field of discussion. We did all this while maintaining an atmosphere of ease, which we were ready to modulate according to the needs and to the emotional tones that could arise from time to time.

Alberto and Rita showed all the time their trust in us and in the path, we were proposing. We believe that this was a determining factor in leading them to the relational adjustments that will somehow increase their resilience as a couple and family, reducing the risk of future conflict.

During the sessions, we tried to honour all the systemic type of strategies: We made use of the positive connotation, to make them reflect on some aspects and opening to possibilities instead of limits. We believe that the positive connotation (Selvini-Palazzoli et al., 1975) was one of the factors that helped the couple to feel more optimistic and even more motivated to act to improve their relationship, thanks to a new reading of the information that was perhaps already present in their minds.

We made use of circular questions (Selvini-Palazzoli et al., 1980), especially at times when we felt there was a communication impediment, or when we felt it was appropriate to involve other members of the system that were not present during the sessions. We tried never to forget that the couple as such is not an isolated universe neither by itself nor by those systems composed of other family members: For this reason, we often brought into session subsystems such as the parental and marital one, but also the siblings and, more generally, their families of origin.

At times in disagreement between us, we also tried to disrupt their schemes of reference when we seemed to read rigid behaviours that were of no utility to the family system.

A special consideration concerns the experience of the DAN prevention model as a couple of therapists: In fact, we believe it was a great chance to have two therapists of different sex, for two main reasons: The first is about the relationship dynamics with the couple, and the second is related to the possibility of confrontation and dialog before, during and after each session. In our case, this proved to be fruitful, full of food for thought and observations and to be a relevant generator of new relational hypotheses.

13.16 Did We Contribute to this Family's Resilience?

The evaluations made by the spouses and the considerations they shared with us suggest that the programme was useful for this couple.

When asked how they lived this experience, both answered in a very positive way. Rita, who initially decided to participate in the research only to please Alberto, found an opportunity to reflect on herself and now she has the desire for a personal journey.

Both spouses recognized this path as a resource for themselves, for the couple and the family. During our meetings, they found time and space only for the two of them. In the therapists, they found two people with whom they could open up without fear of judgement and to whom they could refer to enrich themselves from a relational point of view.

The couple had the opportunity to achieve a greater awareness of themselves and others and to confront. According to Rita and Alberto, during the sessions, they both found time and space to communicate in a more relaxed way. This contributed to the promotion of better communication, greater introspection and better mutual understanding, with positive repercussions on the well-being of the couple and the family in general.

They had the opportunity to reflect as well on the relationships with their children, thanks also to the experience of role reversal and to focus on some dynamics between them as spouses. Alberto's way of handling big and small decisions and Rita's way of accepting them always lost that rigid asymmetry in favour of a more balanced alternation of complementarity and symmetry.

Our point of view is that Rita's search for a new balance was the result of her exposure to the systemic model, that helped emerging and maturing in a structured and 'protected' situation those critical issues that could have been a potential risk factor for the couple and the family in the future. This can be considered as prevention.

They thanked us for our help and for the opportunity we gave them to ponder on their relationship and for showing them also the power of the aspects that we summarize in the acronym DAN. We also thanked them from the bottom of our hearts for having undertaken this path with great commitment and seriousness, for having opened sincerely to each of the proposed activities and for having brought so much of themselves into every session.

13.16.1 …and Then?

In addition to those aspects and information that already emerged during the research, we had the opportunity to meet the spouses out of context, about 3 months later. They told us that they had noticed significant changes in their children's behaviour. Their eldest daughter had become much more autonomous, responsible and serene.

Rita confirmed that she felt the need to work on herself to better cope with future life difficulties and with normative changes and professional relationships, which are especially important for her at the moment. We agreed to start individual sessions at the beginning of the new year.

In conclusion, how can we answer the questions: did we really do prevention? Did we help this couple to be more resilient? The transformations that we saw during the sessions, the ever-increasing involvement of the couple, the moments of confrontation and, finally, the fact that Rita could meet this need seems to lead us to a positive answer.

Even the Score-15, instrument used to measure family functioning at the beginning, in the middle and at end of the journey, showed an improvement in family functioning as perceived by the two members of the couple. Also, the evaluation questionnaire sent after the last session comforts us, because both spouses have expressed a positive opinion on many aspects.

13.17 Conclusion

Looking at the video recordings of the sessions and reflecting on this experience, we inevitably needed to pause to reflect on the meaning of the intervention of manualization and to appreciate its apparent simplicity and transformative power. A real 'systemic challenge'.

Its objective is to help the couple to take time to question, focus on critical issues, but also to achieve a greater awareness of one's own qualities and resources. It is an instrument to become 'relationally more competent', to be able to deal more effectively with daily life, family normative transitions and critical unexpected events.

References

Dazzi, N. (2006). Il dibattito contemporaneo sulla ricerca in psicoterapia. In N. Dazzi, V. Lingiardi e A. Colli (Eds.), *La Ricerca in Psicoterapia: Modelli e Strumenti* (1st Ed., pp. 3–27) Milano: Raffaello Cortina.
Mariotti, M., Bassoli, F., & Frison, R. (Eds.). (2004). *Manuale di psicoterapia sistemica e relazionale*. Sapere Edizioni.
Pote, H., Stratton, P., Cottrell, D., Shapiro, D., & Boston, P. (2003). Systemic family therapy can be manualized: Research process and findings. *Journal of Family Therapy, 25*, 236–262.
Selvini-Palazzoli, M., Boscolo, L., Cecchin, G., & Prata, G. (1980). Ipotizzazione, Circolarità, Neutralità: Tre direttive per la conduzione della seduta. *Terapia Famigliare, 7*, 7–19.
Selvini-Palazzoli, M., Boscolo, L., Cecchin, G., & Prata, G. (1975). *Paradosso e Controparadosso*. Raffaello Cortina.
Stratton, P., Bland, J., Janes, E., & Lask, J. (2010). Developing a practicable outcome measure for systemic family therapy: The SCORE. *Journal of Family Therapy, 32*, 232–258.

Chapter 14
Taking Care of Adoption (TCA): Development of a Treatment Manual for Adoptive Families

Francesco Vadilonga, Barbara D'Avanzo, Gloriana Rangone, and Angelo Barbato

14.1 Introduction

Although poor specification of family therapy interventions has long been recognized as a challenge for process and outcome research (Shadish et al., 1993), at first the family therapy field met the introduction of manuals with mixed reactions and acceptance. Criticisms of manuals mainly focused on failure to reflect the flexibility of family therapy as a relational process involving ecological interventions in natural environments not easily translated into rigid procedures. The first reports of manualized family interventions described therapy models with a behavioral focus. Social constructionist, narrative, and systemic approaches have long been considered less suitable for manualization (Larner, 2004). Recent surveys show that most systemic therapists take an intermediate position on the use of manuals between the more positive stance of cognitive/behavioral therapists and the more critical views of the humanistic/psychodynamic ones (Johnson et al., 2016).

The way toward the validation of treatment manuals related to a systemic model has been paved by the Leeds Family Therapy Research group. The authors described

F. Vadilonga (✉)
Adolescence Therapy Center (CTA), Milan, Italy

IRIS School of Psychotherapy, Milan, Italy
e-mail: fr.vadilonga@gmail.com

B. D'Avanzo
IRIS School of Psychotherapy, Milan, Italy

Istituto di Ricerche Farmacologiche Mario Negri IRCCS, Milan, Italy

G. Rangone
IRIS School of Psychotherapy, Milan, Italy

A. Barbato
Istituto di Ricerche Farmacologiche Mario Negri IRCCS, Milan, Italy

in detail a project aimed at developing a manual for systemic therapy based on the Milan school, including interventions from narrative, reflexive, and solution-focused models (Pote et al., 2003, Chapter 3).

Although some authors still caution against the risk of oversimplification of and restriction of therapists' creativity even in systemic-oriented manuals (Davies, 2019), the development of manuals has become a growing focus of interest also for family therapists working within a systemic framework (Escudero, 2012) and some evidence suggests that the practical advantages of a flexible approach to systemic-oriented manuals are likely to outnumber its risks (Cassells et al., 2015).

A further development in the field has been a shift from manuals addressing broad treatment models, to those targeted to specific problems (Boston & Cottrell, 2016). However, although family therapy is considered as an approach to address the multiple problems of families with adopted children, a recent systematic review of psychological interventions for adoptive parents found just three studies assessing a family systems approach (Ní Chobhthaigh & Duffy, 2019). Moreover, no study used a treatment manual, making the replication of the interventions difficult.

To fill this gap, we present here a model designed for the clinical work with adoptive families together with the outline of a manual to provide the clinicians and the researchers with a guideline describing the treatment steps. The full details of the research project leading to the manualization have been described elsewhere (Barbato et al., 2019).

14.2 The Problems of Adoptive Families

For several years the composition of the adopted child population in Italy has changed. Though the category of infants abandoned at birth is still present, children tend to be older, often close to adolescence, and the proportion of international adoptees is increasing. Moreover, children sent for adoption have now more difficult life histories, in the great majority entailing traumatic experiences. This requires that families are ready to house children with such characteristics. It is critical to adequately prepare parents who apply for adoption. Parents should be ready to get in touch with the child's difficult reality and to experience a "special" form of parenting. Nonetheless, this is not enough: families must also be helped in the post adoption period, and need to be able to access support for a long time in order for parents and children to cope with the burning issues of adoption, which will emerge in different ways at the key points in development. The research in the field highlights that adoptees have a higher risk of developing severe mental disorders in adulthood and are at a greater risk of showing suicidal behaviors compared to non-adopted children of the same age. It has been suggested that adoptive parents approaching international adoption need to be informed and prepared, and that the whole family unit should be supported (Tieman et al., 2005; Von Borczyskowski et al., 2006). The issues of origins, identity, belonging, experiences of rejection and abandonment, abuse, and sexual abuse must be considered in the light of the emotional and cognitive development of the child, even though this experience will be very painful for all people involved.

Although adoption is the best way to recover from trauma experienced in the growth contexts of origin, the complexity of this task represents a burdensome responsibility for adoptive families who welcome children with high levels of attachment disorganization, as defined by the attachment theorists (Crittenden, 1992). When children are moved to a safe family environment, they continue to use the same strategies they developed to survive in situations characterized by abuse and neglect. In the new parent–child relationship adoptees bring their histories, with the associated mental states and behavioral styles that emerged in the first care environment. These strategies, which were adaptive in the original context, are nonadaptive in the new one: the parents are confronted with children who cannot trust them, attack or shut down or freeze. While these strategies may have helped the children to survive in dangerous environments, their use in new conditions means that the children do not have the necessary instruments to draw benefit from good quality care (Stovall & Dozier, 1998).

The encounter with a traumatized child can expose adoptive parents to a high emotional and relational burden, since they can be subjected to disturbed and disorganized patterns that might manifest in a wide range of posttraumatic behaviors (aggressive and challenging acting out, sexualization of relationships). A further risk for adoptive parents is secondary traumatization, or the so-called trauma of the rescuer. Taking care of children with attachment disorders, or with a history of neglect or abuse, might be particularly destabilizing, since the representations of oneself and of the other related to one's own internal working models are challenged, and might even crumble. This would expose caregivers to a level of disorganization that could affect them too.

The child placed for adoption has his/her personal and relational history, which has shaped his perception of himself, others, and the world. He uses relational patterns based on the expectations he/she developed in previous meaningful relationships. As previously noted, adoptees have often internalized disorganized attachment models, and if the adoptive parents as well have internalized insecure or at-risk attachment mental models (confused or disorganized) they are more likely to impact negatively on the unprocessed traumatic events and experiences of their children.

In addition, the conditions characterising the pre-adoptive period, namely the encounter between the child and his new parents, make the process leading to the match between the child and parents highly stressful for both sides. Even if the attachment system maintains its function throughout life, the activation of defense mechanisms typical of any mental model peaks in situations of stress or danger. In the pre-adoption and post-adoption periods, when the parent–child attachment bonds develop, both the parent and the child are in a stressful situation that increases defense mechanisms connected to the mental model, and makes the development of a good attachment bond even more difficult. If the parents do not realise that the child's strategies and behaviors have a posttraumatic origin, they might attribute negative qualities to the child, thinking that he/she is oppositional, evil, or untameable. If the process of development of attachment bonds fails for a second time, offering to the child a negative representation of the self, the outcome might be extremely serious and negative. Therefore, working with the parents is critical, so that they provide a safe base for their children.

14.2.1 The Child's Involvement in Dysfunctional Relational Patterns

The adoptee enters into a family system with a history, and thus into a relational context characterized by consolidated relational pattern, previously defined roles, and preexisting expectations.

We might point out that something very similar happens with biological births as well. In fact, even in this case the child enters a system that already has its own rules, and he might carry the burden of meanings and expectations that can condition his/her development and affect identity. Some children are born to brighten up a dull spousal relationship, to be company for a depressed mother, to fulfill expectations that one of the parents or the siblings did not meet, or to satisfy the demands of a grandmother. While it is true that the presence of a tangle of meanings and expectations is unavoidable, the impact it can have on the child is proportional to the degree of rigidity/flexibility of the relational pattern deriving from it. In other words, can the family relational pattern in progress (Byng-Hall, 1998; Selvini Palazzoli et al., 1989) adapt to create space for the new child with his/her own characteristics, qualities, and inclinations? Or will the pattern produce suffering, severe misunderstanding and even pathology, by co-opting the child into a system of side-taking, coalitions, relational wars, and inappropriate meanings? What happens when the child already carries the burden of a history of traumatic experiences, and needs adults who can attune with him and accompany him through the difficult process of elaborating and repairing his difficult past? In this case, the impact of any dysfunctional family relational pattern on the child will inevitably exacerbate the existing problems, and sometimes add new problems on.

At an early stage of treatment, the first step is to make an accurate assessment of the extended family context, to explore the presence of any dysfunctional relational patterns in the nuclear family or between the nuclear family and the families of origin of the adoptive parents. It is likely that the treatment is compromised or even ineffective if this assessment is not performed correctly. Therefore, it is important to treat and reduce the risk factors connected to dysfunctional relational patterns before broaching the central issues of adoption. In addition, we need to consider that family relational patterns tend to reappear over time in relation to specific events or turning points in the life cycle, and therefore they must always be carefully monitored.

14.3 Theoretical Bases and Assumptions Underlying the TCA Model

The TCA model is based on a systemic family therapy approach integrated with attachment theory (Dallos, 2006; Agnetti et al., 2014) and influenced by the ecological systems theory of Bronfenbrenner (1992), who emphasizes the contextual and interactive nature of human development.

The first comprehensive proposal for the inclusion of attachment theory concepts in a systemic framework was brought forward more than 30 years ago (Wynne,

1984). Wynne outlined an epigenetic model of relational systems involving a sequence of stages, among which the basic one was attachment/caregiving. He stressed that Bowlby had observed that attachment behavior unfolds in a relational context of recursive feedbacks, therefore attachment and caregiving have complementary functions (Bowlby, 1982). However, Wynne addressed this issue from a theoretical standpoint. For many years family therapists remained indifferent to attachment related concepts and focused almost exclusively on patterns of communication and relational games. Adequate attention was not given in clinical practice to the assessment of dyadic relationships and their reflections at an individual level.

The first applications of the Wynne's conceptualization to the clinical work with families were introduced by Doane and Diamond (1994) and Byng-Hall (1995). According to the latter, attachment lies at the core of family life. He drew from attachment theory the construct of internal working models (Crittenden, 1990), defined as the sources of the individual scripts, interweaving to form the family scripts. Further developments along this way proposed models of integration of attachment concepts within a systemic approach: Johnson (1996) with the Emotion-focused therapy, Diamond, in the tradition of the structural therapy (Minuchin, 1974), with the attachment-based family therapy targeted to adolescent problems (Diamond & Stern, 2003) and Dallos (2006), within a constructivist framework.

The need to integrate the systemic concept of psychological suffering into constructs that can satisfactorily explain the individual's functioning stems from a clinical as well as theoretical instance. Beyond the rigid formats of family therapy and starting to use flexible formats, where the individuals can play a more meaningful role, we need categories with a higher explanatory potential. Attachment theory is particularly close to the Bateson's idea of the individual as inherently in relationship. Mind and identity overstep the individual's boundaries. In other words, our identity is the outcome of the meaningful encounters, and their quality, that we had in the lifecourse. One of Bowlby's major intuitions consisted of considering mental events as something primarily interpersonal and hence individual identity as shaped by the early experiences in the relationship with a meaningful caregiver. After that, Fonagy et al. (2004) showed how the self stems from a circular mirroring process involving the adults' and child's minds, in line with Bateson's idea that the mind is born in the relationship with another mind. To summarize, integrating systemic theory and attachment theory allows to view the practice of family therapy through mentalization lenses (Asen & Fonagy, 2012), moving significant steps toward a more satisfactory explanation of complexity, from the particular (the individual) to the general (the system) and vice-versa.

14.3.1 Goals of Therapy

The TCA model was designed to specifically address families with adoptees between 3 and 12 years of age who encounter difficulties in offering protection and reparation for trauma and loss experienced by the children in their context of origin (Farmer & Pollock, 1998; Palacios et al., 2005).

The final goal of treatment is to strengthen or rebuild secure relationships between parents and children, enabling the latter to develop a healthy perception of themselves, trust in others and improved independence, and emotional regulation skills. Therefore, the first treatment focus is *repairing*: promoting parental responses that can offer the child corrective attachment experiences. The treatment aims to help the parents to correctly read and interpret their child's behaviors, to respond in such a way as to disconfirm the negative representations of himself and others, and to structure more useful behavioral strategies. The second treatment focus is *processing*: increasing the ability of the family unit to think and reflect about its own relationships and the adoptive history, transforming information, meanings, and stories so as to support psychological growth (Dallos, 2006; Vadilonga et al., 2012). Despite the fact that difficulties in adoptive families can be manifested in both the reparation and the processing area, there must be a hierarchy in the therapeutic intervention: the family must first be helped to achieve adequate security levels, and at a later stage helped to explore the adoption, supporting the attribution of correct meanings and an appropriate emotional narrative (Vadilonga, 2010).

The aim is to integrate the treatment of traumatized children into the approach to adoptive families, as suggested by research findings summarized by Juffer & Van Ijzendoorn (2007) major meta-analysis revealing a higher percentage of secure attachment in non-adoptees (adoptees 45%, non-adoptees 62%). While the insecure, ambivalent (adopted 10%, non-adopted 9%) and avoidant (adopted 12%, non-adopted 14%) attachment styles don't show significant differences, it is striking that in the adoptee group the disorganized attachment style percentage (33%) is more than double compared to the non-adoptees (15%). As we know, disorganized attachment is associated with traumatic experiences in childhood, and in adulthood to the risk of the onset of psychological disorders. Since adoption is a privileged treatment area for traumatized children, we should be first of all aware that we are dealing with a population of children who have had traumatic experiences, before or after leaving the biological family, which have shaped their adaptive strategies. Therapeutic interventions with adoptees should take into account the knowledge gained in trauma treatment (Hughes, 2004; Porges, 2007).

However, the significant increase in adoptions of children at a later age and with traumatic histories raises new problems for the adoptive parents.

Clinical experience suggests that a significant number of adoptive parents of children adopted at a later age are encountering more relational and behavioral difficulties with them (Howe, 1997) and that, in absence of timely interventions, the difficulties will become even more serious during pre-adolescence and adolescence. Therefore, promotion of an early intervention pattern is necessary in order to prevent crises, and it is critical to facilitate a prompt exchange of information between those in charge of the child's placement and those who will have responsibility for supporting the family after adoption. Even more important is the assumption that parents need detailed report about the adverse experiences and the trauma that the child dealt with, including an explanation of how these experiences can influence the development of children and the different areas of their life. This means facilitating the transmission of information, without omission or censure, from those who have access to it, and who promote the placement, to the adoptive parents. We know that the procedures quite often fail in the transmission of information, but we have to make an effort and ensure that the truth about the story of the child is transmitted comprehensively. Research shows that failure in adoption is not the consequence of a single factor but rather of the sum of many different risk factors (Palacios et al., 2005). If the adoption reaches a deadlock it is necessary to put in place therapeutic processes that enable the adoptive family to adequately support the child in mentalizing the trauma, managing the emotional and behavioral effects, and ultimately developing with greater serenity. Strictly connected with the latter assumption is the need for an ecological approach to the treatment; the adoptive nuclear family as a whole must be considered as the core unit for intervention, since we consider adoption as the first and most important therapeutic intervention, aimed at changing the mental models and representations of the parent–child relationship.

The model, applied to the clinical treatment of adoption, enables us to focus attention on relationships and the mutual influence concerning both the microsystemic level (within the adoptive family) and the mesosystemic level (relationships between the adoptive and biological family, between the adoptive family and the social context, etc.). As regards the strengthening of the reparative aspects of adoption, the TCA model was inspired, as we have already mentioned, by the transactional model of Stovall and Dozier (1998). In this perspective, the treatment aims at generating corrective attachment experiences. Thus, adoption can represent a new experience that modifies the mental organization of the children if the parent's response to the child's behavior allows him to experience new care patterns, profoundly different from his previous experience. The therapeutic work aims at supporting the parents in understanding the meaning of their children's behaviors (including sexualized or challenging behaviors, and attachment difficulties) and facilitating experiences of new ways to fulfill the parental role, so that they become able to respond to the child, disconfirming his negative representations of himself and others. In terms of research about the processing aspects of adoption, Fonagy and Target (1997) studies on the reflective function facilitated the development of interventions aimed at increasing the reflective abilities shown in the adoptive family, which are critical in order to promote the development of a consistent personality and help the adoptee to keep the significant events of life connected and integrated. Lastly, the model was strongly inspired by the concept of communicative openness (Brodzinsky & Palacios, 2005). This concept represents a prerequisite underlying the processing work with adoptive families: without a good level of communicative openness, the attribution of meaning and access to mentalization are impossible, and this is a risk factor for psychopathology (Selvini Palazzoli et al., 1989). The underlying theoretical belief is that if the adoptive parents are able to create and support adequate communicative openness on the issue of adoption, the children might process their experiences and the emotions connected to their trauma.

In summary, the overarching goal of the therapeutic process is to promote changes in family relationships enabling secure attachment bonds, which represent the precondition for the development of an effective reparative process for adoptees who have often developed disorganized attachment styles as a consequence of their traumatic experiences.

14.3.2 Tools and Techniques

The model uses a number of "multipurpose" instruments, often in shortened versions, not only for diagnosis and assessment but also, within a clinical perspective, for offering starting points for the reparation and processing that adoptive families are called upon to carry out. The instruments are shown in Table 14.1, with the indication of their target: child, parents, and child–parent relationships.

A key tool to be used with parents to enhance the reparative aspects of adoption is the Adult Attachment Interview (Hesse, 2008). This semi-structured interview enables the parents to express their mental representations, functioning strategies, any trauma they might have experienced, the level of processing, and the metacognitive skills; therefore facilitating the attribution of meanings to past experiences. This work is useful for the therapist as well, because he/she can understand the person he/she is working with, and for the parents because during the interview they can reflect on their own history of attachment and the influence that this might have on their relationships with the adoptee. The subsequent feedback will focus on

Table 14.1 Instruments used to inform the clinical work

Instrument	References	Type	Target	Focus
Story Stem Assessment Profile	Hodges et al. (2009)	Rating scale based on a narrative technique	Child 4–8 years	Perceptions and expectations regarding the attachment figures
Sceno Test	von Staabs (1971, 1991)	Projective test	Child	Representations of family relationships
Modified Strange Situation	Cassidy et al. (1992) and Solomon and George (1999)	Observational procedure	Child 3–6 years	Response to separation from the parents
Separation Anxiety Test	Klagsburn and Bowlby (1976) and Wright et al. (1995)	Semi-projective test	Child	Response to separation from the parents
Adult Attachment Interview	Hesse (2008)	Semi-structured interview	Adult	Mental representations of attachment and metacognitive skills
Parent Development Interview	Slade et al. (1999)	Structured interview	Adult	Mental representations of child and child–parent relationships
Lausanne Trilogue Play	Fivaz-Depeursinge and Corboz-Warnery (1999)	Structured observation of interaction	Family	Family functioning and child–parent relationships
Indice Osservativo dell'Attaccamento	Attili (2007)	Structured observation of interaction	Family	Child–parent relationships according to attachment styles

limits and resources related to individual and relational skills and strategies. Specifically, personal histories are connected to current adoptive parenting and how that fits together with the child's history of abandonment, loss, and trauma. The goal is to increase mentalization and understanding of the relationship between the parent's functioning and the child's reactions in order to enable the child's representations and strategies to evolve. Later an interview transcript might be read once more, shared, and even modified by the parents, with the advantage of adding elements to the reflections that emerged in the sessions.

A similar tool, more focused on the current parent–child relationship, is the Parent Developmental Interview (Slade et al., 1999). Also in this case the assessment interlaces with the processing work: some of the questions enable an analysis of the adoptive parents' mental representations of the child, to bring to the surface some of the interferences due to the parents' expectations and to specific aspects of adoption, including the pre adoptive history and information and/or fantasies about the family of origin.

For the children, some tools focused on processing the issues of adoption are used. This not only represents a possibility for the clinician to make a child's assessment, but through the practice of sharing and discussing what was brought by the child with the adoptive parents (also through the vision of pictures, video segments, or session transcripts), it also represents a valuable opportunity for the parents to better understand their children's functioning. Moreover, some key issues for adoptees can be addressed: the difficulties of building one's own identity, the "double belonging," the interference of mental representations of the self and others before adoption, the impact of abandonment, loss and trauma on current functioning, and the role of trauma-reactivating factors.

One of these tools is the Sceno Test (von Staabs, 1991). This is a projective test requiring a set of characters made of colored wooden blocks and other accessories for the furniture and scenery, introduced in Italy and adapted to be used in systemic therapy by Selvini Palazzoli (von Staabs, 1971). The child is asked to represent a life scene first with the adoptive family and later with the biological one. Therefore, he/she is actively involved in the assessment of his/her representation of the family relationships. This can give suggestions about possible lines of change to remove relational difficulties in the adoptive family, or to orient the parents' behavior in a focused way.

The Story Stem Assessment Profile (Hodges et al., 2005) is a well-known narrative tool used to enquire about perceptions and expectations regarding the attachment figures. Through the narration and the set-up of stories elicited, the child expresses his/her own functioning, the representations of him/herself and of the caregivers, the expectations for help, protection, comfort, and safety.

The ecological framework of TCA enables these elements to be used to improve the parents' understanding of the child. This is done jointly with video feedback sessions, to increase the parents' awareness of the child's representations and attachment strategies, by stimulating them to give corrective responses that disconfirm the old attachment patterns.

The model follows some of the interventions suggested by Brodzinsky and Pinderhughes (2013), such as the lifebook, the timeline, the imaginary correspondence, in addition to developing an original version of the narration of the family history (Vadilonga et al., 2012). Many of these tools work on identity. The lifebook is a symbolic representation of the children life, built together with them and the parents. It is a way to keep past, present, and future together and create some kind of continuity and consistency using pictures (real – photographies, documents – or reconstructed) of the life of the child. The timelines can create a chronological order in the often chaotic pre-adoptive life of the child, who has frequently changed many places and caregivers. Both the imaginary correspondence and the reconstruction of the family history are narrative instruments. Writing down facts makes it possible to explore the memories, beliefs, expectations, hopes, past, present, and future concerns, building new connections. The imaginary correspondence requires the child or the adoptive parents to write letters to the biological parents (or other significant figures from the context of origin) to which they then try to reply, taking on their "correspondent's" perspective. This intervention facilitates the expression of emotions, thoughts, fantasies, and doubts about what has happened and the attainment of a greater understanding of what underlies the abandonment, trauma, and incapacity to offer care. This can be used with older children or just with parents. The narration of the family history is mainly done by the adoptive parents who write about the complicated, painful and challenging life of their children, with the goal of reading and sharing it during a family session. By writing the story, supported step by step by the therapists, the parents can produce a meaningful narration to be shared with the child. This forces the parents to collect all the known information, create some order in the child's past, and give a structure to the connections between events; it enables the child, often confused and worried about his/her own history and unresolved questions, to benefit from a tailor-made narration (Hodges et al., 2009), which, without diminishing or glossing over past events, gives an explanation of his/her experiences. Three fundamental elements must be coherently integrated into the tale: information known by the parents, memories, and mental representations of the child (Vadilonga et al., 2012).

Besides the interventions focused on the parents' and children's narrations and representations, current relationship patterns are addressed, to connect them and give them meaning when compared with the past, by using the methods outlined in Video Feedback Intervention to Promote Positive Parenting (Juffer et al., 2017). This involves the observation of videotaped play sessions, focusing on meaningful segments and commenting with the parents on resources and promotion of positive parenting.

The vision of interactions, supported by the therapists' interventions, makes it possible to highlight the child's attachment and exploration needs and the positive exchanges with the parents, in order to increase their frequency. The discussion and analysis in detail of expectations, emotions, and thoughts underlying certain behaviors, enables to ascribe a different meaning, which is the essential requisite to change the responses and behavior enacted by the parents.

Lastly, we should also mention some therapeutic rituals (Imber-Black et al., 2003) that work both on the reparation and processing aspects. They provide support for the family in emotionally burdensome moments, allowing the different members to experience and express what they feel, and to communicate crucial messages for the construction and consolidation of the bonds and identity of the adoptee. The inclusion and belonging rituals are built together by the family and the therapist, and then set up during the sessions.

14.4 The Treatment Manual

The development of a manual describing the procedures of family therapy according to the TCA model for adopted families started with a review of available manuals produced within a systemic framework (Barbato et al., 2019).

The second step was the establishment of a focus group of expert therapists skilled in the model. The group consisted of eight clinicians working in the *Centro Terapia dell'Adolescenza*, a private licensed agency in Milan providing support and therapy to adoptive families. The clinicians were six women and two men, mean age 40.6 years (range 31–60), with a degree in psychology and postgraduate training in systemic family therapy and had a mean of 8 years of clinical experience in family therapy (range 2–30 years). The first task of the group was to reach a consensus on a set of core elements, defined as therapist's interventions considered as essential for the model (Waltz et al., 1993), agreeing on an operational definition of each element.

Subsequently, the group was asked to define phases and duration of therapy, timing of interventions, and format of sessions (individual, parental couple, whole family). A draft version of the manual was approved, comprising 29 elements distributed across four phases of therapy, consisting of a number of sessions between 22 and 32: (1) knowledge and alliance building; (2) assessment of the family, couple, and individual members functioning; (3) promotion of change; (4) consolidation and working through. The full list of core elements and their distribution across therapy phases are presented in Table 14.2.

The therapists using this model must be trained both in systemic therapy and in attachment-based interventions. The first phase starts with a brief self-introduction of the therapist, who explains her/his professional background and method of work. Then the therapist starts to collect information about the extended family through specific questions that aim to establish its composition and structure, and through the creation of a genogram displaying family relationships in terms of ties, events, and separations over three generations (Wachtel, 1982). This is followed by an analysis of the history of the couple, of the child, and of the adoption through questions aimed to identify any dysfunctional relational patterns within the nuclear family or in the birth family of the adoptive parents. Circular questions are used to highlight the relationship of the adoptee within the new family.

Table 14.2 Core elements of the model

Basic procedures
Self-presentation of the first therapist
Preliminary contract
Introduction of the second therapist
Explanation of the therapy framework in relation to the adoption
Contract
Closure
Information gathering
Inquiry on extended family
Informative questions
Inquiry on the story of couple, child, and adoption
Inquiry on risk and protective factors
Inquiry on trauma triggers
Monitoring of information given to the child
Inquiry on perceived differences between before and after the adoption
Assessment tools
Genogram
Administration of Adult Attachment Interview or Parent Development Interview
Assessment of child attachment style
Assessment of parent–child relationships
Video feedback
Techniques
Circular questions on adopted child inclusion and his/her relations with adoptive parents
Attachment-related questions
Hypothesizing
Promotion of the child adherence to the therapy
Feedback about Adult Attachment Interview or Parent Development Interview
Reflexive questions
Feedback
Therapeutic dialogue with the child
Therapeutic dialogue with the family
Enhancement of communication openness
Emotional narrative

Then, the therapist asks questions about the development of attachment bonds between the child and parents from the start of the adoption to the present. Specific consideration is given to inquiries about risk and protective factors, through an evaluation of the elements known to influence the outcome of the adoption. Some factors are related to the child: age of at the time of the adoption, presence of behavioral problems and initial attachment difficulties, previous traumas experienced directly or indirectly within her/his birth family or institutional contexts. Others are related to the parental couple: level of education, expectations, presence of other children, support network, motivations for adoption, parental style, and to the services received: pre-adoption assessment, training for adoption, post-adoptive support.

Trauma triggers are then investigated through active research into the antecedents of problematic behaviors or negative emotional states in the child, also considering other information provided by the parents. Once these elements are collected, a preliminary hypothesis about the problems presented by the child in terms of attachment and of functioning is formulated.

After this, during the definition of a preliminary contract, the therapist describes to the parents the model, the goals, the structure, and methods of the therapy, asking for their agreement and willingness to involve the child and to modify any negative behaviors and dysfunctional relational patterns. After this preliminary work, a second therapist is introduced and the monitoring of the information given to the child about the therapy is undertaken. This specific opening serves as an introduction to subsequent enquiries about the differences perceived by the child before and after the adoption, using questions) and nonverbal means of expression. Phase 1 finishes with the legitimization of therapy by the child in the form of a direct request of the therapists to agree to the therapy and to share a contract.

Phase 2 focuses on collecting information about the mental and attachment models of all the family members, and initially requires that parents and child are seen separately. The parents are interviewed using the instruments with a focus on attachment styles and parenting, namely the Adult Attachment Interview and the Parent Development Interview. The first therapist reports to both parents what has emerged from the interviews on attachment styles, highlighting the internal operating models and strategies, presenting some connections between these and the current problems in the parent–child relationship. In addition, the therapist asks both parents some reflective questions designed to promote awareness of their own and the child's mental representations. The second therapist focuses on the child, combining the free drawings with the administration of some of the instruments previously described to assess the child attachment styles and the parent–child relationships.

Then both therapists meet the whole family with the aim of drawing attention to the relationships between the parents and the child through structured observations of interactions.

Phase 3 involves the whole family with variable formats. A first intervention in this phase is the feedback given by therapists to the family, highlighting the connection between the attachment histories that emerged during the interviews, the current relationships between the two parents and between them and the child, highlighting any dysfunctional relational patterns, suggesting a possible explanation of the problems presented, and supporting positive changes.

During this stage, video feedback (Juffer et al., 2017) is used with the parents. The therapists show the parents videos recorded in phase 2, and discuss the child's functioning and his relationship with the parents, with the aim of increasing sensitivity, responsiveness, and reflectivity; facilitating the understanding of the child's functioning in terms of mental representations and strategies; connecting the attachment histories with the current relationships. Some of the sessions are dedicated solely to the child and conducted by the second therapist. A therapeutic conversation with the child uses questions and comments to promote a change in the mental representation of the self, others, and relationships, with the aim of differentiating the current family context from previous contexts. In the therapeutic conversation with the family, using questions, examples and suggestions, the therapists elicit in the parents and the child reflections about the possible consequences of change, and suggest relations and behaviors that might facilitate change, identifying shared relational patterns and strategies to cope with challenges.

In phase 4 all family sessions are conducted by both therapists and are characterized by three interventions: enhancement of communicative openness, emotional narrative, and closure.

To enhance communicative openness the therapists help parents to tell the child the story of adoption and suggest how they and the child can ascribe a meaning to the adverse experiences, to free the child from guilt and clear any interpretative distortions.

In the emotional narrative the therapists help the parents to write the child's history, integrating emotional aspects with information collected in the previous phases.

In the closure the therapists ask the parents and the child what they gained from the therapy, ensuring that they have acquired information and new relational models, and positively reinforcing the learned skills.

The third step of the process of constructing the manual aimed at assessing the validity of the operational definitions of the core elements, by checking whether trained observers were able to identify them by watching therapy sessions. Therefore, five videotaped therapies were taken from the archive of the *Centro Terapia dell'Adolescenza*, in which the model, according to the focus group, was adequately implemented. Twenty-three sessions representing all phases of the process were randomly selected to be assessed by a group of raters.

Fifty-six observers were identified among master-level psychologists attending the postgraduate course in family therapy. They were provided with a glossary including the operational definitions of the 29 core elements of the model and received a brief training on the use of the glossary.

Eleven 4-hour observation sessions were organized between December 2013 and April 2015. The 23 therapy sessions, covering all phases of the treatment, were observed by a number of raters ranging from 12 to 19. The observers were instructed to separately assess the detection of the identified elements by filling a questionnaire at the end of each observed session, following a method used in studies evaluating the treatment process in psychotherapy (Markowitz et al., 2000).

The reliability among the observers was evaluated separately for each component, using the analysis of kappa for multiple raters (Fleiss, 1981). A kappa below 0.60 was considered an indicator of inadequate inter-rater agreement (McHugh, 2012), as suggested by the literature on psychotherapy research (Markowitz et al., 2000). The identification of any element showing kappa below 0.60 was considered to be unreliable. Just one element (informative questions) was deleted for this reason and many elements showed a reliability above 0.80. The final version of the manual was therefore approved (Barbato et al., 2019).

The fourth step addressed the use of the manual in clinical practice. A sample of 14 professionals working at the *Centro di Terapia dell'Adolescenza* were interviewed to assess to what extent they used the manual and found it useful. They were all women, in an age range 29–55, with 2–8 years of experience in the field, few with a consolidated experience of teaching or supervision. All had used the manual, usually in a flexible fashion, as support in single phases of therapies. Few closely followed the manual in the conduction of an entire therapy. They appreciated most the help in planning and giving a structure to the therapy, with a clear distinction of the various phases. Concerning what they thought was neglected, many professionals found that nothing important was missing, with some saying that short explanations of the single phases would be useful, as well as a general framework (at least for those not familiar with the model), examples and how to deal with possible exceptions. One therapist observed that involvement of the larger family including siblings and the assessment of trigenerational patterns were not considered. Whereas the idea of the general structure of the model seemed useful, the need of two co-therapists and particularly the indication of the number of sessions was not appreciated, because these elements were considered too dependent on the specific cases. The components the interviewees found best described were video-feedback, the first phase, and, in general, the definitions of the interventions, while the description of the tools was insufficient. These opinions suggest that the therapists found the manual useful in delivering a systemic therapy model including attachment interventions and that there is scope for an even more thorough tool to guide professionals in the therapy.

14.5 Conclusion

This manual can be considered a small but remarkable bridge between research and practice in the systemic family therapy field, due to the collaboration between a group of clinicians and a research team. However, it should be considered the first step of work in progress, and the more the manual will be used in clinical practice and training, the more a number of refinements will be needed.

The manual provides a practical tool to address the complex treatment needs of adoptive families by offering a systemic intervention model integrated with attachment-based interventions.

Future research developments will need to address the fidelity assessment in delivering the therapy according to the model, the families' experience of receiving the treatment, its dissemination to clinicians and outcome studies to verify the effectiveness of the model.

References

Agnetti, G., Barbato, A., Rangone, G., & Vadilonga, F. (2014). Verso un modello di terapia sistemica integrato con la teoria dell'attaccamento. *Terapia Familiare, 106*, 41–71.
Asen, E., & Fonagy, P. (2012). Mentalization-based therapeutic interventions for families. *Journal of Family Therapy, 34*, 347–370.
Attili, G. (2007). *Attaccamento e costruzione evoluzionistica della mente. Normalità, patologia, terapia*. Cortina.

Barbato, A., D'Avanzo, B., Vadilonga, F., Cortinovis, M., Lombardi, S., Pili, F., Rangone, G., & Visconti, A. (2019). Systemic family therapy integrated with attachment interventions for adoptive families. Development of a treatment manual. *Journal of Family Therapy*. https://doi.org/10.1111/1467-6427.12278

Boston, P., & Cottrell, D. (2016). Trials and tribulations – An RCT comparing manualized family therapy with treatment as usual and reflections on key issues that arose in the implementation. *Journal of Family Therapy, 38*, 172–188.

Bowlby, J. (1982). *Attachment and loss* (Vol. 1, 2nd ed.). Basic Book.

Brodzinsky, D. M., & Palacios, J. (Eds.). (2005). *Psychological issues in adoption. Research and practice*. Praeger.

Brodzinsky, D., & Pinderhughes, E. (2013). Parenting and child development in adoptive families. In M. H. Bornstein (Ed.), *Handbook of parenting 1* (2nd ed., pp. 279–311). Erlbaum.

Bronfenbrenner, U. (1992). *Ecological systems theory*. Jessica Kingsley.

Byng-Hall, J. (1995). Creating a secure family base: Some implications of attachment theory for family therapy. *Family Process, 34*, 45–58.

Byng-Hall, J. (1998). *Rewriting family scripts: Improvisation and systems change*. Guilford Press.

Cassells, C., Carr, A., Forrest, M., Fry, J., Beirne, F., Casey, T., & Rooney, B. (2015). Positive systemic practice: A controlled trial of family therapy for adolescent emotional and behavioural problems in Ireland. *Journal of Family Therapy, 37*, 429–449.

Cassidy, J., Marvin, R. S., & The MacArthur Working Group. (1992). *Attachment organization in preschool children: Procedures and coding manual*. Unpublished manuscript, University of Virginia.

Crittenden, P. M. (1990). Internal representational models of attachment relationships. *Infant Mental Health Journal, 11*, 259–277.

Crittenden, P. M. (1992). Quality of attachment in the preschool years. *Development and Psychopathology, 4*, 209–241.

Dallos, R. (2006). *Attachment narrative therapy: Integrating systemic, narrative and attachment approaches*. Open University Press.

Davies, B. (2019). Critique of manualized therapies: Systemic family therapy manual for adolescent self-harm. *Systemic Practice and Action Research, 32*, 403–409.

Diamond, G. S., & Stern, R. S. (2003). Attachment based family therapy for depressed adolescents: Repairing attachment by addressing attachment failures. In S. Johnson (Ed.), *Attachment processes in couple and family therapy*. Guilford Press.

Doane, J. A., & Diamond, D. (1994). *Affect and attachment in the family*. Basic Books.

Escudero, V. (2012). Reconsidering the 'heresy' of using treatment manuals. *Journal of Family Therapy, 34*, 106–113.

Farmer, E., & Pollock, S. (1998). *Sexually abused and abusing children in substitute care*. Wiley.

Fivaz-Depeursinge, E., & Corboz-Warnery, A. (1999). *The primary triangle: A developmental systems view of mothers, fathers, and infants*. Basic Books.

Fleiss, J. L. (1981). *Statistical methods for rates and proportions*. Wiley.

Fonagy, P., Gergely, G., Jurist, E. L., & Target, M. (2004). *Affect regulation, mentalization and the development of the self*. Karnac Books.

Fonagy, P., & Target, M. (1997). Attachment and reflective function: Their role in self-organization. *Development and Psychopathology, 9*, 679–700.

Hesse, E. (2008). The Adult Attachment Interview: Protocol, method of analysis, and empirical studies. In J. Cassidy & P. R. Shaver (Eds.), *Handbook of attachment: Theory, research, and clinical applications* (pp. 552–598). Guilford Press.

Hodges, J., Steele, M., Hillman, S., Henderson, K., & Kaniuk, J. (2005). Change and continuity in mental representations of attachment after adoption. In D. M. Brodzinsky & J. Palacios (Eds.), *Psychological issues in adoption: Research and practice* (pp. 93–116). Praeger.

Hodges, J., Steele, M., Kaniuk, J., Hillman, S., & Kay, A. (2009). Narratives in assessment and research on the development of attachments in maltreated children. In N. Midgley, J. Anderson, E. Grainger, T. Nesic-Vuckovic, & C. Urwin (Eds.), *Child psychotherapy and research: New approaches, emerging findings* (pp. 200–213). Routledge/Taylor & Francis.

Howe, D. (1997). *Patterns of adoption: Nature, nurture and psychosocial development*. Wiley-Blackwell.

Hughes, D. (2004). An attachment-based treatment of maltreated children and young people. *Attachment and Human Development, 6*, 263–278.

Imber-Black, E., Roberts, J., & Whiting, R. A. (Eds.). (2003). *Rituals in families & family therapy* (Rev. ed.). New York: W.W. Norton & Company.

Johnson, S. M. (1996). *The practice of emotionally focused marital therapy: Creating connections*. Brunner/Mazel.

Johnson, S. U., Hoffart, A., Havik, O. E., & Nordgreen, T. A. (2016). Survey of clinical psychologists' attitudes toward treatment manuals. *Professional Psychology: Research and Practice, 47*, 340–346.

Juffer, F., Bakermans-Kranenburg, M. J., & van IJzendoorn, M. H. (2017). Pairing attachment theory and social learning theory in video-feedback intervention to promote positive parenting. *Current Opinion in Psychology, 15*, 189–194.

Juffer, F., & Van IJzendoorn, M. H. (2007). Adoptees do not lack self-esteem: A meta-analysis of studies on self-esteem of transracial, international, and domestic adoptees. *Psychological Bulletin, 133*, 1067–1083.

Klagsbrun, M., & Bowlby, J. (1976). Responses to separation from parents: A clinical test for young children. *British Journal of Projective Psychology and Personality Study, 21*, 7–27.

Larner, G. (2004). Family therapy and the politics of evidence. *Journal of Family Therapy, 26*, 17–39.

Markowitz, J. C., Leon, A. C., Miller, N. L., Cherry, S., Clougherty, K. F., & Villalobos, L. (2000). Rater agreement on interpersonal psychotherapy problem areas. *Journal of Psychotherapy Practice and Research, 9*, 131–135.

McHugh, M. L. (2012). Interrater reliability: The kappa statistics. *Biochemia Medica, 22*, 276–282.

Minuchin, S. (1974). *Families and family therapy*. Harvard University Press.

Ní Chobhthaigh, S., & Duffy, F. (2019). The effectiveness of psychological interventions with adoptive parents on adopted children and adolescents' outcomes: A systematic review. *Clinical Child Psychology and Psychiatry, 24*, 69–94.

Palacios, J., Sánchez-Sandoval, Y., & León, E. (2005). Intercountry adoption disruptions in Spain. *Adoption Quarterly, 9*, 35–55.

Porges, S. W. (2007). The polyvagal perspective. *Biological Psychology, 74*, 116–143.

Pote, H., Stratton, P., Cottrell, D., Shapiro, D., & Boston, P. (2003). Systemic family therapy can be manualized: Research process and findings. *Journal of Family Therapy, 25*, 236–262.

Selvini Palazzoli, M., Cirillo, S., Selvini, M., & Sorrentino, A. M. (1989). *Family games: General models of psychotic processes in the family*. Norton.

Shadish, W. R., Montgomery, L. M., Wilson, P., Wilson, M. R., Bright, I., & Okwumabua, T. (1993). Effects of family and marital psychotherapies: A meta-analysis. *Journal of Consulting and Clinical Psychology, 61*, 92–1002.

Slade, A., Belsky, J., Aber, J. L., & Phelps, J. M. (1999). Maternal representations of their relationship with their toddlers: Links to adult attachment and observed mothering. *Developmental Psychology, 35*, 611–619.

Solomon, J., & George, C. (1999). The measurement of attachment security in infancy and childhood. In J. Cassidy & P. R. Shaver (Eds.), *Handbook of attachment: Theory, research, and clinical applications* (pp. 287–316). Guilford Press.

Stovall, K. C., & Dozier, M. (1998). Infants in foster care: An attachment theory perspective. *Adoption Quarterly, 2*, 55–88.

Tieman, W., van der Ende, J., & Verhulst, F. C. (2005). Psychiatric disorders in young adult intercountry adoptees: An epidemiological study. *American Journal of Psychiatry, 162*, 592–598.

Vadilonga, F. (Ed.). (2010). *Curare l'adozione. Modelli di sostegno e presa in carico della crisi adottiva*. Milano.

Vadilonga, F., Lombardi, S., Petoletti, S., & Visconti, A. (2012). Il trattamento psicologico: ricostruire e narrare la storia per sostenere l'elaborazione dei traumi di caregiver e bambini. *Minorigiustizia, 1*, 109–128.

Von Borczyskowski, A., Hjern, A., Lindblad, F., & Vinnerljung, B. (2006). Suicidal behaviour in national and international adult adoptees. *Social Psychiatry and Psychiatric Epidemiology, 41*, 95–102.

von Staabs, G. (1971). *Lo Sceno test, traduzione e prefazione di Mara Selvini Palazzoli.* Edizioni O.S.

von Staabs, G. (1991). *Sceno Test manual: A practical technique for understanding unconscious problems and personality structure.* Hogrefe & Huber.

Wachtel, E. F. (1982). The family psyche over three generations: The genogram revisited. *Journal of Marital and Family Therapy, 8*, 335–343.

Waltz, J., Addis, M. E., Koertner, K., & Jacobson, N. S. (1993). Testing the integrity of psychotherapy protocol: Assessment of adherence and competence. *Journal of Consulting and Clinical Psychology, 61*, 620–630.

Wright, J. C., Binney, V., & Smith, P. K. (1995). Security of attachment in 8–12-year-olds: A revised version of the Separation Anxiety Test, its psychometric properties and clinical interpretation. *Journal of Child Psychology and Psychiatry, 36*, 757–774.

Wynne, L. (1984). The epigenesis of relational systems: A model for understanding family development. *Family Process, 23*, 297–318.

Chapter 15
Manualized Family Therapy in a Controlled Study on Childhood Depression: Therapists' and Supervisors' Reflections on the Use of the Manual

Valeria Pomini and Vlassis Tomaras

15.1 Introduction[1]

In 1997, the authors received a proposal from Prof. John Tsiantis to participate in a European multisite, controlled double-blind trial evaluating psychotherapy for childhood depression. He was the coordinator of the Greek team in collaboration with Prof. Issy Kolvin in organizing the entire project. Many issues regarding the project were still to be arranged, but the process was slowly beginning. Our role included the organization and supervision of the family therapy team. A few months later, we were invited to the 25th anniversary of the Milan School of Systemic Therapy, in Pettenasco (Italy). Among the participants, we met colleagues from the UK and Finland[2] who had also been invited to enter the study as family therapists or supervisors. We had a small informal meeting and agreed that participating would provide a challenge to test our psychotherapeutic approach, yielding more evidence to the effectiveness of systemic family therapy in the treatment of childhood depression, as well as offering an opportunity to enter a transnational research process that would create more links and connections among participant services. At the end of

---

[1] The material presented in this chapter has been drawn from personal archives, personal notes, e-mails, manuscripts, and presentations at national and international conferences.
[2] David Campbell and Renos Papadopoulos, from the UK, Jans-Christen Wahlbeck and Helena Lounavaara-Rintala, from Finland.

V. Pomini (✉) • V. Tomaras
Family & Couple Therapy Unit, 1st Department of Psychiatry, National and Kapodistrian University of Athens, Athens, Greece

Training Program in Systemic Family & Couple Therapy, University Mental Health, Neurosciences, and Precision Medicine Research Institute "Costas Stefanis" - UMHRI, Athens, Greece
e-mail: vpomini@med.uoa.gr; vltomaras@gmail.com

© Springer Nature Switzerland AG 2021
M. Mariotti et al. (eds.), *Handbook of Systemic Approaches to Psychotherapy Manuals*, European Family Therapy Association Series,
https://doi.org/10.1007/978-3-030-73640-8_15

the day, we felt that we had already begun to create a "childhood depression study family therapy network".

As expected, many issues emerged from the beginning of the discussion, partly due to the different levels of experience in psychotherapy research among the participants. Furthermore, the five common larger meetings of all the study counterparts conducted by the project leaders in London, Athens, and Helsinki, which took place at different stages of the project, proved to be significant occasions for exchanging reflections from different perspectives, especially with our psychodynamic colleagues. There were two topics for developing a common ground: (a) the importance of parent–child attachment and its transgenerational patterns, and (b) the crucial role of the therapeutic relationship and alliance, assessed through a scale completed by all the therapists.

For both teams, systemic and psychodynamic, a crucial aspect was the use of the two manuals describing the whole psychotherapeutic process. At the end of the 1990s, the argument for the role and function of manuals in psychotherapy had not yet developed. Therefore, the stance of most of the participating therapeutic teams in the three countries towards manualized psychotherapy was ambivalent, at least at the starting phase of the project: On the one hand, everybody was aware of the need for a manual that offered common guidelines and methodology to therapists working in countries presenting many differences (e.g., culture, social context, organization of child and adolescent mental health facilities, educational system) in order to be in some way reliable and comparable for research purposes. On the other hand, therapists as well as supervisors were afraid of the constrictions that manualized therapy might impose to the spontaneity and uniqueness of the therapeutic process. The use of a manual sounded like "heresy" to many therapists from both teams and approaches (Davies, 2019; Johnson et al., 2016; Escudero, 2012). However, in the application of a model, the role of a manual describing the components, techniques and phases of the therapeutic process is essential in providing scientific evidence for the outcome of the specific therapeutic approach and offers an operational method that addresses and enhances the technical, reflective and institutional responsibilities and competencies of the therapists (Pote et al., 2003; Fruggeri, 2012). But these skills are not enough: a relational competence is necessary that *"enables therapists to observe and understand what they are doing together with their clients (...) in an interactional process that produces effects that are not unilaterally determined; the effects are the outcome of joint actions. Not deriving from the intentions and unilateral actions of therapists, the interactional dance may produce unintended consequences. (...) Thus, manuals, in their inevitable fixity, assertiveness and predictability are useful tools for developing technical expertise, but can they be an instrument for developing, enhancing or supporting relational competence?"* (Fruggeri, 2012, pp. 103–104). From this point of view, the capacity of manuals is controversial, and a main research issue arises, regarding the reliability of the intervention, even when manualized, as well as the issue of treatment integrity. In fact, treatment fidelity or integrity in the context of psychotherapy research *"refers to the extent to which the treatment was carried out as it was designed and encompasses three aspects: (a) therapist treatment adherence, the degree to which the therapist utilizes prescribed procedures and avoids proscribed procedures; (b) therapist competence, the level of the therapist's skill and judgment; (c) and treatment differentiation, whether treatments differ from each other along critical dimensions*" (Perepletchikova et al., 2007, p. 829). The issue of therapist competence stressed above refers to a qualitative dimension (how relationally competent and effective a therapist is), whereas treatment adherence can be expressed in quantitative terms (ibid.). Thus, the challenge is poised in the compatibility of these aspects with the epistemological basis of systemic family therapy, i.e. how a manual can implement the continuously reflective position therapists have to maintain on the relational dimensions of the therapeutic process. In order to achieve this purpose, a manual cannot be a mere list of techniques and guidelines on how to conduct sessions in different phases of therapy. On the contrary, it needs to be an *empirical informed guide* (EIG – Escudero, 2012) which functions as a map for therapists, leaving them free to use the guidelines that fit their particular style and adapt to each specific therapeutic circumstance.

In our case, two of the family therapy manual authors, David Campbell and Renos Papadopoulos, were also part of the London team as family therapy supervisors, and they encouraged therapists' critical discussion on the manual, while remaining open to introducing changes in order to better fit empirical practice across the different sites, during the initial phase of the study. As Valentin Escudero would state later: "*such a process is an example of 'putting practice into research and research into practice', that is, it is a circular and dynamic process of connecting the theoretical definition of therapeutic change mechanisms with what is observed in practice*" (Escudero, 2012, pp. 110–111).

15.2 The Research Project BIOMED "Psychotherapy for Childhood Depression"

During the 1990s, a need was expressed for more research in the field of child psychotherapy for clinical conditions often seen in clinical practice. Demand soared for studies conducted in naturalistic settings, by real-world practitioners (Kazdin, 1996). This approach contrasted the boom in the use of psychotropic medications in children and adolescents and promoted effective psychosocial and psychotherapeutic treatments (Escudero, 2012). However, our study was designed as an academic double-blind trial, with exclusion criteria (e.g., suicidal attempts, psychotic-like comorbidity, severe conduct disorders), thus creating a sample that was not representative of real-life cases in child and adolescent mental health facilities.

The research project "Psychotherapy for childhood depression" aimed to assess the effectiveness of two different forms of psychotherapeutic interventions on mild and major depression in childhood/early adolescence, as undertaken by trained therapists under supervision (Tsiantis et al., 2005; Trowell & Miles, 2011). The two modes of therapy used were Brief Individual Psychodynamic Psychotherapy (BIPP) and Systems Integrative Family Therapy (SIFT). The study took the shape of a cross-national European trial implemented between 1998 and 2002, in three clinical settings: The Tavistock Clinic, London, UK, the University Department of Child Psychiatry, Helsinki, Finland,[3] and the Department of Child Psychiatry, Children's Hospital "Ag. Sophia" as well as the Family Therapy Unit, 1st Department of Psychiatry, the latter two belonging to the Medical School of the National and Kapodistrian University of Athens, Greece. Manualization ensured comparability across the three centers (Pote et al., 2003).

The main aims of the study were (Trowell et al., 2007):

- To better understand childhood depression both at individual and family level.
- To explore to what extent psychotherapy can be efficacious for childhood depression and, more specifically, whether SIFT or BIPP is a more effective psychotherapeutic approach.
- To contribute to the knowledge base of how life stressors, interpersonal relationships, and dysfunctional attachment experiences might influence the onset and the maintenance of childhood depression.
- To inform our knowledge of how families with a child presenting depressive symptomatology may function and investigate specific patterns of functioning in these families.
- To experience a transnational, multicenter research process focusing on psychotherapy evaluation.

---

[3] The study was partly supported by the European Community: Concerted action contract No BMH4-CT98-3231 DG 12 – SSMI. BIOMED AND HEALTH RESEARCH PROGRAMME. Central coordination of the Project was by the Tavistock Clinic in London led by Issy Kolvin and later by Judith Trowell. Each center had a national principal investigator.
Participating Centers:

U.K.: Child and Family Department, Tavistock Centre, London.
Issy Kolvin (Central Coordinator), Judith Trowell (Coordinator), Maria Rhode, Anne Alvarez, Margaret Rustin, Gillian Miles, David Campbell, Emilia Dowling, Sarah Barratt, Renos Papadopoulos, Carmen Clemente, Kate Grayson, Vicky Bianco, Susan Bliss, Jane Cassidy, Lois Colling, Carol Desousa, Elspeth Earle, Anna Fitzgerald, Henia Goldberg, Inge Gregorious, Agathe Gretton, Judith Loose, Ryan Lowe, Sue McNab, David Pentacost,
Greece: Department of Child Psychiatry, Athens University Medical School.
John Tsiantis (Coordinator), Dimitris Anastasopoulos, Effie Lignos, Olga Maratos, Vlassis Tomaras, Valeria Pomini, Evi Athanassiadou, Makis Kolaitis, Vasso Moula, Irene Tsanira, Alexandra Alexopoulou,
Maria Belivanaki, Vaso Chantzara, Stelios Christogiorgos, Kostas Francis, Dimitris Georgiadis, Georgios Gritzelas, Terpsi Korpa, Olga Lanara, Dimitris Magriplis, Maria Marangidi, Valeria Pomini, Eleni Stavrou, Marianna Tassi, L. Tsarouhi.
Finland: Department of Child Psychiatry, University of Helsinki.
Fredrik Almqvist (Coordinator), Mika Soininen, Christina Bostrom, Eija Korpinen, Ulla Koskenranta-Aalto, Anna Kuikka, Helena Lounavaara-Rintala, Kaija Mankinen, Pirkko Pingoud, Liisa Pirhonen, Anjaleena Rissanen, Marja Schulman, Esko Varilo, Leena Varilo, Jan-Christer Wahlbeck, Sheila Weintraub, Reija Graeffe, Taru Forst, Reija Graeffe, Susanne Friman, Kaarina Hastbacka, Liisa
Hisinger, Eija Korpinen, Sakari Lehtonen, Kaija Mankinen, Maija von Fieandt, Pirjo Vuornos, Hanna Westerinen.

Following initial assessment, subjects were randomly allocated to one of the two treatment modes. All treatments were conducted at outpatient facilities. Both treatments were described by a treatment manual created ad hoc (Byng-Hall et al., 1996; Trowell et al., 2010) for the aims of the study. Both manuals included commonly used techniques, with clear guidelines in order to ensure adaptability to different cultural contexts but also comparability across the three centers. Treatment was limited to a 9-month period for both groups. For BIPP, this consisted of 30 weekly sessions with the child and 15 sessions of parental support, conducted by different therapists, whereas for SIFT, a total of 14 sessions per family were conducted on a fortnightly to monthly basis (Tsiantis et al., 2005). Supervision for BIPP was offered to the two therapists (child and parent) every 2 weeks by a senior supervisor. The BIPP supervision model did not differ across the three centers. Instead, SIFT supervision was conducted in different ways across the participating centers, as described below. The SIFT manual did not limit supervision implementation in terms of practices used.

SIFT teams functioned as following:

- In London, four family therapists worked in pairs: one interviewing the family, the other offering live supervision from behind the screen. The four therapists met monthly with four senior supervisors as a group to look at tapes and discuss (Campbell et al., 2003).
- In Helsinki, four senior family therapists worked in pairs, one with the family, the other behind the screen or sometimes as co-therapists.
- In Athens, six junior family therapists worked in pairs seeing the family as co-therapists. Each dyad was supervised by either of the two supervisors.[4] Live supervision was offered every other session, and video supervision every fourth session.

In Athens, the supervision model that was utilized for the study drew from the models of "supervision in training" and "supervision as consultation" (Tomaras & Pomini, 2002). The supervisors' role was becoming less and less directive as the project developed.

A total number of 24 cases in each country completed one of the two treatments, equally divided between BIPP and SIFT in London and Helsinki, while in Athens 11 were allocated to the first and 13 to the second type of treatment. Results showed that the change in prevalence of depression over the three time points of clinical assessment (baseline, end of therapy, 6-month follow-up) was statistically

---

[4] The six family therapists and the two supervisors worked in the project as volunteers, giving time after their regular work in their services. Four child psychiatrists, Dimitris Georgiadis, Kostas Fransis, Dimitris Magriplis, and Terpsi Korpa, and two clinical psychologists, Alexandra Alexopoulou and Olga Lanara, worked in pairs (female and male therapists). They were expert clinicians working in child mental health services in Athens. They had completed their training at the four-year training program in Systemic Family and Couple Psychotherapy, chaired by the two authors, of the University Mental Health Research Institute (UMHRI) of Athens, in collaboration with the 1st Department of Psychiatry – Medical School – National & Kapodistrian University of Athens.

significant in the two groups. SIFT showed that 75.7% and BIPP 74.3% of cases recovered at the end of therapy, and, respectively, 81% and 100% of cases recovered at follow-up. Differences were not significant between the two types of treatment (Trowell et al., 2007). Results were similar across the three countries and showed that both psychotherapy approaches were effective for major depression in children and adolescents despite sociocultural differences (ibid.). Notably, SIFT reached positive outcome with almost half the number of sessions of BIPP. Nevertheless, BIPP further improved the clinical outcome reached at the end of therapy during the follow-up period. Furthermore, significant improvements in self-esteem and social adjustment were found on all assessments, independent of the type of treatment (Kolaitis et al., 2011, 2014). Regarding family functioning, it is worth noting that both treatments improved family functioning significantly, across the three centers (Garoff et al., 2012). Family factors were found to influence the outcome both in BIPP and SIFT (ibid.).

15.3 The Manual

The SIFT manual was developed at Tavistock Clinic by John Byng-Hall, David Campbell and Renos Papadopoulos (1996). It provided a format of integrative family therapy widely used and easily implemented by therapists located in different centers and countries. The aim was to focus on the main components of the systemic approach that are shared by most systemic family therapists. An integrative approach was developed on the common ground of systemic family therapy (Byng-Hall & Campbell, 1981; Lebow, 1984, 2016). The main considerations in constructing the manual were the following (Tsiantis et al., 2005):

(a) to create an appropriate research tool,
(b) to provide clear, coherent, and specific guidance for the therapists without restricting their individual styles,
(c) to be flexible and fit to other cultural contexts.

Since the manual was to be used by therapists in three different countries and with families from a wide variety of socioeconomic backgrounds, it needed to allow for cultural and social variations.

The manual explicitly included techniques from the following approaches: Structural, problem-solving, Milan systemic, narrative, transgenerational and life cycle. Techniques not necessarily attributable to specific schools of thought were also included (Byng-Hall et al., 1996). It provided well-defined guidelines in order to ensure comparable treatments; at the same time, it allowed therapists to choose from several options, encouraging creativity and adaptation to the needs of every family in the specific context. As the authors stated: *"the overall aim of the manual was to provide a family therapy which was both consistent enough to be comparable, but could also be exportable"* (ibid., p. 2).

Furthermore, the manual provided a systems theory framework for understanding and addressing childhood depression, according to which the depressive symptoms are conceptualized in interactional terms. The child's feelings and behaviors are viewed as connected to the environment in which they live. Factors related to the onset of depression (stressful life events, losses, parental conflict, family history of depression, etc.) are explored within the family context, as well as maintaining factors (i.e., parental critical attitude towards the child, child behavior as distance regulator between family members, behavior that kept the family involved, etc.), and issues related to the social and cultural context (family social isolation, financial difficulties, peer difficulties, school problems including learning difficulties, bullying, etc.) (ibid.). The manual encouraged the therapists to be active in the therapeutic process, maintaining a stance of open-minded curiosity: "*The therapist acts as a catalyst rather than a social engineer; the aim is not to 'educate' the family or teach them how to do things best, but to empower them to apply their own solutions.*" (ibid., p. 4).

Clear guidelines outlined the time limitations, the structure of the therapeutic process, and allowed for selected techniques by the therapists. The therapeutic process developed in three phases: initial (sessions 1–3), middle (sessions 4–10), and ending (sessions 11–14 sessions). Session frequency could vary from once every two weeks to once a month, depending on the phase of therapy. Families that left treatment after one or two sessions were defined as dropouts, excluded from the research and replaced by the next recruited family, according to the design of the study. During the course of the study, decisions were made regarding early treatment termination (4–8 sessions) and treatment completion (9–14 sessions).

As to the participation of family members, the manual specified that in more than half of the sessions the depressed child[5] and at least one member of his or her family should participate. However, a few sessions with only the child (1–2) or only the parents (2–4) were allowed ("seeing family sub-systems") (ibid.).

The manual techniques were described in detail in 14 subchapters, which also provided other practical guidelines including recommendations on specific aspects of working with children, joining and engagement techniques, narrative approach, exploring gender and cultural issues, family life cycle, circular interviewing, enactments, focusing on strengths and positives, problem-solving and solution-focused techniques, challenging techniques, exploring family history, reframing, assigning intersession tasks, and seeing family subgroups (Table 15.1.) (ibid.).

Other recommendations included avoidance of paradoxical interventions and using parental sessions for marital issues. Inviting to sessions other key persons or relatives (e.g. grandparents) should be occasional. Family sessions were videotaped after informed consent.

A revised manual, informed by the therapy experience, was proposed, but eventually not realized.

---

[5] A wide battery of instruments was used for children's clinical and general functioning assessment (Trowell et al., 2007). Depression was assessed through the *Childhood Depression Inventory* (CDI – Kovacs, 1981), the *Kiddie-SADS* (Chambers et al., 1985) and the *Mood and Feelings Questionnaire* (Angold et al., 1987).

Table 15.1 SIFT manual techniques (Byng-Hall et al., 1996)

1.	Working with children	Attention to useful forms of conversation with children. Use of play material and drawings
2	Joining and engagement	Introduction to the context of therapy. Therapist being in tune with family members, making the family feel comfortable implementing therapeutic alliance, maintaining a stance of neutrality-curiosity and sympathetic, nonjudgmental listening
3	The family tells their story	Encouraging family members to express their views, exploring family narrative of depression, focusing on belief system, encouraging self-disclosure of personal thoughts and feelings
4	Cultural influences	Focusing on gender role and expectations in the specific family, focusing on family ethnic and cultural background, attention to discrepancies and conflicts between different cultural values
5	The family life cycle	Locating the family at the appropriate stage, allowing the family to establish their own important stages, eliciting the problems linked to a particular stage, exploring difficulties in moving from one stage to another, placing problems in a life cycle context in order to normalize them
6	Circular interviewing	Purposive and responsive to feedback interviewing style – circular and reflexive questions, hypothetical questions, questions oriented to the future
7	Enactments	Enacting family interactions during the session, exploring alternative interactions
8	Focusing on strengths and positives	Identifying competences in each family member outlining positive family interactions, discouraging parental critical stances towards the depressed child
9	Problem-solving and solution-focusing	Working on sequences of perceived dysfunctional interactions in order to identifying alternative ways for future events, listing past solutions
10	Challenging	Intensification of an affective component of an interaction, testing boundaries, disrupting monologues
11	Exploring family history	Constructing the family genogram, exploring family scripts, focusing on transgenerational patterns
12	Reframing	Focusing on positive functions of the depressive symptom, proposing alternative meanings of family interaction patterns
13	Intersession tasks, homework	Keeping diary, once a week doing things together, odd days and even days strategies, continuing some of the work initiated in the session
14	Seeing family subgroups	Seeing parents on their own, seeing depressed child, inviting other family members or significant others

15.4 The Athens SIFT Team

As described above, the SIFT manual did not define issues of co-therapy or supervision. Therefore, each center arranged family therapy sessions as in its everyday practice. Therapists and supervisors, however, frequently shared experiences and observations with colleagues from the other centers during and after the end of the

15.4.1 Main Issues Regarding the Therapeutic Process

At the beginning of the project, we were concerned that the child's diagnosis might have a labeling effect. Soon we realized that the depression diagnosis enhanced parental awareness of their child's difficulties, with parents' attitude shifting from "how to cope with a 'bad', un-collaborative child" to "how to help our depressed child". Therapists' next step was to connect the child's depression with the family's dynamics. Children's response to diagnosis was usually: "Finally, somebody understood me" or "I'm not bad, I'm angry and sad". None of the children appeared to understand depression as an illness or declined to take part to the sessions when invited. In several cases, as therapy progressed, children's motivation and engagement increased.

The therapeutic context was more defined than in our everyday clinical work (duration of therapy, number of sessions, goals, etc.). It has been observed that *"the balance between research rigor and 'real life' practice is an inevitable area of tension and requires consideration of both immediate and outcome consequences"* (Boston & Cottrell, 2016, p. 172).

In some cases, there were difficulties linked to referral procedures from the assessment service to the treatment service, although this did not hinder the further families' engagement with the therapeutic team.

The research context increased therapists' and supervisors' motivation in "doing a good job" as well as their concern in "thinking about families with a depressed child".

During the course of the project, team members underwent a gradual learning process; the team was more effective in conducting therapy, families' compliance to therapy improved (e.g., less dropouts and early terminations), and there were fewer difficulties in general.

Positive changes often happened sooner than expected. In some cases, something like a "good result" was achieved already in the middle phase of therapy. In only a few cases, therapists felt that the time limits posed by the study design were tight and that they needed more sessions to ensure the improvement. However, the specific time limits pushed therapists to be more aware of the therapeutic plan, more concentrated in what they were doing, and more effective in building a therapeutic relationship.

---

[6] E.g., the EFTA Conference in Berlin (Germany), 2004 and the AFT/EFTA Conference in Glasgow (UK), 2007.

At the end of the project, the Athens SIFT team agreed that "14 sessions in 9–10 months" was an intensive and viable therapy model for depressed children and their families, which might be expanded to other childhood problems.

15.4.2 Supervision Main Issues

Each of the two authors supervised an equal number of families, offering live supervision and video supervision in monthly meetings with every couple of co-therapists. Supervisors were concerned about:

- Lowering the depressive effect of sessions on therapists who often felt tired or frustrated.
- Supporting therapists' feelings of ineffectiveness, stuckness or risk (e.g. cases presenting suicidal thoughts).
- Supporting therapists facing the depressed mood of the family.
- Warning when therapists sided excessively with the depressed child.
- Helping them cope with family's anger and despair, while maintaining hope (perseverance, patience, empathy but also firmness, see Pentecost & McNab, 2007).
- Encouraging them to limit parental criticism of the depressed child and clarifying the parents' responsibility for the child's safety.
- Advising them "not to substitute the parents" and to trust parents' capacity to understand and cope with their child's problem (enhancing family resilience).
- Helping them to move the family from focusing on facts and behaviors to meanings and feelings.
- Supporting them in acknowledging marital conflicts or parents' unresolved issues, but focusing on parental roles.

15.4.3 Family Features

Some families presented difficulties in engagement from the start of therapy, postponing or missing arranged sessions. The hopelessness and helplessness described by the London and Helsinki teams (Pentecost & McNab, 2007) were rather expressed in Athens as anger, rage, and feelings of injustice. Aggressive behaviors in family life were often reported by parents in the Greek sample and addressed in therapy. All of the families, but one, were homogenous respecting ethnicity, culture, and religion. The therapeutic team contacted other systems (e.g. school) less frequently compared with the other two teams. All of the children attended school regularly, most of them presenting learning difficulties.

15.5 Post-session Notes

From the beginning of the study, the authors of the SIFT manual proposed a common means of recording the impressions of therapist(s) and supervisor(s) after every session. This aimed to assess the use of the manual during the study, thus offering a double description of the therapeutic process and techniques. Post-session notes made it possible to investigate the following issues: (a) which techniques described in the manual were more often reported by therapists, (b) which techniques not included in the manual were also used, (c) the use of techniques and approaches along the different phases of therapy, and (d) how much therapists' and supervisors' recording coincided.

A review of the notes led to the following findings:

Circular questioning, joining, and engagement were the most frequently used techniques. Techniques did not differ among therapists. They mainly focused on building a trusting, empathic relationship with all family members based on active listening and involving everyone in the dialogue, even the absent members (Table 15.2). Joining techniques were not limited to the initial phase of therapy, but continued to be present.

Notably, techniques related to specific work with children were not registered frequently, although in several cases children were asked to draw or they did so spontaneously, as drawing material was always available in the therapy room (Table 15.2). Probably, therapists took those techniques for granted, since all of them

Table 15.2 Most frequently used SIFT techniques

Working with children	Talking and listening to children Use of play material and drawings
Joining and engagement	Empathetically listening, keeping the dialogue alive
Formation of therapeutic alliance both with the child and the parents	Encouraging children's participation, equally allocating time among family members
Circular interviewing	Triadic, ranking, hypothetical, future oriented, reflexive questions
Reframing – positive connotation	Child's behavior, interaction patterns, meanings of clinical symptoms and other behaviors
Focusing on strengths and positives	Focusing on child's and other family members' competence
Exploring family history – mapping genogram	Family life cycle Three generations' history
Problem-solving	Identifying and testing new solutions
Challenging	Changing communication patterns
Dealing with helplessness and hopelessness	Introducing new perspectives
Intersession tasks	New activities, outing, keeping notes
Working with family subgroups	Parents, child alone, mother and daughter, father and son
Reflecting team	Therapists or therapists-and-supervisor dialogue in front of the family

were child-psychiatrists or child-psychologists. Another explanation might be the children's age in the Athens family therapy sample (mostly aged 12–14). In addition to the above-mentioned techniques, reframing and positive connotation (of behaviors, stances, or family interactions) were used frequently in all phases of therapy.

In the sessions during the initial and middle phases of therapy, techniques exploring family history, family life cycle stage and difficulties in moving from one stage to another, life events and their impact on family life (e.g., in single-parent families, after separation or loss), and family genogram were frequently registered. Transgenerational family history received much attention by the therapists, especially traumatic experiences and coping strategies. Therapists paid attention, in line with the manual guidelines, to the meaning of depression within the family, to the presence of depression in previous generations and its impact on family life, as well as to depressive symptoms in one or both parents, their coping strategies and children's responses to them. Notably, within our family therapy sample, in most cases one or both parents presented subclinical depressive symptoms and three parents had received the diagnosis of depression.

Interventive techniques were reported less frequently by all therapists, and they appeared mainly in the middle or final phase of therapy. They consisted of: (a) problem-solving, (b) changing communication patterns (usually criticism by parents), and (c) intersession tasks in order to test alternative ways of behaving, or relating, or simply to collect more information about the family's functioning. Typical structural techniques such as enactment or intensification were seldom registered. Working with family subgroups was preferred by all therapists. In most cases, therapists invited parents separately for 2–4 sessions and in two cases the child was invited alone for 1–2 sessions. In cases of single-parent families, therapists responded to the parent's expressed need to have some space alone for support in his or her parental role. The manual allowed therapists to be flexible on family members' participation, although discouraging individual sessions with the child. Sometimes, in case of divorced parents, therapists divided the session time by meeting certain family members separately and returning to close the session with the entire family.

Regarding collaboration with external systems, in two of the cases therapists contacted the school, after family consent, and had meetings with the teachers.

Narrative techniques were underreported by therapists, although supervisors emphasized their utility. We might assume that for therapists, narrative was more an approach than a technique. Externalization, which is a more specific narrative technique, was adopted only in one or two sessions addressing the child's mood.

It is noteworthy that a technique frequently implemented by all the therapists, although not mentioned in the manual, was the use of reflecting team, transformed into a simpler version of the original concept (Andersen, 1987): towards the end of the session, the two co-therapists turned to each other and had a brief dialogue in front of the family, asking family members not to interrupt them and keep their comments for later. Dialogue focused mainly on the session's main topics, therapists' thoughts and hypotheses about family dynamics, behaviors, the child's symptoms, parental issues, observed changes, as well as the therapeutic relationship or the process as a whole. As a result, at the end of the session, family members had time to give feedback or comment on what the therapists were reviewing. In some sessions, the supervisor joined the therapists and the family, so that the supervisor–therapists dialogue was displaying in front of the family.

As reported above, live supervision in our team occurred every two sessions while video supervision every four sessions. Supervisors filled their post-session notes only after live supervision. In most cases, therapists' and supervisors' notes regarding the use of the manual coincided, although therapists tended to underreport techniques recorded by the supervisors. It is possibly due to the different position of the supervisor observing the session, as compared with the therapists' process of recalling what happened during the session. Furthermore, the considerable agreement between therapists and supervisors might be attributed to the fact that all six therapists had been trained in the past by the two supervisors, who were already familiar with observing them in action. The range of techniques used by the therapists was influenced by the manual but also by the training they had undergone years earlier (Table 15.2.).

15.6 Further Reflections by Therapists and Supervisors

At the end of the project, five out of the six family therapists summarized their experience by answering the following questions: (a) Which in your opinion were the main factors related to child's depression in the families you worked with? (b) Which therapeutic techniques did you mainly use with these families? (c) How do you assess the therapeutic outcome in these families? and (d) Which were the main difficulties you faced during the whole process?

(a) Possible factors related to the child's depression involved their family system, like issues of loss and unresolved grief and separation, as well as the school system. One out of three in our sample was a single-parent family. The mother had been abandoned by the father or she had died. Separated fathers were absent or remote. Mothers' expressed or unexpressed anger towards the father influenced the child's mood. In all families, subclinical or diagnosed depression of one or both parents, greatly influenced the child's mood and feelings. In these cases, children had adopted a parental role and showed great concern for the depressed parent. Financial difficulties, parental unemployment and social isolation, particularly in single-parent families, were factors that negatively impacted the child. A general feeling of emotional isolation, abandonment and inefficacy in everyday life issues was observed in most families, together with open or covert conflictual relationships among family members. Critical stances by parents towards the depressed child were almost the rule. Furthermore, in most of the cases, a position of triangulation of the specific child was observed. Even in single-parent families, the child was overinvolved in the mother's relationships with other relatives or partners. In some cases, depressed mood was observed in siblings, who demanded and received attention in the course of therapy.

In the Athens sample, all but one families did not present ethnic or cultural differences. Transgenerational conflicts linked to internal migration from provincial to metropolitan areas were observed. The role of grandparents in rearing the children was very important in many families, often connected with a loss of boundaries or conflicts about roles. Other common issues presented by the depressed child were difficulties at school, academic and relational (with classmates), and experiences of bullying, either as a victim or a perpetrator.

(b) Therapists underlined the importance of joining techniques along the whole process. The therapists' stances that better fitted the family were nonjudgmental, empathic listening, giving enough time for children to express themselves, use of humor and a playful manner, a respectful position, and active curiosity towards family functioning and history. Circular interviewing was preferred, as well as reframing and positive connotations, problem-solving and other solution-focused techniques, and the use of intersession tasks. Exploring family history and life events, constructing genograms and eliciting transgenerational patterns (e.g. attachment models) also received priority. The same priority was given to the exploration of patterns of depression and other patterns within the family, of the meaning family members attributed to depressive symptoms, and to the co-construction of new meanings of symptoms and family patterns, encouraging and exploring new ways of functioning and interacting. Seeing family subgroups was considered as helpful by all therapists. Challenging techniques were less mentioned. Finally, the reflecting team procedure was very welcome. Although not mentioned in the manual, it was adopted by all the national teams.

(c) A strong feeling of successful ending of therapy was shared by the therapists, despite their preoccupation regarding "what will follow". Only in one case, therapists did not see positive changes. In all the other cases, therapists' feeling of good outcome was prevalent regarding the child's clinical symptoms and overall functioning, as well as the family's emotional climate including the parents' mood and their parental role. Therapists expressed surprise about the speed of the changes observed in certain families, even in the middle phase of therapy. All therapists expressed an overall positive feeling about their experience of participating in the study.

(d) Regarding difficulties faced during the process, therapists mentioned: the heavy or flat emotional atmosphere they felt in dealing with families, particularly during the initial phases of therapy, the initially cautious or suspicious stance of some families regarding the setting (double room with one-way-screen, research context). They also reported their strong efforts for engagement, their difficulty in changing the highly critical parental attitude towards the depressed child, the rigidity of most families, and the explicit or hidden request of parents to focus on their personal or couple issues. All therapists felt uneasy in ending therapy, not only because some families requested further sessions but also because of their reluctance to disengage. In some cases, therapists felt uncertainty over the family's future. It must be mentioned that the therapy frame "14 sessions within 9 months" was quite unusual in the settings where the therapists used to work.

15.7 From the Past to the Present: Further Usefulness of the SIFT Manual

Recently, for the scope of this text, the authors asked the family therapists to recall: (a) what they remember of the manual, (b) how the manual facilitated their study work, (c) if it posed any obstacle in this work, and (d) how much their manualized treatment experience affected their afterwards family work.

Two therapists found it difficult to recall their experiences. Representative answers of the other three are presented:

(a) T1 *"I remember the analytic description of the techniques to be included and those to be avoided, the emphasis on the phases of therapy, as well as the structure of the whole project."*

T3 *"It was for me the first contact with an integrative approach which I adopted in my work, as a further integration of the systemic and the Jungian analytical psychology."*

(b) T2 *"The manual did not limit my personal style, although it provided specific systemic guidelines (...) it was flexible and easy to use."*

T3 *"The manual guidelines were useful as a benchmark and facilitated the therapeutic process. The required recording of the techniques used during each session was particularly helpful, as an exercise of reflection. The three phases of treatment and the description of steps that were appropriate for each phase facilitated the therapeutic work."*

(c) T1 *"The manual limited the therapist's personal style and inspiration; however it was not a disadvantage for me as I gained structure, techniques and scientific methodology."*

T2 *"We were afraid for the treatment outcome if we would not apply all the techniques. Some seemed to be incompatible with Greek reality and culture."*

T3 *"The limited number of sessions for each family put some pressure (...). It was difficult to use the large number of suggested therapeutic techniques. At the same time, the pressure to avoid dropouts was greater than it might have been in another, non-research setting."*

(d) T1 *"It enriched my work both in the diagnosis procedure and in treatment, not only with families with depressed youths but with every dysfunctional family (...) It helped me to mature professionally and be aware of what I' am doing in the therapy room."*

T2 *"When practicing family therapy in a public Child Mental Health Institution (...) such a manual becomes useful in terms of saving time and human resources, especially by applying short-term psychotherapeutic interventions (...), also in other mental disorders such as conduct disorders, school refusal, eating disorders, psychosocial problems, etc."*

T3 *"I don't think the use of this manual particularly affected my subsequent clinical practice. However, (...) it influenced the eclectic approach I use widely in my current clinical work, combining systemic and psychodynamic approaches."*

15.8 Concluding Remarks

Adherence to the treatment manual was assessed on the basis of therapists' and supervisors' notes after the sessions. Thus, it was a subjective, self-evaluation process by the therapists reflecting upon what they did during the session, choosing from a list of techniques included in the manual. On the other side, the supervisors' notes after the session, from their perspective of live supervision, confirmed in several cases the therapists' perspective, and in other cases added new information on the use of the manual. The research methodology did not provide for external evaluation of adherence to the manual, also defined as treatment fidelity and treatment integrity (see Perepletchikova et al., 2007) e.g., observation of videotaped sessions by a rater using an instrument (Weisman et al., 2002; Marvin et al., 2016). Since all family therapy sessions in the three countries were videotaped and this material is still available, other aspects such as differences in approaches and techniques among the three centers might be useful to be explored.

From the supervisors' point of view, adapting to a "Procrustean bed" was a demanding task for all of us. Supervisors had to be constantly alert in order to avoid deviations from the manual guidelines, such as psychoeducation or individual instead of relational dialogue. In a few cases, frustration resulting from the agreed short duration of therapy was discussed and metabolized between therapists and supervisors. In cases of early termination, the supervisors supported the therapists by underlining the right of every family to end the therapy when they felt they had gained what they expected.

Furthermore, the specific time limits pushed the therapeutic system to be more aware of the therapeutic plan and the assessment necessity, and more concentrated in what they were doing.

In conclusion, we believe that SIFT provides an intensive, effective therapy model for depressed children and their families, which could be also applied for other childhood psychological problems. After the end of the study, the SIFT manual has been adopted as one of the texts provided to our trainees, as we overtly encourage them to promote the model in their facilities.

Acknowledgments We are thankful to: Prof. Issy Kolvin, who initiated the study and passed away during its implementation, Prof. Judith Trowell, who succeeded him as coordinator, Prof. John Tsiantis, who coordinated the Athens teams, the authors of the SIFT manual, John Byng-Hall and David Campbell, who passed away after the completion of the study, and Prof. Renos Papadopoulos for their valuable support, all the family therapists and supervisors from the three centers for sharing their time, thoughts, and reflections, the colleagues of the psychodynamic teams for their openness and interest in exchanging experiences with their systemic colleagues, all other scientists who worked for the project and the families who participated. Last but not least, we are thankful to the six family therapists of the Athenian team.

References

Andersen, T. (1987). The reflecting team: Dialogue and meta-dialogue in clinical work. *Family Process, 26*, 415–428. https://doi.org/10.1111/j.1545-5300.1987.00415.x

Angold, A., Costello, E. J., Pickles, A., et al. (1987). *The development of a questionnaire for use in epidemiological studies of depression in children and adolescents*. Institute of Psychiatry, London University.

Boston, P., & Cottrell, D. (2016). Trials and tribulations – An RCT comparing manualized family therapy with treatment as usual and reflection on key issues that arose in the implementation. *Journal of Family Therapy, 38*(2), 172–188. https://doi.org/10.1111/1467-6427.12118

Byng-Hall, J., & Campbell, D. (1981). Resolving conflicts in distance regulation: An integrative approach. *Journal of Marital and Family Therapy, 7*, 321–330. https://doi.org/10.1111/j.1752-0606.1981.tb01384.x

Byng-Hall, J., Campbell, D., & Papadopoulos, R. (1996). *Manual: Systems Integrative Therapy (SIFT) – The basis for an integrative approach*. Tavistock Clinic.

Campbell, D., Bianco, V., Dowling, E., Goldberg, H., McNab, S., & Pentecost, D. (2003). Family therapy for childhood depression: Researching significant moments. *Journal of Family Therapy, 25*(4), 417–435. https://doi.org/10.1111/1467-6427.00259

Chambers, W., Puig-Antich, J., Hirsch, M., et al. (1985). The assessment of affective disorders in children and adolescents by semi-structured interview: Test–retest reliability of the schedule for affective disorders and schizophrenia for school-age children, present episode version. *Archives of General Psychiatry, 42*, 696–702. https://doi.org/10.1001/archpsyc.1985.01790300064008

Davies, B. (2019). Critique of manualized therapies: Systemic family therapy manual for adolescent self-harm. *Systemic Practice and Action Research, 32*(4), 403–409. https://doi.org/10.1007/s11213-018-9462-y

Escudero, V. (2012). Reconsidering the 'heresy' of using treatment manuals. *Journal of Family Therapy, 34*, 106–113. https://doi.org/10.1111/j.1467-6427.2011.00581.x

Fruggeri, L. (2012). Different levels of psychotherapeutic competence. *Journal of Family Therapy, 34*, 91–105. https://doi.org/10.1111/j.1467-6427.2011.00564.x

Garoff, F. F., Heinonena, K., Pesonena, A. K., & Almqvist, F. (2012). Depressed youth: Treatment outcome and changes in family functioning in individual and family therapy. *Journal of Family Therapy, 34*, 4–23. https://doi.org/10.1111/j.1467-6427.2011.00541.x

Johnson, S. U., Hoffart, A., Havik, O. E., & Nordgreen, T. A. (2016). Survey of clinical psychologists' attitudes toward treatment manuals. *Professional Psychology: Research and Practice, 47*, 340–346. https://doi.org/10.1037/pro0000108

Kazdin, A. E. (1996). Developing effective treatments for children and adolescents. In E. D. Hibbs & P. S. Jensen (Eds.), *Psychosocial treatments for child and adolescent disorders: Empirically based strategies for clinical practice* (pp. 9–18). American Psychological Association. https://doi.org/10.1037/10196-028

Kolaitis, G., Giannakopoulos, G., Tomaras, V., Christogiorgos, S., Pomini, V., Layiou-Lignos, E., Tzavara, C., Rhode, M., Miles, G., Joffe, I., Trowell, J., & Tsiantis, J. (2014). Self-esteem and social adjustment in depressed youths: A randomized trial comparing psychodynamic psychotherapy and family therapy. *Psychotherapy and Psychosomatics, 83*, 249–251. https://doi.org/10.1159/000358289

Kolaitis, G., Pomini, V., Tomaras, V., Maratos, O., Lagios-Lignos, E., & Tsiantis, J. (2011). Psychodynamic and family psychotherapy for children and adolescents with major depression: Preliminary findings on the effects on social adjustment and functioning. In J. Trowell & G. Miles (Eds.), *Childhood depression: A place for psychotherapy* (pp. 221–225). Karnac.

Kovacs, M. (1981). Rating scales to assess depression in school aged children. *Acta Paedopsychiatrica, 46*, 305–315.

Lebow, J. L. (1984). On the value of integrating approaches to family therapy. *Journal of Marital and Family Therapy, 10*(2), 127–138. https://doi.org/10.1111/j.1752-0606.1984.tb00003.x

Lebow, J. L. (2016). Integrative approaches to couple and family therapy. In T. L. Sexton & J. L. Lebow (Eds.), *Handbook of Family Therapy* (pp. 205–227). Routledge. https://doi.org/10.4324/9780203123584

Marvin, S. E., Miklowitz, D. J., O'Brien, M. P., & Cannon, T. D. (2016). Family-focused therapy for individuals at clinical high risk for psychosis: Treatment fidelity within a multisite randomized trial. *Early Intervention in Psychiatry, 10*(2), 137–143. https://doi.org/10.1111/eip.12144

Pentecost, D., & McNab, S. (2007). Keeping company with hope and despair: Family therapists' reflections and experience of working with childhood depression. *Journal of Family Therapy, 29*, 403–419. https://doi.org/10.1111/j.1467-6427.2007.00408.x

Perepletchikova, F., Treat, T. A., & Kazdin, A. E. (2007). Treatment integrity in psychotherapy research: Analysis of the studies and examination of the associated factors. *Journal of Consulting and Clinical Psychology, 75*(6), 829–841. https://doi.org/10.1037/0022-006x.75.6.829

Pote, H., Stratton, P., Cottrell, D., Shapiro, D., & Boston, P. (2003). Systemic family therapy can be manualized: Research, process and findings. *Journal of Family Therapy, 25*, 236–262. https://doi.org/10.1111/1467-6427.00247

Tomaras, V., & Pomini, V. (2002). The interlocking of therapy and supervision: The Athenian experience from the viewpoint of supervisors and supervisees. In D. Campbell & B. Mason (Eds.), *Perspectives on Supervision* (pp. 81–90). Karnac. https://doi.org/10.4324/9780429478208

Trowell, J., Joffe, I., Campbell, J., Clemente, C., Almqvist, F., Soininen, M., Koskenranta-Aalto, U., Weintraub, S., Kolaitis, G., Tomaras, V., Anastasopoulos, D., Grayson, K., Barnes, J., & Tsiantis, I. (2007). Childhood depression: A place for psychotherapy. An outcome study comparing individual psychodynamic psychotherapy and family therapy. *European Child & Adolescent Psychiatry, 16*(3), 157–167. https://doi.org/10.1007/s00787-006-0584-x

Trowell, J., & Miles, G. (2011). *Childhood depression: A place for psychotherapy*. Karnac.

Trowell, J., Rhode, M., & Hall, J. (2010). What does a manual contribute? In J. Tsiantis & J. Trowell (Eds.), *Assessing change in psychoanalytic psychotherapy of children and adolescents. Today's challenge* (EFPP book series) (pp. 55–92). Karnac.

Tsiantis, I., Kolvin, I., Anastasopoulos, D., Trowell, J., Tomaras, V., Miles, G., Papadopoulos, R., Almqvist, F., Soininen, M., & Bostrom, C. (2005). Psychotherapy for early adolescent depression (PEAD): A comparison of two psychotherapeutic interventions in three European countries. In E. D. Hibbs & P. Jensen (Eds.), *Psychosocial treatments for child and adolescent disorders: Empirically based strategies for clinical practice* (pp. 267–295). American Psychological Association. https://doi.org/10.1080/10503309812331332337

Weisman, A., Tompson, M. C., Okazaki, S., et al. (2002). Clinicians' fidelity to a manual-based family treatment as a predictor of the one-year course of bipolar disorder. *Family Process, 41*(1), 123–131. https://doi.org/10.1111/j.1545-5300.2002.40102000123.x

Chapter 16
Working Alliance, Attachment, and Mentalization as Relational Indexes for a Systemic Manualization of Psychotherapy

Franco Baldoni

16.1 Effectiveness and Manualization of Psychotherapies

Are psychotherapies really effective? Are there differences in efficacy between the different forms of psychotherapy and the different mental disorders? What makes psychotherapy effective? What influence does the therapist have on the outcome of a psychotherapy? Following a systemic perspective that pursues a biopsychosocial vision, in the manualization of a therapeutic protocol, what are the conditions that need to be considered?

In an attempt to answer these questions, it is necessary to consider that a correct assessment of the effectiveness of a psychotherapy implies a regular follow-up activity and the conduct of randomized controlled trials (RCT) which confirm the effectiveness of the treatment from an evidence-based perspective. In this perspective it is necessary to carry out research on *efficacy* (to demonstrate experimentally that a treatment acts on a specific disorder excluding the influence of other factors), on *effectiveness* (to evaluate the outcome of psychotherapeutic interventions as they are used in the reality of clinical contexts), and on *efficiency* (to evaluate the efficiency of the treatment in terms of cost-benefits and real applicability). These studies require a specific methodology and often the manualization of therapeutic protocols. RCT research data are usually reworked in a meta-analysis which calculates the effect size (the difference in standard deviations between experimental and control groups) which provides a general measure of the amplitude of the phenomenon (a Cohen d value of 0.2 corresponds to a limited effect, 0.5 moderate, 0.8 wide, and 1.0 excellent).

Psychoanalysts have for years shown a certain reluctance to subject their clinical work to validation research, but in recent years, under the pressure of the numerous

F. Baldoni (✉)
Department of Psychology, University of Bologna, Bologna, Italy
e-mail: franco.baldoni@unibo.it

papers published on the effectiveness of cognitive-behavioral therapy (CBT), many RCT studies have been organized on large samples of patients subjected to different psychotherapeutic techniques, short- and long-term psychodynamic ones included (Shedler 2010, 2018). Research into the effectiveness of systemic treatments, despite their complexity, the difficulty of manualizing them, and the number of subjects involved, has also developed considerably since the turn of the century (Carr 2009). This applies to both family, individual, and couple systemic treatments for adult-focused problems (Carr 2014, 2018a; Stratton 2016; Ochs et al. 2020) and for child-focused problems (Carr 2018b).

Collectively, the results of evidence-based research on the outcomes of psychotherapy (especially considering individual psychotherapies of different orientation but neglecting couple, family, or group ones) are set out in an official document of Division 29 of the American Psychological Association (APA 2012) entitled *Recognition of Psychotherapy Effectiveness*, based on many sources concerning RCT studies, and can be so summarized:

1. Effects of psychotherapy are confirmed and largely significant.
2. They are demonstrated for many mental disorders with variations that are influenced (a) by the severity, chronicity, and complexity of the disorder, rather than by the particular diagnosis and (b) by the characteristics of patients and clinicians and context factors (such as social support), rather than the type of treatment.
3. The beneficial effects of psychotherapy tend to persist and increase over time even after the end of treatment.
4. Efficacy tends to be comparable or superior to that of psychopharmacological treatments, with significantly lower costs and side effects.
5. Psychotherapies reduce disability, morbidity, hospitalizations, and mortality, increasing working skills. This entails a clear reduction in healthcare costs (by 20–30%, with a 17% reduction for patients undergoing psychotherapy compared to a 12.3% increase for those not treated psychologically, leading to a saving, in chronic disorders, of $ 10 for every dollar spent).
6. A strong link between psychological and physical health has been demonstrated, and the validity of programs that consider psychotherapy within basic healthcare has been confirmed.

The same document underlines that psychotherapy is fundamentally based on a valid therapeutic alliance (or working alliance, WA).

The effectiveness of psychotherapy has been demonstrated for a variety of psychological and medical disorders in children, adolescents, adults, and the elderly: depressive disorders, anxiety disorders (panic disorders, generalized anxiety disorders), stress disorder, PTSD, alcohol-related disorders and other addictions, personality disorders, (most) childhood disorders (depression, anxiety, ADHD, conduct disorder) (APA 2012; Wampold 2014).

Data of evidence-based research, therefore, indicate that the different models of psychotherapy, as a whole, produce largely positive results (overall effect size on 475 studies: 0.85) and higher than those of antidepressant pharmacotherapy (Effect size: 0.17–0.31) (Shedler 2010), but that no psychotherapeutic technique has demonstrated a particular superiority over the others (APA 2012; Wampold 2014). In studies where slight differences emerge, the results tend to correspond to the researcher's preferences and theoretical training rather than to real effects due to the treatment. In particular, empirical research shows that "evidence-based" therapies are weak treatments (Shedler 2018), their benefits are trivial, few patients get well, and even the trivial benefits do not last.

The most related factor to patient satisfaction and the psychotherapy outcome also appears to be the quality of the working alliance (WA) or therapeutic alliance (Safran and Muran 2000; Ardito and Rabellino 2011), a construct derived mainly from the psychoanalytic clinic that refers to non-neurotic or non-transference-related aspects of the psychotherapeutic relationship and that has been defined as a reality-based collaboration between patient and therapist (Greenson 1965). Bordin (1979) described three dimensions: (1) the agreement on the goals of the therapy (goals); (2) the agreement on the tasks to be addressed (tasks); (3) and the development of a bond between patient and therapist based on mutual positive feelings (bond). The latter element is the one most valued by researchers for its similarity to the concept of attachment relationship. WA is perhaps the most studied aspect of the therapeutic process and is recognized as an important nonspecific factor common to many forms of therapy (Shedler 2010, 2018; Ardito and Rabellino, 2011; APA 2012; Baldoni and Campailla 2017).

Other factors associated with higher psychotherapeutic efficacy are also related to the quality of the clinical relationship and the psychological characteristics of the therapist, rather than to the technical aspects (see Fig. 16.1): empathic abilities, sharing of objectives with the patient, taking a positive attitude, and being consistent and authentic. The various meta-analyses of the evidence-based literature (Wampold 2014; Wampold and Imel 2015) have clarified that these are the determining

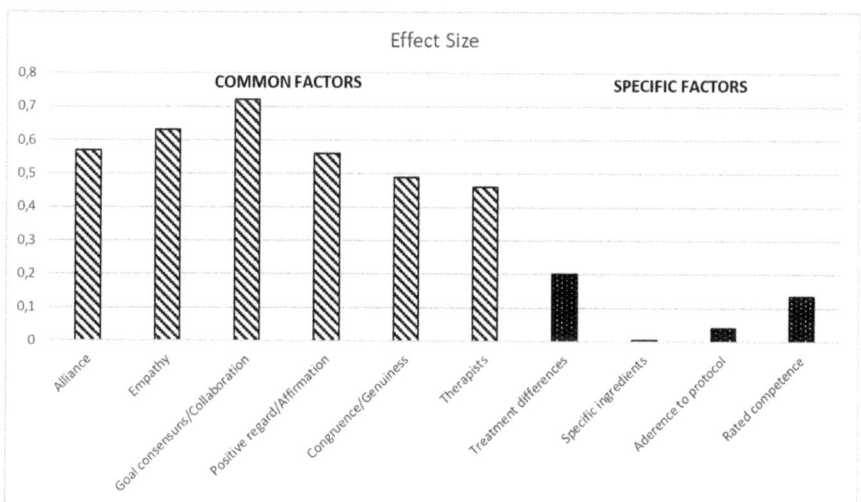

Fig. 16.1 Factors that influence the outcome of psychotherapies. (Source: Wampold, 2014, with the author's permission)

elements (their effect size is higher than 0.2), while, on the contrary, the type of treatment, the adherence to a manualized protocol, or being competent about a particular technique seems to play a decidedly secondary role.

According to Bruce Wampold (2007, 2012, 2014; Wampold and Imel 2015), one of the most authoritative experts in this field and member of APA division 29, the common factors influencing the effectiveness of psychotherapies are related to some human characteristics (which together constitute the humanistic component psychotherapy), in particular:

1. The tendency to attribute meaning to the world (through interpretation, explanation, attribution of a causal effect, mentalization of oneself and others, organization of experience in the form of narration)
2. The tendency to influence and be influenced by others (i.e., to live in relationship with other people, to act on them, and to be subject to social influence)
3. The tendency to change over time through:

    (a) A significant relationship (in particular attachment bonds, such as that between parents and children, between partners of a romantic couple, or between psychotherapist and patient)
    (b) The creation of expectations (which explains the therapeutic influence of suggestion, placebo effect, and rituals)
    (c) Acquiring a new ability (mastery) (i.e., developing a sense of self-efficacy and control towards events, internal ones in particular, linked to emotional reactions such as fear, anger, anxiety, and depression)

In more recent years, the growing interest in attachment theory has favored the use of this construct as a key for interpreting and measuring the therapeutic relationship (Wallin 2007; Obegi 2008; Holmes and Slade 2018; Baldoni 2018). Research data agree in indicating the safety of the clinician as the greatest predictor of a good therapeutic alliance, while insecure attachment, particularly the one concerned, is related to greater difficulties (Baldoni and Campailla 2017). The particular *matching* (i.e., the combination) between the attachment pattern of the patient and that of the therapist, which influences the quality of the relationship, the areas explored, the interventions used, and the therapeutic process, and its outcome also plays an important role (Romano et al. 2009; Hill 2015; Baldoni 2008, 2018).

To conclude, evidence-based research has demonstrated the efficacy of psychotherapy in a wide range of pathologies, but for the purposes of treatment, the characteristics of the therapist and the quality of the relationship assume greater importance than the therapeutic technique and the specificity of the diagnosis. However, we need to repeat the caution (above) that very few of the comparisons in the research literature have included systemic couple and family therapies.

It can be legitimately assumed that clinicians who show greater empathic and relational skills develop a solid and lasting working alliance with their patients and are better able to conduct different types of therapies adapting to the personal needs of the different patients, therefore, the most effective beyond their theoretical preparation.

16.2 Manualization in a Systemic Perspective

How is it possible to use evidence-based research data to develop an appropriate methodology in the study of the effectiveness of treatment and in manualization of psychotherapy? In particular, in a systemic perspective, which methodology should be used in this process? Research data indicate that the quality of the relationship between patients and psychotherapists (in terms of working alliance or attachment safety) is a determining factor, the one most associated with the positive outcome of treatments and the satisfaction of patients and their families. From a systemic perspective, a manualization of a treatment should therefore guide the psychotherapist focusing on these aspects. Some considerations are possible, regarding working alliance, attachment, and mentalization.

16.3 Assessing Working Alliance and Attachment Matching Between Therapist and Patient

The manualization of a treatment should include tools for assessing working alliance and attachment, considering both patients and psychotherapists. Some useful tools that can be used for this purpose are (Baldoni and Campailla 2017):

1. For the assessment of the WA, self-report questionnaires can be used such as the *Working Alliance Inventory* (WAI), the *California Psychotherapy Alliance Scale* (CALPAS), and the Pennsylvania (Penn) Scales (Ardito and Rabellino 2011) completed by the therapist alone, by the patient only, or, more rarely, by both or independent external observers.
2. For the assessment of the attachment of therapists and patients (including their matching), the most used tools are (a) the *Adult Attachment Interview* (AAI) (George, Kaplan, & Main, 1984–1996; Steele & Steele, 2008), a semi-structured interview for the evaluation of the attachment configuration of the therapist and patients; (b) the *Patient-Therapist Adult Attachment Interview* (PT-AAI) (Diamond et al. 1999), a modified form of the AAI that collects detailed information on the interaction of attachment patterns of therapists and patients; and (c) some self-report questionnaire, like the *Experiences in Close Relationships Scale* (ECRS) (Brennan et al. 1998) or the *Client Attachment to Therapist Scale* (CATS) (Mallinckrodt et al. 1995).

Unfortunately, almost all of these tools have been developed for individual assessment. They can therefore be indicated for individual or couple therapies, but they are not specific tools for family or group therapy. One of the few therapeutic models that provide for the assessment of attachment in all family members in a systemic perspective is the *Dynamic-Maturational Model of Attachment and Adaptation-integrative family system treatment* (DMM-FST) (Crittenden et al. 2014) which pursues the study of attachment in system family therapy, considering different assessment tools in life span. Again, however, the attachment of the therapist is rarely considered (Baldoni 2018).

16.4 Assessing Mentalization in a Systemic Perspective

The terms *mentalization* and *mentalizing* refer to "the mental process by which an individual implicitly and explicitly interprets the actions of himself and others as meaningful on the basis of intentional mental states such as personal desires, needs, feelings, beliefs and reasons" (Bateman and Fonagy 2004, xxi) or, more simply, "the capacity to understand ourselves and others in terms of intentional mental states, such as feelings, desires, wishes, goals and attitudes" (Allen et al. 2008). The term *reflective functioning* (RF), introduced by Peter Fonagy (Fonagy et al. 1991, 1998), represents the operationalization for research purposes of the concept of mentalization. From a clinical point of view, mentalization and reflective functioning can be considered synonyms. These faculties are acquired in the context of the first attachment relationships and are fundamental for the organization of the self and the affect regulation and give meaning to one's own and others' behavior.

Mentalization involves a *self-reflective component* (relating to the representations of the Self) and an *interpersonal component* (linked to the representation of others). There is also an explicit and an implicit mentalization (Allen et al. 2008).

Explicit mentalization corresponds to "thinking and speaking of mental states," both one's own and others', is conscious, linked to verbal language, and tends to take on the character of a narrative. It can be more easily learned culturally (through social models and stereotypes) or with experience (in family, with friends, at school, at work, or in psychotherapy), but it can also be imitated or falsified through only apparently mentalizing attitudes.

Implicit mentalization is an intuitive, procedural, automatic, and unconscious mentalization (Allen et al. 2008) and concerns both oneself (sense of self, mentalized affectivity) and others (e.g., manifesting itself by changing shift in conversations or when you spontaneously react to other people's emotions). An example is when spontaneous nonverbal behavior occurs (a meaningful gaze, a particularly expressive gesture such as caressing or touching one part of the other's body, for example, the face, a shoulder, a hand, or a leg, with a clear intention to communicate one's own mental state or an understanding of the other's mental state. Not all emotional states entail an implicit mentalizing (in some cases one can be overwhelmed by an emotion), and there is no defined border between explicit and implicit mentalization.

Pseudo-mentalization is the apparent ability to reflect which lacks the essential characteristics of true mentalization. The pseudo-mentalizing statements at first glance may appear reflexive, but they are the result of a modality of pretending (ideas seem to have meaning, but in reality they are without depth, they are not connected to each other and the states of minds are not really felt or superficial and stereotyped thoughts or manipulative attitudes (Bateman and Fonagy 2004; Allen et al. 2008; Fearon et al. 2006). They tend to be very selective and selfish.

In conclusion, reflective functioning (mentalization) is the basis of empathy (i.e., awareness of the mental states of the other) and allows to go beyond the external attitude to get to grasp the psychological state that motivated a certain way of acting. In the absence of these functions, therefore, one's own and others' behavior remain insignificant. Moreover, mentalization fosters the psychological representation and symbolization of inner states and is therefore crucial for the regulation and control of effects and impulses (including the physiological states related to them) (Bateman and Fonagy 2004).

The concept of mentalization is particularly useful for understanding the clinical process in psychotherapy (Baldoni, 2010). In many cases it is essential that the therapist, by carrying out a reflective functioning, makes the patient perceive that he is reflecting on him considering him in terms of mental states. In the most serious patients, this reflective attitude is more important than interpretation. The patient, reflecting in the thoughts of his therapist, can recognize his mental processes by reaching a higher level of awareness and developing in turn a better reflexive ability. Promoting mentalization in patients and their families is a common goal of most psychotherapies (Michels 2006), and the concept of mentalization therefore offers a key to understanding psychotherapeutic mechanisms and opens new perspectives in the therapy of patients who manifest self-structuring disorders, pathological aggression, empathic difficulties (patients with personality disorders, antisocial and violent patients, alexithymic subjects), and psychological trauma (Holmes 2001; Bateman and Fonagy 2004; Allen et al. 2008; Baldoni 2016).

Specific integrated therapeutic protocols have recently been proposed that promote mentalization using attachment theory as a paradigm and combining psychoanalytic, cognitive-behavioral, and systemic techniques with a possible pharmacotherapy (Jurist et al. 2008; Sadler et al. 2006; Baldoni 2010), such as the *Brief Attachment-Base Intervention* (BABI) (Holmes 2001), the *Mentalization Based Therapy* (MBT) (Bateman and Fonagy 2004, 2008; Allen et al. 2008), and the *Short-term Mentalization and Relational Therapy* (SMART) or *Mentalization-Based Family Therapy* (MBFT) (Fearon et al. 2006), a mentalization-based protocol for systemic family therapy.

It should also be considered that psychotherapeutic treatments, including those based on mentalization, inevitably aim to increase explicit mentalization abilities above all (Allen et al. 2008; Michels 2006). Because of its spontaneous, unconscious, and procedural nature, in fact, the implicit one is more difficult to identify and modify through direct verbal interventions of an interpretative or cognitive-behavioral type.

The mentalizing or reflective processes have been studied in a psychoanalytic and cognitivist perspective above all as individual characteristics. Peter Fonagy (Fonagy et al. 1998) developed a procedure known as the *reflective functioning scale* (RF) that measures the subject's overall reflective capacity in a single dimension (from -1 to 9) based on the analysis of the transcription of the *Adult Attachment Interview* (AAI) or others similar semi-structured interviews derived from the AAI like the *Parent Development Interview* (PDI) or the *Current Relationship Interview* (CRI).

Although it has been studied mainly in a psychoanalytic and cognitivist perspective, particularly within the theoretical framework of attachment, mentalization and reflective functioning can be considered systemic concepts (Baldoni 2007, 2009), as they (1) involve a clear interpersonal component (decentralization, understanding of the mind of the other, affective mirroring) and (2) refer to the cybernetic concept of feedback (positive and negative) and to mental states, behaviors, and faculties developed within a relationship as a response to the other. These functions are therefore the expression of a relationship within a system (attachment bond, couple, family, psychotherapy). Pasco Fearon (Fearon et al. 2006), a Fonagy collaborator, has in fact used these concepts to develop a specific mentalization and attachment-based systemic family treatment (SMART or MBFT).

Mentalization can therefore be studied not only as a characteristic of a subject but also as an expression of a system of relationships. The reflective skills manifested by a patient, a family, or a couple are in fact important for the maintenance of well-being, the resolution of conflicts, and the ability to adapt, while their lack can be considered a negative prognostic factor for relationship difficulties and psychological, behavioral, and somatic disorders manifested by the members of the family during their life (Baldoni 2016).

For this reason, the manualization of a treatment in a systemic relational perspective must consider these aspects for the study of the therapeutic process and as proof of the efficacy of the treatment itself. Considering that fostering mentalization processes is an objective of most psychotherapies, why not measure this dimension in the reality of the clinical relationship?

16.5 The Reflective Function in the Family (RFF)

It is clear to everyone that the mentalization processes are not stable (like an IQ) but vary significantly according to the different relational contexts (work, family, friends, psychotherapy). The *Reflective Function in the Family* (RFF) (Baldoni 2007, 2009) is a new tool for mentalization assessment during a consultation or family therapy session that can be considered in the systemic manualization of a treatment. RFF aims to measure mentalization not as an individual characteristic but as an expression of an interactive system over time. It provides a useful guide for the clinical intervention and for the study of the therapeutic process and effectiveness during treatment, at the conclusion of this and on the occasion of follow-up sessions.

RFF is the specific version for family therapy of the *Mentalization Assessment in Psychotherapy* (MAP) (Baldoni 2014) a tool currently under study that evaluates the reflective skills manifested by patients and therapists within a consultation or psychotherapy session (individual also). MAP and RFF are both compatible with various theoretical guidelines and can be used in different theoretical contexts (systemic, psychoanalytic, cognitivist, or cognitive-behavioral).

The assessment of reflective skills (mentalization) through RFF is based on the systematic analysis of verbal (and partially nonverbal) communication as shown in the *verbatim* full transcription of the audio-video recording of a family therapy session. In this way, family therapy sessions videotaped in the past can also be analyzed. The purpose of the RFF (and the MAP) is not the measurement of the individual mentalization level (for which assessment-specific methodologies like the RF/AAI based on semi-structured interviews have been developed) but is to assess the expression of mentalization within a relationship by detecting the mentalizing statements expressed by therapists and patients during a psychotherapy session.

For the detection of reflective (mentalizing) statements and nonverbal mentalizing expressions, different criteria were taken into consideration:

1. Those indicated by Peter Fonagy, Mary Target, Howard Steele, and Miriam Steele for the assessment of the reflective self (RS) (Fonagy et al. 1995) and of the reflective functioning (RF) (Fonagy et al. 1998; Steele and Steele 2008) through the analysis of the transcripts of the Adult Attachment Interview (RF/AAI)
2. The criteria used by Arietta Slade (Slade et al. 2005) for the assessment of the Parental Reflective Functioning through the Parent Development Interview (Aber et al. 1985) (RF/PDI)
3. The criteria for the assessment of metacognition in a psychotherapy session using the Metacognitive Assessment Scale (MAS) (or Scala di Valutazione della Metacomunicazione, S.Va.M.) (Carcione et al. 1997; Semerari et al. 2003)

The criteria for coding reflective statements with RFF can be summarized as follows:

1. Specific references to one's own or others' mental states
2. Explicit attempts to interpret behavior based on mental states
3. Awareness of the complex nature of mental states
4. Awareness of possible changes in mental states over time
5. Sensitivity towards the other person's mental states
6. Procedural manifestations of sensitivity towards mental states (implicit mentalization, expressed with nonverbal behavior)

In cases relating to criteria 1 and 2, the reflective statement, to be counted as valid, must:

(a) refer to a subject (the self, the other or both) who experience the mental state;
(b) highlight a non-generic mental state;
(c) refer to a specific situation.

To be considered mentalizing, statements about the complex nature of mental states (criterion 3) and its evolutionary aspects (criterion 4) must be used in order to interpret, explain, or clarify the meaning of a behavior within a specific situation, contributing to the understanding of the event in a nontrivial or generic way. In these cases, it is particularly important to consider sufficiently large sections of the transcript (clusters).

For the application of these criteria, it is necessary to consider that:

(a) The reflective statement must be explicit and complete. An incomplete, interrupted, or partial statement is indicated in parentheses and not counted.
(b) It must refer to specific mental states and contexts and not be generic ("In the family I feel rejected" must not be considered reflective, while "When my parents behave this way, I feel rejected" is to be considered reflective).

(c) It must refer to representations of mental states, not to non-mentalizing judgments or descriptions. Affirmations about thoughts, behaviors, or emotional reactions, if not accompanied by the representation of the subject as thinking, are not considered reflective ("At that time I was desperate" is not considered reflective, because it is not clear if it is a posteriori judgment, while "At that time I felt desperate" is reflective).
(d) Statements that merely repeat another person's statement are not to be considered reflective (e.g., a family member who repeats a reflective hypothesis formulated by a therapist).
(e) Pseudo-mentalizing (i.e., apparently mentalizing) statements are counted in a specific subscale and do not contribute to the calculation of reflective statements.
(f) The statements referring to mental states current and pertinent to that specific situation are to be considered reflective even if one does not explicitly refer to the awareness of the mental state, since the representation of the self as thinking is implicit (e.g., a mother who during the session addresses her son saying: "I am very angry with you!"). They must manifest themselves as fresh and spontaneous expressions referring to their mental states and can be accompanied by comments regarding their mental functioning and by their awareness of the complexity of their thinking and their discrepancies and contradictions (*Metacognition*).
(g) The context of the speech must be assessed, considering the previous and subsequent sentences (e.g., if the statement is in relation to a question from the therapist).

In RFF the assessment scores of the reflective functioning statements are distributed in subscales, scales, and total scores (see Fig. 16.2). They are indicated with the letter S (self) if referring to the self, with the letter O (others) if referring to other people, with the initials U (us) if referring to both the self and other people (as in the case where a therapist or family member expresses himself in terms of "we"). The initials H (hypothesis) are added to the reflective statements of the therapists expressed in the form of hypotheses or reflective or circular questions.

The T (therapist and possible co-therapist), M (mother), F (father), S (son, 1, 2, 3), and O (other, like grandparents, uncles, friends, new partners) scales are composed of the sum of the scores of two subscales: the Sp (spontaneous) subscale, related to the reflective statements that emerge spontaneously, and the Rq (on request) subscale in which the answers provided to specific requests are counted, usually by a therapist (as in the case of a reflective question). The total scores respectively indicate the total of the therapists' reflective statements expressed in the form of hypotheses or questions (H) and finally the reflective capacity expressed overall by the family (RFF), by the therapists (TT), and by the therapist/family system (C) in that specific session. The RFF/C index refers to the percentage of total reflective affirmations of the family (RFF) compared to the total of the session (C) and expresses the overall reflective capacity of the family in relation to therapeutic interventions.

Date			Family							
	T_1	T_2	M	F	S_1	S_2	S_3	S_4	O_1	O_2
Code	Sp Rq	Sp Rq	Sp Rq	Sp Rq	Sp Rq	Sp Rq	Sp Rq	Sp Rq	Sp Rq	Sp Rq
Subscales										
Scales										
Self										
Other										
Family	Sp		Rq		Sp/RFF		Comments:			
	S		O		S/RFF					
RFF	π			H		C		RFF/C		

Fig. 16.2 RFF coding card (Baldoni 2010)

Nonverbal expressions of implicit mentalization (*Analogical Implicit Mentalization*, AIM) are usually detected through a careful viewing of the videotaped session (or in its transcription when the nonverbal aspects have been accurately reported) and are counted in the RFF coding card as mentalizing expressions concerning the self (S/AIM) or the other (O/AIM). Pseudo-mentalizing statements are not considered reflective and are not counted.

Reflective statements, scales, subscales, and total ratios are noted in the RFF coding card (see Fig. 16.2 and 16.3) and transferred in Excel format (Table 16.1) and graphics (Fig. 16.4).

The final version of the coding criteria was developed considering the experience of the group of researchers of the Attachment Assessment Lab (Department of Psychology of Bologna) headed by me, who used the pilot version of the RFF in the 3-year period 2009–2011 (Veronica Amadori, Clelia Angelastri, Flavio Casolari, Lucia Colangelo, Sara D'Alessandro, Francesca Del Fabbro, Margherita Dilorenzo, Mattia Minghetti, Laura Nannucci, Micol Natali, Samanta Sagliaschi). The use of the RFF required almost 2 years of training to achieve a coding reliability equal to or greater than 70% (14 family therapies were analyzed, 3 sessions for each therapy). From 2012, the RFF was used in research carried out by the Attachment Assessment Lab in collaboration with the ISCRA Institute of Modena. The results were presented in papers presented at different international congresses (Baldoni 2007; Bassoli et al. 2013).

Date	8-7-2018			Family				Rossi										
	T₁		T₂		M		F		S₁		S₂		S₃		S₄		O₁	O₂
Code	Dott. X		Dott.ssa Y		Alessia				Mirko PD		Rino		Marisa (assente)		Paolo			
	Sp	Rq	Sp	Rq	Sp	Rq	Sp	Rq	Sp	Rq	Sp	Rq	Sp	Rq	Sp	Rq	Sp	Rq	Sp	Rq
	OH OH O OH OH SO SO O				S S S				S S S	S S S			S		S O	S S O S S				
Subscales	8				3				3	3		1			2	6				
Scales	8				3				6		1				8					
Self	2		0		3				6		1				6					
Others	8		0		0				0		0				2					
Family	Sp		8		Rq		10		Sp/RFF		44%		Comments: session 7							
	S		16		O		2		S/RFF		88%									
RFF	18		TT		8		H		4		C		26		RFF/C		18/26 (69%)			

Fig. 16.3 Example of RFF coding completed card. (Baldoni 2010)

Table 16.1 RFF data table in Excel

Session	Sp	Rq	S	O	RFF	TT	H	C
Session 1	7	5	11	1	12	3	2	15
Session 7	8	10	16	2	18	8	4	26

16.6 An Example of Systemic Family Treatment Assessed with RFF

The Green family[1] requested treatment presenting the problem of the eating behavior disorder of their daughter Lucy, 20 years old. Lucy had been suffering from anorexia since the age of 13 and has been treated for years by an individual psychotherapist who suggested that the family undergo systemic family therapy. Lucy, a student, had a boyfriend at the time but had dropped out of school to pursue sports with her mother.

The first session was attended by the mother (48 years old, employed and semi-professional sportswoman), the father (50 years old, musician), Lucy, and her sister Anne (23 years old, employed).

---

[1] Names and personal details have been changed to preserve anonymity.

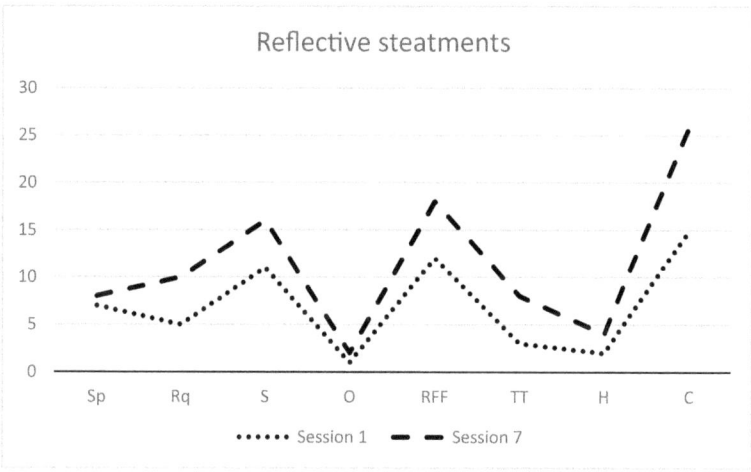

Fig. 16.4 Two family sessions compared with RFF graphics

The therapy was conducted by two therapists (Dr. X and Dr. Y), for a total of 11 sessions on a monthly basis and ended following the significant symptomatic improvement of Lucy and the lesser concern of the parents. The sessions were videotaped and evaluated using the RFF by two reliable coders (trained in a specific course at the Department of Psychology of the University of Bologna). The analysis with the RFF highlighted interesting aspects of the therapeutic process (see Fig. 16.5) and of the techniques adopted by the therapists.

Some key sessions from the beginning to the end of the treatment (I, II, V, and XI), with some transcriptions of video recordings and related RFF coding examples:

Session I (present: mother, father, Lucy, and Anne): it was characterized by very few reflective statements from both the family (RFF: 1) and the therapists (TT: 0). Usually this session is dedicated to describing problems and introducing family members.

Session II (father is missing): there is an increase in reflective statements from the family (RFF: 6), often at the request of therapists, who however do not make reflective statements throughout the session.

T1: *Hmm ... And you know what concern mom and dad have?*

Anne: *Yes, surely their concern stems from the fact that they hear me and see me less, because I no longer live with them, so they feel less controlled and more worries arise.* [Rq, O, 1a] (reflective statement on demand that concerns the self, 1a criterion).

Session V (the whole family is present): the reflective statements increase significantly, both those of the family (RFF: 7) and those of the therapists (TT: 3), and the total score of the session (C) is therefore 10. We are in the middle of therapeutic interventions, and therapists use thoughtful and hypothetical questions (Tomm 1988).

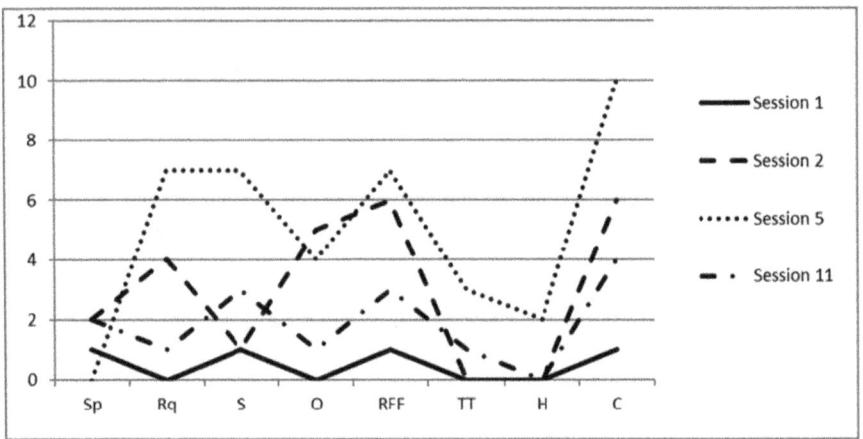

Fig. 16.5 Family Green – four family sessions compared with RFF graphics

T1: *That you can't even understand where they come from. With you it is more about hearing things than understanding. You have already tried so much (the mother laughs) that perhaps it is better to follow the track of how you are and how you feel; dad feels more serene because he sees Lucy more serene, Anne feels more serene because she discovered things in Lucy that she didn't expect, mom is perhaps the one who most difficult accepts the idea that there may be this improvement, this change perhaps because it is due to these ups and downs, to these illusions and perhaps he prefers this change.* [Sp, O, 1a, H] (spontaneous and hypothetical reflective statement about self, 1a criterion).

Mother: *I struggle.*

T1: *What about Lucy? Let's try to get Lucy off the pedestal and put her in the middle. How does Lucy feel?*

Lucy: *I feel, as my mom said, more convinced and to continue the path I am taking and ...* [RQ, S, 1a]. (reflective statement on demand, regarding the self, 1a criterion).

Session XI (conclusion of the treatment, the whole family is present): the total reflective statements (C: 4) and those of family members (RFF: 3) and therapists (TT: 1) decrease significantly. Lucy no longer manifests worrying symptoms or behaviors, has gradually become autonomous, and continues individual treatment. Sister Anne is dating a boy, mother and father are more serene, and therapists prepare the family for discharge.

T1: *We have made a path for which I believe this transformed history should be seen ..., let's say, compared to how it was described at the beginning, when you came, in short, it is not a story that at any moment turned upside down (...). Um, I saw you completely changed, didn't I?* [Gen] (generic reflective statement).

Based on this and many other sessions assessed with RFF, some clinical considerations regarding mentalizing in systemic family therapy and the technique of therapists are possible (Baldoni 2007; Bassoli et al. 2013):

1. The first sessions tend to be not very mentalizing, as are dedicated to gathering information on the family and the problem presented.
2. The intermediate sessions are often characterized by a greater number of mentalizing expressions both by the therapist and the family members. Reflexive and hypothetical interventions are frequent. The therapeutic process is underway, the reflexivity between therapists and family increases (Tomm 1988). and the family system tends to change.
3. In the final sessions, dedicated to the restitution of a more adaptive narrative and to the end of the treatment (Sluzki 1992), the mentalizing expressions tend to decrease.

16.7 Conclusions

Evidence-based research data on the effectiveness of psychotherapies (mainly derived from research on individual treatments) indicate that the factor most associated with the outcome of the treatment is the quality of the clinical relationship. Therefore, a manualization of a treatment, in a systemic perspective, should include tools for the assessment of this dimension (in terms of working alliance, attachment of patients and therapists. and mentalization processes manifested in therapy). Unfortunately, most tools assess these dimensions as individual characteristics. RFF is one of the few tools to evaluate mentalization from a systemic perspective. and its integration in the manualization of a therapeutic protocol can provide very useful information for therapists and to study the effectiveness of treatment.

References

Aber, J. L., Slade, A., Berger, B., Bresgi, I., & Kaplan, M. (1985). *The parent development interview: Manual and administration procedures*. Barnard College, Department of Psychology.
Allen, J. G., Fonagy, P., & Bateman, A. W. (2008). *Mentalizing in clinical practice*. American Psychiatric Press.
APA, American Psychological Association (2012). *Recognition of psychotherapy effectiveness*. http://www.apa.org/about/policy/resolution-psychotherapy.aspx.
Ardito, R. B., & Rabellino, D. (2011). Therapeutic alliance and outcome of psychotherapy: Historical excursus, measurements, and prospects for research. *Frontiers in Psychology, 2*(Art. 270), 1–11.
Baldoni, F., & Campailla, A. (2017). Attachment, working Alliance and therapeutic relationship: What makes a psychotherapy work? *Giornale Italiano di Psicologia, XLIV*(4), 823–846. https://doi.org/10.1421/88770
Baldoni, F. (2007). La Reflective Function in the Family (RFF): una procedura di valutazione della funzione riflessiva in terapia familiare. In *Proceedings National Congress of the Italian Psychology Association* (AIP) (Perugia Sept. 28–30, 2007) (pp. 1–9). Perugia: AIP.
Baldoni, F. (2008). L'influenza dell'attaccamento sulla relazione clinica: collaborazione, collusione e fallimento riflessivo. *Maieutica, 27–30* (June 2007–June 2008), 57–72.

Baldoni, F. (2009). *Reflective function in the family (RFF), Manual* (v. 1.2). Unpublished manuscript. Department of Psychology, University of Bologna.

Baldoni, F. (2010). *Mentalization, clinical relationship and therapeutic process*. Paper presented at the *International Congress Rehabilitation processes: affects and neuroscience* (Bologna, Nov. 6, 2010).

Baldoni, F. (2014). *Mentalization Assessment in Psychotherapy (MAP). Manual* (v. 1.0). Unpublished manuscript. Department of Psychology, University of Bologna.

Baldoni, F. (2016). Psychological trauma and somatization processes: A complex relationship. *Mediterranean Journal of Clinical Psychology MJCP, 4*(Suppl. 2 A), 51.

Baldoni, F. (2018, June). The clinical matching: interactions between patient's and therapist's attachment strategies in a DMM perspective. Paper presented at *IASA's 10-Year Celebration* (Florence, June 12–14, 2018).

Bassoli, F., Baldoni, F, & Campanella, V. (2013, Sept.). Funzione trasformativa e mentalizzazione in terapia familiare: un modello di valutazione del processo terapeutico. Paper presented at the *Second Congress of the Italian Society of Psychotherapy* (SIPSIC) (Paestum, 26–28 September 2013).

Bateman, A., & Fonagy, P. (2008). 8-year follow-up of patients treated for borderline personality disorder: Mentalization-based treatment versus treatment as usual. *American Journal of Psychiatry, 165*, 631–638.

Bateman, A., & Fonagy, P. (2004). *Psychotherapy of borderline personality disorders: Mentalization based treatment*. Oxford University Press.

Bordin, E. S. (1979). The generalizability of the psychoanalytic concept of the working alliance. *Psychotherapy: Theory, Research & Practice, 16*, 252–260.

Brennan, K. A., Clark, C. L., & Shaver, P. R. (1998). Self-report measurement of adult attachment: An integrative overview. In J. A. Simpson & W. S. Rholes (Eds.), *Attachment theory and close relationships* (pp. 46–76). Guilford.

Carcione, A., Falcone, M., Magnolfi, G., & Manaresi, F. (1997). La funzione metacognitiva in psicoterapia: Scala di Valutazione della Metacognizione (S.Va.M.). *Psicoterapia, 9*, 91–107.

Carr, A. (2009). The effectiveness of family therapy and systemic interventions for adult-focused problems. *Journal of Family Therapy, 31*, 3–45.

Carr, A. (2014). The evidence base for couple therapy, family therapy and systemic interventions for adult-focused problems. *Journal of Family Therapy, 36*, 158–194. https://doi.org/10.1111/1467-6427.12033

Carr, A. (2018a). Couple therapy, family therapy and systemic interventions for adult-focused problems: The current evidence base. *Journal of Family Therapy, 41*, 492. https://doi.org/10.1111/1467-6427.12225

Carr, A. (2018b). Family therapy and systemic interventions for child-focused problems: The current evidence base. *Journal of Family Therapy, 41*, 153. https://doi.org/10.1111/1467-6427.12226

Crittenden, P., Dallos, R., Landini, A., & Kozlowska, K. (2014). *Attachment and family therapy*. Open University Press (McGraw-Hill Education).

Diamond, D., Clarkin, J., Levy, K., Levine, H., Kotov, H., & Stovall-McClough, C. (1999). *The patient therapist adult attachment interview (PT-AAI)*. Unpublished manuscript, New York: The City University of New York, Department of Psychology.

Fearon, P., Target, M., Sargent, J., Williams, L. L., McGregor, J., Bleiberg, E., & Fonagy, P. (2006). Short-term mentalization and relational therapy (SMART): An integrative family therapy for children and adolescents. In J. G. Allen & P. Fonagy (Eds.), *Handbook of mentalization-based treatment* (pp. 201–222). Wiley.

Fonagy, P., Steele, H., Moran, G. S., Steele, M., & Higgitt, A. (1991). The capacity for understanding mental states: The reflective self in parent and child and its significance for security of attachment. *Infant Mental Health Journal, 13*, 200–217.

Fonagy, P., Steele, M., Steele, H., Leigh, T., Kennedy, R., Mattoon, C., & Target, M. (1995). Attachment, the reflective self and borderline states. In S. Goldberg, R. Muir, & J. Kerr (Eds.), *Attachment, theory social, development and clinical perspectives* (pp. 233–278). Analytic Press.

Fonagy, P., Target, M., Steele, H., & Steele, M. (1998). *Reflective-functioning manual, version 5, for application to adult attachment interviews.* University College.

George, C., Kaplan, N., & Main, M. (1984-1996). *Adult Attachment Interview Protocol.* Unpublished manuscript. Berkeley: University of California, Berkeley.

Greenson, R. R. (1965). The working alliance and the transference neurosis. *Psychoanalitic Quarterly, 34*, 155–179.

Hill, D. (2015). *Affect regulation theory: A clinical model.* W. W. Norton.

Holmes, J. (2001). *The search for the secure base: Attachment theory and psychotherapy.* Routledge.

Holmes, J., & Slade, A. (2018). *Attachment in therapeutic practice.* Sage.

Jurist, E. L., Slade, A., & Bergner, S. (Eds.). (2008). *Mind to mind. Infant research, neuroscience, and psychoanalysis.* Other Press.

Mallinckrodt, B., Gantt, D. L., & Coble, H. M. (1995). Attachment patterns in the psychotherapy relationship: Development of the client attachment to therapist scale. *Journal of Counseling Psychology, 42*, 307–317.

Michels, R. (2006). Epilogue: Thinking about mentalization. In J. G. Allen & P. Fonagy (Eds.), *Handbook of Mentalization-based treatment* (pp. 327–333). Wiley.

Obegi, J. H. (2008). The development of the client-therapist bond through the lens of attachment theory. *Psychotherapy, Theory, Research, Practice, Training, 45*(4), 431–446.

Ochs, M., Borcsa, M., & Schweitzer, J. (Eds.) (2020). *Systemic research in individual, couple, and family therapy and counseling.* European Family Therapy Association Series, Switzerland: Springer.

Romano, V., Janzen, J., & Fitzpatrick, M. (2009). Volunteer client attachment moderates the relationship between trainee therapist attachment and therapist interventions. *Psychotherapy Research, 19*(6), 666–676.

Sadler, L. S., Slade, A., & Mayes, L. C. (2006). Minding the baby: A Mentalization-based parenting program. In J. G. Allen & P. Fonagy (Eds.), *Handbook of Mentalization-based treatment* (pp. 269–288). Wiley.

Safran, J. D., & Muran, J. C. (2000). *Negotiating the therapeutic alliance. A relational treatment guide.* Guilford Press.

Semerari, A., Carcione, A., Dimaggio, G., Falcone, M., Nicolò, G., Procacci, M., & Alleva, G. (2003). How to evaluate metacognitive functioning in psychotherapy? The metacognition assessment scale and its applications. *Clinical Psychology and Psychotherapy, 10*, 238–261.

Shedler, J. (2010). The efficacy of psychodynamic psychotherapy. *American Psychologist, 65*(2), 98–109.

Shedler, J. (2018). Where is the evidence for "evidence-based" therapy? *Psychiatric Clinics of North America, 41*, 319–329. https://doi.org/10.1016/j.psc.2018.02.001

Slade, A., Bernbach, E., Grienenberger, J., Levy, D., & Locker A. (2005). *Addendum to Reflective Functioning Scoring Manual (Fonagy, Steele, Steele & Target, 1998). For use with the Parent Development Interview (PDI; Aber, Slade, Berger, Bresgi, & Kaplan, 1985; PDI-R; Slade, Aber, Berger, Bresgi & Kaplan, 2003) (Version 2.0).* Unpublished manuscript. The City College and Graduate Center of the University of New York.

Sluzki, C. E. (1992). Transformations: A blueprint for narrative changes in therapy. *Family Process., 31*(3), 217–230.

Steele, H., & Steele, M. (2008). *Clinical applications of the adult attachment interview.* The Guilford Press.

Stratton, P (2016). *The evidence base of family therapy and systemic practice.* Association for Family Therapy, UK.

Tomm, K. (1988). Interventive interviewing: Part III. Intending to ask lineal, circular, reflexive or strategic questions? *Family Process, 27*, 1–15.

Wallin, D. J. (2007). *Attachment in psychotherapy.* Guilford Press.

Wampold, B. E. (2007). Psychotherapy: The humanistic (and affective) treatment. *American Psychologist., 82*, 857–873.

Wampold, B. E. (2012). Humanism as a common factor in psychotherapy. *Psychotherapy, 49*(4), 445–449.
Wampold, B. E. (2014, Sept). What makes psychotherapy work? The humanistic elements! Paper presented at *X National Congress SPR Italy Area Group* (Padua, Sept. 12–14, 2014).
Wampold, B. E., & Imel, Z. E. (2015). *The great psychotherapy debate: The evidence for what makes psychotherapy work* (2nd ed.). Routledge.

Chapter 17
A Manual Developed Through a Variety of Online Resources: The SCORE Index of Family Functioning and Change

Peter Stratton

17.1 Introduction

A particular form of manualisation has arisen during the work to create a recording of quality of family functioning: the SCORE. It has become an alternative form of manualisation in which the manual is progressively evolving and distributed among a variety of Web contexts, a process that has only become possible through the availability of internet facilities. Manuals in this form might be becoming quite common when, for example, the materials of a training course are progressively developed. This trend is bound to escalate in future as therapists are more frequently moving to online working with patients (Borcsa et al., 2020) and is not confined to systemic family therapy (SFT). As just one example of manualisation in a different field, a search for cookery recipes on the web finds many that are accompanied by a video of the process and discussions contributed by users on their experiences in using the recipes, sometimes in a dialogue with the chef. We have extended this by creating translations in many different languages the process of which is described below.

The initial basic manualisation was made freely available through the website of the Association for Family Therapy (AFT) in order to make it widely, and freely, available (www.aft.org.uk). The website has been continually developed over the past decade and now includes a variety of resources beyond the descriptions and guidance, including six videos, and formats in Excel for recording and analysing data. It includes the full set of 32 translated versions, a listing of again freely available material in other

---

The original version of this chapter was revised. The correction to this chapter is available at https://doi.org/10.1007/978-3-030-73640-8_34

P. Stratton (✉)
Emeritus Professor of Family Therapy, Leeds Family Therapy and Research Centre, University of Leeds, Leeds, West Yorkshire, UK
e-mail: p.m.stratton@ntlworld.com

sources, a listing of over 30 publications and an invitation to register for the Google discussion group. These developing resources amount to a distributed manual on the Web and are described in this chapter, leading to indications of potential for future enhancements to the manual and the lessons we would draw for development of manuals in this way as we move to ever greater online facilities.

17.1.1 The SCORE: What It Is

The SCORE was developed to provide a measure of progress and outcome in family therapy, designed for the realities of systemic practice both in terms of the wide range of systemic approaches in use and of the variety of difficulties that families bring to Systemic Family Therapy. As an outcome measure it has been fully validated (Hamilton et al., 2015, O'Hanrahan et al., 2017, Stratton et al., 2014). It has been taken up extensively internationally with some 30 translations, all using a rigorous standard protocol for culturally sensitive translation and checks on reliability and validity. This work is being overseen by Reenee Singh and Judith Lask. In the course of making the SCORE available internationally it became apparent that as well as measuring progress in the therapy it was being used just as often as an interactional tool with clients, to support the therapeutic process (Stratton et al., 2020). This move to clinical use necessitated more guidance and that work is currently in progress with the web material being correspondingly updated.

When we started out to create a new instrument that would provide therapists and researchers with a way to measure progress and outcome in each therapy, we recognised that we needed consideration of what systemic family therapy is trying to achieve. There is no simple answer to this question, and the fact that many clinics see a wide range of families bringing a wide range of concerns makes it unlikely that a symptom-based measure would have any general application. We also felt that it was important to develop a self-report measure rather than rely on therapist ratings. And that the level of agreement that family members expressed about general value statements such as "we have a good relationship" would be neither reliable nor informative about processes in the family.

In searching for a strategy, we considered that there are two stances that therapists might adopt about family processes. Some systemic therapists are interested in how symptoms develop in an attempt to cope with the way the family has operated its relationships. Others are more focused on building the underused capabilities of patients/clients and their families. Whichever position systemic family therapists prioritise, all believe that healthy family processes will help a designated patient to overcome their difficulties and maintain therapeutic change. So the ways the family members describe their life at home should be a crucial indicator of the relational resources the patients have available. We therefore created a set of items that were quite concrete descriptions of aspects of family life. The aspects were chosen by experienced therapists by a process of reducing many possible items to a manageable 15 questions, which were thought to be most likely to be relevant to the life, the interactions, within the family that might indicate the quality of their relationships, their ability to resolve problems that arise, and ability to support each other through difficulties.

The final form of SCORE-15 is a self-report outcome measure designed to be sensitive to the kinds of changes in family functioning that systemic family and couples therapists see as indications of useful therapeutic change. It is intended to be serviceable in everyday practice: short, acceptable to clients and usable across the full range of our work. That is, whatever the presenting problems, the situations and characteristics of the clients, and the formats of work: at least, individual, couple and family (Stratton, 2014a). It can be read in terms of second-order change; structural change; change in the stories the family members have about their family; change in systemic processes within the family; as being within an orientation to solutions; improvements in relation to hopefulness, agency, hostility, risk, blaming, well-being, happiness and so on. All in 19 questions which can be printed on two sides of an A4 sheet. A final criterion from the outset was that in order to maximise its usefulness to systemic therapies it should be free for therapists to use in all contexts.

The process is as follows: The SCORE-15 should be administered to each family member individually at or just before the start of the relevant sessions. Arrangements may be made so that each person fills it in privately and their completed SCORE is not seen by other family members. This reduces the risk of influence from other family members and is essential when data are collected for research purposes. When the therapist intends to discuss specific answers with the family as part of the therapy, initial guarantees of confidentiality would be unethical and must not be offered. Discussion about these aspects of the process takes place prior to filling in the questionnaire.

A note on nomenclature: The SCORE took its name from a suggestion that, as its development was inspired by and to some extent followed the process of development of CORE (Clinical Outcomes in Routine Evaluation, Evans et al., 2002) but was designed for systemic work we should call it SCORE. The name stuck. Some early papers therefore called it the Systemic Clinical Outcome and Routine Evaluation (Cahill et al., 2010). Rather quickly it came to be used for a variety of purposes both research and clinical practice and we adopted the broader title of the SCORE Index of Family Functioning and Change (Stratton et al., 2014). One intermediate paper had the title "SCORE: Systemic Clinical Outcome and Routine Evaluation Index of Family Functioning and Change: Using the SCORE-15" (Stratton, 2014b). Because the name SCORE is not very informative and may even in certain circumstances create a misleading impression, it is useful to add a subtitle though it seems appropriate that the full title should reflect which of the evolving uses is most relevant for that report.

17.1.2 Processes of Development

There was an extensive process of developing pilot versions, followed by progressive testing and refinement until we had a workable version of 40 items. Contributions to the process came from clinicians, other research groups, for example, Alan Carr's group (Cahill et al., 2010) and the Maudsley Hospital User's group who completed the SCORE-40 and gave feedback. Versions were presented at workshops and on SFT training courses with all participants invited to complete the SCORE for their own family and discuss the feedback generated by the group. We therefore collected new data from 510 members of 228 families in therapy along with a non-clinical sample. In this format every participant was invited to identify any specific items that they felt were uninformative about their own family, or alternatively, especially informative. The SCORE-40 worked well but was too long to use routinely in therapy. We then worked with these data until we had created a proven version with just 15 items describing different ways that relationships in the family are operated, and a small set of self-descriptions provided by the family members (Appendix A). The SCORE-15 was created through a data-driven process integrating psychometrics with clinical judgement and feedback from the various sources (Stratton et al., 2010). It is designed to enable family members to report on aspects of their interactions which have clinical significance and are likely to be relevant to therapeutic processes. The extensive consultations were used to obtain simple and unambiguous items that would be meaningful to families from a wide variety of cultural, ethnic and socioeconomic backgrounds.

This process of development of the SCORE-15 is described in detail in Stratton et al. (2010). As an indication of one aspect of the process, the following are the first seven items on which clinical families were found to be most different from the non-clinical (control) sample:

- We seem to go from one crisis to another in my family
- It feels miserable in our family
- We find it hard to deal with everyday problems
- Things always seem to go wrong for my family
- In my family we blame each other when things go wrong
- People in the family are nasty to each other
- We feel hopeful about the future

We have now completed the phase to test whether it is valid as a measure of therapeutic change. The 15-item version (SCORE-15) was administered to a new sample of 584 individual family members at the start of therapy. 239 of these participants provided data at both first and fourth therapy sessions. Consistently statistically significant change ($p < 0.001$) was found in the overall score using a variety of statistical analyses. The amount of change correlated with therapist judgement and independent rating by family members of their problems (Stratton et al., 2014). It is now offered as a comprehensively validated measure. It was then made available internationally with encouragement to make a translation following a procedure developed for the purpose. The protocol and its usage are described below.

17.1.3 Content and Form at Different Stages/Locations

The SCORE was developed initially to be a resource for outcome research. Instructions for its application were first developed by the original team of Julia Bland (Chair) Peter Stratton (AFT Academic and Research Development Officer), Judith Lask, Emma Janes and Chris Evans. After refinement based on the experiences of the first two major samples and consultations as described above, a pack of all available resources was created. This pack constitutes the first phase of the manualisation of SCORE and was made available on the AFT website www.aft.co.uk as well as emailed to therapists and researchers who expressed an interest in using it.

Even the instructions to participants on the SCORE form can be seen as part of the manual (Appendix A). Its intended role in supporting work to generate an evidence base required being concrete about the quality of family processes so that it should be relevant to all forms of family psychotherapy. But research requirements meant that we had to make an effort to ensure that the family that a participant rated at the start was the same constellation of people as those rated at later sessions. There is also guidance specifically on how to deal with negatively phrased items, though I did once have a man at the start of therapy who said he did not know how to answer, and his wife helpfully said "try reading the instructions dear".

The first item of the Pack that was put online at AFT and also mailed to everyone who requested information is a guide to the material so that users could orient to what they needed. It is provided here, adapted for the purposes of this chapter.

17.2 A Guide to the SCORE Material

There will be more than you want in the pack. This guide is to help you identify what you need to look at and in what order.

- *SCORE AFT web* is an overview that will include links to the other material. The most recent version is on ww.aft.org.uk in the research section. We now have a set of six videos that introduce SCORE-15, demonstrate data entry as described in the attached documents and demonstrate administering SCORE to a family. There is also a recent video interview of Peter Stratton by Martin Gill on Youtube to accompany the publication of a comprehensive review of SCORE in Family Process (Carr & Stratton, 2017).
- *Administering measures to families,* prepared by the AFT Family Therapy Outcomes Advisory Group, Convener Peter Stratton with Marcus Averbeck, Iris Corrales, Liz Forbat, Gill Goodwillie, Judith Lask, David Low, Nicola McCarry, Lynne McCandless, Jeanette Neden, Jan Parker, Gary Robinson, Reenee Singh and Yang Yang Teh. This document was compiled by experienced users to give guidance on issues that arise specifically when applying progress measures to families (Stratton, 2014b). It was created by the group for inclusion in the CAMHS Outcomes Research Consortium (CORC) and Children and Young

People's Improving Access to Psychological Therapies (CYP IAPT) initiative Practitioners Guide to Forms, Feedback Tools and Outcome Measures. It was produced by the CAMHS Evidence Based Practice Unit (EBPU), Anna Freud Centre and University College London, available at http://www.ucl.ac.uk/ebpu/publications.
- *Introduction and scoring SCORE-15* is a practical guide to administering it, using it for research, and also clinically.
- *Instructions for Excel group data entry* and the *SCORE-15 data entry Excel* files are for entering group data and having the essential averages calculated. We also have an SPSS template available on request.
- *Score-15 scoring template guide* and the *Score-15 scoring template* are for entering the data of a single respondent and automatically calculate averages. These are most likely to be helpful for supporting clinical work with a specific couple or family or for therapists wanting to check whether they are making progress after a number of sessions.
- *Outcome monitoring with couples and families* is a practical guide for using any outcome measure when families or couples are being seen together.
- Then there are the versions of SCORE-15. The final score-15 is the main clinical version. The score-15 non-clinical version is for the normative comparison sample. A child version for ages 8–11 years, and a couples version are developed specifically for use with LGBT couples.

After this stage the guidance started to take the form of a distributed manual with material becoming available in different kinds of resources either to elaborate on and update the core information or to provide guidance on new or specialised uses as they develop. The AFT Web pages are progressively updated with the examples of content included in this chapter coming from the current update which went live in December 2020. Information for researchers and therapists in European countries was provided on the EFTA web research pages.

17.2.1 Procedures for Translation

As soon as the SCORE-15 was fully functioning in 2009, it became a significant project of the EFTA Research Committee (Chair Peter Stratton, SCORE project leader Luigi Schepisi). The first step was to create a standard protocol for all translators to ensure the quality and consistency of its use in each country or minority language group. The current protocol for translation of SCORE drew on the successful CORE protocol and was developed by the original team in collaboration with an EFTA National Family Therapy Organisations research group led by Mina Polemi-Todoulou. It is provided here:

Translation Protocol for SCORE

The SCORE-15 is a self-report questionnaire which is in stage 2 of its development. The development team is enthusiastic about encouraging translations into other languages. It has developed a protocol for translation which should maximise the possibility of developing versions which demonstrate clinical sensitivity. Following translation it is hoped that research will be undertaken to see if the different language versions remain sensitive to the aspects of family processes and relationships that had been found to be most important during the English language Phase 1 of the SCORE project.

Effectiveness of SCORE in other cultures will not best be achieved by linguistically accurate translations, but by rewording of each item in that language, in a way that is sensitive to the values and definitions of close relationships in that society.

Although we are privileging culturally sensitive adaptation above linguistically accurate translation, we do want to research the extent to which the SCORE-15 is functional as a measure of therapeutic change in different societies. This means that we will stay close to the meanings and intentions of the existing 15 items.

Undoubtedly, cases will arise in which there are aspects of family life that are more important than certain SCORE items for that society. But these will have to be noted for possible incorporation into a subsequent version.

At present, the power and value of this research is in being able to compare versions of SCORE-15 across different societies.

Steps for undertaking the translation:

1. Contact the Score translation subgroup through Judith Lask (judelask@icloud.com) to indicate your intention to translate Score-15. A consultant on matters of translation will be appointed to you. There is no value at this point of many different translations in the same language; it may be possible to pool resources if more than one group wishes to undertake a translation. The Score translation subgroup will keep a data base of translations and their progress.
2. Draw up a local protocol and plan for translation, to show how you will meet the guidelines in your local situation.
3. Commission 5 translations from the English version by fluent English speakers who have the target language as their first language (or one of their first languages). These 5 should include:
    (a) at least one professional with systemic training
    (b) at least one lay person
    (c) someone who has significant experience of translation.
4. Hold a meeting with as many translators as possible to talk through the versions and discuss and resolve differences. A consultation should be sought with the appointed Score translation consultant to discuss the process and ask any advice.
5. Organise 2 back- translations into English by a mental health professional and a lay person who have not seen the original translation.
6. The local SCORE research group decides on the final version in collaboration with the appointed SCORE translation consultant.
7. The final non-clinical version is administered on a test, retest basis (at interval of 2-4 weeks) to 20 individual non clinical family members. The sample should consist of one representative from each family and across the 20 people, have approximately the same demographics (age, gender, ethnicity if relevant) as the clinical sample. This is to test for reliability. Moreover, this group can form part of the comparison sample of non-clinical families described below.
8. The final version should be sent to the Score translation team for incorporation in the data base of translated versions.

    Please keep a detailed record of the experiences and any difficulties in your translation process. At the end we will need to report on the translations, and a comparison of the experiences of different countries will be an interesting study, so please tell us about your experiences.

Please note that this translated version cannot be recommended as a valid measure until it has been administered to a minimum 80 clinical and 40 non-clinical families with similar demographics and is shown to differentiate between them.[1] Our full requirement has been 200 clinical and 80 non-clinical in order to fully replicate the dimensional structure etc. By this stage every fully tested translation has met the criteria and so we are allowing the smaller samples where necessary, especially in countries with limited provision of systemic couple and family therapy.

Colleagues who are undertaking translations should do so in collaboration with the SCORE translation subgroup.

Using this protocol, translations into 24 languages have been completed and made freely available to provide versions that adapt the items to a form most meaningful in that culture. Furthermore, another nine have been prepared according to a rigorous protocol, but not the AFT/EFTA protocol above, for languages widely used by minority ethnic groups in the UK, which are also available for use in the home country or elsewhere. In some cases essential parts of the manualised guidance have also been translated.

So far, the most substantial detailed applications of translated versions have been in Portugal, Italy, Poland, Spain, Germany and China. These are described in some detail in Stratton et al. (2020). The English version has been used most extensively in Ireland by Alan Carr and his team and has also been used in the US, Australia and Tasmania. We have learned much about the ways SCORE has been used through conversations with users in many different countries during conferences and workshops, through many email queries and through surveys reported below.

One outcome of the international work has been findings of cultural differences. Although the original questions were piloted with people of different ethnicities in the UK, the much more varied international applications have made greater demands for universal items. It is testament to the quality of careful work by the translators that they have generally found culturally sensitive ways of expressing the intention of each item, as would be understood by users in their country. In a few cases users have suggested ways in which they feel the translation could be improved for use in their country. These have been arbitrated by Judith Lask and Reenee Singh in collaboration with the original (official) translator for that country.

---

[1] The original requirement was for 200 clinical and 80 non-clinical. As translated versions in several countries have found that their data closely replicate the original findings including the factor analysis generating the three dimensions, we judge that the SCORE is proven to be robust in translated form and we currently reduce the requirement to a more realistic level for countries with smaller numbers of families in therapy.

17.2.2 Publications That Provide Guidance on Implementing SCORE

Considerable material is available in published sources such as journals and textbooks. While independent practitioners and training courses that are not linked to Universities will have limited access to material that belongs to publishers, there are often draft versions of the publications on free access websites, particularly ResearchGate. Other publications are available without charge on the Web.

One of the most comprehensive is the Guide to Using Outcomes and Feedback Tools with Children, Young People and Families (Law & Wolpert, 2013). Because it is freely accessible, none of the content is reproduced here but the headings in the guide indicate the areas on which it makes detail available:

CONTENTS
    RELATIONSHIPS WITH OTHER MEASURES
    ADMINISTRATION OF THE SCORE-15
    PRACTICALITIES OF ADMINISTRATION
    FIRST MEETING
    FINAL SESSION
    SOME SUGGESTIONS FOR CLINICAL USE
    DISCUSSING THE RESULTS AND USING THEM TO INFORM THERAPY – WORKING WITH COMPLEXITY
    INTEGRATING THE "MAPS" FOR ASSESSMENT, REVIEWS AND CLINICAL USE
    SCORING AND DATA RECORDING
    SCORING BY HAND
    SCORE-15 INDEX OF FAMILY FUNCTIONING AND CHANGE
    REFERENCES

A Sample of Recent Formal Publications
Two kinds of usage have emerged in journal and book publications over the decade. The majority of journal publications have a focus on the quantitative outputs and their interpretation especially as indicators of progress and outcome in therapy (Stratton, 2014a; Carr & Stratton, 2017). Clinical applications are generally subsidiary in such publications other than some book chapters even though survey responses indicate substantial creativity and experience of these uses.

The most comprehensive survey and evaluation is by Carr and Stratton (2017) which summarises SCORE publications from 2010 onwards. With an accompanying Family Process YouTube of PS interviewed by Martin Gill.

The most extensively reported translated versions are Portuguese (Vilaça et al., 2014, 2015, 2018), Spanish (Relvas et al., 2015), Polish (Józefik et al. 2015), Italian (Paolini & Schepisi (2020), Stratton et al., 2020), German (Borcsa & Schelenhaus, 2011), Swedish (Zetterqvist et al., 2020), and Thai (Limsuwan & Prachason, 2018). These experiences could be collated for the benefit of others using SCORE (and other outcome measures) in translated version. Most go beyond the quantitative uses of SCORE and discuss experiences of using it in that culture, while some offer qualitative analyses of the descriptions provided by families. Another contribution is describing how translations produced for one country function when transported into a different cultural context: for example the Portuguese translation used in Angola and Brazil, and the Spanish translation used in Mexico (Relvas et al., 2015).

The issues of cultural relevance and transferability are taken up by Stratton and Low (2020) in a chapter that explores the cultural sensitivity of measures: "In practice, therapists have found that as well as measuring effectiveness, both types of measure (*the SCORE and the Outcome Rating Scale/Session Rating Scale*) can powerfully influence the therapeutic process when used interactively in the session with clients. The evidence of wide applicability and acceptability to clients is supplemented by examples of cultural variation. These extensive experiences demonstrate the potential of measures with a proven cross-cultural applicability to enhance the cultural sensitivity of therapists, enable countries with limited resources and provision of family therapy to draw on strong empirical support and ensure that linguistic minorities can be fully included in research" (p. 77).

Some publications arose directly from requests that therapists have made, in particular the version for younger people aged 8–12 years (Jewell et al., 2013); and couples especially those from the LGBT community (Teh et al., 2017). Both of these initiatives are described below. Some are freely available such as Stratton (2014a) reporting on Experiences in Measuring the Functioning of UK Families, deriving from an EFTA Symposium in Istanbul 2013 (Human Systems website http://www.humansystemsjournal.eu/home and ResearchGate).

Another available resource is a number of articles in Context, the Newsletter of AFT. These are available on the AFT website with titles like *"SCORE 15: A tool that just keeps on giving!"* by Gary Robinson and *"Just how effective is systemic therapy? Can SCORE help?"* by Peter Stratton. And in the edition *How do we know we are helping? Measuring and evaluating our systemic practice*, edited by Lindsey Hampson and Danny McGowan View December 2017, Context Issue 154.

17.3 Feedback from Surveys of Users

We have been getting feedback from many therapists who have used SCORE, and here are some examples of what therapists have said about the administration of SCORE. Note the comments reported here were selected to indicate the range of different kinds of reaction to SCORE, so generally, frequently repeated answers and simple evaluations have not been included. Such answers were overwhelmingly positive but we suspect that most of the therapists choosing to respond to the survey were those who felt it was a worthwhile instrument.

While some had started off cautious about possible negative effects on the therapy, very few that had used the SCORE found any difficulties.

Administering the SCORE became easier after the first few attempts. A subsidiary question asked how many times of administering was required before it became an "unproblematic routine". The most common response was four times, with one saying it never did become easy.

Several requested an electronic version that would generate results that would be easily understandable by the family, discussed below under "Future Options".

A survey of EFTA users found that while most (88%) used it to measure outcomes, 75% also used SCORE to support the process of therapy.

17.3.1 A Sample of Specific Responses in the EFTA Survey

General Comments

I work independently

They are more accustomed to use the visuo-analogical scales which are more simple, and even easier to use. SCORE is challenging in routine evaluation as a tool of systematic feedback.

I generally don't use measuring.

The majority of my clients have accepted SCORE as a useful tool for reporting feedback about their change, a useful tool for becoming aware about some aspects of change, and also a tool which sometimes has the effect on increasing responsibility towards effort for change.

From your point of view, what will be the future of SCORE?

It depends on research results and its dissemination by prestigious journals in our field and others

I think the SCORE future is to be recognised as an important therapy tool, both in research and clinical practice, through different European contexts/countries.

As far as I can see it, SCORE is one of the better forms to get a measurement of how the family members experience their relationship. With even better ways to convey the results Score can be even more interesting to use actively in the family therapy.

It can be used to agree and develop family therapy in Europe

To become one of the widely used instruments within systemic community in Europe and outside, supporting outcome research and research generally

It will be nice to have it more developed

Given its statistical properties and the fact that so many European countries translated it and the number of practitioners who use it could increase, I hope SCORE will became a widely used instrument.

Can you tell us some ideas about the utility or possible use of SCORE?

Supervision and group

Routine tool in clinical practice, as other scales we use in other fields

I believe that it is an important measure, particularly for family therapy, in terms of investigation, practice and supervision. It can be administered not only in family therapy contexts but also in the context of other psychological interventions. Also, I believe it represents an essential diagnostic to discriminate community from clinical population.

Referring to the previous question, I miss the possibility to display the results with a graph where one can see the similarity and differences between family members at the start of a therapy. I would also like to be able to use the results at the end of a therapy (after several therapeutic meetings) and display how they see the development in the family. It needs to be more graphic than it is now.

It could be useful for the therapist team to check and analyse family members' answers to SCORE before starting the next session.

Besides its use in family therapy and research, I believe that it is an important tool to evaluate the efficacy of parental training programs.

To create comparable data on clinical as well non-clinical population in European Countries, to improve outcome research in systemic family therapy, to support the efficacy of systemic family therapy and its development

Aside the clinical field it could help to asses also other fields of work with families, for example, school psychology and counselling.

Our team, having recently examined the Child version of SCORE (Jewell et al., 2013), were wondering about this form's suitability for all families. Many of our families have difficulties with literacy. The Child version, which seeks the same information, seems to have greater visual clarity and appears easier to respond too.

Recognise some aspects of change (sometimes both in the case of client and clinician) – sometimes to establish a better focus for the sessions. Could be used to encourage client to express discontent towards the therapy process, to identify specific problems. Differences between clients' perceptions about their functioning could be uncovered.

In my opinion, SCORE is not a sensitive instrument to be used for couple therapy

Do you want to elaborate your answer?

Referring to question 15, I experience the way the outcome form is made, it is mainly for the therapist and needs to be worked with to be truly relevant for the family (both parents and children). It is not easy to read the development.

Need to do so more consistently as a team. This would occur if SCORE was adopted formally by CAMHS Team and FTT.

I routinely ask my clients about the utility of psychotherapy process. Using SCORE and their feedback, I can test my hypotheses about the perceived usefulness of the therapeutic process.

How do you use it?

Going back with the family to some of the points raised in the questionnaire

Talking with the family about SCORE items

We use this questionnaire (therapists and client versions) to evaluate the course of therapy and later for research purposes.

I obtained from the SCORE and from the after administration and after scoring dialog information regarding: therapeutic change, dis-content, what is important to bring in and maintain in focus.

17.3.2 UK Survey Responses

In a project funded by AFT (Association of Family Therapy) we invited all the UK users that we knew about to complete an internet survey. This was a self-selected sample of just 29 users but we found the responses illuminating. As with other feedback the ideas are being progressively incorporated into the evolving web-based manualisation:

What Would Be Your Thoughts about Starting to Use SCORE?

- It was short and family oriented but also seemed problem focused
- It is time to have a good reliable measure in our own field that can reflect the complexity of families and change
- I had mixed feelings and was pleased to have the opportunity to give it a go as part of the research without having to commit to using it
- I thought it might interrupt the engagement process

Experiences with Using SCORE-15
- The "tick" columns are cumbersome, the headings for each column are too long
- It allows me to see which families are best suited to a systemic approach of therapy
- I work in an area where literacy levels are extremely low and many families found it really hard to understand
- My concerns about the effect on engagement didn't seem to be borne out
- Clients with medical/illness understandings react negatively to be asked about family relationships
- SCORE needs to be used in conjunction with tools that measure symptom change

What Were Your Clients' Feelings about Whether an Outcome Measure Would Affect the Therapy
- They appreciated being able to give feedback that acknowledges change
- This has improved as I have become better at administering it,
- Clients generally felt fairly neutral about the effect on therapy,
- OK for measures that are meaningful to their purpose of therapy.
- Clients generally understand that we need to validate the work that we do in order to progress and continue.
- They have only occasionally questioned the request to fill in a questionnaire.
- I don't think anyone expressed the idea that filling out the form was going to affect therapy
- One family highlighted fears around how I would view their comments, another confidentiality
- Generally tend to see them as a separate useful or needed aspect of good practice

Where possible, these comments have been used to upgrade the material describing SCORE in its different contexts.

17.3.3 *Material on Google Groups, Q&As*

A form of communication available to everyone has been the Google Group set up by AFT in 2010. All of my correspondence about SCORE has included in the signature the invitation to "Join our discussions by emailing aftSCORE+subscribe@googlegroups.com". Informally, we have an impression that people find these discussions helpful when they relate to that therapist's practice or research but relatively few of the 124 members post responses, or new items. It may well be that other media of communication would encourage livelier debate.

Taken all together, the questions and comments would be another component of a distributed manual. However, one thing the experience has shown is the great variety of contexts and forms in which SFCT (Systemic Family and Couples Therapy) has been applied. So answers to these specific queries might have limited relevance to other workers, and the accumulated material is not an efficient way for a therapist to achieve the guidance they need in their context.

17.3.4 Feedback Offered by Users Individually, by Email and on Google Groups

Most discussions of issues in using SCORE have been through personal email discussions with Peter Stratton. The process of responding has created a volume of personal responses that have provided guidance to individual therapists and researchers. Up to 2020 PS has a record of 5650 emails personally received and sent since 2014. These exclude those with limited information, which have been deleted. Many of those deleted can be summarised as either "thank you for your very helpful response" or "you have not responded to my previous email". Other discussions have taken place on Skype or Zoom both with individual users and for training workshops.

One suggestion offered in a training workshop was "Should we administer it just before and just after Xmas dinner". In fact the Covid-19 crisis, which has resulted in many families spending greatly increased time at home together, is an important opportunity for an "experiment in nature". We already know that there has been an exacerbation of domestic violence and a less documented increase in tender caring of family members but it would be of great interest to know the pattern of how the quality of life together has changed for families during Covid time. We hope to use the internet to collate data from those who have been routinely using SCORE to survey the changes in family functioning during this time.

Because it is very widely distributed, and designed for a wide variety of uses, it generates feedback about issues that users encounter as well as confirmation from the great majority that the SCORE worked for them similarly to the UK sample. Some representative examples:

> It sometimes feels strange to be given a choice of who is family. In some cultures the invitation to specify who is to be included as family seems strange and disconcerting. 'I do not exactly understand what do you mean by letting me decide who my family members are? Family is family and is given. My children's nanny is like a family member, but certainly not a family member'. 'Yes, definitely I can say that I consider Tante (Aunt) Rosalie (a dear neighbour) a family member, much more than my mum. But my dear neighbour is not a family member, my mom is'. (Romania)

A different issue in choosing who to report is when households vary in composition: "Sometimes, young persons prefer to give two answers to the questions, one for the household of each parent. (It is quite common in Denmark for divorced families that the child lives equal amount of time in each home, e.g. a week at a time.)".

Then there is the issue of how to present questions about family processes in countries where couples do not see themselves as a family.

A message from Europe: "Thank you for your effort to create a research network among family therapists in Europe. Without doubts, SCORE is a worthwhile instrument, easy to manage. An issue is that it is addressed to families and some adjustments are needed in order to be used with couples. We faced the same difficulties with FAD (....). Couples answer differently when they think to themselves as a 'family' and when they focus on their relationship. A couple version of SCORE, with some changes, would be useful."

The call for a couples version has been repeated in several forums. There is already the version created by Yang Yang Teh (2017) but oriented to people in LGBT relationships and not yet validated. We have a group of couples therapists working to create a broad couples version so the work is underway but not yet completed. Once the couples version is tested and refined, it will be necessary to duplicate the validation process along the lines of the work done with SCORE-15 and SCORE-28 in both the original and in many of the translated versions. This process will rely on the existing networks of SCORE users to generate the data in defined conditions and will hope to be able to rely on participation especially by therapists in countries where references to "your family" are problematic or difficult when seeing a couple.

> We have found it helpful in families in generating motivation to engage in family therapy, improve family communication and/or functioning and overall to share the 'problem'. (Australia)

> Many of our families have difficulties with literacy. The Child version, which seeks the same information seems to have greater visual clarity and appears easier to respond to (Tasmania)

"In our sample of 2931 7–12 year olds, boys scored higher (more problematic) than girls in all but one of the 15 items". (China). Reports of differences from data collected with the English versions raise questions about whether they are primarily cultural differences or differences in how therapy is practiced in those countries. This unanswered question applies to all of the cultural differences encountered so far.

17.3.5 Examples of Specific Feedback from Users Shared Through Various Media

Concerns were raised on the AFT Google list (see below) by solution-focussed therapists that SCORE contains negatively phrased statements. These might destroy the work to focus exclusively on positives.

Peter Stratton offered a detailed response on the list (which can be summarised as "we chose those items that worked best") but concluded with the following statement:

> Monitoring one's therapy is now accepted practice and is known to have an overall beneficial effect on therapy. So while every therapist and agency should decide which indicators to use, my view would be that a decision to not use any independent measure, and so to deprive your clients of the known benefit of regularly checking progress, would need to be counter-balanced by an alternative demonstrable benefit.

A recent email directly to PS in response to a request on the Google group is representative of many that I have received:

Briefly to share my experiences of using the Score 15 as an intervention: I almost always use it in a first session, as it 'warms the context' for what family therapy (FT) is likely to be discussing, as so many families seem to have not been accurately informed or have 'forgotten' about what FT is by the time they've had the long wait between the assessment and therapy starting in CAMHS.

A very common experience is that whether the SCORE is used purely as an outcome measure or interactively with the family as a contribution to the therapy, its use at the start of the first session can usefully reorient the family towards how the family lives its life together and perhaps interrupts a problem-saturated story.

I tend to look at the Score 15 element away from sessions, as would take too long to go through in sessions, and instead focus on the back page in the initial sessions(s). I tend to make this into a bit of a 'quiz' as to who knows each other the best in the family and ask circular questions to the family collectively 'what they think mum would have said' to describe the family, 'what dad would have said the problems are', and 'who would have said the family is coping the best', and 'who is most hopeful about FT'. This works very well with younger children particularly. All families seem really curious about what other members have written/scored.

You immediately get into 'the differences' and this helps shape the goals of the therapy from the beginning for me.

The potential value of the more qualitative and analogue items on Page 2 have perhaps been seen as subsidiary to the quantifiable Page 1, so it is good to find that they are now coming into greater prominence, and detailed analyses of the verbatim material are starting to be published (Józefik et al., 2015).

Going back to the Score during/at end of therapy can also be an intervention in seeing from a circular perspective who thinks change has happened or not/who thinks the most change has happened etc.

There has been much ingenuity applied to finding digestible ways of presenting changes in SCORE to families during and at the end of therapy but these have not yet been coordinated into being part of the evolving manual.

I've found the Score essential when working both in a 6 session tier 2 CAMHS model, and in a tier 3 CAMHS longer model.

This is characteristic of feedback we have had from users in a great variety of therapeutic situations.

17.4 Future Options

There is work still to do, especially to share and support clinical applications.

Several users have suggested changes that they would like to make to SCORE. A common suggestion was to change the analogue scales on page 2 so that positive ratings had the high score (10) and negative ratings 1. In a workshop, German users pointed out that this is how scales are used throughout their school system so responders often use it in this direction leading to misinterpretation of the results. Participants from other countries agreed and this suggestion has been taken up by the SCORE team. There is a risk that data using the old direction may get combined with the revision, leading to confusion, but the current plan is to brand the version with the proposed changes as SCORE-15 2021 and provide advice on the AFT website component of the manual about how to integrate the two versions including a version of the Excel spreadsheet that will reverse the order as required. More generally, other suggestions have been made which would be more substantial changes. The problem especially with changes to the Likert scales is that the extensive research findings on the validity and reliability of the current version could not be assumed to apply to any different version. We do not prohibit use of a modified version but require that it does not represent itself as being the same as SCORE; the results from its use cannot be compared directly with those from the existing version; and it cannot claim reliability and validity until it has undergone a full validation research process.

Many have requested an IT version that can be used in session and provide quick feedback to family members. Others have made specific suggestions, for example that histograms are much more easily interpreted by clients than the line graphs often favoured by researchers. This is a very active project of the Tavistock-based Systemic Family Therapy Research Centre (FTSRC https://tavistockandportman.nhs.uk/research-and-innovation/research-centres/family-therapy-systemic-research-centre/) led by Charlotte Burck and Astrid Winkler.

We expect to make such a version available through the AFT website during 2021 along with instructions for its usage.

The need for a version specifically for couples is discussed earlier. We have a group working on such a version starting from the version by Teh et al. (2017). There have also been several requests for a version for adults with a learning disability but it has been more difficult to convene a group to take this on.

Calls for research projects on a variety of topics and ideas for clinical applications have been made on websites, in publications, and presented in workshops. We hope that some of these will be taken up especially as many would be a suitable project for a trainee or a group of trainees. We have an exemplary early project by three training therapists undertaking a research project for their MSc degree in LFTRC. They formed a practitioner research network to share fieldwork in which each interviewed experienced therapists about an early version of SCORE and then each independently conducted a qualitative analysis of the shared material (Stratton et al., 2006).

Of the many possible research projects perhaps the four most urgent are:

1. To investigate the issue of non-independence of couple and family samples. Most published research has treated all data as if it was from an independent sample but if there is a significant tendency for family members to answer similarly, this practice becomes questionable. First stage would be to analyse existing data to find out how much concordance there is between family members. And interestingly, does the concordance increase or decrease over the course of therapy.

2. Gathering and collating data from the many users in varied countries and therapeutic contexts to discover and interpret the main sources of variation. Essential for:
3. Establishing norms and clinical cut-off levels for different populations.
4. Collating and coordinating all of the existing material to create a comprehensive manual in a form that allows for progressive elaboration, promulgated on the internet, as both research and clinical practice develop.

We are currently exploring ways of applying for a grant for a research project that would include at least these issues. Particularly important is to get full ethical approval for procedures to collate data from different sources.

17.5 Conclusion

When the first stage of the SCORE manual was made available on the Web in 2009, there was not a plan to build a diversified set of guidance. Partly because the current range of web resources were not widely available at that time and also because we did not envisage the many creative ways that SCORE has been used since it became available.

Writing this chapter I have come to realise just how distributed the information about how to use SCORE in different contexts has become. In particular for the clinical applications because these had not been a direct objective in the origins of SCORE, just an aspiration that with people's usage became progressively more salient. In fact towards the end of the EFTA Volume 4 chapter (Ochs et al., 2020) we had stated "Another project could be to pull together all of the ways that SCORE has been used clinically and create a small manual for use in training and established practice". (Stratton et al., 2020, p. 381). In fact pages 381–382 of that chapter list 15 research ideas that could usefully be explored.

The extensive individual correspondence raises an issue of manualisation: the value of a manual is to make the information available to all and to open it to critical commentary and improvement. How to do this with the wealth of such material and what forum to put it on?

A conclusion that is likely to be relevant to other Web-distributed manuals: SCORE needs central coordination to curate the current and progressively developing material into an authoritatively sanctioned (though not rigidly prescribed) form. As the project grows it becomes essential to set up long- term funding either through a research grant, or supplied by a consortium of therapy organisations. The implications from our experience for anyone planning to create a web-based manual is that it will be important to plan in advance how the manual will be made available through different resources; how these different aspects will be coordinated so that each contains the links to make other, perhaps more specialised, resources easily available; and what coordination will be set up so that future developments in usage and in widely available web resources can be moderated and incorporated.

We hope that the SCORE experiences described here, of generating a manual that is available entirely through online resources, with the exceptional capacity this provides of continuous progressive updating, will be useful to others who are developing their own manuals in this form. We are thinking of the range from fully specified training courses to specifications and guidance for particular approaches, which are progressively being created online and could thereby be coordinated and made available to a much wider audience.

Appendix. The SCORE-15

Site Code ☐☐☐ Family Number ☐☐☐ Family Position ....

Describing your family   Date....................

We would like you to tell us about how you see your family at the moment. So we are asking for YOUR view of your family.

When people say 'your family' they often mean the people who live in your house. **But we want you to choose who you want to count as the family you are going to describe.**

For each item, make your choice by putting ☑ in just one of the boxes numbered 1 to 5. If a statement was "We are always fighting each other" and you felt this was not especially true of your family, you would put a tick in box 4 for "Describes us: not well".

| | | ✓ | |

Do not think for too long about any question, but do try to tick one of the boxes for each question.

For each line, would you say **this describes our family**:	1. Describes us: Very well	2. Describes us: Well	3. Describes us: Partly	4. Describes us: Not well	5. Describes us: Not at all
1) In my family we talk to each other about things which matter to us					
2) People often don't tell each other the truth in my family					
3) Each of us gets listened to in our family					
4) It feels risky to disagree in our family					
5) We find it hard to deal with everyday problems					
6) We trust each other					
7) It feels miserable in our family					
8) When people in my family get angry they ignore each other on purpose					
9) We seem to go from one crisis to another in my family					
10) When one of us is upset they get looked after within the family					
11) Things always seem to go wrong for my family					
12) People in the family are nasty to each other					
13) People in my family interfere too much in each other's lives					
14) In my family we blame each other when things go wrong					
15) We are good at finding new ways to deal with things that are difficult					
	1.	2.	3.	4.	5.

Now please turn over and tell us a bit more about your family.

What words would best describe your family?
....
....
....

What is the problem/challenge that brought you to therapy?

The main problem is...
....

How severe is it? Please mark your answer on the line below:

no problem at all	really bad
0 1 2 3 4 5 6 7 8 9 10	

How are you managing as a family?

Very well	very badly
0 1 2 3 4 5 6 7 8 9 10	

Do you think the therapy here will be / has been helpful?

Very helpful	unhelpful
0 1 2 3 4 5 6 7 8 9 10	

Some basic information about you:

Age

Gender

Ethnicity

Education achieved

Main occupation

People living in your household (type, such as 'daughter age 12', no names please).

THANK YOU FOR YOUR TIME

References

Borcsa, M., Pomini, V., & Saint-Mont, U. (2020). Digital systemic practices in Europe: A survey before the Covid-19 pandemic. *Journal of Family Therapy.* https://doi.org/10.1111/1467-6427.12308

Borcsa, M., & Schelenhaus, S. (2011). Der Fragebogen zur Erfassung der Wirksamkeit von Systemischer Therapie SCORE 15. Ein Werkstattbericht. *Systeme, 25*(2), 137–140.

Cahill, P., O'Reilly, K., Carr, A., Dooley, B., & Stratton, P. (2010). Validation of a 28-item version of the systemic clinical outcome and routine evaluation in an Irish context: The SCORE-28. *Journal of Family Therapy, 32*, 210–231.

Carr, A., & Stratton, P. (2017). SCORE family assessment questionnaire: A decade of progress. *Family Process, 56*, 285–301. https://doi.org/10.1111/famp.12280

Evans, C., Connell, J., Barkham, M., Mellor-Clark, J., McGrath, G., & Audin, K. (2002). Towards a standardised brief outcome measure: Psychometric properties and utility of the CORE-OM. *British Journal of Psychiatry, 180*, 51–60. View Abstract 297.

Hamilton, E., Carr, A., Cahill, P., Cassells, C., & Hartnett, D. (2015). Psychometric properties and responsiveness to change of 15- and 28-item versions of the SCORE: A family assessment questionnaire. *Family Process, 54*, 454–463. https://doi.org/10.1111/famp.12117

Jewell, T., Carr, A., Stratton, P., Lask, J., & Eisler, I. (2013). Development of a children's version of the SCORE index of family function and change. *Family Process, 52*(4), 673–684. https://doi.org/10.1111/famp.12044

Józefik, B., Matusiak, F., Wolska, M., & Ulasińska, R. (2015) Family therapy process – Works on the Polish version of SCORE-15 tool. Psychiatria Polska. https://doi.org/10.12740/PP/OnlineFirst/42894. http://www.psychiatriapolska.pl/uploads/onlinefirst/ENGverJozefik_PsychiatrPolOnlineFirstNr24.pdf. Accessed on 28 Aug 2015.

Law, D., & Wolpert, M. (2013). *Guide to using outcomes and feedback tools with children young people and families* (pp. 120–128). CORC. Accessed at: https://www.corc.uk.net/resource-hub/?type=Guidance

Limsuwan, N., & Prachason, T. (2018). The reliability and validity of the 15-item systemic clinical outcome and routine evaluation (SCORE-15) Thai version. *Journal of Family Therapy.* https://doi.org/10.1111/1467-6427.12248

O'Hanrahan, K., Daly White, M., Carr, A., Cahill, P., Keenleyside, M., Fitzhenry, M., Harte, E., Hayes, J., Noonan, H., O'Shea, H., McCullagh, A., McGuinness, S., Rodgers, C., Whelan, N., Sheppard, N., & Browne, S. (2017). Validation of 28 and 15 item versions of the SCORE family assessment questionnaire with adult mental health service users. *Journal of Family Therapy, 39*, 4–20. https://doi.org/10.1111/1467-6427.12107

Ochs, M., Borcsa, M., & Schweitzer, J. (2020). *Linking systemic research and practice – Innovations in paradigms, strategies and methods* (European family therapy association series, Volume 4). Springer.

Paolini, D., & Schepisi, L. (2020). The Italian version of SCORE-15: Validation and potential use. *Family Process.* https://doi.org/10.1111/famp.12495

Relvas, A. P., Vilaça, M., Rivas, G., & Pereira, R. (2015). *SCORE-15: Datos portugueses y españoles.* Communication presented at the III Iberian Congress of Family Therapy, Cáceres, Spain.

Stratton, P. (2014a). Experiences in measuring the functioning of UK families. *Human Systems: The Journal of Therapy, Consultation and Training, 25*, 166–177. http://www.humansystems-journal.eu/home

Stratton, P. (2014b). SCORE: Systemic Clinical Outcome and Routine Evaluation index of family functioning and change. Using the SCORE-15 (with contributions from Judith Lask, Gary Robinson, Marcus Averbeck, Reenee Singh, Julia Bland and Jan Parker). In D. Law & M. Wolpert (Eds.), *Guide to using outcomes and feedback tools with children young people and families* (pp. 120–128). CORC. Accessed at: https://www.corc.uk.net/resource-hub/?type=Guidance

Stratton, P. (2017). Just how effective is systemic therapy? Can SCORE help? *Context, 154,* 41–43.

Stratton, P., Bland, J., Janes, E., & Lask, J. (2010). Developing a practicable outcome measure for systemic family therapy: The SCORE. *Journal of Family Therapy, 32*, 232–258.

Stratton, P., Carr, A., & Schepisi, L. (2020). The SCORE in Europe: Measuring effectiveness, assisting therapy. In M. Ochs, M. Borcsa, & J. Schweitzer (Eds.), *Linking systemic research and practice – Innovations in paradigms, strategies and methods* (European family therapy association series, Volume 4) (pp. 367–384). Springer.

Stratton, P., Lask, J., Bland, J., Nowotny, E., Evans, C., Singh, R., Janes, E., & Peppiatt, A. (2014). Validation of the SCORE-15 index of family functioning and change in detecting therapeutic improvement early in therapy. *Journal of Family Therapy, 36*, 3–19. https://doi.org/10.1111/1467-6427.12022

Stratton, P., & Low, D. (2020). Culturally sensitive measures of systemic family therapy. In K. S. Wampler (Ed.), *Handbook of systemic family therapy* (M. Rastogi & R. Singh, Associate Editors. Vol. 4. Systemic family therapy and global health issues). Wiley.

Stratton, P., McGovern, M., Wetherell, A., & Farrington, C. (2006). Family therapy practitioners researching the reactions of practitioners to an outcome measure. *Australian and New Zealand Journal of Family Therapy, 27*, 199–207.

Teh, Y. Y., Lask, J., & Stratton, P. (2017). From family to relational SCORE-15: An alternative adult version of a systemic self-report measure for couples and LGB people. *Journal of Family Therapy, 39*, 21–40. https://doi.org/10.1111/1467-6427.12103

Vilaça, M., de Sousa, B., Stratton, P., & Relvas, A. P. (2015). The 15-item systemic clinical outcome and routine evaluation (SCORE-15) scale: Portuguese validation studies. *Spanish Journal of Psychology, 18*(e87), 1–10.

Vilaça, M., Relvas, A. P., & Stratton, P. (2018). A Portuguese translation of the systemic clinical outcome and routine evaluation (SCORE): The psychometric properties of the 15- and 28-item versions. *Journal of Family Therapy, 40*, 537–556. https://doi.org/10.1111/1467-6427.12197

Vilaça, M., Silva, J., & Relvas, A. P. (2014). Systemic clinical outcome routine evaluation (SCORE-15). In A.P. Relvas & S. Major (Coord.) *Instrumentos de Avaliação Familiar – Funcionamento e Intervenção* (Family assessment instruments – Functioning and intervention (Vol. I)) (Vol. I, pp. 23–41). Imprensa da Universidade de Coimbra.

Zetterqvist, M., Hånell, H. E., Wadsby, M., Cocozza, M., & Gustafsson, P. A. (2020). Validation of the systemic clinical outcome and routine evaluation (SCORE-15) self-report questionnaire: Index of family functioning and change in Swedish families. *Journal of Family Therapy*. https://doi.org/10.1111/1467-6427.12255

Part III
Uses of Manuals in Clinical Practice

Chapter 18
Intergenerational Couple Therapy

Maurizio Andolfi and Anna Mascellani

18.1 Introduction

Couple therapy only started to emerge as a specific treatment independent of family therapy in the beginning of the 1980s. In recent decades, three methodologies have grown significantly: cognitive behavioural couple therapy (Dattilio, 2010; Baucom & Epstein, 1990), psychoanalytic couple therapy (Sharff & Sharff, 2003; Bartholomey & Horowitz, 1991) and emotionally focussed couple therapy based on the integration between gestalt and system and attachment theories (Johnson, 2004; Gottman & Gottman, 2015). These therapeutic methods seem to be very effective on changing couple's dysfunctional dynamics, distorted communicational patterns or focusing on the language of the emotions. However, all of the couple therapy treatments ignore or dismiss the possibility of enlarging the frame to include in therapy other significant family members by inviting to the session members from both partners' families of origin or their children.

Partners in a couple are in a reciprocal intimate relationship and, at the same time, are children in regard to their parents, with whom they might have still unfinished business or incomplete or conflicting separation. Once they start their own family, the partners will, in turn, become parents and we know well how the presence of children can unite and increase harmony or, at the contrary, can become a destabilizing event in couple's life. This complex network of functions and roles is structured along two dimensions. The vertical dimension comprises the various

---

M. Andolfi (✉)
University of Rome, Rome, Italy

Accademia di Psicoterapia Familiare in Rome, Rome, Italy
e-mail: mauriandolfi@gmail.com

A. Mascellani
Accademia di Psicoterapia Familiare in Rome, Rome, Italy

hierarchical levels – grandparents, parents and children – and is fundamental to observe and evaluate the quality of the intergenerational bonds. The horizontal one outlines the quality and the strength of the couple as a unit, which we call their *We-ness* as well as the sibling alliance and the system of friends. The main ingredients of this special bond based on an implicit pact (the couple alliance) are mutual respect, trust and intimacy and they seem to disappear when a couple is in a deep crisis or close to separation. Restoring respect, increasing trust and rediscovering intimacy are the major goal of any couple therapist regardless of his/her major orientation.

18.2   Enlarging the Frame of Observation

We have experienced that the more we enlarge the frame of our observation, the more we help the couple to overcome their difficulties. Through many years of clinical work, we learnt to appreciate the symbolic presence of family of origin (parents and siblings) in the session, often introduced (or pushed in) by one or the other partner from the very beginning of therapy as well as the centrality of their children in the middle of their issues. Instead of considering these presences intrusive or inappropriate for the goal of couple therapy, we encouraged and expanded all these presences, considering them as special resources in order to see the full picture of the family and, by doing that, to help partners to better identify themselves (Andolfi & Mascellani, 2019).

The description of each partner's *genogram* has been a special tool in therapy to explore developmental history and major events in each person's family world in order to understand and evaluate his/her family functioning and individual identity and personality traits. This is even more useful with mixed couples, when the story of emigration and family cut-off of one partner is deeply experienced in the session. In fact, couple's conflicts can be "interrupted" or reconsidered, if we give space to each partner to explore the map of his/her family life and personal growth without any intrusion or prejudice. Giving back individual agency to each partner is a first step to restore mutual respect and appreciation of the life experiences of the other one (Andolfi, 2015). Metaphorical objects and photos are other tangible and concrete tools, highly evocative, which might introduce curiosity and reduce competition and conflicts. For example, we can ask to both partners to bring into therapy the most significant photos of their respective families when they were children, or personal objects, such as a pendant, a bag and a musical instrument, that have a great affective value with regard to a deceased parent or a special grandparent or a sibling far away. It is like introducing a parallel process in therapy from which each partner can learn something very meaningful, often painful, about the other one in a collaborative way, allowing both partners to share a moment of intimacy. Once the family is symbolically present in the session, via images, metaphorical objects and intergenerational questions (Andolfi, 2015), it will be easier for both the therapist and the couple to request the families of origin to come to a joint consult.

18.3 Presence of Families of Origin

The presence of each partner's family of origin for a special session is presented as a great opportunity to re-visit the past, to repair still open wounds and to forgive feelings of neglect or abandonment (Bowen, 1978). Therefore, we spend time to prepare well this session, clarifying to both partners that the couple's conflicts or crisis are not in the agenda of these meetings and that parents and siblings are invited to help the therapist to understand better how they grew up in their families. Re-evoking the past travelled together allows its significance to be re-read from other points of view, but above all it allows the possibility of saying to each other (parents and children and sibling to sibling) what has never been said in a non-judgemental and blaming manner.

Even more important is finding the strength to invite distant or absent parents, since this allows to confront the issue of rejection. *"He/She will never come to help me, he/she never did it in all the years we lived in the same house"!* are some of the justified resistances of an adult in re-opening a dialogue with a no-caring parent. Rather than remaining in a sort of emotional limbo or chronic rage for the rejection of the past, we encourage the adult to try and make the invitation with an open heart. The response is often surprisingly positive, allowing to have a new understanding of the present moment, without being guided by the negative experiences of the past and open to the possibility of an intergenerational reconciliation (Framo, 1992).

A collective memory with multiple generations in the same room has an enormous restorative potential and has a transformative effect at the level of individual growth of each partner, with positive reverberations within the entire family of origin and indirectly in the couple dynamics (Williamson, 1991). For this reason, we have chosen to have both partners present in the special meeting with their respective families of origin, making clear that the "other partner" is invited at the session only as an attentive observer without interfering in the process.

The interviews of a long-term research on follow up of couple therapy (Andolfi et al., 2000) have shown that none of those interviewed stated that they felt a sense of embarrassment or uneasiness in the meetings where the other partner's family was present. On the contrary, the presence of the partner at the session was seen as an important emotional support in the face of an undertaking perceived as difficult and painful. Further, there was a feeling of agreement in that the other partner had to go through the same experience. These positive effects were reported despite the fact that many of these couples had come to therapy as a result of a high level of couple conflict.

When we talk about meetings with family of origin, we do not refer only to parents; and the invitation of brothers and sisters to attend a session might be even more complicated, in particular, if in the past there have been rigid triangulations and favouritism with respect to one child over another. Episodes of rivalry and long-standing cut-off between adult siblings are often the result of distorted roles played from the time when the children were very young, causing very painful emotional distance (Boszormenyi-Nagy & Spark, 1973). Inviting siblings may allow developmental phases relative to the sharing of important growth experiences to be retraced. Such an invitation may also repair any relational distortions tied to rigid roles played in the family and to the difficulty in building or maintaining a generational alliance between siblings.

18.4 Presence of Children

Children are the most precious thing and the strongest bond between two partners, especially when both wanted to have and grow children together. While inviting members of the family of origin to a session can be a complicated undertaking and might generate strong resistance in the couple, it is generally easier to request the children's presence to help the therapist get to know the family better. However, there might be a certain worry on the part of parents, who fear that children can become too involved and have a protective attitude towards them, above all if they are little. Parents are even more reluctant to accept the therapist's request when they are in the process of separating and the children have been in some way involved in the hostility and forced to take the side of one parent or the other. The feeling of guilt and embarrassment in relation to a judgement on the part of children, especially if they are adolescents, can prevail and represent an obstacle to exposing themselves in front of the children. Therefore, it is important to get the timing right and reach a full agreement from both parents.

The presence of children in therapy creates a context that is open to playfulness and creativity. We often use a *magic wand* and ask a child to wave it and do a "magic trick" so that harmony in the family will return. In this way we give a voice to the hope for change and the desire to end hostile or violent behaviour between partners. It is incredible to observe children's capacity for imagination and the emotional responses of their parents, who are able to participate in a creative game, as if it were the reality. At times, we create, together with little children, a *fairy tale* with a general script, which begins with the words: "*Once upon a time there was a happy family…*", then parents and child have to move on, describing what happened to make everyone sad or angry, to discover at the end that the path can go in a different direction and allow everyone to go back to "*living happily and contentedly*". The parents, through the fairy tale, can free themselves of the burden of rigid and defensive positions and transmit implicit messages of change to each other as a couple, to their children and to the therapist.

In other cases, a *drawing* can be used as a projective tool, asking children to draw the main figures of the family and the world that surrounds them. Generally, from the drawing will emerge how children view family relationships. Using their imagination, for example, anger can be represented by an erupting volcano or anxiety as a little snake that engulfs itself around all the members of the family. We can then ask the parents how much they see themselves in the images produced by their children. The drawing could be hung in the kitchen, so everyone can reflect on how to avoid the volcanic eruption and how to keep the snake at a necessary distance.

18.5 Presence of Friends

Friends represent the most important social network within which each of us grows and creates lasting and important relationships, starting from early childhood to late adulthood and old age. Friendships are chosen and renewed over time, even if generally the more genuine and available friends are those with whom we have shared experiences in our developmental stage. Friendships are an outstanding resource in the relational life and growth of couples, it strikes us that so little has been written in the international literature in relation to friends being involved in couple therapy. Russell Haber was the first to underline the importance of friends in family therapy in the book entitled *Please help me with this family: Using consultants as resources in family therapy* (Andolfi & Haber, 1994). We were inspired by his ideas and clinical experience in order to introduce friends as special resources in couple therapy. The presence of friends in the room facilities a change of context of the session, moving from private issues to social bonds. With friends, common experiences and parallel developmental processes can be shared: from early age at school, to becoming a couple, to the birth of children, etc. Friends are special witnesses of each partner's development and they can add their wisdom and care in the process of couple therapy.

As can be evinced from what we have discussed until now, there are many positive results from the meetings with family of origin, children and friends in the dynamic of the couple's relationship and their capacity to handle conflicts. One of the most important outcomes is without doubt the increased solidarity within the couple, even in situations of open contrasts. It is as if taking personal risks with each other's family of origin or bringing in their own children unexpectedly produces a greater authenticity and a sense of benevolence on the part of one with the other. Often this closeness is perceived also through affectionate gestures and looks of encouragement and mirroring of one in the other's story. A second outcome is the increased curiosity and appreciation of one with regard to the other's history of development. Much information on life events, or losses, is not new, and it may have even been the subject of discussion, exchange or even a quarrel within the couple. What is new is the collaborative context in which the family narrative takes its form now.

By remembering experiences of abandonment, mourning and suffering together with privileged witnesses of their development, be parents, siblings, uncles or aunts, or their own kids or their friends, each partner can acquire a greater awareness of *"Who am I"* and of the couple's relationship and have a better awareness of boundaries and identities: my own self, the we-ness of the couple and the intergenerational bonds.

18.6 Conclusion

Intergenerational couple therapy opens the focus on a larger system of relationships, belongings and resources, indicating to couples in crisis the pathway to follow in order to rediscover mutual trust, intimacy and care.

References

Andolfi, M. (2015). *Multigenerational family therapy*. London: Routledge.
Andolfi, M., & Haber, R. (Eds.). (1994). *Please, help me with this family*. New York: Routledge.
Andolfi, M., & Mascellani, A. (2019). *Intimità di coppia e trame familiari*. Milano: Cortina.
Andolfi, M., Angelo, C., & D'atena, P. (2000). *La terapia narrata dalla famiglia*. Milano: Cortina.
Bartholomey, K., & Horowitz, L. (1991). Attachment Style among Young Adults. *Journal of Personality and Social Psychology, 61*(2), 226–244.
Baucom, D. H., & Epstein, N. D. (1990). *Cognitive-behavioral marital therapy*. New York: Brunner-Mazel.
Boszormenyi-Nagy, I., & Spark, G. (1973). *Invisible loyalties*. New York: Harper&Row.
Bowen, M. (*1978*). *Family therapy in clinical practice*. New York: Jason Aronson.
Dattilio, F. M. (*2010*). *Cognitive-behavioral therapy with couples ands families*. New York: Guilford Press.
Framo, J. (*1992*). *Family therapy- An intergenerational approach*. New York: Routledge.
Gottman, J. S., & Gottman, J. (2015). *Ten principles for doing effective couple therapy*. New York: Norton.
Johnson, S. M. (2004). *The practice of emotionally focused couple therapy. Creating connections*. New York: Brunner/Routledge.
Sharff, D. E., & Sharff, J. (2003). *Psychoanalitic couple therapy: Foundation of theory and practice*. London: Karnac.
Williamson, D. S. (1991). *The intimacy paradox*. New York: Guilford Press.

Chapter 19
From Treatment Models to Manuals: Maudsley Single- and Multi-Family Therapy for Adolescent Eating Disorders

Julian Baudinet, Mima Simic, and Ivan Eisler

19.1 The Development of Systemic Treatment Approaches for Young People with Eating Disorders

Systemic approaches to eating disorders started to be developed in the 1970s. At this time psychological therapies began to target patterns of family interaction, making them a central focus of treatments. Prominent was the work of Minuchin (1975) and Selvini Palazzoli (1974), who actively began to involve families in the treatment of their child's eating difficulties. This pioneering work tended to focus initially on exploring the function of the eating disorder behaviours in the context of the family system, with treatment interventions aimed at disrupting or blocking these 'unhelpful' patterns and dynamics. It was at this time that the idea of the 'psychosomatic family' was developed (Minuchin et al., 1978), a hugely influential view that there is a particular family context that interacts with a specific individual vulnerability in the child that leads to the development of anorexia nervosa.

While systemic approaches and focusing on supporting the family around the young person have remained at the forefront of adolescent eating disorder treatments, the field has developed significantly beyond this point. Most notably, the

---

J. Baudinet (✉) · I. Eisler
Maudsley Centre for Child and Adolescent Eating Disorders (MCCAED),
South London and Maudsley NHS Foundation Trust, London, UK

Institute of Psychiatry, Psychology and Neuroscience (IoPPN), King's College London, London, UK
e-mail: Julian.Baudinet@slam.nhs.uk; Mima.Simic@slam.nhs.uk

M. Simic
Maudsley Centre for Child and Adolescent Eating Disorders (MCCAED), South London and Maudsley NHS Foundation Trust, London, UK
e-mail: ivan.eisler@kcl.ac.uk

© Springer Nature Switzerland AG 2021
M. Mariotti et al. (eds.), *Handbook of Systemic Approaches to Psychotherapy Manuals*, European Family Therapy Association Series,
https://doi.org/10.1007/978-3-030-73640-8_19

notion of the psychosomatic family has found little empirical support (Eisler, 2005; Konstantellou et al., 2011). Instead, the focus has shifted to the way in which the process of caregiving and the stress of living with a potentially life-threatening illness impacts the family, and how family dynamics reorganise in ways that become unhelpful and may contribute to maintaining the disorder (Eisler et al., 2015; Blessitt et al., 2020).

19.2 Maudsley Family Therapy for Adolescent Eating Disorders

The Maudsley Family Therapy model was initially developed for the treatment of adolescent anorexia nervosa in the context of a series of treatment studies at the Maudsley Hospital and Institute of Psychiatry in London in the 1980s and 1990s (Dare et al., 1995). Although the early trials at the Maudsley were small, the results were promising (Russell et al., 1987; Le Grange et al., 1992; Eisler et al., 2000), gaining attention as an evidence-based treatment, supported by findings from other studies using a similar approach (Robin et al., 1994, 1999; Lock et al., 2005), as well as data from follow-up of the early studies showing stability of the good outcomes over four to five years (Eisler et al., 1997, 2007; Lock et al., 2006).

Maudsley family therapy, from its early development to its current use, has undergone a number of changes (Eisler et al., 2015), but its central tenets have remained broadly the same. These basic principles (Dare et al., 1990; Dare & Eisler, 1997) are consistent with what has become known as family based treatment, or FBT (Lock et al., 2001), and also apply to eating disorders focused family therapy (FT-ED) in general (Eisler, 2013). They can be briefly summarised as follows:

(a) From the beginning there is a focus on understanding the family in the context of a potentially life-threatening illness. When observing or exploring family relationships and interpersonal dynamics, the purpose is to gain an understanding of the impact of the illness on the family, rather than searching for aetiological explanations of why the illness developed. There may of course be aspects of family functioning that are unhelpful and may have become part of what maintains the illness which need to be addressed in treatment.
(b) The family is seen as a key resource to help the child recover (rather than the cause of the illness), although the family themselves may, at first, mostly not see themselves as having that role. The therapist has to purposefully look for and identify genuine examples of what works or has worked well in the past that is specific to each family, and recognise what gets in the way of the family being able to use these strengths.
(c) Early in treatment there is a strong emphasis on behavioural change around eating and resulting weight gain (Le Grange et al., 2014). While the young person is typically reluctant to engage in such a task at first, the parents are strongly encouraged to take a lead in managing their child's eating in the early stages of

treatment using their understanding of their child to help them overcome their reluctance. The therapist makes it clear that this is a temporary role for the parents, with the aim of getting the young person back on track to manage their future life in the way they want it to develop.
(d) Externalisation of the eating disorder is used to reduce guilt and blame and to help the family find ways to come together to overcome the illness.
(e) The early focus on behavioural change and weight gain is replaced later in treatment to address broader issues of adolescent and family life cycle development.

19.3 Changes in the Model Over Time

The team at the Maudsley Centre for Child and Adolescent Eating Disorders (MCCAED) has continued to evolve its treatment model (Eisler, 2005; Eisler et al. 2016a, b; Simic & Eisler, 2019), incorporating, among other things, findings from randomised controlled trials (RCTs) summarised in systematic reviews and clinical guidelines (Downs & Blow, 2013; Fisher et al., 2019; Jewell et al., 2016; NICE, 2017), research on the neurobiology and temperamental predispositions to developing an eating disorder (Kaye et al., 2013; Frank et al., 2019), findings from attachment research and theoretical developments in attachment theory (Jewell et al., 2016; Luyten & Fonagy, 2015; Holmes & Slade, 2019) and clinical and theoretical developments in the family therapy field (Asen & Scholz, 2010; Diamond et al., 2003; Hoffman, 1985, 1998; Lebow, 1997; Rolland, 1994; White & Epston, 1990). The following are some of the key developments:

19.3.1 Changes in the Definition of the Phases of Treatment

The Maudsley model emphasises the phased nature of treatment, differentiating between the early focus on managing the illness and achieving steady weight gain, and the later task of addressing broader issues of adolescent and family development when the young person is making healthier choices around food and eating (Dare et al., 1990; Lock et al., 2001). The current model has extended the early definition of three treatment phases by adding more detail of both the early (engagement) and late (ending) stages of treatment:

Phase 1 – Engagement and development of the therapeutic alliance
Phase 2 – Helping families to manage the eating disorder
Phase 3 – Exploring issues of individual and family development
Phase 4 – Ending, discussion of future plans and discharge

19.3.2 The Changing Nature of the Therapeutic Relationship Over the Course of Treatment

An important shift in the model has been the development of a more dynamic view of the way the therapist stance and therapeutic alliance interact and change across the course of treatment. This is evident in two distinct ways. Firstly, there has been a move away from the essentially strategic position whereby therapeutic authority was used to convey the gravity of the illness, as a way of mobilising the family to take action (Lock et al., 2001) and use their combined resources to combat a dangerous illness. Instead, the current model now more clearly describes the process of developing a therapeutic alliance with all members of the family that aims to provide containment and a sense of a secure base for treatment (Byng-Hall, 2001). The eating disorders expertise of the therapist and the multi-disciplinary team (MDT) is used purposefully to provide psychoeducation about the behavioural and psychological effects of starvation, as well as knowledge about the predisposing neurobiological and temperamental factors that underpin the development and maintenance of eating disorders. Medical assessment of the severity of the illness and discussions around the management of physical risk are an important part of the MDT engaging with the family to contain anxiety and foster hope. The focus of early sessions on developing a structured and predictable meal environment at home also aims to create a containing context. This helps to ameliorte the low tolerance of uncertainty typically seen in young people with anorexia nervosa (Brown et al., 2017).

The second shift has been the foregrounding of a change in therapeutic relationship across treatment. Moving from phase 2 to phase 3, the therapist purposefully moves away from an expert stance to being more reflective and questioning. This process of shifting therapist stance is mirrored by the changes required of the parents with their recovering child. A move from a place of a temporary, relative dependence to independence; or safe certainty to safe uncertainty. Therapists' self-reflections and discussion in supervision play a key role at this stage to ensure that the relationship does not remain static. This can inadvertently block progress by missing opportunities for experimentation and calculated risk taking by the adolescent and family, and indeed the therapist. In order to promote autonomy, the therapy process has to move to positions of safe uncertainty (Mason, 1993), which is mirrored in the therapist's shifting stance across the four phases of treatment.

19.3.3 Emphasising the Meaning of Parental Management of Eating as Caring Rather than Controlling

The initial development of the model was informed by strategic and structural family therapy concepts. While the core conceptualisation within family therapy of engaging families as a treatment resource (working *with* a family rather than *treating* the family) was in keeping with shifts in thinking in the family therapy field of the time (Hoffman, 1985, 1990), the language (taking control, winning battles, combatting anorexia, etc.) remained the language of strategic and structural family therapy. The focus on control draws on a very narrow aspect of what is effective parenting and takes little account of the importance of nurturing, empathy and attachment (Collins et al., 2002). For the adolescent, being able to control their eating (or rather not eating) is seen by them as trying to achieve a sense of stability and security (Nordbø et al., 2006). For the parents, the battle metaphors (albeit aimed at 'combatting anorexia') can leave them feeling they must never let up, leading to a sense of exhaustion and helplessness (Wufong et al., 2019). The risk of using the language of control is that the child experiences parental firmness and boundary setting around food as punitive and lacking empathy. This can lead to escalations and an increasing sense of isolation and invalidation, which reduces trust and relational containment (Wallis et al., 2017).

Emphasising the meaning of the parental tasks as caring and helping the child to overcome their fear of eating provides a much firmer basis for the family to feel that they are 'on the same page'. This can open up conversations about the aims of treatment on which both the child and the parents can agree, giving a sense of having a shared purpose in the treatment process. This has been shown to be a key element of therapeutic engagement in family therapy (Friedlander et al., 2011). The aim therefore is to help parents to create an environment in which their child can trust them, feel contained and feel more secure, in spite of this being a distressing time for the parents and young person. Shifting away from the language of battles and control to one of care and support can, at times, be a subtle and nuanced difference. However, the change in meaning softens the conversation and often results in a shift in the engagement, formulation and emotional tone of treatment.

19.3.4 Engaging the Adolescents and Siblings

Over time there has been a general shift in thinking about the importance of the therapeutic alliance, particularly with the adolescent. Engaging an adolescent with an eating disorder has often been described as challenging due to the apparent ego syntonic nature of the illness and apparent lack of motivation to recover (Westwood & Kendal, 2012). Given the emphasis placed on the role of parents in a young person's recovery, early descriptions of the model often focused on engaging parents. The need to engage the young person was often deemphasised, as they were often thought to be cognitively too ill to engage in treatment. While engaging and supporting parents remains central to the model, connecting with the young person and understanding their emotional world has become much more of a priority. This has been influenced by research findings of lower treatment satisfaction for adolescents compared to parents (Krautter & Lock, 2004) and clinical experience and research findings of studies comparing conjoint and separated family therapy (Le Grange et al., 1992; Eisler et al., 2000), which showed that it was possible to engage even severely ill adolescents (Dare et al., 1995). The latter demonstrated the benefits of separated treatment for some people and the importance of trust between the therapist, parents and adolescent when navigating distress and difficult family dynamics. This shift in the model is reflected in our clinical work and the structure of our treatments. A recent service audit demonstrated that around 73% of adolescents with anorexia nervosa and nearly all with bulimia nervosa are seen individually over the course of therapy as part of FT-ED.

Similarly, emerging evidence that clinical outcome is not related to the presence or absence of siblings in treatment (Ellison et al., 2012; Hughes et al., 2019) supported a reconceptualisation of the role of siblings. Though sibling attendance remains important, it is now not required at every session. Usually, sibling attendance is planned in advance, and the focus is primarily on addressing the needs of the sibling and helping them to understand the illness that their sister or brother is struggling with.

19.3.5 The Role of Parental Anxiety

Raising parental anxiety as a technique to mobilise parents was a key concept in the early descriptions of the Maudsley approach, which was strongly influenced by structural family therapy (Dare et al., 1990). This early thinking was based on the assumption that raising parental anxiety about their child's health would overcome their concern about making the child more distressed and would activate them to take charge of their child's eating. It was also seen as a structural intervention. By bringing the parents together the parental subsystem would be strengthened, leading to increased parental and child differentiation (Dare et al., 1990). See quote below from an early description of the model:

> .... [the technique of] anxiety induction is a powerful way of developing a focus within which the parents are consistently addressed as the responsible, executive subsystem of the family. This facilitates the development of an appropriate hierarchically structured control system within the family. At the same time, the parental couple also differentiate themselves from the child or children subsystem [...] achieved when the parents are able to take control of their daughter's eating (Dare et al., 1990, p 53).

More recently, empirical findings cast doubt on this assertion for several reasons. Firstly, research shows that parents of people with anorexia nervosa are typically highly anxious (Zabala et al., 2009). Secondly, increased levels of anxiety in parents have been found to be associated with a reduced sense of self-efficacy (Stillar et al., 2016), as well as higher levels of criticism (Duclos et al., 2014) and accommodating to illness behaviours (Flessner et al., 2011; Storch et al., 2015). Moreover, raising anxiety is likely unhelpful (particularly in individuals who are already anxious) because it interferes with learning, emotion regulation and mentalisation (Coan, 2018; Holmes & Slade, 2019). This may result in parents who are less emotionally available, containing and effective when supporting their child. The model is now more focused on ensuring that parents feel contained and supported themselves, to ensure effective problem solving, emotional warmth, validation and calm persistence in the face of their child's distress. Differentiating between anxiety about the child's illness and anxiety about the child's distress is still an important distinction but the focus in our current conceptualisation is on containing the latter ('your child is bound to be distressed and will need your support when things are feeling really difficult') and validating the former ('your parents are right to be worried, this is a serious illness and you will need their help to overcome it').

19.3.6 Broadening the Concept of Externalisation

The concept of externalisation was not well developed in the early model. It was used mainly as a way of addressing guilt/blame and as a strategy to help unite the family to combat the illness. Influences from narrative therapy (White & Epston, 1990; White, 1989) broadened the concept and therapeutic techniques. A major shift in our understanding of externalisation (Eisler, 2005) came from our clinical experience of providing families with information about the physical and psychological effects of starvation (Keys et al., 1950; Allen, 1991) and the role of temperament and neurobiological factors that predispose and maintain the development of an eating disorder (Kaye et al., 2013; Frank et al., 2019). For example, in response to a young person complaining that they cannot eat because they feel full for a long time after their last meal, the therapist will explain that this is due to delayed gastric emptying due to starvation (Robinson et al., 1988). This gives new meaning both to the experience of the young person and the family's understanding of what they, until then, thought of as illness behaviour. This validates the young person's experience and allows more helpful narratives to emerge. In the multi-family therapy (MFT) context, a similar and often even more powerful intervention is the enactment in role plays, or family sculpts, of anorexia as an oppressive voice. The use of these more powerful techniques also highlights the potential pitfalls of externalisation (Eisler et al. 2016a, b; Blessitt et al., 2020). A significant minority of young people can feel invalidated and patronised. For others, externalisation can lead to unhelpful objectification, or even demonisation, of the illness, and the misattribution of non-illness behaviours to the illness, resulting in a lack of agency and/or taking responsibility.

19.3.7 Use of the Family Meal Session

The family meal session in eating disorder focused family therapy has been described in the literature since the 1970s (Rosman et al., 1975). As the Maudsley model was being developed, a meal session was included in the treatment and was part of the early research studies. The meal was an enactment (Minuchin, 1974) to enable the therapist to observe the family interaction around food and to see the extent of the family's flexibility in responding to the therapist's interventions that disrupt their usual patterns. It also had a key strategic aim of parents experiencing the success of getting their child to eat and supporting their child not give in to their eating disorder thoughts. If the child ate spontaneously, this was sometimes seen as a negative outcome depriving the parents of the experience of success (Lock & Le Grange, 2012). Despite the family meal being written into treatment manuals (Lock et al., 2001; Le Grange & Lock, 2007; Eisler et al. 2016a, b) and remaining a prescribed component of family based treatment, as early as the mid-1990s, clinicians at the Maudsley were questioning the role of the meal session, saying it was not always needed and could be talked about instead (Dare et al., 1995). By the late 1990s/early 2000s, the meal was already beginning to be deemphasised in clinical practice at the Maudsley (Eisler, 2005) and alternate ways of supporting the young people and families with the practical tasks of food and eating were being implemented. This included providing meal support and meal-related activities in a multi-family context, the use of the 'mini-meal' during assessments (Eisler et al. 2016a, b) and the introduction of meal plans to guide parents at the beginning of treatment as a prescription of 'food as medicine'.

The shift away from using the meal session with every family was gradual and influenced by several factors. Clinicians and families have long been polarised by it, often reporting it to be stressful and confrontational. Its necessity was cast into doubt by evidence that treatment outcomes are similar when treatment is offered as separated family therapy (Eisler et al., 2000), more general systemic family therapy (Agras et al., 2014) and parent-only treatment (Le Grange et al., 2016), none of which included a meal session. A recent, small RCT comparing FBT with and without the meal session did not find a difference in outcome (Herscovici et al., 2017).

Even though the meal session may not be necessary for a good outcome, it still has a useful role to play with many families. Joining the family for a meal session is an opportunity for the therapist to share some of the most difficult experiences the family has to face and may have a positive impact on the therapeutic alliance, both with the parents and the young person (Assis da Silva, 2013). Practically supporting families at meals can be a powerful exercise, and not to be abandoned because it is difficult. Clinicians are encouraged to use the meal session when the family is finding progress difficult and agree that they could benefit from additional support. In other words, the family meal sessions should be used in a way that is targeted and meets a specific treatment need. The way it is carried out will be informed by the shared formulation and may vary.

19.3.8 Treatment Context and Intensity: Multi-family Therapy

Multi-family therapy (MFT) for anorexia nervosa is conceptually based on the same principles as FT-ED, but extends the model by increasing treatment intensity and significantly shifting context. In MFT-AN, up to eight families work together as a group with a team of clinicians for a four-day block of intensive treatment with up to six further single days offered over the following six–nine months. MFT-AN, as used at the Maudsley, is not a stand-alone treatment, rather an adjunct to FT-ED and can improve outcomes for adolescent anorexia nervosa (Eisler et al. 2016a, b). MFT for bulimia nervosa (MFT-BN; Stewart et al., 2019) is a more recent development and is also showing promise. MFT-BN is less intensive than MFT-AN, incorporates key elements from cognitive behaviour therapy and dialectical behaviour therapy. MFT-BN addresses the specific needs of young people with bulimia nervosa, including managing emotional dysregulation and containing family environmental factors, such as high expressed emotion.

The aims of both MFT models are for families to learn more about the illness, to support and learn from each other, reduce isolation, build skills and try out new behaviours. The unique group setting is a powerful way of supporting shifts in treatment and engendering hope. Rather than offering more sessions of FT-ED, offering inpatient treatment, or changing treatments, MFT allows families to work within the same model, but access greater support. Families can share and learn from the different perspectives of other group members, who all have lived experience of similar difficulties.

The experience of the intensive context of MFT and the relationships that clinicians and families develop over the course of the group has had a major impact on our understanding of how families cope, manage and overcome an eating disorder. Many of the changes described above are a direct result of such experiences.

19.3.9 One Size Does Not Fit All: Differentiating (or Adding to Model) for Different Sub-Groups

Families with High Levels of Criticism / Hostility

A consistent finding over the past three decades has been that raised levels of expressed emotion, particularly criticism, within families at the beginning of treatment are associated with poorer treatment engagement (Szmukler et al., 1985; Allan et al., 2018) and worse outcome (Eisler et al., 2000; Le Grange et al., 2011). Research has demonstrated that separated family therapy is more effective for this group of young people (Eisler et al., 2007; Allan et al., 2018). These findings have significant implications for our understanding of the change mechanisms within the model, as well as its limitations (Simic et al., 2020). These finding have contributed to a number of changes in the model described above, in particular, the emphasis on engaging the adolescent more, containing parental anxiety and the role of emotional safety in the task of re-feeding. More specifically, in addition to having more separated sessions, the model is being specifically adapted for this sub-group of families to focus more on promoting trust, repair any current or historic relationship ruptures and focus more on the intention, meaning and desired impact of behaviours. In addition to the research findings, these developments have also been influenced by theoretical advancements in attachment concepts (Holmes & Slade, 2019) and their practical application drawing on attachment based family therapy model (Diamond et al., 2016).

Bulimia Nervosa and Young People Who Are Emotionally Dysregulated

The place where the model has changed most is for young people with bulimia nervosa and those who are very emotionally dysregulated. The core principles of the model, as described above, remain the same, however, the content and structure have changed so significantly that we have developed new manuals and trainings for family therapy (FT-BN) and multi-family therapy for bulimia nervosa (MFT-BN). This is influenced by research trials demonstrating that outcomes in RCTs are comparatively poor (Schmidt et al., 2007; Le Grange et al., 2007, 2015) and a growing body of research demonstrating how distinctly different the bio-temperamental profile is of people with bulimia nervosa compared with anorexia nervosa. Research over the past few decades has demonstrated that anorexia nervosa is typically associated with a profile characterised by high levels of perfectionism, low reward sensitivity, cognitive rigidity, suppression of emotional expression and reduced emotional closeness to others (Hempel et al., 2018). Bulimia nervosa, on the other hand, tends to be associated with a profile characterised by emotional lability, higher reward sensitivity and emotional disinhibition (Atiye et al., 2015; Rotella et al., 2018; Claes et al., 2015).

Newer iterations of family treatments for bulimia nervosa have been modified to account for these differences. Adolescents and parents are offered to be seen separately initially, to reduce criticism and hostility, help the young person identify core emotions such as shame and guilt, understand the function of bingeing and purging in regulating emotions and develop a formulation. Parent sessions concurrently focus on psychoeducation, validation and skill building around emotion coaching. Once re-joined, the formulation is collaboratively revisited and individual and family skills introduced systemically in a developmentally sensitive manner.

Highly Anxious and Demoralised Families

One reason for intensifying the model by extending it to the multi-family context was to try and offer more support to highly demoralised families. In the face of extreme distress and exhaustion, it is not uncommon for families to feel burnt out, hopeless and isolated, particularly when progress is slow. In these circumstances, some families feel that the therapist does not understand that the task they are being set feels impossible and feel invalidated by the therapist's encouragement. These families often require more intensive support early on in treatment, which may include more frequent outpatient sessions with targeted family meal support sessions, meeting other parents in a parent group or MFT, or attending a brief intensive day treatment programme (Simic et al., 2018). Each of these enhancements target the family's sense of profound isolation and demoralisation through mutual sharing of insider experiences, learning and experimenting with new behaviours, and receiving input from different people of varying backgrounds and disciplines. It also addresses the need for more intensive input from professionals offered in a way that helps to gradually restore the families' confidence in their own abilities to help their children. Together this stimulates hope, helping families to persist when things feel at their worst.

19.4 From Models to Manuals

19.4.1 The Development of Family and Multi-family Therapy Manuals for Eating Disorders

As with any new treatment in its infancy, the early studies at the Maudsley did not use treatment manuals. They relied on relatively brief treatment protocols outlining the key therapeutic principles at different stages of treatment (Dare et al., 1990) and used training workshops and close supervision by the model developers to ensure consistency of the approach. Robin and colleagues (Robin et al., 1999) used a modification of a behavioural systemic manual (unpublished) developed originally for adolescent conduct problems (Robin & Foster, 1989), which was conceptually similar to the Maudsley approach (Eisler et al., 2015).

The first published manual for family therapy for anorexia nervosa appeared in book form in the early 2000s (Lock et al., 2001), formalising the approach of the early Maudsley studies. Now in its second edition (Lock & Le Grange, 2012) and generally referred to as family based treatment (FBT), it has been highly influential in promoting the dissemination of evidence-based treatment for adolescent anorexia nervosa. A treatment manual for family therapy for bulimia nervosa followed, written by the same group (Le Grange & Lock, 2007). The Maudsley group developed their own (unpublished) family therapy manuals for adolescent bulimia nervosa and anorexia nervosa to guide treatment delivery in research trials (Schmidt et al., 2007; Eisler et al. 2016a, b), as well as a training resource and a guide to routine practice. All the above manuals can be considered examples of FT-ED (Eisler, 2013), which are rooted in the key therapeutic principles described earlier and are informed by research evidence on eating disorders.

The development of MFT manuals has followed a slightly different course. Early work at the Maudsley Hospital, London (Dare & Eisler, 2000), and at the Child and Adolescent Service at Dresden University in Germany (Scholz & Asen, 2001) pioneered multi-family work with young people with eating disorders. Both groups developed unpublished draft manuals with the purpose of supporting clinicians within their services to deliver the treatment and to build staff competence. The manuals have also been made available to all teams attending MFT trainings to support skills development and the management of the complex process issues that arise during MFT. A similar manual has also been developed at the University of California San Diego Eating Disorders Centre for a one-week intensive MFT (Knatz et al., 2015). Like FT-ED, the MFT manuals have evolved over time, informed by clinical experience, research and theoretical developments. Only recently has a MFT manual been published (Simic et al., 2021).

The conceptual developments of the treatment approach described above have required several revisions of the treatment manuals (see Eisler, Simic, Blessitt et al., 2016a, for the most recent iteration of the Maudsley service manual available online). A key aspect of these revisions has been the primacy of the conceptual principles underpinning therapeutic interventions, making the manual less prescriptive than many other manuals and allowing flexibility to meet the specific needs of individual families. The therapy is, thus, guided by the general principles of the approach, as well as the clinical formulation developed collaboratively with the family and the multi-disciplinary team, the use of in-session process issues and the use of supervision.

Changes in the manuals raise an inevitable question: if the manual has changed, is it still the same treatment? And can we still claim that it is evidence based? Before we try to answer this question, we need to consider what is meant by evidence-based treatments, evidence-based practice and what role treatment manuals have in delivering effective treatments.

19.4.2 The Role of Manuals in Delivering Effective Treatments

A significant part of the debate on evidence-based practice has focused on how the term should be defined. Many of the prominent proponents of evidence-based practice have argued that the definition is often too narrow, with the notion of evidence is limited to findings from RCTs. This excludes a broad range of available quantitative and qualitative evidence and takes little account of the role of considered clinical judgement, or client and family values and preferences (Sackett et al., 1996; Kazdin, 2008; Rawlins, 2008).

Advocates of the use of treatment manuals argue that they are essential, as they ensure treatments are delivered in line with the empirical evidence, protected against therapist preconceptions and bias (Mansfield & Addis, 2001a, 2001b). Conversely, critics maintain that manuals do not fit the real-world clinical setting, where complexity is higher than in research trials. It is argued that manuals dampen creativity, are too restrictive and place too much emphasis on content and technique rather than engaging the client (Carroll & Nuro, 2002). Manual sceptics also take the view that psychological treatments cannot be reduced to, or constrained by, clearly specified guidelines or a series of specific tasks (Mansfield & Addis, 2001b).

At the centre of this debate are important assumptions that might not always hold true. The key assumption is that the closer a clinician adheres to a treatment manual, the more effective the treatment will be. Research investigating the relationship between adherence to manuals and treatment outcomes is, however, quite mixed. Some studies have demonstrated that adherence is associated with improved outcomes for specific treatments (e.g. Henggeler et al., 1997; Sexton & Turner, 2010), whereas others have found a more complex, curvilinear relationship between adherence and outcome (Hogue et al., 2008; Barber et al., 2006). Some studies have found no relationship at all (Hartnett et al., 2016; Bloomquist et al., 2013).

Systematic literature reviews and meta-analyses also suggest that, overall, adherence may have a fairly limited impact on treatment outcomes (Webb et al., 2010; Collyer et al., 2019). In a recent meta-analysis on treatment adherence in child and adolescent psychotherapy, Collyer et al., (2019) found that adherence was a statistically significant predictor of treatment outcomes; however, in their review, it only accounted for 1% of outcome variance. Collyer and colleagues caution against drawing hard conclusion from these findings because of the significant limitations of adherence research including how adherence is assessed, who assesses it and over what period of treatment. Studies on adherence are often part of carefully controlled efficacy studies, where therapists are specifically selected, trained and supervised to adhere as closely as possible to the manual and the limited variance in adherence may itself result in low correlation with outcome. Moreover, such studies often do not control for potential confounders or variables that may moderate the effect of adherence, such as therapeutic alliance, clinician experience, treatment setting, client motivation and symptom severity. For instance, there is evidence that strong adherence may predict poorer outcome in clients with low motivation (Huppert et al., 2006) and similarly that the effect of adherence is moderated by therapeutic alliance, such that when alliance is strong, adherence is associated with improved outcomes, whereas when alliance is weak, adherence is associated with poorer outcomes (Barber et al., 2006; Castonguay, 2011).

Probably the most important constraint on adherence research is the limit of our knowledge of the mechanisms of change that underpin the process of therapy. This means that while some components of a treatment manual may be essential to bring about change, others may be neutral or even have a negative effect in some contexts (Shechtman & Leichtentritt, 2010). The effectiveness of these mechanisms may vary at an individual and/or relational level. For instance, when treating anorexia nervosa, focusing on individual change in eating behaviours and weight gain early on in treatment (Madden et al., 2015) may be effective in the context of positive family relationships but may be ineffective or even counter-productive where there are critical or hostile relationships (Simic et al., 2020).

If evidence-based practice is defined narrowly as the adherent use of empirically supported (manualised) treatments, there is another assumption, which is that manualised treatments are more effective than the same treatment delivered without the use of a manual. As with the findings on adherence, the data on this are mixed. A recent systematic review of 31 studies concluded that the hypothesised superiority of manualised treatments was not supported by the evidence (Truijens et al., 2019). Again, caution is needed in accepting these conclusions because of the variability between different studies and significant methodological limitations of a number of them.

The above research primarily addresses the binary question 'do manuals lead to better outcomes', which may be too narrow a question.

19.4.3 Treatment Models Are Not Static, So Why Would a Manual Be?

Most manuals have been developed for use in the context of carefully controlled efficacy trials (where adherence is important). However, their use in everyday practice, or in the context of training or treatment dissemination, may be different Carroll and Nuro (2002) argue that different contexts and settings require different types of manuals. They describe three clear and distinct types of treatment manuals that map onto the typical course of treatment development; namely, a pilot manual (stage I), a research manual for testing efficacy (stage II) and, finally, a manual for wider scale dissemination and general effectiveness testing (stage III). These stages closely reflect the way both FT-ED and MFT manuals have needed to adapt and develop over time in order to be relevant. While the FT-ED manual for anorexia nervosa is currently being updated for wider dissemination, MFT is still in the process of being empirically tested across a range of settings and has needed to be written with this different purpose in mind.

We agree with Carroll and Nuro (2002) that manuals should change as treatments evolve through the different stages. They need to evolve to include new evidence, new clinical experiences and new understandings of mechanisms of change. We would add that the process of writing and revising manuals is part of what shapes the evolution of a treatment model through crystallising ideas and specifying how these apply to different parts of the treatment process. Many of the changes in the Maudsley model we described earlier, emerged in the context of team discussions of revising the manuals. The endeavour of writing manuals contains an inherent paradox. For the manual to be useful as a guide to other clinicians, it is necessary to operationalise significant aspects of the treatment process, specifying how the conceptual ideas translate into clinical interventions. The more specific the manual becomes, the more intelligible it will be for the clinician. Simultaneously, it becomes more prescriptive and potentially constraining. This is entirely appropriate for manuals suitable for Carroll and Nuro's stage I and stage II type manuals. In the context of efficacy studies, treatments need to be specified as accurately as possible. What the research on adherence shows, however, is that beyond the RCT, in everyday clinical practice, there is also a need for flexibility to meet the specific needs of individuals and families.

If a manual is to be used to support and guide clinicians, teams, supervisors and trainers in the principles and delivery of a treatment, it has to allow flexibility to meet the complex needs that one meets in everyday practice. The manual needs to be a base from which clinicians can build upon their existing strengths, knowledge and experience of applying a treatment model. It also needs to be something that people find useful to come back to. This might be to refresh thinking, to reformulate or to troubleshoot. Ideally, it should provide a clear guide to clinicians new to the model, while also serving as a useful reference point for experienced clinicians. This poses a difficult challenge, as there needs to be a balance between offering enough specific content for less experienced clinicians, whilst not being too prescriptive for more experienced clinicians. This can leave experienced clinicians feeling constrained, disempowered and unsupported to think for themselves or to be able to draw upon process issues occurring during therapy. This requires finding the right balance between a providing a clear exposition of the theoretical underpinning of the treatments with examples of how this might be achieved, without dictating a particular set of tasks in a rigidly held order.

For example, holding in mind a core principle of FT-ED that parents do not cause their child's eating disorder, the particular way a conversation is had, or with whom it is had in session, can then be at the discretion of the therapist. This will be based on in-session process issues, rather than a provided script of what to say.

The recent revisions of the Maudsley manuals aim to provide both guidance on the structure and content of treatment, but also how to tackle a variety of process issues, such as treatment pace, effective affect management and working with in-session dynamics. This has been particularly applicable in the development and use of the MFT manuals. The complexity of working with up to eight families and a number of clinicians facilitating the group brings multiple challenges beyond the content of the treatment. In addition to providing guidance and skills for how to work closely with a colleague to co-facilitate therapy, there are also descriptions of steps therapists can take to ensure the level of affect within the group is pitched at a safe level. This guides the therapist to simultaneously provide containment for the group and facilitates change.

At a broader level, the flexibility of applying a treatment model also requires having a good understanding of each client and their family. This occurs through the collaborative development of an individual formulation and its revision during the course of treatment.

19.4.4 Formulation in Manuals

An important lesson from the experience of disseminating FT-ED and MFT is that the content of manuals and trainings needs to include more on practically helping clinicians to build skills and confidence with formulation. In the broadest sense, formulating is the process of collaborative sense making (Harper & Moss, 2003), which means, all clinicians are formulating constantly whether they are doing this in a formal way or not. Intentionally describing and being structured about the process of formulating adds an important dimension to a manual. Most clinicians are familiar with the general principals and need to formulate; that is, that formulations should be developed collaboratively, be dynamic and change over time. Formulations clarify hypotheses, guide our questioning and planning of future interventions, and also have an important role in engaging families and reducing clinician/team bias (Butler, 1998; Baird et al., 2017; Dallos & Vetere, 2018). Many manuals discuss formulation but the practical steps involved and the process of formulation are not always emphasised.

A collaborative formulation that incorporates evidence, theory and experience, and changes over time can be a complex task. Clinicians report finding it hard to define and document at times (Christofides et al., 2012) and multi-disciplinary teams can face challenges when formulation happens across different professions (Mohtashemi et al., 2016; Craven-Staines et al., 2010). Formulations vary by discipline and model of therapy (Johnstone & Dallos, 2013) and treatment manuals therefore need to specify the *what* and the *how* of the formulation that is consistent with the specific model of treatment. By focusing more on teaching and supporting the process of formulation, clinicians and teams are more likely to feel confident in practically incorporating it into their practice and team working. By emphasising and teaching the role of a comprehensive and constantly evolving formulation, FT-ED has the greatest chance of being specific, relevant, acceptable and most effective for families. Ensuring formulation extends to the team, not just individual clinicians, is also helpful in promoting a shared team treatment philosophy and improving understanding, bringing together thinking from different disciplines and clarifying treatment plans (Johnstone, 2019; Hollingworth & Johnston, 2014). Based on the formulation, clinicians and teams can build confidence in FT-ED around when to add or modify the treatment (e.g. the family meal session; individual or separated session), when to review (e.g. lack of engagement; trust lacking within the family), when to be directive vs. reflective, how to be more culturally sensitive, or when to change treatment.

FT-ED and MFT models have been in clinical and research settings for over 40 years. If these models (and manuals) had stayed the way they were when first developed, they would be archaic and irrelevant by now. Both models have changed and been modified based on the experience of the families we see, feedback from clinicians and colleagues using the model and, of course, from the ever-growing broad body of research.

19.4.5 Think Teams: No Clinician Is an Island

Within the field of child and adolescent eating disorders, it has been demonstrated that the service context of treatment, that is, the when, how and by whom it is provided, is at least as important as the model of treatment. The emerging evidence shows (House et al., 2012; Byford et al., 2019; Schmidt et al., 2017) that young people with eating disorders referred directly to community-based specialist services have less complicated treatment pathways, significantly fewer hospital admissions and their treatment is more cost effective compared to those initially referred to generic child and adolescent mental health services. These findings have been a turning point in the delivery of treatment in the United Kingdom that sparked a nationwide overhaul of eating disorder services for young people in England, the development of clinical standards (NHS England, 2015) and establishment of over 70 multi-disciplinary teams for young people with eating disorders that were provided national training at a team level (Eisler et al., in preparation).

There is good evidence that training teams, rather than individuals, is the most effective way of disseminating evidence-based practice (Greenhalgh et al., 2004). What applies at a dissemination level is also relevant to how treatment is delivered within a service. The Maudsley manuals emphasise the importance of the role of the multi-disciplinary team across the different stages of treatment. Multi-disciplinary training and clear supervision structure within the team have had several important implications. Most notably, having a shared team understanding of a model helps to ensure new treatments are actually offered by staff and accessed by clients because (a) staff feel more supported to try out new things; (b) individuals will have the support of colleagues to formulate and problem solve within a model when things are not progressing; (c) clinicians are likely to be more confident as they will feel less isolated in their practice and (d) the team will have mechanisms for model-specific peer supervision if they cannot access external supervision.

This emphasis on team development is one thing that may be difficult to replicate in every service and can sometimes be seen as the privilege of specialist services. An important lesson for future developments of FT-ED and MFT models is to include more guidance within the manuals on the role of supervision, and how the model can best be applied in different service context. This will vary in the availability of team and supervisory input and how to problem solve resourcing and incorporating consultation into treatments to support teams, not just individuals, in treatment implementation.

19.5 Conclusions

We have argued that in considering the value of treatment manuals it is important to go beyond their role in carefully controlled efficacy research studies. While manuals are an important part of evidence-based practice, this does not mean that clinicians should deliver treatments in a way that narrowly adheres to the way the manual was used in the relevant RCTs. In clinical practice, manuals have an important role in informing clinicians as to what has been tested empirically, however, the actual treatment delivery also has to be integrated with the clinicians' understanding of how it applies to the particular client or family and their specific context. Clinicians also have to be open to ongoing feedback, both in the here and now as it relates to a specific family, and cumulatively over time. This will help to ensure that our models and manuals keep evolving and are informed by the experience of their use in practice. Equally, the 'evidence' in evidence-based practice should not be simply refer to findings from RCTs, albeit such findings are hugely important. Our understanding of the applicability of the Maudsley family therapy model for eating disorders has been informed by a broad range of research findings including research on the applicability of the treatment approach to different subgroups, on the neurobiological factors that predispose and maintain the development of an eating disorder, on potential psychological and family perpetuating mechanisms that need to be addressed in treatment as well as research on adherence to treatment manuals, alliance research or research on the neurobiology of attachment and mentalisation. We need to continue to be looking for and getting feedback, as well as questioning our ideas, to ensure that we can refine and modify our treatments in the light of new research findings and new understandings.

Manuals also have an important communication role in training and clinical practice. In training they provide the language to explain the conceptual ideas that are important in treatment and how the theoretical concepts link to specific therapeutic treatment interventions. As trainers we particularly value delivering trainings in different contexts to colleagues working in different clinical settings, diverse cultural backgrounds and other contexts that are likely to challenge our assumptions and preconceptions. In the context of a diverse multi-disciplinary team, manuals can also provide a useful tool to have a shared team understanding of our clinical practice, case management and supervisory discussion.

References

Agras, W. S., Lock, J., Brandt, H., Bryson, S. W., Dodge, E., Halmi, K. A., Jo, B., Johnson, C., Kaye, W., Wilfley, D., & Woodside, B. (2014). Comparison of 2 family therapies for adolescent anorexia nervosa: A randomized parallel trial. *JAMA Psychiatry, 71*(11), 1279. https://doi.org/10.1001/jamapsychiatry.2014.1025

Allan, E., Le Grange, D., Sawyer, S. M., McLean, L. A., & Hughes, E. K. (2018). Parental expressed emotion during two forms of family-based treatment for adolescent anorexia nervosa: Expressed emotion and family-based treatment. *European Eating Disorders Review, 26*(1), 46–52. https://doi.org/10.1002/erv.2564

Allen, J. (1991). *Biosphere 2: The human experiment*. Viking.

Asen, E., & Scholz, M. (2010). *Multi-family therapy: Concepts and techniques*. Routledge.

Assis da Silva, A. (2013). *Families with an adolescent child with anorexia nervosa: The impact of the family meal on the development of the therapeutic alliance and the relevance of families' attachment styles*. [MSc dissertation]. King's College London.

Atiye, M., Miettunen, J., & Raevuori-Helkamaa, A. (2015). A meta-analysis of temperament in eating disorders: Temperament in eating disorders. *European Eating Disorders Review, 23*(2), 89–99. https://doi.org/10.1002/erv.2342

Baird, J., Hyslop, A., Macfie, M., Stocks, R., & Van der Kleij, T. (2017). Clinical formulation: Where it came from, what it is and why it matters. *BJPsych Advances, 23*(2), 95–103. https://doi.org/10.1192/apt.bp.115.014670

Barber, J. P., Gallop, R., Crits-Christoph, P., Frank, A., Thase, M. E., Weiss, R. D., & Beth Connolly Gibbons, M. (2006). The role of therapist adherence, therapist competence, and alliance in predicting outcome of individual drug counseling: Results from the National Institute Drug Abuse Collaborative Cocaine Treatment Study. *Psychotherapy Research, 16*(2), 229–240. https://doi.org/10.1080/10503300500288951

Blessitt, E., Baudinet, J., Simic, M., & Eisler, I. (2020). Eating disorders in children, adolescents and young adults. In K. S. Wampler, R. B. Miller, R. B. Seedal, L. M. McWey, A. J. Blow, M. Rastogi, & R. Singh (Eds.), *The handbook of systemic family therapy*. Wiley.

Bloomquist, M. L., August, G. J., Lee, S. S., Lee, C.-Y. S., Realmuto, G. M., & Klimes-Dougan, B. (2013). Going-to-scale with the early risers conduct problems prevention program: Use of a comprehensive implementation support (CIS) system to optimize fidelity, participation and child outcomes. *Evaluation and Program Planning, 38*, 19–27. https://doi.org/10.1016/j.evalprogplan.2012.11.001

Brown, M., Robinson, L., Campione, G. C., Wuensch, K., Hildebrandt, T., & Micali, N. (2017). Intolerance of uncertainty in eating disorders: A systematic review and meta-analysis: Intolerance of uncertainty in eating disorders. *European Eating Disorders Review, 25*(5), 329–343. https://doi.org/10.1002/erv.2523

Butler, G. (1998). Clinical formulation. In A. S. Bellack & M. Hersen (Eds.), *Comprehensive clinical psychology*. Pergamon.

Byford, S., Petkova, H., Stuart, R., Nicholls, D., Simic, M., Ford, T., Macdonald, G., Gowers, S., Roberts, S., Barrett, B., Kelly, J., Kelly, G., Livingstone, N., Joshi, K., Smith, H., & Eisler, I. (2019). Alternative community-based models of care for young people with anorexia nervosa: The CostED national surveillance study. *Health Services and Delivery Research, 7*(37), 1–78. https://doi.org/10.3310/hsdr07370

Byng-Hall, J. (2001). Attachment as a base for family and couple therapy. *Child and Adolescent Mental Health, 6*(1), 31–36. https://doi.org/10.1111/1475-3588.00318

Carroll, K. M., & Nuro, K. F. (2002). One size cannot fit all: A stage model for psychotherapy manual development. *Clinical Psychology: Science and Practice, 9*(4), 396–406. https://doi.org/10.1093/clipsy.9.4.396

Castonguay, L. G. (2011). Psychotherapy, psychopathology, research and practice: Pathways of connections and integration. *Psychotherapy Research, 21*(2), 125–140. https://doi.org/10.1080/10503307.2011.563250

Christofides, S., Johnstone, L., & Musa, M. (2012). 'Chipping in': Clinical psychologists' descriptions of their use of formulation in multidisciplinary team working: Formulation in MDTs. *Psychology and Psychotherapy: Theory, Research and Practice, 85*(4), 424–435. https://doi.org/10.1111/j.2044-8341.2011.02041.x

Claes, L., Islam, M. A., Fagundo, A. B., Jimenez-Murcia, S., Granero, R., Agüera, Z., Rossi, E., Menchón, J. M., & Fernández-Aranda, F. (2015). The relationship between non-suicidal self-injury and the UPPS-P impulsivity facets in eating disorders and healthy controls. *PLoS One, 10*(5), e0126083. https://doi.org/10.1371/journal.pone.0126083

Coan, J. A. (2018). Toward a neuroscience of attachment. In Cassidy, Jude, Shaver, & R. Phillip (Eds.), *Handbook of attachment: Theory, research, and clinical applications* (3rd ed., pp. 242–269). Guilford Press.

Collins, W. A., Madsen, S. D., & Susman-Stillman, A. (2002). Parenting during middle childhood. In M. H. Bornstein (Ed.), *Handbook of parenting: Vol. Volume 1: Children and parenting* (2nd ed.). Lawrence Erlbaum Associates.

Collyer, H., Eisler, I., & Woolgar, M. (2019). Systematic literature review and meta-analysis of the relationship between adherence, competence and outcome in psychotherapy for children and adolescents. *European Child & Adolescent Psychiatry*. https://doi.org/10.1007/s00787-018-1265-2

Craven-Staines, S., Dexter-Smith, S., & Li, K. (2010). Integrating psychological formulations into older people's service-three years on (Part 3): Staff perceptions of formulation meetings. *PSIGE Newsletter, 112*, 16–22.

Dallos, R., & Vetere, A. (2018). *Working systemically with families: Formulation, intervention and evaluation*. Routledge.

Dare, C., & Eisler, I. (1997). Family therapy for anorexia nervosa. In D. M. Garner & P. E. Garfinkel (Eds.), *Handbook of treatment for eating disorders* (2nd ed., pp. 307–324). Guilford Press.

Dare, C., & Eisler, I. (2000). A multi-family group day treatment programme for adolescent eating disorder. 15.

Dare, C., Eisler, I., Russell, G. F. M., & Szmukler, G. I. (1990). The clinical and theoretical impact of a controlled trial of family therapy in anorexia nervosa. *Journal of Marital and Family Therapy, 16*(1), 39–57. https://doi.org/10.1111/j.1752-0606.1990.tb00044.x

Dare, C., Eisler, I., Colahan, M., Crowther, C., Senior, R., & Asen, E. (1995). The listening heart and the chi square: Clinical and empirical perceptions in the family therapy of anorexia nervosa. *Journal of Family Therapy, 17*(1), 31–57. https://doi.org/10.1111/j.1467-6427.1995.tb00003.x

Diamond, G., Siqueland, L., & Diamond, G. M. (2003). Attachment-based family therapy for depressed adolescents: programmatic treatment development. *Clinical Child and Family Psychology Review, 21*.

Diamond, G., Russon, J., & Levy, S. (2016). Attachment-based family therapy: A review of the empirical support. *Family Process, 55*(3), 595–610. https://doi.org/10.1111/famp.12241

Downs, K. J., & Blow, A. J. (2013). A substantive and methodological review of family-based treatment for eating disorders: The last 25 years of research: Eating disorder treatment. *Journal of Family Therapy, 35*, 3–28. https://doi.org/10.1111/j.1467-6427.2011.00566.x

Duclos, J., Dorard, G., Berthoz, S., Curt, F., Faucher, S., Falissard, B., & Godart, N. (2014). Expressed emotion in anorexia nervosa: What is inside the 'black box'? *Comprehensive Psychiatry, 55*(1), 71–79. https://doi.org/10.1016/j.comppsych.2013.10.002

Eisler, I. (2005). The empirical and theoretical base of family therapy and multiple family day therapy for adolescent anorexia nervosa. *Journal of Family Therapy, 27*(2), 104–131. https://doi.org/10.1111/j.1467-6427.2005.00303.x

Eisler, I. (2013). Family therapy for adolescent eating disorders: A special form of therapy or family therapy with a specific focus? *Journal of Family Therapy, 35*(S1), 1–2. https://doi.org/10.1111/1467-6427.12013

Eisler, I., Dare, C., Russell, G., Szmukler, G. I., Le Grange, D., & Dodge, E. (1997). Family and individual therapy in anorexia nervosa: A 5-year follow-up. *Archives of General Psychiatry, 54*, 1025–1030.

Eisler, I., Dare, C., Hodes, M., Russell, G., & Dodge, E. (2000). Family therapy for adolescent anorexia nervosa: The results of a controlled comparison of two family interventions. *Journal of Child Psychology and Psychiatry, 41*(6), 727–736.

Eisler, I., Simic, M., Russell, G. F. M., & Dare, C. (2007). A randomised controlled treatment trial of two forms of family therapy in adolescent anorexia nervosa: A five-year follow-up. *Journal of Child Psychology and Psychiatry, 48*(6), 552–560. https://doi.org/10.1111/j.1469-7610.2007.01726.x

Eisler, I., Wallis, A., & Dodge, L. (2015). What's new is old and what's old is new. In K. L. Loeb, D. Le Grange, & J. Lock (Eds.), *Family therapy for adolescent eating and weight disorders* (1st ed., pp. 6–41). Imprint Routledge.

Eisler, I., Simic, M., Blessitt, E., Dodge, L., & MCCAED Team. (2016a). Maudsley service manual for child and adolescent eating disorders. 164.

Eisler, I., Simic, M., Hodsoll, J., Asen, E., Berelowitz, M., Connan, F., Ellis, G., Hugo, P., Schmidt, U., Treasure, J., Yi, I., & Landau, S. (2016b). A pragmatic randomised multi-Centre trial of multifamily and single family therapy for adolescent anorexia nervosa. *BMC Psychiatry, 16*(1), 422. https://doi.org/10.1186/s12888-016-1129-6

Ellison, R., Rhodes, P., Madden, S., Miskovic, J., Wallis, A., Baillie, A., Kohn, M., & Touyz, S. (2012). Do the components of manualized family-based treatment for anorexia nervosa predict weight gain? *International Journal of Eating Disorders, 45*(4), 609–614. https://doi.org/10.1002/eat.22000

Fisher, C. A., Skocic, S., Rutherford, K. A., & Hetrick, S. E. (2019). Family therapy approaches for anorexia nervosa. *Cochrane Database of Systematic Reviews*. https://doi.org/10.1002/14651858.CD004780.pub4

Flessner, C. A., Freeman, J. B., Sapyta, J., Garcia, A., Franklin, M. E., March, J. S., & Foa, E. (2011). Predictors of parental accommodation in pediatric obsessive-compulsive disorder: Findings from the pediatric obsessive-compulsive disorder treatment study (POTS) trial. *Journal of the American Academy of Child & Adolescent Psychiatry, 50*(7), 716–725. https://doi.org/10.1016/j.jaac.2011.03.019

Frank, G. K. W., DeGuzman, M. C., & Shott, M. E. (2019). Motivation to eat and not to eat – The psycho-biological conflict in anorexia nervosa. *Physiology & Behavior, 206*, 185–190. https://doi.org/10.1016/j.physbeh.2019.04.007

Friedlander, M. L., Escudero, V., Heatherington, L., & Diamond, G. M. (2011). Alliance in couple and family therapy. *Psychotherapy, 48*(1), 25–33. https://doi.org/10.1037/a0022060

Greenhalgh, T., Robert, G., Bate, P., Kyriakidou, O., & Macfarlane, F. (2004). Report for the National Co-ordinating Centre for NHS Service Delivery and Organisation R & D (NCCSDO) April 2004. 426.

Harper, D., & Moss, D. (2003). A different kind of chemistry? Reformulating 'formulation'. *Clinical Psychology, 25*, 6–10.

Hartnett, D., Carr, A., & Sexton, T. (2016). The effectiveness of functional family therapy in reducing adolescent mental health risk and family adjustment difficulties in an Irish context. *Family Process, 55*(2), 287–304. https://doi.org/10.1111/famp.12195

Hempel, R., Vanderbleek, E., & Lynch, T. R. (2018). Radically open DBT: Targeting emotional loneliness in anorexia nervosa. *Eating Disorders, 26*(1), 92–104. https://doi.org/10.1080/10640266.2018.1418268

Henggeler, S. W., Melton, G. B., Brondino, M. J., Scherer, D. G., & Hanley, J. H. (1997). Multisystemic therapy with violent and chronic juvenile offenders and their families: The role of treatment fidelity in successful dissemination. *Journal of Consulting and Clinical Psychology, 65*(5), 821–833. https://doi.org/10.1037/0022-006X.65.5.821

Herscovici, C. R., Kovalskys, I., & Orellana, L. (2017). An exploratory evaluation of the family meal intervention for adolescent anorexia nervosa. *Family Process, 56*(2), 364–375. https://doi.org/10.1111/famp.12199

Hoffman, L. (1985). Beyond power and control: Toward a 'second order' family systems therapy. *Family Systems Medicine, 3*(4), 381–396. https://doi.org/10.1037/h0089674

Hoffman, L. (1990). Constructing realities: An art of lenses. *Family Process, 29*(1), 1–12. https://doi.org/10.1111/j.1545-5300.1990.00001.x

Hoffman, L. (1998). Setting aside the model in family therapy. *Journal of Marital and Family Therapy, 24*(2), 145–156. https://doi.org/10.1111/j.1752-0606.1998.tb01071.x

Hogue, A., Henderson, C. E., Dauber, S., Barajas, P. C., Fried, A., & Liddle, H. A. (2008). Treatment adherence, competence, and outcome in individual and family therapy for adolescent behavior problems. *Journal of Consulting and Clinical Psychology, 76*(4), 544–555. https://doi.org/10.1037/0022-006X.76.4.544

Hollingworth, P., & Johnston, L. (2014). Team formulation: What are the staff views? *Clinical Psychology Forum, 257*, 28–34.

Holmes, J., & Slade, A. (2019). The neuroscience of attachment: Implications for psychological therapies. *The British Journal of Psychiatry, 214*(06), 318–319. https://doi.org/10.1192/bjp.2019.7

House, J., Schmidt, U., Craig, M., Landau, S., Simic, M., Nicholls, D., Hugo, P., Berelowitz, M., & Eisler, I. (2012). Comparison of specialist and nonspecialist care pathways for adolescents with anorexia nervosa and related eating disorders. *International Journal of Eating Disorders, 45*(8), 949–956. https://doi.org/10.1002/eat.22065

Hughes, E. K., Sawyer, S. M., Accurso, E. C., Singh, S., & Le Grange, D. (2019). Predictors of early response in conjoint and separated models of family-based treatment for adolescent anorexia nervosa. *European Eating Disorders Review, 27*(3), 283–294. https://doi.org/10.1002/erv.2668

Huppert, J. D., Barlow, D. H., Gorman, J. M., Shear, M. K., & Woods, S. W. (2006). The interaction of motivation and therapist adherence predicts outcome in cognitive behavioral therapy for panic disorder: Preliminary findings. *Cognitive and Behavioral Practice, 13*(3), 198–204. https://doi.org/10.1016/j.cbpra.2005.10.001

Jewell, T., Blessitt, E., Stewart, C., Simic, M., & Eisler, I. (2016). Family therapy for child and adolescent eating disorders: A critical review. *Family Process, 55*(3), 577–594. https://doi.org/10.1111/famp.12242

Johnstone, L. (2019). *Team formulation: Applications of current models to reduce restrictive practice*. Association of Clinical Psychologists, UK. Retrieved from: https://acpuk.org.uk/team_formulation/.

Johnstone, L., & Dallos, R. (2013). *Formulation in psychology and psychotherapy: Making sense of people's problems* (2nd ed.). Routledge.

Kaye, W. H., Wierenga, C. E., Bailer, U. F., Simmons, A. N., & Bischoff-Grethe, A. (2013). Nothing tastes as good as skinny feels: The neurobiology of anorexia nervosa. *Trends in Neurosciences, 36*(2), 110–120. https://doi.org/10.1016/j.tins.2013.01.003

Kazdin, A. E. (2008). Evidence-based treatment and practice: New opportunities to bridge clinical research and practice, enhance the knowledge base, and improve patient care. *American Psychologist, 63*(3), 146–159. https://doi.org/10.1037/0003-066X.63.3.146

Keys, A., Brožek, J., Henschel, A., Mickelsen, O., & Taylor, H. L. (1950). *The biology of human starvation* (Vol. 2). University of Minnesota Press.

Knatz, S., Murray, S. B., Matheson, B., Boutelle, K. N., Rockwell, R., Eisler, I., & Kaye, W. H. (2015). A brief, intensive application of multi-family-based treatment for eating disorders. *Eating Disorders, 23*(4), 315–324. https://doi.org/10.1080/10640266.2015.1042318

Konstantellou, A., Campbell, M., & Eisler, I. (2011). The family context: Cause, effect or resource? In J. Alexander & J. Treasure (Eds.), *A collaborative approach to eating disorders*. Routledge.

Krautter, T., & Lock, J. (2004). Is manualized family-based treatment for adolescent anorexia nervosa acceptable to patients? Patient satisfaction at the end of treatment. *Journal of Family Therapy, 26*(1), 66–82. https://doi.org/10.1111/j.1467-6427.2004.00267.x

Le Grange, D., & Lock, J. (2007). *Treating bulimia in adolescents: A family-based approach* (1st ed.). Guilford Press.

Le Grange, D., Eisler, I., Dare, C., & Hodes, M. (1992). Family criticism and self-starvation: A study of expressed emotion. *Journal of Family Therapy, 14*(2), 177–192. https://doi.org/10.1046/j..1992.00451.x

Le Grange, D., Crosby, R. D., Rathouz, P. J., & Leventhal, B. L. (2007). A randomized controlled comparison of family-based treatment and supportive psychotherapy for adolescent bulimia nervosa. *Archives of General Psychiatry, 64*(9), 1049. https://doi.org/10.1001/archpsyc.64.9.1049

Le Grange, D., Hoste, R. R., Lock, J., & Bryson, S. W. (2011). Parental expressed emotion of adolescents with anorexia nervosa: Outcome in family-based treatment. *International Journal of Eating Disorders, 44*(8), 731–734. https://doi.org/10.1002/eat.20877

Le Grange, D., Accurso, E. C., Lock, J., Agras, S., & Bryson, S. W. (2014). Early weight gain predicts outcome in two treatments for adolescent anorexia nervosa. *International Journal of Eating Disorders, 47*(2), 124–129. https://doi.org/10.1002/eat.22221

Le Grange, D., Lock, J., Agras, W. S., Bryson, S. W., & Jo, B. (2015). Randomized Clinical Trial of Family-Based Treatment and Cognitive-Behavioral Therapy for Adolescent Bulimia Nervosa. *Journal of the American Academy of Child & Adolescent Psychiatry, 54*(11), 886–894.e2. https://doi.org/10.1016/j.jaac.2015.08.008

Le Grange, D., Hughes, E. K., Court, A., Yeo, M., Crosby, R. D., & Sawyer, S. M. (2016). Randomized clinical trial of parent-focused treatment and family-based treatment for adolescent anorexia nervosa. *Journal of the American Academy of Child & Adolescent Psychiatry, 55*(8), 683–692. https://doi.org/10.1016/j.jaac.2016.05.007

Lebow, J. (1997). The integrative revolution in couple and family therapy. *Family Process, 36*(1), 1–17. https://doi.org/10.1111/j.1545-5300.1997.00001.x

Lock, J., & Le Grange, D. (2012). *Treatment manual for anorexia nervosa: A family-based approach* (2nd ed.). Guilford Press.

Lock, J., Le Grange, D., Agras, S., & Dare, C. (2001). *Treatment manual for anorexia nervosa: A family-based approach* (1st ed.). Guilford Press.

Lock, J., Agras, W. S., Bryson, S., & Kraemer, H. C. (2005). A comparison of short- and long-term family therapy for adolescent anorexia nervosa. *Journal of the American Academy of Child & Adolescent Psychiatry, 44*(7), 632–639. https://doi.org/10.1097/01.chi.0000161647.82775.0a

Lock, J., Couturier, J., & Agras, W. S. (2006). Comparison of long-term outcomes in adolescents with anorexia nervosa treated with family therapy. *Journal of the American Academy of Child & Adolescent Psychiatry, 45*(6), 666–672. https://doi.org/10.1097/01.chi.0000215152.61400.ca

Luyten, P., & Fonagy, P. (2015). The neurobiology of mentalizing. *Personality Disorders: Theory, Research, and Treatment, 6*(4), 366–379. https://doi.org/10.1037/per0000117

Madden, S., Miskovic-Wheatley, J., Wallis, A., Kohn, M., Hay, P., & Touyz, S. (2015). Early weight gain in family-based treatment predicts greater weight gain and remission at the end of treatment and remission at 12-month follow-up in adolescent anorexia nervosa: Early weight gain in adolescent anorexia nervosa. *International Journal of Eating Disorders, 48*(7), 919–922. https://doi.org/10.1002/eat.22414

Mansfield, A. K., & Addis, M. E. (2001a). Manual-based psychotherapies in clinical practice part 1: Assets, liabilities, and obstacles to dissemination. *Evidence-Based Mental Health, 4*(3), 68–69. https://doi.org/10.1136/ebmh.4.3.68

Mansfield, A. K., & Addis, M. E. (2001b). Manual-based treatment part 2: The advantages of manual-based practice in psychotherapy. *Evidence-Based Mental Health, 4*(4), 100–101. https://doi.org/10.1136/ebmh.4.4.100

Mason, B. (1993). Towards positions of safe uncertainty. *Human Systems: The Journal of Systemic Consultation & Management, 4*, 189–200.

Minuchin, S. (1974). *Families and family therapy*. Harvard University Press.

Minuchin, S. (1975). A conceptual model of psychosomatic illness in children: Family organization and family therapy. *Archives of General Psychiatry, 32*(8), 1031. https://doi.org/10.1001/archpsyc.1975.01760260095008

Minuchin, S., Rosman, B., & Baker, L. (1978). *Psychosomatic families: Anorexia nervosa in context*. Harvard University Press.

Mohtashemi, R., Stevens, J., Jackson, P. G., & Weatherhead, S. (2016). Psychiatrists' understanding and use of psychological formulation: A qualitative exploration. *BJPsych Bulletin, 40*(4), 212–216. https://doi.org/10.1192/pb.bp.115.051342

National Institute for Health and Care Excellence (NICE). (2017). *Eating Disorders (NICE Guideline ng69)*. Retrieved from: https://www.nice.org.uk/guidance/ng69.

NHS England. (2015). *Access and Waiting Time Standard for Children and Young People with an Eating Disorder: Commissioning Guide (Version 1)*. https://www.england.nhs.uk/statistics/statistical-work-areas/cyped-waiting-times/

Nordbø, R. H. S., Espeset, E. M. S., Gulliksen, K. S., Skårderud, F., & Holte, A. (2006). The meaning of self-starvation: Qualitative study of patients' perception of anorexia nervosa. *International Journal of Eating Disorders, 39*(7), 556–564. https://doi.org/10.1002/eat.20276

Rawlins, M. (2008). De Testimonio: On the evidence for decisions about the use of therapeutic interventions. *Clinical Medicine, 8*(6), 10.

Robin, A. L., & Foster, S. L. (1989). *Negotiating parent adolescent conflict*. Guilford Press.

Robin, A. L., Siegel, P. T., Koepke, T., Moye, A., & Tice, S. (1994). Family therapy versus individual therapy for adolescent females with anorexia nervosa. *Developmental and Behavioural Pediatrics, 15*(2).

Robin, A. L., Siegel, P. T., Moye, A. W., Gilroy, M., Dennis, A. B., & Sikand, A. (1999). A controlled comparison of family versus individual therapy for adolescents with anorexia nervosa. *Journal of the American Academy of Child & Adolescent Psychiatry, 38*(12), 1482–1489. https://doi.org/10.1097/00004583-199912000-00008

Robinson, P. H., Clarke, M., & Barrett, J. (1988). Determinants of delayed gastric emptying in anorexia nervosa and bulimia nervosa. *Gut, 29*(4), 458–464. https://doi.org/10.1136/gut.29.4.458

Rolland, J. S. (1994). *Families, illness, and disability: An integrative treatment model*. Basic Books.

Rosman, B. L., Minuchin, S., & Liebman, R. (1975). Family lunch session: An introduction to family therapy in anorexia nervosa. *American Journal of Orthopsychiatry, 45*(5), 846–853. https://doi.org/10.1111/j.1939-0025.1975.tb01212.x

Rotella, F., Mannucci, E., Gemignani, S., Lazzeretti, L., Fioravanti, G., & Ricca, V. (2018). Emotional eating and temperamental traits in eating disorders: A dimensional approach. *Psychiatry Research, 264*, 1–8. https://doi.org/10.1016/j.psychres.2018.03.066

Russell, G. F. M., Szmukler, G. I., Dare, C., & Eisler, I. (1987). An evaluation of family therapy in anorexia nervosa and bulimia nervosa. *Archives of General Psychiatry, 44*(12), 1047. https://doi.org/10.1001/archpsyc.1987.01800240021004

Sackett, D. L., Rosenberg, W. M. C., Gray, J. A. M., Haynes, R. B., & Richardson, W. S. (1996). Evidence based medicine: What it is and what it isn't. *BMJ, 312*(7023), 71–72. https://doi.org/10.1136/bmj.312.7023.71

Schmidt, U., Lee, S., Beecham, J., & Perkins, S. (2007). A randomized controlled trial of family therapy and cognitive behavior therapy guided self-care for adolescents with bulimia nervosa and related disorders. *American Journal of Psychiatry, 8*.

Schmidt, U., Sharpe, H., Bartholdy, S., Bonin, E.-M., Davies, H., Easter, A., Goddard, E., Hibbs, R., House, J., Keyes, A., Knightsmith, P., Koskina, A., Magill, N., McClelland, J., Micali, N., Raenker, S., Renwick, B., Rhind, C., Simic, M., … Treasure, J. (2017). Treatment of anorexia nervosa: A multimethod investigation translating experimental neuroscience into clinical practice. *Programme Grants for Applied Research, 5*(16), 1–246. https://doi.org/10.3310/pgfar05160

Scholz, M., & Asen, E. (2001). Multiple family therapy with eating disordered adolescents: Concepts and preliminary results. *European Eating Disorders Review, 9*(1), 33–42. https://doi.org/10.1002/erv.364

Selvini Palazzoli, M. (1974). *Self-starvation: From the intrapsychic to the transpersonal approach to anorexia nervosa*. Human Context Books.

Sexton, T., & Turner, C. W. (2010). The effectiveness of functional family therapy for youth with behavioral problems in a community practice setting. *Journal of Family Psychology, 24*(3), 339–348. https://doi.org/10.1037/a0019406

Shechtman, Z., & Leichtentritt, J. (2010). The association of process with outcomes in child group therapy. *Psychotherapy Research, 20*(1), 8–21. https://doi.org/10.1080/10503300902926562

Simic, M., & Eisler, I. (2019). Maudsley family therapy for eating disorders. In J. Lebow, A. Chambers, & D. C. Bruenlin (Eds.), *Encyclopedia of couple and family therapy*. Springer.

Simic, M., Stewart, C. S., Eisler, I., Baudinet, J., Hunt, K., O'Brien, J., & McDermott, B. (2018). Intensive treatment program (ITP): A case series service evaluation of the effectiveness of day patient treatment for adolescents with a restrictive eating disorder. *International Journal of Eating Disorders, 51*(11), 1261–1269. https://doi.org/10.1002/eat.22959

Simic, M., Jewell, T., & Eisler, I. (2020). Beneath the surface of expressed emotion: The clinical relevance of possible mechanisms underlying EE in eating disorder. In R. R. Hoste & D. Le Grange (Eds.), *Expressed emotion and eating disorders*. Guilford Press.

Simic, M., Baudinet, J., Blessitt, E., Wallis, A., & Eisler, I. (2021). *Multi-family therapy for anorexia nervosa: A treatment manual*. Routledge, UK.

Stewart, C. S., Baudinet, J., Hall, R., Fiskå, M., Pretorius, N., Voulgari, S., Hunt, K., Eisler, I., & Simic, M. (2019). Multi-family therapy for bulimia nervosa in adolescence: A pilot study in a community eating disorder service. *Eating Disorders*, 1–17. https://doi.org/10.1080/10640266.2019.1656461

Stillar, A., Strahan, E., Nash, P., Files, N., Scarborough, J., Mayman, S., Henderson, K., Gusella, J., Connors, L., Orr, E. S., Marchand, P., Dolhanty, J., & Lafrance Robinson, A. (2016). The influence of carer fear and self-blame when supporting a loved one with an eating disorder. *Eating Disorders, 24*(2), 173–185. https://doi.org/10.1080/10640266.2015.1133210

Storch, E. A., Salloum, A., Johnco, C., Dane, B. F., Crawford, E. A., King, M. A., McBride, N. M., & Lewin, A. B. (2015). Phenomenology and clinical correlates of family accommodation in pediatric anxiety disorders. *Journal of Anxiety Disorders, 35*, 75–81. https://doi.org/10.1016/j.janxdis.2015.09.001

Szmukler, G. I., Eisler, I., Russell, G. F. M., & Dare, C. (1985). Anorexia nervosa, parental 'expressed emotion' and dropping out of treatment. *British Journal of Psychiatry, 147*(3), 265–271. https://doi.org/10.1192/bjp.147.3.265

Truijens, F., Zühlke-van Hulzen, L., & Vanheule, S. (2019). To manualize, or not to manualize: Is that still the question? A systematic review of empirical evidence for manual superiority in psychological treatment: TRUIJENS ET AL. *Journal of Clinical Psychology, 75*(3), 329–343. https://doi.org/10.1002/jclp.22712

Wallis, A., Rhodes, P., Dawson, L., Miskovic-Wheatley, J., Madden, S., & Touyz, S. (2017). Relational containment: Exploring the effect of family-based treatment for anorexia on familial relationships. *Journal of Eating Disorders, 5*(1), 27. https://doi.org/10.1186/s40337-017-0156-0

Webb, C. A., DeRubeis, R. J., & Barber, J. P. (2010). Therapist adherence/competence and treatment outcome: A meta-analytic review. *Journal of Consulting and Clinical Psychology, 78*(2), 200–211. https://doi.org/10.1037/a0018912

Westwood, L. M., & Kendal, S. E. (2012). Adolescent client views towards the treatment of anorexia nervosa: A review of the literature: Adolescent client views. *Journal of Psychiatric and Mental Health Nursing, 19*(6), 500–508. https://doi.org/10.1111/j.1365-2850.2011.01819.x

White, P. A. (1989). A theory of causal processing. *British Journal of Psychology, 80*(4), 431–454. https://doi.org/10.1111/j.2044-8295.1989.tb02334.x

White, M., & Epston, D. (1990). *Narrative means to therapeutic ends*. W. W. Norton.

Wufong, E., Rhodes, P., & Conti, J. (2019). "We don't really know what else we can do": Parent experiences when adolescent distress persists after the Maudsley and family-based therapies for anorexia nervosa. *Journal of Eating Disorders, 7*(1), 5. https://doi.org/10.1186/s40337-019-0235-5

Zabala, M. J., Macdonald, P., & Treasure, J. (2009). Appraisal of caregiving burden, expressed emotion and psychological distress in families of people with eating disorders: A systematic review. *European Eating Disorders Review, 17*(5), 338–349. https://doi.org/10.1002/erv.925

Chapter 20
Suggestions for a Creative Manual: The "Intervention for Change" and the Therapeutic Relationship. The Floating Therapies and Working on the Self

Lia Mastropaolo

20.1 Introduction

This chapter outlines the innovations, theoretical contributions, and most significant systemic interventions, stemming from the original "Milan Approach" model. The aim is to highlight how theory, technique and therapeutic relationship are the determining elements that integrate and compose the therapeutic process, in the same way as the synergy of different instruments creates a melody in an orchestra.

As a member of the Milan Approach, I refer to the guidelines outlined by Boscolo and Cecchin. Over time, the Milan Approach has increasingly proven to be a model in constant evolution and, whenever an attempt to define a synthesis of thought and clinical practice was made, this was challenged by new premises and new methods of working. Thus, we shifted from first-order to second-order cybernetics, which views systems as being in continuous evolution and the therapist who is part of the observed system as "affecting it, whether they like it or not." In the Milan Model, recursivity, curiosity, irreverence, transparency, narrative coherence, and attention to resources rather than problems have become fundamental concepts in the second generation of the Milan Approach. Rather than to a model, we have referred to an epistemology, to a systemic way of thinking in complexity. Experimenting has become our keyword. The consistency of the fundamental principles and the basic concepts of the Milan Approach have remained through the transformations that have taken place over time. As Ceruti (1986) states, "concepts circulate, they move

L. Mastropaolo (✉)
Il Metalogo – Genoese Systemic School- Mediation, Counseling, Therapy, Genova, Italy

Centro Milanese di Terapia della Famiglia, Milan, Italy

Genoese Center of Family Therapy, Genova, Italy
e-mail: liamastropaolo7@gmail.com

to problematic fields, they enrich themselves and change their nature, they generalise, disguise themselves, disappear, are reborn."

20.2 What Is Meant by Thinking Systemically to Act Systemically

Researching with families to create a manualized system to work better with clients as well as working with students in schools, I greatly value thinking systemically to act systemically. (Table 20.1) This is the theoretical and practical foundation of different practices presented in this paper both with the court and therapies.

It is the complexity (Bocchi & Ceruti, 1985) that gives meaning to actions and that allows us to be attentive to the ideas and to the complementarity of different points of view (Step 0).

Through circular questions, the use of hypotheses and narratives constructed with families, a change of premises is provoked in their way of thinking, of being, of understanding situations, overcoming the dichotomies of a linear perspective

Table 20.1 Toward a possible manualization: Thinking systemically to act systemically

SYSTEMIC THINKING
THINKING IN A COMPLEX WAY
ABILITY TO PASS TO THE META-LEVEL
KNOWLEDGE OF ONE'S PREJUDICES
Complex thinking (Step 0)
Attention to ideas
Changing preambles
From a linear vision to a circular complex vision
Ability to shift to the Meta-level (Step 0.1)
To Observe and Observe oneself
Knowledge of one's prejudices (0.1.1)
Prejudices cannot be avoided the best way of working is to be actively conscious of them
Acting in a systemic way (0.1.2)
Deconstruct to build (learning and changes occur through a crisis)
To observe and observe oneself
Formulating hypotheses, circular questions, providing one's own point of view comparing it with that of the family
Therapist-family relationship
Goals and abilities (0.1.3)
Positive and not guilty view of the pathology and of the conflict
Ability to pay constant attention to the contents' relational processes
Interlocutor's ability to maintain possibilities for active self-observing, through an adequate conversation management
Ability to keep an active self-observation, to be able to self-adjust with respect to the current relational process

(reason-fault, right-wrong, guilty-not guilty) and shifting to a circular understanding of relationships: this is an authentic epistemological change. Circularity and complexity are closely related. The therapist's role is not to give indications of an instructive nature, for instance, telling the family "you need to do this and the other"; yet, their role is to facilitate a process of change that allows the system to find its own solutions, through original answers, and to evolve. The use of circular, hypothetical, triadic questions allows people to ask themselves questions and to find answers that are different from the obvious and repetitive ones that have so far maintained the pathology or conflict. This represents a way for the therapist to attribute to self-reflection and self-care their importance once again, contributing to patients' and families' self-healing (Table 20.1).

To realize this change, a metalevel shift is necessary, that is, to observe and observe themselves. (Step 0.1) This allows the family and the therapist to reach a deeper perception of the self and the other. It means to experience how we are in relation and to know our prejudices about both actions and thoughts. Prejudices cannot be avoided, so the best way of working is to be actively conscious of them. (Step 0.1.1). We cannot avoid prejudices but, as Cecchin et al. (1997) suggested, the best we can do is to be sharply aware of them. This is better than to try unusefully to shake them off. The only thing we can do is to try to understand the family before investing them also with our prejudices.

The knowledge stems from action. If you want to know act, says von Foerster (1985). Epistemology is a theory to build experience strictly linked to our actions.

To act systemically means to deconstruct premises (Step 0.1.2) that bind the system to build new premises: change goes through the crisis.

Quoting the ethical imperative of Heinz von Foerster (1987): "Act in a way to increase your and others choices" (Step 0.1.3). This is another gift from second-order cybernetics: the observer-therapist not more aseptic, but bringing feelings, emotions and recursively interacting with the family.

20.3 Part A. Working with the Courts

In this first part, I would like to underline that we can be therapeutic not only in a clinical setting but also in institutional context as the court. In the next paragraphs we present a possible manualizable declination of systemic thinking, introducing innovations and building up specific methodologies in order to cause a change. During the last years, this model was used in courts provoking a deep transformation of the old way to consider the court only a place to be judged toward the idea that the court may be the best place to promote a positive change for conflictual families: This approach had been taught at Barcelona University H. Sant Paul during 6 editions each of 1500 hours, as well in Masters in Oviedo, at Universidad Nacional de Educacion de Espana (UNED); in Colombia, Messico, Ecuador, Peru, Brasile, Argentina, as well as in Italy, Genoa University for Law and Social services. Many Italian centers use this method.

20.4 Working with the Courts: An "Intervention for Change"

I am here referring to court situations in which we are called to advise a judge – that is to say, to carry out an assessment, to formulate an expert opinion, a diagnosis on the most appropriate parent in cases of judicial separation or abuse.

In the work with institutions such as the court, the diagnostic task that is entrusted to us simplifies and reduces our possibility of providing an intervention within an assessment. An assignment not only outlines the problem to be solved but also implicitly gives indications on how to solve it, and our client often is not the one to benefit from this intervention.

In this case, I wondered if the frame of the obligation or the request of the client truly are such overbearing elements as to mark a context and prevent us from using the tools at our disposal to structure a therapeutic relationship.

It is my intention to show how systemic thinking, a thinking style that is attentive to ideas, to complexity, determines a way of acting that goes from the deconstruction of a linear intervention to the construction of an intervention to change relational dynamics, even in a context such as that of the court. I am referring to the specific area of competence of working with the courts in judicial separations with highly conflictual couples, whereby the judge asks an expert for an assessment of parenting skills, child custody, even in the case of an abuse, etc. In general, the answer to the judge's question is an assessment, a diagnosis.

Over the past years, my reflections have led me to create a model that should be manualized. I have called this Manual "Intervention for Change," in which I accept and define the context of the judge expert. Within this expert framework, I propose the transformation of the assignment of diagnosis into a pathway for overcoming conflicts and changing family relationships, despite the initial constraints of a "forced" assignment. In this case, differently from when they seek to request therapy, families are sent by a judge, for a diagnostic procedure, forced to meet with the judge expert and to undertake a series of assessments. The couple, feeling in a context of control and judgment, becomes defensive, and both individuals strive to prove the validity of their own account, as opposed to that of the other, and to illustrate how one is an unreliable parent compared to the other. The question was how to overcome, together with the family, the tangle of a "forced assignment," to break out of the control/therapy, right/wrong dichotomies, and to introduce a turning point for a possible change of the relational dynamics (Mastropaolo, 1989). Thus, I effectively constructed a context that would allow me to enter into the expert field, to accept it fully, but at the same time to negotiate with all the parties involved, and with the family itself, the possibility of transforming it into a space for processing conflicts and changing relational dynamics.

Table 20.2 Toward a manual for court experts: the double bind between court-court expert/public service and between public service/expert and family

The double bind between court and public service/court expert
Judge mandate:
* be independent but I give you the limits
*be autonomous but be a social controller instead of me
* be a social controller but also a therapist…before the term I assign to you
The double bind between service expert and family:
"Tell us your problem…then we tell everything to the court."

The first step in this methodology toward a Manual was identified in the 1980s through the first research project I carried out with my team, which was the analysis of the court-service/expert macrosystems, which identified the double binds and typical characteristics of paradoxical injunctions (Bateson, 1977, 1978; Cronen et al., 1982) (Table 20.2).

This research has allowed me to move from the confusion and overlapping of roles to the identification of the respective competences between the two systems with respect to power, functions, and languages. At the same time, it allowed me to identify double-bind situations between Service and Family (Mastropaolo et al., 1985).

This context analysis has provided clarity on an institutional level and has provided me the opportunity to build a context of consensus in which the judge, lawyers and experts adhere to my project so that I can attempt to carry out "within the expertise, an intervention that allows the couple to overcome the serious conflict, in order to reclaim a two parent context, avoiding the triangulation of children."

This meant proposing to a judiciary-legal system a change of premises – that is to say, to leave the logic of judgment and to move from a linear perspective to a complex circular understanding, allowing me to carry out a "therapeutic" intervention. I outline with transparency to the family the context of the CTU (the "forced assignment," the lack of professional secrecy, the report I will send to the court); however, through a sort of "pact with the devil," I propose to use the same space and time assigned by the judge, rather than for a diagnosis, to deal with the problems together and looking to overcome the conflictual relationship of ex-spouses, so that they can take back control of the parenting role, which is at this time delegated to the judicial authority. This means that redefining the premises with all the systems involved opens up a new hierarchy of actions.

Let us follow step by step the methodology of the manual about the "Intervention for Change" I use in my work with couples (Table 20.3).

Table 20.3 Working methodology

Toward a manual for court experts working methodology with conflicts in separations
Work with couples:
Inviting both parents
Leaving aside the children involved in the separation
"Handling" the couple's conflict, "only dealing with the bare minimum"
Encouraging communication to separate the couple's story from the parents' story
Breaking away from the game of responsibilities
Constructing the third story, a relational explanation
Agreements on the children
Why it is necessary to invite children to the first session:
To evaluate the effect of the parents' separation on the children
For an effect of resonance on the parents of what the children think and express about the situation of separation
To understand the family context
For the idea of evolution in the family. The narration of the family story as a common thread in the continuing family relationship
To inform children, by making sure they understand
That they can pull themselves out of third parties in the conflict because the parents decide to start a process of mediation and therefore they can return to their role as children without being involved in the couple's game

With this diagram (see Fig. 20.1), I would like to illustrate how the conflict held up by a confrontational, resentful couple, focused on themselves and their own resentment, can be transformed into a constructive bottom-up agreement. The transition from conflict to agreement allows for the identification of oneself as a person and as a parent.

The diagram identifies two axes: number 1: present, past, and future (Boscolo & Bertrando, 1993); number 2: premises that determine some consequences (Mastropaolo, 2011a). Conflict arises in the past and continual memories maintain the expectations of the relationship of a disillusioned couple, causing a perverse game in which the only interest is to attribute culpability and responsibility to the other. Grudges, anger, and resentment keep the conflict in place at this stage: the couple is so focused on their resentment that they lose the sense of parenthood and at this time, they do not even realize they are not giving space to or considering their children. In this conflict, both parties have constructed a narrative of the end of the relationship, ruminating about how the other person is guilty. The role of the judge expert is like a role of mediator that helps them break away from the game of responsibilities and, through the construction of a third narrative elaborated by them, to help provide a different explanation which takes into account the perspective of the other and allows each person to see the situation from the other's point of view, reprocessing it, accepting it, and moving on. The agreement is built in the present time and allows us to project ourselves into the future on new premises: "stories can change, our couple's story is over but that of us as parents can continue

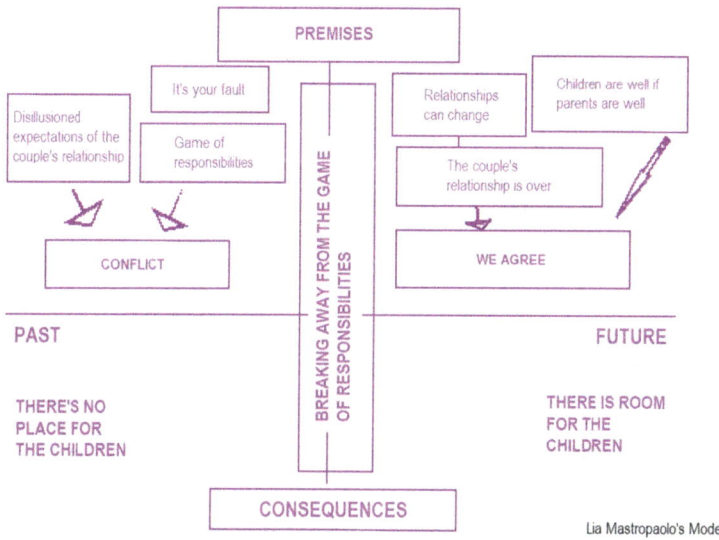

Fig. 20.1 Toward a manual for court experts. Breaking away from the game of responsibilities

Table 20.4 Toward a manual for court experts

The intervention for change:
The "forced assignment" is defined
The context is redefined
Within the assessment, I propose a transformation, rather than a diagnosis
A sort of "pact with the devil": Using the time and space to understand the conflict and regain the parenting role, delegated to the judge
The report to submit to the judge contains:
The history of the family according to a systemic reading: Systemic hypothesis
An outline of the procedure that was followed throughout the interview sessions
The agreements on the custody of the children, decided and written by the parents, and included in the report
The answer to the judge's question

or even reaffirm itself, because now we can take care of our children." Therefore, only if premises change, consequences may change.

Following this reflection, I shall return to the "Intervention for Change" and to the methodology of working with the court (Table 20.4).

20.4.1 The Use of the Methodology and the Manualization

Applying this systemic theory in a judicial context, broadening its perspective, has meant proposing an original restructuring in a system in which I felt constrained. The starting point was the analysis of macrosystems. This allowed me to transform a seemingly limiting factor into a powerful resource for bringing concrete help to families. What is given to the family and to the judge is a hypothesis, rather than a diagnosis, it is an opportunity I offer to the couple and parents to regain a position of awareness of their own story, if the premises that fueled the conflict have changed.

It is relevant the work on emotions and, starting from the request made to the expert as a consultant to diagnose a couple, it is possible to provide the judge a third story, constructed by the parents themselves in which there are no guilty parties. It is a new way of expressing oneself and telling one's story that modifies relationships and furthermore allows to change the judge's understanding of the family. (Mastropaolo, 2019).

For example, in one case, although the parents had been separated for 2 years, when, at the first interview, the separation was mentioned, the children seemed amazed, uncomfortable, and there was a mood of embarrassment and silence. As a matter of fact, the situation was uneasy, what was "unsaid" reigned supreme, and the tension was high. By not saying anything, the parents made the separation look like a simple house move.

Thus, in the first session, a sort of "spell" was discredited: parents and children were freed, as if they had awakened from a long sleep.

What do we say to the judge? We have to convey a systemic hypothesis in narrative form, in which we highlight how the "secret," built and maintained for years and finally dissolved within the court procedure, has influenced the separation process in this family.

> *It is meaningful to underline the damages provoked by untold words and scenic fictions and to comment how it is relevant to this family to get out from the taboo of unspeakable divorce to start the conversation about their relations.*

In this work with the courts, introducing circularity, irreverence, curiosity has meant shaping a new way of thinking and working that has turned the tables and has provided everyone with a new perspective. It modified the initial premises of all the systems involved, providing a new meaning to our work as a court-appointed expert, transforming a task that seemed immutable, based on judgment alone, into a job that favors the taking of responsibility by individuals, overcoming conflicts and changing relations, notwithstanding the therapist's ability to shift to a meta-level, to reflect, observing/observing oneself, being aware of their own prejudices. That is to say, including themselves in the process.

20.5 Part B. Therapies in a Clinical Setting

The second part stems from the same general principles generated by the Milan school. The laws of the context are the prominent concepts that allow us to adapt tools and theories to the epistemologies and vice versa.

The attempt to manualize our intervention as a development of the Milan model will deal with the topic of the clinical field, that is to say, therapies voluntarily requested by families or individuals,

Systemic therapy, according to the Milan Model, was born as a therapy that included the whole family. Only subsequently these assumptions were questioned and the possibility to conduct individual therapies with a systemic approach (Boscolo & Bertrando, 1996) was reconsidered, the peculiarity of which is to present the absent members and to explore the individual's relationships with the people who are significant to them. With time, this dichotomous choice (family or individual therapies) no longer seemed sufficient to move within the intricate space of therapeutic responses.

Demands changed together with therapeutic responses, which had to keep up with the times, as well as with the social, cultural, and technological changes taking place.

The cases presented were of families with children, adolescents, young adults, couples in crisis, recomposed families, homosexual couples, adoptive parents, etc. that expressed serious conflicts or discomforts with different modalities compared to the previous experiences. We had to learn to treat them differently. The same symptoms found a new mode of expression by demonstrating how social, cultural factors, and time influence the dynamics of the individual.

For example, in the case of young adults, I wondered: "is Hikikomori only Japanese?"

> Does staying indoors, surfing the Internet twenty-four hours a day, creating a parallel virtual identity, living a fictitious reality, allowing oneself a social life only in telematics networks (on social networks, adolescents often seem to have hundreds of friends, Facebook at times suggests millions of friends while young people often live isolated), and fleeing to their room/den, where their whole daily life takes place, represent a form isolation that is the same as depression and anorexia, which find different forms of manifestation than in the past? (Mastropaolo, 2011b)

Moreover, in a liquid society (Bauman, 1999) like the current one, where boundaries and social references are lost to the advantage of more blurred boundaries, not marked by continuity but by discontinuity with an interchangeability of roles (Fruggeri, 2005) and where the variety of families has replaced the uniqueness of the patriarchal family, it is obvious and natural that demands have changed, and that times and ways of intervening on people have also changed, whether they be individuals or members of a group.

Inevitably, intervention methods had to change, as well as the language used in therapy.

20.6 Fluctuating Therapies

The need for greater flexibility has prompted me as a therapist to use a method that respects the whole system, but at the same time enhances the possibility of autonomy and individuality of the individual or subsystems. Thus, the definition of "fluctuating therapies" is born, defined in this way as they allow to move with ease between the different levels of complexity of the system by convening, from time to time, the people with whom the therapist considers it most appropriate to work in that moment (Mastropaolo & Gaspari, 2008). It is like observing all angles of reality: like in a kaleidoscope, one can visualize different compositions of crystals, in the family one can broaden and narrow the gaze on the family system, "fluctuating from the individual to the system and from the system to the individual within the same therapy." The manualization this chapter describes defines which frame to outline with the family, evaluating from time to time which parts of the system at that time it is better to work with: with the individual, with the couple, with the family, with the brothers, with the grandparents, etc. The basic concept is that therapies can develop in different ways: they do not arise and end up as individual or family therapies, but they can find different configurations and branches, depending on the problem areas they encounter. For example, in an individual therapy, it is possible to agree with those in treatment with us to include significant people in certain sessions. In the same way, we shift from the family group to the different subsystems – for example, parents and children-siblings, who are seen separately by the therapist, at the same time. Also in the case of couples, there can be individual sessions, in order to provide the individual with a space to face their problems. In the individual sessions, the confidentiality that had previously been communicated to both as a dedicated space, bound to professional secrecy must be preserved. Only when the subsystems meet again can they decide to communicate what they intend to share with the other about their own experience.

For example, in the case of Christian (Fig. 20.2), after three sessions with the whole family, dividing the system into two subsystems, offering separate simultaneous meetings with Christian and with the two parents allowed, like in the field of photography, a zoom and a wide angle, to open one dilated space on the self of the young adult, facilitating his identification, something that in exclusively family

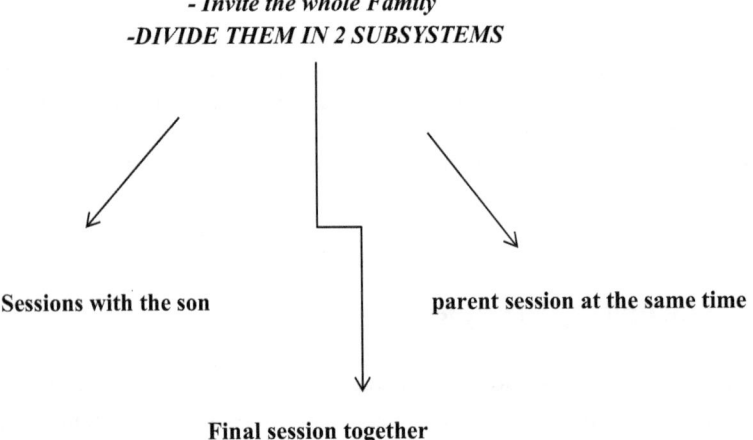

Fig. 20.2 Toward a manual for clinicians: Fluctuating therapies

therapies would have remained unexplored. Working with couple also allows a redefinition that remained neglected in traditional family treatments.

This mode facilitates a clearer definition of generational boundaries. Dividing into subsystems implicitly communicates several messages: the idea that family members can evolve independently is highlighted; we shift from the idea of a family that often finds itself merged like in an amalgamation, to the possibility of separating and finding one's own identity; it allows to make clothes from rags, marks the boundaries, and at the same time introduces the idea of sharing and trust that is recovered in the final session. This multimodal intervention safeguards the general systemic project.

The reunion of the different parts of the system in the last session gives everyone the opportunity to communicate their journey: everyone presents their "new self" to others, making sure not to discuss the aspects they wish to keep to themselves.

In fluctuating therapies, space and therapeutic time is used as a continuum, where in the alternation of people in each session, in the presence-absence of members, it is important that the set of all family members is clear in the therapist's mind, while remembering that when working with the two subsystems, simultaneously but separately, the therapist must not refer to what emerges in the sessions with another member, safeguarding and respecting the two therapeutic paths.

20.7 Working on the Self

In the "fluctuating therapies," one sometimes works on situations of serious conflicts between family members (parents and children), sometimes on situations of obstruction, in order to favor a process of differentiation and autonomy, other times to get out of the bubble, from the igloo that someone in the house has built. "Walls of incommunicability" as Christian's father called them: "For two years now he has locked himself in the house, he doesn't go out, he stopped his studies, he doesn't see friends anymore, sometimes he comes to eat with us. What does he do all the time? He is on the computer at night... he sleeps during the day..."

Elisa's mother says: "Every time I passed that door that was always closed, locked like a fortress, I felt sick, I felt a lump in my throat and my stomach twisted, sometimes I ignored it, sometimes I shouted all sorts of things, in the end I learned to shut up."

How do I treat these forms of strike from life? Forms of passivity and inactivity, a renunciation, a retreat, for some time, an event that happened which the young person feels incapable of opposing, an occasional reason (an act of bullying that was sustained, ending a course of studies, a wild night out), episodes that become the trigger to a final closure...

In individual sessions, I try to make people recognize the complexity and versatility of their self and to unravel the narrative threads that make up the intricate skein of his being. The narrative threads intersect, like in a frame, to give shape to the fabric of the self. But if the threads are knotted and intertwined in an intricate skein, they lead to confusion and internal conflicts. (Mastropaolo & Gaspari, 2008). The recognition of the different narrative threads as part of the self promotes an awareness of opposite needs and allows for more informed choices. A narrative thread is formed including a narrating self. In unrolling the yarn, in identifying new narrative threads, in this process of constructing the plot, the function of the therapist is highlighted. The process of constructing the relationship takes place in the interactions through verbal and analogical language, through the narrations it reflects on one's own emotional experiences.

20.8 The Therapeutic Relationship

The therapeutic encounter is the encounter between two "narratives," that of the system and that of the therapist, which takes place with a continuous exchange of information, in a way that contributes to building the therapeutic reality and constructs a new and unpredictable narrative. (Caillé & Rey, 2009).

To make a connection with a family or a patient, the first step is to create an alliance: everything that happens in the therapy room or in a systemic intervention happens because a significant relationship has been structured between therapist and patient; but if everything that happens can happen because there is a therapeutic relationship, it is also true that techniques can facilitate a therapeutic relationship and make it possible. Thus, it is the therapeutic relationship that becomes a prerequisite and consequence and is an indispensable prerogative for solving the problem and for treatment.

20.9 Examples

I will now present examples of fragments of therapeutic conversations between me and a young adult, Christian, a Hikikomori who has locked himself in the house and who has isolated himself, living an exclusively virtual reality.

Christian (in individual therapy): *"I live in the void, I am in nothingness…"*
T: *"It's like you're covering up everything, everything is suffocated inside. It is as if your words represented nothing."*
C: *"By being too sentimental we risk being weak."*
T: *"All things considered, you're acting like a dead body. I don't understand why you do it."*
C: *"To defend myself."*
T: *"To defend yourself from what? Why do you have to put on a fake character?"*
C: *"I've always been like this."*
T: *"What are the advantages of this situation?"*
C: *"I don't know, I've always behaved like this. When I showed myself for what I was, I got hurt. In the past I exposed myself too much with a girl and suffered. At school I was teased when I showed myself too much."*

This is an example of an incisive dialogue that touches deep chords through a provocative dialectic in which, on the one hand, the hottest themes of a malaise are highlighted, and, on the other, a relationship is structured, made up of pressing questions and responses with penetrating tones, like playing a game of foil. Between meta-communication and provocation it is relevant to use a strong, even touching language that strikes with the intention of shaking Christian to get him out of the block of marble in which he is imprisoned. The therapist tries to make his emotions come out of what he is so carefully hiding behind the mask he built himself. It is a work on the perception that Christian has of himself and the introduction of a visualization technique of the different masks that he wears during the day, without ever asking himself what he really feels or thinks; how can he approach his emotions and give meaning to what he feels out of the fictions he has imposed on himself?

Luca was another Hikikomori who locked himself up at home living an exclusively virtual reality.

On a nonverbal level, Luca is closed in himself, his arms folded motionless, tied like a straitjacket. The analogical language does not display anything, while I am stretched toward him.

In response to my pressing questions, there is no movement, his face betrays no emotion, he is silent

> *In an attempt to bring out his opinions, the therapist provoke him, asking: "How long have you decided to hibernate for and how long do you plan to stay in this freezer?"*

Again the therapist uses strong and deliberately provocative words to create a reaction.

Creating a therapeutic relationship with Luca meant accepting his game: "If I act like this, the therapist will leave me." The therapist played along, maintaining a nonjudgmental approach, respectful, empathic, spotting and recognizing the suffering behind his closure, as well as the attempts to break free from the family.

In our dialogue, through the use of metaphors and key words, the therapist emphasizes the state of strong discomfort to provoke a reaction and break down the silence.

It is the relational framework that allows to use provocation: "You decided to bury yourself alive." It is precisely the provocation that gives strength to the intervention, which disrupts Luca's communicative scheme.

20.10 The Access Routes to the Right Hemisphere: How to Talk to Emotions

- **Images in therapy**
- **Metaphors**
- **Joint family drawing**
- **The voices**
- **Role-playing**

Through the illustration of case studies, I will present some of the techniques the manual suggests to facilitate a therapeutic relationship, which are useful tools to evoke and guarantee to the person, with words or images, a different way of expressing themselves and representing emotions and experiences.

Techniques that use **images in therapy** are more immediate and allow us not only to do a quicker job but are more useful, as they pass through a completely different access route. While verbal communication goes through the left hemisphere and appeals to reason, images go directly to the right hemisphere and affect the emotional aspects. For example, when a couple bring their collages and then give an interpretation, a mutual reading, there is an immediate understanding.

The therapist's role is to make people recognize their own emotions:

> *In one case, a couple spoke like they were reading out of a book: everything was rationalized. I asked: "What are the emotions behind these words?" The woman replied: "Before I would say 'I love you' with my brain, I felt split in two... On the one hand the things I said, on the other... where were my emotions? I ignored it and I only now recognise it as displeasure... I blocked out my emotions... then I felt the pain again... After years I decided that I could not always be angry and wake up seeing everything negatively. Now I feel I have the chance to talk about it... Before it was like the Three Monkeys: 'I don't feel, I don't see, I don't speak."*

In the therapeutic relationship, it is important to find out what the access route is, what the useful language to build a shared space is.

The language of metaphors, symbols, mental images tends to establish a fluid and intense emotional climate that facilitates therapeutic change (Boscolo et al., 1991).

For example, the use of **metaphors** worked between me and Veronica:

> *Veronica is a three-year-old girl and her two parents are in constant conflict.*
>
> *In one session I propose to them to create a **joint family drawing**, saying to Veronica: "Make a drawing with mum and dad." The girl initially uses two sheets and draws a picture with each of her parents. I have to go back to the therapy room, giving them a second assignment specifying that the sheet must be the same. Only then does Veronica manage to draw with both, the mood becomes less tense and she finally speaks with ease. This work represents the first experience the child has with both parents. I suggest that they make two photocopies of the drawing and hang one in one house and one in the other.*

At the end of the meeting I conclude with a metaphor that emphasizes Veronica's position:

> *"You are used to doing things either with dad or with mum. A bit like when you go to the beach and you have two buckets, and in one there is a little fish with shells and seaweed. You know, the buckets with the water when you play at the sea... when you play with one bucket deal with what's in that bucket and when you play with the other you deal with the things of the other; the water in one bucket does not follow you when you move from one bucket to another, do you understand what I mean? Today your parents have come here together and maybe a little bit of water can come with you when you go from one bucket to another; but for now they are still moving you with a fish net, not allowing any water to move with you."*
> *Veronica listens to me with interest, imitating a little fish with her mouth.*

As can be deduced, through the ideas given to me during the session, I constructed an intervention, in the form of an immediate and simple metaphor, understandable even for Veronica, who acts on an emotional level, allowing the representation of a possible different relationship modality. The strength of the metaphor is to create new structures and connections with high emotional intensity.

Another technique is that of "**the voices**" (Stone & Winkelman, 1999).

This particular methodology allows a person to listen to their internal voices, to distinguish them, recognize them and accept them as their own. It then allows them to communicate with each other, encouraging a dialogue between them, without identifying with one or the other, but discovering a possible coherent, sensible, and original recomposition of the two contradictory instances, immobilizing positions to find their own individuality.

Often the "voices" come from the internalization of one's most significant relationships, sometimes they belong to others and pass from generation to generation. In identifying the voices of oneself and others, I suggest attributing an image to each opposing party, allowing each one to express their feelings, their emotions, including anger and resentment. The person introduces a difference between their conflicting and confused voices.

Mario recognizes a voice that represents the values transmitted by the family, and in particular, the myth of autonomy emphasized by the parents ("I will see you as a responsible adult only if you leave home, otherwise you will always be a child..."), and another voice that concerns his need to find his own individuality. The contradiction experienced between these two instances determines a situation of immobility for Mario, who neither identifies with his parents' vision, nor can he find his own, providing dignity to his way of being.

These two centrifugal forces merge. Like in a tornado, the different objects are no longer recognizable, so Mario does not identify them but perceives them as if they were in a whirlpool. The natural consequence is to find the only escape route in the passive acceptance of the ineluctable. The work on these two voices has allowed Mario to identify them, to diversify them, to promote a discussion between them to decide, in a sort of review, what to leave, what to keep, what to add to characterize his current self.

The aim of therapy is "family well-being."

The therapist, in the presence of a pathology and of an unresolved and radicalized conflict, favors a restructuring of family relationships, and calls into question with the family the relational and individual modalities that are not working, facing the conflict more deeply. The solution identified by the family is original and free, it does not lie in predefined schemes.

What emerges inside the reported examples is the model, the hypotheses, the techniques that are completely separable from my way of relating. I am referring to that particular category, creating a relationship, which cannot be described but which is a basic condition transversal to all theories, to all models, but is neglected because it is difficult to translate into words. It is about being and not doing, it is about seeing the other, a condition experienced by all therapists but difficult to describe; it escapes description because it is part of feeling rather than reasoning.

Another way to relate to young people is by **using role-playing in therapy**. In this digital age of ours, the use of video games by young people forced me to "modernize care provision through a new language" and to get closer to virtual communication forms previously unknown to me. I entered Luca's game to discover with him the opportunities of his solipsistic game, to change it into a relational game to share with others. Using video games was not just about using a technique, it was also a way of showing curiosity, interest, and attention; but above all. it became the way I built with Mario or Luca to open the way for change.

To summarize, in this section, I focused on the description of the theories and techniques, but it also seemed interesting to investigate the aspect of building a therapeutic relationship, despite the difficulty encountered in describing it.

20.11 What Ways of Relating Are Successful with Each Family?

When choosing what tools to use, I evaluate which is the most constructive way to build a relationship with a certain family or individual. Is it more useful to use a metaphor or a provocation? In a natural way, I shift the attention from the diagnosis of a patient's pathology to the diagnosis of what may be the most appropriate access route to their emotions. If someone responds well to a sarcastic joke I make or seems to connect well, this becomes a valid piece of information for me. What will be a possible access route with this patient, with this family? If I do not find an answer, if I do not receive any feedback, if humor is not their preferred access route, it means that I have to change the plan and find another way to access the right hemisphere, the emotions, the feelings, and the way in which a family expresses them.

In this part of the chapter, I have tried to reflect on how to build a therapeutic relationship that is helpful and effective. Reviewing videos of therapy sessions and re-reading what happened in the interaction between me and my patients, I tried to rattle off the different components that make up the therapeutic process and to provide dignity to the different elements that, like concentric circles in an equal and complementary way, enter into play, with equal significance, within the therapy: theory, technique, and the therapeutic relationship that, like in a dance, intertwine, integrate – one exists because the other allows it. Teaching those principles, techniques, tools to the students the idea to manualize became an important issue.

Patients arrive with a narrative that they believe to be true and unique. The therapist job is to add other points of view, introduce complexity, help them deconstruct the premises that are immobilizing them, blocking and impeding the evolution of the system. More and more I think that overly abstract and verbal techniques are not helpful in therapy and that people do not need to intellectualize, which they already do enough; yet, in order for a change to occur, they need to "feel what is happening," not only on a rational level but also on an emotional level. For this reason, the manual uses more experiential techniques, such as simulations, sculptures, collages, and joint family drawings.

If we look at the relationship, I am more and more convinced that the context of therapy is not defined solely by words. Therefore, I focused on those elements that allow us to find a way to access emotions and feelings, that is to say, the "right hemisphere" of an individual. I have paid particular attention to the way in which a particular family expresses their emotions, I look for the best access route to build a therapeutic alliance so that our interactions gain meaning and consistency. For this, the use of humor, sarcasm, provocation, and the use of metaphors and keywords represents a chance of access, which is measured and calibrated to the communication style of an individual client or family which, together with the therapist, builds an alternative story, simple but accessible, based precisely on the communication modalities of the two subsystems, in order to become in tune with each other.

Analogical communication is not only nonverbal. The analogical is in words, in connections, in metaphors, in analogies, in the stories told: in therapy, in the thread that is woven between what the therapist says and hears, and what the client says and hears, we find the notions of recursion, circularity, and above all, the curiosity that is seen at the end as what differentiates the therapeutic conversation from other conversations.

In the therapeutic relationship, the initial subtle thread that links therapist and family thickens and takes on color to become a particular "relational yarn," which is connoted by the interaction of a particular therapist with a particular family.

References

Bateson, G. (1977). *Steps to an ecology of mind*. Jason Aronson Inc. Publishers.
Bateson, G. (1978). *Mind and nature: A necessary Unity*. E. P. Dutton.
Bauman, Z. (1999). *Liquid modernity*. Wiley.
Bocchi, G., & Ceruti, M. (Eds.). (1985). *La sfida della complessità*. Feltrinelli.
Boscolo, L., & Bertrando, P. (1993). *I tempi del tempo*. Bollati Boringhieri.
Boscolo, L. & Bertrando, P. (1996). Terapia sistemica Individuale. Cortina editore.
Boscolo, L., Bertrando, P., Fiocco, M. P., Palvarini, R. M., & Perreira, J. (1991). Linguaggio e cambiamento: l'uso di parole chiave in terapia. *Terapia Familiare, 37*.
Caillé, P. & Rey, Y. (2009). *Les Objets flottants. Méthodes d'entretiens systémiques (Psychothérapies créatives)*. Fabert.
Cecchin, G., Lane, G., & Ray, W. (1997). *Verità e pregiudizi*. Raffaello Cortina.
Cronen, V., Johnson, K., & Lennamann, J. (1982). Paradoxes, double binds, and reflexive loops: An alternative theoretical perspective. *Family Process, 21*.
Fruggeri, L. (2005). Diverse normalità. Carrocci editore.
Mastropaolo, L. (1989). Ridefinire la coazione: terapeuta sistemico e Tribunale. *Ecologia della Mente, 18*.
Mastropaolo, L. (2011a). Crisi e conflitto: mediazione familiare, "intervento per il cambiamento" e terapia. Percorsi differenti della Scuola Genovese. In P. Chianura, L. Chianura, E. Fuxa, & S. Mazzoni (Eds.), *Manuale Clinico di Terapia Familiare vol. II* (pp. 105–140). Franco Angeli Edizioni.
Mastropaolo, L. (2011b). Nuove patologie adolescenziali o nuove emergenze sociali? L'hikikomori è solo giapponese? *Terapia Familiare, 97*.

Mastropaolo, L. (2019). Dentro la perizia: l'"Intervento per il Cambiamento" nelle Consulenze Tecniche d'Ufficio capitol. In P. Barbetta & U. Telfner (Eds.), *Complessità e Psicoterapia. L'eredità di Boscolo e Cecchin vol. II* (pp. 105–140). Cortina editore.

Mastropaolo, L., & Gaspari, G. (2008). Le terapie individuali, le terapie "fluttuanti" Riflessioni di due psicoterapeute sistemiche sulla loro pratica clinica. *Connessioni, 20.*

Mastropaolo, L., Pesenti, E., Rizzo, P. E., & Daglio, R. (1985). L'interazione Consultorio Tribunale Strategie sistemiche operative. *Terapia Familiare, 17.*

Stone, H., & Winkelman, S. (1999). *Voice dialogue*. A tool for transformation.

von Foerster, H. (1985). *Sicht und Einsicht*. Vieweg.

von Foerster, H. (1987). *Sistemi che osservano* Ceruti & U. Telfner (a cura), trad.it. Bernardo Draghi, Casa Editrice Astrolabio –Ubaldini Editore, Roma.

Chapter 21
"Triangular Mirroring" in Teaching, in the Clinic and in Research: A Procedure to Evaluate the Outcome of the First Session in Infant Systemic Psychotherapy

Mariarosaria Menafro, Rossella Aurilio, Maura Ruggiero, and Ferdinando Ivano Ambra

21.1 Theoretical Premises

"Triangular mirroring" is a method of "structured intervention" used during the first infant systemic psychotherapy sessions. The sessions undergo "systematic observation" (from the other side of a two-way mirror and through videorecording), which is carried out by a team of researchers trained in this specific method. This practice has also been integrated into the study program offered by the Psychotherapy Specialisation School, where specialising students have the opportunity to participate in "observation for research purposes" alongside a research team.

This working method was perfected at the I.Te.R* (Institute of Relational Therapy) in order to collect data specific to the evaluation of the outcome of the first session and acts as an "*operational protocol*" and as a premise to the future development of "experimental research".

The definition "triangular mirroring" was conceived to describe the multiple relational levels implied in the context created specifically for the *operational protocol*. The mirroring, with the underlying reflective function (Fonagy & Target, 2001) and the triangular dimension (Bowen, 1978; Haley, 1963; Boszormenyi-Nagy & Spark, 1973) can be attributed to all the subsystems involved.

M. Menafro (✉) · R. Aurilio
I.Te.R. - Istituto di Terapia Relazionale, Scuola di Specializzazione in psicoterapia ad indirizzo sistemico-relazionale, Naples/Caserta, Italy

S.I.P.P.R. Società Italiana di Psicologia e Psicoterapia Relazionale, Naples, Italy
e-mail: m.menafro@alice.it

M. Ruggiero
Dipartimento di Studi Umanistici Università degli Studi di Napoli Federico II, Naples, Italy

F. I. Ambra
Scienze Motorie e Sportive Università degli Studi di Napoli Parthenope, Naples/Caserta, Italy

The adopted methodology has benefitted from the creation of a context made up of multiple interconnected systems: the family with its subsystems, including three-generational subsystems, the research group, including just as many further subsystems, such as therapist/teacher and specializing student/researcher. The team has therefore also been committed to uncovering the isomorphic dynamics between the various subsystems generated by the active involvement of all the components.

The study of the first infant systemic psychotherapy sessions originated from a hypothesis: starting from the dynamics activated during the very first session, significant aspects of family functioning can emerge, which could reveal both the quality and typology of relationships as well as possible changes.

These considerations are consistent with the theoretical constructs derived from research on the effects of the adult–child relationship, highlighted by Malagoli Togliatti and Mazzoni (2006).

Therefore we felt it was necessary to create a "standardised interactive sequence", or "manualisation of the procedure", to be able to highlight the characteristics of the family dynamics, the quality of the adult/child relations and the possible changes during the first session.

Our current work specifically deals with open dialogue between the clinical/formative context and research. Accordingly, we propose a methodology aimed at integrating the various contextual levels to offer a future scientific contribution on the effectiveness of psychotherapy.

The selected sample is characterised by a clinical population consisting of 40 families with children aged between 4 and 11 years of age.

Furthermore, direct observation, as well as indirect observation through the recording of the sessions (a method often used in an educational context), was used specifically to broaden and extend the study of the relationships, from the principally diagnostic aspects to those evaluative of family functioning.

From the existing literature on the subject, the value of the data and the additional worth of direct observation have been clearly demonstrated by scholars who deal predominantly with research and the creation of coding systems. This further validates the systemic approach. Indeed, historically, this methodology formed the theory and practice of the systemic model. Among others, we can cite Minuchin (1974), who applied systemic theory to the study of family relationships and is counted among the scholars who have made the greatest and most significant contributions.

Along with direct observation, the study of the family as a *unit* (Kerig & Lindhal, 2001) is of equal importance and should be considered a conceptual legacy of the systemic model, which lends itself so well to the understanding of the complexity that characterises relational dynamics. The realisation that the family system is much more than, and quite different from, the sum of its parts (Bertalanffy, 1968), and that the quality and specificity of each single relationship conditions, and is conditioned by, the others has led many researchers to develop observation methods specifically aimed at understanding the value of the family as a "unit".

21.2 Observational Experience for Research Purposes

The research we outline is the continuation of work that began in 2008 and was previously published (Aurilio & Menafro, 2011). The work was carried out with the use of a table created during the operative phase, specifically for the purpose of recording the data, termed "observational experience for research purposes".

During the research guided observation was carried out using videorecorded clinical material of first sessions with children aged 3–5 years old. The premise for the observations came from the recognition that significant modifications in family dynamics could already emerge during the first session, and accordingly the key objective was that of ascertaining/evaluating in what terms and in which ways relational changes presented themselves. In fact, the definition of the child offered by the parents generally corresponded to the way in which the child defined themself through their behaviour. However, if, during the course of the session, the therapist redefined the parents' affirmations (attributing relational significance to the child's behaviour), not only did the parents modify their point of view, but also the child aligned itself to the parents' expectations expressed in the "here and now" of the session (Aurilio & Menafro, 2011).

Some reflections emerged from our observations (Aurilio & Menafro, 2011). Firstly, we recognised the importance of the presence of the parents with the child during therapy, and the fact that dyadic observation would not have captured the complexity, which cannot be reduced to the sum of dyads: for family therapists, the triangle is the minimum unit for observation and therefore, if this basis is valid for clinical therapy, it is also valid for research.

Giving further value to the centrality of the triangular dimension and the need for the parents to be present at in the session, Andolfi affirms the importance of considering the child the "expert" of the family dynamic and placing them in a trigenerational prospective. (Andolfi, 1990).

The child "belongs to a system" (Whitaker, 1989) and is a product of at least three generations. It actively participates in the family dynamic with relational control, and it presents a spontaneous tendency to interact with others while respecting and modifying pre-existent rules or introducing new ones. The child is the custodian of truths and secrets, stories and remote myths as well as sentiments and emotions, of its own and those of the other members of the family (Menafro, 2006).

The concept of the child in systemic theory allows the child to be considered, also for research purposes, a precious resource, through which the functioning of the family can be understood by attributing meaning to its behaviour and value to its competences.

This objective is pursued in the clinic with different techniques from those used in adult therapy. Some techniques are applied with more flexibility, for example, "interaction management through the use of specific relational rules", (relationship control), (Menafro, 2006), and the focus is on the opportunity for the child to understand the "sense" of its behaviour through the therapy: the parents' new perceptions of the behaviour should be the right contribution to enable this to take place.

Systemic theory pays particular attention to the parents' response with a view to understanding the evolution of the child's interaction with their environment (Cancrini & La Rosa, 1991). Infant psychotherapy should value the child's special qualities through a process of "reciprocal recognition", not so that the child becomes what the parents want it to be, but so that the child is perceived for who it really is. (Menafro, 2019).

The focus of the observation carried out during the "observative experience for research purposes" was on how the parents viewed the child, how the child felt perceived by the parents and how the therapist's redefinitions may have modified the reciprocal perceptions of each participant.

Therefore, the main task was to observe the parents' means of defining the child's disorders and, more specifically, to compare those means to those used by the child itself to define its disorder and, therefore, define itself.

From the observations it emerged that the children examined demonstrated a precocious ability to recognise the therapeutic context (Aurilio et al., 2015) and were able to express a definition of the following relational aspects: reason for the request (for therapy), their parents' definitions (of their disorders) and their own definition of themselves.

Accordingly,

(a) The child can define itself in relation to the reason for the request (for therapy), even independently from what it is told by its parents;
(b) The child's definition surprises the parents who start to perceive the child differently;
(c) This new perception of the child constitutes the premise for change.

21.3 Triangular Mirroring: A Teaching, Clinical and Research Procedure

Considering the results of this experience we have created a procedure *"triangular mirroring"*: a structured intervention applied during the first infant psychotherapy session, which requires the presence of both parents with the child. The therapist conducts the meeting in the usual way while carefully ensuring the following "sequence:"

– The therapist addresses the child and asks what the child knows, thinks or imagines – or what its parents have explained to it – is the reason for the session (item A);
– Each parent expresses a definition of his or her child's difficulties at the request of the therapist, who asks: "could you tell me in your opinion which behaviour prompted you to ask for today's consultation?" (item B)
– The therapist

- highlights the child's behaviours that are coherent/incoherent with their descriptions during the immediate interaction (item C)
- uses different strategies (for example, the redefinition of the behaviour regarding its relational significance) to reshape the parents' perceptions (item D)
- emphasises the consequent changes in the child's behaviour (if present) (item E)
- underlines (verbally or analogically) the relational patterns used by the parents, when confronted with their child's new behaviour in the "'here and now" of the session (item F).

The work, which lasted approximately 4 years, involved 41 sessions with children aged between 4 and 11 years old.

A group of specialising students/researchers participated in the collection of data. Their task was to directly observe each session, behind a two-way mirror, to carry out an initial *global analysis,* and subsequently observe the videorecordings to identify relevant interactions, which are the following:

1. The child's definition of the reasons behind the request for the meeting,
2. The definitions expressed by each parent regarding their child's difficulties
3. The coherent/incoherent behaviour of the child with the descriptions of its parents during the immediate interaction
4. The therapist's "strategies and interventions to reshape the parents'" perceptions
5. The (possible) consequent changes in the child's behaviour
6. Relational patterns employed by the parents in response to their child's new behaviour in the "here and now" of the session.

The observation tasks are carried out as follows.

The group of specialising students and researchers were trained so that each could choose to identify a specific pattern during the direct observation: therapist/child, therapist/father, therapist/mother, father/mother, mother/child, father/child, parents/child.

The opportunity to be present in the "here and now" of the dynamics in progress, even from behind a mirror, amplified the emotional effects and enabled the group to perceive some specific characteristics of the sentimental atmosphere beneath the relations activated during the session.

This first phase, defined as *global analysis,* permitted the observers to create an initial map of the family dynamics and take note of the significant elements, in order to later verify the items listed above, required by the research. Subsequently, in the second phase, during the observation through the videorecordings, what had come up and been noted during the first phase was examined more carefully.

In this second phase the flow of the interaction could be interrupted, at the discretion of the group, when it was necessary to report relevant elements regarding the research ITEMS.

Therefore, everybody took part in the collection of data during the indirect observation (videorecording), whereas in the first phase, each participant had concentrated on a specific pattern. This methodology of subdivision into a first and second phase, as well as the assigning of specific patterns to individual participants, presented didactic, clinical and research advantages.

Firstly, it allowed the observers to identify discrepancies between what was observed and noted during direct observation, as well as omissions/distortions verified during indirect observation.

The feedback for each member of the group was an opportunity for the self-evaluation of their abilities to pay attention, concentrate and, above all, their capacity for relational "reading" and management of their own emotions.

Furthermore, the observation of a specific pattern during the first phase (direct observation) and the observation of the entire therapy system in the second (indirect observation) gave the group the opportunity to confer. Even if each participant had a greater understanding of one particular pattern, the selection of valuable elements for research purposes was a decision shared by the whole group.

21.4 Analytic Description of the Items

Analysis of each ITEM:

Item A

The therapist addresses the child and asks what the child knows, thinks, or imagines – or what their parents have explained to them – is the reason for the session.

> This item is especially important, to communicate the objectives and the meaning of the meeting to the child and their parents at the same time. It acts as a kind of relational "informed con-sent", which transmits information as a difference. (Bateson, 1972)

It is also necessary to consider that the child is not always able to say what it really thinks, or does not have the cognitive, linguistic instruments to express itself effectively.

An example follows:

It refers to a family made up of two parents and a five-year-old boy.

The reason for requesting the therapy session is the behaviour of the child that is not appropriate for his age, above all in unfamiliar contexts. The child is too dependent on the father, with whom he also uses a specific lexis that only he understands.

When the therapist asks the child what he knows about the reasons for the meeting, the child runs to hide behind his father's chair and then moves around him and asks to sit on his lap. While the mother asks him to say his name, the little boy closes his eyes almost as if pretending to be asleep. He then stretches out his arm and reaches for his father's hair, which he rolls delicately between his fingers, while putting the thumb of his other hand in his mouth. The mother appears obsessed with baby-talk and starts to use a series of neologisms invented by the child, almost ridiculing him, while asking the therapist, every so often, whether it is normal to still not know how to speak properly. At that point, the little boy begins to sniffle, saying that he wants to leave. He gets down from his father's lap, tugs on his jacket and heads for the door, followed by his father.

This case is emblematic of how a child can find a way to answer the therapist's question.

In other cases in the selected sample, the observation of the child revealed that, even if the child was initially silent, or a little shy, throughout the course of the session, it became clear that the child was actually perfectly aware of what was worrying their parents. During our research, the keen eye of the observer has been able to recognise indicators in the "reactive" behaviour of the child in response to the therapist's question. These indicators reveal how much the child actually "already knew" about the reasons for the consultation, but they may only have become clear at the end of the meeting. During indirect observation, not only was it possible to "pause" the video on the more significant interaction of the direct observation, but the observation group could also confirm the importance and usefulness of that interaction for their work together.

Item B

Each parent expresses a definition of their child's difficulties.

Clinical experience has corroborated the systematic interpretation, which recognises that the presence of the child has a specific role in a couple's relationship.

The child, who is trapped in the triangular dynamic, can fulfil various functions (Minuchin, 1974): deviation of conflict between the couple, who consider the child the only element of disturbance in the supposed marital "harmony;" coalition with one parent at the exclusion of the other; serious confrontation that distances all members of the family, possibly with violent behaviour. In all these hypotheses, it is clear that, when the family requests help, they are not aware of the real underlying significance of their child's behaviour.

At the request of the therapist, who asks, *"could you tell me, in your opinion, which behaviour prompted you to ask for today's consultation?"*, the parents should define themselves, and it is like asking them to reveal their hand at cards. Firstly, they may discover, during the meeting, that they do not share the same view and secondly, because they are required to precisely describe what they have noticed about their child's behaviour and what has particularly struck them. It is like photographing invisible machinery and it is up to the therapist to understand how much of the child's behaviour is caught up in the cogs of the family relationship systems' wheels.

Group consultation amongst the observers has enabled them to identify the analogical, and even verbal, details during the indirect observation, which confirm, or not, the therapist's understanding, which is subsequently recounted to the couple within the here and now of the session.

An example follows.

A couple comes to our attention due to the phobic/obsessive social avoidance behaviour and night-time enuresis of their nine-year-old daughter. The child's mother initially praises her daughter by describing her artistic talent before defining the problem, which evidently causes her embarrassment. The father, on the other hand, consults the therapist in an irritated manner, to explain that it is inconceivable to him that a young girl, who is almost a young woman, has difficulties that most two-year-olds have overcome. The mother intervenes, by pointing out that he has been unable to stop smoking, to which her husband responds by saying that if it bothers her so much he would willingly distance himself from their home and take his unhealthy habit to a bar where he can enjoy it with a coffee and a chat with his friends.

It became clear that the aggressive component underlying the little girl's difficulties came under "family functioning", where an ill-concealed mother/daughter coalition emerged, at the exclusion of the father.

Item C
The therapist highlights the child's behaviours that are coherent/incoherent with their descriptions during the immediate interaction

This is the most complicated part, which benefits most from "double observation".

It has been noted that when the parents are on the verge of describing their child's disturbed behaviour, (perhaps the very behaviour that prompted the request for the consult), the child becomes agitated and assumes particular postures before the behaviour has been verbally expressed. Indirect observation benefits from the attention of the whole group to identify predictive signs of what the parents then confirm. In some cases, it was also possible to note the extent to which the child's behaviour was synchronised with the words of one or both parents.

In one of the cases observed, this synchronised aspect was of particular interest.

It is the case of an eleven-year-old girl accompanied by her parents to the consult because of self-harm behaviour (cutting). At a certain point of the interview, while the mother was about to describe what worried her most, the girl, who was already biting her nails, tore a piece of skin off, perhaps inadvertently, and her hand began to bleed. The father coldly hands her a tissue, while the mother silently looks at the therapist and then, almost crying, says that her daughter really does not "love herself".

Item D
The therapist uses different strategies (for example, the redefinition of the behaviour regarding its relational significance) to reshape the parents' perceptions.

In this case indirect observation was again extremely useful, as a means of recuperating further elements that broadened the vision of the family system.

In fact, the speed at which the interaction flows during the session does not always permit the therapist to identify all the elements needed to translate the relational meaning and mechanisms underlying the child's behaviour.

It has, however, been observed that in all the families in the research sample a change took place in the parents' perceptions. In some cases, it was the parents themselves who, by using the therapist's "key", enriched the relational significance of the child's behaviour.

An example follows.

A family with an eight-year-old son, who comes to the consult due to speech disfluency, severe inhibition, and a social avoidance tendency. At a certain point of the session the therapist affirms that the child has found a way to keep the family shut away at home and to make them listen to him, because the disfluency meant that he needed time to completely express his thoughts.

The therapist then hypothesises that the being shut away at home is, perhaps, on some level, a need of one of the parents, who does not have the courage to tell the other. The child's mother immediately answers that she does not love going out much, mainly because her husband wants to take the family to his parents' home, where his mother, after the death of his father, now lives alone.

The child then intervenes, saying that he loves his grandmother, but he prefers speaking to her on the phone. The father interrupts to say that the child has his grandfather's name, who died exactly a month after he was born, and that, for his grandmother, to see him and to hear his name is a great comfort. The child's mother, slightly resentfully, explains to the therapist that her mother-in-law had almost come to live with them, and that the joy of the birth of her son had not only coincided with their mourning for his grandfather, but also a conflict between the couple regarding the question of her mother-in-law coming to live in their home, an issue that still comes up between them.

During direct observation, the observer who had the task of noting the child's behaviour, noticed that the child moved his chair nearer to his mother, putting his hand on her bag, immediately after the therapist's redefinition. The other observers noticed that the father, sat up straight and markedly crossed his arms. During indirect observation the group discussed how the mother and son sided with each other on the one side, leaving the father closed off in opposition on the other, forming the "war" set up that the child had grown up with. Furthermore, when the child stated that he loved his grandmother, but preferred to speak to her on the phone, he had had no hesitation and his speech disfluency had not emerged. The group considered that this "mediatory" position between his father and his mother, expressed through this phrase, alleviated the anxiety that accompanied the rest of his life.

Naturally, the implementation of item D, in this case, was considered satisfactory.

Item E

The therapist emphasises the consequent changes in the child's behaviour (if present).

In this case the double observation enables the observers to re-watch the child's behaviour at the beginning and in the central/final sections of the session. This is a very delicate part of the therapy, as, however clear the transformation may be, the parents may have difficulty recognising it.

This is the case with the following example.

The family is made up of two parents and a five-year-old girl. The consult has been requested due to antagonistic and provocative behaviour, which is resistant to scolding or punishment. The session starts with a request by the little girl to sit on the sofa at the back of the room. The parents sit down together and look at each other as if to confirm to each other that the insubordinate attitude of their daughter had immediately emerged. The therapist watches them.

The conversation flows quite easily and when the parents insist on the little girl coming to sit with them, the therapist intervenes saying that there is no need, that it is fine if the child stays where she is. There are another couple of antagonistic episodes, with requests that are unsuitable to the context, particularly at the moment in which the parents define the reasons for the consult.

In light of some elements that emerge, the therapist suggests creating a kind of sculpture. She asks the parents to imitate a kind of swing by embracing their daughter and then delicately letting her swing side to side, while one holds her hands and the other her feet. The family begin to enjoy the game and the little girl even laughs and jokes with them. At the end of the sculpture the parents retake their seats and the little girl goes to sit between them. Further "treasure hunting" continues for a little while, as they identify the similarities that the little girl has to each parent.

The therapist's redefinition was that the child was curious to know who was in charge in her home, and the only way to discover that was by being disobedient. So as not to show a preference for either parent, the child had made sure not to ever pay attention to either of them. In the meantime, the child was asked to get a box of coloured pencils and choose each of her parents' favourite colours. She was then asked to draw whatever she wanted with those colours and to give the pictures to her parents. As she was giving her parents the pictures, the therapist said that deep down she was much more docile than she tried to appear, and that she seemed more like a little fairy than a little witch. As the therapist petted the little girl, the parents' expressions were sceptical, they then added that they already knew what would happen as soon as they were out the door.

The group of observers, in this case, noted more changes in terms of quantity and quality than in the other cases. The fact that the parents did not recognise these changes lead them to hypothesise that the parents were too upset that the therapist had had more influence on the course of the child's behaviour than they had, and therefore, according to the therapist's redefinition, was "in charge". Furthermore, the parents seemed particularly disorientated and perhaps felt guilty for not having recognised their daughter's real potential. The therapist added that their fear of not being able to "control" their daughter could finally be balanced with the hope that it was possible.

Item F

The therapist underlines (verbally or analogically) the relational patterns used by the parents, when confronted with their child's new behaviour in the "here and now" of the session.

This is the conclusive frame and it is the litmus test of the entire session for the group of observers. It enables them to connect the results of all the previous items and verify their coherence.

The following is an example, in which the parents appeared surprised and participative regarding the changes that took place during the session.

A family come to the session with their very shy little girl of about six. The parents are worried because of the child's persistent mutacic behaviour. They had hoped that when their daughter had started primary school, she might have got over it, but after three silent months of school, the teachers had suggested a consult.

For the entire session, the little girl had studiously avoided looking at or speaking directly to the therapist, but she sometimes murmured requests in her mother's ear. At a certain point, the therapist asked the parents to sit more closely together and to hide behind their daughter, and then to talk in turn about things that had to do with her. As the couple also had an older son, the first thing the mother talked about was the way her brother kindly helped her with her homework. The father added to this that when he took his son to the gym to train for competitions, he had tried to involve his daughter, but she had flatly refused. The mother then intervened on her daughter's behalf to say that the sport she liked did not exist in any gym. The therapist provocatively said that their statements seemed to be covering up their doubts regarding their daughter's motives, as she had chosen "something that did not exist" or that was too difficult to find. The father added that she really could have chosen so many sports, but this "blessed skating", which they had been unable to find. The mother explained that it was also a dangerous activity, it was quite easy to fall over in skates, and she was actually glad that it had not been possible. The little girl suddenly broke the silence by saying to her father:

<< You wouldn't have deliberately not found it, would you?>>

<<Let's just say that we didn't try very hard ... >>

The little girl reacted to this: <<You'll go all the way to Bologna for my brother's competitions, but you aren't willing to do anything for my dream ... >>

The therapist had gradually distanced herself in the meantime, so as to exclude herself from the ongoing confrontation. The parents started to move apart so that the little girl could sit between them. The therapist intervened saying that there was no need to argue and that perhaps the little girl did not enjoy speaking because her requests were not met. The father smiled and said that he would like to have a hundred arguments if it meant hearing his daughter express herself in the presence of a stranger and the mother explained that her comments regarding the danger of skating were meant jokingly, but given the results she had used the provocation well, because her daughter had finally stopped behaving like a baby. Meanwhile the child reservedly went back to her original position, holding on to her mother, but by now her "shyness" seemed a bit of an act, and anyway her approach had changed since the beginning of the session. The therapist assured her that she would help her parents find her a skating rink, which made the little girl smile and hug her parents.

In the 40 cases observed the parents modified their approach and all the children began to behave differently in a recurrent circular dynamic.

We should highlight that if the new approach is really the result of the new perspective with which they view their child, it is also true that if the child's "new" behaviour becomes constant, then the "new" perspective will also stabilise, and vice versa. All components should become progressively aware of their methods of communication and the underlying dynamics of their relationships. However, this change was not supposed to be observed by our research group, as their task was to concentrate on the first session.

21.5 The "Operative Protocol"

Here we present one of the cases from the sample to illustrate each item and recount the interactive sequences.

The family is made up of two parents and a 7-year-old boy.

Item A
The child hid behind his mother, then behind a pillar, so as not to be seen by anyone. Even if both his parents call him, he spends some time "appearing and disappearing" from everyone's sight.

This attitude forms part of the "difficulties" that prompted the parents to request this meeting.

Item B
The parents express themselves coherently regarding the reasons for the request: both explain that their son behaves "bizarrely", avoids interlocuters he does not know, "as if he were shy", says the father. The mother adds that her son says often says things that are out of place and that he never lets go of his mask, which he wears in inappropriate situations (at school, for example). The father insists that his son is "unusually reserved", that he avoids eye contact and tends to retreat within himself.

Item C
In the immediate interaction the child's behaviour is coherent with the description given by the parents. Consequently, the therapist notes that:

The boy initially hid behind his mother and then behind a pillar, the precise spot in the room from where he could see everyone without being seen; he nearly always wore the mask and the little he added to his parents' remarks was quite out of place. For example, while his mother was stating that he couldn't let go of his mask, he had added that his mobile phone was ultra-modern. While his father explained that he hid when strangers arrived at the house, he said that his father worked a lot.

Item D
The therapist redefines, explaining that when the child plays "hide and seek", he pushes them to look for him continually, as if he wants to test to what extent his parents notice he is there. The father immediately answers that this is possible, as his son often asks him if he loves him, as if he were afraid of being abandoned. The father then adds that this is part of his son's strange behaviour, because his son has no reason to fear such a thing. When the mother asks how she should go about getting her son to remove the mask, the therapist answers that the parents need to manifest fear, the fright that the *horror* mask intends to provoke. The mother answers that she is not able to play the game, because of how worried she is. The therapist explains that her reaction to her son's playful behaviour is too serious and the father adds that she should do what he does. The mother immediately answers, resentfully, that he is never there… The therapist points out that their son has found the right way to make them consider who, apart from him, is playing hide and seek…

Item E
While the father says that his son fears being abandoned, the child leaves his hiding place and places himself between his two parents, still trying not to be seen by the therapist. While the father continues to talk, the mother gives her son her attention and caresses him, as if to reassure him. The child takes off his mask and tells the therapist that his parents love him and that his sisters are very nice and often play with him. The therapist gathers from the description that the sisters are much older, and the mother adds that her son was born 12 years after her second daughter. The child says to his father that, even if he is the youngest of the family, he is the man of the house. While he says this, he puts his mask back on and returns behind the pillar. The father asks his son to come back and sit with him, and the therapist agrees, but he answers that the therapist can continue to ask his parents questions while he is hiding. The therapist then tells the child, that if he is not present, she will talk to his parents about what the family was like before he was born. The mother puts her hands to her face, as if she were upset and the child goes to her, hugs her, takes off his mask and tells her not to be afraid.

Item F
The therapist asks the father why the child went to his mother when she tried to talk about the family before he was born. The father answers that it had been a difficult time for the family, because just before their son's birth and then a year later, they had suffered two important losses, his father and his uncle, to whom he was very close. The mother adds that, even before her father in law's death, the couple had been going to separate when she became pregnant. Meanwhile, the child returns behind the pillar. The father explains that he had been very shocked by both losses, but, in particular, by the tragic death of his uncle, and, as a consequence, had not participated very much in family life. He felt that he had definitely neglected everyone. The mother plays down the situation and says that he was simply a bit down, and anyway, she had been there to look after the children at the time. The father adds that she is too protective of the child and that, from that time onwards, she had been too attached to the child. The child comes out from hiding place at this point and goes towards the therapist and tells her that his father looks like a monkey. His father laughs and tries to hug him, but the child avoids his embrace and moves to the end of the room. The father asks the therapist why his son does not allow anyone to hug him, his father, in particular. The therapist answers that this is an interesting question that may be connected to the use of a mask, intended to frighten and distance others.

21.6 Conclusions

From the video material collected over 4 years with 40 families during the "operative protocol" it is possible to observe:

Item A

In 25 out of 40 cases the "behavioural reaction" of the child corresponded with the contemporary and/or subsequent descriptions of their parents: in 14 cases the child verbalised, in a more or less efficient manner, the real reason for the consult, 11 expressed a combination of the real reasons and fantasy, possibly imagining the involvement of their school at some level.

In 15 cases the children expressed fear and anxiety, not having understood that the context of the session would be clinical and the therapist's question to them disorientated them a little: in 3 cases the children reacted aggressively towards the parents because they had lied, in 7 cases they asked the parents why, and in 5 cases they simply stated that they were completely in the dark regarding the reasons for the consult, while studiously avoiding looking at their parents.

Item B

Out of 40 cases 27 couples had corresponding definitions of their child's difficulties that were expressed right at the beginning, usually by the parent who had requested the therapy. Of the other 13 cases, 5 couples were in total disagreement (for example, the father found the therapy unnecessary, whereas the mother found the child's behaviour very worrying) and 8 were in partial disagreement (for example, each parent found different aspects of the child's behaviour more significant). Of the 27 cases in which the parents' descriptions corresponded, there were variations in the descriptions regarding the intensity and frequency of the "difficult" behaviour. One parent may have felt that the difficulties were particularly persistent and interfered with the child's life, and the other may have downplayed the consequences on the child's other activities. For 13 couples it became clear that they used the child's difficult behaviour to accuse each other of failing in their educational duties and/or their participation in family life.

Item C

In 11 cases out of 40 the child's immediate way of behaving was quite coherent with the parents' descriptions, in fact, while the parents were defining the "disturbed behaviour", the child behaved exactly as was being described; in 24 cases there was clearly a high/medium amount of unease during the parents' descriptions: The children showed signs of anxiety (for example, suddenly interrupting the conversation, stopping playing, looking through their mothers' bags, scratching their heads, moving physically nearer to one of their parents); in 5 of the cases the children behaved "indifferently" during their parents' descriptions, as if their parents were not talking about them.

Item D

In 34 out of 40 cases the therapist's redefinitions induced a change in the emotional environment of the session, noticeable in both the parents and the child. The redefinitions facilitated access to the play area, in fact, in 12 cases the parents started playing with the child spontaneously, in 6 cases expressions of affection emerged towards the child and in 17 cases positive and praising descriptions of the child followed. In 5 cases the parents continued, in different ways, to feel personal discomfort regarding the difficulties manifested by their child.

Item E
The behaviour of the child changed after the therapist's redefinition of the child's behaviour in all 40 cases. An increase has been observed regarding initiative in interaction, graphical representation and spontaneous narrations concerning the other components of the family, as well as more physical closeness to both parents, a growing command of the therapeutic space and coherence of behaviour.

Item F
The parents demonstrated more emotional closeness with their children in all 40 cases. The emphasis of the therapist enabled the parents' awareness of their own interactive patterns: in 18 cases the parents compared the interaction patterns used previous to and at the time of the change in the child and established some self-criticism. In seven cases one of the parents was evidently emotional (cried or hugged the child tightly) or both parents expressed their own feelings of guilt. In five cases the same parents as in item C continued to express their personal discomfort, but balanced it with the advantage posed by their child's emotional contribution. In 10 cases new relational modalities emerged in the "here and now" of the session, some aimed at encouraging the child in their ways that had become more appropriate during the meeting.

The methodology has made the observations repeatable. We have, in fact, managed to gather precisely the same data for all 40 of the observed sessions. The therapist was also able to repeat, for the most part, the same itinerary for all the families and the observers noted the useful elements at the end.

The possibility of using the procedure for research without significantly impacting on the ordinary clinical intervention safeguards both the research and the therapy: the research has been able to extract data concerning the clinical population and the clinic has been able to offer its contribution in order to observe the changes that take place in therapy.

The operative protocol has also made it possible to highlight the aspects that are lacking in the parent–child relations, while precisely identifying the dysfunctional patterns more systematically than is ordinarily done in the clinic.

In conclusion, the experience has been extremely significant and allows us to imagine the clinic and research operating together at the same time and in the same space.

References

Andolfi, M. (1990). Il bambino-problema come coterapeuta. In C. Loriedo & A. Bianchi di Castelbianco (Eds.), *Il bambino e i suoi sistemi* (pp. 155–166). Roma.

Aurilio, R., & Menafro, M. (2011). Itinerari diversi per una stessa meta: formazione clinica e ricerca. In P. Chianura, L. Chianura, E. Fuxa, & S. Mazzoni (Eds.), *Manuale clinico di terapia familiare* (Vol. III, pp. 59–73). Franco Angeli.

Aurilio, R., Menafro, M., & De Laurentis, M. G. A. (2015). *La terapia sistemico-relazionale tra coerenza e strategia: Apprenderla e praticarla*. Franco Angeli.

Bateson, G. (1972). *Steps to an ecology of mind*. Chandler Publishing Company. (Trad. it. *Verso un'ecologia della mente*. Milano: Adelphi, 1976).
von Bertalanffy, L. (1968). *General system theory: Foundations, development, applications*. Penguin. (Trad. it. *Teoria generale dei sistemi: Fondamenti, sviluppo, applicazioni*. Milano: Mondadori, 2004).
Boszormenyi-Nagy, I., & Spark, G. (1973). *Invisible loyalties*. Harper and Row. (Trad. it. *Lealtà invisibili*. Roma: Astrolabio, 1988).
Bowen, M. (1978). *Family therapy in clinical practice*. Jason Aronson.
Cancrini, L., & La Rosa, C. (1991). *Il vaso di pandora*. La Nuova Italia Scientifica.
Fonagy, P., & Target, M. (2001). *Attaccamento e funzione riflessiva*. Raffaello Cortina.
Haley, J. (1963). *Strategies of psychotherapy*. Grune & Stratton. (Trad. it. *Le strategie della psicoterapia*. Firenze: Sansoni, 1974).
Kerig, P. K., & Lindhal, K. M. (Eds.). (2001). *Family observational coding systems: Resources for systemic research*. Lawrence Erlbaum. (Trad.it Sistemi di codifica per l'osservazione delle relazioni familiari. Milano: Franco Angeli, 2006).
Malagoli Togliatti, M., & Mazzoni, S. (Eds.). (2006). *Osservare, valutare e sostenere la relazione genitori-figli: Il Lausanne trilogue play clinico*. Raffaello Cortina.
Menafro, M. (2006). La psicoterapia infantile sistemica: l'uso relazionale della fiaba inedita. In P. Gritti & E. L. Di Caprio (Eds.), *Le nuove prospettive della psicoterapia sistemico-relazionale*. Armando.
Menafro, M. (2019). Il bambino allo specchio: il Sé riflesso nella relazione di coppia. *Terapia Familiare, 121*, 27–47.
Minuchin, S. (1974). *Families and family therapy*. Harvard University Press. (Trad.it. *Famiglie e terapia della famiglia*. Roma: Astrolabio, 1976).
Whitaker, C. A. (1989). *Midnight musings of a family therapist*. W.W. Norton & company. (Trad. it. *Considerazioni notturne di un terapeuta della famiglia*. Astrolabio, 1990).

Chapter 22
The Treatment of Mutual Demonization in Post-separative Conflict

Renzo Marinello and Davide Sacchelli

22.1 Introduction

The phenomenon of post-separation conflict has grown exponentially, to the point that it has catalysed the attention as a complex new area for exploration. Mental health manuals fail to offer explicit diagnostic reference frameworks for conflictual separations. Diagnosis has usually focused on individuals, hardly ever on relationships. Malfunctions in relationships are generally attributed to a deficit in individual conduct.

And yet as we see it, we are today faced with an out-and-out "disease of relationships", a black hole into which couples may slip, dragging their children along behind them.

When we talk about conflictual divorces, we refer to those situations where a couple with children, after the separation, start a war that can be carried on for many years. The objects of the legal dispute are usually child custody and patrimonial matters. Often these families face very substantial economic difficulties mainly due to the need to bear the costs of war (lawyers, specialists, family mediators, psychotherapists, etc.): very often these families fall into poverty, even starting from comfortable economic initial conditions. On an individual level, people develop symptoms that can range from anxiety disorders (mainly generalized anxiety and obsessive ideation) to psychosis (persecutory and paranoid symptoms), passing through depressive mood disorders. The children, in turn and as objects of the dispute, suffer greatly and can develop various types of symptoms, the best known of which is the complete refusal of one of the two parents.

R. Marinello (✉)
Psychologist, Centro integrato di counseling familiare, SIRTS past president, Milan, Italy
e-mail: renzomarinello17@gmail.com

D. Sacchelli
Psychologist, Centro Milanese di terapia della famiglia, Milan, Italy

In Italy, this type of cases accesses the work of specialists mainly through the social service, involved by the judicial authority that defines the compulsory taking charge of the case with the aim of protecting the rights and health of the children.

In this paper, we shall be focusing on the phenomenon of demonization and its treatment with a manualistic approach. We shall, however, be omitting our observations on children (we merely outline them) and the methods we normally adopt to include them in the treatment.

The word *manual* derives from the Greek word "encheiridion" (Epictetus manual) and indicates an object to keep close at hand, an object that has important contents to keep in mind when dealing with a certain kind of problem. In this paper, we refer to one of our recent publications Marinello and Sacchelli 2018 in which we deal with the issue of post-separative conflicts both by carrying out an analysis of the phenomenon and identifying what we believe to be its main features and by proposing a method of treatment consistent with our premises theoretical. This publication is, in all respects, a manual as *a book that broadly and comprehensively exposes the fundamental information about a certain topic*. It is not, however, a "user manual", or a sequence of indications on how a certain instrument must be used correctly, because we believe that in this matter the effects of each instrument are irreparably linked to four objects: the user, his characteristics, and its therapeutic style; the recipients of the intervention with their character peculiarities, with their ideas and their attitudes; the relationship between the user and the recipients of the intervention, which is unique and unrepeatable each time; and the context within which a certain action can be accomplished. We believe, in this sense, that every intervention carried out on human systems has the characteristic of being largely unpredictable with respect to its consequences.

It seems important to us to add that the model evolved out of an approach based on dialogue and trying out solutions. We have progressively developed this through our daily work with divorced couples caught up in high levels of conflict. Each time we have encountered a problem, we have discussed it and tried to work out what was happening and what we could do to get past that problem. Over the years, we have often had occasion to question what we know or have learned about human systems and relationships between and with the people with whom we work. It is our belief that this approach – one that G. Cecchin, Barbetta, Telfener, 2019 referred to as "irreverence" – has served us well, providing an excellent key for opening the door to different views on common issues and often achieving positive results.

It is consequently our wish to start this paper by inviting the reader to adopt a similarly irreverent approach towards the paper itself: only by doing this it seem to us possible to continue asking questions as we strive to come up with new hypotheses that serve as the foundation for building new, ever-more effective courses of action.

22.2 Differences Between Post-separation Conflicts and Intra-Family or Gender Violence

In many cases, the phenomenon of post-separative conflict is mistaken for infra-family or gender violence. With post-separative conflict, however, physical aggression is sporadic, or belongs to the past, to the phase of coexistence of the couple. We use accordingly the terms "post-separative conflict" to indicate those situations in which the former partners have already physically separated living in different houses. In post-separative conflicts, the violence is perpetrated above all through third parties, such as lawyers, social workers, and psychology professionals, not to mention the children, and exercised through socially approved tools such as criminal and civil legal proceedings. In this paper, therefore, we are talking about the hundreds of cases in which a complaint to judicial authority of violence against children followed a criminal trial, investigations, and, finally, an end to the proceedings due to inconsistency of the facts.

Another distinction must be made to understand the difference between intra-family violence and post-separative conflicts, and it concerns the shape of the phenomenon: when we talk about conflict, as usual, we have to deal with the description of an observer. Here we are talking about the cases of relationship between two persons engaged in a mutually aggressive behaviour and thus conceptualized by an observer. While in post-separative conflicts the dynamic we can observe consists in a continuous exchange of victim and executioner positions, in intrafamilial and gender violence, we see a systematic assumption, over time, of the same victim and executioner positions by the same actors.

In addition to differences in the form of the phenomenon, there are also significant differences in the contents of the narratives typically observed: when we face violence unilaterally exercised by a person on a victim, more often the latter develops narratives based on identification with the aggressor according to Ferenczy's conceptualization. On the other hand, in cases of high post-separative conflicts, each of the contenders perceives himself, and exclusively, as a victim of the other.

Finally, circularity and linearity are two different ways to observe a phenomenon and built explanations; when we use linearity, we observe causal relationships; otherwise, when we use circularity, we observe processes. Our approach with the phenomenon does not want to affirm prevalence of circularity on linearity but propose to look to objects usually thought as causally related as processes. In intra-family and gender-based violence, indeed, it is essential to take a linear observing position that allows to clearly identify the responsibilities of the events, both for the interventions to protect the victim and for the sanctioning measures that must inevitably follow. On the contrary, in cases of high post-separation conflict, we passionately believe that the use of a linear vision of the cause-effect type and the impossibility of observing the phenomenon as a circular process are on the basis of the problem and contribute to maintaining it over time, with consequences disastrous for both the protagonists of the story, the former partners, and for their children.

22.3 Part One: The Phenomenon of Post-separative Conflict

22.3.1 Separation as an Onset of Trauma

Philippe Caillé (2004) defines the "couple's absolute" as a shared representation that partners have of their bond, the central hub around which their sense of belonging is structured. In post-separation conflict, the couple's absolute, which we may simplify by defining as the mutual celebration of the two partners' love, has ceased to exist, and it seems that both members of the couple have drawn a veil over it, "excising" everything that existed prior to the conflict.

When couples talk about the moment of separation, we often observe how, in couples that are going through post-separation conflict, the separation was experienced as traumatic rather than merely painful, whether it be the sudden discovery or revelation of one partner's extramarital affair, one of the two partners suddenly leaving the family home, or sometimes physical (more often psychological) violence.

As is the case with traumas triggered by macroscopic events (for instance, an earthquake), the event often occurs in such a wholly unexpected manner that it creates a caesura in the normal flow of events – a caesura that generates a discontinuity, making it impossible to maintain a chronological connection between "before" and "after". This discontinuity seems to prevent maintaining that "third party", the couple's absolute, which is the basis for mutually recognizing one another, identifying one another, and belonging. The narrative, the shared story is lost. This appears to create a sense of meaninglessness that leaves space for a new "third party".

It is this that we call "mutual demonization".

22.3.2 The Schismogenetic Transacting Couple: Mutual Demonization

Applying a concept put forward by G. Bateson (1972), we may say that the conflicting partners' relational structure is configured as schismogenetic if it is characterized by sequences of cumulative interactions that generate a progressive differentiation between the parties involved, up to the point where, in certain cases, the whole system collapses.

The fulcrum of this structure is constituted by what we have defined as "mutual demonization", a circular and recursive process that accompanies the partners in building a specular narrative in which the Other is hated more and more because they are feared more and more. In this process, the Other ceases to have human characteristics: they become a "demon". The Other's attacks and harassments are perceived as actions designed to destroy them. This leads to a situation in which both parties consider themselves to be the "victim" of a powerful and mythicized tormentor; they feel they have the right to defend themselves by launching their own attacks and aggressions that, first and foremost, are oriented towards ensuring their own survival. In such circumstances, even though very few people are prepared to admit it, the prevailing feeling is that of fear. People who experience this condition feel as if they are being hunted down; they live in a condition of constant danger that is confirmed by the other person's acts of aggression (which, in actual fact, are also deployed as acts of self-defence). It may be ventured that the schismogenetic process removes any chance of mentalization[1] of the partner, catapulting each member of the schismogenetic couple into egocentric, survival-oriented behaviour.

If, as we have indicated, separation entails the death of the couple's absolute, the narrative within which each of the two recognized themselves and found an identity and meaning for their own existence, demonization acts as a replacement absolute, perpetuating the system through time. We have no doubt that each of the two ex-partners would wish to see the other defeated and destroyed or that each of them wishes to separate from the other. These desires and feelings, nevertheless, seem to us to act as incredibly powerful "bonds"; indeed, over the years, we have found that what binds people together is not so much love but feelings, including feelings of fear and hatred. We consequently consider a couple in conflict as a couple that has not yet given up on their bond; rather, they have transformed it. To borrow Paul Bohannan's words, these couples have failed to achieve the "psychic divorce" necessary to enter into a real dissolution of the system.

Whereas on one hand demonization keeps the system alive, on the other it entails a whole series of systemic impoverishments, first and foremost by blocking generativity. By generativity (Marinello and Sacchelli 2018), we mean the ability to build new narratives that make it possible to give reality meaning. Embroiled in the morass of their relationship, the parties lose their own freedom, becoming unable to construct alternative descriptions of what is happening. The couple system ends up forfeiting the ability to reinvent itself, remaining in the inferno of everything staying the same, as well as the chance to apprehend the new, which can no longer even be glimpsed.

A second impoverishment in the demonization phenomenon is development of a progressive process of distancing the self from responsibility. Having delegated to the other responsibility for initiating and perpetuating the conflictual dynamic, both partners believe they have no chance of intervening to attenuate the conflict. After all, each partner's attention is wholly focused on what the other is doing, on one arc of the relational circuit rather than on the process as a whole. When all is said and done, in a relationship with another person, we are almost never aware of our own behaviour, especially when that behaviour is conditioned by aggression or violence. It follows that we are often unable to perceive the behaviour of the other person as a reaction to our own behaviour; we prefer to decode their behaviour through the representations, ideas, and preconceptions we have of the other – representations that almost never have anything to do with the actual reality of the person opposite

---

[1] By mentalization, we mean the ability to "represent one's own and other's minds," in other words, "internally representing mental states" regarding oneself and others. The ability to mentalize therefore implies the possibility of understanding others' behavior as the outcome of their mental or emotional content. The concept was introduced by Peter Fonagy.

us. Thus, conflict is not perceived as the result of a circular and relational process but rather as the outcome of the monstrous characteristics we have attributed to the other person.

A third systemic impoverishment, as we briefly mentioned on the topic of trauma at the beginning of this paper, is a suspension of time. This impoverishment entails abolishing the past and the love story the partners experienced. No element from this story survives; on the contrary, it appears to be replaced by a hollowed-out sense of the future, one that is relegated to an ever-more-constricting horizon of legal and administrative proceedings.

Of course, the children are also affected by this demonization process. Children can potentially adapt in many different ways to conflict, albeit often through the development of symptoms. One of the best-known adaptations and, from our point of view the most stable, is the child's refusal to meet with the parent who has left the family home. In a systemic review of the concept of parental alienation, we refer to this as a Systemic Condition of Family Alienation (SCFA) (Camerini et al. 2016).

22.3.3 The Macrosystemic Effect of Amplifying Schismogenesis

Although mutual demonization may be conceived as a process that takes over the couple system, a schismogenetic structure is maintained through crossovers between the couple system and the other systems that are drawn in by the conflict. Families of origin, lawyers, official or external consultants, judges, social workers, and psychologists are all elements that, in interaction with the couple system, can maintain and amplify schismogenesis. The more the relational dynamic is intensified by amplification circuits, the more schismogenesis takes on a multiplier function, in a chain reaction weakening the opportunity to break this process or change direction. For amplification to occur, the interaction of at least two structurally coupled circuits is required. Expanding on the idea of structural coupling developed by H. Maturana and F. Varela (1984) we suggest conceiving the couple and the systems implied in the conflict (the legal system, clinical system, families of origin, etc.) as autopoietic units whose internal organization produces and reproduces the system itself. As in the case of living systems, in which the structural coupling of the organism and its environment keeps it alive, in a couple undergoing post-separation conflict, the schismogenetic process may be kept alive only through interaction with the context in which it exists – a context that we define as its "macrosystem".

An additional element of amplification within the nuclear family consists of adaptations children adopt to survive the conflict – adaptations that are necessary to overcome the conflict of loyalty to which they have been exposed.

22.3.4 The Semantic and Structural Homology Between the Couple System and the Legal System

For amplification to occur, the two systems (the couple and the macrosystem) must share a structural homology, that is to say they must be made up of the same material, of homologous structures. It is our belief that a structural homology may be found in similitudes within the narrative constructs that exist in the various systems. For instance, the way that the legal system is organized appears to be based on a dualistic approach of right/wrong, legal/illegal, and, above all, victim/perpetrator, an approach that perfectly fits with the conflictual couple's way of thinking. In the approach to litigation, each member of the couple is identified as a "party", and each of the parties fights to prevail over the other, in a competitive approach oriented towards winning the lawsuit, acknowledgement of blame, and the doling out of penalties to the adversary. The judge is the referee of this competition, delegated the functions of assessing each party's claims and deciding who should prevail over whom, ultimately acknowledging who may lay claim to victimhood status.

Similar expectations apply to the clinical system. Here, the expectation is often that the other party obtains a "correct" diagnosis from a clinician, an expert opinion that categorizes and acknowledges the other in their natural position as an abject individual, a mentally ill person, a dangerous individual...in a word, a "demon". Such expectations run even higher when parents and their child/children are on a pathway to assess the general situation and/or recommendations as to which parent is best suited to take custody and predominantly look after the child.[2]

If, on one hand, to a former partner's mind, a clinician – particularly a clinician assigned through a public service – does not seem to be a healthcare professional but rather a direct emanation of the legal authorities, on the other the rulings of these authorities that provide the framework for the clinical system are expressed through the same dualistic logic that pits right against wrong, guilt against innocence, and victim against perpetrator. As P. Barbetta notes, a Judge's provisions that bind the clinical system take the form of "'compulsory therapy' both for the persons indicated by the Court, and for the therapists brought in to do the job..." The clinical system therefore runs the risk of being invaded by homogeneous and dualistic approaches, not only by each party from the couple in conflict but by the legal system too, in as much as the judge's request, which often concerns choosing which parent is the most suitable, is merely a reflection of the demand the couple has obsessively been asking. Within this perspective, handing off assessment and identification of the most suitable parent to the social services means embedding this dualistic approach into the clinical system, which is akin to converting it into an additional amplifier of the conflict.

---

[2] Recently, some court appointed experts (CAEs) have sought to structure their work through treatment rather than assessment, fully aware of the risks involved in the latter approach. Lia Mastropaolo defines CAEs' working methodology as "seeking interventions for change."

Clinicians' operating practices often include a series of redundancies that are, we might say, typical and that inevitably bring the clinical world close to the legal world, to the point that it risks being construed as similar. This means that no type of work oriented towards introducing new meanings is any longer possible.

The main redundancies we have observed over the years are:

- The paradox that clinical work consists of giving an unwell person the chance to show that they are healthy. This means that the only people who can be treated are those who show that they are capable of adapting to the norms and rules of the institution that provided access to the treatment.
- The more professionals perceive the strength and destructive nature of the conflict, the more they may strive to avoid any possible meetings between the partners.
- The decision to consider the portrayal offered by one of the two parties as a representation of reality, thereby forfeiting their neutrality.
- A distancing from the problem because of the clinician's sense of failure resulting in "phantom treatment".

22.3.5 The Difficulties for the Parents

A separation implies the existence of a significant series of stressful elements associated with everyone's change in status and becoming part of a conflictual dynamic. Almost always, this equates to economic impoverishment (two homes rather than one), not to mention paying legal fees and spending on "technicians" (psychologists and psychotherapists), working hours-related difficulties if the separation affects a single-income family, and, often, the non-payment of alimony. Where children come into the equation, in many cases each parent must come to terms with rebuilding an individual relationship with the kids – a relationship no longer mediated by the other parent's presence. Lastly, in many cases the separation of the two partners implies that at least one of them is forced to return to their family of origin, which may trigger or rekindle intergenerational conflict or dynamics associated with periods preceding their emancipation as adults.

This highly stressful situation is exacerbated by the psychic content associated with the existence of the conflictual dynamic: as briefly noted earlier, for each of the two individuals involved, the demonizing narrative generates a permanent and constant state of fear caused by the existence of a persecutor with almost supernatural powers. As well as this being a way of attributing meaning to events, because the persecutor is mythicized, their dangerousness and power is magnified further still. Some of the most widespread fears in such circumstances are a fear of being unfairly convicted in the proceedings underway; a fear or losing or having the children taken away; a fear of being plunged into economic hardship; and, in the most serious cases, a fear of being killed or that the partner may kill or destroy the child.

In such cases, we have observed the development of many different symptomatologic expressions which we believe to be directly associated with a separation-related event and the emergence of a state of conflict, from anxiety-related disorders in their various guises to mood disorders of a depressive nature. What, however, seems to occur most frequently within post-separation conflict is the presence of obsessive ideation associated with the implicit threat of potential acts by the demonized persecutor. Over time, such ideation seems to resolve into persecutory experiences that, in turn, take on an increasingly significant and bizarre dimension, up to and including veritable paranoiac symptoms and delirium.

We know that the continuation and perpetuation of vexatious environmental conditions that on their own an individual is unable to modify may generate significant changes in feelings of self-efficacy that can lead to learned helplessness and depression. In such cases, we encounter another critical issue: the dynamic is based on a schismogenetic context that the person is unable to end, as a result of which they are constantly prompted to mount a personal defence. We have excellent reason to believe that such situations may, in many cases, also be considered a key element in the etiopathogenesis of a psychotic disorder.

22.4 Part Two: The Triggering Generativity Intervention

The purpose of our intervention is to trigger a recovery of generative capacity, an ability overshadowed by the demonizing narrative. The desire is to recover generativity to give the people involved in what is happening the opportunity to apportion new meaning to events, to their own actions, and to the behaviour of their ex-partner and their children, in line with what Heinz von Foerster (1987) refers to as "acting to increase the options for choice".

Because it works on the system rather than on the couple alone, this is a complex intervention. Although it is true that within a family the mere presence of a therapist can sometimes be a disturbing element for the system sufficient to generate change, in the case of conflictual separations, we must deal with "assimilative systems" endowed with enormous homeostatic abilities. Within such systems, individual elements are often redundant; in other words, a function may be carried out by several elements, none of which on its own is indispensable – the lawyers and psychotherapists could be changed, sometimes even the judges and competent courts. For this reason, a psychotherapist or social worker can easily be assimilated into the system, resulting in their presence generating absolutely no change at all.

A methodological approach characterized by sufficient elasticity is required to be able to adapt the intervention to the specific situation of the family with which we are working. It is especially necessary to entertain the idea of a varied setting, depending on needs open to the option of conducting individual, couple, and whole-family sessions. It is, it seems, almost always necessary to involve the families of origin, defence lawyers, and any new partners of the separated ex-spouses during the treatment phase.

22.4.1 The Intervention Context: Safeguarding the Clinical Space

In a legally framed competitive, litigation-based approach, the legal system engages a new system that makes it possible to convert the polarities of true/false and right/wrong into sound/unsound of mind, that is to say the sphere of the clinical system. Given that within the legal framework it is impossible to establish which of the two partner's narratives most closely corresponds to the criterion of true or false, an additional judgement is sought based on the criteria of health and sickness.

In such circumstances, the clinical system is faced with the issue of how to proceed without renouncing its treatment-oriented vocation, in a compulsory intervention not requested by the people involved because of an external judicial authority's provisions.

As far as we are concerned, safeguarding the clinical system as a treatment-based place does not mean rejecting compulsory work, it means doing what it takes to avoid the same dualistic and linear approach that characterizes the couple and the juridical system. We consequently believe that for the clinical system, the key priority throughout treatment must be to avoid presenting itself as an element that amplifies the schismogenetic structure characteristic of the couple's relationship. The model we are proposing hence focuses closely on a few principles, for example, not apportioning blame to the individuals involved, transparency during the various stages of the process, and combatting a fragmentation of interventions that, very often, can result in more psychologists than family members at the table.

22.4.2 Implementation of Collaborative Practices and Setting Up a Working Party

The transition from defensive and competitive practices to collaborative practices, entailing a frustration of the former partners' demands for justice, requires putting together a cohesive working party out of the elements that constitute the macrosystem. Each element must be committed to achieving the goal of attenuating the schismogenetic drift. This is therefore a quite different kind of intervention from classic family therapy: it acts not just on the parental couple but directly on the systems with which they interact – systems that, as we have seen, tend to have a multiplier function on the conflict.

The working party consists of the parents, their children, defence lawyers, any new partner, the family of origin, and even friends willing to take on a communications advisor role. When assembling this working party, it seems to us preferable that during the meeting with the parents and at meetings in which members of the macrosystem are present, the professionals declare their intentions in a comprehensible manner, laying out their "worldview "on the conflictual phenomenon.

22.4.3 Methodology

The triggering intervention for generativity relies on a different intervention format that, in certain phases, is pushed forward on parallel fronts. The formats used are work with the macrosystem; work with the couple; work with the children; and work with the parents and children together. Within these various formats, a variety of different actions are undertaken at different times.

During the introductory phase of macrosystem work, we first meet with the couple and their children and then with the defence lawyers. It must be said that in a few cases, this sequence is inverted if one or both of the former partners request that the defence lawyer interact with the clinical system. After this initial stage, work continues by meeting the families of origin and, if there are any, current partners of the former couple, and their friends.

Having set terms for the work we are about to embark upon and a limit to the number of meetings, we move on to the meetings with the family. In the initial phase of this work, the parental couple and children are seen separately but in parallel. One of the first goals when initiating the treatment is the option of meeting the separated couple, as a part of the macrosystem, together. Although it is often difficult to achieve this, a dual presence must therefore be a part of the working arrangements, as agreed by the former partners and their lawyers.

Particularly in cases of parental alienation, children attending meetings with the couple can potentially make it very tough to move through the various stages that, we believe, are necessary for both parents to go through, in as much as such sessions tend to catalyse all of the attention onto the child's often dramatized rejection of one of the two parents. The parallel parental and children's work pathways converge towards a continuation of the work in joint parent/children meetings.

Where possible, we have observed that it is useful to involve the children in homogenous groups that give them a chance to understand their experience is not unique but, on the contrary, shared by contemporaries who are going through wholly analogous experiences.

All these different treatment formats naturally imply a significant amount of work. Ideally, the meetings in their various forms should be led by the same professionals. It seems to us that at least a "therapeutic couple" co-present at the various meetings is a good way of coping with a workload that may involve remarkably high levels of emotional intensity.

22.5 Work with the Macrosystem

22.5.1 Meeting the Defence Lawyers

When the parties ask for their respective lawyers to intercede, it is often the lawyer who contacts the healthcare professional or shows up at the first meeting. Often, healthcare professionals experience this as an unwelcome annoyance; in fact, it is a huge opportunity. The meeting with the parties' lawyers is invaluable because, frequently, defence lawyers have become confidantes of the former partners, and as such they have their clients' ear. During such meetings, it can be possible to agree the terms of a legal truce.

By "legal truce", we mean a jointly agreed period of time during which a commitment is made not to pursue further legal action and, if admissible under the legal system, to withdraw previously lodged accusations if they prove to be groundless.

Where possible, withdrawing accusations is a vitally important initial and tangible step in weakening the schismogenetic dynamic.

From our experience, we have learned that it is not possible to play "the same game on different tables": what may seem to be a positive intervention in the clinical sphere, leading to an attenuation of conflict and a recovery of trust between the former partners, can reveal itself to be fragile when one of the partners, unbeknownst to the other and even to the clinicians, has submitted an appeal or initiated new legal proceedings.

If both partners are called upon to comply with the agreement that has been reached, their lawyers are tasked with helping their clients delay lodging any further lawsuits.

22.5.2 The Initial Meeting with the Family

Once the option of combined action has been established after meeting with the parties' defence lawyers, it is possible to move on to the first meeting with the separated couple. In such circumstances, it is good practice to carefully assess the option of setting up an initial meeting with the children present, in other words a first meeting attended by the whole nuclear family. This approach is motivated by a number of good reasons:

- It enables direct observation of relational dynamics between parents and children.
- It tangibly presents a system (the united family) that existed in a prior phase, during which the couple's absolute strove to maintain their bonds. Bringing the family back together offers elements of continuity for their shared story.
- Including the children constitutes an action that combats the phenomenon of their marginalization (children are rendered unseen because the conflict has taken priority).

- Presence of the children enables each parent to "see" the child in interaction with the other parent, presenting this relationship between these two to the third party in attendance.
- It means that each parent benefits from an important spectator of the conflict, namely, the child. This situation often leads to the parent limiting their conflictual conduct and exploring the possibility of more restrained interaction with their former partner.
- Should conflict erupt within the family session, each of the two parents may be prompted to observe their child's reaction to the row as it happens.
- Through direct therapist interaction with the child, it is possible to bring out content about their experience that, as a third party and, provided parental alienation has not occurred, may significantly contribute to presenting the conflict to parents who have been incapable of seeing it.

Should it not be possible to conduct a meeting with the whole nuclear family in attendance – for example, if, in the case of parental alienation, the child refuses – then we move on to meeting the couple. During this first meeting, it is particularly important for the terms of engagement to be laid down: a detailed explanation is given of the work we are about to undertake, the attendees are made aware of what might happen, and they are asked to be prepared to put up with their ex-partner expressing direct conflict.

The issue of neutrality is a topic that can be particularly tricky for the therapist. When conflict is in evidence, to the participants' eyes, the third person cannot remain neutral: as far as they're concerned, it is almost always a case of "either you're with me or you're against me". For the therapist, losing that neutrality, however, means being assimilated into the schismogenetic dynamic and unexpectedly becoming a participant in conflict implementation. It is therefore necessary to act in such a manner as not to bolster the interlocutors' perception that we are taking the other party's side. We believe that in situations of conflictual separation, there are two types of antidote to a loss of neutrality:

- To give preference to meeting the couple or the family rather than taking individual meetings, to ensure that everything is said in the presence of the other interlocutor. This is something that can help maintain sufficient transparency.
- The therapist maintains a strong focus on the job in hand. The therapist must actively work to obtain an alliance with all members of the separated family as members of the same working party, to strive to resolve a common problem. The therapist takes on the role of coach, a manager of a team that requires motivation as it learns to work together to separate – something that can only be achieved if there are two teams that are capable of cooperation.

22.5.3 Co-constructing the Rules of the Game: The Rules of Communication

A whole series of practices is defined when structuring post-separation conflict between former partners to ensure that the two parties keep their channels of communication open. These practices are not only functional to maintaining a form of indirect communication that seemingly restricts the possibility of entering into conflict, but they also serve to maintain a record of what is actually communicated. Such practices are often encouraged by each party's lawyers, as they can potentially serve to collect evidence of the other party's unsuitability and subsequently used in court: communications via standard or certified e-mail, via multimedia written message, and recordings of phone calls or parent/child interactions.

Unlike direct communication, all these forms of communication share one characteristic: they sunder the signified from the signifier. In other words, these communications lack the context indispensable for defining and making it possible to share the signified. Such messages may therefore possess the characteristics of ambiguity, lending themselves very well to being misconstrued. In the presence of demonizing content (the context), the recipient's reading and comprehension of the message immediately deviates towards a perception of threatening or destructive content on the sender's part. For example, a simple request to change the time of an arrangement to see the child, perhaps as a result of a work commitment, may in the best of cases be construed as an intentional attempt to create difficulties for the recipient, as a manifestation of a lack of interest in the child, or as a desire to row back on a previously made arrangement. These forms of communication function in subtle but effective ways to keep the conflict going, continuously nourishing the idea of the other as a persecutor, against whom the only defence is attack.

It is vitally important to ensure that communications between the two former partners take place directly or, at the very least, via normal phone conversations. The two parties should be given responsibility for engaging in direct conflict during these communications, making it explicit that clashes will take place and that, despite this, they should not be particularly concerned because such things are a standard part of the process. We strongly believe that distance (an anti-generative event) can keep conflict going for a much longer time than proximity, in as much as it maintains a sense of potential menace without leading to a "collision" (a generative event) between the individuals, which brings with it the consequent potential for subsequent resolution.

22.5.4 Meeting the Families of Origin, New Partners, and a Significant Friend

A meeting between each partner and their family of origin offers a chance to see the family dynamic in action and helps us to reconstruct the family's viewpoint about the separation event now in their lives.

In the majority of cases, we observe the family of origin taking their own child's side. Sometimes, parents blame their own child for the separation and expect that once they are single again, they will dedicate themselves exclusively to looking after their offspring. In such cases, the person going through the separation experiences great isolation and feelings of guilt.

The session with the family of origin is useful for two additional reasons: it serves to obtain the wider family members' approval of the intervention, meaning that they may subsequently be of help; and it makes it possible to find out which members of the nuclear family of origin may be given the vital function of consultant to the family member caught up in the schismogenetic spiral.

Should it be preferable not to undertake a dedicated meeting, new partners may also be invited to the session with the family of origin, to verify whether they may become involved in a help and support function. Often, the bond of trust that develops within the new couple relationship leads to an acritical sharing of the demonizing narrative; equally often, the new partner manages to maintain a position that is sufficiently external to retain a rather objective view of the conflict.

We have also observed the importance of involving a particularly significant friend for each partner in the working party in an advocacy role.

22.6 Working with the Family

As noted earlier, after an initial presentation at which we ask that the children attend, working with the family proceeds through parallel but separate meetings with the parental couple and children. In this paper, we shall be focusing on the work that concerns the parental couple (Table 22.1).

22.6.1 Step 1: Presentification of the Conflict

As we can see on Table 22.2, the first step at the meetings with the parental couple is the act of presentifying the conflict. Usually, neither of the two is willing to admit that a conflict exists. What is required is a step change, an epistemological shift. Neither of them feels responsible for what is happening. Rather, and this is important to remember, they simply feel that they are a victim of the other's harassment.

Table 22.1 Caption

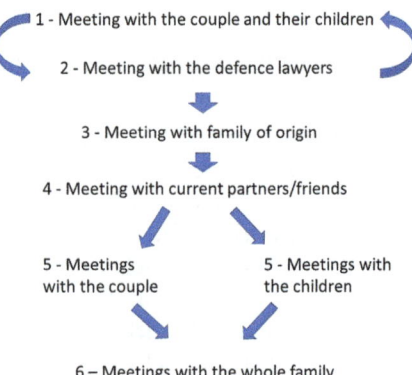

Table 22.2 Caption

Steps in working with the family
1 - Presentification of the Conflict
Introducing the idea of "conflict";
2 - Externalization of the Conflict
Conflict is therefore put forward as a "third party" toward which it is necessary build together new coping strategies;
3 - From Alienated Responsibility to Responsibility for the Conflict
Bereavement process for the loss of one's innocence and reaching a meta-position;
4 - Intervention to Break the Bond: Recovering the Past
Recovery continuity between before and after;

Therefore, when the word "conflict" is used, we hear our interlocutor say, "What conflict?". To admit that there is a conflict implies responsibility for being a part of and nourishing that conflict. Each of the two parties believes that the actions that keep the conflict going are legitimate acts of self-defence to ensure their own and their children's survival. At this stage, the therapist's task is to help each of the two people to see and accept the fact that their own behaviour has consequences on the other people involved, including the children. It goes without saying that this is extremely tough, given that to a greater or lesser extent each of the two interlocutors is living within what we may define as a narcissistic bubble, fed continuously by the need to face up to mortal dangers: just like pain, fear pushes an individual into an egocentric position in which neither empathy nor, less still, mentalization is possible. Imbuing what they are experiencing with meaning by introducing the idea of conflict, on the contrary, makes it possible to construct a meaning framework for potentially understanding the other's behaviour and actions and, albeit with greater difficulty, one's own emotional reactions and actions.

22.6.2 Step 2: Externalization[3] of the Conflict

Given that what comes before reification is an undue transformation of the label into a causal element ("I'm sad because I have depression"), the establishment of a taxonomic or diagnostic category pursues an end purpose of classification; in other words, it serves to give an over-arching name to an ensemble of events. However, in addition to the causal inversion, the process of reification transforms the meaning of the intention of the person who creates the taxonomic or diagnostic category by generating another major semantic event: externalization (it is depression that is making me sad). Identifying the element of discomfort as a factor external to the individual is a renouncement of responsibility. In a conflictual separation, this may be a necessary step to enable the people involved to begin acknowledging that conflict exists: "it is conflictual separation that is making me suffer". Here, the therapist has the option of conveying the concept that the couple and its constituent individuals are "victims" of a destructive relational dynamic, rather than of the other person. The presentified conflict is therefore put forward as a "third party", as a process co-created through interaction of the partners that has taken on a life of its own and is trapping them. It is pointed out that all members of the family have become victims of this mechanism which, by self-replicating, continues to wield its strength and generate anger, fear, and suffering.

What is necessary is therefore a three-way alliance that may be extended to all of the other actors involved (families of origin, lawyers, and other professionals) in a bid to find effective strategies for tackling this "new" demon.

22.6.3 Step 3: From Alienated Responsibility to Responsibility for the Conflict

Acknowledging responsibility for the conflict is the step that comes after externalization. This step cannot be taken immediately, because it requires both main parties involved to have developed sufficient faith in the therapist: what in common parlance is known as the "therapeutic alliance".

Identifying the conflict as the demon responsible for the long-term misfortunes that have befallen the family and its individual members may appear to be dangerous because it maintains and confirms the process of reification. Yet, it is necessary for the people involved to take back responsibility, to win back a sense of self-efficacy regarding their own actions. To make the transition from alienated responsibility to responsibility for the conflict requires going through a process of bereavement: after their innocence has died, the moment arrives to develop an ability to live with their own guilt. To use a metaphor, this step may be depicted as

---

[3]The concept of externalization was developed by Michael White, a family psychotherapist of Australian origin and a leading figure in the narrative-based clinical approach.

being ejected from paradise on earth. Afterwards, the time of innocence gives way to taking on the original sin that characterizes the human condition.

Taking responsibility for the conflict is achieved by gaining an awareness about the content of one's own demonizing narratives. Each of the two participants should be helped to reach a "meta" position with respect to the conflictual dynamic within which they have been acting, allowing them to become capable of observing it from the outside in order to gain an overview that we may term "systemic", as opposed to their customary way of seeing things. Active self-observation of this kind makes it possible to bring the mechanisms that generate the conflictual behaviour out into the open. In other words, it makes it possible to accept the link that exists between former partners' fear, aggressive behaviour, and retaliation that confirms their role as demonized objects. Although by no means the only option, one useful tool for fostering self-observation from the outside is video feedback, applying this technique to couples' sessions and then using it later for individual work.

22.6.4 Step 4: Intervention to Break the Bond: Recovering the Past

As we have seen, the couples we work with have transformed a bond of love into a bond of antagonism.

In a significant number of cases (but by no means all), the existence of such a bond may lead the couple to swing between periods of varying length characterized by separation and bellicose actions, and periods of varying length characterized on the contrary by rapprochement, sometimes including a sexual level.

It is always exceedingly difficult when we start working with a couple in a state of post-separation conflict to gain access to their past history. The two former partners appear totally focused on the present, or else on the past immediately after separation – a recent past consisting of clashes, reciprocal accusations, vilification, attack, and defence.

At this stage, a necessary part of the work is to try and patch up the tear in the story to enable a recovery of a degree of continuity between the before and after. To achieve this, depending on the situation, the therapist must first choose the most appropriate format for the story, for reconstructing what it was before, including the moment and motives for the decision to separate – a decision that in many cases has never properly been understood either by the person who took that decision or the person to whom it was presented as a fait accompli. Individual or couple sessions are the potential options available for tackling this transitional process. The therapist should be guided in their choice by their assessment of how useful it would be to ally themselves with the decision to separate or with the sphere of the couple. Working with the couple's love story is another way to potentially bring about a rapprochement. This does not per se suffer from any particular negative side effects, apart from the partners taking rash, not sufficiently well-thought-out choices that might have truly perilous effects on the children should the chance of an imminent relapse into conflict exist.

22.7 Conclusions

We wanted to present the reader with a model of intervention on a theme, that of conflictual separations, still little discussed in the environments of psychology and psychotherapy, with the aim of sharing the knowledge acquired so far and the experience of the work done. We believe that being able to create points of reference through the manualization of knowledge represents an opportunity because each point of reference gives the traveller the opportunity not to get lost but also the opportunity to choose a starting point to embark on a new journey of exploration.We firmly believe that there is no freedom without the possibility of considering constraints and that this concept can also be applied to our profession: if it is true, as G. Bateson said when quoting Korzybski, that "the map is not the territory", it is also true that a representation of the territory is really the only tool we have that allows us to prepare for exploration, guaranteeing us the great opportunity to continue moving, and learning.

Good job!

References

Allen, J. G., Fonagy, P., & Bateman, A. W. (2008). *Mentalizing in clinical practice*. American Psychiatric Publishing.

Andolfi M., & Russel H. a cura di (1994), *Please help me with this family*. New York: Brunner/Mazel. (*La consultazione in terapia familiare. Una prospettiva sistemica*. Milano: Raffaello Cortina Editore, 1995).

Barbetta, P., Telfener, U., & A cura di. (2019). *Complessità e psicoterapia. L'eredità di Boscolo e Cecchin*. Raffaello Cortina Editore.

Bateson G. (1972). *Steps to an Ecology of Mind*. San Francisco: Chandler Publishing Company. (trad. it. *Verso un'ecologia della mente*. Milano: Adelphi, 1978).

Bateson G. (1979). *Mind and nature. A necessary Unity*. New York: Hampton Press. (trad. it. *Mente e Natura*. Milano: Adelphi, 1984).

Benasayag M., & Del Rey A. (2007). Éloge *du conflit*. Paris: La Découverte. (trad. it. *Elogio del conflitto*. Milano: Feltrinelli, 2008).

Berger, B., & Berger, P. L. (1983). *The war over the family – Capturing the middle ground*. Anchor Press/Duobleday. (trad. it. *In difesa della famiglia borghese*. Bologna: Il Mulino, 1984).

Bohannan, P. (1973). *The six stations of divorce in love marriage and family: A developmental approach*. Scott e C.

Caillé, P. (2004). *Un et un font trois! Le couple d'aujourd'hui et sa thérapie*. ESF. (trad. it. *Uno e uno fanno tre. Quale psicoterapia per la coppia di oggi*. Roma: Armando Editore, 2007).

Camerini, G. B., Pingitore, M., & Lopez, G. (2016). *Alienazione parentale. Innovazioni cliniche e giuridiche*. Franco Angeli.

Castelbarco A., Comelli I., Marinello R. (2012), Il bambino ostaggio del conflitto, una forma di maltrattamento relazionale e i dispositivi di intervento. *Minori e Giustizia*, 1, 154–159. : Franco Angeli.

Cigoli, V. (1998). *Psicologia della separazione e del divorzio*. Il Mulino.

Cigoli, V., Galimberti, C., & Mombelli, M. (1988). *Il legame disperante*. Raffaello Cortina Editore.

Dell'Antonio, A. (1993). *Il bambino conteso. Il disagio infantile nella conflittualità dei genitori separati*. Giuffrè.

Giddens, A. (1992). The Trasformation of intimacy. In *Sexsuality, love end eroticism in modern societies*. Polity Press.

Marinello, R. (2017). *Un modello di intervento nelle separazioni conflittuali. L'esperienza di un centro pubblico di terapia familiare* (*Connessioni*, 36). Centro Milanese di Terapia della Famiglia.

Marinello, R., & Sacchelli, D. (2018). *Separazioni conflittuali. Conflitto, demonizzazione e paradossi nelle coppie in fase di separazione*. Edra.

Mastropaolo, L. (2019). Dentro la perizia: l'"Intervento per il Cambiamento" nelle Consulenze Tecniche di Ufficio, in Barbetta P. e Telfener U. a cura di *Complessità e psicoterapia. L'eredità di Boscolo e Cecchin*. Milano: Raffaello Cortina Editore.

Maturana H. *The biological foundations of self consciousness and the physical domain of existence*. Manoscritto inedito, Santiago Universidad de Chile. [trad. it. *Autocoscienza e realtà*. Milano: Raffaello Cortina Editore, 1993].

Maturana, H., & Varela, F. J. (1980). *Autopoiesis and cognition. The realization of the living*. Reidel Publishing Company. (trad. it. *Autopoiesi e Cognizione – La realizzazione del vivente*. Padova: Marsilio, 1985).

Maturana, H., & Varela, F. J. (1984). *El árbol del conocimiento: las bases biológicas del entendimiento humano*. Editorial Universitaria. (trad. it. *L'albero della conoscenza – Un nuovo meccanismo per spiegare le radici biologiche della conoscenza umana*. Milano: Garzanti, 1992).

McHale, J. P. (2010). *La sfida della cogenitorialità*. Raffaello Cortina Editore.

Saraceno C., Pradi M., a cura di (1991), I figli contesi – L'affidamento dei minori nella procedura di separazione. : Unicopli.

Von Foerster, H. (1987). *Sistemi che osservano*. Astrolabio.

Von Foerster, H., & Pörksen, B. (1997). *Wahrheit ist die Erfindung eines Lügners: Gespräche für Skeptiker*. Bild-Kunst. (*La verità è l'invenzione di un bugiardo. Colloqui per scettici*. Roma: Meltemi, 2001).

White, M., & Epston, D. (1990). *Narrative means to therapeutic ends*. WW Norton & Company.

Chapter 23
Basic Model of a Couple's Crisis: A Manual for Couples' Therapy

Virginia Ioannidou and Christina Lagogianni

23.1 Working with Couples

Couples usually seek therapy when they face a crisis, during a transitional period, when the old state no longer exists, and a new state is not yet formed. The past state of stability is no longer satisfactory, and growth through which a new state might arise is still not achieved. A possibly successful therapeutic process combines those two notions: stability and growth. The therapist helps to cultivate in the therapeutic system a feeling of emotional safety in the here and now, a meta-stability, promoting opportunities for progress and growth (Welter-Enderlin, 1998). The eagerness to learn and proceed with personal change, requires for the individual to feel safe and become curious and interested.

When therapists show stability, openness and creativity, they offer this meta-stability to both partners and promote their interest for development. To respond to such challenge, therapists need to feel confident in their role. This is not easy, because couples usually bring a lot of information and intense feelings. It is common that each partner tries to convince the therapist of his or her side. Listening, reflecting on emotions, making suggestions and individual sessions are not enough to get along with the complexity.

V. Ioannidou (✉) · C. Lagogianni
Institute of Systemic Therapy of Thessaloniki (ISTT), Thessaloniki, Greece
e-mail: ioannidou@istt.gr

© Springer Nature Switzerland AG 2021
M. Mariotti et al. (eds.), *Handbook of Systemic Approaches to Psychotherapy Manuals*, European Family Therapy Association Series,
https://doi.org/10.1007/978-3-030-73640-8_23

We regard couples' therapy as a journey, on which the couple invites the therapist and on which she[1] needs equipment to stay confident and show multidirectional partiality (Simon et al., 1999), in order to be helpful. What she needs is a manual. We agree with Stratton that "a well-constructed manual can be a supportive structure for the therapist and thereby free them to open up choices for their own activities and for their clients" (2013, p. 182).

We regard the model presented in this chapter as a manual, which helps the therapist organize the large amount of information couples usually share in the first sessions and develop with them an understanding about what is going on in their relationship. A feeling of acceptance and safety, a common language is created. This is how the presented manual impacted Virginia's practice, when she first met Hans and Margarete Jellouschek in Thessaloniki in 1993. Virginia started their training a year after in Germany and was strongly inspired and influenced by their work and attitude. In 1995 Hans Jellouschek encouraged her to start giving training in couples' therapy in Greece, which she did many years after. He has supported her ever since and he gave a speech in Thessaloniki, when her book *The Art of Being a Couple. A Systemic Approach* was published in 2012, long after Margarete had died.

With reference to the model, the therapist makes hypotheses, which she may offer to the partners as tentative and incomplete alternative perspectives. The same hypotheses enable her to ask insightful questions about behaviors, sequences of behaviors, and meanings these may have to each of the partners. Thus, new associations emerge, misunderstandings are solved, and a new narration is constructed.

Since the words we use are determined by the way we think, therapists using this manual talk in a comprehensive way without any notion of psychopathology (von Schlippe & Schweitzer, 1997). Adapting to clients' own language and vocabulary allows partners to feel understood on an emotional and on a mental level. The therapist shares her dilemmas and ideas openly. This helps clients, even skeptic ones, to feel safer and trust the therapeutic process.

Although the model helps the therapist feel confident and structure the session, it is suggested that she does not insist on her hypotheses or ideas (Cecchin et al., 1992). It is clear from the beginning that no one knows the correct answer to the couples' unique story, but there is space for exploration of alternatives. This space for dialogue promotes open communication between partners. In some cases, when the difficulty of the couple is described in a comprehensive way during the session, the therapy is brief, one to three sessions may be enough.

More recently in the context of Open Dialogue sessions, in the presence of two therapists, we have been sharing our thoughts during reflection in front of partners. Previous research has shown that during co-therapists' reflections, couples tend to have a high autonomic systemic response, pointing to the fact that their therapists' ideas and thoughts seem highly meaningful to them (Seikkula et al., 2018). Bearing this in mind, the language that we use when talking to clients about our [therapists'] ideas is very open and respectful.

---

[1] For the purposes of the present chapter we will refer to the therapist in the female gender.

We have been applying this manual since 1994. The feedback from clients is that they are thankful not only to be heard but also to understand their difficulties in a few sessions and to feel they can take matters into their own hands.

Virginia has been training mental health professionals in couples' therapy since 2004, and they confirm that this manual is a useful framework to understand a couple's crisis. Trainees have recognized it as helpful in pointing out subjects, which are essential to the partners' stories, while at the same time offering ideas that are relevant to the complexity of couples' narratives.

We want to emphasize that we do not propose that the therapist acts in a manualized way. Acquiring the manual can be useful in understanding complexity but can act as a threat in appreciating couple's experiences, as clinicians can limit themselves to the framework provided. Theories determine the way we speak and thereby the conclusions that we draw. In this way, the manual may shape our thoughts and questions. Still, therapy is a collaborative process. Therapists are invited to use the manual with sensitivity, to further explore feelings, ideas, and embodied reactions that they may have in the therapeutic encounters. The relationship with the therapist is the prerequisite to use the manual, as it is the basis for every therapy.

23.2 Relationship with the Therapist

During the therapeutic process, the aim is for each partner to experience himself or herself being seen, being accepted, and understood. The therapist takes on both partners' perspectives, her stance is characterized by multidirectional partiality, which is relevant to neutrality (Selvini Palazzoli et al., 1980). This does not mean that the therapist is cool and distant. On the contrary, she understands the narratives of both partners, no matter how different these are. Neutrality thus, characterizes the perspective of the therapist and not her feelings towards the clients (Brown, 2010). It reflects that the therapist can work with multiple truths and not align herself with a single one. This attitude can be achieved for example, by maintaining eye contact with each of the partners, even when she is in dialogue with the other partner.

For the partners to feel safe, curious, and willing to proceed with change, it is encouraged that the therapist engages in the following behaviors:

Tension Regulation For example, consider a couple which is arguing, because the wife is referring once again to the discovery of her husband's extramarital adventure through his mobile phone account. It is useful for the therapist to point out the repetitiveness of this argument and help reduce the tension: "I understand that you are very upset about it, that it was a very difficult time for you. However, we have mentioned it before, and it seems to me not helpful to continue discussing it now." The therapist may speak for a few minutes separately with each partner, asking the other partner to wait in the next room. She may further point out that they can try something different in therapy, to the usual fights that they have at home.

Many couples consider the continuation of dialogue a great advantage of the therapy, as if the therapist was not present it is likely that one partner would interrupt the discussion or there would be an escalation of tension.

Mutual Emotional Regulation The therapist attunes herself to her clients verbally and nonverbally through questions, tone of voice, facial expressions, gestures, and body posture (Seikkula et al., 2018). For example, she may soften her voice, if one of the partners cries.

Reflection of Emotions The therapist listens carefully and names the feelings the clients express, for example: "you felt hurt," "it annoyed you."

Containment The therapist can act as a "container" within which clients can temporarily place their negative feelings of fear, frustration, hopelessness, etc. The therapist is present, and does not abandon the clients in this difficult emotional state that they are in. She is present to support them and can tolerate the difficulty, even when nothing can be done.

The therapist demonstrates unlimited curiosity and maintains a not-knowing attitude to explore the meanings of the clients who are experts in their lives (Anderson, 2008). The therapist talks with people rather than about them.

Resonance This is not a mere repetition or imitation of what the client has said, but a narration by the therapist, who is attuned to the client's state. The therapist's goal is to show understanding, recognition, and appreciation to both partners and their efforts to address difficulties so far, and to invite them to view difficulties from another perspective (de Shazer, 1991; von Schlippe & Schweitzer, 1997).

For example, the therapist might say to the couple: "You have been troubled with work and financial problems for many years and have had no time or energy for your relationship. Maybe now is the time to focus on the ways you communicate, pay attention to your personal needs, etc."

Or in another case: The husband, a young doctor, is studying for his internship exams, the wife is working, and they have two young children. The wife has discovered her husband's extramarital adventure. They have big fights. The therapist may say: "You are experiencing a stressful situation. Perhaps the other relationship worked for the husband as a safety valve, at a time when he could not burden his wife with his anxiety, while she devoted herself to their children and work. Despite these difficulties, the fact that you are here shows that you want to meet as partners again. We just have to find the way."

According to Anderson (2008), clients wonder what their therapist is thinking, what is behind her questions; they feel naked in front of her. Therefore, it is helpful that the therapist engages in dialogue and talks about her ideas with clients (Andersen, 2007). In this way, the therapist can further attend and reflect upon her inner dialogue (Olson et al, 2012; Rober, 2011). Goolishian argued that you never know what you think, until you have said it (Anderson & Goolishian, 1988).

When the therapist approaches clients in such ways, a relationship with the clients (structural coupling) is created and maintained, allowing the topics discussed to act as stimuli for them. Clients can be receptive to ideas that emerge during the sessions, which may then be processed according to their own structures. Indications that this therapeutic relationship exists are for example when the therapist and the couple laugh together, when they shake their heads together, when there is a sense that what is said touches everyone. If the therapist and the couple do not achieve this contact, it is unlikely that their collaboration can bring about any change.

23.3 Couple in Crisis

Each couple is thought to construct reality according to each partner's past experiences, social norms, and the particular context in which they live. That is, partners have their own construction, their own lenses, with which they see reality. When a construction contributes to the system's (the couple's in this case) survival, working in the given environment, then it is characterized as viable and resembles a key that fits into a lock. "This matching is a quality of the key, not of the lock" (von Glasersfeld, 1984 in Simon et al., 1999, p. 182). There are many keys that can open the same lock. Correspondingly, there are many constructions that enable a system to survive, many solutions to a problem.

Usually partners state they have a problem when the construction, the solution, and the way that they have been using is not useful anymore, when the old state no longer exists, and a new state is not formed yet. A couple is in crisis when an internal need or an external event acts as perturbation, which the couple is unable to counterpoise on its own based on the capacity provided by its structure.

In other words, the crisis is caused by the fact that familiar behaviors are not enough for the requirements of the present situation, and new behaviors are needed. According to Watzlawick et al. (1967), it is not a change in the repertoire of behaviors the family has utilized so far, but a change in the repertoire itself. For instance, when two partners become parents, they must adopt novel behaviors to meet the demands of the new situation: they may remain sleepless at night, have limited time to rest, have concerns about their child, need to rely on other people's help, etc.

A crisis in a couple can be triggered, as mentioned earlier, by an external event or by an internal development of one or both partners. An external event can be a problem at work, a relocation, a change of residence, an illness, a death in the close family environment, etc. It is an event that affects the daily life, the habits, and the feelings of the partners.

An internal development can refer to either a newly recognized need or one that becomes more intense in a given period of time. It may be a need for greater engagement with the partner, clearer boundaries with others, having a child, professional development, creative expression, etc.

For example, a couple could start having difficulties, in the case where only one of the partners develops the desire for a child, following a period when both felt content in their relationship. In another case, difficulties may arise if one partner wants more distance from their families of origin, while the parents of the other partner need further caring.

Whether it is an external event or an internal development, those changes entail something new that disturbs the existing balance of the system. Systems usually resist novelty (perturbations), resulting in communication problems, psychological or psychosomatic symptoms in family members. For instance, a husband felt intense physical pain shortly after his wife started working and engaging in a new hobby. In the past, the wife was devoted to their children and the household. It took more than 2 years of medical assessments, until the doctors concluded that his pain was psychosomatic, and the couple sought psychotherapeutic help.

Hence, the initial crisis in a relationship may be disguised by some symptom or illness. The therapist is asked to explore with the partner or both partners the initial crisis, holding an attitude of neutrality and curiosity. Every crisis, however unpleasant and painful it may be, can be seen as a transition from one phase of relative stability to another, as a condition for growth. The questions that arise are the following:

- What resources does the system (partner, couple) have to overcome the crisis?
- How can the therapist contribute so that these resources are activated?

For example, when a married woman says she has "depression," the therapist can discuss with the couple the effects of "depression" on their relationship. It is often the case that the husband treats his "depressed" wife with greater interest, takes on more responsibilities within the family. At the same time the woman herself values her needs more and starts expressing her wishes. In this way, "depression" is the reason for finding a new balance between the partners, a balance that would not have been achieved, if there had not been the weight of the "disorder." This example illustrates why, when the symptom is isolated and treated with medication alone, the opportunity for change in people's relationships and lives can be missed (Gergen & McNamee, 2000).

Every crisis is therefore a challenge for system members to adopt new behaviors and create a new structure. This is why the goal of the psychotherapeutic process is to explore the meaning of the crisis. As a result, the therapist does not act as an authority, but as an expert in asking questions, facilitating reflection processes. The therapist can be considered the expert in approaches, while clients are the experts in their lives' content. Different models may influence the therapist's thoughts and attitude. Being flexible and not committing to a specific model, is, according to Cecchin et al. (1992), a prerequisite for the therapist to respect her clients.

In each case, the therapist constructs a new reality with the couple, according to the needs of the partners in each session and the therapist's own understanding. At times, this new construction, the new perspective, may offer relief, while at other times it may intensify the emotions associated with the crisis. For example, the suggestion that an extramarital relationship may be the trigger for a more meaningful dialogue may alleviate and provide the starting point for changes in the relationship, or it may lead to the painful recognition that one of the partners no longer has feelings towards the other, and separation is inevitable.

23.4 A Basic Model for Understanding a Couple's Crisis

Working with couples is more complex, because the therapist must attune to two people, who may have different or even conflicting needs. The German couples' therapist, trainer, and writer Dr Hans Jellouschek (von Tiedemann & Jellouschek, 2000) developed a model, which we consider a useful manual for exploring the meaning of a given crisis and maintaining the engagement of both partners.

Fig. 23.1 (von Tiedemann & Jellouschek, 2000, p. 37) illustrates that a couple in crisis:

- lives in a context in the present (in a particular place, in certain socioeconomic conditions, is going through a specific phase in the life cycle, etc.),
- is influenced by both the shared story and the individual stories of the partners,
- cultivates (or does not cultivate) dreams and plans for the future.

Having all these factors in mind, the therapist makes hypotheses, forms questions, and together with the partners constructs a new narrative of the problem. The problem may concern:

- a dysfunctional communication scheme,
- a difficulty in organizing aspects of adult life,
- a difficulty transitioning from one phase to another in the life cycle,
- an unfinished story from the couple's history,
- an unfinished story from a partner's individual history,
- lack of individual or shared plans for the future,
- or a combination of the above factors.

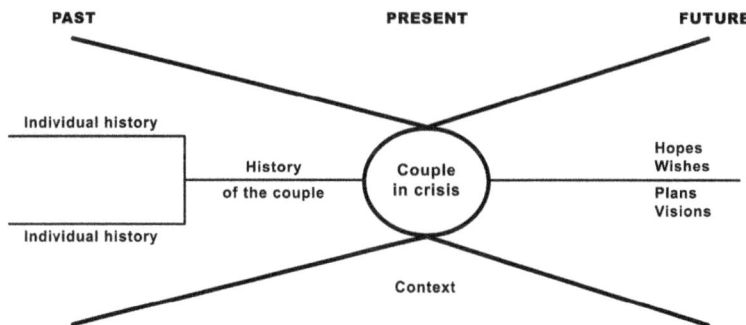

Fig. 23.1 Couple's crisis in the present, past, and future

Before looking at these factors in detail, we want to point out two advantages of the manual:

In the beginning of therapy there is a risk of getting lost in past negative experiences and narrations about the partners' families of origin. If the therapist concentrates on the first three factors, she brings attention to the present context, reduces complexity and enhances partners' agency. Past experiences and the relationships with the families of origin may be discussed later, when the therapeutic alliance with both partners is more stable.

The second advantage is that the therapist may organize quickly the information shared. This is especially important in the beginning of therapy. After the first sessions, the dialogue with the partners may focus on different agendas. If, at some point the partners feel unsatisfied with the progress of therapy, it may be helpful for the therapist to reflect openly on these factors again: where have the partners made progress and where are there still difficulties.

Let us give some examples to explain the above factors:

23.4.1 *Dysfunctional Communication Scheme and Difficulty of Transition*

For example, a couple starts therapy, following the wife's initiative, who is furious because the husband is not paying attention to her. The sessions are their last source of hope, as she has already done two years of individual therapy in the past with another therapist. The context within which this couple operates is that the husband works hard; he is a young physician. She works fewer hours, as she took over her father's practice as a microbiologist. They have a 2-year-old child, signifying that they recently became parents.

In therapy sessions, the wife is aggressive and cries, and the husband is restrained and cold. In their daily lives, they are trapped in a vicious cycle of communication: The man is often absent, and the woman feels neglected and complains. The man feels guilty, lacks understanding, and consequently withdraws himself or is absent. This couple seems to have a dysfunctional pattern of communication and is transitioning from the "young couple" phase to the "couple with children" phase.

23.4.2 *Difficulty in Transition and Issues Around Organizing Adult Life*

Another couple comes for therapy because the husband is having an extramarital affair. The therapist is trying to understand the context of the crisis. This couple had a baby just a few months ago. Consequently, the wife devoted herself to the newborn with the help of her mother and distanced herself from her husband. He was excluded from the mother–child interaction and felt neglected and helpless in his paternal responsibilities. The couple's old balance was lost, and the husband began an extramarital affair, maybe trying to restore his own inner balance (Welter-Enderlin, 2007).

This case also involves a difficulty in transitioning to a new phase "couple with children," as well as coping with adult life issues, for example, give-and-take, relationships with third parties (see further down: Sect. 23.4.6).

We consider it useful to take into account individuals' life cycles, as this offers hope that difficulties are not terminal, a crisis may be temporary. We are constantly evolving.

23.4.3 Unfinished Story from the Couple's History

Partners may be emotionally drained because of financial problems, work difficulties, relocations, or instances where they have hurt each other, either in words, "you are not worthy of becoming a mother," "you are not capable of maintaining a family," or in acts such as:

- a past extramarital relationship,
- when one did not take the side of the other partner, but that of their own parents,
- when the husband was absent or distant during childbirth and the subsequent caring for the children, and
- when a partner purchased an asset only in his or her own name without consulting the other partner.

It is often that such hurtful experiences accumulate, and partners refer to them in their arguments.

23.4.4 Unfinished Issues from a Partner's Individual History

Quite often there are repetitions from the individual past of a partner. For example, the husband did not tell his wife how neglected he felt because of her behavior. He protected her from his needs, in a similar manner to how he used to protect his mother after she and his father divorced. As a result, the wife was not aware of his emotions and his needy side, while experiencing his demands to take care of the children and the household as an attempt to control her, leading to her rebelling against him. In this way tensions were often created.

In another case, the man's desire to rest after work while watching television was translated by the woman as a sign of indifference. As a child she had experienced many occasions when no one cared for her. Whenever her husband was absorbed in watching television, those memories came to the surface and triggered intense negative feelings in her.

23.4.5 Lack of Individual or Shared Plans

When a person has desires and visions and strives to realize them, he or she develops a sense of contentment that further impacts upon his or her relationship. The significance of having a personal prospect in life is evident from the consequences of its absence. When a partner becomes unemployed or when a mother loses her everyday duties because her children have reached adulthood, this gap quite often leads to a crisis in the couple's relationship.

In addition, the lack of shared visions and plans can often be a source of tension in a couple's life. Following the first period of being in love, partners need a shared perspective, to keep their love alive (Jellouschek, 2000). They need common goals that inspire and fascinate both. Usually the common goal is to have and raise one or more children. The issue of having a shared perspective emerges again when children grow older and leave home. Most couples find it difficult to develop a new common interest, a new joint activity that excites them both. This can be the reason why this phase is associated with major problems in many families.

23.4.6 Difficulty in Organizing Aspects of Adult Life

In order to understand the meaning of a couple's crisis and the couple's communication and behavioral patterns in general, it is worth exploring some of the aspects that are central for organizing adult life (Jellouschek, 1992b):

(a) *Autonomy and intimacy:* The need for autonomy is undeniable in today's age. Every person needs his or her own space and time to express his or her self, be creative, and have the feeling that he or she can define his or her life. At the same time everyone has the need to feel that they belong somewhere, to experience intimacy.

The question that arises is whether and how these opposing needs are met within the partnership. An additional difficulty is that the two partners have these needs in different degrees, which are influenced by internal and external factors.

The couple is thus invited to find a changing balance, so that each partner experiences both autonomy and intimacy within their relationship (see below: Sect. 23.6).

(b) *Give and take:* Is there a balance in giving and taking between partners? Is there a shift in roles so that everyone can offer, but also receive interest, help, care from the other? It is argued that the more balanced the giving and taking is among partners (and people in general), the more lively and satisfying their relationship is.

It is common that because of their ongoing obligations partners are so absorbed and tired, that they are not present for each other emotionally. As a result, their intimacy becomes fragile and at risk in crisis situations. What partners need from each other is not difficult or time-consuming: a kind word, a touch, a helping hand.

Some couples have a great imbalance with respect to giving and taking. One partner gives a lot with ease, while the other mainly takes and feels guilty. Over the course of time the former has increasing demands made on them and the latter cannot withstand his or her guilt. The need for balance is intense, and, if not fulfilled, the relationship may break down. When the giving partner has an additional sense of moral pressure to endure any deprivation or injustice, then it is likely that this partner may develop emotional or psychosomatic symptoms.

For example, the wife had a stable job and was responsible for the children and the household. The husband struggled with his professional career in great uncertainty and was not able to offer either emotional or practical help to the family. The wife did not complain but tried to support him. The wife developed symptoms of depression and panic attacks. Through discussing the matter of giving and taking, as well as the difficult external circumstances, the wife began to set her boundaries while the husband started offering practical help. The wife's symptoms gradually disappeared.

(c) *Male and female roles:* How have the partners divided what are considered as male and female responsibilities? How much flexibility do they show in this arrangement? How satisfied are they with their choices?

For example, a couple had divided roles since the beginning of their marriage in the perceived traditional way: the husband made a living and the wife took care of the children and the household. However, she was not pleased with this arrangement. After 10 years, she decided to work and pursue her interests. Her husband accused her of neglecting their children. She got angry that he was trying to control her. She started taking antidepressants and her husband developed severe psychosomatic symptoms. It becomes obvious that they were not able to distribute family responsibilities in a way that satisfied them both.

Dividing male and female responsibilities creates particular difficulties, when the woman has a good job, while the husband has severe work-related problems (e.g. debts, unemployment). In most societies men are socialized to be outside the home, and women inside it. When roles are reversed for reasons that the couple cannot control (e.g. economic crisis), a great deal of flexibility and maturity is needed on the part of the partners, to find a suitable balance.

(d) *Relationships with third parties:* How does the couple find the balance between setting boundaries and permeability in interpersonal relationships? Does the relationship of the partners distinguish itself in terms of intensity and quality compared to the relationships the partners have with other people?

Some couples are looking for an open relationship with no clear boundaries. Partners openly admit to having further sexual relationships, a shared decision that may work well for a while. In the long run however, a problem arises because none of those relationships offer the quality and safety that partners usually expect, resulting in frustration and hurt feelings.

On the other hand, couples that isolate themselves from relatives and friends and try to meet their needs for warmth and closeness solely with each other, usually experience an emotional deprivation that leads to high tensions. The explanation is simple: no one can meet all the needs of his or her partner.

We therefore need a special relationship with a partner, surrounded by a close network of personal friends (Jellouschek, 1992a). Friendships meet important needs of partners and can be extremely valuable in difficult times.

The issue of relationships with third parties also refers to the relationships with the families of origin – a factor, which is quite crucial in countries like Greece, where family members of different generations have very close bonds. The question is to what extent and in which way do partners allow their parents to intervene in their lives and their relationship. How does the family of origin influence a crisis or the growth of the couple?

For example, a young man discussed everything that concerned him with his parents, not with his girlfriend, who felt that her opinion did not mean much to him. She was particularly upset, when he chose the living room furniture for their new shared home with his parents, because they were paying for it. After being together for two years, this couple broke up.

(e) *Division of power:* How much flexibility is there in sharing out power between partners? Do they have assigned roles, so one dominates and the other subordinates? In these cases, the relationship is reminiscent of a parent–child relationship and there is usually a significant negative impact on the couple's sexuality.

When both partners try to impose on each other, there may be constant tension in the couple. They disagree frequently; there is no understanding or willingness to communicate. The causes of recurring arguments may vary: hurt feelings, low self-esteem, lack of autonomy, communication difficulties, diversity/dissimilarity in many aspects, etc.

The most rewarding pattern according to studies cited by Napier (1990) is when there is an alteration of who prevails upon and who follows; when the partners alternate positions, like two children on a seesaw. Everything is openly discussed; there are no taboo issues. There are intense fights, which are not sterile and poisonous, but constructive, as the question is not "who is the strongest" but "which is the best solution for us." Bearing this goal in mind, partners are ready to support their position at times, while at other times they are willing to follow their partner's position. This stance is taken without them feeling inferior but having a sense that they are doing the best for their relationship.

In these cases, there is respect for each partner's individuality and autonomy. Everyone feels responsible for themselves. Partners meet as two separate autonomous individuals.

23.5 Process of a Couple's Therapy

Having explained all the factors of the couples' crisis model, we want to emphasize that it can be very useful for the therapist to keep in mind the following sequence of Fig. 23.2, on where to focus during the therapeutic process (von Tiedemann & Jellouschek, 2000, p. 38):

Depending on where the focus is and how the partners describe their problem, the therapist asks further questions, makes comments and proposals on their narration. She first looks for a dysfunctional communication scheme in the present. If there is not such an obvious scheme, she explores if there is a difficulty in organizing aspects of adult life. A difficulty transitioning from one phase to another in the life cycle may also be a suitable hypothesis. Only if these factors have been explored,

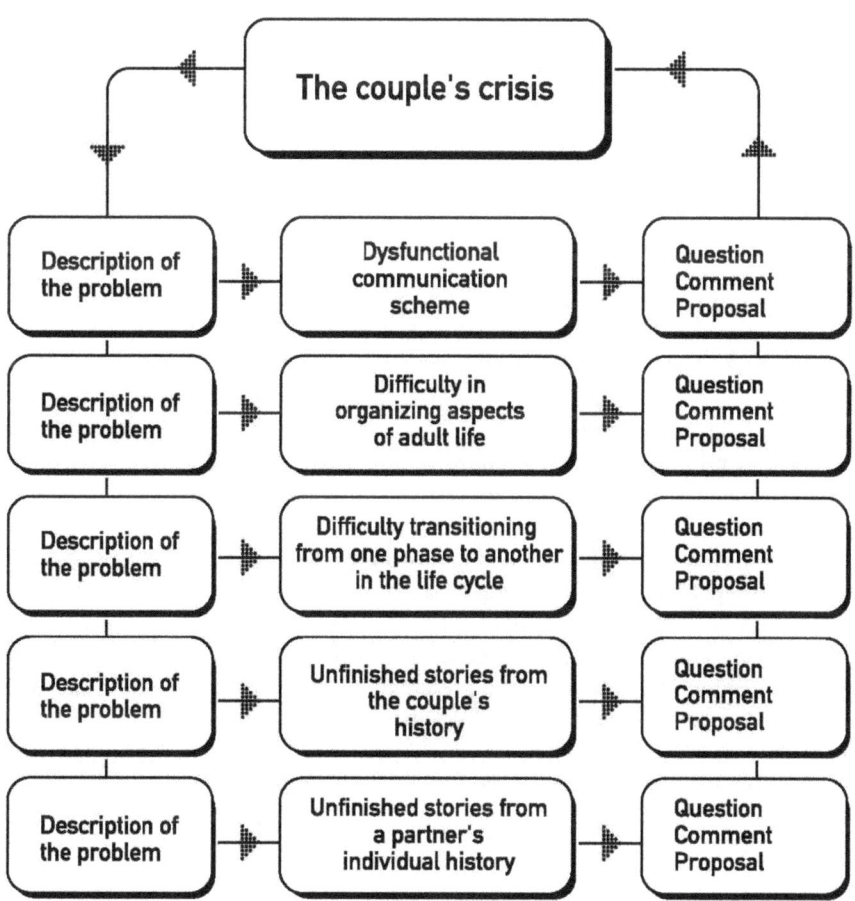

Fig. 23.2 The process of a couple's therapy

is it advisable for the therapist to open up issues from the past of the couple and the partners.

While in the original figure (von Tiedemann & Jellouschek, 2000, p. 38) the therapist's response was coined after "intervention," we feel that this term is rather intrusive and draws an image where the therapist comes from the outside, having the power to intervene in clients' life. In the contrary we value the uniqueness of therapeutic encounters and the space created in between clients (Shotter, 2011). In this way we changed the terminology to "Question, Comment, Proposal" of therapists, to reveal the interaction and engagement of the therapist to what the clients bring with their stories.

From our experience this is a useful manual especially in the beginning of couples' therapy, during difficult phases of the therapeutic process and at the end of therapy to check in with clients' expectations.

For the purposes of the present chapter we explore autonomy–intimacy, the most important factors in couples' relationships.

23.6 Autonomy–Intimacy

According to Bischof (1994) the dipole of stimuli–safety, or otherwise the need for stimuli on the one edge of the spectrum and the need for safety on the other edge, motivate us to come in contact with other people. Social behavior is based on this dipole.

From an anthropological point of view, autonomy is seen as "the power and the will to be responsible for one's own life, to follow one's own path, to take risks, not to use support, and as a result to take no one into account" (Bischof, 1994, p. 353).

As becomes obvious, autonomy is linked to interpersonal distance and the feeling that one has his or her own space and time. At the same time, being responsible for one's own life and following one's own path is connected to recognizing and caring for one's own needs. Autonomy is not a state to achieve, but a process of maturation that lasts a lifetime.

It becomes apparent that not taking anyone into account can only be partially applied, as individuals live in societies – a fact reflecting their need for intimacy.

Intimacy is seen as the need for affection, for contact with a familiar person. It is differentiated from states of dependency (need for help) and sociality (need for company). When intimate there is a preference towards a specific individual with whom one is familiar. This preference goes beyond sexuality and is reciprocal (Bischof, 1994). Intimacy is associated with closeness, emotional connection, having a feeling that one belongs somewhere, that one is sharing things with a familiar other.

23.7 Stages in the Couple's Development

The crucial issue that arises is how to find the balance between the need for autonomy and the need for intimacy (Bischof, 1994). We are constantly on the move like a pendulum between these two poles. It is mastery not to stick to a single pole. If someone gets stuck in intimacy, he or she runs the risk of losing touch with his or her self. At the same time, if one sticks in autonomy, one risks feeling great loneliness. Each partner has these needs to varying degrees. This is why meeting all these needs in a relationship is a complex process. As partners strive for balance between intimacy and autonomy, they go through five phases, Fig. 23.3 (Ioannidou, 2012, p. 67):

1. *Merging*

It is the phase of the first love, the time when partners want to share everything, if possible. Usually, they idealize each other and project their expectations for an ideal partner.

In addition to projections, this stage further encompasses the resources[2] of the relationship, the visions of the partners, and their potential as a couple. Later, in challenging periods they may look back to that initial stage and draw from those

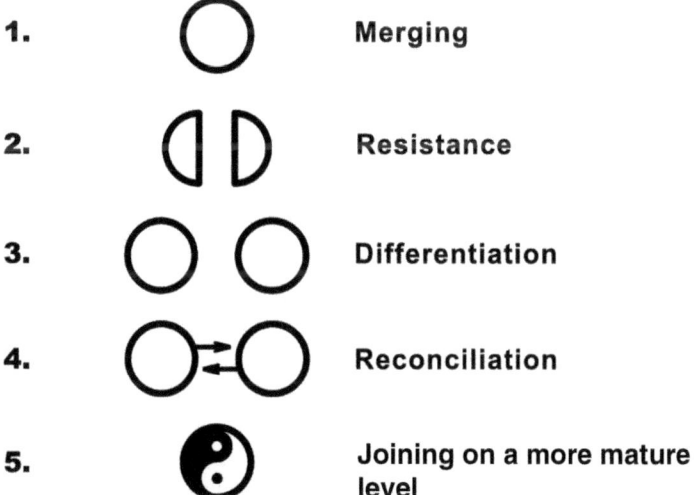

Fig. 23.3 Autonomy–intimacy phases in a couple's life

---

[2] Systemic therapy defines as a resource "any material, mental or emotional potential that promotes the alternatives of a given system and thus improves its ability to survive and solve problems" (Simon et al., 1999, p. 275). Systemic therapists focus on resources rather than on their clients' deficits.

experiences ideas about what they like in each other and what is possible to happen between them in the future.

The merging phase does not last long, because the need for autonomy remains neglected. Some people satisfy their need for autonomy by looking for a new partner every time the merging period ends. In this way they are constantly in love with different partners and seem to avoid becoming autonomous.

2. *Resistance*

Resistance to merging appears in multiple ways, through frequent fights, sexual difficulties, an extramarital affair, depression, psychosomatic symptoms, and more. In this phase one experiences the other as an obstacle. For example, the wife blames the husband because she does not have a job. The husband claims that it is the wife's fault that they have rare sexual encounters.

It is likely that the initially attractive characteristics of one partner now seem annoying, for example, the sociality of the partner. Each partner fights against the other as a danger to his or her self.

Partners feel dependent on each other and they have negative feelings about it, whereas in the previous phase, this dependency was a pleasant experience. They have difficulties being together, and at the same time they find it impossible being apart. They function as two semicircles that are in reference to each other.

3. *Differentiation*

In the third phase, partners neither idealize nor battle against each other. They no longer blame each other for everything that bothers them. Each one focuses on their own dark sides, concentrating on how he or she contributes to the situation that is bothering him or her. The wife admits that it is ultimately her own choice not to work or not to allow herself to relax from time to time. The husband recognizes how his own behaviors impact their sexual relationship, for example, he is in a hurry, acts abruptly, etc.

Everyone takes responsibility for his or her own development and takes care of his or her self. In this stage, the need for autonomy is met to a great extent. It resembles a psychological divorce; partners might experience it as a risk.

4. *Reconciliation*

If partners do not separate during the differentiation phase, if they discover that they value important aspects in each other, then they are likely to feel attracted to each other again. They may come closer in a novel way: they tend to see each other as they really are, and not as they would like each other to be, projections are usually reduced compared to the first phase.

5. *Joining on a more mature level*

If the partners get closer again, then they are likely to move on to the fifth phase. At this stage, each partner retains his or her own autonomy and at the same time creates a new whole with the other. According to Schellenbaum (1993), each partner appreciates something strange and something familiar in the other person. The diversity of the other person is experienced as a challenge for personal growth.

What annoys and irritates one partner in another, may be an indication of a projection. Projections often reflect aspects of our mental world that we have not explored and cultivated yet (Schellenbaum, 1993).

For example, one partner accuses the other of intense sociability. Noticing this, the therapist may ask this partner: How is socializing for you? How do you cultivate friendships? It is common, that this partner finds it hard to establish and maintain social interactions.

These phases, apart from the first, are usually experienced by couples more than once. The reason being that the balance that the couple reaches in the fifth phase may be overturned by an external event or an internal development of one partner. Then partners go through a period of resistance, differentiation, reconciliation, etc. Proximity, distance, proximity... it is a spiral process. The purpose of it is to be constantly evolving, so that the two poles are continually aligning with one another: to experience intimacy within autonomy (the sense one belongs to the other, when they are apart), and to experience autonomy within intimacy (the sense that the partner is different, when they are together). Over time, the phases are not experienced in the same intensity.

In our experience, when we explain these phases to couples, they begin understanding their behavior and that of their partners from a new perspective. Partners gain a sense of relief, as they appreciate that their condition is temporary and that there are options for development. For some of them this is enough, and they terminate therapy with a feeling that their state is normal. For others this information motivates them to stop demanding more closeness and start cultivating their autonomy, since lack of autonomy is quite common in a couple's life, at least in our country.

23.8 Conclusion

Therapists working with this manual, approach couples' difficulties in a way that normalizes them and promotes development on an individual and relational level. A safe and respectful context is created, in which partners are encouraged to reflect on their communication scheme, on important aspects of adult life, like autonomy and intimacy, on their state in the life cycle, on past experiences, on their resources and visions. The therapist explores together with the couple, alternative and more suitable solutions for them. The prerequisite for this is that partners bear feelings for each other, that there are hidden positive feelings behind the tensions, like coals under the ashes (Welter-Enderlin, 1996). In therapy we dig beneath the ashes, as we may find smouldering coals that will eventually ignite.

Therapists using the presented manual feel more confident to work with complicated couples' issues. In the beginning applying it may feel like learning to drive. Later on, one uses it automatically. It helps organize information, make thoughtful hypotheses and insightful comments. The therapist may get back to the manual anytime she feels lost during the therapeutic process. It acts as a framework, which helps the therapist be stable, open, and creative.

References

Andersen, T. (2007). Reflecting talks may have many versions: Here is mine. *International Journal of Psychotherapy, 11*(2), 27–44.
Anderson, H. (2008). *Conversation, language, and possibilities: A postmodern approach to therapy*. Basic Books.
Anderson, H., & Goolishian, H. A. (1988). Human systems as linguistic systems: Preliminary and evolving ideas about the implications for clinical theory. *Family Process, 27*(4), 371–393.
Bischof, N. (1994). *Das Rätsel Ödipus*. Piper.
Brown, J. M. (2010). The Milan principles of hypothesising, circularity and neutrality in dialogical family therapy: Extinction, evolution, eviction or emergence? *Australian and New Zealand Journal of Family Therapy, 31*(3), 248–265.
Cecchin, G., Lane, G., & Ray, W. A. (1992). *Irreverence: A strategy for therapists' survival*. Karnac.
Gergen, K. J., & McNamee, S. (2000). From disordering discourse to transformative dialogue. In R. A. Neimeyer & J. D. Raskin (Eds.), *Constructions of disorder: Meaning-making frameworks for psychotherapy* (pp. 333–349). American Psychological Association.
Ioannidou, V. (2012). *The art of being a couple. A systemic approach*. Published in Greek language. Thessaloniki: Gnosi.
Jellouschek, H. (1992a). *Die Kunst als Paar zu leben*. Kreuz Verlag.
Jellouschek, H. (1992b). Destruktiv – Konstruktiv. Beziehungsmuster bei Paaren. *Zeitschrift Universitas, 2*, 138–149.
Jellouschek, H. (2000). Beziehung und Bezauberung. In *Wie Paare sich verlieren und wiederfinden, gespiegelt in Märchen und Mythen*. Kreuz Verlag.
Napier, A. (1990). Alle Macht für beide. *Psychologie Heute, 7*, 20–26.
Olson, M. E., Laitila, A., Rober, P., & Seikkula, J. (2012). The shift from monologue to dialogue in a couple therapy session: Dialogical investigation of change from the therapist's point of view. *Family Process, 51*(3), 420–435.
Rober, P. (2011). The therapist's experiencing in family therapy practice. *Journal of Family Therapy, 33*(3), 243–255.
Schellenbaum, P. (1993). *Das Nein in der Liebe. Abgrenzung und Hingabe in der erotischen Beziehung*. Deutscher Taschenbuch Verlag.
Schlippe, A. v., & Schweitzer, J. (1997). *Lehrbuch der systemischen Therapie und Beratung*. Vandenhoeck & Ruprecht.
Seikkula, J., Karvonen, A., Kykyri, V., Penttonen, M., & Nyman-Salonen, P. (2018). The relational mind in couple therapy: A Bateson-inspired view of human life as an embodied stream. *Family Process, 57*(4), 855–866.
Selvini Palazzoli, M. P., Boscolo, L., Cecchin, G., & Prata, G. (1980). Hypothesizing circularity neutrality: Three guidelines for the conductor of the session. *Family Process, 19*(1), 3–12.
de Shazer, S. (1991). *Putting difference to work*. Norton.
Shotter, J. (2011). Therapeutic realities and the dialogical: Body, feeling, language and world. *Human Systems, 22*(3), 763–784.
Simon, F. B., Clement, U., & Stierlin, H. (1999). *Die Sprache der Familientherapie*. Klett-Cotta.
Stratton, P. (2013). Manuals: A secure base for playful therapy. *Human Systems, 24*, 181–192.
von Tiedemann, F., & Jellouschek, H. (2000). Systemische Paartherapie – Ein integratives Konzept. *Psychotherapie im Dialog, 2*, 37–44.

Watzlawick, P., Beavin Bavelas, J., & Jackson, D. D. (1967). *Pragmatics of human communication*. Norton.
Welter-Enderlin, R. (1996). *Deine Liebe ist nicht meine Liebe. Partnerprobleme und Lösungsmodelle aus systemischer Sicht*. Herder.
Welter-Enderlin, R. (1998). Was hat Säuglingsforschung mit Therapie und Beratung zu tun? In R. Welter-Enderlin & B. Hildenbrand (Eds.), *Gefühle und Systeme*. Carl-Auer-Systeme.
Welter-Enderlin, R. (2007). *Einführung in die systemische Paartherapie*. Carl-Auer-Systeme.

Chapter 24
Marte Meo and Coordination Meetings: A Systemic, School-Based Intervention

Ulf Axberg, Bill Pettit, and Ingegerd Wirtberg

In Remembrance of Ingegerd Wirtberg
Shortly after the present chapter was finished Ingegerd Wirtberg passed away. Ingegerd was the one who took the initiative for the project (MAC) that was designed to facilitate the development of children who experienced difficulties in school, and how it was implemented and researched. Without Ingegerd's enthusiasm, knowledge and stamina, the project would not have seen the light of the day. Ingegerd will stay in our hearts.
Ulf Axberg
Bill Petitt.

24.1 Introduction

The manual "Marte Meo and Coordination Meetings (MAC)" (Wirtberg et al., 2013) is an integral part of a researched and ongoing school-based intervention (Axberg et al., 2006; Balldin et al., 2019). It models the processes involved in two different interventions which are implemented concurrently in the contexts of the school and the home: the first – Marte Meo (MM) – is an established model that is normative and pedagogic in nature, while the second, coordination meetings (CMs), reflects a language-system and open-dialogue approach (Andersen, 1995; Anderson,

---

U. Axberg (✉)
Faculty of Social Studies/Family Therapy and Systemic Practice, VID Specialized University, Oslo, Norway
e-mail: ulf.axberg@vid.no

B. Pettit
Consultant, Logos A. B., Lerdala, Sweden

I. Wirtberg
Department of Clinical Psychology, Lund University, Lund, Sweden

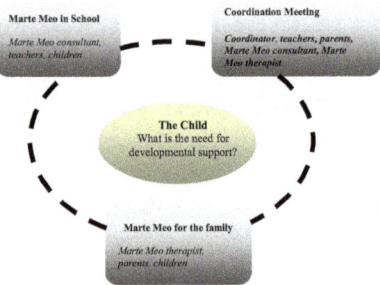

Fig. 24.1 Overview of the MAC model (Wirtberg et al., 2013, p. 18)

1997; Seikkula et al., 2003). The two parts – MM and CMs – are together conceived of as a single, systemic intervention (MAC). An overview of the MAC model is displayed below (Fig. 24.1).

MAC was developed in close cooperation between the research group and the professionals who applied it in schools and families (Wirtberg & Axberg, 2004). One of the goals of the first study was to develop and test the model in a real-world context where it was hoped that it could be of value (Axberg et al., 2006). When this study showed promise, the next stage was to apply MAC in a broader context. It was at this point that the need for a manual became obvious, for two major reasons: firstly to provide a single, clear guide for all of the many different professionals involved in the project and secondly to provide the unifying coherence necessary for an RCT.

MM has previously been manualized (Aarts, 2008), but as it now had to be fitted into the framework of a specific project, a decision was made to create a single MAC manual which would include both MM and CMs, showing how to integrate them into one systemic intervention. This was done in collaboration with the professionals who had participated in the study and who, as they grew in confidence and competence, offered valuable feedback. Important feedback came also from parents, particularly concerning their experience of the CMs. For them it often proved to be a different way of communicating about and reflecting over their relationship to the school and to their children: one parent said: "We can keep doing this until he finishes school" (Wirtberg, 2004).

The description of each step was shared with relevant organizational representatives to ensure that the manual fitted with their needs, routines, and laws.

Two of the authors (UA and IW) were deeply involved with the development of the project and the attendant research program. In the initial phase, they also acted as the supervisor for both the MM consultants and therapists (IW) and for the CM coordinators (UA). The third author (BP) is a family therapist, trainer, and writer. He was not involved in either the intervention or the research. He was asked to participate in writing the manual as he would be able to provide an "outsider" perspective. He was also familiar with MM and had followed the project from the start.

There were three principal starting points for MAC: firstly, the experience that self-reinforcing, problem-affirming systems can quickly be established around what is perceived as a child's problematic behavior; secondly, that children's problematic behavior is often first observed and reported by their teachers and thirdly, that problems can often be attended to in the context in which they are first noted.

A flowchart describing how the intervention is implemented step by step is presented in Fig. 24.2.

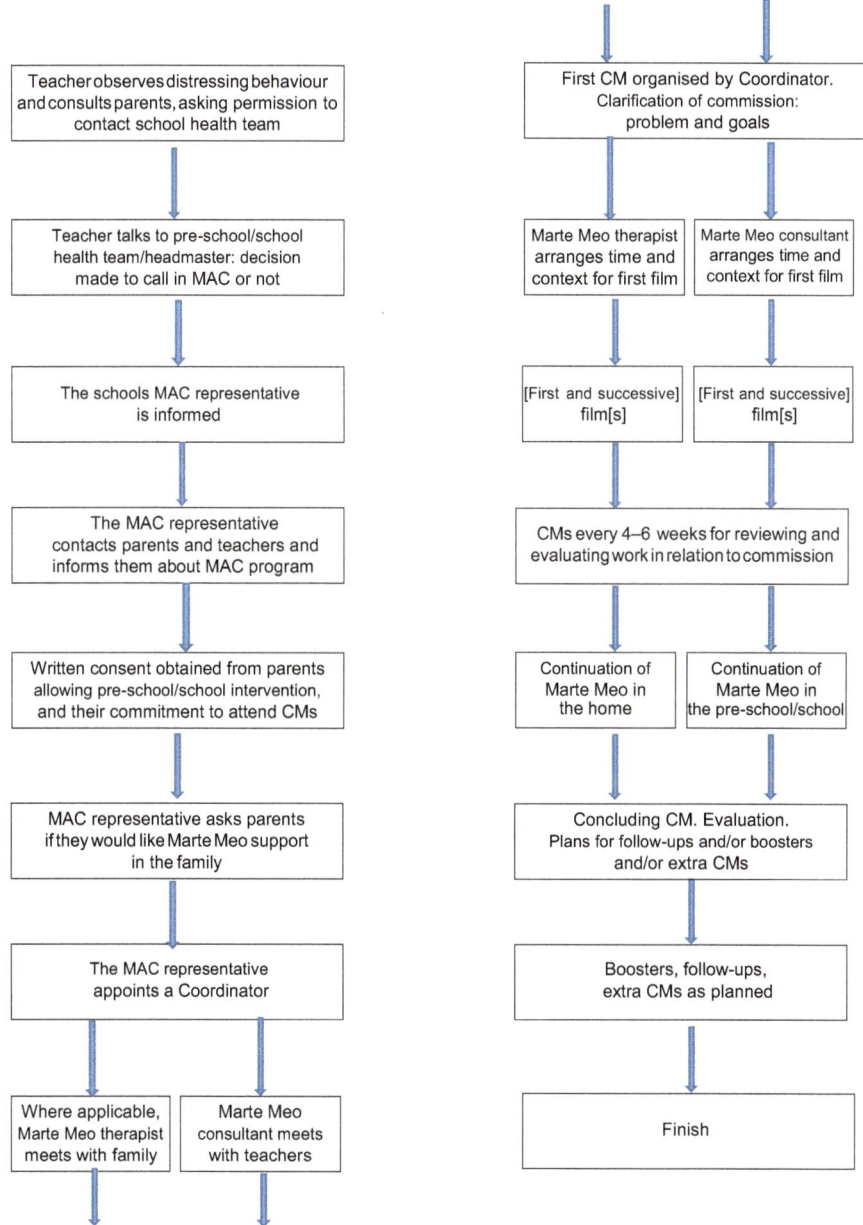

Fig. 24.2 Flowchart describing the MAC intervention (Wirtberg et al., 2013, p. 120)

Following a more detailed discussion of these starting points, the chapter has four sections: firstly, a description of the theoretical frameworks used and the way in which normative and non-normative theories can be combined; secondly, how different narratives describing the child can be supported to co-exist while the possibility of the co-construction of new narratives is created; thirdly, the qualitative and quantitative research findings are presented; finally, some thoughts concerning implementation are offered.

24.2 Starting Points

The present authors are all licensed psychotherapists and work as trainers and supervisors in the public sector. In their work with schools, social work, and psychiatry, they became aware that certain families seemed to "pop up" again and again in the different agencies. Enquiring into the history of the families' contact with these authorities, one particular pattern emerged – for many of them, the first contact could often be traced back to soon after the child began school. In a typical sequence of events, a teacher would be the first "official" to identify a child who displayed what she judged to be problematic behavior. If the school's attempts to help the child failed, then the family would be consulted. If this did not result in the desired changes, the school might then suggest family treatment either at the child and youth psychiatry unit or with the family counseling services agency provided by the local social services. Many families simply declined the suggested help. For others, the help offered proved unsuccessful in terms of influencing the child's behavior in school, and this in turn tended to result in more contact with the authorities – and the longer the contact, the more serious the child's behavior tended to be judged by the school.

At the level of the group, judgments shared by its members are often mutually reinforcing. In social groups that are especially important to the individual, such as the family, the school, and the workplace, these processes contain the possibility for generating positive or negative consequences. For most children, the family, the school, and the peer group are the three social systems that are most influential in growing up and how they are treated in those groups will have a life-long impact. Being a nexus point between the school and the family, the child has to balance two different sets of expectations that are placed on her (Aponte, 1976). While a systems perspective identifies (among other things) the importance of positive and negative feedback loops, a structural perspective reminds us that participation in a triadic set of hierarchically ordered relationships can be challenging.

When members of a hierarchical system cannot cooperate, then this has consequences. In extreme cases, the lack of cooperation can destroy the system; even milder forms may create many different problems. Another factor common to living systems is that they possess many different kinds of homeostatic parameters which, if pushed against or broken, produce negative consequences for the system's continued functioning (Luhmann, 2013; Petitt, 2016; Skyttner, 2005).

In the classroom, the child who displays behavior that deviates too far from generally accepted social norms may become a source of disturbance. The group cannot function in a satisfactory manner if one or more of its members regularly behaves in such a way. The teacher is in a very special position: her experience of many children, coupled with the fact that she sees many children of the same age in groups, means that she may detect quite early those children whose behavior deviates from generally accepted behavioral parameters. This in turn opens the possibility for early intervention, which if successful, could prevent the emergence and development of positive feedback loops that serve only to increase distress (Maruyama, 1963).

Another observation, one that particularly concerns the group that we are discussing here, is that when the teacher informed the parents of the problems that she experienced in the classroom, some responded by stating that there was nothing problematic about the child's behavior when she was at home. Accepted at face value, such an exchange simply confirms the common observation that when an individual is a member of two or more social groups, then she may be perceived and judged in very different ways by members of those different groups. An individual's identity is not something that is absolute in time and space but is to a significant degree dependent on context. The individual might be perceived as following the norms in one group while being perceived as deviant in another. This reflection is at the heart of Bateson's epistemology when he suggests that the ways that we experience things are products of the patterns that connect us to them (Bateson, 1979).

When the parents of a child whose behavior at home is unproblematic meet a teacher who views the same child's behavior in the classroom as problematic, then communication and interaction may become stressed and a conflict may emerge, reflecting their different experiences of the child. This potential for conflict may become exacerbated as each part tries to make sense of a communication that contradicts their own experience: "Why does this teacher complain to me about problems she has in her classroom?" and "Why can't these parents accept that their child has difficulties?" Both parts may doubt the communication, intentions, and competence of the other.

This possibility invites us to consider that members of different systems might possess different epistemologies or worldviews – for example, considerations concerning the nature of social reality and of what is important in life – so much so that meaningful communication might be a challenge. Effective communication requires a form of epistemic trust, in that those who participate in a "conversation" (which literally means to create together) must believe that the other has something of interest and value to communicate if they are to spend the time and energy required to understand what they are trying to say (Thayer, 1972; Fonagy & Allison, 2014).

One of our assumptions is that when there is some form of "epistemic breakdown" between the teacher and the parents, it makes a cooperative relationship difficult to establish. The application of structural and systems perspectives suggests that the child may be in a particularly difficult situation, being the nexus point for both systems. From such theoretical considerations, we identified two clear starting points: firstly, when the teacher reported that a child's behavior was disturbing, we needed an intervention that could be used directly in the classroom to support both child and teacher and secondly, that this should be coupled with a second intervention designed to help reduce potential (and actual) conflicts between school and family. This can be likened to trying to create a kind of "fifth province," a symbolic place where people could meet and talk with each other in a safe way (McCarthy & Byrne, 2008).

The idea of the first intervention is not necessarily self-evident: a common assumption is that a child's behavior is a product of the upbringing provided by her parents. The logical consequence of such a belief is that parents are also perceived as being responsible for the child's behavior even outside of the family. However, it is not uncommon that parents refuse to accept such a position and instead suggest that problems that manifest themselves in, for example, the school belong to the school and should be handled there. Education systems normally have two commissions: the first is educational, while the second is to promote social development. When a child's behavior is experienced as disturbing in the classroom, this can be perceived – by definition – as a signal that the child might need special support to develop her social skills. It also seems permissible to reason that when specific skills are identified as lacking in a specific context, then that lack is perhaps best addressed in that context. MM is a specialized model designed for just such a purpose.

CMs were created to meet the challenge noted above: bound together through a mutual responsibility for the same child, one system (the school) experienced that they had a problem while the other system (the family) often said that they had none. If we were to have a goal to hold the communication lines open between them, then we would need a narrative that was not only acceptable to both parts but also could motivate and support the idea that they should meet and talk with each other.

24.3 Two Sets of Theories, Two Interventions, One System Perspective

One of the fundamental teachings of the systems perspective is that everything is in some way connected. The family and the school can be thought of as two interconnected sub-systems whose function is important for a larger system of which they are a part – the state. Both sub-systems are charged by the state as being responsible for (among other things) the education and upbringing of children. This means that the ways in which both sub-systems interpret and carry out their commission will have a defining effect on how they perceive the nature and functioning of the other. If, for example, the family considers school to be relatively unimportant or the school perceives the family to be subversive in relation to the school's commission, then achieving mutual support and trust between the two systems might be difficult. This perspective provided our starting point: that it was important to try and sustain communication between school and family and to encourage the possibility of establishing epistemic trust.

As a consequence of this analysis, it was decided that two different kinds of interventions were required. MM was a concrete, practical method which teachers could implement in their classroom. MM could also be offered to the family in those cases where the parents experienced that they also had difficulties. CMs were designed to create a social forum in which members from the school and the family could meet and talk.

24.3.1 Marte Meo (MM)

There were a number of reasons for choosing MM. Firstly, the coordinator of the project was qualified as a practitioner of and supervisor for MM. Secondly, the method had already been introduced in the area chosen for the project, so that a number of practitioners were available from the start. Thirdly, there was an established training program available.

MM is a video-based method founded by Maria Aarts (2008). The basic intervention is structured in the following way: firstly, the teacher (or parent) identifies and defines their problem and goals in relation to the child; secondly, a brief interaction (5–10 min) between the caretaker and child in the classroom/home is filmed (we shall use "caretaker" as a generic term for parent or teacher when specification is not important); the MM practitioner then analyzes and edits the film using MM principles; the edited film is reviewed together with the caretaker; the caretaker is then given specific homework to test in interaction with the child – and the sequence is then repeated.

The heart of MM is to identify the child's need of developmental support as observed in the filmed interaction between her and the caretaker and then to identify what kind of response from the caretaker could be helpful in meeting the child's needs in just those situations that are difficult for them both – and such responses are also selected from the film. Finally, the MM practitioner and the caretaker explore together to see if and how using such different behavior might be of benefit.

MM can be classified as a "normative" model in that it identifies principles that are claimed to be effective in supporting the psychosocial development of the child. While it places responsibility on the caretaker, it also shows that she is often in possession of the relevant skills and that the real challenge is how to contextualize them – i.e., of when and where to use them. The heart of the method is the microanalysis of the filmed interaction between caretaker and child which are edited by the MM practitioner and then reviewed together with the caretaker (Wirtberg et al., 2013). The model is used in many countries in Europe as well as in Australia and India and appears to be able to adapt to different cultures.

In constructing the MM section of the manual, we took care not only to describe the practical steps but also to attach them to a broader theoretical base. We considered it important to connect such a "hands-on" model to the wider field, showing where it can be anchored with communication theory, systems perspective, developmental psychology, attachment theory, affect theory, and so on. The manual is then two books in one, with the theoretical considerations clearly separated from the practical steps but inserted at relevant points.

Before starting with MM, it is important to discuss the interests and goals of the caretaker, checking out not only if they are willing to invest their time to try and help the child but also if they believe that they can help the child. This applies to both teacher and parent: so, for example, those parents who did not experience their child's behavior as problematic could normally see no point in receiving treatment. Of importance here is the affirmation of the parent's experience: they were always offered the opportunity to participate in MM, but if they did not wish to do so, their refusal was considered a natural and logical response. This fits with common factors considerations, in particularly the establishment of an alliance (Fife et al., 2014; Shick Tryon et al., 2019; Wampold & Imel, 2015). Another issue that was important to clarify was that even if the parents did not themselves wish MM, could they permit the teacher to get help in order to better support their child in her classroom. In almost all cases, as soon as the parents understood that their child was not being scapegoated and that the goal was for the teacher to get help, they not only accepted the plan but also thought it a good one.

24.3.2 Coordination Meetings (CMs)

While MM may be thought of as a normative and pedagogic model, aimed at supporting the caretaker-child relationship to help the child to learn new psychosocial skills, the theory and purpose behind CMs are very different. In clear contrast, there is no goal of achieving any specific change. There is no intention of delivering any form of treatment at all. There were two major goals: firstly, to maintain the lines of communication between the school and the family while supporting the integrity of both systems and secondly, to ensure that the focus of the meetings remains firmly on the issue of what is the the child's need of developmental support and how it can be met. Systemic practitioners are aware of how conflicts influence relationships. One rule of thumb reflects the observation that the more positive family members experience their relationships, the less conflicts there tend to be concerning the exercise of power. Conversely, when conflicts concerning the exercise of power are frequent, the poorer the members experience the quality of their relationships (Gottman & DeClaire, 2001). In other words, a relationship based on cooperation is generally experienced as being more satisfying than one based on coercion.

The reciprocal power relationship between school and family is not equal, just as the power relationship between adults and children is not. This is often most apparent when relationships break down and conflicts emerge. As noted above, the structural/functional perspective suggests that when the executive aspects of a system work in a mutually satisfying way (i.e., in a way that is experienced as beneficial for all parts of the system), then there will be less of a tendency to question their application. Translated into everyday practice, this implies that if the teacher and the parents generally share the same values and share the same general worldview and each have trust in the other's way to execute their responsibilities, then the child will presumably experience little dissonance in her nexus role connecting the two systems. It also means that the parents and the teacher will be more likely to achieve a working alliance. The working alliance is here thought of as possessing three elements: (1) a relational aspect, which is a function of how all participants experience to what degree they are accepted and respected by the other; (2) a task-related aspect which is a function of how well the participants are able to agree on both the starting point (present state) and the goal (desired state) of the intervention; and (3) how well all parts agree on the means that are to be used to try and achieve the goal (Friedlander et al., 2019). Thus, in the CMs, from the first meeting, it is expected that both teachers and parents will be able to agree about the goals of the intervention in the school. In practice, this means formalizing and affirming the commission (problems and goals) as specified and desired by the teacher(s).

In order to facilitate working alliances, we assumed a need for a third party who is defined as neutral in relation to both systems. Neutrality is conceived of as being equally curious about and affirming of every participant's narrative concerning themselves and others, similar to the concept of "multidirectional partiality" (Boszormenyi-Nagy & Spark, 1973). Again, practitioners trained in a systemic approach are aware of the importance of neutrality in working with group conflict. To define the CMs as neutral from the beginning was to establish the identities of the meetings themselves and that of the CM coordinator. The formal role of the CM was to keep the parents advised of the work of the teachers and the progress of that work and to invite the parents to ask questions or offer advice. They could also share their experience of being parents. At the same time, it was an opportunity for the teachers to report what they were doing and possibly even show a film of their work if they so wished. The "identity narrative" of the CMs as communicated to the parents can be summarized in the following way: "In school, the teachers experience that they needed help in order to support your child and they have applied for that help from the school health team. You have offered your consent to this and we would like you to come to the CMs to follow its progress and discuss it. You may stop the work at any time if you think it is not appropriate."

The role of the meeting coordinator was defined as a facilitator for communication. Her primary job was to affirm the narratives presented by both the school and the parents within the context of the meeting. In order to do this process skills are needed. For this reason, it was decided that the coordinator should be trained in systemic practice. Affirming and protecting the narratives of both the parents and the teachers simultaneously can be a challenging task, especially if there is potential for conflict. The manual specifies that the coordinator should avoid a problem-solving stance and instead maintain a neutral and curious position. So, for example, if a teacher questioned a statement made by a parent (or vice versa), the coordinator would simply affirm the question and then encourage exploration of its meaning and intention. The teacher (or vice versa) would then simply be asked to reflect on what was being communicated, not if they agreed or wanted to refute the statement. The guiding principle was that the teacher and parents were present at the meeting in order to inform each other rather than to argue or to convince. This helps the coordinator to avoid becoming triangulated in any conflict and instead focus both on supporting parallel and different narratives and on the possible creation of new ones (Bowen, 1976; Minuchin, 1974; Rhoades, 2008).

Such a position is central to the language system and open dialogue perspectives and other methods that are based on the use of reflection (Anderson & Goolishian, 1992; Andersen, 1995; Seikkula et al., 2003). This approach could also provide a clear structure for supporting all members. For example, some parents could feel that they were inferior to or of lower status than the teacher – they might for example have had personal difficulties connected to their own school time or might feel that the education of the teacher in some way created a disadvantage for them. On the other hand, some teachers might be nervous in meeting the parents and discussing their problem with their child's behavior and be afraid that they could lose professional status by being open.

24.4 Differences, Information, and Development

While the following discussion is drawn mainly from psychotherapy, we believe it has a great deal of relevance for most planned psychosocial interventions. In our attempts to understand ourselves, we have created three major scientific domains – biology, psychology, and sociology – each of which examines the world from a specific perspective. Psychotherapy is isomorphic to the parent field of the human sciences in that it contains many different models, each of which examines people and their contexts from specific theoretical positions. It is worthwhile remembering perhaps that the theories and the knowledge that the different perspectives generate are seldom competitive in themselves – it is rather people who compete. Generally, in the history and philosophy of science, ideas are thought of as competing only when they attempt to describe a single, specific phenomenon in noncompatible ways. Such differences are usually resolved over time by empirically testing different propositions that the ideas themselves include and generate.

An intervention will usually target one or more of the three human domains, but its success or failure will always be influenced to some unknown degree by all three of them. In psychotherapy, the study of common factors suggests that up to 50% of the outcome effects of any given intervention may be the result of nontherapeutic factors (Wampold & Imel, 2015). A purely psychological intervention will inevitably be influenced by biological and sociological factors and so on. While we are not usually in a position which allows us to tease out the precise ways in which the three domains reciprocally influence each other, we are well aware at a general level that they do so.

Of the two models used, MM is part of a larger video-feedback tradition (Balldin et al., 2018) and is of particular practical value in working with younger children, protecting them from participating directly in a treatment that might generate discomfort for them and instead focusing on helping the caregiver to generate new strategies for helping the child. CMs were developed out of three theoretical models: a system perspective (Petitt, 2016), a structural/functional concept (Minuchin,

1974), and a linguistic systems approach (Anderson & Goolishian, 1988). One set of assumptions that can be derived from these three theories is that facilitating and supporting communication within and between two systems should increase the possibility of cooperation and reduce stress factors. From a structural perspective, supporting the structural integrity of the two systems – in particular the parent's role in the family and the teacher's role in the classroom – predicted that the child might suffer less dissonance in her nexus position.

We see no inherent difficulties in applying different models in the same systemic intervention. The world is complex, and sometimes one specific intervention will not be enough.

24.5 Research Results

The MAC intervention has been tested in two different effectiveness trials, in "real world" settings (Axberg et al., 2006; Balldin et al., 2019). The first trial had a quasi-experimental design with a nonrandomized comparison group that received services as usual (SAU) – the usual intervention offered in the given child's ordinary school settings. The aim of the first study was to develop and evaluate the effectiveness of the MAC intervention as a tool for early detection and intervention in 4–12-year-old children with externalizing behavior. The results of the first study were promising and encouraging. Assessments were made before and 2 years after the intervention. For the parents, a statistically significant decrease in those symptoms closely related to children's externalizing behavior was found. A similar finding was noted from teachers' ratings in the MAC group ($N = 33$). The measures used were two instruments from the Achenbach System of Empirically Based Assessment family of instruments (Achenbach & Rescorla, 2001), namely, The Child Behaviour Checklist (CBCL) and the Teacher's Report Form (TRF). In addition, Conners' Parents Rating Scale (CPRS) (Conners, 1973; Goyette et al., 1978) and Conners' Teacher Rating Scale (CTRS) (Conners, 1969) were used. The pre- and post-effect sizes were in the medium and large range, following Cohen's operationally defined values for small (0.20), medium (0.50), and large (0.80) effect sizes (Cohen, 1992). In addition, a clinically significant change was found in 50–54% of the children – the proportion of children who had a pre- and post-improvement exceeding 30% (Webster-Stratton et al., 1989) according to parents' and teachers' ratings. No significant pre- and post-changes were found on the parents' ratings in the comparison group ($N = 16$), and the effect sizes were close to zero. A clinically significant decrease in parents' ratings was found in 23–33%. Teacher ratings had to be dropped in the comparison group since some of the schools were disinclined to allow their teachers to fill in the different measures because it took too much time from their regular work.

Even if the results were promising, they should be taken cautiously due to limitations in the study. However, one incidental result that is of interest was that there were no dropouts in the intervention group, which is remarkable since dropout rates from interventions directed at children displaying externalizing behavior problems and their parents are usually as high as 45–65% (Chacko et al., 2016; Gould et al., 1985; Lai et al., 1997).

The second trial was a randomized controlled trial (RCT). The aim of the study was to compare the manualized MAC intervention with SAU among 3–12-year-old children displaying externalizing behavior problems or difficulties in social interaction in school as defined by their teachers. Besides using a more rigorous research design, the trial was conducted in four separate municipalities different from that where the intervention was first developed and tested. The intervention developers were involved in the research team and in the training and supervision of the professionals who conducted the intervention, but not directly in the intervention itself. Primary outcome variables were derived from teachers' ratings of children's externalizing behavior. The measures used were the TRF and the Sutter-Eyberg Student Behaviour Inventory – Revised (SESBI-R) (Eyberg & Pincus, 1999). Assessments were made before the intervention started (baseline) and 8 months post-baseline. Within-group differences were analyzed for the MAC ($N = 47$) and the SAU ($N = 44$) groups, respectively. There was a statistically significant decrease (effect sizes small to medium) in the former group but only on the SESBI-R in the latter (effect size was small). Between-group difference analysis revealed a statistically significant difference in outcomes between the groups in favor of MAC. To assess clinically significant change, the Reliable Change Index (RCI) was used (Jacobson & Truax, 1991). The RCI makes it possible to assess change at an individual level. Approximately 41–57% of the children in the MAC group displayed a significant positive change according to the teachers' reports derived from the different measures. In the SAU group, a positive change was reported for 25–39% of the children. The parents' reports showed a statistically significant decrease in externalizing behavior problems in four out of six variables, while a statistically significant change was found in only one of the variables in the SAU group. The effect sizes were mainly small, and there was no statistically significant difference between the groups. The dropout rate was also very low (10%) in the second study. No one dropped out from the intervention per se, but attrition was due to such issues as withdrawal of consent (though not from the intervention), replacement of teachers, and change of school or municipality.

In a master's thesis titled "Coordination meetings – pure luxury," Tarnow Håkansson and Hansson (2015) explored teachers' and parents' experience of the CMs. The approach used was Inductive thematic analysis (Braun & Clarke, 2006). The analysis resulted in the presentation of four main themes. Two of these themes were called, "From silent and cautious to open and relaxed" and "Leadership designed to include everyone." The first theme refers to how participants in the CMs describe how they progressed from being silent and cautious participants in the beginning to gradually become more open and relaxed. This process was influenced by two factors: firstly, if the teachers and parents had a good relationship before the intervention began and secondly, if the coordinator was able to maintain a respectful and non-blaming style throughout the meetings.

The second theme was found in the way the informants described how the coordinator continually offered support to both parents and teachers, taking the lead in creating a climate and a structure which meant that everyone's voice was heard.

The authors conclude from their analysis of the interviews that the CMs seem to be necessary in the sense that they facilitate communication and strengthen the link between home and school. In another study that investigated teachers' experience of receiving Marte Meo supervision (Carlsson & Thorp, 2013), the teachers stressed the importance of getting concrete support that focused on their interaction with the pupils, while at the same time being helped to become more aware of the child's need of support in everyday situations. They also noted the positive effects Marte Meo supervision had in creating a learning environment for both teachers and pupils and of how discussing and practicing the new skills helped them to develop their school team.

24.6 Notes on Implementation

One special aspect of MAC is that it is implemented simultaneously in different sovereign domains such as the school, the family, and even sometimes the social services. In these three domains, influential contextual factors such as law, praxis, leadership, responsibility, training, and history are often very different. In implementing MAC, meticulous care has to be taken to meet and respect the specific prerequisites of each domain. In addition to cooperating as part of the "school-home system," representatives of the different domains have to preserve the integrity of their own system. One simple example: since it is the headmaster who is formally responsible for all decisions concerning what may or may not happen within her organization, it is she who decided how to seek consent from the parents in any given class or group so that filming could take place. Typically, this was done by informing everyone concerned that filming was designed to improve the quality of teaching and inviting anyone who had questions or objections to contact the school to discuss the issue. Another example was when the social services provided Marte Meo therapists for working in the home: the therapists informed the families of the nature of their own professional rules and responsibilities. Additionally, within the project the school and the social services always collaborate with a specific family in which the parents are legally responsible for their children – and who can terminate the intervention at any point without having to provide any explanation.

Both the MAC intervention and its implementation involve a series of processes which are sensitive because they are carried out within two or three very different social systems. In the school, for example, attention has to be paid to the organizational demands involved in teaching and learning. Many teachers experience their work as stressful, so the introduction, implementation, and operation of a new routine such as MAC must be done in such a way that it is not experienced as yet another source of stress.

To better the chances of successful implementation and operation, attention has to be paid to the fit between staff and the nature of the project. They will need appropriate training (pre- and ongoing), coaching, and consultation, which also is subject to an organizational level (Fixsen et al., 2005). In addition, communities and consumers should be fully informed and involved in the selection and evaluation of programs and practices. Finally on a societal level, it is important that the state and its funding systems, policies, and regulations permit an environment that facilitates and promotes the implementation of the intervention (Fixsen et al., 2005). The implementation process and the nature and quality of the intervention are two distinctly separate issues, existing independently each from the other (Fixsen et al., 2009). However, the implementation process is a strong determinant of how well the intervention will succeed. It is possible to conclude that no intervention is better than its implementation – that a high-quality intervention might be of little use when badly implemented. An example of this is given by Wilson and Lipsey (2007) in their meta-analysis of school-based interventions for aggressive and disruptive behavior. They recommend that due to the small differences in effects between different evidence-based interventions, it is better to choose the intervention that has the best chance to be implemented properly in the identified setting. One of the reasons for choosing MM as the specific method in the MAC intervention was that it was already being used in some schools and was appreciated by the specially trained teachers who implemented it.

24.7 Some Final Reflections

Hollis (2002) suggested that it would be practically impossible to write a manual for social work, as every other sentence would have to read, "Use your own judgement." In many ways the same can be said of all intervention manuals: whoever implements a given intervention must continually adapt the principles and spirit of the manual to the unique client she has before her. However, to do research, there must be some form of order in line with the principle of ceteris paribus (all things being equal) – the researcher must try to control as many variables as possible. This inevitably creates a form of tension between being faithful to the manual (fidelity) and responsive to the client (empathy, alliance, etc.). This is interesting as there is little evidence as yet to support the idea that a high degree of fidelity significantly improves outcomes (Wampold & Imel, 2015; Collyer et al., 2019).

However, if one wishes to test one specific method rather than, for example, one specific therapist, there is little choice. Manuals also have other values: the MAC manual is available to everyone and thus offers the possibility of transparency – this is how we think, and why, and this is what we do, and why. In complex social settings such as the one identified here, a manual also offers a common map or guide which offers specific pathways to everyone – it can possess a unifying effect.

Another value of a manual is that, when it has been tested, it offers credibility to a certain specific intervention, often in a specific kind of context. Evidence-based or evidence-supported interventions are surely of value to the practitioners in the field – no one should have to recreate the wheel in every new situation. Finally, MAC shows the possibility of mixing models from different disciplines in the service of the client.

References

Aarts, M. (2008). *Marie meo: Basic manual* (2nd ed.). Aarts Production.
Achenbach, T. M., & Rescorla, L. A. (2001). *Manual for the ASEBA school-age forms & profiles*. University of Vermont.
Andersen, T. (1995). Reflecting processes; acts of informing and forming: You can borrow my eyes, but you must not take them away from me! In S. Friedman (Ed.), *The reflecting team in action, collaborative practice in family therapy* (pp. 11–37). Guilford Press.
Anderson, H. (1997). *Conversation, Language and Possibilities: A Postmodern Approach to Therapy*. Basic Books.
Anderson, H., & Goolishian, H. (1992). The client is the expert: A not-knowing approach to therapy. In S. McNamee & K. J. Gergen (Eds.), *Therapy as social construction*. Sage.
Anderson, H., & Goolishian, H. A. (1988). Human systems as linguistic systems: Preliminary and evolving ideas about the implications for clinical theory. *Family Process, 27*, 371–393.
Aponte, H. J. (1976). The family-school interview: An eco-structural approach. *Family Process, 15*, 303–311.
Axberg, U., Hansson, K., Broberg, A. G., & Wirtberg, I. (2006). The development of a systemic school-based intervention: Marte Meo and Coordination Meetings. *Family Process, 45*, 375–389.
Balldin, S., Bergström, M., Wirtberg, I., & Axberg, U. (2019). Marte Meo & Coordination Meetings (MAC): A systemic school-based video feedback intervention – A randomized controlled trial. *Child and Adolescent Social Work Journal, 36*, 537–548.
Balldin, S., Fisher, P. A., & Wirtberg, I. (2018). Video feedback intervention with children: A systematic review. *Research on Social Work Practice, 28*(6), 682–695.
Bateson, G. (1979). *Mind and nature: A necessary unity*. Fontana.
Boszormenyi-Nagy, I., & Spark, G. M. (1973). *Invisible loyalties: Reciprocity in intergenerational therapy*. Harper & Row.
Bowen, M. (1976). Theory in the practice of psychotherapy. In M. Bowen (Ed.), *Family therapy in clinical practice* (pp. 337–387). Jason Aronson.
Braun, V., & Clarke, V. (2006). Using thematic analysis in psychology. *Qualitative Research in Psychology, 3*, 77–101.
Carlsson, I. & Thorp, H. (2013). *Pedagogers uppfattning av barn i behov av särskilt stöd och Marte Meo handledning*. Examensarbetet vid lärarutbildning vid Högskolan i Skövde [Teachers' conceptions of children with special needs and Marte Meo supervision. Examination as part of teacher training at Skövde College of Further Education]. University of Skövde.
Chacko, A., Jensen, S. A., Lowry, L. S., Cornwell, M., Chimklis, A., Chan, E., & Pulgarin, B. (2016). Engagement in behavioral parent training: Review of the literature and implications for practice. *Clinical Child and Family Psychology Review, 19*, 204–2015.
Cohen, J. (1992). A power primer. *Psychological Bulletin, 112*, 155–159.
Collyer, H., Eisler, I., & Woolgar, M. (2019). Systematic literature review and meta-analysis of the relationship between adherence, competence and outcome in psychotherapy for children and adolescents. *European Child and Adolescent Psychiatry*. https://doi.org/10.1007/s00787-018-1265-2
Conners, K. C. (1969). A teacher rating scale for use in drugs studies with children. *American Journal of Psychiatry, 126*, 884–888.

Conners, K. C. (1973). Rating scales for use in drug studies with children. *Psychopharmacology of Children, 9*, 24–29.

Eyberg, S. M., & Pincus, D. (1999). *ECBI Eyberg Child Behavior Inventory and SESBI-R Sutter-Eyberg Student Behavior Inventory: Revised professional manual*. Psychological Assessment Resources.

Fife, S. T., Whiting, J. B., Bradford, K., & Davis, S. (2014). The therapeutic pyramid: A common factors synthesis of techniques, alliance, and way of being. *Journal of Marital & Family Therapy, 1*, 20–33.

Fixsen, D. L., Blase, K. A., Naoom, S. F., & Wallace, F. (2009). Core implementation components. *Research on Social Work Practice, 19*, 531–540.

Fixsen, D. L., Naoom, S. F., Blasé, K. A., Friedman, R. M., & Wallace, F. (2005). *Implementation research: A synthesis of the literature*. University of South Florida.

Fonagy, P., & Allison, E. (2014). The role of mentalizing and epistemic trust in the therapeutic relationship. *Psychotherapy, 51*(3), 372–380.

Friedlander, M. L., Escudero, V., Welmers-van de Poll, M. J., & Heatherington, L. (2019). Alliances in couple and family therapy. In J. C. Norcross & M. J. Lambert (Eds.), *Psychotherapy relations that work. Vol. 1: Evidence-based therapist contributions*. Oxford University Press.

Gottman, J. M., & DeClaire, J. (2001). *The relationship cure: A 5 step guide to strengthen your marriage, family and friendships*. Three Rivers Press.

Gould, M. S., Shaffer, D., & Kaplan, D. (1985). The characteristics of dropouts from a child psychiatric clinic. *Journal of the American Academy of Child Psychiatry, 24*, 316–328.

Goyette, C. H., Conners, K. C., & Ulrich, R. F. (1978). Normative data on revised Conners Parent and Teacher Rating Scales. *Journal of Abnormal Child Psychiatry, 6*, 221–236.

Hollis, M. (2002). *The philosophy of social science: An introduction* (Rev. ed.). Cambridge University Press.

Jacobson, N. S., & Truax, P. (1991). Clinical significance: A statistical approach to defining meaningful change in psychotherapy research. *Journal of Consulting and Clinical Psychology, 59*, 12–19.

Lai, K. Y., Chan, T. S., Pang, A. H., & Wong, C. K. (1997). Dropping out from child psychiatric treatment: Reasons and outcome. *International Journal of Social Psychiatry, 43*, 223–229.

Luhmann, N. (2002). *Einführung in die Systemtheorie*. Carl-Auer-Systeme Verlag. English edition: Luhmann, N. (2013). *Introduction to systems theory* (Trans. Gilgen, P.). Cambridge: Polity Press.

Maruyama, M. (1963). The second cybernetics: Deviation-amplifying mutual causal processes. *American Scientist, 52*, 164–179.

McCarthy, I. C., & Byrne, N. (2008). A fifth province approach to intra-cultural issues in an Irish context. In M. McGoldrick & K. Hardy (Eds.), *Revisioning family therapy: Race, class, culture and gender in clinical practice* (2nd ed.). Guilford Press.

Minuchin, S. (1974). *Families and family therapy*. Harvard University Press.

Petitt, B. (2016). *System, context and psychotherapy*. Create Space.

Rhoades, K. A. (2008). Children's responses to interparental conflict: A meta-analysis of their associations with adjustment. *Child Development, 6*, 1942–1956.

Seikkula, J., Arnkil, T. E., & Eriksson, E. (2003). Post-modern society and social networks: Open and anticipated dialogues in network meetings. *Family Process, 42*, 185–203.

Shick Tryon, G., Birch, S. E., & Verkuilen, J. (2019). Goal consensus and collaboration. In J. C. Norcross & M. J. Lambert (Eds.), *Psychotherapy relations that work. Vol. 1: Evidence-based therapist contributions*. Oxford University Press.

Skyttner, L. (2005). *General systems theory: Problems, perspectives, practice* (2nd ed.). World Scientific.

Tarnow Håkansson, P., & Hansson, A. (2015). *Samordningssamtal, en ren lyx. Föräldrars och pedagogers upplevelser av samordningssamtal inom interventionsmodellen Marte Meo och Samordningssamtal*. Göteborg: Master's thesis, University of Göteborg, Department of

Psychology. [Coordination meetings, a pure luxury. Parents' and teachers' experience of coordination meetings in the intervention "Marte Meo and Coordination Meetings (MAC)"].

Thayer, L. (1972). Communication systems. In E. Laszlo (Ed.), *The relevance of general systems theory*. George Brazillier.

Wampold, B. E., & Imel, Z. E. (2015). *The great psychotherapy debate: The evidence for what makes psychotherapy work*. Routledge.

Webster-Stratton, C., Hollinsworth, T., & Kolpacoff, M. (1989). The long-term effectiveness and clinical significance of three cost-effective training programmes for families with conduct-problem children. *Journal of Consulting and Clinical Psychology, 57*, 550–553.

Wilson, S. J., & Lipsey, M. W. (2007). School-based interventions for aggressive and disruptive behavior: Update of a meta-analysis. *American Journal of Preventive Medicine, 33*(Supplement 2), 130–143.

Wirtberg, I. (2004). Fält och forskning och om konsten att sam-värka. Samordning och Marte Meo som redskap att hjälpa barn som uppvisar samspelssvårigheter i skolan. *Psykisk Hälsa* (1), 43–56. [Field and research and the art of working together. Coordination and Marte Meo as tools to help children who reveal difficulties with social skills in school].

Wirtberg, I., & Axberg, U. (2004). *Marte Meo and collaboration meetings. The development of a school-based intervention*. Paper presented at the 5th European congress of family therapy and systemic practice, Berlin.

Wirtberg, I., Petitt, B., & Axberg, U. (2013). *Marte Meo and coordination meetings: MAC. Cooperating to support children's development*. Palmkrons.

Part IV
Training as a Basis for Development of Manuals and a Context for Their Application

1.1 Introduction

Across the world, vast differences still exist on how best to teach psychotherapy. Many international associations provide guidelines for educating psychotherapists and family therapists (e.g., World Council for Psychotherapy, International Family Therapy Association, Asian Academy of Family Therapy, European Family Therapy Association (EFTA), American Family Therapy Association, American Association for Marriage and Family Therapy), and yet the rules to become a psychotherapist differ significantly.

In some contexts, the work of psychotherapy can only be done by a psychologist or physician with specific specialization. In others, one can enter the field of psychotherapy with any degree. For some, psychotherapy is just a magic trick; for others, it is science. The European Psychotherapy Act was adopted from the European Association of Psychotherapy (EAP) Governing Board on April 30, 2018. This Act states that *psychotherapy* is an independent profession from psychology, psychiatry, and counselling. A psychotherapist usually has a graduate degree followed by a professional highly specialized training. EAP promotes the recognition of common standards of training. The same is done, speaking specifically about systemic therapy and family therapy, by EFTA. Nevertheless, each country has its own legislation, and perhaps the Italian law for psychotherapy is one of the oldest and asks more requirements.

In Italy, the 1989 "Law Number 56" provided a specific frame or the teaching of psychotherapy. A decade later, the "Regulation D.M. 11712 n.509" mandated precise rules to activate training courses of psychotherapy. This led to 344 Italian schools being recognized as authorized to teach psychotherapy. Only those with a degree in psychology or in medicine are allowed to attend the training; no other degrees can obtain the specialization in psychotherapy. This regulation has practical implications. To work in the national health system, the Italian government requires psychologists to have the title of psychotherapists. Some of the requirements include the following: (a) during the 4-year curriculum, there must be at least 2000 hours;

(b) the internship must have a minimum of 600 hours; (c) trainees must be exposed to theory which should be about 30% of the total curriculum and decreasing in number of hours from the first to the fourth year; and (d) trainees exposition to clinical practice must be about 70% of the curriculum and increasing from the first to the fourth year. One of the key requirements is that each school must have its own manual and each year must report to the Minister of Education, University, and Research (MIUR) the results obtained. During 2020, the MIUR licensed a new digitalized protocol to help schools verify monthly if they are following the prescribed rules and giving specific procedures to adhere to during the Covid-19 pandemic. The MUIR gave all the schools 25 recommendations necessary to obtain the training approval during this time.

This processual guide to the manualization of the Italian schools of psychotherapy allows students coming from different roots of psychotherapy to have the same amount of theory, practice, and internship. While all Italian schools must follow the national requirements, they can include additional training to further bolster the skills of psychotherapists. For example, the Istituto di Psicoterapia Sistemica e Relazionale di Modena e Cesena (ISCRA) not only offers an excellent program that adheres to the government regulations but also requires a solid curriculum in research. Camillo Loriedo in this section provides an excellent example of how another school enacts the Italian government's regulations.

Obviously, this handbook aims to demonstrate that only evidence-based manualized training could accomplish the dramatic task to create a professional able to help people in their daily relational, affective, personal-family-mental-based problems. Not easy...but we will succeed. From Freud to now, we have travelled a long and fruitful trip. In this part of the book which focuses on the use of manuals in training, the reader should understand the differences and the similarities in preparation that systemic trainees will meet on their way to become psychotherapists. The following section will introduce the reader to a fantastic forest of knowledge, and experiences full of possibilities, of creativity but with solid reference to the science in the training of systemic clinicians through processual manualization.

Chapter 25
Image, Family, and Clinical Practice: Image and Family of Origin as Tools for Training the Family Therapist

Rodolfo de Bernart and Mauro Mariotti

25.1 Introduction

Rodolfo passed away on Monday, 18th of February 2019. We had been eagerly looking forward to the chapter he had planned for this Handbook, as well as many more years of collaboration. However, all of us have all been deprived of his

Dr. Rodolfo de Bernart 1947–2019 President of EFTA until his untimely death

R. de Bernart
Florence Family Therapy Institute, Florence, Italy

EFTA, Florence, Italy

M. Mariotti (✉)
Iscra Institute, Modena, Italy
e-mail: dottmauromariotti@gmail.com

© Springer Nature Switzerland AG 2021
M. Mariotti et al. (eds.), *Handbook of Systemic Approaches to Psychotherapy Manuals*, European Family Therapy Association Series,
https://doi.org/10.1007/978-3-030-73640-8_25

precious presence. In this chapter, we present the contributions he made to the systemic and relational field of family therapy. He was an incredible weaver, connecting family and systemic therapists of Asia, America, Australia, and Europe at the most important level. To include a greater number of international colleagues, he ensured that our journals had summaries written in Chinese, Japanese, and Russian. He was the master of using images, collages, movies, and metaphors as main tools for therapy. Always he reminded us that the brain builds 80% of its connections and ideas based on images. Beginning in the 1980s, he accepted and promoted collaborations among the various roots of systemic practices: the epistemologic, the strategic, and the structuralist. Furthermore, he was able to connect psychodynamic with attachment and systemic theory and promoted the fundamental relationship among the various scientific societies. Having risen to the presidency of most of those organizations testifies to his great capacity to create bonds and bridges, while avoiding barriers and fragmentations.

On Saturday, December 22nd of 2018, we, the editors, were emailing one another about this Handbook. Peter was saying to George "Just got this from Rodolfo so he is in action. He has been very supportive … publishing his work in Human Systems so maybe the invite should be a joint one…" As president of the European Family Therapy Association, he was inviting us to share our experience with manualization and the progress on gathering a wide representation of systemic therapists to contribute their work, at the Naples EFTA conference in the fall of 2019. In June of that year the three of us, Maria Borcsa and Rodolfo, had all planned to meet to discuss the Handbook. Of course while we met without Rodolfo, his lovely memory was still present.

Our (MM and RDB) friendship began around 1980; we shared a lot. Our Institutes were founded during the same period; we were the main organizers of the international conference "Children and their systems" in Rome. We invented and created the International Association of Systemic Mediators, AIMS, the major Italian organization of systemic and family mediation. We ran the European forum of mediation and worked together for 10 years for EFTA. At the end of the 1980s, we held the first training in Palermo with Umberta Telfener, Fabio Bassoli, and Camillo Loriedo. We shared thousands of mails to organize our agendas, working together in Italy, Europe, and America, where we ran conferences at the University of California, San Francisco, Harvard, and Columbia University. We founded and shared the direction of two journals: Maieutica and Mediazione familiare sistemica, which are still in circulation with more than 50 issues.

In 2009, he became the president of the European Association of Psychotherapy (EAP), taking the position from our dear Mony Elkaim, who we also lost in the Fall of 2020. Rodolfo's idea for his term of office was to keep the wisdom of people who worked for the EAP for many years and at the same time be open to new projects and developments. For him the most successful event during his presidency was the European Conference on the political and legal situation of psychotherapy in the European Union, where the EAP succeeded in bringing together psychotherapists and politicians from all of Europe to share their views.

Pertinent to this Handbook, Rodolfo, did considerable work to advocate for the principle of manualization! In fact during his presidency. The EAP Board approved a project to establish the Professional Competencies of a European Psychotherapist. This project set out to define and establish the professional competencies of a European psychotherapist, with the intention of allowing this project to act as a set of principles or guidelines for ministries of health; national associations of psychotherapists in various countries; other professional psychotherapy associations (often representing a modality or method of psychotherapy); psychotherapy training organizations; and all other individuals and associated bodies in relation to the professional practice of psychotherapy, in all its various forms, across Europe.

"We are now starting to develop the actual Core Competencies within a number of various 'Domains' – and we explain in detail exactly what these are on the website. We anticipate that much of this part of the work will be done through the spring and summer of 2011, and we will be posting these results up on the website over the next few weeks and months. We are now asking you for your feedback on this project and the details of these Core Competencies." *1 "Liquid Modernity": An Interview with Zygmunt Bauman Edited by Helga Hanks and Peter Stratton, Leeds Family Therapy and Research Centre, (LFTRC), U.K. and Rodolfo de Bernart, Istituto di Terapia Familiare di Firenze (ITFF), Italy; "Liquid Communication": An audiovisual stimulus prepared by Rodolfo de Bernart, Giuseppe Ruggiero and Daniela Ferrone.*

The collaboration with Peter had been also very useful both during the Efta meetings and in many other occasions: the collaboration with his journal *Human Systems,* sharing the TIC and EFTA adventures, and taking part in many conferences, among which I recall the one with Bauman. The opening session featured a videotaped interview with the renowned Polish sociologist Zygmunt Bauman who was based in Leeds in the UK. This was a collaborative venture which involved various colleagues including Allan Holmgren, Peter Stratton, Helga Hanks, Paolo Bertrando, Barbara Józefik, and Rodolfo de Bernart from three countries. Some were interviewers, some editors, and some brought audiovisual skills to bear on the material. The result was a provocative and intellectually stimulating opening presentation entitled "Liquid Modernity".

In addition, he fully embraced the systemic approach to revolutionize the field of medicine. On many occasions, he presented with George Saba, on the application of the biopsychosocial model to health and illness, the collaboration between systemic therapists and physicians and the need to train systemic physicians who can care for families in the context of their medical practice.

25.2 Rodolfo, EFTA, and the Need for Manuals

Rodolfo was the president of EFTA, the European Family Therapy Association. During his presidency the TIC (Training Institutes Chamber) wrote this manifesto that well represents the need we professionals have to promote Manuals as the best way to promote the family welfare:

> Welcome to the European Family Therapy Association Training Institutes Chamber (Efta-Tic). Why do we need a European Chamber of Training Institutes?

We have witnessed the field of family therapy in Europe evolve into a strong scientific modality encompassing increasing diversity in recent years. This process has contributed to the founding of a substantial number of family therapy training institutes. Many of these institutes are now members of EFTA-TIC-125 institutes in 28 countries. The prospect of promoting further enriching developments through the networking of institutes emerges. What are our challenges?

1. Legislation: Given the inevitable development of laws by national governments regarding the training and practice of psychotherapy, we need to develop a broad consensus on the European level, which respects the diversity and creativity of training in our field. We will then be in a strong position to negotiate.
2. Training in Training: The many diverse training approaches developed throughout Europe offer a major resource for experiential learning through professional and personal communication among trainers. We aim to create a process of interaction where we, as trainers, learn from each other and thereby contribute to the maturing of our profession of training as a whole.
3. Sharing Specialists' Expertise: Colleagues from European training institutes have developed high levels of expertise in specific areas of our field. We wish to organize regular events across Europe where the acquisition and sharing of this expertise will be enhanced.
4. Exchange of Students: Professional mobility throughout the EU will be enhanced through undertaking training in institutes in other European countries. We hope to coordinate a framework of exchange to facilitate students' experience through their participation in the training activities of other institutes.
5. Research: With current pressure for evidence-based practice and our own need to monitor the effectiveness of training programmes, it is crucial that we share evidence and, where possible, co-ordinate research efforts. Furthermore, an expanding and more diverse Europe increases our need for research in cross-cultural processes regarding family dynamics, therapy, and training.
6. Internet Newsletter: The access to information on the activities of the Chamber is of importance. Our web-pages (www.efta-tic.eu) are being developed to provide an ongoing forum for the sharing of ideas and experiences." (Newsletter EFTA europeanfamilytherapy.eu).

Rodolfo wrote books and hundreds of papers and chapters, and his contribution was seminal regarding the use of analogic tools in family therapy. I remember for instance his presentation in Brussels "New images for family therapy training." Or the seminar we ran together in Istanbul, "Images and words in family therapy", or the session I gave with him and Cristina Dobrowolski. They acted as a couple of clients, and I used the tridimensional genogram. He was so impressed by the instrument that he asked me to present the 3d genogram to his institute, where he told participants that the 3d genogram was one of the most challenging tools along with his photographic genogram.

The institute founded by Rodolfo and Cristina in December 1981 was so well manualized that from there sprang 30 different institutes. Now the AITF, the association he founded has in Italy 50 centres of systemic family therapy!

For the 30th anniversary of the foundation he wrote: "Dear friends and colleagues… Our program shows how our Institute is a kind of craft workshop that inherited from great Italians and non-Italian maestros new ways to do and teach family and relational psychotherapy. Some of our main 'assets', our original products such as the use of images, the liaison with psychodynamic and attachment theory are well known. The conference will develop around such keywords as **memory, desire, beauty, solidarity, time and future**."

During the conference Rodolfo presented the photographic genogram he developed and I, with Kyriaki Polichroni, and Alain Ackermans, tried to develop the keyword "desire".[1]

Many seminars have been held following his trip to the infinity. At Iscra, we were expected to run a seminar with him just a month after he had died. We decided to hold the seminar with one of his four children and all our staff; it was an unforgettable ceremony of celebration of the life after death. Maurizio Andolfi dedicated to his seminar to the loving memory of Rodolfo. Maurizio, presenting the conference, told to us: "we honor him through the images, a pathway for him to the clinic and teaching. We will present a video collage done through a careful research of his professional work as well his rich personal life." I have to say that I'm personally grateful to Maurizio who inspired me to take part in his next annual conference in July 2020 and certainly this will not be the same….

Among related publications, a must read has been written by his wife, Daniela Giommi, and Eugenio Roberto Giommi. In this book it is possible to have a full panorama of his production. In the first issue of Maieutica, the journal we jointly created in 1993, Rodolfo clearly emphasizes the importance to be creative as well as systematic. In this number he asserted: "Our story began during 1973. We were mental health workers joint in a research about family systems…two years later we decided to go to Rome for training with Maurizio Andolfi and Carmine Saccu, meanwhile working with families inside public services. We made seminars with Minuchin, Bowen, Haley, Madanes, la Perriere, Scheflen, Bolch, Zwerlin, Boscolo, Cecchin, Selvini, Boszormenyi-Nagy, Elkaim, Cancrini, Singer, Whitaker, Resnik, Ackermans, just to name some…." In a move that reflects Rodolfo's goal of bringing

---

[1] The photographic genogram (Del loewenthal ed- Phototherapy and theraèeutic photgraphy in a digital era (Routledge 2013).

communities together, Maeutica will now become the journal of CNSP, the society of societies of psychotherapy in Italy.

While there are many therapeutic approaches and methods of training, both systemic and otherwise, that Rodolfo found important to build connections, what is our main feature? are we different? how do we communicate what we share and what we differ on? and how do we communicate it to our trainees and students, so they are clear on what they are learning. This was important to Rodolfo and to me. So let us begin to reflect on the process of manualizing as it relates to training and to the multiplicity of approaches.

25.3 Common Ground and the Importance of Training

Our common ground is the systemic theory, the research on systems communication. Today we feel to be distant from the systemic-strategic approach and we love the study of the normal family from a sociological, structural, and analytic point of view. We consider three main roots of family therapy: systemic-strategic, psychoanalytical, and structural-experiential (Minuchin and Whitaker with a particular emphasis towards family history (trigenerational approach of Boszormenji-Nagy and Andolfi)). We are not used to working with strategic assets and we value more the therapeutic alliance, the relationship between family and individual and between them and the internal world of the person.

Our training underlines the great culture coming from the psychoanalytical studies on groups, and the true characteristic of our training model is the study of images that we use from the very beginning of the training.

The training is based on relational observation and on the evolution of the normal family, and the theoretical part is mixed with experiences that they have with images, movies, and analogic techniques.

A particular emphasis is to give to the family images through the use of movies or video or family pictures proposed by teachers to the students. The goal is to enlarge and deepen the idea of family history and to increase the knowledge the pupil has of his/her own history. To give to him/her the expertise as observer of his/her family and to understand and manage the analogic communication.

25.4 Training at Our Institutes

Our trainings are properly organized and manualized:

20% of the time is used to work with group relational exercises and activities.
20% is used to work on pupil and his/her family;
20% on theory, lectures, and supervision on the clinical work of the pupils;

40% is used for behind the mirror work, directly supervising pupils during the family session held by the institute.

We have many working tools: genograms, collages, videorecording, role playing, and so on.

This method allows the students to manage the systems theory by doing, using the relational approach for diagnosis, daily work, using the group as a learning tool.

Our training is based on the work on the person that we begin a year before in our PTR, the pretraining year. This allows the student as well as the teacher to know each other better and to start the training with the right motivation and knowledge.

The second year is the beginning of the training and only motivated and selected people enter the training. From this point and for the third and fourth year the clinical activity is the centre of the training.

Supervision and clinic being the two main activities held.

To be more clear, the following are what we expect from our students:

- to learn the use of the images,
- to learn the therapeutic relationship,
- how to use the self,
- how to relate with individuals inside the family,
- how to integrate differences in theory and approaches.

Students will follows many therapies during the training and they will defend their dissertation during and at the end of the process. They are strongly invited to connect with other realities in different regions and nations to enlarge their point of view. Recently we waived a net of our institutes opened by our past students in different towns: Treviso, Padova, Este, Parma, Siena, Lucca, La Spezia (now this net, called AITFF has 50 centres). At the International level ITFF is part of EFTA, recently born in Paris from the stem of European network, born in 1986 and in which three of our teachers were taking part."

Rodolfo remembers "I was also founding member during 1979 of the American Family Therapy Association" and we were together also in this occasion. He ended his presentation saying "When Mauro Mariotti and Fabio Bassoli proposed to us to share this adventure with the goal to publish the work of our pupils, we gladly accepted. We hope our students will get a push to write more. In fact a limit of our training, based on analogic, was the faible push to an active theorization" that is may be too much represented inside the Milan Model (my quote). "Finally, as systemics we believe we grew up through differences and we believe and hope that readers will use at best the evident difference between contributions from Modena and from Florence."

And actually it happened from 1993 to today. Maieutica grew up representing many Italian schools of psychotherapy and the last number of Maiutica is called le fil rouge…the wire that connects practice and theory.

A brief excerpt of the analogical tools: he collected 40 analogical tools and worked to let them be recognized and usable for all therapists. He was asserting that analogical systemic therapy was much more reliable, easy and effective than the so-called spoken therapies:

> Among the 40 techniques he considers the best analogic practices, we remember the genogram, the photographic genogram, the 3d genogram, the object letter, the heraldic shield, the videocollage, the collage, drawing the house, joint drawing, 10 line draw, the train trip, the pot of emotions, the 40 Matisse cards, the blind role playing, building a family, the family sculpture of the past, the present, the future and desired ones, the test art's images, the trilogue play etc.

Many of those techniques came from the work of pioneers, and his work had been to create some, to catologue and order others, to push us towards a creative manualization and order all those tools promoting in this way the easiest way to create a family therapy based on shared experiences. For us coming from the Milan root, used to the spoken world of therapy as he called us, the connection with him represented the way to create the DAN model that is presented in this book. A model in which the analogic, the digital, and the narrative are mixed to obtain the maximum effect with the minimum effort requested of the family.

Thanks Rodolfo. You are still with us.

25.5 Rodolfo—In His Own Words

We conclude this chapter with edited extracts from papers of 2008 in which Rodolfo describes his approach as it focusses on non-verbal channels. It describes the ways he has manualized the approach and the first phase of his research to validate it. These are edited versions of articles he wrote for *Human Systems* keeping his own words.

Image and Family of Origin as Tools for Training the Family Therapist
Rodolfo de Bernart & Cristina Dobrowolski
Istituto Di Terapia Familiare Di Firenze, Italy
Human Systems Volume 19, 2008. pp. 222–239

According to Daniel Stern the Implicit Relational Knowing (IRK) is Nonverbal, non symbolized, unnarrated, non conscious (unconscious but not repressed or removed). The vast Majority (80% maybe) of all we know about how to be with others (including the Transference) is implicit. So this part of communication heavily influences our relation with other people.

But the most important reason is that the verbal channel is too much saturated. We should use a non-verbal channel, which is less controlled by patients and can allow us to enter into the internal image of the family. A way to enter it is by using a metaphorical language (built through images). The power of metaphor stays clearly in her capacity to get to the affective component of the personality which normally is too much defended to be got. Memory and historical and cultural identity are preserved through images. Representation is the time-space, through which absent becomes present, not only through a magic evocation but also through a real substitution of the object. Another important element is that a human being has two types of intelligence: Holistic and Sequential. The first one is generic, not defined, global, simultaneous, and not sequential. The second one is analytic, structured, referential, and sequential. We used the first for centuries before the "invention" of the writing and reading (first phase). Then we developed the second in order to read. For this purpose, in fact, we need to see letter by letter, then word by word, then sentence by sentence, analytically. Only through this sequential intelligence can we read using the left brain (at least in the western world; of course in Eastern World things are sometimes different because there they use ideograms and use partially also the right brain). Since 500 years (after invention of Press) our Western world had an increasing prevalence of the sequential intelligence, because people learned more and more through reading (second phase), but for the past 10–20 years our children learned again, like before, more through seeing (TV, computer, movies, etc.) We can use here the distinction by Sartori between Homo sapiens and Homo videns. Homo sapiens learns by reading, decodificates signs, is auto-driven, and has immediate emotions. Homo videns learns by seeing, looks at images, is etherodriven, has immediate emotions, and uses simultaneous intelligence (holistic). This is another important reason to develop tools which use the non-verbal, visual channel in therapy.

The principal tools based on the use of images in family therapy and in training are photographic genograms, sculptures, conjoint family drawings, metaphorical objects, collages, art pictures, and films. We have already spoken about some of these techniques in other meetings (for example, the collages in the meeting of Barcelona and Photographic Genograms later in Glasgow Conference). So in the second part of the workshop in Rhodes we decided to describe the Conjoint Family Drawing and we have engaged the group in two practical exercises to make the participants experience how we use this technique and how we observe the dynamics of the family during the process of drawing to make hypotheses about family relations and functions.

In the Conjoint Family Drawing we make in fact two types of observations: static and dynamic observation. In the first one we include how participants choose the spaces, divide it and put the borders, include present and absent members, put distance and closeness, and give meanings and interpretations of the contents of the drawing. In the second one we include level of collaboration during the project, levels of participation during the making of the drawing, levels of sharing, erasing, and redrawing.

Observing the conjoint family drawing, we make symbolic interpretation of the drawing of each person, of the complete drawing and of the relation between drawing and final comments given by participants. But for us one of the most important aspects of the conjoint family drawing is opportunity to look at the family interactions in the "here and now" of the session and in the playful atmosphere, which does not arouse individual and family defences. So, we can note how people begin to draw, who follows and how, who touches and develops the same theme, who intervenes in other's drawing, who finishes the other's drawing, and who differentiates him/herself. We can also observe the degree of participation and avoidance of the individual members, how each one stops or increases his/her activity in drawing, and we have an idea of the closeness and exclusion of the members of the family through the position of the paper and on the paper itself, the movements of the persons, and the choice of a common theme or of different themes.

Comparing the results of the conjoint family drawing with the verbal information we have received from the family, we can often understand the differences between the level of consciousness the family has about some relations and the effective relations themselves. For example, the mother of a seven of years old boy had explained to us how she tried in every way to encourage her son to be independent from her and how disappointed she was by the behaviour of the father who refused to participate in the growth and education of the boy. During the conjoint family drawing we saw at least four times the mother stopping the work of the son, correcting him with decision and making with her body a kind of "wall" to avoid the father being able to enter in relation with the son.

The static observation was introduced by Bing in 1971, while we are responsible for introducing the Dynamic observation in reintroducing this technique in Family Therapy in Evaluation for Courts and in Family Mediation. Different contexts demand of course different ways of using the technique. For example, we used to discuss the meaning of the drawing with the whole family in therapy, we avoid that and discuss only with other expert in Court Evaluation, we discuss later only with parents without the children in Family Mediation. We have used different kinds of tools over time. Before, we used a paper support on a table. The need to videotape the entire procedure in order to observe the dynamic part made us move to a paper poster, then the need to allow changes through erasing and redrawing convinced us to move to a white erasable board.

During a CFD with a separated couple and a girl 12 years old, the mother was drawing in half of the white board three ducks, clearly representing the original, now separated, family: mother, father, and daughter. Father and daughter were drawing in the other half of the board. Father having drawn himself on a bench looking at the girl who was drawing herself with her dog. Both parents were remarried and had each a newborn son from their new marriages.

So, it was clear what the mother meant when she, invading the other half of the board, tried to draw a fourth small duck! The immediate reaction of the girl was to draw a vertical line (a border?), but also the mother reacted dramatically and quickly erasing the border and the small duck while saying "no, no, no…". All the sequence lasted more or less 15 s but was clear enough to help us understand many things about the relationship between girl and mother. These 15 s were indeed more important than the rest of the drawing and could be seen just because we allowed the possibility to erase and redraw, which could be observed only in the dynamic process not looking at the product drawn.

We hope these two examples will help our readers to understand the CFD tool, even if we are aware that writing on these procedures is a little contradictory. Images would help much more. We anyway trust in the capacity of using fantasy and the right brain (that is the Holistic intelligence) of our colleagues…

The final section of the paper, by Donata Millón, Raquel Negrete, & Rodolfo de Bernart (pp 228–238) presented results from a research project into the training based on Rodolfo's approach: "On the Development of the Accomplishment Skills of Relational Hypotheses During the Years of Training in Family Psychotherapy. A Cross-sectional Study in the Institute of Family Therapy of Florence."

In presenting this research they provide an indication of the structure of the manual:

> The present research aims at assessing the development process of the capacity of accomplishment of relational hypotheses during the training in Family Psychotherapy. The training is based on the Relational-Systemic model. We define the accomplishment of "relational hypotheses" as the capacity to carry out conjectures on how a family system works and to see the relations among the members.

The hypothesis of this study is that the capacity of accomplishing relational hypotheses varies throughout time: people with a greater number of years of formation should be able to make more trustworthy hypotheses. We have thought that carrying out accurate relational diagnoses can help to construct more focused therapeutic processes, which can increase therapeutic success in the clinical cases. During the complex process of accomplishment of the relational hypotheses, we have decided to limit ourselves to some aspects that we considered basic, on which we have developed the questionnaire of evaluation used in this investigation.

Training in the Institute of Family Therapy of Florence is structured in 4 years. Our sample consisted of 44 students distributed in the following way: 12 (27%) in the first year, 13 (29%) in the third and 19 (43%) in the fourth year, four trainees in training, and one supervisor. We have not been able to collect data from subjects of the second year. In order to carry out the work we availed of the collaboration of the students of the institute who attend the specialization courses. The selection of the students is based on their presence at the course on the day of the application of the questionnaire.

Instrument of evaluation: The questionnaire is made up of 11 items. We selected: family triangulations, mandates, circular patterns of behaviour, affective responsibility in the couple, alliances, separation from the extended family, adoption of cultural models in the family, parental roles of the children, and emotional relationships between siblings.

Here the authors presented data from the study, available in the original paper (De Bernart & Dobrowolski, 2008). They concluded that they have observed that there are no great nor significant differences between the levels of training in recognizing the types of relationship within the families. Only in some tactical missions, like the identification of the type of triangulation, the identification of the life cycle moment, the separation from the extended families, and the adoption of a cultural model, we remark some differences between the students of the first year and the rest of the groups, showing greater variability in the answers. According to these results we can claim that for 4 of the 11 items, trainees in the first year present a greater difficulty in answering, considering that greater variability in the answer is an index of greater difficulty. We indicated that the students of the third and fourth year do not show any significant differences in identifying the relational patterns and they do not display as well any significant difference compared to the trainers in training nor to the group of trainers-supervisor. We can conclude saying that data from the second year's training group will obviously improve our investigation. Our purpose is to add data also from more supervisors to be able to have more accurate results and coordinated comparisons.

References

De Bernart, R. (1990). Video Et Therapie Familiale, Bulletin De Psycologie, Tome Xliii, N.395, pp. 564–568.
De Bernart, R., & Dobrowolski, C. (2008). Image and family of origin as tools for training the family therapist. *Human Systems, 19*, 222–239.

Chapter 26
A Manualized Systemic Family Therapy Training Program

Camillo Loriedo

The idea of a manualized training program essentially came to my mind because of a state of necessity.

The Istituto Italiano di Psicoterapia Relazionale (IIPR) was approved in 1998 by the Italian Ministry of Education, University and Research in five different locations and with many faculties (around 60). Unfortunately, the expectation of having a unique training program shared by all the different venues of the Institute was certainly in the Ministry's indications, but even if using a common canvas the creativity of the faculty was so wide that, we were close to having 60 different interpretations of the general program.

In a strange way, at the same time, we received complaints because some teachers repeated themes already covered by others.

The first hypothesis was that, in order to have a unified program, we should decide to detail and clarify the theoretical premises inspiring the faculty interpretation of the training program.

Initially, the change did not consist only in carefully listing each different matter of the program, as the Ministry required, but included as well a detailed little map of the different topics to be covered by the teachers during their lessons.

Despite the expectation that the Faculty could protest a too restrictive organization of their teaching or of an imposed orthodoxy they did not like, we received considerable appreciation from the teachers for making the program more clear and helpful.

A positive response was received as well by the trainees, who gave us appreciative comments through the Training Evaluation Form (TEF), a survey students can

---

C. Loriedo (✉)
University of Rome, Rome, Italy

Istituto Italiano di Psicoterapia Relazionale, Rome, Italy
e-mail: camillo.loriedo@gmail.com

use to evaluate and comment on various aspects of the teaching activities at the end of each lesson.

The TEF responses also indicated a strong reduction in the amount of repetitions and overlapping of the teaching topics.

At this point, the students declared themselves as more satisfied with the teaching activities; their only remaining request was to have more time dedicated to the practical and experiential teaching.

The fact that psychotherapy trainees regularly complain about not having enough time dedicated to practical experience seems to be common among the great majority of the Institutes providing a psychotherapy training.

Although in the past 20 years our teachers received, at the beginning of every Academic Year, the recommendation to spend at the least half of their teaching time utilizing practical and experiential activities, this was not considered sufficient by the trainees.

My faith in self-correcting systems was stronger than the fear of receiving some heavy criticism. So, at this point I decided to bring a radical change to the training program and to introduce the *Practical Learning*, in our model that we defined *Systemic Experiential Model*.

The main inspiration came from Minuchin's book "The Craft of Family Therapy: Challenging Certainties" (Minuchin et al., 2014). In the Prologue to the book, the authors say:

> Currently, new practitioners in family therapy are trained in university settings, rather than in institutes. Learning comes from textbooks for classes that try to provide a wide foundation for the field, so that people have the knowledge designated as necessary by state licensing boards. The brunt of learning comes in the classroom rather than in the therapy room. Students are expected to digest a variety of approaches, and then are asked to use one or more of these theories as a guideline for their practice when they begin to see families.
>
> The current process represents a shift from an inductive mode of understanding to a deductive mode. It seems to us that the loss of an inductive process for becoming a family therapist has severe consequences for the quality of a student's work in the therapy room. For that reason, we have decided to write this book. We are promoting an inductive method of learning how to become a family therapist, and exploring through illustration, how learning comes from doing. (pp. ix–x)

The discovery that both the trainees and Minuchin agreed on the concept of giving to the inductive methods a central role in the Family Therapy training, was certainly tempting, and influential on the decision to return back, as Minuchin was suggesting, to the times in which practice was much more important than theories.

However, in the new project we did not decide to minimize the theoretical teaching. The theories, and particularly the Systems Theory, as well as the Complexity model and the Organization principles, as applied to Family Therapy, should be considered a derivation of the inductive knowledge acquired in the therapy room after more than 60 years of family therapy practice.

Perhaps, it is possible to explain why the inductive methods' abandonment did not allow anymore the return to the philosophy of doing if we try to apply the *Experiential Learning Cycle* proposed by Kolb (1984) to the development of the Family Therapy movement.

Describing the Experiential-Learning Cycle, Kolb considers the passage to the "Concrete Experience" as necessary to activate the "Reflective Observation," and then a new "Abstract Conceptualization" that should be tested in an "Active Experimentation."

Family Therapy began with a phase of Active Experimentation followed by a period of Concrete Experiences (the period of inductive methods emphasized by Minuchin). Then if the following Abstract Conceptualization does not proceed again toward the Active Experimentation, the Cycle stops and the new passage to the Concrete Experiences is not allowed (see Fig. 26.1).

On basis of this theory, if we do not go through Active Experimentation followed by Concrete Experiences, we cannot complete the Learning Cycle. According to Kolb, under these conditions of incomplete learning, it becomes difficult to develop a new thinking.

Many theoretical assumptions prevailing in the 50's and 60's of last century, such as the "schizophrenogenic mother," blaming of the parents, or confusing the marital with the parental role, have been inquired by extensive research programs (e.g.: Double Bind, Parental Child, Enmeshment, and so on) corrected mainly by the strong impact of the direct experience family therapists made in the therapy room.

Thanks to that direct experience the family therapist of today believes much more on the importance of activating the family's own healing potential. Asking for the family system's resources, instead of distributing guilt among the family members, is now a fundamental acquisition for both teachers and students of family therapy.

The new training path that was instituted in 2017 and named *Practical Learning* is based on some principles of the *Systemic Experiential Model* that the Italian Institute of Relational Psychotherapy intends to propose as useful at all levels of training, for an increasingly advanced and practical development of systemic knowledge.

Practical Learning (PL) is based on an experiential and not speculative-type conception of the Systemic Thinking which privileges learning through a clinical approach.

Doing becomes the essential part in the training process, as was basically the case in the pioneering era, before the birth of the great theories that led relational-systemic psychotherapy toward a predominant deductive attitude.

Fig. 26.1 The development of family therapy and the blocked transition

26.1 The Manual

How to structure the training process based on doing, and above all how to make common guidelines available to all of the Institute teachers?

At this point, the idea of the *manual* came in, thanks above all to the stimuli of the Pote et al. (2003) paper that offered the proof that *"Systemic family therapy can be manualized."* The authors opened the door to the fact that manualization was not only applicable to Cognitive-Behavior approaches.

We realized soon that the clinical application to family therapy is different from the systemic family therapy training process and considered useful in our case to simplify the manualization structure.

Gradually, the image of the *Road Map* (see later) developed, and a series of steps were set in order to reach the goal of offering detailed (but not too strict) instructions both to the teachers and to the students of our training program.

To perform *learning by doing* What we wanted was to have a manualized Practical Learning, but the question was: where to take from some easy prescriptible tasks that should be taught to the trainees?

We decided for the option of setting our *Learning Outcomes* (what specific ability the student is expected to learn) and then to build around each one of them the correspondent *Practical Learning*.

Since we already had a basis of conceptual issues that constitutes the *Theory* of our approach, we asked in the related systemic family therapy literature for all the key concepts *(Theoretical Teaching)* that could be phrased as Learning Outcomes and immediately after in the Practical Learning tasks. Therefore, the core elements that constitute our Manual are: *Theoretical Teaching* (The Principles), *Learning Outcome* (The Expected Ability), and *Practical Learning* (The Task).

Since is essential for them to know in order to prepare their experience, the Manual is given at the beginning of every training year, both to the teachers and to the students.

26.1.1 Practical Learning

Practical Learning is articulated in first-person activities, which have the value of having systemic therapeutic expertise acquired directly from experience. It is not only a learning through making, but also an active observation through personal acting under the guidance of an experienced teacher.

It consists of an intensive and dedicated program, made up of 384 *tasks*, each one tailored to the correspondent theoretical premises and aimed to develop in the trainee's specific psychotherapeutic skills.

In our manual project, the major question was how to word each task in a way that it could be enough clear and detailed, but at the same time broad enough to cover all the key concepts we needed to obtain the desired learning outcome we wanted.

In this case, the inspiration came from the taxonomy (or better the philosophy) of Benjamin Bloom, the American educational psychologist who contributed to the theory of *mastery learning,* and above all gave rise to a specific *classification of educational objectives.*

His *taxonomy* (Bloom, 1956) was a system of description and assessment of educational outcomes that opened the door to the Experiential-Learning Model. His system has strongly influenced the development of the education theory and practice around the world.

Bloom's taxonomy has been accepted, applied for years to all sorts of education fields and revised hundreds of times until more recent times (Anderson et al., 2001; Krathwohl, 2002; Plack et al., 2007), but the general philosophy of his approach of categorizing the learning outcomes' *descriptors* and making them more experiential is still alive.

A good reason to use this approach in the Manual is that it can also enable the assessment process providing several measurable and confrontable items. The *key concepts* of the taxonomy are a number of *active verbs* used as descriptors that we will better illustrate in the paragraph dedicated to the Learning Outcomes.

Each one of the verbs describes an *educational objective* that fits with minimal adaptations in our training program and allows us to assess both its functioning and the abilities acquired by the trainees.

With the intent of not only simplifying the complexity of the training process but also of creating a more profound *continuity* in its different steps, we also made the choice of building both the Practical Learning and the Learning Outcomes (what the student is expected to learn) on the basis of the same Key Concepts.

Sharing the same Key Concepts, the wording of each task of the Practical Learning and the correspondent Learning Outcome will appear very similar, and sometimes even coincident.

Actually, this is a reversal of the order usually applied to the dynamic of the learning process: instead of making a program and eventually stating its expected results, we considered Learning Outcomes as the initial basis for developing the Practical Learning programmed tasks.

An example of the comparison between Practical Learning (PL) tasks and Learning Outcomes (LO) will demonstrate their continuity (Table 26.1):

After these general premises, let us see the relational context in which the Practical Learning develops.

The students are first exposed to the theoretical topics of Theoretical Teaching in the morning then, in the afternoon, they are trained by an expert family therapy teacher and requested to apply by doing what they have learned.

Practical Learning tasks are executed by using specific tools that allow to practice directly and in front of the teacher and of the group's each single assignment. Tools are:

Role Played Family Interview (during the first two years)
Live Family Interview (after the second year)
Video playback

Table 26.1 An example of comparison between Practical Learning (PL) tasks and Learning Outcomes (LO)

Normal families and developing resilience factors	
Practical learning (PL) Tasks	Learning outcomes (LO)
Recognize the characteristics of a normal family	Ability to describe the characteristics of the normal family
Demonstrate an interview with a normal family	Ability to analyze an Interview with a normal family
Identify resilience factors in the observed family	Ability to identify resilience factors in an observed family
Amplify the resilience factors identified in the family	Ability to describe the resilience factors and indicate how to amplify them

PL tasks involve both the teacher and the student in the execution of the following steps:

Introduction: The teacher briefly introduces *the essential parts of the theoretical contents that have been presented in the morning.*

Description: The teacher describes *the practical tasks (at least four) that will follow and will allow the trainee to develop specific therapeutic skills.*

Demonstration: The practical activities to be performed are first demonstrated *by the teacher.*

Performing: The student performs *the practical activities as demonstrated by the teacher.*

Instruction: The teacher will give instructions, offer comments and directions *to the performing student during the task execution.*

Group Discussion: Finally, the teacher will open to comments and discussion with the other students about what they have observed and understood.

Through years of experience, we have learned that seeing an expert teacher personally demonstrating the task execution can be much more effective than doing it with all the instructions but without the possibility of observing its exemplification.

For this reason, we consider the *demonstration phase* crucial in the learning the *by doing* process.

These steps are followed and repeated for each and one of the practical lessons the students are receiving during the training program.

Before proceeding to examine the details of the manualized educational process, we consider it necessary to have a better idea of its formal part that constitutes a meaningful context explaining how the teaching develops in time and what the overall structure that contains it is formed.

Table 26.2 summarizes the Family Therapy Training Program of the Institute that, according to the Italian Ministry of Education, University and Research rules, consists of 4 years of postgraduate education, including *500 h* of training per year, reaching a total of *2000 h.*

Table 26.2 General overview of the family therapy training program

FAMILY THERAPY TRAINING PROGRAM

FIRST YEAR
First Semester: TT1.1–TT1.12, PL1.1–PL1.12 — ASSESSMENT
Second Semester: TT1.13–TT1.24, PL1.13–PL1.24 — ASSESSMENT
SUPERVISED RESEARCH
EXERCISES

SECOND YEAR
First Semester: TT2.1–TT2.12, PL2.1–PL2.12 — ASSESSMENT
Second Semester: TT2.13–TT2.24, PL2.13–PL2.24 — ASSESSMENT
SUPERVISED RESEARCH
EXERCISES

THIRD YEAR
First Semester: TT3.1–TT3.12, PL3.1–PL3.12 — ASSESSMENT
Second Semester: TT3.13–TT3.24, PL3.13–PL3.24 — ASSESSMENT
SUPERVISED RESEARCH
ESERCISES
SUPERVISION

FOURTH YEAR
First Semester: TT4.1–TT4.12, PL4.1–PL4.12 — ASSESSMENT
Second Semester: TT4.13–TT4.24, PL4.13–PL4.24 — ASSESSMENT
SUPERVISED RESEARCH
ESERCISES
SUPERVISION

26.1.2 Family Therapy Training Program

The Ministry also requires a meaningful experience (in our case, 150 h per year) of *internship* in accredited mental health services. The Core Curriculum's fundamental part is made by the Theoretical Teaching and by the Practical Learning that together cover the larger part of the teachings and sum up to about *800 h* in the 4 years.

Another important part of the training is the Supervision of Clinical Cases that requires *120 h* per year in the third and fourth year. Together with Clinical Supervision, the *16 h* per year of the Micro-Analysis of Clinical Cases, the *8 h* of Clinical Seminars, and the *16 h* of Clinical Workshops give their contributions to the total amount of practical activities of the Training Program.

To complete the total amount of *500 h* that the trainees are expected to receive every year, there are one annual Congress of the Institute and the General Modules. These Modules include matters and topics that are not directly relevant to Family Therapy (like Psychopathology, General Psychology, Developmental Psychology, Psychodiagnostics, and Other Psychotherapeutic Approaches).

The Core Curriculum finally includes Supervised Research and Exercises. In the Supervised Research hours, the students are helped by one Researcher of the Institute to participate in or to design one or more research projects in the systemic family therapy field. Exercise hours are dedicated to reinforcing the results obtained by the Practical Learning: students are supported by a Tutor to repeat and rehearse their practical experience.

26.1.3 Core Curriculum of the Four Years Training Program

Training activities	Hours	Teaching units
Theoretical learning	384	96
Practical learning	384	96
Clinical seminar	32	8
Workshops	64	16
ACC (Analysis of Clinical Cases)	64	15
Congress	48	12
Supervision of clinical cases	240	60
Supervised research	72	18
Exercises	72	18
Assessment	24	8
General modules	28	8
Internship	600	120
Total	2012	475

Lesson days are a compound of two Units of *four hours* each, and they are combined in a way that every Unit of Theoretical Training (TT) is followed by one of Practical Learning (PL).

Some examples of the topics treated by TT and of the consequent tasks of PL will clarify the relations between the two different Units. We will illustrate here (maintaining their original coded numbers) four excerpts of four lessons each, containing 8 Units (4 TT and 4 PL), and each excerpt is taken from one of the 4 years of training.

EXAMPLE OF THE TT's AND PL's TOPICS
(Excerpts taken from each of the four year of training)

FIRST YEAR
LESSON SEVEN
Morning
TT1.7 INFORMATION THEORY
How to distinguish communication from information. Information and difference. Informational value of communication. The *relational relevance* of information: a key concept in understanding communicative flows in families. The transmission of information. Information and cybernetics
Afternoon
PL1.7 PRACTICAL LEARNING PL1.7 – INFORMATIVE AND NON-INFORMATIVE COMMUNICATION
Distinguish communicative messages from informative messages.
Identify individuals' and system's responses to communication not conveying information.
Identify individuals' and system's responses to communication conveying information.
Illustrate the effects of the therapist's informative communication on the system

LESSON EIGHT
Morning
TT1.8 GENERAL SYSTEMS THEORY I: GENERAL PRINCIPLES
The System as a descriptive language. The concept of System. The Part and the System. The concept of Level. Different Level types. System levels. Hierarchical levels. Complexity levels. Systems, subsystems, and components.
Afternoon
PL1.8 PRACTICAL LEARNING PL1.8 – SYSTEM'S DESCRIPTION AND ANALYSIS
Describe the System as a whole.
Describe the System in its Subsystems and Components.
Analyze System's relationships with the higher and lower Complexity Levels.
Identify how the Suprasystem influences the System, and how the System's influence its Components.

LESSON NINE
Morning
TT1.9 GENERAL SYSTEMS THEORY II: STRUCTURE AND FUNCTION
The System's laws. System's Structures and Functions. The effects of Feed-back and Feed-Forward mechanisms, and their role in the System's functioning. Internal and External Boundaries.
Afternoon
PL1.9 PRACTICAL LEARNING PL1.9 SYSTEM AND THERAPEUTIC INTERVENTIONS
Observe a System and Describe the laws of its functioning.
Observe and Describe the Structure of the System with its Internal and External Boundaries.
Note the effects of the System's Feed-Back on the therapist's interventions.
Prepare and deliver therapeutic interventions to produce a meaningful change of the System and its regulation mechanisms through a Feed-Forward change.

LESSON TEN
Morning
TT1.10 GENERAL SYSTEMS THEORY III: STRUCTURE AND ORGANIZATION
The organization of the System. Positive and Negative Emerging Qualities. Autopoiesis. The development of self-organization principles: order from order, order from noise, complexity from noise.

26 A Manualized Systemic Family Therapy Training Program

PL1.10   **PRACTICAL LEARNING PL1.10 - EMERGING QUALITIES AND COMPLEX TRANSFORMATIONS**
Identify Positive and Negative Emerging Qualities that develop when a Therapeutic System is formed.
Learn how to use Positive and Negative Emergencies to obtain a System's restructuring.
Distinguish disorganizative (noise) from organizative (complexity) aspects of the System.
Design and execute interventions that allow to transform disorganization into complexity.

SECOND YEAR
LESSON EIGHTEEN
Morning

TT2.18   **FAMILY THERAPY MODELS I: STRATEGIC THERAPY**
Strategic Family Therapy. The philosophy of the strategic model. The setting of strategic therapy. Problem solving therapy. The main techniques of strategic therapy. Indications of Strategic Interventions

Afternoon

PL2.18   **PRACTICAL LEARNING PL2.18 – STRATEGIC THERAPY**
Conduct a Strategic Interview with the family.
Comprehend the indications for Strategic Interventions in a family.
Apply to the family the most common Strategic Interventions.
Assess the strategic interventions' results in the family.

LESSON NINETEEN
Morning

TT2.19   **FAMILY THERAPY MODELS II: STRUCTURAL THERAPY**
structural therapy. the structural modeland the useof structural maps.
differences with other models. the influence of the structural model in family therapy. the main structural interventions.indications of structural interventions.

Afternoon

PL2.19   **PRACTICAL LEARNING PL2.19 – STRUCTURAL THERAPY**
Conduct a Structural interview with the family.
Evaluate the indications for Structural Interventions in a family
Apply to the family the most common Structural Interventions
Assess the Structural Interventions' results in the family.

LESSON TWENTY
Morning

TT2.20   **FAMILY THERAPY MODELS III: SYSTEMIC THERAPY**
The Systemic Therapy of Mara Selvini Palazzoli. Hypothesizing, neutrality and circular interview. From paradox to invariant prescriptions. Games and psychotic processes.

Afternoon

PL2.20   **PRACTICAL LEARNING PL2.20 – SYSTEMIC THERAPY**
Conduct a Systemic Interview with the Family.
Evaluate the indications for Systemic Interventions in a family.
Apply to the family the most common Systemic Interventions
Assess the Systemic Interventions' results in the family.

LESSON TWENTYONE
MORNING

TT2.21 — FAMILY THERAPY MODELS IV: SYMBOLIC EXPERIENTIAL
Carl Whitaker's symbolic-experiential therapy. Experiential play therapy. Therapy of the absurd. Carl Whitaker's multigenerational vision, and approach.

PL2.21 — PRACTICAL LEARNING PL2.21 – SYMBOLIC-ESPERIENTIAL THERAPY
Conduct a Symbolic-Experiential Interview with the family.
Evaluate the indications for Symbolic-Experiential Interventions in a family.
Apply to the family the most common Symbolic-Experiential Interventions
Assess the Symbolic-Experiential Interventions' results in the family.

THIRD YEAR
LESSON ONE
MORNING

TT3.1 — FAMILY ASSESMENT III: HYPOTHESES
Cognitive value and clinical utility of Hypotheses. Morphostatic and morphogenic Hypotheses. Construction of the Hypothesis. Evaluating, correcting and verifying Hypothese.

PL3.1 — Afternoon
PRACTICAL LEARNING PL3.1 – THE CONSTRUCTION OF HYPOTHESES
Construction of Morphostatic and Morphogenetic hypotheses about the symptom function in a family.
Verifying and correcting the hypotheses.
Hypothesis for the intervention construction.
Active control of hypotheses for the construction of the intervention.

LESSON TWO
MORNING

C3.2 — THEORY AND PRACTICE OF FAMIL PSYCHOTHERAPY I: THE FAMILY REFERRAL
The family referral. Functional referrals. Dysfunctional referrals. Therapist attitude toward the referring person. Solutions for the dysfunctional referrals and dysfunctionality prevention in the relationship with the referring person.

AFTERNOON

PL3.2 — PRACTICAL LEARNING PL3.2 – DYSFUNCTIONAL REFERRALS AND THEIR SOLUTIONS
Conduct an interview with a dysfunctionally referred family
Find the proper attitude to prevent dysfunctional referrals.
Use different attitudes with each type of dysfunctional referral.
Apply the correct strategy to solve the dysfunctional referral.

LESSON THREE
MORNING

TT3.3 — THEORY AND PRACTICE OF FAMILY PSYCHOTHERAPY II: THE FIRST CONTACT WITH THE FAMILY
The first contact. The first phone call with the family. Notes from the first phone interview. Delimiting the family system. Convening the system and its problems.

AFTERNOON

PL3.3 — PRACTICAL LEARNING PL3.3 – MANAGING THE FIRST CONTACT AND REQUESTING
Role play a first phone call with one family member
Take notes about the family information in the phone conversation.
Decide which family members need to be included in the initial session
Convening the Problem-Determined system and related techniques.

LESSON FOUR
MORNING

 TT3.4 THEORY AND PRACTICE OF FAMILY PSYCHOTHERAPY III: THE FAMILY THERAPY SETTING
the systemic setting. defining the setting rules.collaborative context and therapeutic alliance with the family system. the problem of extra-therapeutic communication and the therapist attitude.

AFTERNOON

PL3.4 PRACTICAL LEARNING PL3.4 – SETTING DELIMITATION AND BREACH RESOLUTION
Defining the setting rules during the family interview.
Establish a collaborative context and a therapeutic alliance with the family and its individual members.
Interview with a family member who offers or ask for extra-therapeutic information.
Interventions to solve the problem of extra-therapeutic information

FOURTH YEAR
LESSON THREE
MORNING

 TT4.3 THEORY AND PRACTICE OF THE THERAPUTIC PROCESS I: PSYCHOTHERAPY AND PLAY
Play: Definitions and Rules. Play-therapy: The use of the Play in Family Psychotherapy. The message "this is a game". Family games and therapeutic games.

AFTERNOON

PL4.3 PRACTICAL LEARNING PL4.3 – USING PLAY-THERAPY IN THE FAMILY CONTEXT
Propose a Play Therapy session to the family.
Choose the type of play and adapt it to the family.
Introduce playing to all the family members
Understand the individual and family responses to the playing experience

LESSON SIX
MORNING

 C4.6 THEORY AND PRACTICE OF THE THERAPUTIC PROCESS II: THE METAPHOR
Indirect communication in psychotherapy. The metaphor: definition and construction. The communicative value of metaphor. The metaphor in psychotherapy. Choice and calibration of the metaphor. Family metaphors and therapist metaphors. Therapeutic value of metaphor. The use of stories and anecdotes.

AFTERNOON

PL4.6 PRACTICAL LEARNING PL4.6 – RESEARCH AND USE METAPHORS
Identification of spontaneous metaphors used by the family.
Prepare metaphors and deliver them in family therapy.
Choosing and calibration of the metaphor based on the degree of tension most suitable for the family.
Evaluate of the response to metaphor by the system and its components.

LESSON SEVEN
MORNING

 C4.7 THEORY AND PRACTICE OF THE THERAPUTIC PROCESS III: THE INTERVIEW WITH THE FAMILY SYSTEM
Conducting the family interview. Direct interview and indirect interview. Family questions and therapist's questions. The circular interview. Circular questions and other forms of questions.

AFTERNOON

PL4.7 — **PRACTICAL LEARNING PL4.7 – CONDUCT THE INTERVIEW WITH THE FAMILY SYSTEM**
Use direct and indirect methods of conducting family interviews.
Choosing the right interview method for the family.
Conduct a circular interview.
Use different forms of questions, and justify the choice.

LESSON EIGHT
MORNING

 THEORY AND PRACTICE OF THE TERAPEUTIC PROCESS IV: THE MULTIGENERATIONAL INTERVIEW

The role of generations. The indications and contraindications. Problems of convening the extended family. Respect for generational levels. The change of the nuclear family's generation and of the grandparents' generation. Grandparents as special consultants. How to participate. Specific techniques. Guidelines.

AFTERNOON

PL4.8 **PRACTICAL LEARNING PL4.8 MULTIGENERATIONAL APPROACHES**
Convening the extended family. Criteria and Modalities.
Make an interview with the extended family.
Grandparents as consultants to the therapist.
Criteria for choosing multigenerational therapy.

| PL1.7 | **PRACTICAL LEARNING PL1.7 – INFORMATIVE AND NON-INFORMATIVE COMMUNICATION**

KNOWLEDGE
LO1.7.1 – Ability to Distinguish communicative messages from informative messages.
PLt1.7.1 - Distinguish communicative messages from informative messages.
Q1.7.1 - List two differences between communicative and informative messages
SKILL
LO1.7.2 - Ability to Identify individuals' and system's responses to communication not conveying information.
PLt1.7.2 Identify individuals' and system's responses to communication not conveying information.
Q1.7.2 - Describe one possible response of the individuals and one of the system as an effect to non-informative communication
SKILL
LO1.7.3 - Ability to Discover non-informative communications of the therapist
PLt1.7.3 - Discover non-informative communications of the therapist
Q1.7.3 - Describe three possible non informative communications of the therapist

RELATIONAL ABILITY
LO1.7.4 - Ability to Illustrate the effects of the therapist's informative communication on the system
PLt1.7.4 - Illustrate the effects of the therapist's informative communication on the system
Q1.7.4 - Explain one possible system's response to the therapist informative communication.

| PL2.18 | **PRACTICAL LEARNING PL2.18 – STRATEGIC THERAPY**

RELATIONAL ABILITY
LO2.18.1 - Ability to Conduct a Strategic Interview with the family.
PLt2.18.1 - Conduct a Strategic Interview with the family.
Q2.18.1 - Illustrate three key points to design a Strategic Interview with the family.

KNOWLEDGE
LO2.18.2 – Ability to Comprehend the indications for a Strategic Interventions in a family
PLt2.18.2 Comprehend the indications for a Strategic Interventions in a family.
Q2.18.2 List three indications for a Strategic Interventions in a family

RELATIONAL ABILITY
LO2.18.3 - Ability to Apply to the family the most common Strategic Interventions
PLt2.18.3 Apply to the family the most common Strategic Interventions.
Q2.18.3 – Explain how to apply three Strategic Interventions.
SKILL
LO2.18.4 - Ability to Assess the strategic interventions' results in the family.
PLt2.18.4 - Assess the strategic interventions' results in the family.
Q2.18.4 – Describe how to assess the strategic interventions' results in the family

In this work, it is not possible to include all of the teaching units of the Institute Training Program that are part of the manual (they are in total 472); yet, these excerpts, used as examples, provide an idea of the standardized task we use for the Practical Learning, and of the continuity they have with the Theoretical Teaching.

However, in order to understand to which extent PL can be effective as a way of *learning by doing*, we should examine the relationship that this form of teaching has, not only with TT, but also with the rest of the more complex structure of the entire training program.

We offer now a brief presentation of the manual steps (Educational Components) that the students entering the Program will go through. As we have anticipated, among these Components there is one, the Learning Outcomes that, by our choice, influences directly and indirectly all the others.

26.1.4 Learning Outcomes (LO)

Learning Outcomes have been defined by Suskie (2018) as "knowledge, skills, attitudes, and habits of mind that students take with them from a learning experience" (p. 40).

It can look like a simple definition, but can also become complex when considering the level of detail needed in the manual to compile meaningful learning outcomes. In fact, descriptions that are too detailed can be confusing, as well as descriptions that are too general may result in becoming meaningless.

We should distinguish LO from the Educational Objectives, which, "in general, state what the institution plans to 'achieve' rather than what students will learn as a result of a course or other learning experience" (Buckley & Michel, 2020).

What has been learned is generally more relevant because the acquired knowledge, skills, and abilities will concur to form specific competencies for the family therapy student.

In terms of *competence,* we embraced the definition given by the European Qualifications Framework (EQF), a system developed by the European Commission with the aim of making possible the confrontation of the different professional qualifications among the European Citizens.

EQF defines competence as the ability to use *knowledge*, *skills*, and *social/relational abilities* (European Commission, 2011).

Following this principle, in order to establish and evaluate the student's acquired competence, we will consider three different sets of Outcomes:

Knowledge
Acquisition or understanding of facts, principles, and concepts.

Skill
Acquired ability to take actions and decisions, to describe, to distinguish.

Social/Relational Ability

Ability to intervene in relationships to activate change.

In order to make it easier to recognize the different types of Learning Outcomes acquired, we enclose in Table 26.3 a list of Action Verbs (Descriptors) that usually accompany the three categories of ability.

As mentioned before, the use in the manual of Verbs as *Descriptors* of active actions that correspond to the Learning Outcomes has been and continues to be adopted by the great part of the Experiential-Learning studies.

Our choice has been to use them as descriptors not only of *Learning Outcomes*, but of *Practical Learning* and *Learning Method of Assessment* as well. In order to maintain continuity, correspondence, and alignment between these variables, the descriptors should either be the same or belong to the same category.

In other words, if we want to evaluate the achievement of an LO belonging to the SKILL category (e.g., Observe), we will teach it with a PL task and assess it with an instrument that will be either based on the same descriptor (Observe) or on a descriptor belonging to the same category (e.g., Describe or Identify).

The fact that Active Verbs and their belonging to one category vary from one study to the other, it is not so surprising if we consider that their meaning depends on the type of Learning Outcome to be explored and on the general purposes of the Institution.

As an example, the verb "Interpret" can belong to Knowledge if used in a high school program, but it will be considered part of the Skill category in a psychotherapy institute.

Table 26.3 Examples of the action verbs that describe the three categories of learned ability

Knowledge	Skill	Social/relational ability
Acquire awareness, insight	Acquire skill, instruments	Act
Analyze	Assess	Apply
Classify	Choose	Conduct
Comprehend	Describe	Deliver
Criticize	Discover	Demonstrate
Define	Emphasize	Develop
Distinguish	Evaluate	Discuss
Knowledge	Hypothesize	Empower
Learn	Identify	Explain
List	Implement	Illustrate
Name	Interpret	Indicate
Order	Judge	Produce change
Outline	Note	Prescribing
Realize	Observe	Promote
Recognize	Propose	Refraining
Summarize	Select	Suggest
Understand	Utilize	Transform

Therefore, Descriptors and their categorization should be adapted to the different perspectives they will be part of. Of course, verbs like *Reframe* or *Prescribe* have a specific place in the Family Therapist's toolbox, while they represent an ability that is not required in other learning contexts.

Sometimes, verbs can have an ambiguous meaning, and their meaning can be clarified only when they stand by a substantive, as in the case of Acquire awareness, insight, and Acquire skill, instruments.

According to Morss and Murray (2005), words like "appreciate" and "understand" do not help students because there are too many interpretations of their meaning.

Although to comprehend their correct meaning is not always easy, we found that using the active verbs and subdividing LO into the three categories is of great value since it allows to find out more easily in what area of their learning experience students can demonstrate more weak points and in what area, more resources.

Anyhow, to use a more sensitive approach to the LO, we prefer to bind together the Practical Learning and the Learning Outcome. That means that a Practical Learning task is tailored to the Learning Outcomes and this choice guarantees *coherence* and *continuity* between what is needed and what is given.

The general philosophy of this manualized approach is to focus above all on *observable behavior*, to describe categories of learning, to enhance practical learning in every type of teaching context, and to offer a measurement tool that can sustain a manualized training program.

What is essential for us is the *congruence* of the most qualifying Educational Components: Theoretical Teaching, Practical Learning, Learning Outcomes, and the Assessment Method that validates them. Educational Components based on the same principles make it possible to trace a coherent *road map* to become a qualified family therapist.

26.1.5 The Road Map

We see the steps that in this manualized approach connect Learning Outcomes, Theoretical Teaching, Practical Learning, and Assessment as a Road Map that gives a step-by-step support to the general learning process and offers a frame for a better understanding and reaching the required achievements.

The *alignment* between the various steps helps to make the overall learning experience more coherent, transparent, and meaningful for learners (Biggs, 2005).

Morss and Murray (2005) emphasize the importance of this aspect they define as Constructive Alignment:

> …is the deliberate linking within curricula of aims, learning outcomes, learning and teaching activities and assessment. Learning Outcomes state what is to be achieved in fulfilment of the aims. Learning activities should be organized so that students will be likely to achieve those outcomes. Assessment must be designed such that students are able to demonstrate that they have met the learning outcomes.

......
> The concept of aligning aims, outcomes, assessment, and learning and teaching strategies seems so simple that some might say this is just a fancy name for "joining up the dots." The trouble is, very often it does not happen in practice (p. 20).

26.1.6 The Theory

A general presentation of the Theory is the first step of the manual. Every program varies depending on the theory that supports it. In a training of psychotherapy, the basic and the more advanced principles of the perspective should be learned, for both their theoretical and practical aspects.

The IIPR institute considers Systems Theory as the main orientation. The Strategic approach of Jay Haley (1973, 1977), the Structural model of Salvador Minuchin (1974; Minuchin & Fishman, 2004), the Symbolic Experiential orientation of Carl Whitaker (1989: Whitaker & Bumberry, 1988; Whitaker & Napier, 1978), and the Milan Systemic perspective of Mara Selvini et al. (1989, 1994) are considered the basic fundaments for teaching.

At the same time, we have developed a specific model called the Resource-Based Family Therapy (RBFT) (Loriedo, 2006; Loriedo & Angiolari, 2015) that centers on the family strengths and is committed to the development of the functional parts of the system, and gives particular relevance to learn by doing and the active role of the therapist.

Theoretical Teaching
The manual summarizes all the general principles that are part of the Theory and are offered by interactive frontal lessons. Their definitions are sufficiently illustrated, but their level of abstraction allows only limited standardized assessments that will be included in the evaluation of Practical Learning, under the category *Knowledge* of Learning Outcomes.

The Key Position of Learning Outcomes in the Road Map
Not unlike many other learning institutions, we have decided to give to Learning Outcomes the *central role* of representing and explain more clearly to trainees what they are expected to achieve during their curricula.

In the manual, they put emphasis on the student and have written it particularly as a recommendation to the teacher to develop in the student the ability to do something.

However, we consider not less fundamental for the teachers to access such a clear and structured knowledge of what is expected they should offer to the students.

In the Road Map described by the manual, Learning Outcomes are necessarily *in close and reciprocal connection with the Theory* that suggests to them its *basic and advanced principles*.

These same principles are translated into *Theoretical Teaching* and then by the Learning Outcomes and through the *active verbs* they become *Practical Learning*.

According to Kennedy et al. (2009), Learning Outcomes should have the following Seven Characteristics:

1. *They are "achievements," clearly identifiable (written in the infinitive).*
2. *They must be achievable within the training environment.*
3. *They are feasible for students.*
4. *They must have an observable behavior.*
5. *They have to be measurable.*
6. *As a consequence of 3, 4, and 5, they can be assessed.*
7. *They establish an educational level and are related to a specific skill and competence level.*

Thanks to these characteristics, LO help to define more effectively the Assessment Criteria.

Practical Learning

As said, this is the part of the manual that includes all the standardized tasks that are part of the three categories of Learning Outcomes: Knowledge, Skill, and Social/Relational Ability.

Because of our choice of tailoring it on Learning Outcomes and, being the most relevant and detailed part of the official program, it is considered a reliable guide both for the students and for the teachers.

General Assessment

According to Huba and Freed (2000), assessment is the process of gathering and discussing information from multiple and diverse sources in order to develop a deep understanding of what students know, understand, and can do with their knowledge as a result of their educational experiences.

Since we have designed the practical part of the training program in terms of Learning Outcomes, we must now find out if the trainees can get from this program their intended practical achievements.

With this aim, we have established during the 4-year training, a *check* every semester module for a total of eight checks.

Two *oral exams,* one at the end of the second year and the last exam that will include the discussion of the thesis after the end of the entire training program, will complete the students' evaluation.

Exams require a committee of three experienced teachers and will consist of the discussion of both theoretical principles and of the presentation of two clinical cases treated by the trainees and discussed on the basis of a written report and samples of their video-recorded sessions.

Admission to the conclusive exam at the end of the training course is submitted for acceptance to the positive opinion of the trainees' Supervisors that evaluate their clinical work.

At this point, we have described the different steps of the manualized Family Therapy Training Program defining it as the Road Map concluding with the general information about the assessment that is the last stage of the route.

Summarizing it here briefly, the manual that we call Road Map is presented to the *teachers* at the beginning of every teaching year in the form of a 100-page manual including, after a brief Introduction, the five steps of the Road Map description:

Theory
Theoretical Teaching
Learning Outcomes
Practical Learning
Assessment

At the beginning of their training year, students receive a limited version of the manual in the form of a very detailed program, including all the first four steps (Educational Components) but excluding the assessment that will instead be administered to them at the end of each semester.

We will soon describe the Assessment part of the Learning Outcomes and its standardization in more detail, but we would like to emphasize since now how the end of the program reconnects with its beginning.

And in fact, we intend to continue to use the assessment results as an endless contribution to the development of the training activities.

As a self-organizing system, the manualized Program uses feedback from the Learning Outcome achievements and from the Training Evaluation Form to correct its contents as well as its same evaluation process.

Here, we have a graphic description of the Family Therapy Training Program Road Map that summarizes all the different Educational Components and their complex intersections, including this important feedback mechanism (Table 26.4).

26.7.1 Learning Outcomes Assessment

The Learning Outcomes will be evaluated by summative assessment in every single check at the end of the semester, on the basis of a written test, in order to measure the progress made in the last 6 months' module.

The Grades received by the trainee in each module will sum up in the 4 years of training with the other evaluations and will generate the final assessment reported in the conclusive exam (Table 26.5).

Table 26.4 Family therapy training program road map

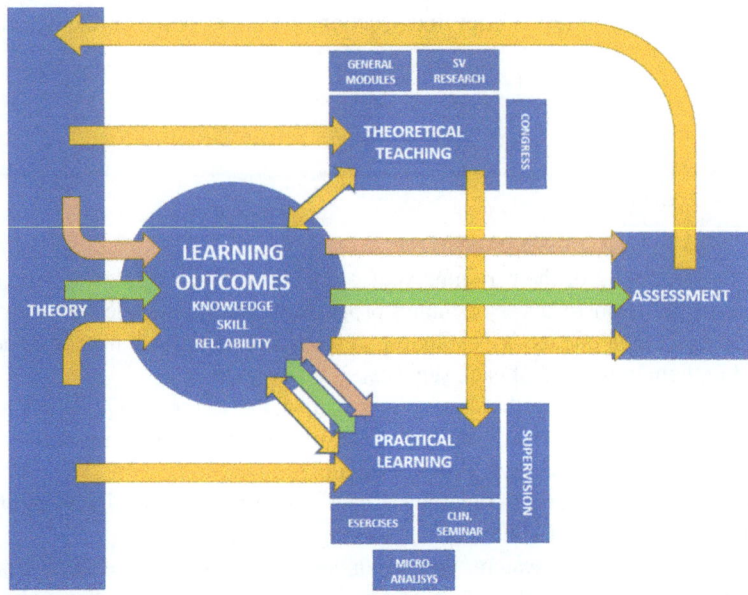

Legends: Arrows represent the Learning Outcomes connections, subdivided into the three categories of Knowledge (yellow), Skill (green), and Social/Relational Ability (red)

In every module, the trainee will receive 24 Units of Practical Learning, and at the end of the same module, the trainee will be assessed to verify what the achieved Learning Outcomes' extent was.

Assessment Criteria

The *Seven Characteristics* proposed by Kennedy et al. (2009), and already described in page 21, are certainly important criteria to be followed.

Apart from that, we considered a priority a *clear alignment* between the Learning Outcomes and the associated assessment methods used.

For this reason, we decided to apply to the assessment method the same or similar *descriptors* that have been used both in compiling the Learning Outcome and in describing the Practical Learning.

Table 26.5 Learning outcome assessment

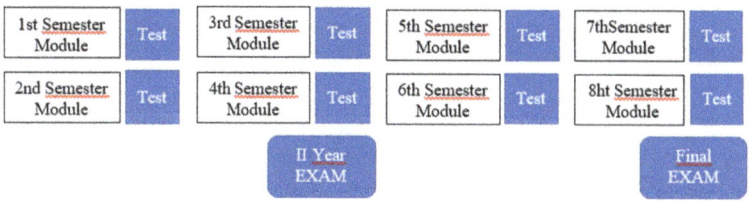

The questionnaire we have adopted contains 96 questions for every Semester Module, but every question uses either one descriptor pertaining to the same descriptors' category of Learning Outcomes or even the same descriptor.

A similar criterion of alignment of the descriptors is followed by the greatest parts of institution organizing training programs, then this option demonstrated so far to guarantee, *coherence and continuity*, better than any other possible method.

Another important point was *not to have a simple set of "yes" or "no" questions*. We rather preferred to have a grading tool with more complex responses, and then either to sum them up as a whole or dividing them according to the three categories to obtain peculiar students' *profiles*.

The Questionnaire

The Practical Learning Assessing Method is made by a questionnaire, containing *Open-Ended Questions* of the Objective Type, one for every single task that has been performed in order to assess the related Learning Outcome.

In order to improve the possibility to measure the students' achievement, we have included, whenever possible, numbers to count and graduate the acquired ability.

Here, a couple of questions' examples will help to understand this aspect:

Describe three different interventions aimed to subtract the child from involvement in conflicting dynamics between parents.
Illustrate three critical factors or three moments of the therapeutic relationship that in your experience have led to significant changes.

It is very useful to realize how the questions are in direct continuity with the Practical Learning and the Learning Outcomes.

Here, we show together the Learning Outcomes (LO) with the category of descriptors (Knowledge, Skill, and Relational Ability) they belong to, the Practical Learning Task (PLt) as described in the Training Program, and the relative Question (in blue) aimed to evaluate the achieved outcome.

The Responses of the trainee to the Questions are supposed to indicate their level of Knowledge, Skill, and Relational Ability. Every response will receive 1–3 points (Excellent, Good, Poor) or no point if it is completely wrong or missing.

Every three points will calculate one grade. Grades coming from the Learning Outcomes Evaluation will sum up with other forms of assessment (Exams, Thesis, Clinical Work, etc.) and will generate the final assessment that will conclude the Training program.

Learning Assessment, and the grades obtained by the students, could produce a profile with three different vertical bars: one indicating the student's Knowledge, one for the Skill, and one for the Social/Relational Ability.

Here in Fig. 26.2 we have two graphic representations showing an excellent general profile and another profile in which Relational Ability is much more relevant than the rest.

26.8 Some Preliminary Results

After the first 2 years of the manualized program application, we have observed the following results:

26.8.1 Effects on the Students

Since we collect from the Students their evaluation of the training program through the Training Evaluation Form at the end of each year, we can compare the results with the ones of the previous year.

Here are the items of the Form that showed the more meaningful grades given by the students:

(a) *Clarity and Comprehensibility of the Training Program*
 2018: +2,8%–2019: +7,6%
(b) *Organization of the Training Program*
 2018: + 6.9%–2019: + 12,0%
(c) *Level of new knowledge received by the Training Program*
 2018: −4,7%–2019; +18,2%
(d) *Utility for my usual work*
 2018: + 15,3%–2019; +24,2%

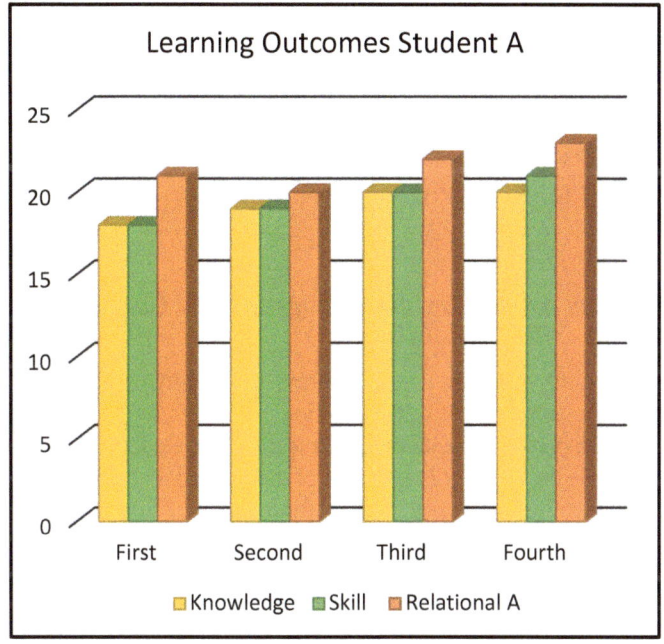

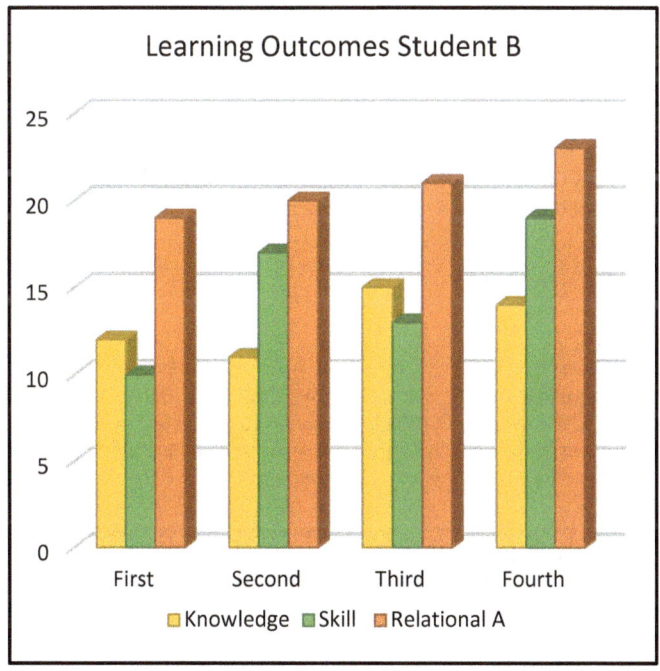

Fig. 26.2 Learning outcomes of two trainees

26.8.2 Effects on the Teachers

Unfortunately, at present we do not have Teacher Satisfaction questionnaires, so we can only report some of the teachers' verbal comments. The most common was: "Now I can understand better if my teaching is effective" and "I see my students much more active in the therapeutic process."

26.8.3 Effects on the Training Program and Conclusion

The main goal of this program was to improve the quality of teaching, through an ongoing circular mechanism of self-correction.

In this sense, a partial but encouraging result in our students' assessment at the end of each year is the *Median Evaluation* of the students' abilities.

Analyzing the comparison with the preceding year, we found in 2018 an improvement rate of +3,6% and in 2019 + 18,3%.

We judge as very useful the indication coming from every semester assessment that tells us where the students are successful and where they are lacking. It can also suggest whether the learning abilities are growing, so that some of the teaching can be adapted to the student with individually tailored education paths.

Indication can also emerge of where and how to modify the teaching program and a correction of the assessment process itself is needed.

We strongly believe that a circular self-correcting model can be at the same time structured and flexible and that a similar approach is more than a measurement tool.

It could serve as a common language about educational goals to facilitate the student-teacher cooperation in order to put the same emphasis on *learning processes* that has been up till now given to teaching.

References

Anderson, L. W., Krathwohl, D. R., Airasian, P. W., Cruikshank, K. A., Mayer, R. E., Pintrich, P. R., Raths, J., & Wittrock, M. C. (2001). *A taxonomy for learning, teaching, and assessing: A revision of Bloom's taxonomy of educational objectives* (Complete ed.). Longman.

Biggs, J. (2005). *Teaching for quality learning at university (2003)*. Open University Press. ISBN 0335211682.

Bloom, B. S. (Ed.). (1956). *Taxonomy of educational objectives: The classification of educational goals*. David McKay Company, Inc.

Buckley, J. B., & Michel, J. O. (2020, January 3). An examination of higher education institutional level learning outcomes. *Innovative Higher Education, 2020*. issn: 1573-1758. https://doi.org/10.1007/s10755-019-09493-7

European Commission. (2011). *Using learning outcomes – European qualifications framework series*: Note 4 Luxembourg: Publications Office of the European Union 2011. ISBN 978-92-79-21085-3. https://doi.org/10.2766/17497.

Haley, J. (1973). *Uncommon therapy. The psychiatric techniques of Milton H. Erickson* Norton.
Haley, J. (1977). *Problem solving therapy*. Jossey Bass.
Huba, M. E., & Freed, J. E. (2000). *Learner-centered assessment on college campuses. Shifting the focus from teaching to learning.* Allyn & Bacon.
Kennedy, D., Hyland, A., & Ryan, N. (2009). Learning outcomes and competences. In *Bologna Handbook, introducing Bologna objectives and tools*, B2.3 Tools, B2.3–3, 1–18.
Kolb, D. A. (1984). *Experiential learning: Experience as the source of learning and development.* Englewood Cliffs.
Krathwohl, D. R. (2002). A revision of Bloom's taxonomy: An overview. *Theory Into Practice, 41*(4), 212–218. https://doi.org/10.1207/s15430421tip4104_2
Loriedo, C. (2006). Vincoli e Risorse: la trasformazione silenziosa della Psicoterapia Relazionale-Sistemica. In A. De Francisci & T. Piersanti (Eds.), *La famiglia tra vincoli e risorse: percorsi terapeutici complessi* (pp. 13–22). Franco Angeli.
Loriedo, C., & Angiolari, C. (a cura di) (2015). *Dagli Interventi paradossali alle narrazioni molteplici. 40 anni di psicoterapia relazionale sistemica.* Franco Angeli. ISBN 978-88-917-1420-6; ISSN 2420-9201.
Minuchin, S. (1974). *Families and family therapy*. Harvard University Press.
Minuchin, S., & Fishman, H. C. (2004). *Family therapy techniques*. Harvard University Press.
Minuchin, S., Reiter, D. M., & Borda, C. (2014). *The craft of family therapy: Challenging certainties*. Routledge/Taylor & Francis.
Morss, K., & Murray, R. (2005). *Teaching at university. A guide for postgraduates and researchers.* Sage Publications. ISBN 1412902975.
Plack, M. M., Driscoll, M., Marquez, M., Cuppernull, L., Maring, J., & Greenberg, L. (2007). Assessing reflective journals on a pediatric clerkship using a modified Bloom's taxonomy. *Ambulatory Pediatrics, 7*, 285–291.
Pote, H., Stratton, P., Cottrell, D., Shapiro, D., & Boston, P. (2003). Systemic family therapy can be manualized: Research process and findings. *Journal of Family Therapy, 25*(236–262), 0163-4445.
Selvini Palazzoli, M., Cirillo, S., Selvini, M., & Sorrentino, A. M. (1989). *Family games: General models of psychotic processes in the family* (p. 1989). H. Karnac Books.
Selvini Palazzoli, M., Boscolo, L., Cecchin, G., & Prata. (1994). *Paradox and Counterparadox: A new model in the therapy of the family in schizophrenic transaction.* Jason Aronson. ISBN 13: 9781568213057.
Suskie, L. (2018). *Assessing student learning: A common sense guide*. Jossey-Bass.
Whitaker, C. A. (1989). *Midnight musing of a family therapist*. Norton & Company.
Whitaker, C. A., & Bumberry, W. M. (1988). *Dancing with the family. A symbolic-experiential approach.* Brunner-Mazel.
Whitaker, C. A., & Napier, A. Y. (1978). *The family crucible*. Harper and Row.

Chapter 27
Healing Relationships: A Manualized Curriculum for Systemic Primary Care Physicians

George Saba

> "Great teachers and therapists avoid all direct attempts to influence the action of others and, instead, try to provide the settings or contexts in which some (usually imperfectly specific) change may occur (Bateson, 1987, p. 254)."

27.1 Introduction

Seventy percent of medical problems have a significant psychological or behavioral component (American Psychological Association, 2017; Strosahl & Robinson, 2020). Primary care physicians are in a unique position to treat both the biomedical aspects of disease and to address patients' psychosocial context. However, because the dominant model of medical treatment and physician training in the United States is reductionistic and prescriptive, physicians frequently learn to treat patients out of the context of their families and primarily focus diagnosis and treatment on individuals. Because this biomedical model also promotes algorithmic and protocol-driven thinking, manualization of both treatment and training tends to focus on content and procedures and encourages rigid adherence by physicians.

Training primary care physicians to think and act systemically requires a radically different approach to training and the process of manualization. I will describe what a systemic family physician is, present the context of our training and treatment of families who are culturally diverse, experience economic poverty, and have limited access to health care, discuss our approach to manualizing, and present an overview of our manual. Then, I will present quality improvement studies and

G. Saba (✉)
Emeritus Professor of Family and Community Medicine, University of California, San Francisco, San Francisco, California, USA
e-mail: George.Saba@ucsf.edu

research related to our manualized approach and discuss the evolution of our manualization, which focuses on processes rather than procedures and attempts to balance rigor with the creative imagination essential to addressing the complex needs of faculty, learners, and families who have been marginalized by society.

27.2 Evolution of Medicine in the United States

Until the 1960s, general practitioners had been the cornerstone of American medical care. These physicians delivered babies, treated chronic disease, made home visits, and cared for the whole family as they lived and died. However, in the 1960s, the field of medicine began to change dramatically. Because of the rapid increase in new information about diseases, a surge in medical technology, increased pharmaceutical sophistication, and aggressive marketing strategies, medicine evolved into a number of subspecialties. Specialists became highly trained experts on a specific body part or organ system, and Americans wanted their expertise to ensure they received the best treatment. These changes generated considerable hope that medical science would discover cures for everything from cancer to the common cold. The dominance of germ theory, the development of antibiotics, and the creation of vaccines had become the heroic innovations that would control many of the infectious diseases that had plagued humanity for generations (polio, typhoid, smallpox). The American public soon believed they could live longer and healthier. They viewed pain and stress as daily inconveniences of modern life that could be eradicated by new medications, such as analgesics and tranquilizers. The medical-industrial complex was born.

At the same time that biomedicine flourished, the United States was in the midst of major societal challenges. The post-war generation had grasped the implications of the atomic bomb, watched the horrors of the Vietnam War televised daily, witnessed the violence of racism and the struggles of the civil rights movement, and understood the damage we were doing to the environment. Their vision of the world began to shift from a collection of disconnected nations, classes, and races to that of an ecosystem inextricably linked and in need of change.

In this context, disenchantment with biomedicine also grew. Cures for colds and cancers failed to materialize. The valuable doctor-patient relationship, a hallmark of the general practitioner era, was lost. A revolution among patients and physicians was brewing. A new medical specialty emerged to give physicians the breadth of training to deal with the substantial advances in modern medicine and to recapture the relational and holistic aspect that was so essential for health care. In 1967, the specialty of Family Medicine was created to train systemic physicians to care for the individual, family, and community. Similar changes also occurred in the mental health field leading to the birth of family therapy. Family therapists became natural collaborators with family physicians in developing clinical approaches and training programs (Bloch, 1983; Doherty & Baird, 1983; Saba & Fink, 1985).

27.3 Family Medicine

In the United States, training in the specialty of family medicine requires 4 years of medical school followed by a 3-year residency, during which doctors learn the broad spectrum of medicine: pediatrics, adult medicine, women's health, intensive care, emergency care, inpatient medical care, obstetrics, general surgery, and palliative care. They learn to practice medicine in both outpatient and inpatient settings. They become primary care physicians who provide continuity care for families, deal with most health issues, and only refer to other specialists when needed. Because 70% of medical problems have a significant psychological or behavioral component, family physicians also learn psychotherapy. To be clear, however, systemic family physicians are not psychotherapists or psychiatrists. Rather, they provide both biomedical and psychosocial care from a biopsychosocial perspective.

27.4 UCSF SFGH Family and Community Medicine Residency

In 1977, a group of systems-oriented physicians and family therapists, including Carlos Sluzki and Don Ransom, created a family medicine residency program at the University of California, San Francisco (Ransom & Vandervoort, 1973). They designed a 3-year residency curriculum that provided the requisite training in medicine and surgery. Within that program, they included a behavioral sciences curriculum that trained residents in systemic/relational therapy to care for families who are impoverished and marginalized (Sluzki, 1974).

Since its inception, our residency program has operated in a publicly funded clinic and hospital that cares for an urban underserved, multi-ethnic, multi-racial community that includes many refugees and immigrants, who often do not speak English. Most of our families have low health literacy, live in poverty, experience food insecurity, and have multiple, complex medical, and psychosocial problems. Many struggle to find affordable housing or live on the streets. These families exist on the margins of our society.

In the United States, physicians often learn medicine by treating people who have no other choice receiving their health care for public institutions. However, many of these physicians prefer then to care for insured patients upon graduation from residency training. Fundamental to our program's mission, we recruit physicians who choose to care for the families and communities we serve throughout their career. We train our physicians to expand their scope of treatment beyond the walls of the exam room and work toward healing their community, society, and world. They gain expertise in community health and political advocacy to address broad issues that influence health such as racism, poverty, violence, and climate change. They are committed to working for all forms of justice (e.g., social, racial, sexual, gender, and economic). Therefore, the 3-year curriculum teaches these physicians to work systemically at multiple levels to maximize the healing process. We ask residents to consider "What is the pattern that connects" the beta cells of a child to the emotions of a father to the communication between the parents to the food insecurity of the family and community, to national immigration policy, and to the physician and team involved in their care?"

27.5 Behavioral Sciences Curriculum

Once the family medicine residency was created, Carlos Sluzki became director of its Behavioral Sciences curriculum. This curriculum focused on specific training for the intimate relational therapy work with individual, couples, and families who comprised the residents' primary care medical practices. From 1977 to 1982, he trained residents in the therapeutic approach he had helped create at the Mental Research Institute, and began to draft proto-manuals for that curriculum to assist residents in working therapeutically with couples.

Howard Liddle became director of the Behavioral Sciences curriculum in 1982, and I joined the faculty the next year. Together, we expanded the therapeutic model that residents learned to encompass the structural-strategic approach that we had been developing (Liddle & Saba, 1985; Schwartz et al., 1985). This approach was rooted in our training by and work with Salvador Minuchin, Braulio Montalvo, and Jay Haley. In addition to building the curriculum on the concepts of the structural-strategic model, we began to apply findings from two research projects that we were simultaneously conducting in the residency's outpatient clinic. One project explored families' experience with chronic illness and health, and the other was a National Institute of Health-funded randomized control trial on adolescent substance use and family therapy from a structural-strategic approach. This latter project was an incubator for Liddle's development of the highly effective, manualized Multidimensional Family Therapy model.

In 1986, I became the director of the Behavioral Sciences curriculum and began to grapple with codifying our therapeutic and training models. Over the next few years, we began to write more formal manuals that were specific to particular components of the curriculum. These focused manuals took the form of paper handouts which were distributed at the start of the particular curriculum.

27.6 Manuals, Epistemology, and Pedagogy

Articulating our epistemologic and pedagogic foundation was a necessary first step to more formally codifying our work. From the beginning of our residency, we had grounded our behavioral science curriculum in a systemic and relational epistemology. When Gregory Bateson's posthumous work *Where Angels Fear* appeared (Bateson and Bateson, 1987), it provided a new shift in our work. To counter the mechanistic interpretations that people were making regarding systems (i.e., a system is an object that can be tinkered with), Bateson introduced the epistemology of the sacred. In the burgeoning field of systems-based medicine, we had experienced the same phenomena. The biopsychosocial model (Engel, 1977) was often interpreted as a guide for seeing the individual in context rather than multiple interconnected subsystems. Bateson's focus on the sacred seemed a valuable correction that we needed in our treatment and training.

Bateson described the sacred as the larger immanent mind, the pattern that connects, with its vast network of interconnections, circuitry of feedback, branchings and communication patterns of information wrapped up in a beautiful organized whole. He believed the sacred could repair the Cartesian tear in the fabric of life. However, by its very nature, the sacred eludes simple definition, because as Bateson believed "we never see in consciousness that the mind is like an ecosystem - a self-corrective network of circuits. We only see arcs of these circuits" (Bateson, 1979, p.8). Yet the sacred is available for our experience and awe, as it holds multiple dimensions of organization in its gaze and allows us to focus on the beauty of organizational process even in the face of pain, suffering, and death.

In addition to Bateson's work, we were also influenced by other systems thinkers whose work was pertinent to the community we serve. As our mission has always been to care for those families and communities which are historically disenfranchised and underresourced, we wanted to explicitly address how our physicians would interact in a just manner that would counter the oppression these families experience and not replicate oppression in our care of them. Paolo Freire's (1970) *Pedagogy of the Oppressed* and bell hooks' (sic) (1994, 2013) *engaged pedagogy* became influential in developing our anti-oppression and anti-racist therapeutic and educational approaches. The work of two systems thinkers and researchers, Chris Argyris and Donald Schön, also became a valuable resource for training physicians to engage in recurrent sequences of action and reflection (Argyris & Schön, 1974; Schön, 1983, 1987). All of these systemic and relational influences presented well-developed models of learning that aligned well with one another and emphasize learning is always a mutual process in the context of relationships that include ourselves, our learners, and the families and communities we serve.

In the 1980s, we also began the process of codifying the training program. An early step involved formally delineating specific goals and objectives for the various components of the 3-year training. We then transposed the research manuals of the structural-strategic treatment approach developed in our chronic illness and substance use studies to inform a curricular manual. This information provided an evidence base for our manualized clinical model.

Residents frequently requested a "how to" cookbook for a step-by-step approach to care for families. At this time, a substantive literature on the growing field of family systems medicine emerged. Don Bloch (1983) created the journal *Family Systems Medicine* (now *Families, Systems, & Health*) which served as a forum for mapping this new territory. Doherty and Baird (1983) offered a perspective of collaboration between the family therapy and family medicine fields, and followed with a volume of case studies demonstrating it in practice (Doherty & Baird, 1987). McDaniel et al. (1990) published *Family Oriented Primary Care: A Manual for Medical Providers*. They discussed how primary care physicians could implement a family systems approach to various topics including conducting a family meeting, treating a couple, focusing on chronic illness, and life cycle stages, and ended each chapter with step-by-step protocols.

We found these resources useful supplementary material to our teaching, as they provided residents multiple examples of how physicians could conceptualize and treat families. However, we faced a continual challenge when residents read these publications. Frequently, the discussion and examples in this literature maintained an exclusive focus on the family, and did not demonstrate how to think of the multiple, interconnected systems inside and outside the skin of those in the family. Residents were vulnerable to the reductionistic approach common in the tendency of biomedical training, and were applying it to this literature. They were interpreting a more reductionistic perspective to the work (e.g., the family, not the individual, was now the object for assessment and treatment; the assessment did not include themselves, and understanding or intervening in social, political, and discriminatory systems was not part of their work).

Similarly, we faced a challenge from some of the literature emerging from the family therapy field that focused primarily on a narrow definition of family, an implied mandate to only seeing whole families in treatment, and a content-focused approach to clinical issues. For example, the cross-cultural literature of this time often involved delineating the typical behaviors of Black families or Asian families. Development literature described how families move through discrete, predictable life cycle stages, regardless of class, race, or other sociopolitical factors. While this literature offered important information and lent itself to being manualized and offering algorithms and protocols, such as the key things to know about treating Latino families or the stages of therapy with people who are refugees from a war zone (Hoang & Erickson, 1982; McGoldrick et al., 1982), the guidance was not systemic, could lead one toward a deficit rather than strength focus, tended toward overgeneralization and was unable to deal with the uniqueness and complexity of the families who came to us for care (Liddle & Saba, 1982; Saba & Rodgers, 1989; Saba et al., 1990). In any attempt to manualize our training, we knew it would require a format that was process rather than content oriented. For example, rather than talking about the expected changes in life cycle stages (e.g., leaving home), we shifted to asking: "How does the family I now care for move through this particular time of change, adapting and learning to internal and external demands?" Questions replaced statements. Rather than borrowing the emerging "how to" approaches, we needed to actively contextualize the literature on "family" to help residents recognize that the family was one key system and not the only one to consider in their systemic care (Saba, 1985, 2002a). It became important for us to develop a means of providing a systemic guide to the work of the family physician that was process oriented rather than protocol oriented, to counter the tendency to follow a mechanistic, algorithm for how to treat the families we served.

Shifts in therapeutic approach. In the late 1980s, based on our clinical experience, increased research on the physician/patient/family relationship, and Bateson's epistemology of the sacred, I moved away from a strict structural-strategic approach and developed a systemic and relational treatment approach. This approach orients physicians toward acknowledging they are participants within the systemic mind, that is, within the sacred, and involved in a process of healing within a living organism, rather than acting as an outward agent who enters to cure disease. Adopting this stance requires physicians to radically and continuously remain vigilant to function "as a part of" rather than "apart from." The therapeutic effort includes asking everyone in the system (physician/family/others) to search for patterns, sequences, and interactions; identify strengths; co-create stories and reframes; engage in mutual learning, support reflection and action; think and act systemically; manage complexity and uncertainty; maintain humility; and work actively against oppression (Saba, 1987). Because of the tendency to learn an approach and apply it, we knew that a manual served the vital role of reminding residents of their correct place within the organism.

As we further drafted the manual, we reinforced that this approach was appropriate both for seeing couples and families and also applicable to any level of the system (within the individual; the community; the health care team; the training program; and larger social and political systems). Residents needed to see the connections among the multiple systems and decide whether at a particular moment in care they prescribe medication for asthma, work with the patient and partner who are in conflict, and/or write the landlord to ask for a move from the fifth floor to a first-floor apartment.

We also became conscious of how the language in the manual could unwittingly reinforce a more mechanistic way of talking about systems and systemic treatment. We needed to be careful that the explication of concepts and strategies did not lead to discussing families as if they were gears in a machine that should be tinkered with and manipulated. Therefore, we adopted more formally the language of the sacred, emphasized every person and family's uniqueness, focusing on the mutuality of the interaction, and used examples to help physicians envision a living organism that they and families were co-creating.

27.7 Manuals and the Sacred

In 1990, our Behavioral Science faculty shrank from three to one, due to severe budget cuts. I took this opportunity to write the first comprehensive and complete training manual to communicate the goals and processes of our curriculum and to externalize its development outside of me. This manual was the by-product of the mutually influencing activities of training, our clinical approach, and our research that had been co-evolving up to this point.

Working from an epistemology of the sacred raised its own challenges in the process of manualizing. According to Bateson, the sacred is not an object or a "thing" that can be delineated; it is a vast unconscious that cannot and should not be brought wholly into consciousness. Can we, therefore, manualize an approach to training and therapy that is grounded in the sacred? How do we ensure the rigor needed to consistently teach physicians in our approach and also foster the creativity and beauty needed for learning and healing?

For us, manualizing is a methodology to guide residents and faculty to provide these contexts. Manualizing does not simply produce a written document nor a list of directives that uni-directionally tells the physician what to do to a family, at certain points in treatment, that must be rigidly adhered to in order to guarantee consistency. Rather manualizing serves as an anchor to help us rigorously keep our gaze on the sacred, rather than drifting into extreme reductionism. It serves to reorient us to the correct position in the systemic mind. Our manualizing is a living process, which provides a nodal point that reflects the co-learning within the relationships of the physician, supervisor, family, and the training program. It coevolves in an iterative fashion between theory and praxis, and in a sense, represents an ongoing research methodology. By manualizing, we are forced to state what we do, define it, and recognize its limits. The manual not only reflects what we teach, but is also an intervention, that impacts the faculty, the residents, the families, and other systems with whom we were interconnected.

Initially, we developed separate manuals—one for the therapeutic approach with families, another for the training of residents, and third for the training of faculty. However, we realized that all three activities were isomorphic and interconnected, as they were all based on a systemic perspective on learning and change (Liddle & Saba, 1985). Therefore, we moved from three discrete manuals to one meta-manual that could then be applied more specifically to each activity. For example, the meta-manual discusses the importance of mutuality of learning or the importance of recurring acting and reflecting. Then we have provided guidance on how those concepts operate in the encounter between the physician and the family, or between the faculty and the resident.

The manual is in constant flux and revision. Feedback from all three of these groups shape changes in emphasis or content. Changes in the needs of the community we serve may require a shift in what physicians may focus on at a particular point in time. For example, changes in immigration policy may result in some families becoming more fearful to engage in treatment and require physicians to focus primarily on relationship building and/developing specific skills that communicate an attempt to create as safe an environment as possible. Increased messaging in medical school for a particular generation of physicians that individually oriented therapies and/or antidepressants are the gold standard requires further attention to explicating the systemic epistemology and debating its clinical value. While clearly the manual is a map and not the territory, our process of manualization has always reflected the complex dance between the map, territory, cartographers, and travelers.

27.8 The Manual

Throughout the 3-year residency program, our physicians receive 300 h of training in our systemic and relational therapy approach. Teaching methods include lectures, seminars, live supervision, video review, and group reflection (see Table 27.1). The

Table 27.1 Number of hours of behavioral science curriculum for each resident

	Outpatient clinic	Classroom	Inpatient hospital	Hours
PGY 1	Linkage 60 h	Lectures and seminars 10 h	Behavioral health rounds 20 h	90
PGY2	Linkage 20 h Family care unit 55 h	Lectures and seminars 25	Behavioral health rounds 10 h	110
PGY3	Linkage 10 h Family care unit 55 h	Lectures and seminars 25	Behavioral health rounds 10 h	100
Hours	90	170	40	300

Table 27.2 Goal of behavioral science curriculum

To increase the capacity to rigorously assume and maintain a correct position in relation to the sacred that will ground learning of a systemic and relational approach to family medicine. To increase capacity, we need to:
1) Create liberating rather than oppressive relationships;
2) Experience the interconnectedness of life in which we are a participant in the ecosystem;
3) Search for the patterns that connect;
4) Engage in and encourage continual action and reflection within the system;
5) Foster respect, awe and humility;
6) Catalyze interactional processes that will link dislocated or disrupted relationships back to the systemic mind, the sacred.

manual is distributed to all residents at the beginning of their training and again at the start of each main component of the curriculum. Much of the training is done in small groups, so that the relationships among the learners and with the faculty and family become an added dimension that is addressed in the manual. The synergy among peers as they use the manual and see how they interpret it variably in practice often helps to inform needed changes in the approach. Residents are provided with an overview of the manual at the start of their training. The complete manual has moved from paper handouts to an electronic format and we introduce the manual progressively as they begin each component of their training over the 3 years.

The manual begins with stating the goal of the curriculum—to build physician's capacity to rigorously assume and maintain a correct position in relation to the sacred that will ground their learning of a systemic and relational approach to family medicine. To increase their capacity, physicians need to engage in a number of experiences that, as Bateson notes, are essential to learning and healing—become adept at catalyzing interactional processes that will link dislocated or disrupted relationships back to the systemic mind, the sacred. Table 27.2 highlights some of the experiences physicians will need to increase their capacity. We delineate how systemic physicians do not structure their practice as systemic therapists do. Therapists typically begin work with an individual, couple, or family focusing on a problem already identified by them or another professional, spend on average an hour for each session, and have a limited time frame for treatment. Family physicians see people in continuity over years, in appointments that often last 20 min and can focus on multiple physical, emotional, and behavioral issues. Family physicians' relationships with families are built through various avenues (caring for a parent's diabetes; attending the delivery of a baby) and trust to address mental health issues is often already developed by the time they emerge; in addition, they can focus on preventing relationship problems in addition to treatment. Treatment strategies tend toward maintaining the physician-family relationship in order to allow families access to come for the breadth of care. Residents do not set ultimatums with patients (e.g., "If you are not ready to deal with your problems (e.g., depression, substance use, diabetes) please come back into care when you are ready."). Rather they learn to make small changes while working on other health issues and being ready to intervene when the time is right. Therefore, the manual clarifies that residents are not learning a twelve week, one hour per week, therapy model which is focused on a particular presenting problem. Rather it helps them learn systemic therapy principles and strategies to use in each visit. The manual provides guidance on how to be systemic whether the visit is twenty or 40 min and whether the strategies combine treatment of diabetes and family communication or have an emphasis of one over the other at any given time.

The manual then presents the core beliefs about the systemic medical model (Table 27.3) and the objectives of the Behavioral Science Curriculum (Table 27.4). Systemic-centered medical care expands beyond curing disease to include healing. Rather than seeing the physician as the expert who transfers knowledge to a passive family, it views both physician and family as having expertise. In biomedical care, the physician and the family unilaterally try to control the treatment process and protect themselves; the systemic approach envisions mutuality—of control, responsibility for the outcome, and protection. The goal of treatment is to optimize the mutual learning, growth, adaptation, and healing of multiple interconnected subsystems (e.g., family, physician, and training system).

Table 27.3 Core beliefs of behavioral science curriculum

Core beliefs about the systemic medical model include:
1) Refusing to participate in and maintain oppressive, racist structures and relationships to actively challenging them and creating ones that are collectively liberating;
2) Moving from a pathology, deficit-based assessment to a more strength and resilience-based approach;
3) No longer using reductionism as the only way to understand the disease, but including it as one tool alongside more complex, contextual methods;
4) No longer privileging dichotomous thinking or linear cause and effect, but moving toward both/and thinking, circularity, and complexity;
5) Recognizing the limits of certainty and accepting uncertainty, ambivalence, and ambiguity;
6) Valuing emotions as much as rational thinking;
7) Expanding beyond the bio-organic and physiologic processes within the patient's skin to exploring the social and interpersonal determinants of health, in particular appreciating the oppressive structures and institutional racism that negatively affect health;
8) Moving away from an external objective observer/intervener to a participant within the system.

Table 27.4 Objectives of behavioral science curriculum

1) Develop caring and trusting relationships that are collectively liberating rather than oppressive
2) Understand the influence of and address the socio-cultural determinants of health (racism, oppressive systemic structures, poverty, unstable housing, food insecurity, cultural beliefs)
3) Create contexts that foster mutual learning, development, adaptation, and resilience of the interconnected family, therapeutic, and training systems (e.g., deutero-learning)
4) Assess inter and intrapersonal interfaces and patterns related to health and illness
5) Construct a meaning-centered narrative
6) Foster reflective, engaged participation within the system
7) Learn relationship-oriented strategies for learning-joining, reframing, enactment, between session tasks
8) Utilize digital and analogic communication
9) Collaborate as a team, and specifically learn to work in an integrated way with therapists

27.9 Examples of Objectives from the Manual

The manual next delineates how one can develop competency within each objective and offers clinical examples. For example, for the objective of **"Develop caring and trusting relationships"** we have identified three areas of foci: (1) What skills will facilitate a patient/family's trust in the physician? (demonstrating empathy, offering support, instilling hope, expressing one's openness to questions and disagreement; following through on promises; acknowledging mistrust); (2) What skills are necessary to establish and maintain effective communication patterns? (revealing one's assumptions, using professional interpreters rather than family members, assessing health literacy). (3) What skills will convey that the physician cares about the family (overtly expressing their concern; active listening)? One of the clinical examples describes a family who expresses concern about receiving care at a public hospital. The family is African American and well aware of the historical experimentation on Blacks in the United States for scientific research. They wonder if the physician is only interested in them for learning rather than truly wanting to help. The systemic physician says, "I know that you are mistrustful of me, and that is understandable. I want to earn your trust. I truly care about you. Please let me know if at any point you believe I am not working towards your best interests."

Another objective in the manual: *Foster a Reflective, Engaged Participation within the System* also has three specific foci: (1) What skills will enhance everyone's consideration of each other's perspectives (reflect what one hears from each family member; circular questioning; double listening); (2) How can we focus on observable data that allows reflection, agreement, and disagreement about what we see and how we interpret? How can we identify the "difference that makes a difference" occurring in observable data, rather than at a distant point of inference? (3) What will foster a mindful presence in the encounter? (4) What skills will stimulate "reflection on action," which is the ability to reflect on something that has just happened (inquiring about thoughts and feelings regarding what family members have just enacted; involving an observation team of colleagues)? and (5) What will stimulate "reflection-in-action" (reflect on one's own and/or other's actions)? One example involves a single parent and her 16-year-old daughter with retractable migraines which has resulted in missing school. The mother is recently unemployed, and the daughter has received a scholarship to transfer from the worst school, in San Francisco to the best, because of her intelligence and hard work. They are African American, and the mother wonders if the teachers are racist. The physician asks them to discuss together the daughter's concerns that her teachers are not supportive when she misses school or turns her homework in late. As they talk together, the mother becomes angry, saying she will go to the school to confront the teachers. The daughter becomes visibly nervous, touches her mother's hand and tells her to calm down. The mother raises her voice, reasserting she will go and defend her daughter. The daughter again tries to calm her down. The physician intervenes, describes what he sees, and asks what they were thinking and feeling.

Another objective, **Utilize Digital and Analogic Communication**, encourages physicians to engage in verbal discussion as well as art, music, dance, poetry, and rituals. Physicians historically have the experience of verbal communication through conveying information and nonverbal communication primarily through physical touch. However, beginning to engage in more creative activities within a medical exam can be conceptually difficult to imagine. The manual provides guiding questions and multiple clinical examples. Questions include: What do you enjoy/or have you enjoyed doing? Who do you enjoy doing this with? How often do you engage in that activity now? Can we engage in that activity now during our visit (draw, sing; write a story/poem, look at pictures of loved ones, ask children and parents create a game (theme and rules), and then play at home/future visit. Various rationales are provided to suggest how analogic modes can be effective (access other dimensions of consciousness; change the tone in the interaction; connect patients/families to their strengths). The physician is caring for a woman from Cuba who has worsening diabetes. Their visits typically involve the physician talking about diabetes, medication, and recommendations to eat better and walk, and the patient agreeing. This visit the patient tells the physician that she was too tired to walk more and her husband, who is in the visit, agrees. The physician shifts to ask her what she used to do when she was more active. She replies that she and her husband regularly went salsa dancing. The physician, also a salsa dancer, begins to play a song on her IPhone and asks the patient to dance with her. As they begin to dance, the physician motions for the husband to join them. The couple then dances to another song. The patient smiles, saying, "We have not danced together for years; I now know we can." The couple begins to dance weekly and her diabetes improves.

27.10 Value of Our Manualized Training

How do we know if this manualized training and therapy approach is beneficial? And how can research inform the evolution of the manual? The experience of our graduates in practice provides real-world feedback for the manual. The American

Council on Graduate Medical Education, the national accrediting organization for medical specialties, independently contacts our physicians 3 years after graduation and inquires about the full range of the training (obstetrics; pediatrics), including psychotherapy. Annual surveys from 2016 to 2020 have found that 90% of our residency graduates have said they were well-prepared to provide psychotherapy compared to 86% of the graduates in family medicine in the United States who responded to the survey; also 87% of our graduates were still actively involved in providing psychotherapy therapy compared to 85% of the national respondents.

As part of our ongoing quality improvement process, we continually review the therapy training clinic experience (Family Care Unit) which then also shapes the manual. For example, once our physicians complete their rotation in this clinic, they continue to provide the patients and families systemic therapy and/or co-follow their therapy with our clinic's therapists. Resident's evaluations of the clinic reveal that the vast majority of patients and families they care for during this training clinic are substantially improved, and nearly all of the physician-patient/family relationships are improved. They note that they prescribe approximately 15% of their clinic patients' psychiatric medications. While this is low compared to 70% of those patients receiving medications in the national studies (Abed Faghri et al., 2010; Gill et al., 2010). This percentage has risen slightly in the last 2 years; residents attribute it to guidelines they learned prior to medical school and our county's health systems' metrics which are tied to funding. This trend has shaped the manual to include further focus on the risks and benefits of following current evidence-based guidelines regarding psychiatric medication which we have introduced at the beginning of their training.

Qualitative research also provides information to shape the manual. In a recent study using Stimulated Recall (Thom et al, 2016) families in our clinic identified that the quality of the physician-family relationship greatly affected their capacity for healing. Families said that to engage in the treatment, the physicians needed: (1) to demonstrate that they care for them as people, not just patients, (2) to show a sincere interest in the families' interpersonal context, and (3) to gain their trust to ensure they were not being used for experimental purposes. These findings lead to changes in the manual to highlight how physicians can specifically attend to these issues.

27.11 Recurrent Challenges

Qualitative research with residents about using the manualized approach revealed recurrent challenges they face.

27.11.1 Reductionism

While our physicians choose our training program because they fundamentally believe in a systemic approach, they are still susceptible to thinking reductionistically given that their medical school education remains based on a biomedical reductionistic model. The dominant field encourages them to focus only on the individual level. The health care delivery system requires them to assign diagnoses to the individual, use screening measures and employ individually oriented treatment approaches. Residents said they were vulnerable to protocols that told them what to do when. "I know what to do to start treatment for hypertension; I just follow the algorithm. I know it's not the same, but I sometimes want an algorithm on how to treat depression or what to do in a family meeting. Then I won't make a mistake. Ultimately, I know that isn't possible though." Over the years, residents have wanted protocols for treating diagnoses that become highlighted in the field as important to attend to: trauma, substance use disorder, culturally competent care, interpersonal violence. Early in training, they also acknowledge thinking rigidly that systemic therapy only happens when you have a family in front of you. These concerns are most evident at the beginning of residency and begin to resolve in the third year in which they have more practice with our manual and the systemic approach.

27.11.2 Evidence-Based Treatment

When they hear about new evidence-based treatments (such as the Transtheoretical model, Cognitive Behavioral Therapy, Motivational Interviewing, Serotonin Selective Reuptake Inhibitors), residents report that they feel the urgency to learn about them and incorporate them into a 15-min office visits. The evidence-based medicine movement is a strong force in their medical school training. In residency, evaluation by faculty from other specialty departments, expected answers on their national licensing examinations, externally applied metrics for our clinic's revenues, reinforce what they feel required, that they expect themselves to apply it to the therapeutic realm. Conversely, they also learn that if you do not have a proven treatment, then you should not ask patients about problems you cannot treat. Even if one suspects that there is a psychosocial issue that families are struggling with, if you cannot treat it with an evidence-based approach, you should not broach the topic. They report most influenced by this approach until the middle of their second year, when they have patients who do not fare as well as the research may suggest and as they have more skills themselves to work systemically.

27.11.3 Desire to Fix

Residents reported that the pressure to follow evidence-based treatments is intensified because they have a strong desire to "fix" their patients' and families' many medical and psychosocial problems. They consciously try to fix a problem in a lineal way. These epistemological pressures lead them say to us: "Tell me what should I do, step by step, to fix this problem." They want the type of manualized algorithms or protocols that they see so frequently in their biomedicine for treating hypertension or diabetes. These challenges particularly plague our physicians in the first 2 years of residency. We have increasingly shaped the manual to overtly address this tendency, which Bateson (1982) identified as "conscious purposiveness," that is, the desire to fix problems in a lineal way that often creates new problems. This tendency leads physicians to see only arcs of patterns and conclude that they represent the whole and are the only information needed to resolve health problems. Bateson cautioned that by treating arcs out of context, we risk ignoring other messages in the ecosystem, but by relaxing that arrogance of conscious purpose in favor of creative experience we can optimize the opportunity for real healing to occur.

We have used these findings from research with residents to include extensive discussions and examples of these themes in the manual.

27.12 Program Evaluation

Prior to and after finishing each curricular component of the behavioral science curriculum residents complete self-evaluations and evaluate the usefulness of the manual. Recent resident comments include the following:

- *"It is really great that what we are experiencing is guided by the manual, and also can change it. It's like we are creating the curriculum for the next group." (2nd year resident)*
- *"I really needed the manual at the beginning of 2nd year, just to know I wasn't missing anything; although I realize I was doing what was in the manual and more; so I was reassured. By 3rd year, I think it is just part of me now. I only really rely on it when I have a really challenging situation and feel stuck." (3rd year resident)*
- *"I was glad to see this at the start of training, because I get anxious if I don't know if I am going to learn everything I need to know." (1st year resident)*
- *"Looking back, it's interesting to see how we all act so differently from one another in the room with patients but still seem to be following the same principles. I really learn so much from seeing how differently we can work and still help." (3rd year resident)*
- *"I know what's in the manual, but I don't like reviewing it before the visit. I like doing first, then going back to the manual to put a name for what I was doing. That consolidates it for me." (2nd year resident).*

Comments on the use of the manual over the years reveal that residents vary greatly from those who want to rely on the manual with a methodical application of the approach to those that primarily want to know the principles, engage first with families, and then reflect on their experience by reviewing the manual with colleagues.

On the self-evaluations, the average change in score for residents from prior to and after completing the Behavioral Science curriculum is from 2.75 to 4.80 (on a 5 point Likert scale; 2017–2019). The residency program has an official body that reviews all components of the training annually, including the Behavioral Science Curriculum, in part basing the review on the residents' anonymous of the experience. This review is conducted by the program director, residency faculty, and residents. In addition, our residency clinic has a Patient Advisory Council, which consists of a group of Family Health Center patients whose role includes evaluating the current treatment of patients and families and collaborating with the residency program to ensure training curricula are responsive to patients' and families' needs. Feedback informs any necessary revisions to the training and to the manual. Suggestions based on patient, resident, and faculty feedback have helped evolve the manual to remain relevant and responsive to clinical and educational needs.

27.13 Dissemination of the Manualized Curriculum

Given the continual evolution over the past several decades of a manualized approach and the reluctance of the medical education literature to include manuals, we have not published the manual in its complete form. However, we have disseminated several components of it, particularly once we have been able to research their value (Saba, 2017). Some of these components have also been adopted by other training programs. The Linkage Curriculum training, initiated by Sluzki in 1981, was disseminated (Saba et al., 6) and adopted by a family medicine program in New York City, which formally evaluated it and found it successfully formed trusting relationships with patient, residents, and faculty, effectively taught resident to integrate the family systems approach into patient care and provided a mechanism for faculty to monitor the learning needs of the residents (Williams et al., 2011). The inpatient Behavioral Health Rounds curriculum with qualitative analysis of its process (Saba et al., 2019) has been adopted by five family medicine and pediatric residency programs in the United States. A basic content-oriented toolkit covering 20 key issues for health professionals to consider in clinical care was incorporated into the medical student curriculum at UCSF (Saba et al., 2010), and then revised and included into the training of health psychologists at Università Sacro Cuore in Milan (Saita et al., 2011). Two components of the social justice training, an Anti-oppression curriculum (Wu et al., 2019) and an Antiracism toolkit (Edgoose et al., 2017, 2021), have been used in multiple residencies and health professional teaching programs with significant positive change among the learners. Faculty development programs have utilized the curriculum exploring physicians' model of medicine (Saba, 1999; Rydel, 2009) and the core beliefs and values of the family systems training (Saba, 2000, 2002b; Saba, 2002c; Hepworth, 2003). We plan to submit our complete manual to one of the newer online medical education platforms (MedEd Portal, Family Medicine Digital Resource Library) which have published some of our curricular components previously and may be interested in a disseminating a more comprehensive manualization of a program.

27.14 Manuals and the Pandemic

When the COVID-19 pandemic emerged in the city of San Francisco, our outpatient training clinic and our public hospital were at the center of the health department's response, and we needed to make immediate adaptations. We sheltered in place earlier than other major cities in the United States. Our resident physicians stopped seeing patients and families in person in the outpatient clinic, except for urgent problems and shifted to a telephone visit model of treatment. We moved most of our residents to our inpatient service and other hospital departments to care for patients who had or were presumed to have the virus. We had to drastically alter the behavioral science curriculum, because we no longer could see families in person; and telephone visits were challenging, given the limited technologic resources our families have (lack of phones, many requiring interpreters). As our existing curriculum relied on live supervision and video review of the visits in small groups, we struggled to design a meaningful replacement curriculum. We could not enact much of what we have manualized.

However, we believed that the manual represents a process more than a product and is continually adapting. The pandemic has been an unprecedented test of that hypothesis. Rather than only focusing on what we were unable to do, we returned to the core values and beliefs and then determined how best we could enact them given the current contextual possibilities and constraints (see Tables 27.2 and 27.3). We also actively outreached to our families who were the ones most devastated by the virus in our city. From both of these processes, we reaffirmed that fundamentally we needed to help residents and ourselves find the correct stance within the mind of the sacred, which included the coronavirus. We needed to maintain awe and humility in what we could do, in experiencing interconnectedness of life, and fostering relationships that were collectively liberating rather than oppressive.

We recognized that our families were facing disproportionate effects: Asian American families were facing discrimination for being identified with the cause of the pandemic. The Latin X families had a higher rate of positive test given that they could not easily shelter in place without losing employment and were in jobs that were of high risk, and the African American community was disproportionately hospitalized and having worse outcomes. Systemic racism, which the families we care, have faced for hundreds of years in the United States, was operating at multiple levels, from how it affected economic pressures to an already poor infrastructure to care for families who are marginalized. At the same time as the pandemic, with the deaths of George Floyd and many others, once documented and disseminated publicly, more Americans began to acknowledge the depth of racism in our country and its many adverse effects, none the least are related to health inequities.

While our residency's mission, our therapeutic approach and subsequently our manual have always been focused on creating liberating not oppressive or racist experiences or relationships with the families who come to us for care, we needed to help our residents implement this mission in the context of the social, political, and health issues that our families were dealing with. Our daily work became outreaching to those families and addressing their social needs and stresses. We found an increased ability to talk to family members of patients, previously unavailable due to work, as more were also sheltering in place and available. We could talk to families who might be experiencing stresses of living for an extended time in close quarters (handling conflict in couples, with children, designing ways to safely discussing the risk of/and action physical and emotional abuse). In our group reflection rounds on our inpatient service, although we were in different locations in the hospital rather than in one room, served a much-needed purpose of helping learners deal with the stresses of caring for patients who were COVID-19+ and who could not see family members; fear of their own infection, and the inadequacy of what they expected to be able to do as physicians. In time, we have found ways to have "live supervision" in using a combination of telephone and video platform. We were able to talk much more readily with patients, families, and each other about how racism was affecting our decision-making and the quality of our care, and provide additional examples and considerations in the manual that furthered our anti-racist and anti-oppressive teaching and treatment.

While this remains a work in progress, we have taken the opportunity to identify what ways of clinical care and education we want to change, for the better, and what now feels more valuable than ever, as we are without it. The manual which required explicitness at all stages: values, beliefs, concepts, objectives, content provided a map for where we needed to find our grounding, what we could continue, what we must abandon, and what new possibilities existed. Without it, we would have had a much harder time in the crisis to determine the rapid changes in clinical care and teaching that were essential. Rather than scrambling to enact a rigid set of procedures in the moment of crisis, we found that the manual served its purpose: to resituate us in a correct position in the living organism of the mind, of the sacred, as we cared for those families most in need.

27.15 Conclusion

To provide meaningful treatment for those families who have been marginalized by society, who face many challenges, and who have many strengths, our experience suggests that systemic physicians can benefit from the rigor of manualizing that can focus everyone's gaze on the sacred, while providing the imagination to foster the humility, awe, and love needed for healing.

References

Abed Faghri, N. M., Boisvert, C. M., & Faghri, S. (2010). Understanding the expanding role of primary care physicians (PCPs) to primary psychiatric care physicians (PPCP): Enhancing the assessment and treatment of psychiatric conditions. *Mental Health in Family Medicine, 7*(1), 17–25.

American Psychological Association. (2017). *Psychology in primary care*. Resource document. APA Center for Psychology and Health. https://www.apa.org/health/briefs/primary-care.pdf 2017. Accessed 5 May 2020.

Argyris, C., & Schön, D. (1974). *Theory in practice: Increasing professional effectiveness.* Jossey-Bass.
Bateson, G. B. (1979). *Mind and nature.* Dutton.
Bateson, G. (1982, Winter). They threw god out of the garden. *CoEvolution Quarterly, 62*–67.
Bateson, G. B. (1987). *Steps to an ecology of the mind* (p. 1987). Jason Aronson.
Bateson, G. B., & Bateson, M. C. (1987). *Angels fear: Towards an epistemology of the sacred.* Macmillan.
Bloch, D. (Ed.). (1983). *Family systems medicine journal (now families, systems, & health).* American Psychological Association.
Doherty, W. J., & Baird, M. A. (1983). *Family therapy and family medicine: Toward the primary care of families.* Guilford Press.
Doherty, W. J., & Baird, M. A. (1987). *Family-centered medical care: A clinical casebook.* Guilford Press.
Edgoose, J., Anderson, Q., Brown Speights, J., Bullock, K., Ferguson, W., Fraser, K., Guh, J., Martinez-Bianchi, V., Ring, J., Roberson, K., Rodgers, D., Saba, G., Saint-Hilaire, L., Svetaz, V., White-Davis, T., & Wu, D. (2017). Toolkit for Teaching About Racism in the Context of Persistent Health and Healthcare Disparities, 04-30-2017 16:35. *Society of Family Medicine Resource Library.* https://resourcelibrary.stfm.org/viewdocument/toolkit-for-teaching-about-racism-i.\
Edgoose, J. Y. C., Brown Speights, J. S., White-Davis, T., Guh, J., Bullock, K., Roberson, K., De Leon, J., Ferguson, W., & Saba, G. W. (2021). Teaching about racism in medical education: A mixed method analysis of the need for and outcome of a train-the-trainer faculty development workshop. *Family Medicine*;53(1):23-31.DOI: 10.22454/FamMed.2021.408300.
Engel, G. L. (1977). The need for a new medical model: A challenge for biomedicine. *Science, 196*(4276), 129–136. https://doi.org/10.1126/science.847460
Freire, P. (1970). *Pedagogy of the oppressed.* Herder & Herder.
Gill, J. M., Klinkman, M. S., & Chen, Y. X. (2010). Antidepressant use for primary care patients with and without medical comorbidities. *Journal of American Board of Family Medicine, 23*, 449–508.
Hepworth, J. (2003). Personal communication.
Hoang, G. N., & Erickson, R. V. (1982). Guidelines for providing medical care to Southeast Asian refugees. *The Journal of the American Medical Association, 248*(6), 710–714. https://doi.org/10.1001/jama.1982.03330060050033
hooks, b. (1994). *Teaching to transgress.* Routledge.
hooks, b. (2013). *Writing beyond race.* Routledge.
Liddle, H. A., & Saba, G. W. (1982). Clinical use of the family life cycle: Some cautionary guidelines. In H. A. Liddle (Ed.), *Clinical implications of the family life cycle* (pp. 161–176). Aspen Publication.
Liddle, H. A., & Saba, G. W. (1985). The isomorphic nature of training and therapy: Epistemologic foundation for a structural-strategic training paradigm. In J. Schwartzman (Ed.), *Families and other systems* (pp. 27–47). Guilford Press.
McDaniel, S. H., Campbell, T. L., & Seaburn, D. B. (1990). *Family-oriented primary care: A manual for medical providers.* Springer Verlag.
McGoldrick, M., Giordano, J., & Garcia-Preto, N. (1982). *Ethnicity and family therapy.* Guilford Press.
Ransom, D. C., & Vandervoort, H. E. (1973). The development of family medicine. Problematic trends. *JAMA, 225*(9), 1098–1102.
Rydel, T. (2009). Personal communication.
Saba, G. (1985). Introduction to a contextual refocus of systems therapy: An expansion of role, purpose, and responsibility. *Journal of Strategic and Systemic Therapies, 4*, 1–3. https://doi.org/10.1521/jsst.1985.4.2.1
Saba, G. W. (1987). Bypass surgery in the doctor-patient relationship. In W. J. Doherty & M. A. Baird (Eds.), *Family centered medical care: A clinical casebook.* Guilford Press.
Saba, G. (1999). What do family physicians believe and value in their work? *The Journal of the American Board of Family Practice., 12*(3), 206–213. https://doi.org/10.3122/jabfm.12.3.206

Saba, G. W. (2000). Preparing health care professionals for the 21st century: Lessons from Chiron's cave. *Family, Systems, and Health, 18*(3), 353–364.

Saba, G. W. (2002a). *The biopsychosocial approach:* Maps, myths and models of health and illness. In V. Cigoli & M. Mariotti (Eds.), *The physician, the family and the community* (pp. 25–55). FrancoAngeli.

Saba, G. W. (2002b). The behavioral sciences in family medicine: A history of heroic questioning. *Families, Systems & Health, 20*(2), 135–140.

Saba, G. W. (2002c). Educating the biopsychosocial physician: A curriculum in relationship, reflection, and healing. In V. Cigoli & M. Mariotti (Eds.), *The physician, the family and the community* (pp. 114–122). FrancoAngeli.

Saba, G. W. (2017). On training systemic physicians. *Rivista di Psichotherapie Relazionale, 45*, 5–27.

Saba, G., & Fink, D. (1985). Systems medicine and systems therapy: A call to a natural collaboration. *Journal of Strategic and Systemic Therapies, 4*(2), 15–31.

Saba, G. W., & Rodgers, D. (1989). Discrimination in urban family medicine. *Journal of Psychotherapy and the Family, 6*(1–2), 177–207.

Saba, G. W., Karrer, B. M., & Hardy, K. V. (Eds.). (1990). *Minorities and family therapy.* Haworth Press.

Saba, G., Shore, W., Sommers, P., & Rodgers, D. (1996). Teaching a systems approach to family practice residents: The '2-on-2' curriculum. *Families, Systems & Health, 14*, 151–165. https://doi.org/10.1037/h0089909

Saba, G., Satterfield, J., Salazar, R., et al. (2010). The SBS toolbox: Clinical pearls from the social and behavioral sciences. *MedEdPORTAL, 6*, 7980.

Saba, G., Chou, C. L., Satterfield, J., Teherani, A., Hauer, K., Poncelet, A., & Chen, H. C. (2014). Teaching patient-centered communication skills: A telephone follow-up curriculum for medical students. *Medical Education Online, 25*(19), 22522. https://doi.org/10.3402/meo.v19.2

Saba, G., Villella, T., & Goldschmidt, R. (2019). Behavioral science rounds: Identifying and addressing the challenging issues that residents face on a family medicine inpatient service. *Family Medicine, 51*(7), 603–608. https://doi.org/10.22454/FamMed.2019.726006

Saita, E., Novelli, M., & Saba, G. (2011). Pearls toolbox: The psychological equipment for the doctor. In E. Saita (Ed.), *Thinking about health and illness: Links between mind, body and context of belonging* (pp. 53–67). EDUCatt.

Schön, D. (1983). *The reflective practitioner.* Basic Books.

Schön, D. (1987). *Educating the reflective practitioner.* Jossey Bass.

Schwartz, R. C., Barrett, M. J., & Saba, G. (1985). Family therapy for bulimia. In D. Garner & P. Garfinkel (Eds.), *Handbook for psychotherapy for anorexia nervosa and bulimia* (pp. 270–310). Guilford Press.

Sluzki, C. E. (1974). On training to "think interactionally". *Social Science & Medicine, 8*(9–10), 483–485.

Strosahl, K., & Robinson, P. (2020). Bureau of Primary Health Care: Mountain view Consulting Group, Inc. Integrating Primary Care and Behavioral Health Services: A compass and a horizon. https://www.apa.org/practice/programs/rural/integrating-primary-behavioral.pdf Accessed 9 May 2020.

Thom, D. H., Wolf, J., Gardner, H., DeVore, D., Lin, M., Ma, A., Ibarra-Castro, A., & Saba, G. (2016). Decision making in primary care. A qualitative study of how health coaches support patients in making health-related decisions and behavioral changes. *Annals of Family Medicine, 14*(6), 509–516. https://doi.org/10.1370/afm.1988

Williams, Y., Reich, D., Ladonga, L., Tiburcio, J., & Levine, A. (2011). The 2-on-2 precepting model: A method for enhancing and integrating the biopsychosocial perspective. Research. *Annual Conference.* Society of Teachers of Family Medicine: New Orleans. pp 115–116. https://www.stfm.org/media/1752/11an_program.pdf. Accessed 9 May 2020.

Wu, D., Saint-Hilaire, L., Pineda, A., et al. (2019). The efficacy of an antioppression curriculum for health professionals. *Family Medicine, 51*(1), 22–30. https://doi.org/10.22454/FamMed.2018.227415

Chapter 28
Changing the Trainees' Epistemology in Systemic Family Training: The Manual as a Secure Base

Dubravka Trampuž and Maja Rus Makovec

28.1 Introduction

Over the last 25 years, we have been developing the training course in systemic family therapy in different contexts. We were the first group of systemic family therapists in Slovenia who were trained by trainers from the Institute of Family Therapy London. We started in the context of the newly formed Slovene Society for Family Therapy and organised the first introductory courses in collaboration with the Medical faculty of the University of Ljubljana. Prompted by our teachers and supervisors, we embarked on the demanding journey of setting up a 4-year training course in the context of the University Psychiatric Clinic, Ljubljana in collaboration with the Institute of Family Therapy London. This journey enabled us to develop as trainers and supervisors and empowered us to continue our professional development on our own in the context of the Medical faculty, University of Ljubljana and the Institute of Family and Systemic Psychotherapy, which we founded primarily as a training institute.

Over the years, we have considered shortening the training course to 3 years, as the training course is time consuming and demanding. The participants of the course are mainly psychologists, clinical psychologists, psychiatrists, child psychiatrists, and medical doctors who are enthusiastic enough to join the course in order to enrich their practice and be better therapists. In Slovenia, family therapy (nor any other psychotherapy) is still not recognised as a profession. Very few enlightened

---

D. Trampuž (✉)
Slovenia Institute of Family and Systemic Psychotherapy, Ljubljana, Slovenia
e-mail: dubravka.tramp@siol.net

M. Rus Makovec
Outpatient Psychiatry Center, University Psychiatric Clinic Ljubljana, Medical faculty University of Ljubljana, Ljubljana, Slovenia
e-mail: rusmakovec@gmail.com

© Springer Nature Switzerland AG 2021
M. Mariotti et al. (eds.), *Handbook of Systemic Approaches to Psychotherapy Manuals*, European Family Therapy Association Series,
https://doi.org/10.1007/978-3-030-73640-8_28

institutions are willing to send their employees to such lengthy trainings; so, the majority of course participants have to pay for the training and negotiate the time to attend the course. For this reason, the course is organised on weekends and afternoons. Even though we realise that a 4-year commitment is quite a burden for the would-be participant and his/her family, we cannot shorten the course, since in practice, participants need another 6–12 months to complete all the course requirements and feel prepared for their final assessment. At the end of the fourth year when participants, who by now have developed their competencies and are better aware of their strengths and shortcomings as well as their needs, express their wish for further supervision we readily agree and provide another 6 months of free supervision. As trainers and supervisors, we witness their struggles in applying the systemic epistemology in practice and by the end of the training course, we feel we are all sailing on the same boat rowing hard towards the anchor we all hope will be safe and satisfying for all. The cultural context values achievement and even people coming from other cultural contexts, usually from other parts of what once used to be our homeland, seem to assimilate these cultural values. As we have external examiners for the final assessment, we all share this culturally embedded anxiety of not being good enough, since the trainee's assessment is also an assessment of us as trainers and supervisors. So, it is difficult to say whose need we are satisfying more – our trainees or our own.

From a reflexive standpoint, it seems that we, as teachers, have invested our trainees with our understanding and empathy, sympathising and identifying with their needs and struggles. As teachers, we have been committed and responsible, striving to do our best. We can however ask ourselves what is the meaning of "best", "responsible" and "committed" and think of other ways we could deal with our and our trainees' feelings "of not yet being prepared well enough for the final examination". Our trainees come largely from a clinical context and we wonder if for them, the change of perspective may be more difficult than for clinically less experienced colleagues. From the neurobiological perspective, changing the lens from lineal to circular and systemic is enabled by the brain neuroplasticity; whenever we learn something new, including new attitudes, perspectives, or behaviours, we are changing the physical structure of the brain. Experience alters the brain, even as we age (Fishbane, 2007). Even old dogs can learn new tricks, supported by attention, motivation and repetition in an enriched environment which systemic family therapy training is (Lillard & Erisir, 2011). So, in order to enable change, we need a learning ritual, whose repetition enables new encoding. We thought that our persistence in tracking the trainees' systemic reflective processes in his /her different positions of student, therapist, observer and team member may fulfil the role of such a learning ritual which will introduce change in their epistemology. We have realised that, in line with Bateson (1972), the most important thing for the process of learning is to understand our own processes of learning and change through our own training as well as the training of others.

It seems that we need, in the same manner as our clients and patients, first "to tell our story" about our training course before we can focus on our perception of the possibilities a manual can offer in the process of changing the trainees' epistemology.

28.2 Significant Moments That Organised Us in the Development of Our Training Course

28.2.1 Theoretical Input: Theoretical Narratives and the Training Social and Cultural Context

The field of systemic psychotherapy is like a living system in a state of constant evolution, progressing from cybernetics to linguistic systems, from modernism to postmodernism and social constructivism, from Bateson's myth of power to Foucault's socially embedded power, from mechanics to feelings, from communication theory to the theory of attachment and from technical narratives to political and philosophical narratives. The diversity and richness of theoretical narratives and systemic practices from its pioneering stages to the present day are challenging both for the trainees, who have to cope with a vast array of new ideas, and for trainers who have to find a way to present them in a sensible and digestible way, that will enable trainees to own them and connect them with their previously acquired experiences. The multitude of theoretical concepts the trainees get acquainted with in the interactive theoretical and reading seminars has provoked a challenging feedback from a group of our students: "From all that we have learned and read so far, we seem to know less about what systemic psychotherapy is. How would you define it?" It seemed like an echo of Minuchin's (1998) provocative question of where is the family in the evolving systemic practices. It made us think of the importance of a clear structure, with a hierarchy of theoretical concepts and clear boundaries between the core principles of systemic psychotherapy and the rich pool of ideas inspired by post modernism for every trainee/therapist to develop his/her own creative therapeutic style. Another experience we had that strengthened this belief was the observation of trainers and supervisors that some trainees seemed to be adopting an uncritical position towards social constructionist ideas, particularly the concept of conversational therapies and the ideas of Anderson et al. (1986) about "problem determined systems" and the "not-knowing position" (we use Gergen's (1985) term "constructionism" to represent the whole spectrum of relativistic perspectives, which includes also radical constructivism). Some trainees seemed to be taking these ideas too literally: that in therapy anything goes – you just have to talk with the family and see what happens. If the family members do not talk about addiction or physical or sexual abuse or some other hidden family agenda that may be crucial for the therapeutic process, it is not their responsibility to explore it and they do not have to use their expertise since it is the family who knows and is the expert. The problems we encountered in challenging these positions and beliefs in supervision might be in part stemming from our social and cultural context. Slovenia is a small and "adolescent country", only recently separated and developing its autonomy. It has a history of serving different masters, adopting a servile attitude outwardly and a position of rebellious pride inwardly, which was bred on its national language, kept and developed by its literary men. But it is a language of only two million people. Situated at the border of Eastern and Western Europe, it has developed a dual set of values – overvaluing the West and devaluing the East. For the working immigrants from the East, it has functioned as a melting pot of acculturation to Slovenian values. On the other hand, it aspired towards Western values to which it eagerly and uncritically adapted. These tendencies are still deeply rooted in our culture and we think it might be one of the reasons that, although we encourage both our trainees and ourselves to cherish a critical position towards the ideas we present and the texts we read, which are mainly in English and the authors are from the West, we still often miss a wider perspective with different views.

28.2.2 The Application of Theory in Practice: The Formation of Therapeutic Teams

We observed that trainees became more critical of us as trainers in the course of the training which the trainees experienced as particularly stressful and the most stressful time for trainees is the start of live supervision when they form therapeutic teams, usually of four trainees-supervisees. One group of trainees became at that point in the training course extremely dissatisfied with us and they criticised us for not having provided them with a clear, how to do, step-by-step therapy manual. Exploring this issue with the group a safe enough space opened up for the expression of their fears of being seen as incompetent by their peers which made it difficult for them to form therapeutic teams. At that time, trainees were expected to bring their own cases to live supervision, and they expressed fears that their patients will not be willing to come to a therapy context where they will be observed by a team and supervisor, or that they will not be willing to invite other family members. The anxieties of being exposed, of one's work being displayed on stage in front of peers and evaluated by supervisors was overwhelming and it made us wonder what could we do differently in the future to ease these anxieties before they escalate to such a degree as this.

28.3 Diversity of Therapeutic Experiences During the Course of Training

One of the requirements of the training course is that during the course, trainees get an experience of working with families, including couples, with diverse problems. At the time when trainees brought to live supervision families or couples from their working contexts, we realised that some trainees will have a problem fulfilling this, since in their working contexts they do not see patients with a variety of problems. Another shortcoming was that often the therapeutic team could not follow the therapeutic process since the therapeutic work went on in between the supervisions or the trainee, for different reasons, brought another family to the next supervision.

28 Changing the Trainees' Epistemology in Systemic Family Training: The Manual...

Table 28.1 The general training specifications for the 4-year training course

Year	1	2	3	4
Interactive Theoretical input Interwoven with personal & professional Development & Training skills	208 h	126 h	125 h	125 h
Reading seminars	12 h	14 h	14 h	14 h
Group consultations	10 h			
Work in dyads		40 h		
Group supervision		40 h	40 h	40 h
Work in teams			40 h	40 h
Experiential median group		36 h	36 h	36 h
Live supervision		90 h	90 h	90 h
Projects & written assignments	Interview with well-functioning family	Application of systems thinking in working context	Theoretical paper Professional development	Dissertation Professional development

These critical moments influenced the reshaping of our training course to better fit the cognitive and emotional needs of both the trainees and trainers and support both in containing the uncertainties in the process of training and therapy.

Embedded in the belief that a manual may lessen creativity we have overlooked that the development of the capacity to tolerate uncertainty may be encouraged by a clear structure and helpful strategies (Peters et al., 2017; Mason, 2002).

The general training specifications for the 4-year training course that presently inform our trainees are summarised in Table 28.1.

28.4 Professional Development: The Journey from the Individual Perspective to Systems

The training starts as an assembly of individual members, some of whom have already met in other contexts and others who meet for the first time. Since systemic training has not adopted the requirement of personal therapy and the trainers belong to a generation embedded in individual and group analytically oriented psychotherapy, that values personal experience, we find personal development extremely useful to bridge this gap. We have not set it as a separate module as described by Judy Hildebrand (1998), but have it interwoven throughout the training course in different degrees and with different aims (Table 28.2).

Table 28.2 Professional development

Year	1	2	3	4
Aims: To promote To explore To experiment with	Group cohesion Personal contexts Different roles	Cooperation Individual learning styles Risk taking	Containing capacity Personal/emotional issues influencing therapy Positioning	Tolerating uncertainty Personal/emotional Issues influencing impasse Positioning
Means	Genograms Drawings Sculptures Role plays	Work in dyads Metaphors Role plays Reflections from group	Role plays Reflections from team & supervisor Deconstruction & externalisation Protocols	Role plays Reflections from team & supervisor Deconstruction & externalisation Protocols

In the first year of the training, its aim is to promote group cohesion and enhance feelings of trust that allow trainees to share their personal stories in different settings: dyads, small groups, and the median group (we have not had groups exceeding 25 candidates). Trainees in the first year of the course are encouraged to explore their personal contexts: relationships in their primary and secondary families, intergenerational scripts and family stories that had influenced their values, beliefs, prejudices and their choices of how and what they want to be as persons, professionals and in relationships with others. To this end, we use the exercises described by Hildebrand to which we have added our own, often stemming from situations that arise in the group. Having extensive experiences in working analytically with groups, it is impressive to experience how easily the group connects and develops a trusting environment and a sense of belonging. In their feedbacks, trainees, including those who had personal therapy, value this opportunity to explore their personal stories in a different way than in therapy.

Through role plays, the trainees' exploration of personal stories is expanded by the interpersonal. Feedback from the group enables trainees to explore the congruency (or lack of it) between how one wants to be seen and how he/she is seen. Trainees are first exposed to feedback from the group on their performance, as interviewers to a role-played family system of their own choice: how they approach the family, the language they use, to whom they connect with greater ease and empathy, what beliefs and prejudices they may have and how these affect the interview and their curiosity. These role plays are aimed to help trainees in their first-year project to interview a well-functioning family system (that means a family that is not seeking expert help) of their own choice, they would be interested to learn more about. This means that the trainee has to find a family, make contact with it and has to explain to the family why he/she would like to have the opportunity to interview them at their home. In the process of preparing for the project through role plays, trainees get the opportunity to explore their beliefs about diverse family systems of different ethnicity, social and cultural backgrounds and sexual orientation. It also enables them to experiment with positioning themselves differently, as non-expert, curious interviewers. This seemingly undemanding task, which does not expose their professional competencies, role played in a context that has by now become safe enough, opens up the space for playfulness. As eloquent professionals, dealing with many difficult situations in their working contexts, they are surprised and amused as they observe themselves and their peers getting stuck in their attempts to get the families consent to be interviewed. This first experience of acting on stage as a curious researcher of a family system whose permission, trust and collaboration they have to win and of being the recipient of reflections from their peers and trainers, which does not threaten their professional self, seems to be, from the feedback we receive, a valued experience by trainees that helps them in overcoming the fears of exposing themselves as professionals at later stages of the training process.

At the beginning of the second year, trainees form consulting pairs, in order to consult each other on the cases from their working contexts. The consulting pairs bring some of the cases they discuss to the group which includes two supervisors. One of the supervisors has a conversation about the case with the presenting therapist and about the consulting process with the presenting consultant. Following this, the rest of the group is invited to give their reflections. The presenting consultant pair then gives their feedback on what they found useful. The focus of the second year, on applying the relational contextual lens of systemic practice in their own working contexts, allows trainees to choose when, how and to what extent will they include systemic concepts and techniques they are learning on the course. It gives them freedom to move at their own pace in finding ways to connect the newly acquired experiences with the once they already have. The role of the peer consultant encourages them to rely on the wholeness of their experiences, both from the past and from the present. Group supervision opens the space for the exploration of the choices they make and how these connect with their professional and personal contexts and preferred ways of using their therapeutic selves. Trainees are encouraged to take risks both in the context of teaching and skill development in role plays and in the context of supervision in applying the systemic lens in practice. Trainees describe as significant moments in their learning process, situations when they experience the trainer/supervisor as encouraging and allowing enough time in role plays for the training therapist to risk leaving his/her comfort zone and experiencing how this resonates with the role-playing family and the observers. In the second half of the second year, each trainee has a presentation of his/hers experiences with introducing the systemic perspective in their working contexts – in what ways is their everyday practice affected, what changes they perceive themselves and what changes are reported or they think are seen by their patients and colleagues.

28.5 Mapping the Territory: A Guide for the First Session

With this, step-by-step progress from the personal to the interpersonal, from individual contexts to relational, social, cultural and political contexts, from reporting about one's practice to exposing it publicly, trainees seem to be less apprehensive of organising themselves into therapeutic teams and starting with live supervision. For the majority of trainees, this is the first time they meet with families in a therapeutic context and the experience may be overwhelming. To ease the first anxieties, we devised an unwritten protocol for the first session, a sort of guide that has been developing in the interactive contexts of teaching, skill development and supervision that trainees found helpful and that we are now, for the first time, putting on paper:

1. Introduce the therapeutic team and the therapeutic context.
2. Negotiate the therapeutic contract and ask the families permission to video tape the session which is helpful to you during the treatment process and which will be erased after the end of the therapeutic encounters.
3. Join the family members and learn how they would like to be addressed. Inquire about other family members that may not be present and be curious if any of the family members think it would be good if they were.
4. Give the family members permission to inform you if they feel that your questions are too intimate or exposing or are opening a theme, they are not yet ready to discuss.
5. Explore the families' understanding of their referral to family therapy and how did this organise the family. If it was the family's or couple's decision to come, be curious about what brought them to this decision.
6. Explore the family's expectations of family therapy.
7. Explore how family members will know that the therapeutic encounters were useful to them.
8. Inquire about what each family member thinks the therapist should know about them, that will help you and the therapeutic team be useful to them.
9. A provisional area of exploration, left to you to decide when and whether to open it or not, is the exploration of what would you have to do for the family members to feel that therapy was of no use to them (Mason, 2005).

The team behind the screen observes and reflects to the therapist how they saw him/her join the family and position himself/herself with different family members. Since trainees had the opportunities to role play this when learning therapeutic skills from different schools of family therapy, the first sessions usually (but not always) leave the therapist and team members with a feeling of satisfaction. This feeling eases up the tensions and opens the space for reflections and hypothesising that might be helpful to the therapist in organising his/hers thinking: which hypothesis to test, on what theoretical concepts to rely, which therapeutic skills to use, how to use the team and the supervision. The supervisor encourages self-reflection and the development of double vision by inquiring about the therapist's feelings during the conversation with the family and while listening to the team's reflections. Whose voice it was easier to hear and understand? Which experiences, personal or professional, might this be connected with? Which past experiences might be helpful or unhelpful in working with this family?

28.6 Witnessing the Family Drama: Containing Emotions

Following the "successful" first sessions in the beginning of live supervision, we experienced that trainees often started to experience in practice, what till then they knew academically – that the family's pressure on the therapist may be overwhelming, blocking their curiosity and ability to use the systemic lens. They appear to be drawn by the content of the families' preferred stories, already told and retold in other therapeutic contexts. Most families that come to the Institute are referred by psychiatrists and child and adolescent psychiatrists. Usually, they have a history of prior therapeutic encounters in different contexts. The therapeutic team, in this nascent phase, attempts to be supportive and empathic with the struggling therapist, but seems similarly lost and confused, relying on the supervisor for direction, thus providing the therapeutic team with the experience of isomorphism. To help the trainees retain the systemic perspective, we have found useful Minuchin's concept of externalisation (2014), so we added it to our protocol as a guiding principle for the therapeutic encounters, although it might be confused at first with the technique of externalisation from narrative therapy:

10. Externalise the leading problem from the identified patient to the relational context of the family.

    "I borrow from Michael White (2007) the term "externalisation" but I give it a different meaning..........as one in which the therapist pushes the symptom out of the symptom bearer and helps the family members to see the family's participation in the construction and maintenance of the symptoms in the symptom bearer" (Minuchin 2014).

Instead of using the term "externalise" we could have used "contextualise", but it seemed both to us and to the trainees that the concept of externalisation is a better reminder that the problem is not in the individual system but in the web of relationships that are influenced by different contexts.

Sitting with the family and witnessing their stories, their sorrows and their pains can be for the therapist emotionally much more overwhelming than in the individual setting. Therapists may react with physical discomfort, emotional withdrawal, or may allow the family's emotions to overflow them. They may feel more empathic and understanding towards some family members and blaming towards others. They may feel frustrated with a family member and angry with another. The observing team with the supervisor contains the therapist and helps him/her with their reflections and reflective questions to differentiate between those that belong to him/her and can be connected with his/her personal stories from those that feel alien as they belong to the members of the family system. This helps the therapist to regain his/her capacity to be empathic and understanding and enables him to use these new pieces of information in his/her further work with the family. In our experience, therapists usually find it helpful to role play the difficult family member. For example, role playing the mother, experienced as annoying and hard to reach, the therapist became overwhelmed with feelings of sadness and loneliness and was eager to meet the family again. Having the experience of how strong emotions incapacitate the therapist's ability to think and his/hers containing capacity helps trainees to better understand distressed families who are similarly incapacitated by their inability to contain their emotional struggles. This helps them to develop better therapeutic relationships with the families they work (Flaskas, 2002).

28.7 The Experiential Median Group

From our experience, trainees, in general, have no problems understanding the systemic paradigm academically but they struggle with adopting the systemic lens in practice, especially when they meet with the pressures of a distressed family system. Learning to use the multileveled perspective to connect the diverse contexts in which the family relationships are embedded and at the same time developing double vision that enables the therapist to keep track of his inner and outer dialogues and to connect his way of being with the family with the multi-layered contexts from his past and present, that he brings to the therapeutic system, is an emotionally demanding process. As in analytically oriented psychotherapies, the therapist witnessing the family drama is expected to develop the capacity to contain his/her own self and the uncertainties that are the unavoidable companion of the therapeutic process. The containing context of the median group, conducted by a group analyst who is otherwise not connected to the course, that runs from the second year till the end of the course on a fortnight base, opens a safe place for trainees to give voice to their fears and anxieties and work through some of the emotional stress that arises in the different contexts of the training course. This at least was the aim of introducing the median group to the training course, as a secure context in which trainees can be free of the anxiety of being evaluated. Since the median group is closed to trainers and supervisors, we do not really know what use the trainees make of it. The only information the conductor of the median group gives the course organisers are the lists of attendance. Trainees gave a positive feedback and regard it as a valuable addition to the structure of the course.

28.8 Changing the Trainees' Epistemology

28.8.1 The Relational Context of the Therapeutic Team and Group Supervision

During the first half of the third year, therapeutic teams start to consolidate, each developing its own culture, style of communication and relational network. As in any other developing system, members are assigned different roles and positions. So, a member may take a nurturing position taking care of the group, or a position of a "difficult child" challenging the rules and not attending regularly. Some members may compete as to whose voice will be heard while others recede into a silent observing position, giving voice to their ideas and thoughts only if asked directly. The supervisor is a visiting member to the team since the teams work also without the presence of the supervisor and the supervisors change, usually a team has two rotating supervisors. Tensions that may arise in the teams may affect their ability to think, to be curious and creative. Consultations aimed at exploring the relational context of each team have been described as helpful by trainees who reported that, following such consultations, they felt their collaboration improved and they felt less restrained and freer to take different positions in the team.

Group supervision that trainees attend in their second year continues till the end of the course. Unlike the second year, when trainees mainly present cases with their individual patients, in the last 2 years of the course, they are expected to present cases with families or couples. They are encouraged to invite members from their team to attend the sessions if their working contexts allow this. Group supervision affords more time for group reflections and role plays aimed at enhancing trainee's professional development and self-reflection. In group supervision, trainees, apart from presenting cases as already described, bring written transcripts of chosen parts of a session (Table 28.3), to present their therapeutic interventions and their understanding of the family system, as well as the theoretical concepts that organised their thinking.

In the context of group supervision, some sessions are reserved for the therapeutic teams to present how they organised themselves, what they found works best for them, what kind of feedback they find helpful and from whom, what strengths they see in each other, what metaphors would they choose for the team and its members. Time is also taken to reflect on the supervision process and their experiences with different supervisors. When they find supervision to be more and when less helpful? What would have to change for them in the supervision process for them to feel more encouraged to take more risks? Group supervision allows more time for the discussion of written protocols (Mason, 2002) trainees keep for each session both as therapists and as members of the team for both supervised and unsupervised therapies (Tables 28.4 and 28.5).

Table 28.3 Specifications for written transcript

1. Present your systemic understanding of the family and therapy system
2. Describe how your thinking and understanding of the family/therapy system got organised – In particular in planning the intervention you choose to present
3. Present the theoretical frame that supported your thinking
4. Write a transcript of the intervention and the family's reaction
5. Describe your understanding of the impact of your intervention
6. What impact did it have on your understanding of the family/therapy system?
7. Reflect on personal/professional issues that might have been helpful/unhelpful

Note: intervention is meant in a broad sense, it can be deconstruction or challenging a belief, exploring an issue or relationship you see as important, exploring or challenging an interactional pattern, using any therapeutic intervention from any of the family therapy schools

Table 28.4 Protocol for therapist

Focus & feed-back & reflections regarding:		
Therapist	Family	Session
Pre-session: Systemic understanding of the family system: Understanding of the therapy system and my positioning in it: Theoretical concepts that have been organising me: Working hypothesis and plan for present session: Theoretical concept I will rely on: Use of the therapy team: Use of supervision:	Session: Final message (if given): Reflecting team (if used):	Post-session: The impact of the session on my understanding of the family system: The impact of my positioning in the therapy system: Therapy skills used: Inner conversation: Personal /emotional issues that were helpful/unhelpful: Important issues for supervision: Important reflections from the team and supervisor: Reflections on supervision: Reflections for the next session:
Genogram		

Table 28.5 Protocol for team member

Focus & feed-back & reflections regarding:		
Therapist:	Family:	Session:
Positioning in the team:		
Important theoretical issues about therapy and/or families:		
Important/personal/emotional issues:		
Reflections on the process of therapy:		
Reflections on the process of supervision:		

Keeping a written record of therapy sessions has a manifold function. It is a formalised way of keeping a record of the number of sessions trainees have in the role of therapist and team member and the diversity of family systems trainees work with, either as therapist or as team member. Their aim is also to help trainees follow the therapeutic process, giving them a clear overview of how their understanding of the therapeutic system and their positioning in it changed over time, how their thinking developed and what theoretical concepts they found useful, what constraints and challenges they experienced, particularly as therapists, how they managed them and what new personal and professional learning experiences these enabled. Trainees report of their experiences in filling these protocols, what they found helpful and what was restraining in the format of the protocol. This opens the space for negotiating changes that would better fit the needs of both trainers and trainees. The latest change was the addition of recording the therapists internal dialogue (Rober, 1999), which the trainees suggested.

We devised a similar protocol for supervisors to help them keep record of the process of supervision (Table 28.6).

Table 28.6 Protocol for supervisor

Focus & feed-back & reflections regarding:			
Supervisor	Therapist:	Family	Session
The therapy system:			
What sort of system is the therapist co-creating with the family:			
How the therapist wants to be seen by the family:			
How does the therapists engage with the family:			
How does the therapist use his/hers self:			
How does the therapist follow his/hers plan for the session:			
How does the therapist deal with emotions:			
Supervisor's view of therapist's self-reflexivity:			
Supervisors understanding of the therapist s dilemmas:			
The impact of supervisor's interventions on the therapy system:			
The supervision system:			
Supervisor's thoughts during supervision:			
Issues brought up in supervision by supervisor:			
Issues not voiced in supervision:			
Important issues in supervisors view for next supervision:			
The impact of supervision on supervisee:			
Supervisor's dilemmas:			
Impact of supervision on supervisor:			
Personal/emotional issues helping/hindering supervision:			
Feedback from supervisee:			

28.9 Encouraging Creativity – Integrating Diverse Theoretical Concepts

The philosophy of our training course is that the essential component of systemic psychotherapy is the exploration of the multi-layered interdependence of contexts and relationships. To this end, we teach our students the theoretical concepts of various schools of systemic family therapy and the distinctions between first- and second-order principles of therapy. Social constructionism has certainly widened the systemic perspective, by underlying the importance of the power embedded in the dominant social, cultural and political discourses and for training therapists, we would also add the dominant theoretical discourses. During the training course, we encourage the trainees to experiment with different theoretical concepts and therapeutic skills that will enable them to cherish their creativity and develop their own therapeutic styles, which may include both first- and second-order principles. We teach them that there is not one right way to do therapy and not one method of therapy that fits all. There are times when we can frame the therapy process in the narrative and not knowing metaphors which are as old as psychoanalysis and there are times the therapist feels that a systemic frame would be more helpful. It was, after all, the reason some psychoanalysts widened their perspective to include contexts that enable the therapist to explore how the patient's different contexts interrelate with his/her difficulties. What they missed to see is that they are part of the picture and that, what they brought to the therapeutic system was the whole of their experience and knowledge. While including the patient's contexts, they simultaneously excluded the therapists. One may wonder how this splitting happened. As psychoanalysts, they were well aware the therapist is part of the therapeutic system and both impacts and is influenced by it. From this stems the requirement for personal therapy and supervision. Was this denial of the need to include the therapist's self and the accompanying tendency to denigrate psychoanalysis and analytically oriented psychotherapy the integral part of the process of separation and identity formation? Due to this, a few decades had to pass before allowing the return of feelings to the therapeutic encounter and the recognition of the importance of the therapeutic relationship. This we found liberating, since when starting the training courses, we felt blasphemous when inquiring about feelings and addressing the therapeutic relationship. We have included in our training theoretical concepts from child and adolescent development as we feel it helps training therapists to better understand and contain their frustrations when working with families with children and adolescents, so that they might find it easier to resist the temptation to exclude them from therapy as it happened in one of our beginning training courses.

Trainees report that they value the ways we attempt to weave a net of interconnected stories between the individual and his/her contexts of relationships and they find this helpful in connecting their new knowledge and experiences with the once they have already acquired. From their feedbacks and their work, we get the feeling that we are heard when we teach them not to push their patients/families into the Procrustean bed of their preferred theoretical concept or constructed narratives and that they monitor the power delegated to them as mental health professionals and/or therapists.

28.10 Safe Uncertainty: Constructing a Secure Base in Training

The majority of our trainees respond well to the neurobiological metaphor and the common explanations of their feelings of uncertainty in training. It seems that the explanations from neuroscience can serve as an externalizing intervention, enabling the reframing of the experience of not knowing. It may seem paradoxical to instruct trainees to tolerate uncertainty better if there is no clear strategy how to cope with uncertainty in the context of training. In times of uncertainty, the brain computes the probabilities for each available strategy that will safeguard future well-being (Peters et al., 2017). The anterior cingulate cortex (ACC) assesses the degree of certainty/uncertainty of future outcomes (Liljeholm & O'Doherty, 2012). The assessment of uncertainty triggers the emotional-amygdale transmission pathway and intensifies distress. The capacity of patients and healthcare professionals to tolerate uncertainty can affect the extent to which both parties form therapeutic relationships, seek and exchange information, and engage in shared decision-making (Hillen et al., 2017). Aversive aspects of uncertainty are fear, worry and anxiety, perceptions of vulnerability and avoidance of decision-making. We cannot be mindful during distress. It seems that the development of the capacity to contain uncertainty is of utmost importance for the trainees to be able to process new information and use it in the therapy session. It has been proposed that for a useful change to happen, we sometimes need to become less certain of the positions we hold; from such a position, we are more likely to become receptive to other possibilities (Mason, 1993, 2019). The concept of safe uncertainty enables us to be more comfortable with not knowing, enhances our creativity and enables us to be more in tune with the needs of our patients. The experiential median group has been created as a complementary secure base for trainees.

28.11 Deconstruction of the Meaning of Manual

We have been aware for a long time of the ambivalences regarding manualised therapies in the psychotherapeutic community (Cook et al., 2017). Manuals as a path to evidence-based therapies have been of great importance "to demonstrate that systemic therapies are effective, acceptable to clients, and cost effective for a sufficient range of conditions to give confidence that the wide application in current practice is justified and could be extended usefully" (Stratton, 2016). One of the dilemmas has been how to make the manuals designed for research acceptable and useful to practitioners (Pote et al., 2003). While fidelity is a crucial component of successful evidence-based psychotherapy practice, implementation with flexibility is also necessary (Cook et al., 2017). The dilemma has been well bridged by Mason (2019), who thinks that frameworks, guidelines, manuals and checklists can help us but they do not do the work for us; they are helping us as an aid to use creativity in the therapeutic relationship.

Recently, our trainers have been invited to train systemic supervisors in a different training context in one of the republics of former Yugoslavia. Despite the notion that we have all been trained in the systemic paradigm, the perceptions of how to use the acquired knowledge and which concepts to apply in sessions were very different and heterogeneous to such an extent that it supported our view that structured feedback protocols can be a common factor or common ground that may connect different training contexts. This experience strengthened our belief that the structured reflexive feedback following every session is a good foundation for the development of safe uncertainty and connectedness, which could be perceived as a manual. The ongoing, structured, contextual (self) reflexivity for several years could be experienced as a manualised support for trainees in the process of their epistemological shift to systems.

28.12 Conclusion

Through the narrative of our training course, our understanding of manuals changed. We started to perceive the usefulness of a manual in the process of systemic training. We widened our view of manuals that need not serve only as a foundation for evidence-based research. From our point of view, systemic training needs a comprehensive, primarily stable and structured teaching tool used in a repetitive way which acts as a secure base that enables metaperception and enhances the ability to cope with the uncertainties of the systemic perspective. A repetitive and persistent use of such a teaching tool helps to introduce changes in trainees' perceptions which are neurobiologically founded as they promote neural plasticity. To this end, we use the structured reflexive feedback to be filled after every session by therapists, observers and supervisors. This feedback summarises the reflections on the referral, the hypothetical constructs of the family system, the relevant topics and theoretical concepts, as well as personal issues and dominant discourses. Together with the first session scenario, it ritualises the training process that, in our view, helps to change the trainees' epistemology.

References

Anderson, H., Goolishian, H. A., & Windermand, L. (1986). Problem determined systems: Towards transformation in family therapy. *Journal of Strategic & Systemic Therapies, 5*(4), 1–13. https://doi.org/10.1521/jsst.1986.5.4.1
Bateson, G. (1972). Social planning and the concept of deutero learning. In G. Bateson (Ed.), *Steps to an ecology of mind* (pp. 159–176). Jason Aronson.
Cook, S. C., Schwartz, A. C., & Kaslow, N. J. (2017). Evidence-based psychotherapy: Advantages and challenges. *Neurotherapeutics, 14*(3), 537–545.
Fishbane, M. D. (2007). Wired to connect: Neuroscience, relationships, and therapy. *Family Process, 46*, 395–412.
Flaskas, C. (2002). *Family therapy beyond postmodernism: Practice challenges theory*. Brunner-Routledge.
Gergen, K. (1985). Social constructionist theory: Context and implications. In K. Gergen & K. Davis (Eds.), *The social construction of the person*. Springer-Verlag.
Hildebrand, J. (1998). *Bridging the gap: A training module in personal and professional development*. Karnac Books.
Hillen, M. A., Gutheiil, C. M., Stroul, T. D., Smets, E., & Han, P. (2017). Tolerance of uncertainty: Conceptual analysis, integrative model, and implications for healthcare. *Social Science & Medicine, 180*, 62–75.
Liljeholm, M., & O'Doherty, J. (2012). Contributions of the striatum to learning, motivation, and performance: An associative account. *Trends in Cognitive Sciences, 16*(9), 467–475.
Lillard, A. S., & Erisir, A. (2011). Old dogs learning new tricks: Neuroplasticity beyond the juvenile period. *Developmental Review, 31*(4), 207–239.
Mason, B. (1993). Towards positions of safe uncertainty. *Human Systems, 4*, 189–200.
Mason, B. (2002). A reflective recording for supervisors and trainees. In D. Campbell & B. Mason (Eds.), *Perspectives on supervision* (pp. 54–58). Karnac Books.
Mason, B. (2005). Relational risk-taking and the therapeutic relationship. In C. Flaskas, B. Mason, & A. Perlesz (Eds.), *The space between: Experience, context and process in the therapeutic relationship* (pp. 157–170). Karnac Books.
Mason, B. (2019). Re-visiting safe uncertainty: Six perspectives for clinical practice and the assessment of risk. *Journal of Family Therapy, 41*, 343–356.
Minuchin, S. (1998). Where is the family in narrative therapy? *Journal of Marital and Family Therapy, 24*, 397–403.
Minuchin, S., Reiter, M. D., & Borda, C. (2014). *The craft of family therapy: Challenging certainties* (p. 19). Routledge.
Peters, A., McEwen, B. S., & Friston, K. (2017). Uncertainty and stress: Why it causes diseases and how it is mastered by the brain. *Progress in Neurobiology, 156*, 164–188.
Pote, P., Stratton, P., Cottrell, D., Shapiro, D., & Boston, P. (2003). Systemic family therapy can be manualized: Research process and findings. *Journal of Family Therapy, 25*(3), 236–262.
Rober, P. (1999). The therapist's inner conversation in family practice: Some ideas about the self of the therapist, therapeutic impasse and the process of reflection. *Family Process, 38*(2), 209–228.
Stratton, P. (2016). *The evidence base of family therapy and systemic practice* (p. 1). Association for Family Therapy.

Chapter 29
Trainee-Focused Training: A Second-Order Approach in the Making of Therapists

Elena Ceuca

29.1 Introduction

Trainee-focused training (TFT) emerged from a constant concern to attune the training process and content to the philosophies fostering contemporary approaches in systemic therapy. This concern emerged both from the trainer's direct experience and from reflections on a blend of familiar concepts in the field such as Virginia Satir's *congruent communication* (Satir, 1988), Harlene Anderson's *collaboratives* with the client (Anderson & Gehart, 2007), Tom Andersen's *generation of multiple perspectives* (Andersen, 1991), John Shotter's *intermingling movements* (Shotter, 2011), and the interrelational concept of *isomorphism*. These concepts, and others, were catalysts for a training approach where students acquire knowledge and know-how in a way that is coherent with the core philosophy of the therapeutic approach, and the trainee is in the center of the training process similar to client centrality in the therapeutic process.

This chapter will present the process of systemic family training in TFT, both general specifications regarding the training as a whole and particular specifications at each stage, i.e., theoretical training, personal growth, supervision, and educational therapy. Context and principles framing TFT, as well as the purposes directing the process, will be briefly described.

E. Ceuca (✉)
Institute for Couple and Family, Independent Mental Health Care Professional, Iasi, Romania
e-mail: ceucaelenaiasi@gmail.com

29.2 Why Speak About a Second-Order Cybernetics Approach in Therapy Training?

The second-order cybernetic perspective describes the observer as a part of that which is observed, and consequently any explanation of the one named *observer* is self-referential (Hoffman, 1985). As being an observer is one of many therapist's roles, by implication, a therapist is part of the system created together with the client in therapy. For therapists who embrace the second-order cybernetic theory, the question might become how to act congruently with it. For me, the cybernetics of the observer had become a question: *How should a trainer or supervisor conduct a training where he/ she proposes the practice of a second-order cybernetics therapeutic approach?* With TFT, I propose an alternative paradigm for training in family therapy based on second-order cybernetics (or cybernetics of the observer theory).

29.3 My Background

I believe that making the author visible as a person in her or his text might give deeper insight to the message. What do you think? If you do not think the same, you may skip the part below.

In writing this introduction, I came to see myself producing a new narrative, different from the one I initially wrote for various lectures at conferences and congresses, because factually talking to people and learning their questions and reflections differs from writing to them: I select new episodes, "prune" others, and make them construct a new dominant story (White, 1988, 1989). This reference to narrative theory in therapy is a way of positioning myself relative to this piece of writing, as I believe that where a story evolved, there are many others to be constructed on the same topic but with different plots and where there is one truth imagined, there are many others to be imagined, as well. The abovementioned theory is the one developed by Michael White and David Epston and is based on the assumption that a person's lived experience can be "re-authored" in new narratives with each telling and retelling of one's story (Epston, David & White, Michael, 1990).

In the following I will link together a series of elements to form a narrative about my background, which I consider to be a significant bias for TFT: my training and my practice as a medical doctor, the life in a country under communist dictatorship, being trained in Romania by Dutch trainers to become a systemic family and couple therapist, and my years of practice as a trainer and supervisor for systemic family and couple therapists.

In all my practice as a medical doctor, I guided myself bearing in mind the maxim: "First, do not harm." Also I came to be at ease when accessing people's privacy and making inquiries, I developed the tendency to scrutinize all natural facts, including human behavior, through the lenses of the fundamental laws of biology, and I learned that neurobiology is reliable when it comes to evaluating concepts and theories tackling issues of the human mind.

I have lived all my life in Romania: the first 25 years in a communist society and the last 30 years in a postcommunist society. After many years of reflection and self-inquiry, I am still surprised at my new understanding of the deep influence the communist regime and its impact on everyday life has had on what I can be today. I will share here only one aspect which to me seems relevant. And this is my striving for congruence between the thinking, the saying, and the doing. I could understand it as a consequence of the years when all systems I was part of, either the larger society, the school, or the family, were functioning with an obvious discrepancy. What we were seeing was different from what was said to be happening and what we felt and thought often had to be hidden. And I think that in developing TFT, I have taken into it this concern to align what is said to what is thought and what is acted.

Later after the fall of the communist regime, the systemic family and couple therapy training exposed me to systemic thinking, circular causality, reflexivity, and the social constructionist theory of knowledge. In addition, I encountered the Dutch culture, which was intriguingly different in terms of values and ethics from the one I was accustomed to, the Romanian culture. I learned about the value of individuality, while before I had been preached the value of the masses. I discovered that ethics is present in everyday interactions, not something written in books, subordinated to politics and generating ambiguity. By that time I was in my thirties, and all this experience was tremendously influential; there was something I was waiting for without knowing it.

I began my practice as a trainer and supervisor for systemic family and couple therapists soon after I started my practice as a therapist. My colleagues and I were the first generation of systemic family therapists in Romania; we had been trained for free and told that we were expected to disseminate this profession among other people in our country. I took that as a mission. Besides my private practice, I work in a Romanian Institute for the training of systemic family and couple therapists. Together with my colleagues, we deliver a 4-year program to parttime students learning to get their free practice license as therapists. Our students are people who graduated in psychology, pedagogy, medicine, theology, social work, or sociology. Experiential teaching is the method of choice in this training institute where, as in most European institutes of this kind, students are introduced and accustomed to utilizing a variety of therapeutic models and approaches. They begin with a historical modernist model, the structural family therapy model, which is more concrete and easy to understand, and they end by studying social constructionist approaches. At the end of the theory course, they are free to choose and create an integrative or an eclectic combination of one or several models. Those students who had opted for a social constructionist approach in their supervised practice were the mirrors in which I – as a trainer – saw there was an incongruity between the content I was teaching and the teaching process itself. Henceforth I started thinking of other ways to do training for social constructionist therapists.

29.4 Theoretical Sensitivity

This part is for those of you eager to find an alternative story making sense of the worldview fostering TFT.

Since I started to notice certain peculiarities in my practice as a trainer and supervisor, I have become aware that there are different philosophical theories and paradigms informing my ideas, nurturing or altering them. I could compare these philosophical theories with a circle of older and of more recent companions, creating an inspiring context for my work.

Socratic thinking is among the oldest companions. As a teenager in the late 1970s, I read about Socrates' life and Plato's *Socratic dialogues*. I was quite relieved to find that such a fruitful conversation is possible, a conversation where people may come to unexpected ideas and perspectives. Until then, living in a communist society and having an authoritarian father, I was not able to think beyond conversations where you only say what you have learned you are allowed to. I was fascinated about the possibility *to* direct conversation by using questions to bring new ideas to life. Aporia was, and still is, a concept of a particular interest to me. This is how it was called; the state reached by Socrates' interlocutors thanks to his questions, a state when they were still not knowing what to say about the debated topic, but they knew that what they had believed in at the beginning of the debate was not absolute truth, and it was not completely reliable. It is a state when people may start thinking that ideas are not to be taken for granted. I think that when a conversation, or interview, allows for new directions besides repetitive pathways and new hypotheses to be set, theories are taken into account and valued, and then new possibilities may reach the level of awareness. This awareness is not about prereflectivity (van Manen, 2007) but about the transformative potential of maieutic conversational relationships. Originally, the Socratic debate, named also maieutic questioning, stops when a thesis is demonstrated to be unreliable; I, however, consider the debate should become an open, endless process. This is how I imagine the difference between Socrates' approach on knowledge and the social-constructionist knowledge-making theory. It is a great challenge to present a definition for the latter, because there are very many definitions; besides, the term "social *c*onstructionism" is sometimes used interchangeably with social constructivism or merely constructivism (Hoffman, 1990, Sommers-Flanagan & Sommers-Flanagan, 2012). Nonetheless, it is largely accepted to be described as a theory proposing an epistemological perspective concerned with how knowledge is constructed and understood, with emphasis on current interactions, or on social interchange, where language is used to construct (describe, explain, or account for) everyday life realities (Gergen, 1985, Burr, 2003). Due to the social constructionist shift from facts to negotiated constructions, I have reconsidered maieutic questioning, and I abandoned any intention to reveal a fact and retain only the aporia, the friendly and serene attitude the character Socrates shows in Plato's dialogues.

Later, I started to integrate social constructionism into my way of making sense of things. Beginning with the 1980s, social constructionism significantly infused family therapy theories, which until then had been developed around general systems theory, communication theory, and cybernetics, and were circumscribed by modernism. According to Lynn Hoffman, modernism corresponds to a spatial metaphor, the metaphor of "timeless circles," while social constructionism corresponds to a temporal metaphor, "rivers through time" (Hoffman, 1990). It seems to me that the two metaphors do not exclude each other and both are useful when a practitioner strives to make sense of human functioning.

Beyond the systemic metaphor rooted in biology and cybernetics, systemic family therapy theories are characterized by the focus on relationships and the disposition to explore the process rather than the content. Being familiar with thinking about systems in the human body as in the field of biology, I easily adopted the systems' metaphor to make sense of people's relationships. Furthermore, I discovered that there are "certain forms of thought" (Lang et al., 1990) in systemic practice considered as desirable, for example, not generalizing judgments; being concerned with multiple perspectives; being aware of the influence of the context; and being open to consider the individual aspects and equally the larger systems, such as the social order. Considering these features of social constructionism and of systemic family therapy theories, I think there is some affinity between the two of them. Thus, for many therapists and theoreticians, the transition from one to the other was possible, even though it took a while as systemic therapy moved from first to second-order cybernetics (Flaskas, 2002). I mention the example of Anderson and Goolishian who juxtaposed concepts from both perspectives and came up with the following proposal: "The therapeutic system is a linguistic system," or "Change is the evolution of new meaning through dialogue" (Anderson & Goolishian, 1988, p. 1).

While I was already performing as a trainer, I added dialogism to Socratic thinking, social constructionism, and systemic family therapy theories. For many years, the dialogic perspective has been a rich and comprehensive resource for me when searching for existential answers, when imagining solutions to doubts, or when building meaning for issues in my everyday professional practice. In this paper, I consider dialogism only through the lens of Mikhail Bakhtin's theory, narrowing all down to some of the many Bakhtinian constructs. Dialogic relationship is, from Bakhtin's point of view, the relationship between ideas or thoughts when they are juxtaposed, as opposed to monologue where ideas fall into two categories, either true, i.e., important, or untrue, i.e., indifferent (Bakhtin & Emerson, 1984). He used terms from music to designate some of the concepts he elaborated. For example, he used counterpoint as an adverb, contrapuntally, to illustrate the fact that in dialogic relationships, ideas not only juxtapose but they also combine harmonically while retaining their individuality. Another concept named with a musical term is polyphony, which draws attention to the multiplicity of voices or ideas to be taken into account. It is polyphony that guarantees the open-endedness of dialogical relationships, while on the contrary, monophony displays "material within the framework of its own monologic understanding" (Bakhtin & Emerson, 1984, p. 18). As a practitioner, I make use of these concepts when I wonder how to position myself in order not to objectify people, not to treat the person as a commodity or an object, disregard her/his individual interest, seek on the contrary to be curious, and learn together with them about their thoughts, about their meanings. It is actually ideas like these ones that make me stay aware of the nonfinite nature of my understanding. Aside from considering Bakhtin's elaboration on contexts which facilitate dialogue and contexts which are a limitation to it, such as military contexts, I have also directed my attention to my work and reflected upon the measure in which my training approach enables our dialogic nature. So it was that precisely reflection process became one of my main resources for the TFT's inception.

29.5 Trainee-Focused Training (TFT)

Trainee-focused training is an approach developed as an attempt to align training methodology to the theory and know-how delivered to students who are trained to practice systemic psychotherapy in a social constructionist paradigm. It is addressed both to trainers and students. In the next pages, you will find a narrative about the context into which TFT emerged and my views on the subject.

29.6 TFT in Romanian Context

In Romania, most psychotherapy trainings use input-based methods, with some using experiential learning – acquiring knowledge by direct experience – as well. Most of the trainers adopt a directive stance. There are no studies reported on these issues, and the information about how therapy training is practiced in Romania is based on my direct observation as a very active professional in the field for over 20 years. TFT is an approach developed to attune training for systemic family therapy to the contemporary worldview and theories in the field. TFT is something I have developed, I am still developing in my practice as a trainer and supervisor for systemic family therapists in Romania and expanding in my activity as a facilitator for continuous education for psychotherapists in my homeland and abroad.

Due to distance and, at that time, lack of convenient remote communication means I could not have my activity as a novice trainer working in Romania supervised by Dutch trainers. Moreover, I could not rely on peer supervision, as I was among the first generation of Romanian trainers and we were all novices and, most probably, owing to the individualistic Romanian mentality where: "you should do it on your own," "asking for support is a sign of weakness," "when people associate, trouble results." So, being on my own was one of the Romanian's contextual features. Hence, I turned toward the trainees to get feedback and started to attend professional events abroad where I could meet experienced trainers and learn about others' practices. Another trait of the Romanian context is the one-sided authoritative attitude of the teacher at all levels in education, with learning heavily based mainly on the simple reproduction of the information delivered by acknowledged experts (teachers, educators, professors, trainers). In order to outline the local context for developing TFT, I will also include the lack of updated information. I used to have limited access to some books and journals, most of them published 15–20 years before, donated by Dutch therapists to our young association's library. It is in the last 3–4 years that I have gained some access to up-to-date literature in training in systemic psychotherapy. This is why I could place TFT only recently into an international context.

29.6.1 TFT in an International Context

There are many studies dedicated to understanding systemic family therapy training. An example of an early study that attempted to evaluate the effectiveness of systemic family therapy training by Tucker and Pinsof (1984) concluded that "three attributes were expected to change with training: (a) clinical cognition (theoretical perspective); (b) in-therapy verbal behaviour (technique); and (c) personal skill (self – actualization)" (Tucker & Pinsof, 1984, p. 439). The strength of this study was that it valued the trainee's personal skills and put them on the same level as theory. Meanwhile the study's perspective raised concerns about the case when a therapist does not fit the standardized attributes. Therefore the study contrasts with Simon's work (2006) which demonstrates that one should place "the self of the therapist at the centre of family therapy research and training" (Simon, 2006, p. 331).

Based on my current observation, I very much concur with opinions such as Mason's that there are contradictions between what trainees and supervisors' claim and how they act in training sessions (Mason, Barry, 2010). The author illustrates his statement with an example about the differences between teaching second-order cybernetics and not performing it. I too have noticed, not only in Romania, but in international workshops and lectures as well, an incongruence of the same kind in other relational issues: teaching about a *not knowing* stance while with an expert position or teaching about *withness* and *non-othering* the others and meanwhile constantly overlooking them. In my view, this is one of the reasons why I started to imagine solutions to establish congruence between what I teach, my beliefs, and how I act and interact with trainees and supervisees. Likewise, I endorse Biever and Gardner's observation that: "Translating social constructionist theory into practice of psychotherapy is often difficult for students. The shift from theory to practice is made more difficult when the process of supervision contradicts the ideas which have been taught to students" (Biever & Gardner, 1995). I am concerned not only with the supervision, but with the teaching of the theory alike. The authors propose the use of a reflecting team as a solution to overcome this difficulty. In TFT we use the reflecting team, too, but I consider it not enough, and the model is based mainly on the trainer/supervisor's congruence to the teaching's content. In the late 2000s, there was a movement meant to clarify, describe, and prescribe the features of clinical competence in systemic family therapy. New models were created to accomplish this kind of scope, for example, the learning-centered and outcome-based methods proposed by Gehart to replace input-focused methods (Gehart, 2011). My point is that this direction in research overlooks the trainee as a person with unique and unpredictable talents. Sutherland et al. questioned the competency-based supervision in its traditional form, claiming their preference for the term *orientation* instead of *competence*, and elaborated a list of orientations a therapist should prove to have (Sutherland et al. 2012). I particularly mention one of the orientations they pointed out in the paper the therapist's collaborative stance. This is largely defined with respect to the relationship in therapy, whereas there is no indication about collaborative stance in the supervision relationship itself. I shall take as an example London and Tarragona's chapter concerning collaborative therapy and supervision. They quote:

"We decided we would approach each of our clients and their families as we would normally do: trying to avoid preconceptions about them, being curious about their lives and experiences, attempting to understand their dilemmas […] We encouraged our students to position themselves in the same way" (London & Tarragona, 2007, p.256). And further on, "We invited our students to use their *not-knowing* as a way to get to know people." (ibidem)

When engaging a dialogue with this excerpt, my inner voices were saying "Why wouldn't trainers try to avoid preconceptions about trainees?!" and "What if trainers would be genuinely curious about the trainees' experiences, their preferences, their beliefs, instead of asking them to replicate a certain way of acting?!" and "What would it be like to deliver training from a not-knowing stance?!", "How is it for the student when asked to practice an unfamiliar kind of being with the others?"; "How exactly is avoiding preconceptions instrumented?", or "In what degree a novice feel at ease when asked to use a not-knowing stance by someone who implicitly performs from a knowing position- knowing that not-knowing stance is effective in therapy?". In TFT, these rhetorical questions become operational because TFT is based on guiding principles such as viewing learning as an interactive, mutual process; the trainer's thoughtful concern for the trainee's worldview; building comfort into learning; and the trainer's continuous preoccupation to change in order to cope with genuine circumstances generated in the training process.

The person of the therapist training (POTT) is built around an original concept: "signature themes" (Aponte et al., 2014) which designates the therapist's personal unresolved issues presumed to negatively influence the therapeutic relationship. POTT's goal is to teach therapists how to use themselves to enhance therapeutic effectiveness (Aponte, 2009). This and other models and papers (i.e., Karam, 2010, or Storm et al., 2001) create indirectly an image which evolves discreetly that the therapist is used as an instrument, which to me, to a certain extent, may appear as counter-collaborative, and not so appropriate.

Something all these models and papers have in common is a perspective in which the trainee tends to be objectified, while the trainer is remaining invisible to scrutiny. I call "objectified" the fact of imposing on novice therapists an expected list of competencies and even evaluating them in this Procrustean bed. On the contrary, in TFT it is the trainee with her or his abilities and unique capabilities that is the main focus of concern.

In the following underlined lines, I will present in another form the above text. The idea of an alternative story appeared precisely from being as receptive as possible to editors' feedback regarding the first draft of the chapter: "At times though, as a reader, we felt your contrasting of your thinking and your model to other approaches a bit dismissive." The input that I could thusly receive was absolutely fantastic. It challenged my view about myself and inspired me as to reposition and reconsider my stance. That being said, this below is the alternative in writing.

The person of the therapist training (POTT) is built around an original concept: "signature themes" (Aponte et al., 2014) which designates the therapist's personal unresolved issues presumed to negatively influence the therapeutic relationship. POTT's goal is to teach therapists how to use themselves to enhance therapeutic effectiveness (Aponte, 2009). This and other models and papers (i.e., Karam, 2010 or Storm et al., 2001) go into details and approach from various angles the attributes a therapist should have in order to be effective. My inner dialogue emerging from the encounter with the abovementioned models was about: what happens if a trainee has other qualities than those listed by a certain theoretical training model; or what if the student – and future therapist – does not believe in a proposed beliefs system; how could a training process support the trainee to shape a distinctive therapeutic approach using her/his unique capabilities; what would mean efficient qualities in the trainer's or supervisor's case; how to translate collaboration into the training process; and so on. The constant comparison of TFT to other existing therapy training models actually helped me conceptualize it.

29.7 TFT Specifications

The editors asked me to talk about any ways in which TFT could be regarded as a manual. In my understanding, a manual is a material providing instructions on how to do something, like the first aid manual, or on how to use something, like the car owner's manual. Bearing this understanding in mind, I felt stuck, thinking it would be an inconsistency to manualize a process which is intended to minimize instruction. It is as difficult as to teach about the not-knowing stance which implicitly assumes a knowing stance. Perhaps I should rather talk about TFT in terms of specifications concerning this approach where we strive not to manualize and present suggestions instead of instructions. Specifications are meant to be subject to debate, amendment, and any other intervention of further construction, deconstruction, and re-construction of TFT. What should one know if interested to perform like a TFT trainer? Or how could a student expect a TFT trainer to do?

29.7.1 General Specifications

I intend TFT to be just a suggested frame for doing systemic therapy training, guided by distinct specifications. All its features are thought to orient and inspire, and not to be adopted as such.

TFT is free of outcome-oriented standards and of competency-based scaffolding. I would say that these competency-based trainings operate with *linear causality* and rely on the modernist assumption that there is an absolute truth about reality, which can be discovered, and this would be somehow outside the social constructionist paradigm.

TFT does not use input-focused methods, because methods which favor theory and skills transfer from trainer to trainee have the tendency to be monological. This feature, as well as the one above, emerges from one of TFT assumptions: training should emerge congruently with its theoretical content and with its epistemological leanings; to put this another way, the therapeutic model should inform supervision. Therefore, TFT stays congruent not only with postmodern, social constructionist but with dialogic views as well. Flaskas considers that: "The idea that practice is based on theory is an illusion..." (Flaskas, 2014, p 283). Based on my experience with very many supervisees, I can confirm it is an illusion to believe that practice is based on theory. I never dare to say it frankly, not even in my mind, but I was driven by this belief; therefore I am concerned to help students to become aware not only of the fact that they can produce theory, but that they do this anyway. They just have to be prepared to see themselves as being able to produce their own valuable practice and relevant conceptualization. In TFT, theory is important, but it is not the unquestionable authority. When compared to POTT, TFT similarly lays the emphasis on the future therapists' personal growth. Yet, the aim is not to make the therapist effective in using his/her own person as if this would be a mandatory task. In this respect, in TFT there are mainly two goals: to support the novice therapist in the process of becoming aware about her/ his worldview and for the trainer to keep her/ his openness toward that unique worldview. These goals are both about having a trainee-focused training.

One more assumption of TFT is that training for a humanistic profession should be concerned not only with the interest and welfare of clients but with that of trainees as well.

Another component of TFT, not really an assumption but a kind of statement, is the use of the term *training*, instead of *learning*. According to dictionaries, *learning* is concerned with acquiring knowledge or skills in a new activity or on a new topic, and does not necessarily envisage outcomes to be performed in any way, while *training* is about preparing to perform, which is the case in any professional training.

TFT relies now on tenets such as:

- Performing training for systemic psychotherapy is an ongoing process of flexible practices.
- Systems metaphor applies in the context of training as *training system*.
- The trainer is part of the training system according to second-order cybernetics theory.
- The training should not harm the trainees' trust in their own worldview but should provide opportunities and options when remodeling this worldview.
- The trainer's stance should be the *not-knowing* one while the trainee is the expert in becoming a therapist.

29.7.2 Theoretical Training Specifications

To this stage in TFT, students are regarded as potential founders of new therapeutic schools. Consequently, they are empowered to have their own view about how emotional/behavioral/cognitive or relational problems arise, about how these problems are resolved (or solved), and about what role should the therapist assume in the therapeutic process. It is desirable that trainees get to coherently use systemic thinking and are able to describe, for any of the presented family therapy models, the logical connection between the philosophy, the explanatory theory, the therapeutic intervention, and the position of the therapist in this process. The trainer should be humble when presenting knowledge such as explanatory theories or techniques, and he or she can do this if, for instance, as a lecturer softens her/his without-question stance.

29.7.3 Specifications for the Supervision Stage

Supervision is designed together with the supervisees. The goal is to make future practitioners who will optimally harness their own potential, talent, and inclinations. From the TFT perspective, the supervisor should cultivate tolerance for multiple perspectives and polyphony; use the Socratic method to reveal ideas through dialogue but retain the relationally responsive systemic reflexivity; show sensitivity for the trainee's need for guidance; use isomorphism to conceptualize; and learn about the interdependence between the different contexts involved, i.e., supervision, therapy, trainee's personal life, trainer's personal life.

29.7.4 Specifications for the Personal Growth Stage

In this stage as well as in previous ones, the training focuses on the trainee. The general aim is to enhance skills and attitudes that enable future therapists to interact effectively with clients. Using exercises based on role-play, peer fish bowl, or projective techniques, participants find out which skills might be useful to develop. Once the individual priorities are discovered, we proceed to the personal growth process itself.

29.8 The Present Stage of TFT Model

In general, despite an abundance of studies, books, and articles dedicated to the topic of systemic family therapy training, supervision included, I could not find any study discussing the trainees' perspective, the focus being only on what works in general, not on how a certain training approach works for them. One such study dedicated to what trainees in family therapy consider their most and least meaningful learning experiences reports that family therapy graduate students "appreciated collaborative teachers and supervisors who valued them and what they had to say, and did not appreciate those who cut them off" (Piercy et al., 2016, p 11). This study indirectly validates the importance TFT gives to a collaborative stance. It does not, however, explore a specifically social-constructivist approach. How social constructionism provides different trainings of social constructionist models of psychotherapy?

At the present stage of development, the model has accumulated practical experience but lacks a systematic production of knowledge about it. Therefore, one could say that the description of the model is monologic, based on its author's view and intentionality. TFT it is not a training model with a scientific outcome study to support it. It would be worth a qualitative study to make room for trainees' voices about training this way and to validate or invalidate the abovementioned specifications.

There is room for a robust story about how TFT works alike for trainees and for trainers, one that could be used as a basis for reconsidering and improving current aspects in the TFT model and for making this model more transferable to other trainers and trainees. A story that honors the individual uniqueness both of trainees and trainers.

References

Andersen, T. (1991). *The reflecting team: Dialogues and dialogues about the dialogues*. Norton.
Anderson, H., & Gehart, D. (Eds.). (2007). *Collaborative Therapy. Relationships and Conversations that make a Difference*. Routledge.
Anderson, H., & Goolishian, H. (1988). Human systems as linguistic systems: Evolving ideas about the implications for theory and practice. *Family Process, 27*, 371–393.
Aponte, H. J. (2009). Training the person of the therapist in an academic setting. *Journal of Marital and Family Therapy, 35*(4), 381–394. https://doi.org/10.1111/j.1752-0606.2009.00123.x
Aponte, H. J., et al. (2014). "If I can grapple with this I can truly be of use in the therapy room": using the therapist's own emotional struggles to facilitate effective therapy. *Journal of marital and family therapy, 340*(2), 152–164.
Bakhtin, M. (1992). *The Dialogic Imagination: Four Essays*. University of Texas Press.
Bakhtin, M., & Emerson, C. (1984). *Problems of Dostoevsky's Poetics*. University of Minnesota Press.
Beresford, P. (2013). From 'other' to involved: User involvement in research: An emerging paradigm. *Nordic Social Work Research, 3*(2), 139–148.
Biever, J. L., & Gardner, G. T. (1995). The use of reflecting teams in social constructionist training. *Journal of Systemic Therapies, 14*(3), 47–56. https://doi.org/10.1521/jsyt.1995.14.3.47
Burr, V. (2003). *Social Constructionism*. Routledge.
Epston, David & White, Michael (1990). Narrative Means to Therapeutic Ends. New York: W.W. Norton
Flaskas, C. (2002). *Family Therapy Beyond Postmodernism: Practice Challenges Theory*. Routledge.
Flaskas, C. (2014). Teaching and learning theory for family therapy practice: on the art and craft of balancing. *Australian & New Zeeland Journal of Family Therapy., 34*(3), 283–293.

Gehart, D. (2011). The core competencies and MFT education: Practical aspects of transitioning to a learning-centered, outcome-based pedagogy. *Journal of Marital and family Therapy, 37*(3), 344–354. https://doi.org/10.1111/j.1752-0606.2010.00205.x

Gergen, K. J. (1985). The social constructionist movement in modern psychology. *American Psychologist, 40*(3), 266–275. https://doi.org/10.1037/0003-066X.40.3.266

Hoffman, L. (1985). Beyond power and control: Toward a "second order" family systems therapy. *Family Systems Medicine, 3*(4), 381–396. https://doi.org/10.1037/h0089674

Hoffman, L. (1990). Constructing Realities: An Art of Lenses. *Family Process, 29*(1), 1–12. https://doi.org/10.1111/j.1545-5300.1990.00001.x. PMID 2178969

Karam, E. A. (2010). The Research-Informed Clinician: A Guide to Training the Next-Generation MFT. *Journal of marital and family therapy, 36*(3), 307–319.

Lang, P., Little, M., & Cronen, V. (1990). The systemic professional: domains of action and the question of neutrality. *Human systems: The journal of systemic consultation and management, 1*, 39–55.

London, S., & Tarragona, M. (2007). *Collaborative Therapy* and Supervision in a Psychiatric Hospital. In H. Anderson & D. Gehart (Eds.), *Collaborative Therapy: Relationships and conversations that make a difference* (pp. 251–268). Taylor and Francis, Ltd..

Mason, Barry (2010). Six aspects of supervision and the training of supervisors, Journal of Family Therapy, Vol. 32, Issue 4, p. 436–439. https://doi.org/10.1111/j.1467-6427.2010.00525.x

Piercy, F., et al. (2016). A cross-national study of family therapy training: A collaborative pilot project. *Contemporary Family Therapy., 36*(2). https://doi.org/10.1007/s10591-014-9300-z

Satir, V. (1988). *The New People Making*. Science and Behavior Books.

Shotter, J. (2011). Gergen confluence, and his turbulent, relational ontology: The Constitution of our forms of life within ceaseless, unrepeatable, inteemingling movements. *Psychological Studies, 57*(2) Doi: 10.07/s12646-011-0127-5.

Simon, M. G. (2006). The heart of a matter: a proposal for placing the self of the therapist at the centre of family therapy research and training. *Family Process, 23*, 437–456.

Sommers-Flanagan, J., & Sommers-Flanagan, R. (2012). *Clinical interviewing*. Wiley.

Storm, C. L., et al. (2001). Gaps between MFT supervision assumptions and common practice: suggested best practices. *Journal of marital and family therapy., 27*(2), 227–239.

Sutherland, Olga; Fine, Marshall; Ashbourne, Lynda (2012). Core competencies in Social Constructionist Supervision? Journal of Marital and Family Therapy. Vol.39, Issue 3/ p. 373–387. https://doi.org/10.1111/j.1752-0606.2012.00318.x

Tucker, J. S., & Pinsof, M. W. (1984). The empirical evaluation of family therapy training. *Family Process, 23*, 437–456.

van Manen, M. (1997). From meaning to method. *Qualitative Health Research, 7*(3), 345–369. Sage Publications, Inc.

van Manen, M. (2007). Phenomenology of Practice. *Phenomenology& Practice, 1(1), 11–30*.

White, M. (1988/89). The externalizing of the problem and the re-authoring of lives and relationships. *Dulwich Centre Newsletter,* Summer.

Chapter 30
Family Therapy Training in the Greek Public Sector: The Manualization of an Experiential Learning Process Through Personal and Professional Development

Katia Charalabaki, Kia Thanopoulou, and Athanasia Kati

> *The states of mind we call 'free will'... are achieved through a process that we can equate with "learning to learn". (Bateson, 1972, p. 166)*

> *The ultimate goal, the main purpose of adult education, is to help people realize their potential, become more empowered, socially responsible and self-sufficient learners – that is, to make more conscious choices by thinking more critically. (Mezirow, 2007, p. 68)*

30.1 Introduction to the Theoretical Context of the Training Program of the Family Therapy Unit

The Family Therapy Unit (FTU) of Attica Psychiatric Hospital was founded in 1994, by two psychiatrists Katia Charalabaki and Fotis Kotsidas. Inspired by systemic family therapy, their interest in practicing family and couple psychotherapy, and their common vision of psychiatric reform, they established the Family Therapy Unit. The fact that the FTU belongs to a psychiatric hospital, mainly an asylum, made providing psychotherapy a difficult and challenging endeavor – one of the earliest of its type in the history of the Greek health services – because it demanded a transition from asylum practices to psychotherapy ones.

The Family Therapy Unit's main body of work consists of providing psychotherapy and education. Both clinical and training work has been based on the systemic principles of the Living Human Systems (LHS) (Gournas, 2019), as they are

---

K. Charalabaki (✉) · K. Thanopoulou · A. Kati
Family Therapy Unit, Psychiatric Hospital of Attica, NHS, Athens, Greece
e-mail: katiacharalabaki@hotmail.com; kthanopoulou@gmail.com; athkati@gmail.com

introduced by Yvonne Agazarian in "Systemic centered Group Therapy" (2004). In accordance to this theory, Living Human Systems define a hierarchy of isomorphic systems which are self-organizing, self-correcting, and goal directed:

(a) Systems organize energy, based on their ability to distinguish and compile differences. Through this process the LHS survive, develop, and transform. The organization of energy defines the function of the system, its ability to produce work, or particularly its ability to work to achieve its objectives.
(b) Systems are self-correcting. They remain "stable," constantly changing in the context of a world, which changes through reception, inclusion, and integration of information. Conflicting (noisy) communications make them unstable. Systems regain their stability through the resolution of conflicts, either by cutting off some of the differences that disrupt the existing situation (defenses, forces against change) or by taking time to contain the conflict, until they are able to integrate the differences. Systems survive due to their ability to approach and resolve problems that appear on their way to a goal.
(c) Systems are directed toward specific goals. Within all LHS there are primary and secondary goals. The primary goals of a system are survival, evolution, and transformation, and these are the goals that constitute the primary driving force in all groups. The secondary goals are the predetermined tasks or the apparent goals posed by the system, the tasks of solving the problems set by the environment. All secondary goals can only be achieved when aligned with the primary systemic goals. These primary goals of survival, evolution, and transformation are achieved through a process of distinguishing and integration of differences.

According to our own experience, when a public organization wants to establish a training program in systemic psychotherapy, it should take under consideration the principles of self- organization, self-correction, and goal direction:

1. *Self-organization:* Every system, every group is built and organized upon a goal. The Family Therapy Unit was born from a new concept through the vision of psychiatric reformation and was based on:

    (a) The human values and the principles of denying commercialization and trying to maintain genuine care for people under therapy and training
    (b) The coexistence of therapists/trainers upon the maintenance of common principles
    (c) A common theoretical systemic background which later on was subjected to revisions

2. *Self-correction:* The theory has been modified in depth, based on vast experience, with changes concerning:

    (a) Education, e.g., gradually making it more experiential, by blending theory with personal experience and personal development of trainers and trainees and connecting it with the professional identity for all kinds of mental health professionals

(b) Therapy, by changing the manner of intervention, e.g., from the one-way mirror to a more "self-revealing" role for the therapists, living the difficult experience of coevolution

(c) Cooperation with other units and institutions (e.g., School of Philosophy of the University of Athens, Greek Ministry of Justice), in Greece and in Europe

3. Goal direction (in brief):

   (a) "Public psychotherapy," individual, couple, and family therapy, at the level of public institutions, responding to severe or urgent problems with registered social dimension and offering the opportunity of free access
   (b) "Public education" for mental health professionals, primarily working in the public sector, cultivating trainees' personal development, deeper social consciousness, and responsibility and professional skills, in the field of supporting vulnerable individuals and families
   (c) The introduction of systemic principles and practices into community mental health services, enabling change from restrictive biomedical views and interventions to a holistic approach (Marketos, 2008)

These characteristics drove the FTU to follow the notion of irreverence introduced by Cecchin and his colleagues (Cecchin et al., 1992). According to this the therapist (and the trainer we could add) is urged to not adhere to the safety of his theoretical constructs but to be ready to revise them, promoting uncertainty, questioning preconceptions, and being open to human experience. Irreverence essentially prevents the therapist (and the trainer) from adhering to the dominant ideology of his scientific model or the facility in which he works and urges him to remain alert to the true needs of his clients (and trainees) and provides alternative viewpoints and meanings.

So, we have come to understand learning as a continuous process of questioning, reflecting, and challenging what we know and how we know it. The learning process is an interactional process, which means that the interactions between trainers and trainees determine the outcome. According to Anderson and Swim (1993, p. 150), learning is a coevolutionary process in which the teacher and student are jointly engaged. Knowledge is not something the teacher gives the student. The creation of new knowledge is not standardized; it is created through the process of conversation and relationship. It is the kind of knowledge that Shotter (1993) refers to as "knowing of the third kind" (knowing from), "a kind of knowledge one has from within a situation, a group, a social institution, or society" (p. 190). This knowledge comes from lived experience, is closely connected to emotions, and is present only in moments of interaction.

We agree with Kolb (1984) that learning is defined as "knowledge created through the transformation of experience," while knowledge "results from the combination of grasping and transforming experience" (p. 41). In this way, learning is constructed as continuous, reflexive, and interacting processes stimulated across multiple levels through connections between inner and outer contexts of experience (Neden & Burnham, 2007).

30.2 The "Synthetic, Systemic-Experiential" Program

The educational program starts with the creation of the educational group. The synthesis of the group is very important to us. Since the Unit belongs to the public sector, there are no tuition fees and this fact determines the choice of the participants. Every year we accept a great number of applications (about 150) from which we have to choose 20 participants. We give emphasis on diversity of clinical work settings, professional specialties (psychiatrists, psychologists, social workers, psychiatric nurses, etc.), and professional experience level, since one of our criteria is that candidates should have clinical employment.

Our program is called "synthetic, systemic-experiential" program because it includes the following axes:

- Theory and experience of systemic approach and family therapy. Theoretical knowledge is linked to the trainees' personal experiences and feelings through exercises.
- Practice through observing family sessions behind a one-way mirror or monitoring and editing therapeutic sessions via DVD.
- The construction of genogram – the most experiential part of training – where members of the educational group turn toward their own family history and share stories with the rest of the group.
- The supervision group which is mainly concerned with the clinical cases that trainees deal with in their own workplace.

The content of our theoretical framework is structured over 3 years. The first year is introductory to both the content and the relationship building process of the group. The first lessons describe the systemic way of thinking through the presentation of theory but also through experiential exercises. Following the first academic year, always through a combination of theory and experiential exercises, we present the basic schools of systemic thinking (structural, strategic, Milan school, narrative, etc.) and specific topics (e.g., function and meaning of symptom, family triangles and differentiation, couple therapy, morality and ethics in therapy). Also, during the first year, the team studies and presents a number of articles and a book, organizing how they will distribute and discuss the material. This process is also embedded in the dynamics of the group, as the way in which they choose to share and present the learning material reveals their interrelationships which may be unrecognized and worthy of being highlighted. Finally, in the first year, trainees present clinical cases that arise in their workplaces. The presence of the trainer usually creates a sense of security within the group that allows this process to evolve.

The second year is more clinically oriented and focuses on clinical entities or issues arising in family psychotherapy. Topics addressed in the second year include myths and rituals in family and healing, family mourning processes, family psychotherapy in which a member exhibits symptoms (such as psychosis, eating disorders, or serious physical illness), and the concept of emotional attachment to psychotherapy, systemic group psychotherapy.

Also, during the second year, in order to gain a deeper theoretical understanding, the team is invited to study and present a number of books from systemic literature. The process followed is equivalent to that of the first year, that is, the team members themselves assume the responsibility of sharing and presenting the project. The books presented are some of the classic or more up-to-date family therapy books, and team members work in subgroups to present them to the whole group. These are very creative moments in the life of each team as trainees are mobilized and engaged in a teamwork and collective effort.

In addition to the theoretical deepening in systemic thinking, the team is also called to delve deeper into therapeutic issues. So, in the second year, team supervision continues in cases brought by trainees from their workplaces. Furthermore, the philosophy of our therapeutic and educational work is based on the use of the self of the therapist, which is why we focus on issues such as resonance, self-reference, and the therapist's genogram.

The second year prepares the team members to present their personal genogram in the third year. Creating and presenting the personal genogram to the team is one of the key processes of education and one of the key moments in the personal development of our trainees. Realizing the patterns of their own family relationships, they are invited to deepen their understanding of systemic thinking, as well as to shield themselves from the influence that their own family history has on their therapeutic work. In the third year, trainees are also invited to write a thesis of a clinical case combined with relevant systemic theory.

After the completion of the first 3 years of the training, program trainees are involved in at least a 2-year-long supervisory group, as supervision is recognized as a key tool for development, support of young psychotherapists, and a process of training and feedback. It gives space to very complex processes within the team, through the acceptance and support of each member, and it facilitates communication and awareness among supervisors. The supervisor-supervisee relationship is by definition a hierarchical one. The supervisor has the experience, knowledge, and oversight of the supervisee's work, with the ultimate goal of assisting others in their work. Both the supervisor and the supervised can contribute to the supervisory process, from different viewpoints and with different responsibilities

The supervisor feels safe to comment on his/her intervention and think about how he/she can be helpful and supportive and facilitate treatment and management. The process is based on a fruitful dialogue between the members, and not just the supervised member, under the direction and guidance of the supervisor, without focus on evaluating right and wrong. Supervision is primarily a learning process, but also offers case management guidance, and its success rests on the supervisor's ability to facilitate transformative learning, a process by which data is redefined to make it more open and more thoughtful. It is more than just transmitting technical information or clinical skills. It is a space for reflection and transformation through dialogue (Moschakou, 2018).

Jay Haley (1987) was quite convinced that there is isomorphism between therapy training and therapy itself since he claims that therapy training changes only when theories of how to implement therapy change, meaning that a theory of therapy is almost synonymous with a theory of training.

However, all theories of therapy are interconnected, so there are different variables that a training theory depends on. Even with changes in the social context and epistemological "paradigm shifts," many changes in both therapy and training have occurred over time.

30.3 Basic Topics as a Manual for the Development of a "Synthetic, Systemic-Experiential" Program

30.3.1 The Goals and Objectives of the Training Program

A major issue in education is how meaningful learning experience is produced. Not only as therapists but also as trainers, we seek and form networks of relationships and meanings. Education as a learning process is a role model. It is not only about the level of content but also about the process, the relationships between the people involved in education. We believe that the academic content and the personal relationships form a dialectic relationship – the one emerges from the other but also already contains the other. According to our philosophy and principles, we aspire our trainees' group to be a safe, transitional space of experience and reflection that is open and in constant evolution for all participants (Thanopoulou, 2018).

The Unit trains mental health professionals, who mainly work in the public sector and thus are people who have relevant experience in the field of work. We are, of course, always open to adjust to current social needs, for example, in the context of the socioeconomic crisis we have experienced during recent years, we have accepted unemployed people who fulfilled the conditions to the training program.

One of our principles is that we don't offer therapy to our trainees, because we strongly believe that this is a way of maintaining clear boundaries. It is the trainees' responsibility to decide the time and the type of their personal therapy, the integration of which is a prerequisite for becoming a therapist. Some of our trainees decide not to become therapists and get the knowledge and experience they need to continue their work in a more creative way. What is important for the procedure is for it to become a meaningful and important experience for all types of mental health professionals.

30.3.2 The Training Group Is Not a Therapeutic One

The experiential nature of education often raises the question for our trainees of whether it is a therapeutic group or a training group. We often say that the education we provide is more than education and less than therapy (Charalabaki, 2008).

There is no group that has not asked this question in some phase of its life. A few years ago, on the last day before the summer holidays, we set a task to a group that was at the end of their first year: it was a simple family story about a father, mother, son, and daughter, leaving for summer vacations. The group divided into four subgroups, each one in one of the family roles, and had to discuss and write down some thoughts about the other family members. To our surprise, this apparently innocent task triggered sharp conflict within the group. Working through the issues of the conflict unveiled that there had been a latent scapegoat process and that if it was to remain unrevealed, some members of the group were to be "ostracized."

Then in another group, again at the last meeting before the summer holidays, two members unexpectedly brought their young children with them. So, in this way it was ensured that the group would not talk about separation and would say good-bye but not "discuss good-bye."

The team creates an environment that facilitates and supports the learning process through experience, as it provides a framework for understanding oneself in relationships. It also offers the experience of feeling and giving meaning to a variety of intense emotions within interpersonal relationships. This may seem obvious, even "banal," but we must admit that the story of each center is "local" and the developmental stages do not necessarily coincide with general assumptions. Each member identifies personal myths, types of transactions, commands, beliefs, and values brought from their own past, through the whole transaction with the team. This process helps the members come closer, to the point where they are ready, as Campbell would say, to pursue their "personal blessing," understanding that everyone is a complement to the others but also that the whole other world is in us (Sakkas, 2018). As Bakhtin (1984, p. 287) reminds us, "….to be means to communicate to be means to be for another, and through the other, for oneself. A person has no internal sovereign territory, he is wholly and always on the border; looking inside he looks into another's eyes or with another's eyes."

A very important part of our educational program is to carefully observe the processes of the group: the interconnection and relationship of the group as a whole with each individual member, the give and take, the competition, inclusion and exclusion, evolving group roles and being preoccupied with gender roles, the evolution of roles within the group, and their relationship to the gender role. As one of our graduates of the program put it, "getting involved in the group process of a learning community is a simulation of engaging in a rather family-like system that has a basic structure and a specific life cycle (three years), functions, roles and role models, alliances, triangles, etc." (Petta, 2018).

We have observed three phases in the training groups' life cycle:

(a) It is a group of good students, eager to learn. They usually take notes and ask for more theory and bibliography. Trainers are idealized.
(b) As members come to know each other, several triangulation processes take place, group roles are formed, and coalitions appear. There are fears about personal exposure and trust within the group is tested. It is at this stage that questions about the nature of the group, such as "Are we a training or therapeutic

group?," appear more often. The "contract question" becomes prominent, and its linguistic slip of calling trainers "therapists" begins to appear sporadically. There are also attacks on the procedures, for instance, if there are absent members or if members arrive late and do not want to leave on time. At this phase trainees feel very happy to work on book presentations, which creates and "tests" bonds between members; there is enthusiasm and competition among subgroups in an ambition of great creativity. "Teenage uprisings" against the educational context make their appearances, differing in intensity. As an example, one group was due to present G. Bateson's *Steps to an Ecology of Mind*; however, the subgroup that was responsible for the presentation refused to do it (they considered it too difficult and had forgotten to do it on time), and the whole group presented great solidarity in the rebellion. So, the group had to discuss what it is to be a group again and had to leave theory aside.

(c) As the program is in its final stage, which includes the presentation of each member's family genogram, there is great relevance to the usefulness of this objective. It is a kind of "to be or not to be" period, and the linguistic slip of calling the trainers therapists is more common.

As Petta (2018) rightly remarks, "in the third year, we are changing our life cycle of education and preparing for "leaving home", our educational home. The presentation of the genealogies at this stage invites us to a substantial self-disclosure, in a quest to find our position in two different systems: on the one hand, in the search for our place in our family system and on the other hand, at the same time, in our search for our position in a twenty-member group system. The team presentation process does not serve as a one-dimensional utility guide for any future system work. Rather it functions as a hint, a hint,of the complexity that every personal story has; the need to grasp the totality of relationships and to avoid linear interpretive patterns. There are multiple levels that the therapist is called upon to keep in mind and at the same time to forget so as not to be confined to close-ended interpretations."

Despite initial reservations about the final presentation, eventually the outcome is quite optimistic. There has been no single group not to complete the program successfully. Each has achieved in its own way, some with their own wounds, mainly as a result of arbitrary departures of group members or sometimes "communicating" messages to trainers (which is taken seriously). The aftermath of a group's life also presents all the characteristics of group dynamics. Members apply for the next cycle of the program, which is supervision, asking for personal appointments with trainers, referring family members to therapy, and giving promises of "eternal fidelity to the group" or, more realistically, staying in touch.Below is an experiential imprint of the genogram by a group of our trainees:

> The genogram is a search of our line through time, our mnemonic traces; the inevitable connection of the past, the present and the future. If you do not dive into the past, you cannot understand the present and differentiate, exist and create or co-create the future. A topography of experiences full of memories of relationships, marriages, births, death, a cycle of climbing and pruning. A photograph of our existence, of our story that becomes alive as it revives. We are a small part of it all, a small chain link but important. There is so much more to his image than the eye can see – absenteeism, traumas, silences, secrets …

> Hearing our family life narratives we struggle to put our own personal punctuation because as we're growing, we grow so deep.

30.3.3 The Role of the Team of Trainers and the Trainer-Trainee Relationship

As the very nature of this latter relationship is asymmetrical and hierarchical, we did not really concern ourselves about this issue. However, being an expert has less to do with knowledge or experience (which is also an important aspect, as people come to learn) and more to do with the ability to identify resonances. In the end, if one wants to meet the group's needs, for educational purposes, the group is really the expert. Can this be accomplished without having a democratic spirit and sincerity?

Group members are not at all indifferent about the trainers' relationships. How do they cooperate? Do they agree but at the same time want to stab one another in the back? Are women subordinating to men and vice versa? Who is friendly and who is "cold" and how do all these differences influence their integrity as a team? Here again this is latent among their "teachers" and is often expressed in a very apocalyptic way. For example, if there is a latent competition or conflict among trainers, the trainee group may pose direct or indirect questions, make remarks, or present anxiety. The included-excluded fears are activated; people are curious, provocative, or protective. To be aware of this is of great value for the efficacy of the educational program on the whole.

There is a strong tradition in our field of having very bright, talented, and charismatic personalities as trainers. However, this also left a guru or "narcissistic" model of trainers as a legacy for the new generations. Self-development includes this aspect, of finding our own way of being trainers, incorporating only those of our teachers' qualities that we can assimilate, avoiding the temptation of imitating them.

Goethe said, "What you inherited from your father must first be earned before it's yours." A dialectical tension exists between inventing oneself freshly, on the one hand, and creatively using one's emotional ancestry on the other hand (Gabbard & Ogden, 2009). We believe that in our clinical practice as therapists, the most important tool is our self and our capacity to make use of what is unique to our own experience and that our knowledge is sought to be transmitted to our trainee (see also Thanopoulou, 2019). Minuchin and Fishman (1981) compare the training of a therapist with that of the samurai swordsman who must spend a lot of time learning skills and techniques. After intensive training, the apprentice is instructed to retire to the mountains where he meditates. When he has forgotten all that he has learned, then he can return and become the sword.

30.3.4 The Nuclear Philosophy

Every therapist or trainer works differently in different circumstances, depending on his or her personality. We believe that integration processes within each space are a complex undertaking and bear specific, unique historical features. This story creates the unique identity of each training center that goes hand in hand with the theoretical and individual development of the trainers, the specific characteristics of each training group, and the rules of the wider system where they fit. Through its 25 years of operation, we want to believe that the Family Therapy Unit has managed to create a "crack" within the public mental health system by providing "public psychotherapy" to families, couples, and individuals with severe or urgent problems, by training mental health professionals from diverse professional backgrounds – mainly public – and cultivating trainees' personal development, deeper social awareness, and responsibility and professional skills, in the work of supporting vulnerable individuals and families and "introducing systemic principles and practices into community mental health services, enabling the shift from restrictive biomedical views and interventions to a holistic approach" (Marketos, 2018). Over the years, we have remained a vibrant, open system that has sought to redefine its organization and function by maintaining our belief in human values and principles that are concerned with genuine care for both our patients and trainees. The way our training groups perceive and respond has changed over the years as a result of the evolution of both instructors and trainees.

30.3.5 The Therapist's Therapy

For many decades, most systemic schools responded negatively to the question of whether the personal therapy is mandatory for the therapist. Our position is identical to that of Bowen (a therapist whose work connects with us and whose theories we use in our curriculum). According to Bowen (1978, p. 468), the family therapist usually has the same problems in his own family that are present in families he sees professionally, and he has a responsibility to define himself in his own family if he is to function adequately in his professional work. So, we see the fact that during our training many group members are sensitized to start personal therapy (60% of our trainees) very positively. Our global view regarding therapy and therapists' training makes us believe this is a major benefit. Personal needs for therapy can vary widely.

Thus, there is no unique format for family therapists' therapy. It could be individual or group therapy, systemic, psychodynamic, gestalt, or psychodrama. This diversity will not necessarily be muddling or cause chaos. On the contrary, it can be very enriching. The unifying element would be knowing one's self in relationships better. Resonance, a nuclear concept proposed by Elkaim (1989), is central to our understanding of team life. Thanks to the concept of resonance, the self-referential paradox ceases to be a limit and becomes possibility, if and only if the therapist has learned to use himself as a therapeutic instrument: if he has learned to work in the intersection between the constructs of the world of the family system members and his own constructs, utilizing the systemic function of resonance to generate new possibilities for that system. Using, that is, the emotions or perceptions of his own personal history, which the system evokes and amplifies, in such a way as to avoid the mutual strengthening of the world constructs of all the members in the therapeutic system (Chouhy, 2008, p. 248).

Further elaborating on this notion, it is used as a tool to bring aspects of group education and inner life into proportion. We try to bring facts, thoughts, and emotions into the here-and-now of the learning process of the group's life, and sometimes we do so by using information drawn from our past. Any peculiarity, difficulty, or creative takeoff from the perspective of the educational point goes hand in hand with interactions between members. It is impressive how differently the same "lesson" is "learned" and "taught" in each group, or even within the same group at different moments in time, but also how a lesson can teach many more important things about the group itself, about its abilities and anxieties. We do not consider the differences that exist in members' scientific jargon to be an obstacle or pose any special problems. In the group's storytelling, there are always different languages of origin (cultural, family, personal, or scientific), and there is no risk of creating Babel.

30.3.6 The Group Has the Potential to Integrate Different Idioms

We never undertake therapy for group members, even though requests are received quite often. The reasons are organizational limitations, but also the rule of not taking too much responsibility over trainees, which creates an omnipotent type of teacher-therapist or "master"-type role, in a context that infantilizes and transforms them to noncritical followers. This is an important aspect as opposed to the phenomenon that appears in many training institutions (systemic as well as psychoanalytic) of the so-called training therapy. In our view, the institutionalization of therapy for qualifying reasons may be a result of a bureaucratic view of therapy and can eventually lead to self-development becoming subordinate to educational achievements.

There are also many questions regarding qualification formats. Is it possible that the evaluation of a therapist or trainer is based on impersonal data (hours, years of training) that are collected in a widespread "diploma market"? This may include the risk of validating pseudo- or "as if" therapies. In any case, one cannot control the social process that leads to the expansion of psychotherapeutic perspectives, nor is it our mission to judge and act as moralists. We ourselves are responsible for choosing "virtues" and "sins" for ourselves, our way of being therapists and trainers, even though this can never happen out of context. We find this an essential feature of personal-professional development. Carl Whitaker (1972) revealed that he went through his pornographic period, his medical phase, and he was maternal, paternal, authoritarian, cooperative, and all this while having five personal therapy experiences.

It is very important for our trainees to be aware of the way they relate to others and the way they relate in their inner world and to be able to reflect on themselves. We consider that training to become a psychotherapist has important similarities to the growth and psychological maturation of the patient under the care of the psychotherapist. Our profession invites us to an exploration of the inner life of both the therapist-trainee and the patient, which is never-ending. An exploration that is always open to what we are and what we are becoming. According to Pinsof (2005), who you are as a psychotherapist is a product not only of education, training, and personality but also more importantly of your own experience as a patient in psychotherapy over the course of your life. All of the above, in our opinion, have an impact on our understanding of clinical practice and psychotherapy theory, and what we do in our clinical practice has the potential to influence our values, beliefs, theory, and personal style in a reflexive way.

30.4 Epilogue

In this chapter we presented the synopsis of the manual of the "synthetic, systemic-experiential program" of the Family Therapy Unit. Since the family therapy training program has been developed over the last 25 years in the public sector, utilizing some important aspects of our experience, we have identified several points that could, hopefully, work as possible guidelines for further systemic training programs:

- Learning is a coevolutionary process for both trainers and trainees. The trainer, like the trainee, is always in the process of learning.
- Theoretical knowledge of systemic approach and family therapy is better understood when linked to the trainees' personal experiences and feelings.
- The synthesis of the team is of great significance: complementarity, diversity, and clinical employment enhance the learning process.
- The structure of the training program's curriculum has an evolutionary character, which prepares the trainees for deeper knowledge and integration of the theory and practice in systemic therapy: starting from main theory and bonding of the members, continuing with experiential tasks and the presentation of the genogram, and concluding with clinical supervision.
- The team functions as a safe, transitional space of experience and reflection for all participants, an environment that facilitates and supports the learning process.
- Emphasis is given on the process of the group.
- The continuous supervision and therapy for becoming a therapist is of great importance.

In conclusion we would say that it is a great pleasure for us when, at the end of their training, many of our trainees report their experience to the training team as a milestone in both their personal and professional lives. As one graduating group said: "Three cycles, three years, three generations .... A group of vivid restless expectations, excitement and diversity. Now emotion, hugs paused. Not the end though. Growth and evolution. Together and apart. Is it an end or a start? This basic training seems small but is complete. You leave full of rich experience. It closes and finishes but continues, not only as an education, but also as an internalized process that you take with you. It offers links to emotional reflections, stimuli, information openings and a frame to hold onto. It starts with completely different people wondering how they were chosen, but in the end, have discovered bridges and continuity. You look at them and they no longer look different, but familiar. You start with anxious tension and maybe when it finishes something has subsided and been reassured as it has experienced maturity. I sit and listen to what I feel, without haste. When one manages to do so, then maybe one can properly say goodbye. I listened, I thought, I felt .... now sorry for saying goodbye. I'm growing up we're growing up."

References

Agazarian, Y. (2004). *Systems-centered therapy for groups*. Karnac Books.
Anderson, H., & Swim, S. (1993). Learning as collaborative conversation combining the student's and teacher's expertise. *Human Systems: The Journal of Systemic Consultation & Management, 4*, 145–160.
Bakhtin, M. (1984). *Problems of Dostoevsky's poetics*. University of Minneapolis Press.
Bateson, G. (1972). *Steps to an ecology of mind: Collected essays in anthropology, psychiatry, evolution, and epistemology*. Chandler Publishing.
Bowen, M. (1978). On the differentiation of self. In *Family therapy in clinical practice*. Jason Aronson.
Cecchin, G., Lane, G., & Ray, W. A. (1992). *Irreverence: A strategy for therapists' survival*. Karnac Books.
Charalabaki, K. (2008). Personal professional development within a family therapy training institute: "More than ... less than". Development of the therapist as part of a social process. *Human Systems: The Journal of Therapy, Consultation & Training, 19*, 260–267.
Chouhy, A. (2008). Developmental parameters in family therapy training: The matching process of the therapist's family history. *Human Systems. The Journal of Therapy Consultation and Training, 19*(3), 240–259.
Elkaim, M. (1989). *Si tu m'aimes ne m'aime pas*. Editions du Seuil. Greek edition: Elkaim, M. (2008). *If you love me don't love me* (N. Hristakis, Trans.). Athens: Kedros (in Greek).
Gabbard, G. O., & Ogden, T. H. (2009). On becoming a psychoanalyst. *The International Journal of Psychoanalysis, 90*, 311–327.
Gournas, G. (2019). Book presentation: Family Therapy Unit, Psychiatric Hospital of Athens: Memories and reflections. *Electronic Journal of Systemic Thinking and Psychotherapy, 14*, 70–77. Retrieved from http://hestafta.org/
Haley, J. (1987). *Problem solving therapy*. Jossey-Bass Publishers.
Kolb, D. A. (1984). *Experiential learning*. Prentice Hall.
Marketos, N. (2018). *The family therapy unit's relationship to the wider setting*. In K. Charalabaki, M. Borcsa, & K. Thanopoulou (Eds.), *Family Therapy Unit and Attica Psychiatric Hospital: "Recollections and reflections"*. Korontzis. (in Greek).
Mezirow, J., & Associates. (2000). *Learning as transformation*. Jossey-Bass. Greek edition: Mezirow, J. (2007). *Transformative learning* (G. Koulaouzidis, Trans.). Athens: Metaihmio (in Greek).

Minuchin, S., & Fishman, H. C. (1981). *Family therapy techniques*. Harvard University Press.

Moschakou, G. (2018). Supervision in a training setting. In K. Charalabaki, M. Borcsa, & K. Thanopoulou (Eds.), *Family Therapy Unit and Attica Psychiatric Hospital: "Recollections and reflections"*. Korontzis. (in Greek).

Neden, J., & Burnham, J. (2007). Using relational reflexivity as a resource in family therapy teaching. *Journal of Family Therapy, 29*, 359–363.

Petta, S. (2018). Apprenticeship in the genogram: Charting the past, changing the present. In K. Charalabaki, M. Borcsa, & K. Thanopoulou (Eds.), *Family Therapy Unit and Attica Psychiatric Hospital: "Recollections and reflections"*. Korontzis. (in Greek).

Pinsof, W. M. (2005). A shamanic tapestry: My experiences with individual, marital, and family therapy. In J. D. Geller, J. C. Norcross, & D. Orlinsky (Eds.), *The psychotherapist's own psychotherapy. Patient and clinician perspective*. Oxford University Press.

Sakkas, D. (2018). Utilizing the myth of Iphigenia in experiential learning. In K. Charalabaki, M. Borcsa, & K. Thanopoulou (Eds.), *Family Therapy Unit and Attica Psychiatric Hospital: "Recollections and reflections"*. Korontzis. (in Greek).

Shotter, J. (1993). *Conversational realities: Constructing life through language*. Sage.

Thanopoulou, K. (2018). Experiential learning experiences from training in the Family Therapy Unit. In K. Charalabaki, M. Borcsa, & K. Thanopoulou (Eds.), *Family Therapy Unit and Attica Psychiatric Hospital: "Recollections and reflections"*. Korontzis. (in Greek).

Thanopoulou, K. (2019). Some reflections on becoming a therapist. *Electronic Journal of Systemic Thinking and Psychotherapy, 15*, 25–37. Retrieved from http://hestafta.org/

Whitaker, C. A. (1972). Commentary, a longitudinal study of therapy styles. *Family Process, 11*(1), 13–15.

Chapter 31
"From Mind to Culture": Developing a Treatment Plan Manual for the Enriched Systemic Psychotherapy Model
SANE-System Attachment Narrative Encephalon®

Athena Androutsopoulou, Tsabika Bafiti, and George Kalarritis

31.1 Introduction

In the last few decades, integration of treatments within psychotherapy in general and within family therapy in specific has become a widespread movement (Lebow, 2003). There have also been several important influences in the field of systemic therapies. The first is the influence of the narrative turn that psychology and consequently psychotherapy took in the late 1980s (Bruner, 1990; Sarbin, 1986) leading an increasing number of systemic therapists to place emphasis in the organization of experiences by storytelling. From a narrative perspective, therapy is perceived as an exchange of stories in dialogue, both external and internal, where therapists seek to help clients form coherent and meaningful narratives (Angus & McLeod, 2004; McLeod, 1997, 2004). A second influence in the field of psychotherapy in general, and systemic therapies in specific, has been the increasing influence of attachment theory and relevant research evidence that has provided systemic therapies with a theoretically compatible developmental theory. Systemic therapists who have informed their clinical and training work by attachment theory include Dallos (2004, 2006), Dallos and Vetere (2009), Fishbane (2001), Hughes (2007), and Johnson et al. (2001). Finally, a third influence in the field has been the impact of affective (Armony & Vuilleumier, 2016; Damasio, 2018; LeDoux, 2019) and social (Cacioppo & Berntson, 2005; Todorof et al., 2011) neuroscience findings and specifically those from interpersonal neurobiology (Schore, 1994; Siegel, 1999). Interest in ways to incorporate such findings in training models is growing (Sluzki, 2007).

A. Androutsopoulou (✉) · T. Bafiti · G. Kalarritis
"Logo Psychis" – Training and Research Institute for Systemic Psychotherapy, Athens, Greece
e-mail: athena@androutsopoulou.gr

Over a decade ago, Fishbane (2007) pointed to the importance of linking all three influences with systemic practice. However, creating a coherent model provides an important challenge. A most interesting example in combining systemic, attachment, and narrative ideas constitutes the work of Dallos (2004, 2006). Other theorists/therapists have combined attachment theory, narrative psychology, and neuroscience (e.g., Cozolino, 2015; Siegel & Solomon, 2003), but to our knowledge there is no other model to date that combines all four into a single coherent model. An extra challenge derives from the effort to create such a link for systemic therapy irrespective of treatment duration or type of session and to provide a general treatment manual that can benefit clients irrespective of individual differences and even symptoms. We have developed an enriched systemic outlook which is "therapist-centered" rather than "prescriptive" (Lebow, 1997). The "therapist-centered" outlook allows for a personal – but *guided* – synthesis of ideas, interventions and techniques, types of sessions (individual, family, and group), and contracts (short and long). In contrast, a "prescriptive" integrative model would provide an organized set of strict practice directives.

We begin this chapter by outlining our theoretical assumptions regarding the benefits of multiplicity and the usefulness of all four perspectives presented. After providing a brief outline of the therapy setting, we describe the process of therapy in four parallel stages, including therapy goals for each stage. Ways to help conceptualize a case are discussed, including guiding questions. We focus on the role of the therapist which is extremely important in our enriched model and one of the most crucial "common factors" in psychotherapy in general (Sprenkle & Blow, 2007). The qualities of an effective therapist are discussed with emphasis placed in providing reparative attachment experiences through personal growth and gained security. Finally, relevant research on the process and experience of therapy conducted at our Institute is presented in brief, along with research-based tools for assessing progress.

31.2 Theoretical Assumptions

31.2.1 *A Multiplicity of Perspectives*

Our approach enriches systemic therapy with attachment theory, basic premises from narrative/dialogic psychology and psychotherapy, and relevant findings from interpersonal neurobiology (Androutsopoulou et al., 2014; Bafiti, Androutsopoulou, & Kalarritis, 2017; Bafiti, Androutsopoulou, & Kalarritis, 2018). First, let us take a brief, separate look at each perspective that enriches our basic systemic outlook.

John Bowlby's (1988) theory of attachment, shaped through careful long-term experimental and observational research (Cassidy & Shaver, 2016), offers a developmental theory of the way personality is formed and of reasons for later life difficulties (Parkes et al., 1991). It relates such difficulties and/or symptoms to family functioning without blaming the family: specifically, it detects transgenerational patterns that transfer emotional insecurity to children and points to ways that this insecurity influences adult relationships. In the words of Byng-Hall (1995), one of the first and most important figures who introduced attachment theory to family therapists, "attachment theory suggests an overall aim of increasing the security of the family base, thus helping all family members to be self-sufficient" (p. 8). In his opinion, many different family therapy techniques can be used at the appropriate moment:

> In other words, attachment theory provides a framework that can integrate several ways of working, as opposed to providing a school of family therapy with set premises and specific techniques. It has the potential to offer something to all therapists. (Byng-Hall, 1995, p. 8)

A key to the transgenerational nature of emotional security-insecurity is narratives – told in different voices – and their level of coherence (Byng-Hall, 2008; Main, 1991). Secure relationships are associated with coherent narratives and vice versa. Coherent narratives are told by parents who are in touch with emotions, their own and those of their child, and are appreciative with the child rather than indifferent or strict. A child's sense of self is constructed in dialogue with the narrating parents, and this dialogue is internalized and carried through adulthood as inner dialogue of different parts of self or voices (Hermans & Dimaggio, 2004). An inner dialogue of good quality does not tend to become monologue (Penn & Frankfurt, 1994); it allows for many inner voices to be heard rather than one dominant voice (e.g., the internalized voice of a strict parent).

Finally, findings from neurosciences in regard to the brain, the most complicated system known to us, emphasize the imprinting of early and later experiences, positive and negative, on our neural circuits. Researchers place particular emphasis in the importance of early attachment bonds and of narratives as the means of shaping the brain. Even specific contemporary concepts, such as *unique outcomes* (White & Epston, 1990) or of *internal dialogues* (Hermans & Dimaggio, 2004) in dialogical approaches, to name just two, are now explained by or associated with specific brain structures (Beaudon & Zimmerman, 2011; Lewis & Todd, 2004). Luckily, we now know that our brain continues to be shaped throughout our lives and can develop in a positive direction through corrective social interactions and particularly by corrective relationships, such as those offered in the psychotherapy setting.

31.2.2 Combining Perspectives

The Treatment Plan Manual is the product of both readings and experience, and its scope is to provide guidelines for clinical practice. We draw from readings of authors such as *Daniel Siegel* (Siegel, 2007, 2010; Siegel & Solomon, 2003), *Louis Cozolino* (Cozolino, 2006, 2015, 2017), *Alan Shore* (Schore, 2003, 2012), and *Joseph LeDoux* (LeDoux, 2002) for their brain studies and proposed links to narrative and attachment: *Jeremy Holmes* (Holmes, 2001) and *David Wallin* (Wallin, 2007) for their comprehensive applications of attachment theory; *John Byng-Hall*

(Byng-Hall, 1995, 2008) for his writings on the importance of connecting family therapy with attachment theory and research; *James Pennebaker* (Pennebaker, 1997) for his studies of expressive writing, coherent narratives, and health; *Hubert Hermans* (Hermans & Dimaggio, 2004) and *Kenneth Gergen* (Gergen, 1994) for the understanding of self as narrative multiplicity; *Peggy Penn* (Penn & Frankfurt, 1994), who made the idea of narrative multiplicity more approachable for systemic and family therapists combining it with her interest in expressive writing; *Jerome Bruner* (Bruner, 1990) and *Theodore Sarbin* (Sarbin, 1986) who made a major contribution to the narrative turn of psychology; and *John McLeod* (McLeod, 1997) for the comprehensive history and importance of narrative in psychotherapy, which is a broad approach much wider than any specific model which includes the word "narrative" in its title (see Angus & McLeod, 2004; McLeod, 2004).

Beyond our readings, the project of enriching systemic therapy was made possible due to our previous training in a synthetic systemic model (Katakis, 1990; Katakis et al., 2011), as well as to our accumulated experience in clinical practice, research, training, and supervision (Androutsopoulou, 2005; Bafiti, 2008, 2009a, 2009b; Bafiti & Kalarritis, 2009; Kalarritis, 2005, 2013, 2016; Kalarritis & Bafiti, 2005).

How are the multiple perspectives combined in our Treatment Plan Manual? A basic premise for this combination is that each perspective directs clinical attention to a different aspect of the therapy process: Attachment theory directs attention to the *therapeutic relationship*, systemic theory to the *content of therapy discourse*, narrative psychology to the *form of therapy discourse*, and interpersonal neurobiology *to the process of therapy* as a long-lasting interchange between progress and impasse.

The Treatment Plan Manual is comprised of:

(i) *Stages* describing the process of therapy, stated in parallel from all four perspectives: systemic, attachment, narrative, and brain. Each stage comes with basic goals.
(ii) *Guiding questions* for clinical practice, phrased from all four perspectives. Guiding questions explicate the goals set in each stage as stated from all four perspectives.

31.3 Process of Therapy

31.3.1 Therapy Setting

Clients come to us with various requests. Some approach us for problems with their children or partners; others come with unresolved traumas, serious psychological difficulties, or requests for "personal growth." We generally embrace the position that systemic family therapy is more about a way of thinking (i.e., posing curiosity questions, exploring alternative perspectives) than a way of doing (i.e., having all family members present), so we use a variety of session types with the following rationale.

We usually begin with short-term contracts conducting an average of five to ten individual and/or couple or family sessions depending on such factors as the nature of the request, the intention of the person making initial contact, and the availability or willingness of family members to attend one or more meetings. Some clients will want to renew their therapy contract even though their immediate concerns have been dealt with, recognizing that other difficulties have emerged which need work at a deeper level. These difficulties affect relationships well beyond the limits of the immediate family environment and block the sense of freedom that allows persons to make the best possible choices for their lives and the lives of their children. To deeply understand such implications – at a behavioral, cognitive, and emotional level – takes time. To be able to deal with old ways of constructing experience and to trust new ways takes even more time. Thus, these clients will embark on a long-term therapy "journey" often to be taken in a highly relational setting provided by a group of other individual clients. More than one family member may embark on such long-term work and will join a different group, often with different therapists.

Groups are open and heterogeneous (various ages, symptoms/requests) usually headed by two co-therapists and comprised of up to ten members. Groups meet for weekly 2-hour sessions. The therapists are responsible for making the whole experience meaningful, including the experience of termination. They are also responsible for dealing with any misunderstandings or obstacles in communication. They "train" new members in providing feedback in sensitive ways, and they contribute their own alternative views. The interaction between the co-therapists and with group members provides a useful model of relating. Members function as both participants and active audiences. As participants, they take turns in recounting events that mostly troubled them (personal, familial, work-related) or thoughts they had during the week. As active audiences, they propose alternative views based on their own life experiences, validate new stories, and offer companionship during the long "journey" as equals. Family members are occasionally invited to a family session or to the group as a validating audience of special significance.

31.3.2 Parallel Therapy Stages and Goals from Four Perspectives (Diagram 31.1)

In the four parallel stages, short-term contracts usually end after completion of stage 1, but may be renewed as long-term contracts to cover stages 2–4.

- Attachment perspective (stages adapted from Holmes, 2001)

    1. *Building a safe therapeutic relationship.* The therapist learns to offer a corrective attachment experience to clients, a safe base for exploring inner and outer experiences that pose a challenge to clients' life.

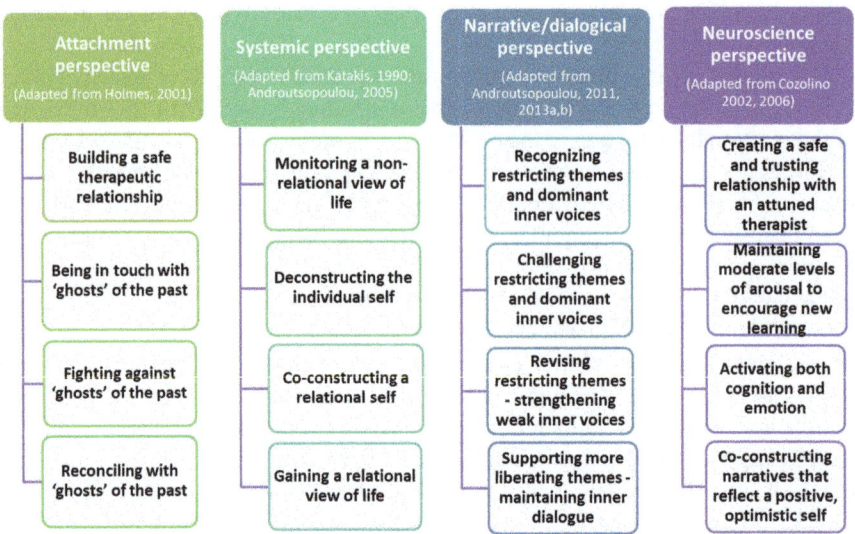

Diagram 31.1 Four parallel stages from the four perspectives of *SANE-System Attachment Narrative Encephalon*®

2. *Being in touch with "ghosts" of the past*. The therapist helps clients detect unresolved attachment issues and their present influence upon their life.
3. *Fighting against "ghosts" of the past*. The therapist learns to provide a safe place for dealing with unsaid emotions; works with "transferences" or – in other words – the "recruitment" of therapist or therapy group members as participants in familiar scenarios.
4. *Reconciling with "ghosts" of the past*. The therapist helps clients accept past experiences and losses based on the idea of transgenerational patterns of secure and insecure attachment; helps the client to "let go" and to minimize such influences on present relationships and to invest on new relationships.

- Systemic perspective (stages adapted from Katakis, 1990; see also Androutsopoulou, 2005)

   1. *Monitoring a non-relational view of life*. The therapist learns to map the rigid emotional-cognitive construction of the individualistic notion of "self," for instance, to monitor non-relational thinking in the clients' narrations; the therapist also examines together with client helpful and unhelpful communication patterns, related to difficulties and/or symptoms.
   2. *Deconstructing the individual self*. The therapist helps clients challenge rigid psychological roles and deal with an unavoidable "inner void" that emerges following the gradual deconstruction of the "individual self."
   3. *Co-constructing a relational self*. The therapist helps clients challenge family myths and dominant cultural values; helps to create together with clients a

sense of differentiated "self" or identity but also helps to co-construct a "relational self."
4. *Gaining a relational view of life.* The therapist helps clients reinvest on life, family, and "self" from a new relational perspective and enjoys with clients an emerging sense of new meaning.

- Narrative/dialogical perspective (stages adapted from Androutsopoulou, 2011, 2013)
    1. *Recognizing restricting life themes and dominant inner voices.* The therapist helps clients name dominant inner voices and the restricting life themes they support; helps clients realize difficulties in using inner dialogue and the negative effects of inner monologue leading to difficulties and/or symptoms.
    2. *Challenging restricting themes and dominant inner voices.* The therapist uses deconstructing questions; helps discover silenced or weak inner voices that need to be strengthened by also discovering openings to more liberating life themes.
    3. *Revising restricting themes – strengthening silenced or weak inner voices.* The therapist encourages the borrowing of voices from supportive others to strengthen weak voices, including the therapist's voice and therapy group members' voices; encourages exercises in compassionate inner dialogue with voices that revise restricting life themes to leave room for more liberating ones.
    4. *Supporting more liberating themes – maintaining a revising/reflexive stance or "authorial" voice.* The therapist helps establish a self-observing position or meta-position that facilitates the maintenance of compassionate inner dialogue, as well as the peaceful coexistence and functional interchange of voices within.

- Neuroscience (interpersonal neurobiology) perspective (stages adapted from Cozolino, 2002)
    1. *Creating a safe and trusting relationship with an attuned therapist.* The therapist uses empathy to "reactivate attachment circuitry making it available to neuroplastic processes" (Cozolino, 2006, p. 308).
    2. *Maintaining moderate levels of arousal to encourage new learning.* The therapist learns to keep clients interested but not too anxious (ibid).
    3. *Activating both cognition and emotion.* The therapist learns to use or improvise multiple means or clinical tools; learns to utilize or seek multiple sources of support; learns the importance of utilizing help from other professionals.
    4. *Co-constructing narratives that reflect a positive, optimistic yet realistic self.* The therapist learns to cultivate ongoing optimism based on his/her personal therapy and on "the physiological reality of ongoing neuroplasticity and neurogenesis" (ibid); explains the healing effects that connecting has for the social brain.

31.4 Case Conceptualization

31.4.1 Teaching the SANE Model

Years of experimenting with teaching the theoretical notions involved in the SANE model have resulted in the following method: Each trainer teaches the model from the position of one perspective (e.g., from the position of systemic thinking or from the position of narrative/dialogical thinking, etc.) based on their own theoretical preferences and research interests. All trainers teach in parallel courses. Trainers place their chosen perspective in a *magnifying* lens, so that its importance for theory and practice is understood in depth, and then proceed to *compose*, pointing to the way the chosen perspective is linked to the other three. Applications begin with life cycle issues in the first 2 years of training (e.g., divorce, birth, death, sexuality, career choices, etc.) and proceed with issues of psychopathology in the next 2 years.

31.4.2 Asking Guiding Questions

In conceptualizing any case, trainees learn to ask themselves a number of guiding questions inspired by the four perspectives.

- Importance of therapeutic relationship – guiding questions inspired by attachment theory:

  1. What sort of attachment pattern do clients appear to be mostly familiar with, deriving from their family of origin? How does this pattern influence their adult relationships, including the therapeutic relationship?
  2. What sort of corrective experiences can I provide in individual, family, and/or group psychotherapy?
  3. What additional steps can I take to make clients feel that our relationship is a "secure base" for facing both their external and their inner world?

- Noticing the content of therapy discourse – guiding questions inspired by systemic thinking:

  1. Do clients understand and practice skills of good communication, do they set protective boundaries for themselves and their family, and do they understand the challenges of their family life cycle and stresses of transitions?
  2. Can they understand their own thoughts and feelings and distinguish them from those of their parental family? Are they able to challenge family and dominant cultural values and myths?
  3. Can they construct a sense of identity that they can recognize as their own? Do they see this identity as helping them be functional, happy, realistic, but also optimistic?

- Noticing the form of therapy discourse – guiding questions inspired by narrative/dialogical psychology:

    1. Do clients' narratives appear coherent? Which stories appear less coherent than others and indicate more emotionally loaded or sensitive issues?
    2. What are the central life themes in clients' narratives? Is there one or more such life themes that appear to restrict their life (e.g., unlovable)? Do they appear to be the protagonist in their stories (e.g., use of "I" pronoun)? Are there openings (unique outcomes) to more liberating stories evident in their narratives?
    3. Is there a voice that appears to be dominant in clients' inner dialogues and narrations? Is this voice strict or rejecting? Whose voice is this? Are there any other, weaker voices, more tender and appreciative, in clients' inner dialogue that I can help strengthen?

- Therapy process as a long-lasting interchange between progress and impasse – guiding questions inspired by findings from neuroscience (interpersonal neurobiology):

    1. What examples, metaphors, or imageries can I use to help clients understand their complicated minds? How can I inform them in a comprehensive way about issues such as brain synapses, explicit and implicit memory, brain laterality and nervous system responses to stress and trauma? How can I explain the idea of brain circuits being reactivated by old traumatic experiences and losses to explain mood disorders, phobias, and so on and to explain the intensity of emotions that may seem disproportionate in the current situation?
    2. How can I help clients appreciate the importance of brain plasticity and keep/create optimism for change joined by realism? How can I support them in becoming more encouraging of themselves rather than being self-critical when facing difficulties in making changes? What is my position or understanding of resistance, and how can my understanding of brain effort in learning new things help me be more encouraging rather than being critical toward clients? How can I keep moderate levels of arousal in the psychotherapeutic process to encourage learning, keep clients interested, and avoid extreme "resistance"?
    3. How can I help clients understand their brain as a social organ which changes through making corrective attachments? If I work with groups in psychotherapy, how can I promote the idea of working with other brains? What dialogues can I help generate to make Cozolino's (2006) phrase "human brains have vulnerabilities and weaknesses that only other brains are capable to mend" (p. 307) have practical value?

31.4.3 Using Skills and Techniques

We mentioned that our enriched systemic outlook is "therapist-centered." As such, it does not offer an organized set of strict practice directives, but rather, it allows for a personal – but *guided* – synthesis of ideas, interventions and techniques, types of sessions, and contracts.

Essential counseling and therapy skills (e.g., attending, paraphrasing, noticing patterns), common to all counselling and therapy models (Nelson-Jones, 2002), form the basis of interventions and are practiced throughout training in role-plays and therapy simulations. Their use is guided by our Qualitative Criteria for Coherence in Narratives (QCCN) tool (Androutsopoulou et al., 2004) described below which aims to help clients narrate coherent stories that provide meaning to experiences. Traditional systemic techniques (e.g., paradox) are taught but are placed in their historical context, a context which did not promote positive expectancy and therapeutic alliance (Sprenkle et al., 2009). Techniques that monitor intergenerational patterns (genograms) of attachment styles and life events are preferred and widely used. Constructionist therapy techniques are promoted, borrowed from narrative therapy (e.g., externalization and unique outcomes) (White & Epston, 1990) and collaborative therapy (e.g., conversational questions) (Anderson, 2012). The methodology of reflecting teams (Andersen, 1987) enriched from additional bibliography for use in supervision (Mason, 2010) forms the basis of role-plays and simulations. Ideas from dialogical self-psychotherapy (e.g., identification of and working with internalized voices) (Androutsopoulou, 2014, 2015; Androutsopoulou & Viou, 2019) and dialogic practices for training (e.g., monitoring therapist inner dialogue) (Androutsopoulou et al., 2016) also inform our practice.

In their final year, trainees embark on writing a case conceptualization. There, they are invited to apply the (teaching) method of *magnifying* one of the four perspectives and *composing* based on personal preferences and style that also match client issues. In presenting their case conceptualization, trainees are encouraged to suggest and develop additional techniques that fit the SANE model. For instance, interesting techniques have been proposed to serve the neuroscience perspective and trauma treatment (Korovilas, 2018). So, it is worth noting that trainees are not just duplicating the treatment approach of their trainers but are developing the ability to think complexly and independently and remain open to challenge in their practice. The idea of a guided synthesis, which is also personal in many ways, is something that trainees greatly appreciate as stated in their yearly assessments of the training program and a reason to recommend it to others.

An important value that trainees learn to respect irrespective of personal preferences in theory and technique is the value of working cooperatively with clients. Cooperative work generally includes (a) posing curiosity questions, (b) exploring alternative perspectives through hypothetical questions, (c) employing reflective listening, (d) drawing meaning-making from the client through careful listening to or reading of personal stories (events, self-descriptions, memories, dreams, diary excerpts, letters), and (e) doing all the above in a tentative manner, which respects client expertise and minimizes resistance. Trainees learn to invite clients to notice alternative perspectives, concerns, and emotions, which appear to emerge directly from their oral and written stories. They also invite clients to (a) understand their identity as a construction through storytelling, (b) develop a capacity to reflect on their self-multiplicity, and (c) appreciate their continuous effort for growth and change.

31.5 Role of Therapist

The role of the therapist and the therapeutic relationship is of paramount importance in this enriched systemic model. Since the early 1990s, more systemic therapists are placing emphasis in the therapeutic relationship or therapy alliance than in the past, with growing emphasis also put on the importance of emotions on both sides (Flaskas, 1997; Greenberg & Paivio, 1997; Sprenkle & Blow, 2007). Since we expect therapists to provide reparative attachment experiences to clients, personal growth and gained security is essential. This is why therapists attend personal long-term psychotherapy (combination of individual, family, and primarily group sessions) as part of their training in our approach.

Several guiding questions inspired by all four perspectives guide trainees' personal growth.

- Guiding questions inspired by attachment theory:

  1. What have I understood in my personal therapy about the attachment patterns in my family?
  2. How is my own history affecting my attunement with my clients, my understanding of their needs, and our relationship?
  3. To what extent does my familial attachment pattern help/does not help my clients have a corrective attachment experience?

- Guiding questions inspired by systemic thinking:

  1. What have I understood in my personal therapy about the functioning of my own family, communication patterns, psychological roles, myths, and values?
  2. Am I engaged in a continuous effort to differentiate my beliefs and emotions from my family of origin, but still be in contact with my family from an equal, adult position?
  3. Do I feel free to question or challenge beliefs/stereotypes of the dominant culture that restrict my life?

- Guiding questions inspired by narrative/dialogical psychology:

  1. What have I understood in my personal therapy about restricting and more liberating themes in my life? Am I the protagonist of my narrations?
  2. What voices are dominant in my inner dialogues?

3. Do I have a strict inner voice that becomes external in the therapeutic dialogue and negatively affects my clients' effort to become more appreciative of themselves?

- Guiding question inspired by neuroscience (interpersonal neurobiology):

    1. What have I understood in my personal therapy about how my own brain works and learns?
    2. Have I personally appreciated the time needed for any changes to occur in my own life?
    3. How do I try to be less critical of myself when facing difficulties in changing old patterns?

31.6 Supporting Research

Several research projects using qualitative methodologies are being conducted to support, specify, and explicate our model. These findings are then incorporated into teaching it and applying it in therapy. Most of these projects are carried out by trainees or with trainees' contribution (cited as authors or co-authors), who learn to conduct qualitative research in action with close guidance and supervision. Engaging trainees in research which ranges from topic selection to conference presentation and/or publishing is a recommended practice that bridges the usual gap between research and practice. Since our Institute's establishment in 2011, several of our trainees' research projects have won poster presentations awards at the European Family Therapy Association (EFTA) conferences 2013, 2016, and 2019 and at the 8th World Congress of Psychotherapy 2017.

31.6.1 Research on the Process and Experience of Therapy

Macro-Level Studies

In one recent study conducted at our Institute, clients were asked to narratively reconstruct their ongoing long-term therapy, and findings were placed into four core categories with three subcategories each: (i) motives (general dysphoric feeling, relationship difficulties, self-disappointment), (ii) processes (getting in touch with painful emotions and needs, taking personal responsibility, strengthening compassion), (iii) means (therapist qualities, group support, self-reflexivity), and (iv) effects (trauma healing, improved relationships, self-development) (Delieza et al., 2019). Table 31.1 additionally presents findings in clients' own words to be read in sequence form.

In other studies, we have explored client and therapist experiences of long-term therapy through *interviews* (Bafiti, Viou, et al., 2017; Christofis et al., 2013) and

Table 31.1 Clients' narrative reconstruction of long-term therapy (Delieza et al., 2019) based on *SANE-System Attachment Narrative Encephalon®*

Motives "What brought me to therapy?"	*General dysphoric feeling*	*I decided to seek help feeling a dead-end, and an endless sense of misery* (Martha)…
	Relationship difficulties	*… I never talked of my own problems and no one knew who I was, not even I* (Jane)…
	Self-disappointment	*… Even though I always used to give promises to myself, how I would motivate myself, I always ended up with a feeling of self-disappointment and self-cheating* (George)…
Processes "What happened?"	*Getting in touch with painful emotions and needs*	*… In the course of therapy, some realizations made me get in touch with a lot of pain* (Catherine)…
	Taking personal responsibility	*… But it also became clear that since I could not change others I had to do something to change myself* (Catherine)…
	Strengthening compassion	*… Of course, I was aware that I had a lot of unresolved issues since childhood, but eventually this realization made me feel more compassion for myself and others* (Helen)…
Means "What helped?"	*Therapist qualities*	*… The moment my therapist said that she believed in me helped me greatly* (Peter)…
	Group support	*… And when my therapist said I could let the group hold some of my burden, I felt lighter!* (Mary)…
	Self-reflexivity	*…I also realized that I can react in any way I want. That was so liberating!* (Cecilia)…
Effects "What changed?"	*Trauma healing*	*… Accepting the pain was hard but it also gave me freedom, like opening a window and letting in the fresh air* (Cecilia)…
	Improved relationships	*… I now have new people in my life that do not leave me no matter what. And it is so comforting to have people that care, even if they are not the ones you had once imagined* (Jane)…
	Self-development	*… Finally, I know that there will always be issues that come up and that I will need to deal with. But I also know that my inner voice will guide me with love, care and safety* (Annie)

post-session recalls of a single group session (Papageorgiou et al., 2017). In a recent study using Interpretative Phenomenological Analysis (IPA), results showed that our clients who reflected back on long-term systemic therapy remembered their therapist as a source of safety, as a parental role model, as encouraging autonomy, as owning therapeutic qualities (e.g., acceptance, caring, sensitivity, respect), and as a person owning authentic feelings (Bafiti et al., 2019a). The experience of clients in therapy and with their therapist is an issue of ongoing research, including experiences of the therapeutic relationship and long-term therapy (Bafiti et al., 2019a, 2019b), experiences of therapists' emotional expression (Viou et al., 2018), and experiences of LGBT clients with heterosexual therapists (Bafiti, Tarasis, & Viou, 2018).

Micro-Level Studies

An interesting qualitative study we conducted monitored how co-therapists and members of a therapy group contribute (e.g., through questions, self-disclosure) to the co-construction and revision of a restricting life theme toward a more liberating one. The importance of essential counselling and psychotherapy skills, along with lexical choice and questions as interventions, was highlighted, together with the importance of client self-disclosure as feedback to other clients in the group. We studied this topic on a micro-level, in a single group therapy session (Poimenidou et al., 2017).

In a study of a single couple therapy session adopting discourse analysis, the importance of the therapist's active role in co-shaping client accounts was indicated. The interventions contributed to the dropping of pathological positions. The therapist argued for the couple's normality: she re-situated the problem from the individual to the interpersonal and transgenerational sphere, rephrased futile dilemmas, and translated "jargon" into emotions (Amplianiti et al., 2017). Finally, theory-building case studies are currently conducted to specify the process of recognizing, revising, and challenging restricting themes and working toward more liberating ones in individual, family, and group sessions (Androutsopoulou, Grypari, & Makarouna, 2019; Bafiti, 2019; Thanopoulou, 2021).

31.6.2 Research on the Progress of Therapy

To assess progress, we rely mainly on the formal aspects of narratives rather than the content of responses (as with more traditional self-report measures). This is because formal aspects "are harder to influence or manipulate" (Lieblich et al., 1998, p. 13). To this end we have both generated and borrowed tools and techniques.

Coherence Enhanced

A narrative assessment tool, the Qualitative Criteria for Coherence in Narratives (QCCN), was formulated by us based on qualitative research and narrative analysis (Androutsopoulou et al., 2004; Androutsopoulou & Bafiti, 2015). It provides a coding system for assessing narrative coherence based on two core categories, each including two criteria: (I) comprehensibility (acknowledging/explaining contradictions, thinking in a relational manner) and (II) evoking empathy (acknowledging/responding to the needs of the audience, being in touch with emotions). The last criterion was broken into 2 more categories (avoiding emotion and regulating emotion) together comprising 20 codes describing linguistic strategies used to deal with sensitive issues. The tool has been applied to monitor both short- and long-term changes in client narratives following our enriched systemic approach (Androutsopoulou, Bafiti, et al., 2017).

Sensitive Stories Turn Less Sensitive

Another narrative assessment tool we use is the "four languages of the unsayable," a research-based tool created by Rogers et al. (1999) (e.g., Androutsopoulou, Bafiti, et al., 2017; Androutsopoulou, Dima, et al., 2019). Both "languages" and the QCCN tool, previously described, are useful for monitoring progress in terms of how sensitive stories are being retold at various times in therapy. Both tools assess progress on the basis of narrative strategies used. Additional research is being conducted by us on the narrative strategies used by clients to deal with sensitive stories in early sessions, highlighting uses of foretelling and escalation in the telling of stories (Amplaniti et al., 2019).

Stories Assessed

The materials we rely on for assessment may be referring to stories of earlier or more recent experiences of relating to significant others, to the self, or even to strangers in a therapy group. Assessed stories may be coming from a number of sources: therapy sessions, autobiographical interviews, and any written material produced by clients: self and family characterizations; letters; diaries; personal summaries of favorite novels, films, or plays; but even dream series as personal narratives that are evolving (see Androutsopoulou, 2001a, 2001b, 2011, 2013, 2015). Intrigued by the reviving of psychobiography, we have recently applied some of our assessment ideas to the writings of famous persons (i.e., Virginia Woolf, Georgia O'Keeffe, Frida Kahlo), who serve as case studies of complete life stories (Androutsopoulou, 2019; Androutsopoulou, Grypari, & Makarouna, 2019; Androutsopoulou, Kalyvopoulos, et al., 2019; Androutsopoulou, Rozou, & Vakondiou, 2019).

We have also experimented with using projective techniques and story lifeline diagrams as triggers for generating storytelling in children attending counselling (Androutsopoulou, Hourmouzoglou, et al., 2017), adolescents in residential care (Papaharalambous et al., 2018), adults with severe psychotic symptoms (Kolomvrezou et al., 2018), and homeless persons (Androutsopoulou & Stefanou, 2018) among others, with the purpose of gaining insight into the process of narration depicting family dynamics and attachment styles and indicating turning points in the lives of various populations.

31.7 Epilogue

In this chapter, we presented a Treatment Plan Manual for the enriched systemic model SANE-System Attachment Narrative Encephalon®. The manual was built to help trainee therapists understand how to enrich the systemic perspective with three additional perspectives, those of narrative/dialogic psychology, attachment theory, and neuroscience, and how to apply this knowledge to treating clients and monitoring progress. The Plan describes parallel therapy stages from all four perspectives and proposes guiding questions to help conceptualize cases and help with trainee therapists' personal growth. The model can be applied to individual, family/couple, and group therapy, in short- and long-term contracts, and to a variety of symptoms/requests. Shorter courses on trauma treatment, child and couple therapy, and lgbtq therapy are now taught based on the SANE model.

It goes without saying that the SANE model reflects our understanding of the complexities of therapy at the present moment. It is put forward as only one suggestion of how to combine four different perspectives and enrich systemic therapy at a time when integration and eclecticism is widely practiced. Other perspectives with a robust theoretical background and relevance to the systemic approach could be potentially incorporated to paint a more complete picture of clients existing within complex micro- and macro-systems, ranging from neurons to neighborhoods (Cozolino, 2006), from mind to culture (Bruner, 1990).

References

Amplianiti, E., Bafiti, S., Dima, E., Gkioni, F., Kandreva, P., Kostala, M., Sanidas, G., & Androutsopoulou. (2017). Is that normal? Discourse analysis of an initial couple therapy session. *Human Systems: The Journal of Therapy, Consultation and Training, 28*, 245–255.

Amplianiti, E., Kandreva, P., Kostala, M., Papageorgiou, S., & Androutsopoulou, A. (2019, September). *Some stories await to be told: Exploring narrative processes in initial sessions of systemic therapy.* In Poster presented at the 10th conference of the European Family Therapy Association, Naples, Italy.

Andersen, T. (1987). The reflecting team. Dialogue and meta-dialogue in clinical work. *Family Process, 26*, 415–428.

Anderson, H. (2012). Collaborative relationships and dialogic conversations: Ideas for a relationally responsive practice. *Family Process, 51*, 8–24.

Androutsopoulou, A. (2001a). The self-characterization as a narrative tool: Applications in therapy with individuals and families. *Family Process, 40*, 79–94.

Androutsopoulou, A. (2001b). Fiction as an aid to therapy: A narrative and family rationale for practice. *Journal of Family Therapy, 23*, 278–295.

Androutsopoulou, A. (2005). Themes in nested stories: A case in family-oriented synthetic therapy. *Journal of Systemic Therapies, 24*, 43–59.

Androutsopoulou, A. (2011). Red balloon: Approaching dreams as self-narratives. *Journal of Marital and Family Therapy, 37*, 479–490.

Androutsopoulou, A. (2013). The use of early recollections as a narrative aid in psychotherapy. *Counselling Psychology Quarterly, 26*, 313–329.

Androutsopoulou, A. (2014). "Many inner authors": Practical comprehension of the polyphonic self in psychotherapy training. *Systemic Thinking & Psychotherapy, 5*. Retrieved from http://hestafta.org/

Androutsopoulou, A. (2015). Moments of meaning: Identifying inner voices in the autobiographical texts of 'Mark'. *Qualitative Psychology, 2*, 130–146.

Androutsopoulou, A. (2019). My broken chrysalis: Narrative processes in Woolf's autobiographical writings of sexual trauma. *Qualitative Psychology*. https://doi.org/10.1037/qup0000139

Androutsopoulou, A., & Bafiti, T. (2015). *Qualitative Criteria for Coherence in Narratives (QCCN) as an assessment and therapy guiding tool*. Working paper series of the training and research Institute for Systemic Psychotherapy, no 2015/3, Athens (in Greek).

Androutsopoulou, A., Bafiti, T., Andriosopoulou, E., Bingou, N., Giannoukakou, F., Koutsaftiki, K., & Papadaki, E. (2017, May). *Gini's stories: A single case narrative analysis of therapy micro-changes using the QCCN tool*. In Poster presented at the 16th National Congress of Psychological Research of The Hellenic Psychological Association (ΕΛΨΕ), Thessaloniki, Greece (in Greek).

Androutsopoulou, A., Bafiti, T., & Kalarritis, G. (2014). The enriched systemic perspective SANE-System Attachment Narrative Encephalon®: Selected training guidelines for clinical practice. *Human Systems. The Journal of Therapy, Consultation and Training, 25*, 161–176.

Androutsopoulou, A., Dima, E., Papageorgiou, S., & Papanikolaou, T. (2019). Constructing Georgia: *Love, play, work* as a central theme in O' Keeffe's early and late memories. In K. Zoltan & C.-H. Mayer (Eds.), *New trends in psychobiography* (pp. 325–342). Springer.

Androutsopoulou, A., Grypari, E., & Makarouna, T. (2019). *Challenging unhelpful voices: A narrative-dialogical sequence analysis of initial sessions with a single client*. Manuscript in preparation.

Androutsopoulou, A., Hourmouzoglou, M., Iliopoulou, E., Kalamaki-Stravoskoufi, K., Korovilas, C., Papandreou, I.-E., & Papanikolaou, T. (2017, July). *More on telling sensitive family stories: An extended narrative analysis of Children's apperception test results*. In Poster presented at the 8th world congress of psychotherapy, Paris, France.

Androutsopoulou, A., Kalyvopoulos, I., Koukidis, E., Koutsavgousti, G., Passa, I., Tarnara, E., & Tsatsaroni, T. (2019). *Not anybody's husband: A narrative inquiry into Frida Kahlo's writings on her husband Diego*. Manuscript submitted for publication.

Androutsopoulou, A., Rozou, E., & Vakondiou, M. (2019). Voices of hope and despair: A narrative inquiry into the diaries, letters and suicide notes of Virginia Woolf. *Journal of Constructivist Psychology*. https://doi.org/10.1080/10720537.2019.1615015

Androutsopoulou, A., & Stefanou, M. M. (2018). Seeking "home": Personal narratives and turning points in the lives of homeless. *The European Journal of Counselling Psychology, 7*, 126–147.

Androutsopoulou, A., Thanopoulou, K., Economou, E., & Bafiti, T. (2004). Forming criteria for assessing the coherence of clients' life stories: A narrative study. *Journal of Family Therapy, 26*, 384–406.

Androutsopoulou, A., & Viou, M. (2019). The guided imagery therapy activity "inner dialogue-child adult meeting" (ID-CAM): Steps and applications. *The Journal of Creativity in Mental Health*. https://doi.org/10.1080/15401383.2019.1624993

Androutsopoulou, A., Viou, M., Nikolaou, N., Moschakis, C., Nikolopoulou, V.-N., Kontoni, N., & Diamantaki, E. (2016). Therapist inner dialogue and first session resolution. Qualitative data from the training activity 'Inner dialogues-therapist observer Client' (ID-TOC). *Human Systems: The Journal of Therapy, Consultation & Training, 27*(1), 65–81.

Angus, L., & McLeod, J. (Eds.). (2004). *Handbook of narrative and psychotherapy: Practice, theory and research*. Sage.

Armony, J., & Vuilleumier, P. (Eds.). (2016). *The Cambridge handbook of human affective neuroscience*. Cambridge University Press.

Bafiti, T. (2008). Systemic approaches in dealing with health and illness. In F. Anagnostopoulos & E. Karadimas (Eds.), *Health and illness: Psychological processes*. Livanis.

Bafiti, T. (2009a). Training in systemic therapy. In T. Bafiti & G. Kalarritis (Eds.), *Systemic approach: Concepts and applications*. Ellinika Grammata. (in Greek).

Bafiti, T. (2009b). Training in systemic diagnosis. In T. Bafiti & G. Kalarritis (Eds.), *Systemic approach: Concepts and applications*. Ellinika Grammata. (in Greek).

Bafiti, T. (2019). *Hearing the polyphonic self: Narrative analysis of a session with a single client in long-term group therapy*. Manuscript in preparation.

Bafiti, T., Androutsopoulou, A., & Kalarritis, G. (2017, December). *The application of the synthetic model of systemic therapy SANE-System Attachment Narrative Encephalon® on supervision: An example*. In Round table presentation at the 8th one-day conference of NOPG-Greece, Athens, Greece.

Bafiti, T., Androutsopoulou, A., & Kalarritis, G. (2018). *'From four angles': The enriched systemic model SANE- System Attachment Narrative Encephalon®*. Assimakis. (in Greek).

Bafiti, T., & Kalarritis, G. (Eds.). (2009). *Systemic approach: Concepts and applications*. Ellinika Grammata. (in Greek).

Bafiti, T., Tarasis, P., & Viou, M. (2018). Stepping up the ladder in safety: An interpretative phenomenological analysis of how LGB clients experience their therapists' sexual orientation. *The European Journal of Counselling Psychology, 7*, 211–223.

Bafiti, T., Viou, M., Moschakis, C., & Nikolaou, N. (2017, May). *Looking back: Clients who have completed their therapy narrate their experience of the therapeutic relationship*. In Paper presented at the 16th National Congress of Psychological Research, Thessaloniki, Greece (in Greek).

Bafiti, T., Viou, M., Moschakis, C., & Nikolaou, N. (2019a, September). *Looking back in therapy: An interpretative phenomenological analysis of clients' experiences of systemic group therapy, years after completion*. In Presentation at the 10th conference of the European Family Therapy Association, Naples, Italy.

Bafiti, T., Viou, M., Moschakis, C., & Nikolaou, N. (2019b). *Therapeutic relationship and systemic psychotherapy: A qualitative study*. Manuscript submitted for publication.

Beaudon, M.-T., & Zimmerman, J. (2011). Narrative therapy and interpersonal neurobiology: Revisiting classic practices, developing new emphases. *Journal of Systemic Therapies, 30*, 1–13.

Bowlby, J. (1988). *A secure base; parent-child attachment and healthy human development*. Basic Books.

Bruner, J. (1990). *Acts of meaning*. Harvard University Press.

Byng-Hall, J. (1995). Creating a secure base: Some implications of attachment theory for family therapy. *Family Process, 34*, 45–58.

Byng-Hall, J. (2008). The crucial roles of attachment in family therapy. *Journal of Family Therapy, 30*, 129–146.

Cacioppo, J. T., & Berntson, G. G. (Eds.). (2005). *Social neuroscience: Key readings*. Psychology Press.

Cassidy, J., & Shaver, P. R. (Eds.). (2016). *Handbook of attachment: Theory, research, and clinical applications*. Guilford.

Christofis, O., Kyriazopoulou, E., Peppa, E., Saliaris, K., & Zeriti, M. (2013, October). *Critical events in the process of long-term systemic therapy from the perspective of individual clients and their therapists*. In Poster presented at the 8th EFTA congress, Istanbul.

Cozolino, L. (2002). *The neuroscience of psychotherapy: Building and rebuilding the human brain*. Norton.

Cozolino, L. (2006). *The neuroscience of human relationships: Attachment and the developing social brain*. Norton.

Cozolino, L. (2015). *Why therapy works: Using our minds to change our brains*. Norton.

Cozolino, L. (2017). *The neuroscience of psychotherapy: Healing the social brain* (3rd ed.). Norton.

Dallos, R. (2004). Attachment narrative therapy: Integrating ideas from narrative and attachment theory in systemic therapy with eating disorders. *Journal of Family Therapy, 26*, 40–66.

Dallos, R. (2006). *Attachment narrative therapy. Integrating narrative, systemic and attachment therapies*. Open University Press.
Dallos, R., & Vetere, A. (2009). *Systemic therapy and attachment narratives. Applications in a range of clinical settings*. Routledge.
Damasio, A. (2018). *The strange order of things: Life, feeling, and the making of cultures*. Pantheon Books.
Delieza, P., Bori, N., Grypari, E., Makarouna, T., Papasimakopoulou, P., & Tolia, M. (2019, September). *Scenes from therapy: A narrative reconstruction of long-term systemic group therapy*. In Poster presented at the 10th conference of the European Family Therapy Association, Naples, Italy.
Fishbane, M. D. (2001). Relational narratives of the self. *Family Process, 40*, 273–291.
Fishbane, M. D. (2007). Wired to connect: Neuroscience, relationships, and therapy. *Family Process, 46*, 395–412.
Flaskas, C. (1997). Engagement and the therapeutic relationship in systemic therapy. *Journal of Family, 19*, 263–282.
Gergen, K. J. (1994). *Realities and relationships: Soundings in social construction*. Harvard University Press.
Greenberg, L. S., & Paivio, S. C. (1997). *Working with emotions in psychotherapy*. The Guilford Press.
Hermans, H. J. M., & Dimaggio, G. (Eds.). (2004). *The dialogical self in psychotherapy*. Brunner-Routledge.
Holmes, J. (2001). *The search for the secure base*. Routledge.
Hughes, D. A. (2007). *Attachment focused family therapy*. Norton.
Johnson, S. M., Makinen, J. A., & Millikin, J. W. (2001). Attachment injuries in couple relationships: A new perspective on impasses in couples therapy. *Journal of Marital and Family Therapy, 27*, 145–155.
Kalarritis, G. (2005). Psychotherapy and neurosciences: New paths in synthesis. In G. Kalarritis & T. Bafiti (Eds.), *Healthy mind in a healthy body*. Ellinika Grammata. (in Greek).
Kalarritis, G. (2013, September). *The neurobiological basis of attachment: Links with systemic psychotherapy*. In Presentation at the 8th continuing education meeting of the Greek National Organization of EAP, Athens, Greece (in Greek).
Kalarritis, G. (2016, September–October). *Our adventures in Brainland. Psychotherapy in the age of neurosciences. Past struggles, present practices, and future hopes*. In Workshop presented at the 9th EFTA congress, Athens, Greece (in Greek).
Kalarritis, G., & Bafiti, T. (Eds.). (2005). *Healthy mind in a healthy body*. Ellinika Grammata. (in Greek).
Katakis, C. (1990). Stages of long-term psychotherapy: Progressive re-conceptualizations as a self-organizing process. *Psychotherapy: Theory, Research and Practice, 26*, 484–493.
Katakis, C., Androutsopoulou, A., Kalarritis, G., & Bafiti, T. (2011). Training in systemic therapy with individuals, groups and families. In P. Assimakis (Ed.), *The training of psychotherapists in Greece*. Assimakis/NOPG. (in Greek).
Kolomvrezou, A., Fragkouli, N., Katsarou, E., Tsolaki, S., & Valma, N. (2018, June). *Just my voice: Narratives of early family experiences of voice hearers*. In Poster presented at the 10th international conference on the dialogical self (ICDS), Braga, Portugal.
Korovilas, C. (2018). *Body on ice: Dealing with panic attacks and chronic trauma revelation from the neuroscience perspective of the SANE model* (Working Paper Series No 2018/1). Logo Psychis: Training and Research Institute for Systemic Psychotherapy (ISSN 2441-2778 online). (in Greek).
Lebow, J. (1997). The integrative revolution in couple and family therapy. *Family Process, 36*, 1–17.
Lebow, J. L. (2003). Integrative approaches to couple and family therapy. In T. L. Sexton, G. R. Weeks, & M. S. Robbins (Eds.), *Handbook of family therapy: The science and practice of working with families and couples* (pp. 201–225). Brunner-Routledge.
LeDoux, J. E. (2002). *Synaptic self: How our brains become who we are*. Viking.

LeDoux, J. (2019). *The deep history of ourselves: The four-billion-year story of how we got conscious brains*. Viking.

Lewis, M. D., & Todd, R. (2004). Toward a neuropsychological model of internal dialogue: Implications for theory and clinical practice. In H. J. M. Hermans & G. Dimaggio (Eds.), *The dialogical self in psychotherapy*. Brunner-Routledge.

Lieblich, A., Tuval-Maschiach, R., & Zilber, T. (1998). *Narrative research: Reading, analysis and interpretation*. Sage.

Main, M. (1991). Metacognitive knowledge, metacognitive monitoring, and singular (coherent) vs. multiple (incoherent) model of attachment: Findings and directions for future research. In C. M. Parkes, J. Stevenson-Hinde, & P. Marris (Eds.), *Attachment across the life cycle* (pp. 127–159). Routledge.

Mason, B. (2010). Six aspects of supervision and the training of supervisors. *Journal of Family Therapy, 32*, 436–439.

McLeod, J. (1997). *Narrative and psychotherapy*. Sage.

McLeod, J. (2004). The significance of narrative and storytelling in postpsychological counselling and psychotherapy. In A. Lieblich, D. P. MacAdams, & R. Jossleson (Eds.), *Healing plots: The narrative basis of psychotherapy* (pp. 11–27). American Psychological Association.

Nelson-Jones, R. (2002). *Essential counselling and therapy skills*. Sage.

Papageorgiou, S., Filia, M., Gkotsi, G., Regli, D., Zougrou, K., & Androutsopoulou, A. (2017). Seeing eye to eye: A qualitative case study of significant moments in a systemic group therapy session. *Human Systems: The Journal of Therapy, Consultation and Training, 28*, 235–244.

Papaharalambous, A., Nikolaidou, N., Karamani, I., & Asilian, E. (2018, September). *And the love you gave me...: Attachment stories of adolescents living in residential care*. In Poster presented at the 7th conference on qualitative research on mental health, Berlin, Germany.

Parkes, C. M., Stevenson-Hinde, J., & Marris, P. (1991). *Attachment across the life cycle*. Routledge.

Penn, P., & Frankfurt, M. (1994). Creating a participant text: Writing, multiple voices, narrative multiplicity. *Family Process, 33*, 217–231.

Pennebaker, J. W. (1997). *Opening up: The healing power of expressing emotions*. The Guilford Press.

Poimenidou, P., Biniori, D., Christodoulaki, C., Zerma, K., & Androutsopoulou, A. (2017). Beyond the dark side of life: Processes of theme co-construction and revision in a systemic group-therapy session. *Human Systems: The Journal of Therapy, Consultation and Training, 28*, 257–268.

Rogers, A. G., Casey, M. E., Ekert, J., Holland, J., Nakkula, V., & Sheinberg, N. (1999). An interpretative poetics of languages of the unsayable. In R. Josselson & A. Lieblich (Eds.), *Making meaning of narratives: The narrative study of lives* (pp. 77–106). Sage.

Sarbin, T. R. (1986). The narrative as a root metaphor for psychology. In T. R. Sarbin (Ed.), *Narrative psychology: The storied nature of human conduct* (pp. 1–37). Preager.

Schore, A. N. (1994). *Affect regulation and the origin of the self. The neurobiology of emotional development*. Erlbaum.

Schore, A. N. (2003). *Affect regulation and the repair of the self*. Norton.

Schore, A. N. (2012). *The science of the art of psychotherapy*. Norton.

Siegel, D. J. (1999). *The developing mind: How relationships and the brain interact to shape who we are*. The Guilford Press.

Siegel, D. J. (2007). *The mindful brain: Reflection and attunement in the cultivation of wellbeing*. Norton.

Siegel, D. J. (2010). *The mindful therapist: A clinician's guide to mindsight and neural integration*. Norton.

Siegel, D. J., & Solomon, M. (2003). *Healing trauma: Attachment, mind, body, and brain*. Norton.

Sluzki, C. E. (2007). Interfaces: Toward a new generation of systemic models in family research and practice. *Family Process, 46*, 173–184.

Sprenkle, D. H., & Blow, A. J. (2007). The role of the therapist as the bridge between common factors and therapeutic change: More complex than congruency with a worldview. *Journal of Family Therapy, 29*, 109–113.

Sprenkle, D. H., Davis, S. D., & Lebow, J. L. (2009). *Common factors in couple and family therapy*. The Guilford Press.

TEDxChania. (2015, October). *Georgios Kalarritis: What is the job of a psychotherapist? or "When I grow up I want to be a psychotherapist"* (in Greek) [Video file]. Retrieved from https://www.youtube.com/watch?v=IoMRQfUM45g

Thanopoulou, K. (2021). Uncovering secret voices in family therapy: A narrative case study based on therapy notes. In C. Monereo, C. Weise & H. Hermans (Eds.), *Dialogicality: Personal, local and planetary dialogue in education, health, citizenship, and research*. International Society for Dialogical Science (ISDS).

Todorof, A., Fiske, S. T., & Prentice, D. A. (Eds.). (2011). *Social neuroscience: Toward understanding the underpinnings of the social mind*. Oxford University Press.

Viou, M., Moschakis, C., & Nikolaou, A. (2018). Love in therapy: A qualitative study of how clients perceive their therapists' emotions. *European Journal of Psychotherapy & Counselling*. https://doi.org/10.1080/13642537.2018.1529692

Wallin, D. J. (2007). *Attachment in psychotherapy*. The Guilford Press.

White, M., & Epston, D. (1990). *Narrative means to therapeutic ends*. Norton.

Chapter 32
Manualising – Personalising – Without Compromising (Either the Manual or the Systemic Approach) Except When …

John Burnham, Nicky Maund, Beki Brain, Ellen Twist, Shila Desai, and Rubina Singh

32.1 From Conflict to Cooperation: A Tale of Two Colleagues

*Picture the scene: It is the first day of a Foundation Training in Non-Violent Resistance (NVR). Two of the authors (Nicky and John) who are both experienced systemic psychotherapists are attending the course. Nicky is experienced in NVR and is leading the training, and John is not experienced in NVR and is a trainee on the course. Nicky feels that NVR is **not** a manualised approach. John is curious since he has in front of him a document called 'NVR a Training Manual'. A difficult interchange takes place, which goes something like 'Oh yes, it is manualised, … Oh no, it's not manualised'. A little while later, the two colleagues discuss this more maturely, and some interesting feelings and attitudes emerged. Nicky loves NVR and regarded the description 'manualised' as somehow critical and not appreciative of its deeply based philosophy. On the other hand, John appreciated the contributions that manualised treatment programmes made to systemic practice and had intended the comment as an appreciation of the substance of the approach. This conversation seemed to be a microcosm of a larger debate in the systemic field between those who appreciate manuals as a scaffold for practitioners in difficult areas of practice and*

J. Burnham (✉) · N. Maund · B. Brain · E. Twist
Inpatient CAMHS, Parkview Clinic, Birmingham Women's and Children's Hospital, Birmingham, UK
e-mail: johnburnham0@icloud.com

S. Desai
Birmingham Women's and Children's Hospital, Birmingham, UK

R. Singh
Forward Thinking Birmingham, Birmingham Women's and Children's Hospital, Birmingham, UK

those who regard following a manual as a betrayal of the systemic approach. Over the next few months, Nicky and John, within the context of a respectful relationship, processed their initial differences from an unhelpful either/or conflict to what has become a both-and position. From these positions we are able to appreciate the ways in which a manual may be used to rigorously scaffold practice to create a secure context in uncertain circumstances. This relatively secure base allows for and promotes imaginative application across contexts.

As Bateson has so aptly said:

we shall know a little more by dint of rigour and imagination, the two great contraries of mental process, either of which by itself is lethal. Rigour alone is paralytic death, but imagination alone is insanity. (1979, p. 233)

This chapter explores how we use both rigour and imagination when introducing manualised treatments into our agency context both within and beyond the systemic department. It seeks to show that both rigorous imagination and imaginative rigour are useful in making the most of a manualised approach.

32.2 Problems-Possibilities and Resources-Restraints (PPRR)

Developments in a particular field sometimes prompt a mixture of responses including challenge, change and controversy and perhaps none more so than the relatively recent introduction and indeed requirement for 'manualised treatments'. As I (John) experienced this a number of times in my own practice over time, I became dissatisfied with a tendency of practitioners (including myself) of following the latest fashion/paradigm and potentially falling into the trap of what has been termed 'theoretical agism' (Burnham & Harris, 2002). Mason (2013) proposes that we work towards creating a 'culture of contribution' as one way to escape the unhelpful aspects of the 'old/new' dichotomy. Over time I developed a model known as PPRR (Burnham, 2021 in preparation). The model/framework of PPRR is designed to enable a practitioner or group to critically appreciate the contribution of an approach, method or technique (Burnham, 1992, 1993) based not only on its age or relative attraction. The PPRR model suggests that the dimensions of Problems-Possibilities and Resources-Restraints can be used to construct the following quadrant (Fig. 32.1).

When considering a particular issue, practice or theoretical concept, a practitioner's habitual, preferred or non-conscious choices may lead the issue, idea or practice to be placed by default into a particular quadrant, and its full potential may not be appreciated. I developed the routine of placing whatever is being considered at the centre of the quadrants and deconstructing its contribution to an individual, team, agency or discipline, using a range of questions. The set of questions I usually begin with are:

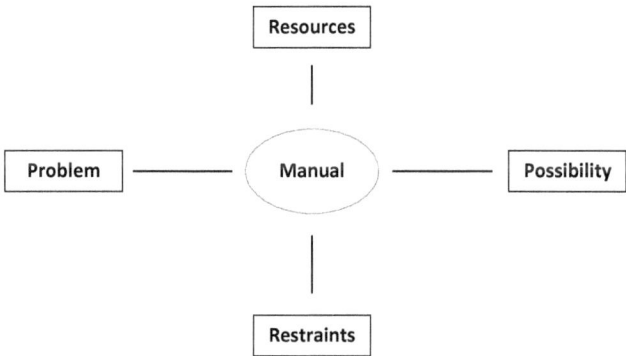

Fig. 32.1 A PPRRactice map for exploring a professional practice

What problems might a manual overcome?
What problems might a manual create?
What possibilities might a manual close down?
What possibilities might a manual open up?
When and how might a manual be a resource?
When and how might a manual be a restraint?

32.3 Level 1: Manualising: The Relationship of Each Team Member with Manualised Approaches

32.3.1 Agency Context

We work in a regional child mental health centre with three inpatient units. We are a small team of five family and systemic psychotherapists who contribute to the work of a multidisciplinary mental health staff service. Between us we have around 150 years of practice, 250 years of life experience, a variety of cultural influences and an unhealthy relationship with chocolate biscuits (well one of us does anyway, and there is no treatment manual!).

In a serendipitous meeting between John Burnham (lead author) and Peter Stratton (co-editor), these issues were discussed, and an invitation to write about our team's experiences of using manualised approaches was extended.

To learn from the rich experience of the five inpatient team members/authors, Nicky Maund, Shila Desai, Beki Brain, Ellen Twist and John Burnham contributed their experiences and views in reflecting on the following ten questions generated by John and based on the PPRR model outlined above (questions 9 and 10 were intelligently contributed by the editor Peter Stratton).

What is your relationship with manualised treatment programmes?

1. Before training in systemic psychotherapy, did you practise within a manualised approach?
2. How many manualised approaches have you trained in and to what level?
3. What resources did I gain from practising in a manualised approach?
4. How did it restrain me as a practitioner (how was it insufficient)?
5. What attracted me to systemic training?
6. Did you experience any tensions between systemic training and the manualised approach?
7. How did I resolve these tensions?
8. What is my current experience/approach?
9. In what ways are you still making use of a manual in your current practice? (How often do you refer to it or did you stop looking at it as soon as you finished training?)
10. Do you have a copy of a manual that you have modified to be more relevant to your practice? If so is this by emphasising some content, adding new material of your own or deleting or rephrasing some material (or maybe that comes later in the 'personalise' section)?

Ellen conducted a thematic analysis of therapists' responses guided by the principles outlined in Braun and Clarke (2012). The responses to these questions generated some common themes, interesting differences and useful learning. The responses have been clustered according to the flow of the themes rather than the order of the questions.

How many manualised approaches have you trained in and to what level? (Question 2)

Within our department we have about 40 years of experience across ten manualised treatment approaches: **Non-Violent Resistance (NVR)** (Omer, 2004; Jakob, 2011), **Dyadic Developmental Psychotherapy (DDP)** (Hughes, 2011), **Multi-Systemic Therapy (MST)** (http://www.mstuk.org/multisystemic-therapy-mst), **Functional Family Therapy (FFT)** (Sexton, 2011; Alexander et al., 2013), **Advanced Integrative Therapy (AIT)** (Clinton, 2010, 2018), **Family Therapy for Anorexia Nervosa (FT-AN)** (Eisler et al., 2016), **Family-Based Treatment for Anorexia Nervosa (FBT)** (Lock & Le Grange, 2012), **Multi-Family Therapy (MFT)** (Asen & Scholz, 2010), **Dialectical Behaviour Therapy (DBT)** (Rathus & Miller, 2015) and **Strengthening Families Programme (SFP)** (Allen et al., 2006; https://guidebook.eif.org.uk/programme/strengthening-families-programme-10-14).

Before training in systemic psychotherapy, did you practise within a manualised approach? What attracted me to systemic training? (Questions 1 and 5)

Of the five therapists who contributed, three therapists had experience of practising as a family therapist for between 3 years and 7 years prior to training in a manualised model. Two therapists were trained in a manualised model prior to engaging in training in family therapy and were attracted to systemic training as it promised to extend their therapeutic repertoire beyond the restraints of the manuals. Overall, therapists have between 4 and 40 years post-qualifying experience practising as family therapists.

What resources did I gain from practising in a manualised approach? (Question 3)

Framework of the Model

The framework for practice provided by manualised approaches was considered to be helpful by respondents, giving therapists '…something concrete and tangible to work with…' (Shila) and '…anchoring…' (Beki) them to the aims of the approach. The structure provided by the manual also had the effect of '…slowing down my thinking in relation to the presentations I was seeing and take a more methodical approach to working through difficulties…' (Beki) and supporting the therapeutic process by giving '…inherent directives for method and techniques provid[ing] a map […] informing therapist orientation, pacing and transition through the model' (Ellen). This was particularly welcomed by therapists during and soon after training in systemic family therapy:

> *It was reassuring to have the structure when my therapeutic skills were still in their early infancy. (Beki)*
>
> *My training in FFT helped me immensely in navigating the unfamiliar terrain of family therapy. The phasic model and specific goals and techniques within this framework enabled a clear focus of 'what to say/do' and 'what to look out for'.… (Ellen)*

In contrast, for those who had already completed family therapy training, manualised models were viewed as '…a map/framework which systemic skills and other approaches fit into/add to when utilised' (Nicky) and '…a useful scaffold to organise existing skills in particular contexts and extend my repertoire beyond the familiar' (John).

Structure in Emotional and Therapeutic Containment

Therapists commented on how the structure of the manualised approach offered containment for clients '…both parents reported feeling calmer and clearer' (Nicky), as well as for therapists and the therapeutic relationship:

> *…when working with families in which there was often a high degree of emotional volatility and unpredictability […] the structure and techniques espoused by the model functioned to support me to contain and regulate my own emotions and external pressures which likely supported the establishment of successful therapeutic relationships and supported family members to feel more contained during therapy. (Ellen)*

John described that 'The manual is often a useful "touchstone" in times when "unsafe uncertainty" (Mason, 1993) creeps in, and it helps to re-orient everyone involved towards the therapeutic endeavour'.

Co-constructing Through Involvement and Language

Therapists reflected on the opportunities that were created for working collaboratively and creating different relationships with families and staff from different disciplines when using manualised models, 'Having something concrete to offer staff in the moments of crises/chaos/unsafe uncertainty gave me a way of creating different relationships with residential staff/families…' (Shila). The framework itself is '…useful in enhancing transparency and explicitly negotiating and re-negotiating the therapeutic relationship' (John). Nicky commented on how delivering manualised model in a group-based format enabled a richer experience: 'Other team members observed the group, went on to co-facilitate the group and have since embarked on more formal NVR training. The "I" became a "we", as the group evolved with contributions from all'.

Therapists also commented on the '…common language that is developed [with the family] to make sense of interactions and responses and experiment with change and difference' (Beki) and deciding with families what aspects of the model might be useful and when '…I suggested going back to the original plan, thinking this might at least help us to prioritise what to focus on going forward. The effects of doing this was far greater than I expected…' (Nicky). 'The manuals often contain memorable mantras expressed in accessible language *(e.g. "Strike when the iron is cold" (NVR)* and *"CCRACON"* (**C**heck in, **C**ompliment, **R**eflect, **A**dvise/suggest, **C**hange (expect it!), **O**ver to you, **N**ow How is it?) from the MFT for Eating Disorders,) that are easy to remember when professionals and families most need them' (John).

Contextual Influence and Influence on Context

Professionals found that within the context of independent contracted work, using a manual created a closer and more explicit fit with the requirements of funding from stakeholders (Shila). Families found that manualised models (specifically NVR) that paid attention to resolving specific problematic episodes may also have an implicative (upward/broader) influence through '…prioritising and enhancing relationships that […] positively influence wider contexts and cultures and provide an antidote for dehumanising systems' (Nicky).

Flexibility/Ease of Integration

Some manuals seem written in ways that promote fidelity, while others were written as if promoting flexibility. Beki stated, 'From the outset the Multi-Family Therapy (MFT) guidance I experienced more as a "toolbox". The objective of the programme remain clear, but the methods (therapeutic activities) […] remain flexible and can be adapted depending on the needs of the group'. Nicky quickly realised that training in the NVR model '...provides a map/framework into which systemic skills and other approaches fit [...] Principles have become incorporated into my overall approach'.

How did it restrain me as a practitioner (how was it insufficient)? Did you experience any tensions between systemic training and the manualised approach? (Questions 4 and 6)

Manualised Models as Rigid and Constraining

At some point in the use of an approach that has been manualised, the majority of therapists experienced following a manual as '...constraining and attending too superficially to presenting issues...' (Ellen). Within several models, this sense of restraint appeared related to '...the direction of the model and the implicit timescale for change' (Beki) with a view to maximising model fidelity and the requirements to produce '...a measurable piece of work with the likelihood of quicker "wins" outcomes wise' (Beki). Pressures in relation to model adherence were experienced by the majority of therapists, directed either by the requirements of the model or the organisation's stakeholders, leading to an experience of limited '...scope/permission to deviate from manualised practices...' (Ellen) or the '...structure [that] fitted the funding context...' in independent practice (Shila). This led to therapists '...feeling prescriptively "pushed and positioned", and isomorphically feeling that they needed to "push" or "position" the family...' (Beki). This appeared to produce a sense of '...frustration with some aspects of the model...' (Ellen) and even '...to resent the model and what I perceived as rigidity of thinking and processes' (Beki), conversely leading to a relationship with the model that resembled a '...dichotomy [...] whereby I thought of the model as "good" or bad", "useful" or "not useful"' (Beki) and paradoxically impacting model fidelity through therapists choosing to be '...irreverent (sometimes overtly and sometimes covertly) to the model...' (Ellen). Beki reflected that she experienced her '...adherence to the guiding principles of these manuals is stronger when I have some individual agency in regard to how I choose to apply the ideas'.

One therapist viewed NVR not being a manualised approach '...I know one of my triggers is being controlled so maybe [I] have seen manualised approaches as restrictive/constraining, which has not been my experience of NVR' (Nicky). John found that those trainers that '...encouraged practitioner creativity within the clear structure of the manual...' enabled him to appreciate the value of the manual without feeling overly restrained. Given this variation, it is perhaps interesting to consider whether all manualised approaches prescribe the same level of fidelity, how any variations may impact therapists' relationship to the approach and how, in turn, these factors may influence measurable and subjective outcomes for families.

Privileging and Subjugating Discourses and Ethical Positioning

When structure and pace were too tightly prescribed, opportunities to attend to significant issues within the work were missed, and it seemed practitioners may adopt a reductionist stance to the problems families were experiencing 'After my initial enthusiasm and positive results, I started to notice the setbacks [...] This did lead to tensions around [whether] we were simplifying the difficulties?' (Shila).

The ethical positioning of some of the models sometimes suggested certain dominant and subjugating discourses:

> *At times I questioned the ethics of the model and the implicit messages of failure being directed at parents (usually mothers) [...] There was a dominant discourse about what 'good parenting' looks like based on a White Western ideal and philosophy that was never questioned....* (Beki)

Shila also highlighted that using the NVR model, she experienced '... a tension in privileging adult voices whilst not really knowing what the [young person]/siblings might be saying/experiencing when used in a very structured way'.

Therapists expressed a lack of clarity regarding the level of agreement or understanding of parents and families when there was a need to work quickly or push to achieve predetermined outcomes, which made therapists concerned about whether they may be asking the '...family to change in ways they were not always consenting to (or at least motivated to)' (Beki) or '...whether parents were really signing up to this or was it desperation....' (Shila).

Structure Leading to Tensions and Pressures

The structure of the model and the context of delivery also led to other internal and external pressures for the therapist. Ellen described her experience of the '...expectations from referring systems' and the '...aware[ness] of these pressures and the way they might position me within my work with families (e.g. fast pacing, oversimplification) and the need to try and contain the impact of these in therapy'. Shila also described her experience of working in a community CAMHS setting in which she '...received [so] many referrals specifically for NVR, that it became a prescription...'.

Set time frames in the manual were sometimes experienced as unhelpful in relation to the family: 'Each family could receive the intervention for a maximum of 5 months, putting pressure on the practitioner to achieve the stated outcomes within that timeframe...' (Beki) and potential to generate negative responses from other systems if change was not realised in time: '...I recall being acutely aware of the potential consequences for the young person and their family, unless we could support them towards change' (Ellen). Additionally, some models imply a '...high degree of therapist-responsibility and accountability...' (Ellen) for the outcomes attained by families, adding another potential layer of pressure for the therapist and the family system.

How did I resolve these tensions? What is my current experience/approach? (Questions 7 and 8)

Integration of Approaches

'The resolution of these tensions occurred over time as I was able to find a way of integrating these two approaches…' (Ellen). Therapists 'blended' ideas from systemic family therapy and manualised models '"Borrowing" principles and elements of one and combining it with the principle or element of another' (Beki). Integration processes varied between therapists. Some find it easier to '…connect with the approach…' (Nicky) and more quickly embed within personal and professional. Others initially focussed on methods and techniques:

> …wanting to 'get to know' the model and seeking out examples of 'pure' practice so that I can 'recognise' and appreciate its form and position on my practice landscape before being able to consider how I would 'weave' or integrate it further. This process is not without its frustrations and doubts, but I have come to accept this as part of the (my) process – a dialogue with the approach…. (Ellen)

Using First-Order Methods in a Second-Order Way

Systemic concepts, such as first and second order, promoted integration '…us[ing] manuals within a systemic approach (to at times use first order methods and techniques from a second order position) […] where these ways of working may provide a better fit for the family, therapist or the practice context' (Beki). Ellen described this as '…systemic thinking/practice being the landscape which can be populated with other ideas/approaches that can be brought in and out of focus while remaining a part of the wider whole'. Shila spoke about blending or finding natural overlap between systemic ideas and those that are meaningful within the model: 'This fits with appreciative ideas – that we have always existed in meaningful relationships before NVR came along and how to use these in different ways that are NVR informed…'.

Creating a Relational Fit Through Collaboration

Delivering manualised models collaboratively with families and other professionals enhanced imaginative fidelity: 'This involved thinking more carefully about the level of collaboration between therapist and client possible within a pre-determined structure…' (Beki) and '…look[ing] at some of the relational aspects of the work and try to find a better fit for different families i.e. what […] methods needed to be foregrounded and at what point' (Shila). Pacing was important: '…taking [therapy] a bit slower – not needing to do everything, […] holding back my own enthusiasm, not trying to force the ideas too much […] discarding some of the methods…'

(Shila), in order to '...create an experience for families that feels like I am offering something that makes sense of, or is led by, their experiences rather than supporting them to map their experiences on to an existing model' (Ellen). John related this to his process of introducing the manual into his work with families:

> It seemed to improve a collaboration with families when 'I 'warmed the context' (Burnham 2005) by explaining: 'This was a new model I am training in and so I would be 'going by the book' to begin with'. Sharing the model explicitly in a visually educative way seemed to help families come on board and feel included in decision making along the way. (John)

Personally Informed Professional Practice

Emerging relationships between a 'model' and the 'personal' informed the positioning of models within a therapist's practice:

> I have now a much 'softer' relationship with NVR [...] I now like listening out for words, phrases, ways of being when NVR methods could fit [...] I have a deeper personal understanding of [...] low mood, trauma self-deprecating stories [...] [this is] something that I take from personal to professional and back again. (Shila)

Nicky shared her personal experience of being '...influenced by my own experiences as a daughter and as a mother who didn't experience or believe in a need for physical chastisement. I became increasingly interested in the principles and began to connect with the approach'. A model's philosophy influenced integration into practice:

> NVR appeals to me on so many levels; its origins from the socio political field, that it's a relational approach that is accessible to all; that its applicable across contexts and provides a way of addressing problems whilst prioritising and enhancing relationships and that it can positively influence wider contexts and cultures.... (Nicky)

Manuals can make it '...clearer to clients how therapist personal experiences were relevant and potentially useful to **their** situation' (John) and create practices that '...felt more authentic to working in a relationally reflexive way...' (Shila), fitting with both personal and professional values and philosophies.

In what ways are you still making use of a manual in your current practice? (How often do you refer to it or did you stop looking at it as soon as you finished training?) Do you have a copy of a manual that you have modified to be more relevant to your practice? If so, is this by emphasising some content, adding new material of your own or deleting or rephrasing some material (or maybe that comes later in the 'personalise' section). (Questions 9 and 10)

Therapists Continuing Reference to Manuals

As therapists practised the manual, they tended to only refer directly to the written manual when facing less familiar applications 'When I am training professionals .... because [I am] less experienced in this aspect...' (Nicky), requiring inspiration '…a resource to return to, especially if I need something quickly…' (Shila), ensuring faithfulness to the model 'avoiding only relying on my "favourite" bits of the manual' (John) and creating handouts and homework for families.

Anchoring and Adaptation

Therapists used manuals to anchor their practice within the approach while allowing them to adapt structure, timing, proportions and language within the model: 'I juggled with the (NVR) structure, so self-care is something I give more space to now…' (Shila). 'I have made notes on the manual, perhaps highlighting or modifying language or considering the order of techniques/aspects of the model' (Ellen). John and Beki spoke of '…manuals beginning as "bibles"…' but worked best when adapted to the working context; 'Admission and Discharge are two significant transitions within an inpatient experience'; adding these transitions to the MFT model makes more sense, is of greater practical value and is much appreciated by families and staff during the process of an inpatient experience.

Ellen adapts manuals in developing useful '…analogies or ways of [making] ideas more accessible to families, […] some of this may also be spontaneous within sessions'. The successful outcomes Nicky observed through using a manual became a bank of practice examples and witnessing '…as my experience has grown; I increasingly share parent stories, testimonials and sparkling moments to illustrate key principles'. Her practice experience enables her to become more agile in presenting/teaching the material to varied audiences.

The above themes, enriched with personal/practical examples, illustrate how the *rigour* provided by manuals was immediately seen as a *resource* offering a range of *possibilities* for systemic practice. As direct experience of using the manuals developed, practitioners recall experiencing *problems-in-use* which became *restraints*. As is often the case, systemic practitioners find ways to use *imagination* in order to overcome these restraints and develop new possibilities, which are described later in this chapter. In the next section, AMT is used to consider how to select and personalise a manual to practitioners, units and organisations.

32.4 Approach-Method-Technique: Making Distinctions and Creating Connections

Deconstructing a manualised approach using the framework of approach-method-technique (Burnham, 1992) may be one way to identify which are the 'bits' that are important to be loyal to and which bits can be personalised.

32.4.1 Approach

Refers to the 'why' of a model, including values, principles, prejudices, politics and premises that overarch or underpin manualised practices. Approach includes theory, but is not limited by any particular theory. It may borrow from several theories that fit and enhance the guiding principles/politics that inspired the developers of this way of working. When the principles/politics of a model resonate with those of the practitioner/team/agency, there is a stronger possibility for a working fit being created.

32.4.2 Method

Refers to the 'how' or the organisational aspects of the approach. Methods embody and enable the enactment of the values and principles and change them from theoretical/passionate ideas into working practices (e.g. how many sessions, length of sessions, who is included in the sessions, position(s) of practitioner in the process of the therapy).

Example 1 (Approach)

Politically speaking, FT-AN, MFT and NVR aim to form a collaborative working partnership with parents in overcoming the difficulties, emphasising, enhancing and extending abilities of the parents. This value is conveyed explicitly including educational sessions and written material for the parents.

Example 2 (Method)

Organisationally speaking, FT-AN has five distinct progressive phases to the work. In each phase the practitioner adopts a particular position; each session should be preceded by weighing the young person; family meals are a focal point of the work; the practitioner positions themselves as coaches of the parents to coach the child, rather than directly coaching the child.

32.4.3 Technique

Refers to the interpersonal practice skills used in sessions. Methods create rich connections between approach and technique. Methods create contexts in which techniques have meaning, purpose and direction. Technique brings an approach alive. Practitioners may feel robotic in using unfamiliar techniques. Persistent and deliberate practice enables practitioners to become skilled, almost human robots. Further on they may well find themselves personalising both the methods and techniques in ways that reflexively extend the development of the model.

Using a manual rigorously enables a coherence at the levels of approach, method and technique. Following only the methods and technique within a manual, without consciously engaging with the values and principles of the approach can become problematic in the longer term. There is little personalisation even when things aren't working, and it can happen that the responsibility for failure is visited upon a practitioner ('I am not skilled enough'), client (not cooperative enough), the context (not supportive enough) or the shortcomings of the manual (not right enough). When difficulties arise, try referring to the level of approach and think about the 'bits' (values and principles) that can help to create more personalised methods and techniques that fit their context and clients.

For example, 'Baskets' is a well-known and valuable method in NVR. Practitioners use three different size baskets to help clients to enact the systemic principle of making 'distinctions upon the distinction' of trouble (prioritising): small basket for 'must deal with now', medium basket for 'important but can wait' and large basket for 'annoying but can live with'. This method offers a tangible relief for clients overwhelmed by trying to tackle too many troubles at the same time. I had no baskets. Tragedy! …. I used three different size envelopes and achieved the same goal and enact the same principle. The family posted the envelopes on the fridge with the contents written on the outside, serving as a visual reminder which baskets may not provide.

Figure 32.2 represents a manual visually at the levels of AMT, suggesting how a practitioner might explore the fit between themselves and any particular manualised model.

Reflections on Level 1: **Manualising and** Then Personalising Without Compromising (Except When…)

We considered emergent themes in the relationships between individual practitioners and **manualised** treatment programmes. When facing clinical problems or learning a new way of working, practitioners valued the rigorous structure of manuals as a resource in scaffolding their practice in situations that seemed unsafe or uncertain. As they became more professionally confident, the methods and techniques specified in the manual could be experienced as something of a restraint that limited their imagination and creativity. However, practitioners continued to find that the principles associated with the philosophical and theoretical approach of the manual guided their efforts in developing broader ranges of practice possibilities that could create a more **personalised** fit with their style or agency.

32.5 Level 2: Implementing a Manualised Approach Within a Single Unit (Eating Disorders)

Manualising and **Then Personalising** Without Compromising (Except When …)

A comprehensive training programme in systemic practice and psychotherapy, supervision training and CPD is embedded within the culture, practice and heart of the service. And yet … there often seemed to be a split/divide between 'Upstairs'

M **A** **N** **U** **A** **L**	**Approach** What are the recurring messages about principle within the manual? What language is used to describe clients? What ethical postures are required to practice? Is it a single theory model or does it draw upon several? Is it respectful towards other ways of working? Is it modest about its achievements? Are the voices of clients evident in the manual and teaching? Are theories accessible? Do I feel I inspired by it?	**P** **R** **A** **C** **T** **I** **T** **I** **O** **N** **E** **R**
	Method Is this clinic based or can it be practised in the community? How many sessions? How much time investment will I need to work with clients in this way? Do I need to work with a team, or can I do it solo? Does it have a mix of instructional and invitational ways of intervening? Are the methods clear and portable enough for me to transfer into my own agency? Will I need to ask my agency for any more resources, or can I work with what we've got? Will I be able to explain the rationale to my clients to get them on board? What materials will I need to make the sessions go well? What is the sequence of the sessions and what shape does each session take? Do I believe I could do this?	
	Technique Do I need to start from scratch? Can I use the skills I already have? What new skills do I need and does the manual give me examples of them? As I read through the techniques and how they are used, do some of my clients and the situations they face come flooding to my mind? Am I already thinking about using it in the next session or would I be thinking I am needing the 'right' client? Can I imagine saying/doing some of the techniques? Am I excited about telling some of my colleagues about this to use in their work?	

Fig. 32.2 Manuals deconstructed through AMT

(staff trained in practising therapy) and 'Downstairs' (staff trained in nursing patients). Nurses and therapists may not get involved in each other's practice, nor be able to explain the detail of those practices and procedures to patients and their families. On admission family members may be in a state of 'unsafe uncertainty' (Mason, 1993), and if the experience 'Downstairs' is quite different to their experience 'Upstairs', then it may amplify the state of 'unsafe uncertainty'. Introducing the Family Therapy for Anorexia Nervosa (FT-AN) manual on the newly created specialist ED unit contributed towards creating a coherent approach, with a common language, a shared familiarity with treatment principles, professional mantras and practice skills around ED. This helped to create if not '**safe**' uncertainty' (Mason, 1993), then probably a '**safer**' uncertainty' for staff and families. It did not reduce the number of therapies available but introduced a coordinating narrative and structure about the stages of treatment. It described the central part that parents, siblings, other family members and friends could and would be expected to play in the treatment programme. Parents were persistently requested to move from being *worried witnesses* to becoming *active agents* in the therapeutic process.

The FT-AN manual had been developed to prevent inpatient admissions. *Personalising* the manual to work in an inpatient unit meant a number of things:

- Being clear to parents that the inpatient team would be working on the first two stages of the manual.
- Organising visiting times so that parents could come in to do supported meals.
- 'Upstairs' therapists who traditionally 'talked' about food and feeding now had to be involved in sessions involving real food.
- 'Downstairs' nurses who traditionally were directly feeding young people were now included in coaching parents to feed their son or daughter.
- Introducing mealtime rules that applied to all inpatients.

The manual became integrated into the unit with great enthusiasm, and the teams seeing families could be described as 'trans-disciplinary' with each discipline contributing towards a unit approach, while continuing to provide what was unique to their discipline.

Over time and perhaps inevitably, staff change, 'culture carriers' move on, training resources are focussed elsewhere and a particular manualised approach can drift and become compromised to the extent that it may be practised thinly or in name only. At this point Beki will pick up the story as an incoming member of staff new to the unit and the manual.

32.5.1 Beki's Experience

On joining the ED unit in my first post as a family and systemic psychotherapist, I read the two family-oriented manuals used on the unit, Lock and Le Grange (2012) and Eisler et al. (2016). I diligently went about arranging to see families with a view to following the session structures within the manuals, often including a family meal in the third meeting. I explored the context of this work prior to my arrival, ascertaining who had previously been delivering the family work, in what format and how the approach had come to be embedded in the treatment philosophy of the unit.

Eight years before my arrival, the clinic had received funding to purpose-build a 12-bed specialist ED unit. All staff who would be working on this unit (nursing and multidisciplinary team) had been trained in Family-Based Treatment (FBT). The ward was designed to facilitate the Multi-Family Therapy (MFT) programme, to be offered to all patients and their families. Pairs of professionals (including the unit psychiatrist, family therapist and numerous nursing staff) offered individual FBT sessions to families on a fortnightly basis, and on the alternating week, all families attended MFT. All nursing staff on the unit (including those not involved in delivering FBT sessions) were trained in delivering the message of the manual, i.e. positioning parents to take the lead in refeeding their child, instructing them to complete weekly menu planning and encouraging them to conduct regular supported meals on the unit.

As experienced staff left, the structure and delivery of FBT changed, and individual family sessions became solely provided by the family therapist allocated to the unit. MFT continued in its fortnightly format. A few weeks into my new role, I was informed that the first-line treatment for anorexia nervosa stated in the NICE guidelines is FT-AN (Eisler et al., 2016) and that family therapy sessions did not necessarily still need to follow the format of the FBT (Lock & Le Grange, 2012) manual to the letter. My requests to attend both FT-AN and MFT training were unsuccessful, in my first year of the post due to funding constraints. Only one member of the unit's senior team had received this training, and only a few of the original nursing team who had this training remained in post. Some of the methods and techniques of FT-AN were still evident in the day to work of the unit, but there was little understanding of the approach (why things were done that way). A number of practices had 'slipped'. The spirit of the manual had become compromised.

Furthermore, the increased capacity of community eating disorders teams to manage young people with AN, and prevent them requiring inpatient care, meant our patient mix had changed. Approximately half of young people on the unit would have a diagnosis of AN, whereas the others would have eating difficulties comorbid with other disorders. Diagnoses may include atypical anorexia binge/purge type or ARFID (avoidant/restrictive food intake disorder). Three separate ED treatment pathways were created. A systemically informed family approach continued to be useful in these situations alongside other manualised approaches such as attachment focus, DBT (Dialectical Behaviour Therapy) or NVR (Non-Violent Resistance) to support parents with understanding, managing and responding to their child's behaviours, including their eating difficulties and escalations around mealtimes. We became a multi-manual unit and the process of creating relationships between the manuals continues.

32.5.2 *Refreshing Rigour Through Formal Training*

In my second year on the unit, I attended the 3-day FT-AN and 4-day MFT trainings, alongside two senior colleagues from psychiatry and psychology which underscored and supported a renewed commitment to the manual. This formal training allowed me to fully appreciate how much of the ethos of FT-AN remained embedded in the unit's approach and which elements had become 'dusty' or 'rusty'. They helped me see that a manual one may be reading and implementing and may not be up to date with the thinking and practice of those who created the manual. We returned and rolled out a 'refresher training' in FT-AN. This allowed me to realise that seeing a manual sitting on a shelf (sometimes gathering dust) may mean that it is not being used; alternatively it may mean that for other members of staff, the manual has become lived practice. It seemed that the principles of FT-AN are embedded in the 'thinking' and 'doing' of all staff on the unit, as opposed to the FBT manual being used as a step-by-step instruction guide for treatment.

Accessing the formal training in FT-AN and MFT both increased my confidence in delivering these approaches/programme and also refreshed the work on the unit. Returning to some of the basics that had been overlooked and refreshing staff enthusiasm about some of the developments in the manual since the unit's specialist EDU conception. I came to realise that if the 'originators' were changing/extending the manual, then we could too as long as we stuck to the philosophy/principles of the approach.

John and Beki began working together using Beki's renewed enthusiasm and updated knowledge, to personalise the practice of the manual to better fit the inpatient context. For example, in a community-based programme, families will be making the transition from therapy to home after each session. In contrast, the transition of discharge from an inpatient unit to home involves a redefinition of several significant relationships (family, friends, school, neighbours and community professionals). Our personalised practice of the FT-AN and MFT manuals includes discharge-focussed sessions with a focus on relational relapse prevention and building bridges.

Bridges are particularly important to build so that families can prepare for the homecoming and families can reconnect with community professionals. Creating a bridge from hospital to home allows for lessons learnt from the manual to be personalised for each family's house, home, living and working context. We learnt from families that those families who relaxed into the 'old normal' as soon as they left hospital tended to struggle somewhat, and confidence sometimes became complacency. Many families were able to maintain the 'rigour' of the manual and still create a 'new normal' through using their 'imagination'. A very recent example of 'imaginative rigour' was a parent using 'Facetime' to be 'with' her daughter during mealtimes at school. This chapter is being completed 2 months into the COVID-19 'lockdown', and in order to maintain clinical services in both community and inpatient services, both professionals and families have shown great imagination in the use of online platforms to maintain the rigour and integrity of the models of working.

32.5.3 Connecting with Community

Building bridges with community professionals is also vitally important, especially if there have been changes in community staffing during the inpatient stay. Rubina Singh, Lead for Community Family and Systemic Psychotherapy, and Dr. Laura Coglan joined an MFT session to offer reflections and coaching to families for reconnecting with community services. Those families who are able to present themselves to the community team in terms of what changes they have achieved, the skills they have developed and the help they think they need from professionals are more likely to remain in the position of 'active agents' in creating the direction and flow of therapeutic change. Likewise, Rubina proposes that community professionals receiving families from inpatient care into the community begin by 'gaining some insight into what stage (of the manual) the family are at by opening space to inquire about the skills and competences the family have acquired. This allows the professional(s) to carefully and cautiously position ourselves in relation to this particular family'. This 'relationally reflexive' approach (Burnham, 1993, 2005) attunes the professional and family to one another, 'personalising' the work and increasing the possibility that a relationship with the potential to be therapeutic is created. Such a relationship is critical whatever manual is being used. Rubina goes on to say: 'Indeed the manual has at times acted as a bridge between the inpatient and community services, creating a seamless transfer (when it works well!) and, at worse, highlighting the challenges (problems and restraints) encountered by some families, which gives clues as to how to best search for resources and possibilities'.

Further 'bridge building' initiatives include Rubina being the external supervisor for the MFT team. This tends to reduce a 'silo' culture and enhances the working relationship between inpatient and community services.

32.6 Level 3: Process of Training the Staff Across All Three Units in the Service in Non-Violent Resistance (NVR)

The previous section is an example of using a purpose-made manual for a particular clinical problem within a specialised unit. This next section is written by Nicky and John and describes the introduction of a manualised approach across all units.

In 2013, the systemic training programme sponsored a training in Non-Violent Resistance (NVR), a systemically based approach to violent interactions, that spanned inpatient and community services, was across disciplines and ensured some staff were trained as trainers. The training included a day focussing on the CAMHS inpatient context facilitated by Nick Goddard, a psychiatrist from De Bascule in Amsterdam, who was reporting some successes after the introduction of ward-based NVR (Goddard et al., 2009).

This first round of training included staff selected from one of the three inpatient units. Following the training and using the manual, the principles and practices of NVR were utilised within the weekly staff support/reflective practice group. Trainers used feedback from initial successes and difficulties to adapt the manual to the inpatient setting. NVR mantras such as 'striking when the iron is cold' and the value of an 'emotionally regulated' team became embedded. As usual some trained staff moved on, but some staff persisted until an NVR parent group was set up. Other pockets of NVR practice continued, ready for what was to come!

Following an absence, Nicky returned as clinical lead for the systemic department. Alongside a clinical nurse specialist (trained in NVR), they created a proposal reviving NVR and in the process potentially breaking down the 'silo' culture between the three wards. Their proposal introduced an NVR approach, across the three wards. It would be central across clinical models and underpin the therapeutic milieu, and most importantly it would address the most worrying issue on all of the wards, responding to very challenging/violent behaviours. While the Eating Disorders manual was problem specific, NVR was more applicable across the wards and promised to enhance other approaches too. Initiatives in breaking down the 'silo culture' and promoting a 'trans-ward' culture was to introduce a 'pan-unit parents group' using NVR principles/practices that would enable parents to enhance their repertoire of parenting positions and skills. The group was co-run by multidisciplines and so was not seen as exclusive to the systemic psychotherapists. Parents attending the group began to spread the word about the immediate usefulness of NVR. NVR might be described as having its own 'language game' (Wittgenstein in Cronen & Lang, 1994) with phrases and mantras that enable theoretical concepts to be remembered and used when you most need them. For example, parents often regret things they do or say in the 'heat of the moment'. Retrospectively, these moments can be deconstructed in all sorts of theories that do not necessarily help a parent behave differently in the next 'heat of the moment'. Theoretically, we might say something like: 'It is better to postpone the enactment of a parental response that has the potential to escalate the very inter-action that you are hoping to decrease or change, until you are feeling calmer and more able to respond in a way that has the potential to produce the kind of inter-action you are hoping to create'. The NVR phrase 'Strike while the Iron is Cold' captures this in a practically memorable way and was found to be useful in a variety of contexts, for a range of reasons by family members and professionals alike. While the NVR manual sets out a strong theoretical base, it converts this base into many practical phrases and mantras, which caught the imagination of staff across all units.

32.6.1 Transferring Excitement into Expertise

Then perhaps the most revolutionary development was a foundation course (complete with manual) across the wards attended by multidisciplines, particularly targeting senior staff in an attempt to recruit organisational 'supporters' and a shared vision for a whole system approach. The training reignited NVR presence within the inpatient service and across the trust and achieved a consensus for NVR to be utilised therapeutically and operationally across the service. Foundation-level training has been completed by 25 members of staff with a further 20 due to be trained. All staff have received some training in NVR, and 1 day of NVR training will be included both in the induction training programme for all new starters and the ongoing staff training programme.

32.6.2 Feedback from the Training

Comments from some of those who have attended the foundation-level training:

'It's all been fantastic…I can't wait to share with the rest of my team tomorrow!'
'Baskets is applicable to every aspect of ward life!'
'I feel understanding parental presence and how vital it is to NVR has been the most useful, also that it is about how "you" respond not the response of the other'.
'It's all been extremely relevant, thoughtfully put together and sensitively delivered throughout'.
'It was all I hoped for…I think NVR can become an underpinning framework for the whole clinic'.
'Listening to the experience of a graduate parent was invaluable'.

This kind of inspired feedback may be found on the websites of a number of different trainings, including systemic models. Generating excitement through training is the beginning of an important process. Transferring that excitement from training into sustainable skills and expertise within a practitioner's own day-to-day work is perhaps the most important step. The way that the NVR training was set up 'warmed the context' (Burnham, 2005) for the approach to become more integrated within the service and making a contribution across the units.

What place does a manual have in this process of transferring excitement into expertise and skills?

Let's revisit the conversation between John and Nicky that we began this chapter with. John was insisting that NVR was manualised, and Nicky (who currently accepts that she uses other manuals such as AIT) maintained that she did not experience it as a manual, even though it is officially. This conversation has continued and developed throughout the writing of this chapter. While the conversation has not come to a definite conclusion, nor is it likely to, some interesting thoughts have emerged along the way about this manual which may be useful for other manual makers.

At first, I suggested to Nicky that perhaps the NVR manual was a good example of a non-manualised manual? But what did I mean by this? Perhaps I could contribute my experience of it, as a student on the course who is more aware of using the manual, than is Nicky for whom it is a richly embedded part of her experience as a practitioner and a person.

The qualities that I found the NVR manual to have and perhaps are common to other successful manuals are (currently):

(a) The components of the manual have been laid out and languaged in 'ordinary' terms that make the practices more available. This fits with John's expression of 'think theory and talk ordinary'.
(b) Essential ideas in the approach are converted into practical tools and popular language that populate the manual. Words such as 'self-care', 'baskets', 'an announcement', 'sit-in' and 'supporters' are used that suggest an action and can be used by the staff and families alike.

I think it becomes a 'living manual' because the contents are living outside the manual in very usable way by both families and professionals. Perhaps, these features may apply to most manuals that are successful.

32.7 Closing Remarks

A practitioner's initial response to a manualised way of working may be to immediately fall in love with it, immediately hate it or somewhere in between. One practitioner may experience a manual as a reassuring structure which they follow with **rigour**, while another may feel they are working in a strait jacket and want to be free to use their creativity and **imagination**. Following Bateson (1979, p. 233) avoid rigour becoming 'rigor mortis' and imagination becoming … well, … something that only you can understand! Bateson proposes a 'both-and' position, and so perhaps we can aspire to be imaginatively rigorous and rigorously imaginative.

Creating a manual is a necessary step towards claiming the status of being 'evidence based'. The notion of 'personalising (without compromising)' addresses a curiosity for practitioners contemplating engaging with the manualised model 'Can **I** make this work', in my agency, with my colleagues and with the families I work with?' As luck would have it, several manuals emphasise that the manual should 'not compromise the creativity of the practitioner' (FT-AN, 2014), 'This is the way I do it …now go and do your own thing' (Peter Jakob, NVR training, 2019).

'Without compromising' heeds the message from nursing staff that if you over-'personalise' the manual, you may severely compromise its effectiveness. Claiming that 'We tried the X model and it didn't work' may be unfair if the essential aspects of the manual were not followed sufficiently. Practitioners might say 'I still use bits'; but, which 'bits' are crucial to follow (fidelity) and which 'bits' can be personalised? The answers may decide whether a practitioner/team/agency/client can use the manual with sufficient fidelity that your trainer would see a 'family resemblance' (Wittgenstein in Cronen & Lang, 1994) to what they trained you to do.

But still, practitioners might worry about 'copying' the practice in a manual or any other model that is set out clearly. It may negatively affect their creativity and they don't want to end up as a mere copy. Even after extensive searches, I have no idea where this quote came from but it seems quite appropriate:

Person 1: 'How is it that we all start off as originals, and we end up as copies?'

Person 2: 'On the contrary, I think we all start of as copies and end up as originals'.

> Example (Drawn from John's Own Experience)
> In my early stages of training, I reverently followed the 'Milan model' (Boscolo et al., 1987). After 2 years, I knew, off by heart, and was word perfect with all of the questions, strategies and interventions from their articles, workshops and live clinical interviews. I watched and rewatched videotapes of interviews and developed something of an Italian accent! At a small training event for our team within our agency, I was showing a videotape of one of my clinical sessions to Luigi Boscolo and Gianfranco Cecchin. I intended to 'show off' how closely I had followed their model. I suddenly realised there was a section coming up on the tape that was not 'Milan'. I did **not** want them to see it. As I left my seat to pause the machine (pre-remote controls), Luigi gently restrained me and said 'Hold on a moment, let's see how this turns out'. I felt 'I'm doomed' and awaited my fate of being exposed as an imposter and diagnosed as 'not sufficiently systemic' (Pearce et al., 1992). However, Boscolo watched and said (after what seemed like a very long time), 'This is a very interesting use of Bateson's concept of a "raid on the random"' (phew!!).
> The Milan team developed their model within a private therapy centre in Milan, Italy. We were working in an NHS regional mental health unit for children and young people in Birmingham, UK. Differences were to be expected and necessary. After my initial sense of relief, our team reflected that we had been following the 'methods and techniques' of the Milan model. Our next stage of development was to read what the 'Milan associates' had read in order to think like they did, as well as do what they do. Bateson became our go-to reading to appreciate the Milan approach. Perhaps this is one of the inspirations in developing the framework of 'approach-method-technique' (Burnham, 1992).

References

Alexander, J. F., Barrett Waldron, H., Robbins, M. S., & Neeb, A. A. (2013). *Functional family therapy for adolescent behaviour problems*. APA.

Allen, D., Coombes, E. L., & Foxcroft, D. R. (2006). *Cultural accommodation of the strengthening families programme 10–14: UK phase 1 study*. Oxford University Press.

Allen, D., Foxcroft, D. R., & Coombes, L. (2006). *Strengthening families programme 10–14 (UK): For parents and youth 10–14*. Oxford University Press.

Asen, E., & Scholz, M. (2010). *Multi-family therapy: Concepts and techniques*. Taylor and Francis.

Bateson, G. (1979). *Mind and nature. A necessary unity*. Wildwood House Ltd.

Boscolo, L., Cecchin, G., Hoffman, L., & Penn, P. (1987). *Milan systemic family therapy: Conversations in theory and practice*. Basic Books.

Braun, V., & Clarke, V. (2006). Using thematic analysis in psychology. *Qualitative Research in Psychology, 3*(2), 77–101.

Braun, V., & Clarke, V. (2012). Thematic analysis. In H. Cooper, P. M. Camic, D. L. Long, A. T. Panter, D. Rindskopf, & K. J. Sher (Eds.), *APA handbooks in psychology. APA handbook of research methods in psychology, Vol. 2. Research designs: Quantitative, qualitative, neuropsychological, and biological* (pp. 57–71). American Psychological Association.

Burnham, J. (1992). Approach – Method – Technique, creating distinctions and creating connections. *Human Systems, 3*, 3–27.

Burnham, J. (1993). Systemic supervision: The evolution of reflexivity in the context of the supervisory relationship. *In Human Systems: The Journal of Systemic Consultation and Management, 4*(3&4), 349–381.

Burnham, J. (2005). Chapter 1: Relational reflexivity: A tool for socially constructing therapeutic relationships. In C. Flaskas, B. Mason, & A. Perlesz (Eds.), *The space between: Experience, context, and process in the therapeutic relationships.* Karnac Publications.

Burnham, J. (2012). Developments in social GRRRAAACCEEESSS: Visible – Invisible and voiced – Unvoiced. In I.-B. Kraus (Ed.), *Mutual perspectives. Culture and reflexivity in contemporary systemic psychotherapy.* Karnac Publications.

Burnham, J. (2021). *PPRR*. In preparation.

Burnham, J., & Harris, Q. (2002). Cultural perspective in supervision. In B. Mason & D. Campbell (Eds.), *Perspectives on supervision*. Karnac Publications.

Clinton, A. (2010). Advanced integrative therapy. In M. C. Folkers, V. Danzig, & P. Martin (Eds.), *AIT: The basics*. AIT.

Clinton, A. (2018). *The AIT core belief book: All the cognitions You'll ever need to promote transformation and healing*. AIT.

Cronen, V., & Lang, P. (1994). Language and action: Wittgenstein and Dewey in the practice of therapy and consultation. *Human Systems: The Journal of Systemic Consultation & Management, 5*, 5–43.

Eisler, I., Simic, M., Blessitt, E., Dodge, L., & Team. (2016). *Maudsley service manual for child and adolescent eating disorders*. https://www.national.slam.nhs.uk/wp-content/uploads/2011/11/Maudsley-Service-Manual-for-Child-and-Adolescent-Eating-Disorders-July-2016.pdf

Hughes, D. (2011). *Attachment focused family therapy workbook*. W.W. Norton & Co..

Jakob, P. (2011). Non-violent resistance to help aggression in young people. *Community Care*, February 2011.

Linehan, M. M. (1993). *Cognitive-behavioral treatment of borderline personality disorder*. Guilford Press.

Lock, J., & Le Grange, D. (2012). *Treatment manual for anorexia nervosa, second edition: A family-based approach*. The Guilford Press.

Mason, B. (1993). Towards positions of safe uncertainty. *Human Systems: The Journal of Systemic Consultation and Management, 4*, 189–200.

Mason, B. (2013). Towards a culture of contribution in supervisory practice: Some thoughts about the position of the supervisor. In C. Burck, S. Barratt, & E. Kavner (Eds.), *Positions and polarities in contemporary systemic practice: The legacy of David Campbell*. Karnac Publications.

Molgaard, V., Kumpfer, K., & Fleming, E. (1997, Revised). *The strengthening families program: For parents and youth 10–14*. Iowa State University Extension.

Multi-Systemic Therapy. http://www.mstuk.org/multisystemic-therapy-mst

Omer, H. (2004). *Nonviolent resistance a new approach to violent and self-destructive children*. Cambridge University Press.

Pearce, W. B., Villar, E., & McAdam, E. (1992). Not sufficiently systemic: An exercise in curiosity. *Human Systems, 3*(1992), 75–88.

Rathus, J. H., & Miller, A. L. (2015). *DBT® skills manual for adolescents*. Guilford Press.

Sexton, T. (2011). *Functional family therapy in clinical practice: An evidence-based treatment model for working with troubled adolescents*. Routledge.

Strengthening Families. https://guidebook.eif.org.uk/programme/strengthening-families-programme-10-14

Chapter 33
Implications of the Handbook for the Future of Manualization of Systemic Therapies

Peter Stratton, George Saba, and Mauro Mariotti

33.1 Introduction

"If you watch any therapist work with one family, you may be amazed that they are spontaneously improvising the therapy in that moment. However, if you watch any therapist working with three different families, you will begin to see the pattern of how they work. They are following a pattern, a model of how they think of families and how to enact change that they then adapt to any individual family." Salvador Minuchin

As we come to review the full set of chapters of the *Handbook of Systemic Approaches to Psychotherapy Manuals: Integrating Research, Practice, and Training* with contributions from across the world, the enthusiasm, and the variety of approaches to manuals is striking. We want to conclude that, so long as we take an open position and avoid restrictive definitions of what constitutes a manual, at least for the 61 authors who have contributed, all in one way or several are using manuals. We suspect this is representative of very many other systemic practitioners, but also know that very often therapists and trainees operate mostly on implicit

---

The original version of this chapter was revised. The correction to this chapter is available at https://doi.org/10.1007/978-3-030-73640-8_34

P. Stratton (✉)
Emeritus Professor of Family Therapy, Leeds Family Therapy and Research Centre, University of Leeds, Leeds, West Yorkshire, UK
e-mail: p.m.stratton@ntlworld.com

G. Saba
Emeritus Professor of Family and Community Medicine, University of California, San Francisco, San Francisco, California, USA
e-mail: George.Saba@ucsf.edu

M. Mariotti
Iscra Institute of Psychotherapy, Modena, Italy
e-mail: info@iscra.it; dottmauromariotti@gmail.com

© Springer Nature Switzerland AG 2021, Corrected Publication 2022
M. Mariotti et al. (eds.), *Handbook of Systemic Approaches to Psychotherapy Manuals*, European Family Therapy Association Series,
https://doi.org/10.1007/978-3-030-73640-8_33

manuals. When manuals are not explicit, we risk thinking that within a particular approach, we are all generally doing the same thing when in fact we often are not. As we know, systems are rule-governed. Manuals represent one articulation of the rules. We would argue that everyone is operating via a manual, just that some are more explicit than others. Explicit conversations of what is in everybody's implicit manuals is a good deal of what happens in the process of mutual learning, change, co-evolution, and study that happens in all our activities, as we ask people to disclose their thinking, perspective, and narrative of any given situation.

This handbook provides numerous examples of the strengths of carefully evolved and tested training with a clear theoretical base. Some authors have not only formalized their manual but have made it publically available, while others are on the way to articulating their process and/or simply need to make the step towards dissemination. For many, the "public" often consist of the trainees and supervisors of the course, but others have taken it beyond their context and published their manuals in both print and/or social media. We hope this handbook demonstrates that a much wider audience would benefit from learning what a particular approach actually does as well as generate useful feedback for improving the manual.

We did not intend to provide a collection of systemic manuals, rather we hoped to consider the current and future issues that arise in the use of systemic manuals. We also tried to maintain both sides of Shotter's (2015) distinction between two forms of inquiry: thinking about systems and thinking systemically. So an early title for this handbook was *Systemic Approaches to Manualization of Psychotherapy.* While some chapters have explicitly addressed ensuring that the process of constructing manuals was a systemic exercise, the great majority have focussed on the systemic manuals themselves; hence, the final title is of *systemic manuals.*

In general, contributors provided just enough description of their treatment, research, and training models to allow readers insight into how they have grappled with various issues of manualization. We believe the result provides all of us with a vast array of what can constitute a manual, the various stages one can go through in developing a manual, and lessons that can serve as a guide for those interested in creating manuals.

The contributions we received fell naturally under four headings which make up the four parts of this handbook. The first, *Issues and Experiences in the Creation of Manuals*, presents a diverse set of perspectives on how the authors developed their established manuals or sources for manualization. Part 2 then reviews some of the *Research Issues in the Use and Evaluation of Manuals.* As we specified at the start, value cannot be claimed for a manual unless there is evidence that practice based on it is effective. So we asked all authors to report the grounds for claiming the effectiveness of their manual, but the chapters in this section have a strong focus on their research base. For Part 3 we move to concentrate on the varied *Uses of Manuals in Clinical Practice.* Here we have more detailed accounts of the ways a manual can be specified to meet the requirements of a particular clinical application. We start to see how we might make a distinction between manuals with a general specification that would be needed in the kind of clinic that sees families with a wide variety of problems and those that provide a specialist service. Finally, Part 4 focuses on *Training as a Basis for Development of Manuals and a Context for Their Application.*

While most chapters in the handbook show the relationship between the manual and the training context for which it is used, these are approaches to manualization that trace a specific derivation from meeting the needs of training courses. The format of the manual explicitly follows the epistemology of the training.

This brings us to the question of what would be required to call something a manual. From this collection, we would propose that a manual should:

- Be a guide to practice, with the underlying theory identified but not elaborated, and linked to references for further background
- Present clear goals and objectives for the activity manualized (treatment, training, research, or all three)
- Provide a specification of core processes
- Be explicit
- Be made publicly available
- Serve as a concise indicator of the therapy being reported on, whether as research or practice in journal articles

33.2 Nine Issues of Systemic Manuals Generated by the Content of This Handbook

Our learnings from working intensively on the contents of this handbook can be grouped under nine headings.

33.2.1 The Status of the Manualization Issue

Manuals are influenced by the local, national, and regional politics, economics, and culture of the context in which they develop. Some countries, such as Italy, require by law very detailed manuals for training institutes. In other countries, poorly funded clinics are often too overwhelmed with mere survival to make more than a basic manual that is shared among the few staff at that site. Research manuals are often more refined, given that funders may require them in proposals or as products from the projects. A country which has lived under an authoritarian government for generations may develop a culture in which some therapists will be cautious in producing manuals that might be misunderstood as an authoritative document requiring unwavering fidelity. Regulations for clinics, hospitals, treatment programs, training sites, and research projects may require formal manuals to be considered for funding. So, not surprisingly, manuals are not an acontextual phenomenon. This also raises questions about how well-manualized treatments developed in one context fit into another context.

As just one example of directly confronting differing understanding of manuals, in Chap. 32 John **Burnham,** Nicky Maund, Beki Brain, Ellen Twist, Shila Desai, and Rubina Singh start with a report of opposite perceptions of manuals in their team, for and against. They then report on how, in practice, the major issues of manualization were experienced over time while being implemented within the unit specializing in eating disorders.

Dubravka **Trampuž** and Maja Rus Makovec in Chap. 28 draw on Mason (2019) to propose that frameworks, guidelines, manuals, and checklists can help us, but they do not do the work for us; they are helping us as an aid to using creativity in the therapeutic relationship.

33.2.2 Different Forms and Formats of Manual-Type Material Among the Chapters

From our array of chapters, the question arises: What constitutes a manual, and perhaps more accurately, what constitutes the process of manualization? Clearly the forms vary: from written to electronic, considerable detail to general specifications; focusing on systemic therapy in general to applying the approach to a specific population; guiding therapists on their first session to elaborating on the entire course of treatment; and from guidance for the conduct of research, to the implementation of therapy, to the process of training, and to the intertwined dialogue among all three.

While we cannot articulate everything we do as systematicians, in at least systemic therapy, we have not had a dearth of people saying what they do—from individual pioneers and institutes publishing multiple texts describing how their model deals relationally with assessment, treatment, and change.... One could ask whether manualization is really different from the tomes that different schools of family therapy (structural, strategic, narrative, etc.) produced and required fidelity to by their therapists, even if there was not a "manual" per se.

YES manualization is different, because a manual needs to be more concise as it describes what to do with a minimum of the theoretical discussions that tomes often include (sometimes in the form of self-justification, vainglorious claims, attacks on other previous approaches), patterns that seem to be compulsory in systemics when one is claiming an advance.

One example of the developmental process of manualization can be seen in Julian **Baudinet**, Mima Simic, and Ivan Eisler's Chap. 19 in which they discuss Carroll and Nuro's (2002) description of three clear and distinct types of treatment manuals that map onto the typical course of treatment development, namely, a pilot manual (stage I), a research manual for testing efficacy (stage II), and finally a manual for wider-scale dissemination and general effectiveness testing.

33.2.3 Variations in How Widely Applied Are Manuals Beyond the Originators' Settings

An important function of a manual is that it should be made public and thereby become available to other users as well as generating feedback from other contexts through which it can be improved.

In Chap. 3, Peter **Stratton** and Helen Pote report on the translations of their English language manual into Spanish and Italian. Both translated versions have been widely used, and the Spanish version which originated in Chile has been used in many Spanish-speaking countries.

In Chap. 15, Valeria **Pomini** and Vlassis Tomaris describe using a manual for research across three European countries while reporting first-hand experiences of doing therapy within a research process.

Julian **Baudinet**, Mima Simic, and Ivan Eisler's Chap. 19 make the important point that, ideally, a manual should provide a clear guide to clinicians new to the model and also serve as a useful reference point for experienced clinicians.

33.2.4 The Epistemological Bases Used for the Manuals

It is plausible to suggest that all work towards creating a manual is based on decisions about an appropriate basis for the therapy.

Mosconi and B. Trotta in Chap. 6 describe an approach securely rooted in hypothesizing and pragmatics, whereas in Chap. 5, Nicholas **Paritsis** argues for keeping our manuals rooted in basic cybernetics and general systems.

Athena **Androutsopoulou**, Tsabika Bafiti, and George Kalarritis in Chap. 31 integrate their approach with neuroscience and consider how to enrich the systemic perspective with three additional perspectives (those of narrative/dialogic psychology, attachment theory, and neuroscience) and how to apply this knowledge to treating clients and monitoring progress.

When integrating different systemic approaches to a single model (Structural-Strategic Therapy; Digital Analogical Narrative Chaps. 12 and 13, Mauro **Mariotti**, Samantha **Miazzi**), how can process manuals help? We wonder how manualization can keep these brilliant insights available and developed for current practice, while countering the rush to embrace the latest idea (epistemology) and promote it with a claim that it makes earlier ideas obsolete. Manualization can serve as an exercise in clarifying one's integrative approach and showing the therapist how such varied perspectives emerge seamlessly in practice. One could argue they are essential so that those using the model will not be confused based on a vague conglomeration of assumptions.

33.2.5 Variations in the Forms That Manuals Are Taking

The manuals presented in this handbook reveal a great variety of forms. Those that describe training programs can range from multiyear detailed curricular content to more basic descriptions of a particular aspect of the teaching. Some manuals provide an overview for the entire course of therapy, while others focus on how to conduct the first phase of treatment. We often see an evolution in manuals over time from a rudimentary presentation of goals and objectives to increasing specificity over time of "what could be done when". Training manuals can begin as a syllabus comprised of mostly content and then transform into more specificity of the processes.

Peter **Stratton** and Helen Pote in Chap. 3 describe a series of six manuals or near-manuals in very different formats that were put into the public domain by a single training and research institute.

33.2.6 The Process of Developing a Viable Manual

These chapters reveal that the originators represent a continuum of manualization. Some fully meet the above criteria for a viable manual. Others are at different stages of articulation, while many who have well-developed manuals have yet to disseminate them. This raises the question of what the incentive is for the originators to take the important but often challenging and time-intensive work to formulate and share their manualization. Learning about the process one has gone through to reach a viable manualization is demonstrated in Chap. 24 in which Ulf **Axberg**, Bill Pettit, and Ingegerd Wirtberg describe a clear process of constructing a manualized intervention.

33.2.7 Relationship Between Competence Specifications and Manuals

There may be a quite useful association between analyses of the competences of systemic therapists and the content of manuals. Competences can offer a useful checklist of the surprisingly extensive specific practices that a qualified and experienced therapist can draw on. Stratton et al. (2011), through analyses of existing systemic manuals, identified a total of 256 specific competences. Lists of competences are necessarily referring to processes, whereas some manuals may primarily specify procedures, which Mauro **Mariotti**, George Saba, and Peter Stratton have, in Chap. 1, argued are less helpful.

Lennart **Lorås**, in Chap. 10, points out that manuals tend to be written for use by trained therapists (or those in training) and often omit some basic skills on the assumption that they are knowledge that therapists already have. *Competences*, on the other hand, refer to the documentation and description of the fundamental elements of systemic therapy that are expected to be mastered by systemic therapists. By drawing on both, the therapists will base their practice on the full range of systemic ideas, adapted to their context.

33.2.8 The Prospects for Future Development of the Manuals

One key issue is whether a manual changes over time or remains basically the same for years. What is the process and rate of feedback, change, and evolution of any particular manual? Do they change based on loops of interaction within a course of therapy (Robert **van Hennik**, Chap. 4)? Do they change when periodically reviewed based on outcomes or required reporting to a funder or accrediting body? Do they change based on users' feedback, do they never change for long periods, and are there multiple versions of a particular manual that are allowed to develop and morph somewhat on their own? One answer to these questions comes from the fact that many manuals relate to the practices of a training clinic. Cigdem **Alper** in Chap. 9 offers a description of how the specification of a training clinic totally matched to their context can provide the framework for the accompanying manual. It becomes clear that, just as trainings evolve and adapt to requirements from above and developments in practice from below, the accompanying manual should also evolve flexibly.

The publication of manuals is challenged by available formats: journal articles are often too brief for much detail, and a published book that only presents the manual is probably not a best seller. So dissemination will be key, particularly as more programs develop systemic manuals.

How will available and new technologies affect the development and evolution of manualization as we have more options than printed journal articles and books? Newer formats offer more immediate dialogue, among a wider network globally, and with a variety of formats (YouTube; websites; podcasts). A number of internet resources used for dissemination of the SCORE manual are described by Peter **Stratton**, Chap. 17.

33.2.9 Future Challenges

Where do we include families and the community in the evaluation and development of manuals? Are they simply the object of the work, do they provide input into the creation, and do they serve as evaluators of effectiveness of both the manual and treatment? It certainly seems likely that the process of constructing a manual will prompt careful consideration of the practice being described which will inevitably and usefully feedback to a careful consideration of that practice.

Camillo **Loriedo**, in Chap. 26, points to the importance of Kolb's concepts of including the adult learner in active experimentation with the material, as distinct from the traditional teacher and researcher stance of the learner being a passive recipient.

Robert **Van Hennick** in Chap. 4 outlines his concept of "Practice-Based-Evidence-Based Practice" which specifies that no therapy would be provided without measuring its effects and no research is done outside of the practice itself. The therapist is both practitioner and researcher and involves clients as co-researchers. Therapist and clients examine the effects of their collaboration. The output of research is input for therapy in the "collaborative learning community" constituted together.

33.3 Conclusion

We believe the authors in this handbook have shown that the process of manualization is one way to articulate what we think—a point of juxtaposition to what we observe that we do, a means of dialoguing about what we learn in our work, and how it helps to then further our effectiveness. There is nothing authoritarian about this way of viewing manualization. And we believe that the common knee jerk reaction to manuals (i.e., "don't tell *me* what to do") becomes a harmful distraction. The current allergy towards manuals in part comes from seeing them as "scriptural": the word of an almighty that requires fidelity, demands defence against alternative sacred texts, and an unchanging set of directives that guarantees ultimate success. This either/or thinking has bred an unnecessarily contentious debate that can too easily devolve into "who is more systemic—the manual deniers or the manual proponents?" This duality emerges in emphasizing one dimension over the other—rigor/creativity, fidelity/use of judgment, and all treatment is the same/every treatment is unique. These are often pitted against each other with valences of positivity or negativity. Manuals that are procedure based are too reductionistic, and those, as shown in this handbook, that are process based do not "chop the ecology". We suggest that there can be a balance of these seeming opposites, and manuals can guide that balance of what we believe is important to do and how do we adapt it to the specific families, learners, and research participants at any given moment.

While this book hopes to open a new path for dialogue, even the current clash we experience is worth reflecting on as it may tell us something important about our epistemology and ourselves. A bit of news being a difference that makes a difference. And learning about this may help systemics to continue to influence practice, training, and research.

33.3.1 Our Guesses/wishes for the Future of Manualization

Evaluation of manualized approaches and dissemination of them are two areas that are underdeveloped. So much time has been spent on developing models of treatment for clinical practice and/or formal research, that little time has been available for evaluating if the manualization of that approach is effective. Perhaps EFTA and other international organizations have a job to do to support communication between clinics to share their knowledge and experience.

Many complex appliances no longer come with a printed manual but simply direct the owner to a downloadable resource. And if the owner has a problem, they can undertake a search for solutions. One of us recently had a problem of the retractable lead of a vacuum cleaner having jammed. On the Web were not just detailed instructions, but a set of videos of step-by-step processes for solving the problem and evaluations and elaborations by people who had used the instructions. A question for the future is which aspects of psychotherapy lend themselves to interactive Web presentation especially given that we can expect a progressively elaborating availability of Web resources. Is this the future of manualization in psychotherapy?

Should we expect to see manuals demonstrated by videos of therapy sessions in which the manual was followed and thereby instruct the viewer not just in the contents of the manual, but how it is used in practice? Of course vacuum cleaners raise few ethical issues of confidentiality which are likely to be a concern when posting actual sessions on the internet.

And more to the isomorphic nature, we would argue that, fundamentally, the epistemology from which one views the world informs how one creates a model of therapy, how they teach it, and how they study it. Thus the process of manualization would begin with the articulation of how one believes that an organism changes, learns, and coevolves, which is a theory underpinning all three activities of practice, teaching, and research (e.g., learning requires enactment; acknowledging the role of self in each of these activities). Then one would develop a meta manual as an umbrella presenting core beliefs, values, and goals. The next step would require developing how these domains are enacted specifically in each of the three activities so that one develops a practice manual, a training manual, and a research manual that are isomorphic and also specific to their particular function. For example, if one believes an experiential approach is fundamental to learning, that would be presented in the meta manual, and then in the practice manual one could discuss enactment; in the training manual one would delineate live supervision; and in the research manual, one would describe the experiential manner of gathering information about the value of the approach. Or if one values the mutuality of learning as key, they would discuss in the meta manual the process of the participants learning together. In the therapy manual, one would describe how to foster a mutual learning experience between therapist and family. In the training manual, there would be descriptions of how to build a community of mutual expertise with a flatter hierarchy, and in the research manual, one might describe a participatory research process of inclusion of research participants and researchers from the beginning of what to study, how, interpretation of results, and mutual participation in what, where, to whom, and how the findings are disseminated. And from this, it is natural to begin to see how families become part of the process, as all involved are participants and manualizers. This would differ from the top-down unilateral, reductionistic, and inaccurate view of how manuals are developed and used, and why when seen from that perspective, fail?

We need to begin to grapple with the multi-layered, multi-contextual nature of processual manuals that are embedded in a particular time, co-evolving within the geopolitical, economic, philosophical, and specialty forces that also considers the families, research participants, communities of foci, therapists, researchers, and trainers. Instead of falling into a reductionistic approach to deal with this complexity and offer a manual that is acontextual and limited in scope, governed by dualism and centring the expert in developing procedures to reach singular goals, we can turn to our multiple tools for guidance, for example, a systemic epistemology, complexity, and chaos theory, returning reductionism as one method for understanding parts and wholes, rather than the only method, and focusing on processes.

And perhaps the debate about manualization is simply a predictable and necessary step in the co-evolution of any field of study where there was once an explosion of ideas, a rapid application, a rise of discrete theoretical schools of thought, the grafting of different approaches (the time of integration). So now manualization is what is needed, as we have increased common footing/factors and yet can identify significant differences. Maybe this dialogue is a required stage in our growth, a formalizing (for this moment) who we are in distinction to who we are not (reductionistic only approaches) in the larger context of our world. We are articulating that to grow towards the needed amount of sun, water and nutrients this tree bends that way, another the other, another will not grow without attending to this and that....

It is time for thanking all the authors for their contribution to our knowledge: learning by writing, learning by teaching, and learning by doing. We want to also thank those individuals, couples, families, learners, and research participants who have helped shape the work offered in this handbook. We began our trip, and there were only three of us, sharing the same ideas that we tried to communicate, and over time we met extraordinary people. Luigi Boscolo, Gianfranco Cecchin, and now Rodolfo De Bernart and Mony El Kaim gave to us inspirations, friendship, and strength. Before them, we were inspired by such people as Gregory Bateson, Heinz von Foerster, Ludwig Bertalanffy, David Cooper, Franco Basaglia, Ronald Laing, Aaron Esterson, Lyman Wynne, Sal Minuchin, Peggy Penn, Lynn Hoffmann, Murray Bowen, Virginia Satir, Jay Haley, Ivan Borszormeni-Nagy, Braulio Montalvo, Luigi Onnis, Mara Selvini Palazzoli, Paul Watzlawich, Michael White, John Weakland, Don Jackson, Milton Erickson, James Framo, Carl Whitaker, Nathan Ackermann, Humberto Maturana, Tom Andersen, Francisco Varela, and many others. We met many of them. We learned with them; we conversed with them. They are still with us. They were teachers, therapists, philosophers, anthropologists, biologists, and more, and now many of them are myths. Did they have written manuals? No. But all of them accomplished the task to transmit powerful ideas and tools to us, and we want everyone to be well-prepared therapists, using methods that are renowned not only because they have been developed by geniuses but also because they have been manualized by those of us working day to day with those who come to us for help and they are recognized as valuable by those families and by science.

The marriage between the myths and ourselves will actualize the paradox we are promoting: the creatively systemic manualization of systemic therapy.

We started as three, and we finished the book as sixty-one. We hope that this exponential progression will lead to a better world in which systemic ideas will increasingly help our wounded humanity.

References

Carroll, K. M., & Nuro, K. F. (2002). One size cannot fit all: A stage model for psychotherapy manual development. *Clinical Psychology: Science and Practice, 9*(4), 396–406. https://doi.org/10.1093/clipsy.9.4.396

Mason, B. (2019). Re-visiting safe uncertainty: Six perspectives for clinical practice and the assessment of risk. *Journal of Family Therapy, 41*, 343–356.

Minuchin, S. (1980). Personal communication, Saba.

Shotter, J. (2015). Psychiatric diagnoses, 'thought styles', and ex post facto fact fallacies. *European Journal of Psychotherapy and Counselling, 17*(4), 1–14. https://doi.org/10.1080/13642537.2015.1094502

Stratton, P., Reibstein, J., Lask, J., Singh, R., & Asen, E. (2011). Competences and occupational standards for systemic family and couples therapy. *Journal of Family Therapy, 33*, 123–143.

Correction to: Handbook of Systemic Approaches to Psychotherapy Manuals

Mauro Mariotti, George Saba, and Peter Stratton

Correction to:
M. Mariotti et al. (eds.), *Handbook of Systemic Approaches to Psychotherapy Manuals*,
European Family Therapy Association Series,
https://doi.org/10.1007/978-3-030-73640-8

This book was inadvertently published with the wrong affiliation of Dr. Peter Stratton. The correct affiliation is:

Peter Stratton
Emeritus Professor of Family Therapy, Leeds Family Therapy and Research Centre, University of Leeds, UK

This has now been amended throughout the book to the inclusion of right affiliation.

The updated online versions of the chapters can be found at
https://doi.org/10.1007/978-3-030-73640-8_1
https://doi.org/10.1007/978-3-030-73640-8_3
https://doi.org/10.1007/978-3-030-73640-8_12
https://doi.org/10.1007/978-3-030-73640-8_17
https://doi.org/10.1007/978-3-030-73640-8_33
https://doi.org/10.1007/978-3-030-73640-8

This book was also inadvertently published without the "Abstracts" and first paragraph which is "Introduction" in chapter 12 which should come after the chapter name. The chapter format has been changed as:

Abstract The current chapter describes the DAN (digital, analogical, narrative) manualized intervention developed over the past two decades at the Iscra Institute in Modena, Italy. The name Iscra means spark, the title of a famous newspaper founded to free the Russian Empire divulgating social democratic ideas. The intervention is aimed at promoting family well-being by applying systemic therapeutic methods through working with couples. Over the years, the DAN model has been perfected by including widely used digital, analogical and narrative tools, and a pilot study has been undertaken by having trainee family therapists carry out the intervention on young families. The tools developed by the Iscra research team, such as the tri-dimensional genogram, the relational style profile couple interview (RSPc) and the better formed tale, are briefly described in this chapter and the reader will find a case report in the following chapter 'The DAN Model in Practice'. It is argued that the manualized DAN intervention provides a simple way of applying important and established systemic techniques that will promote family well-being by helping young couples develop reflexivity and resilience. The SCORE had been adapted avoiding pathological terms and administered three times, having the best result at the end of the process.

12.1 Introduction

Manualization is a way to organize and share meaningful data with methods that have been proved to work. We think of manualization as one of most interesting experiences students should encounter in their training to become psychotherapists. The Iscra Institute began its activity in the field of systemic psychotherapy in 1981, stemming from the Milan School of Boscolo and Cecchin. Up to this date, we have trained more than 1000 psychotherapists, wrote and edited different books as the 'Manual of Systemic and Relational Therapy' (Bassoli et al., 2004), conducted research in the field with our students and prepared a manualization with the use of the best instruments we found or invented during our experience. We called it 'DAN: Digital, Analogical and Narrative Model'. Many tools were invented and experienced in different contexts: The relational style profile (RSP) (Mariotti & Langella, 2011), the tridimensional genogram and the better formed tale (BFT).

Index

A
AccEPT clinic (Accessing Evidenced Based Psychological Therapies), 128, 135
Achenbach System of Empirically Based Assessment family of instruments, 457
Acknowledging responsibility for the conflict, 423
ACL scale, 117, 119
Active self-observation, 374
Adherence protocol, 40, 41, 47, 54
Adoption
  AAI, 270
  abandonment, 271
  adoptive nuclear family, 269
  attachment disorganization, 265
  behavioral problems, 274
  child's involvement, 266
  clinical experience, 268
  clinical treatment, 269
  international, 264
  life histories, 264
  post-adoption period, 265
  pre-adoptive period, 265
  relational patterns, 265
  traumatized child, 265
  treatment of traumatized children, 268
Adult Attachment Interview (AAI), 270, 274, 275, 303, 305
Adult-focused problems, 194, 300
AFT Family Therapy Outcomes Advisory Group, 321
Alienated responsibility, 423
Analogical, 218, 219, 224, 233
Andolfi, Maurizio, 471

Anorexia nervosa (AN), 349, 350, 352, 354, 357–359, 361
Anterior cingulate cortex (ACC), 486, 540
Anti-oppression curriculum, 522
Antiracism toolkit, 522
Approach-method-technique
  approach, 604
  organisational aspects, 604
  organisationally speaking, 604
  politically speaking, 604
  practice skills, 604
Asian Academy of Family Therapy, 465
Asian American families, 523
Asian families, 512
Assessment, WA, 303
Associated abnormal psychosocial situations, 178, 179, 188, 189
Association for Family Therapy (AFT), 317, 321, 328
Attachment-based family therapy, 267, 358
Attachment Interview (AAI), 270, 274, 275, 303, 305, 307
Attachment perspective, 575
Attachment theory, 43, 266, 267, 273, 277, 302, 305, 351, 471, 572, 574, 578, 581, 586, 621
Attending therapy, 202
Attribution, 31, 131, 133, 268, 270, 302
  circularity, 42
  LACSM, 40–44
  in psychotherapy, 42
  recognition of attachment processes in family discourse, 43–44
Authentic epistemological change, 375

Index

Autonomy, 187, 249, 255, 381, 383, 387, 436, 438, 440–443, 529, 583
Autonomy–intimacy, 440, 441
Axis 5, 178

B
Bassoli, Fabio, 468, 473
Bateson's epistemology, 451, 512–513
Beauty, 471
Beck Depression Inventory, 134
Behavioral Health Rounds curriculum, 515, 522
Behavioral science curriculum, 510, 521–523
  core beliefs, 516
  goal, 515
  number of hours of, 515
  objectives, 517
Behavioural couple therapy, 125–127, 134, 135, 343
Behavioural-systemic, 123–138
Beki's experience, 607–608
Better-formed story, 15, 216, 219, 220, 236
Better formed tale (BFT), 215, 217–221, 224, 225, 235, 236, 254–256
Biopsychosocial model, 469, 511
Black families, 512
Borderline personality disorder (BPD), 92, 143, 144
Brain neuroplasticity, 528
Brief Attachment-Base Intervention (BABI), 305
Brief Individual Psychodynamic Psychotherapy (BIPP), 283–286
Brief Strategic Family Therapy, 171, 191
Brief therapy, 29, 93, 161
Bulimia nervosa (BN), 354, 357–359

C
CAMHS Outcomes Research Consortium (CORC), 322
Caretaker, 453, 454
Case conceptualization
  counseling and therapy skills, 580
  guiding questions, 578
  SANE model, 578, 580
CFD tool, 476
Challenging techniques, 287, 288, 291, 294
"Change interpretations", 103
Child and adolescent, 177, 179, 180, 186, 282, 381, 540
Child and adolescent psychiatric disorders/ Axis 5, 178, 179
Child Behaviour Checklist (CBCL), 457

Childhood depression
  research project BIOMED, 283–285
  SIFT (see Systemic integrative family therapy (SIFT))
  systemic family therapy, 281
Child-oriented therapy, 181, 185
Children and Young People's Improving Access to Psychological Therapies (CYP IAPT), 322
Child's disturbed behaviour, 398, 404
Circular interviewing, 287, 288, 291, 294
Circularity, 42, 48, 101, 129, 132, 133, 164, 216, 375, 380, 389, 409
Client Attachment to Therapist Scale (CATS), 303
Client feedback, 127, 183
Clinical cases, 143, 147, 148, 150, 153, 154, 477, 486, 560, 561
Clinical practice, 53, 104, 108, 170, 171, 193, 217, 276, 283, 319, 356, 373, 467–478, 565, 574
Clinical system, 416
Clinicians' operating practices, 414
Coat of arms, 218, 220, 221, 225, 236, 237
Coevolutionary process, 559, 568
Cognitive behavioural couple therapy, 343
Cognitive behavioural therapy (CBT), 6, 39, 125, 127–129, 131, 134, 135, 300, 520
Cognitive science, 86
Collaborative learning, 76
  co-creating
    a collaborative community, 66
    a fluid manual, 67, 68
  collaboration, 67
  contextual forces, 68
  Coordinated Management of Meaning, 68
  feedback-informed systemic practices and collaborative inquiry, 66
  first-order learning, 69
  implicative forces, 69
  levels of learning, 69
  practical forces, 69
  prefigurative forces, 68
  roadmap, 67
  second-order learning, 69
  third-order learning, 70
  zeroth-order learning, 69
Collaborative practices, 64, 66, 74, 416
Collaborative supervision, 550
Collaborative therapy, 181, 550, 580
Collages, 386, 388, 468, 473, 475
Combatting anorexia, 353
Combining perspectives, 573–574

Committed, 528
Common factor (CF), 5, 302, 454, 456, 541, 572
Communication theory, 18, 453, 529, 547
Communist society, 545, 546
Community medicine residency, 509–510
Competences, 41, 56, 57, 494, 550, 622
Competencies, 172, 282, 469, 517, 528, 550, 552, 622
　definition, 494
　metacompetences, 57
　relational competence, 282
　systemic therapy, 56–57, 177–189
　therapist competence, 283
Complexity, 375, 376, 382, 383, 388
Complex systems, 64, 76
Complex thinking, 374
Conflictual dynamic, 411, 414, 424
Congruent communication, 543
Conjoint family drawing, 475, 476
Connectedness, 541
Conners' Teacher Rating Scale (CTRS), 457
Conscious purposiveness, 521
Constructionism, 16, 19, 35, 529
　See also Social constructionism
Constructivism, 6
Consulting pairs, 533
Containing emotions, 535, 536
Containment, 430
Content-focused approach, 512
Contextual awareness, 182
Conversational therapies, 529
Coordination meetings (CMs), 454–456
Core curriculum, 486
Counselling rooms, 162
Countertransference, 143, 152, 153
Couple and family therapy interventions, 201
Couple's absolute, 410, 411, 418
Couples and Family Therapy (CFT), 160, 162
Couples' crisis, 431–434
　life cycles, 435, 439, 443
　model, 439
Couples' interventions, 147
Couples' maintenance cycle, 133
Couples' stages
　autonomy–intimacy phases, 441
　differentiation, 442
　joining at a maturing level, 442–443
　merging, 441, 442
　reconciliation, 442
　resistance, 442
Couples therapy, 11, 427–429
　autonomy and intimacy, 436, 440
　behavioural therapy, 125, 126

clinical experience, 147
couples' crisis model, 439
CTfD, 126
dysfunctional communication scheme, 434
ERG, 127
Exeter Model (*see* Exeter Model)
family therapy, 343
financial problems, 435
friendships, 347
genogram, 344
giving and taking, 436
IAPT, 134
interpersonal relationships, 437
lack of shared visions and plans, 436
male and female responsibilities, 437
metaphorical objects and photos, 344
mother–child interaction, 435
partner's family of origin, 345–346
partner's individual history, 435
presence of children, 346
reciprocal intimate relationship, 343
relational system, 147
relationships with third parties, 438
stages in couple's development, 441 (*see also* Couple's stages)
18 systemic practices in, 17, 18
tension regulation, 429, 430
therapeutic process, 439, 440
"thread", 145
Couple therapy for depression (CTfD), 123–138
Couple therapy training, 545
Couple therapy treatment, 130, 343
Court Evaluation, 476
Courts, 375–377, 379, 380
COVID-19 crisis, 330
COVID-19 pandemic, 11, 523, 524
Creativity, 10, 11, 177, 185, 346, 427, 431, 539–540, 605, 620
Crisis interventions, 151
Critical moments, 68
Critical realist ideas, 187
Cultural context values achievement, 528
Cultural genogram, 135–138
Cultural influences, 288, 595
Culturally embedded anxiety, 528
Culture, 24, 39, 74–76, 323, 324, 326, 330, 594, 605, 607, 610, 619
Culturegram, 135
Current Relationship Interview (CRI), 305
Cybernetics, 3, 4, 6, 87, 89, 547
　first-order, 4, 85, 373
　principles, 81
　second-order, 4, 84, 373, 375, 544, 547

D

DAN (digital, analogical, narrative) model, 474
  aim, 218
  axioms, 217
  BFT, 215, 217
  DAN manual in practice, 219–221
  description, 219
  hypotheses, 218
  and ISCRA training, 238
  manualised therapeutic intervention, 218
  RCT, 241
  RSP, 215, 217
  session structure, 218, 219
  systemic therapy, 217
  tools
    BFT, 223, 224, 235, 236
    coat of arms, 236, 237
    2018 DAN structure, 225
    dichotomies, 227, 228
    2018 format, 224
    genogram, 225–226
    the 'Object and Letter' homework, 232
    RSP, 226, 227
    RSPc, 221
    systemic house drawing, 233–234
    tridimensional genogram, 222, 229–232
  as treatment pathway, 241
  tridimensional genogram, 215
  valuable manualised path, 242
DAN model in practice (case study)
  couple description, 242–243
  eight session
    discharge session, 257–258
    meta-communication session, 257
    Score-15, 257
    trigenerationality, 257
  family's resilience, 260–261
  fifth session
    restitution of the homework, 253–254
    Score-15, 254
  first session
    genogram, 243–244
    Score-15, 244–245
  fourth session, 250
    construct of mentalization, 251
    exercise of communication, 253
    object and letter, 253
    parental approaches, 251
    3D genogram, 251
    3D genogram of the future, 252–253
    3D genogram of the past, 251–252
    3D genogram of the present, 252
  second session
    house of the past, 246–247
    house of the present, 247–248
    RSP, 245, 246
    systemic drawing of the house, 246
  seventh session, 255–256
  sixth session, better formed tale, 254–255
  therapists and spouses, 258–260
  third session
    reversing roles at home, 250
    RSP feedback, 248–250
    workspace, 248
De Bernart, Rodolfo, 467–474, 477
"Demon", 410, 413
Demonization, 408, 411
Demonization phenomenon, 411
Demonizing narrative, 414, 415, 421, 424
Depression, 432
  and anxiety disorders, 126
  Beck Depression Inventory, 134
  behavioural couple therapy, 126
  conducting RCTs, 125
  CTfD, 126
  depressed patients, 128
  health expenditure, 124
  by NICE, 124, 125
Desire, 471
Developmental support, 453, 454
Developmental theory, 572
Diagnosis, 407
Diagnostic Statistic Manual (DSM), 3, 6
Dialogical relationships, 547
Dialogic psychology, 572
Dichotomies, 227, 228
Dichotomy-environment matrix structure, 221
Digital, 218, 219, 224, 229
Direct communication, 420
"Disease of relationships", 407
Disorganized attachment, 268
Double-bind model, 15, 16, 21, 377, 481
Drawing, 45, 71–73, 185, 233, 237, 246, 248–250, 256, 291, 346, 475–476
Dropout rate, 457, 458
Dutch therapists, 549
Dynamic-Maturational Model of Attachment and Adaptation-integrative family system treatment (DMM-FST), 303

E

Eating disorders, 349, 352
Eating disorders–focused family therapy (FT-ED), 350, 354, 357, 359, 363–365
Eating disorders-focused MFT (MFT-ED), 363–365
Educational program, 560
Education systems, 452

Effective communication, 451
EFTA National Family Therapy Organisations research group, 323
Emotionally focussed couple therapy, 343
Emotions, 380, 384–389, 430
Empathic abilities, 301
Enactments, 287, 288, 292
"Encheiridion", 408
Enlightened institutions, 527–528
Epistemic breakdown, 451
Epistemic trust, 451, 452
Epistemologically based systemic therapy, 4
Epistemology, 375
Epistemology change, 528
Epistobabble, 5, 6
Ethical, 182
European Association of Psychotherapy (EAP), 465, 468
European Family Therapy Association (EFTA), 2, 83, 465, 468–470, 473
European Family Therapy Association Training Institutes Chamber (EFTA-TIC), 470
European psychotherapist, 469
The European Psychotherapy Act, 465
Evidence-based medicine, 6
Evidence-based practice (EBP), 360, 361, 365
Evidence Based Practice Unit (EBPU), 322
Evidence-based psychotherapy, 6, 541
Evidence-based research, 300, 302, 541
Evidence-based systemic therapy, 63
Evidence-based treatments, 520
Exeter Model
  AccEPT clinic, 128, 135
  behavioural change, 133
  behavioural-systemic couple therapy, 123
  circularity, 124, 128, 131–133
  creation of manual, 125
  IAPT, 134
  IEM, 124, 134–136
  manualisation, 123, 124
  NICE recommendations, 127
  systemic-behavioural circularity, 131
  trainees and external clinicians, 138
Experiences in Close Relationships Scale (ECRS), 303
Experiential-Learning Cycle, 480
Experiential-Learning Model, 483
Experiential median group, 536, 541
Experiential teaching, 480, 545
Expertise, 377
Expert reference groups (ERGs), 127, 128
Explicit mentalization, 304
Exploring family history, 287, 288, 291, 292, 294

Extensive experiences, 532
Externalization, 292, 355, 423, 535
Externalizing responsibility, 24, 57, 183–184, 199, 200, 206, 292, 355, 423, 457, 532, 535, 540
Eye Movement Desensitization and Reprocess (EMDR), 168

F
Family, 141, 145, 146, 148, 154
Family-based treatment (FBT), 350, 356, 359, 608
Family counseling services agency, 450
Family dynamics, 392, 393, 395
Family functioning, 119, 392, 398
Family intervention, 92
Family life cycle, 287, 288, 291, 292
Family meal session in FT-ED, 355, 356
Family mediation, 476
Family medicine, 509
Family of origin, 414, 416, 421
Family Oriented Primary Care: A Manual for Medical Providers, 512
Family physician, 507–509, 512, 516
Family psychotherapy, 103
Family system, 143–146, 151, 153, 512, 522
Family Systems Medicine, 511
Family therapists, 142, 143, 145, 146, 150, 151, 465
Family therapy, 4, 7, 44–46, 101, 143, 146, 343, 347
  Active Experimentation, 481
  analogic tools, 470, 472–474
  conjoint family drawing, 475, 476
  Court Evaluation, 476
  criticisms of manuals, 263
  EFTA-TIC challenges, 470
  epistemology, 84
  families as treatment resource, 352
  Family Mediation, 476
  holistic and sequential intelligence, 475
  images, 471–476
  instrument of evaluation, 477
  interventions, 263
  manualization (*see* Manualisation (manualization))
  manuals, 470
  non-verbal channels, 474
  parental task, 353
  relational hypotheses, 477
  systemic theory, 472
  therapeutic engagement, 353
  training, 472, 473
  treatment manuals, 263

Family Therapy for Anorexia Nervosa
(FT-AN), 362, 363, 607
Family therapy for bulimia nervosa
(FT-BN), 358
Family therapy teams, 171
Family therapy techniques, 573
Family therapy training program, 499
   Core Curriculum, 486
   overview, 485
   road map, 499
   training, 486
Family Therapy Unit (FTU), 284, 557, 566, 568
   characteristics, 559
   definition, 558
"Family well-being", 387
Feedback, 64, 532
Feedback-informed systemic therapy, 64, 66, 70, 76
Feedback-informed treatment (FIT), 166, 170
Few-sessions therapy, 87, 98
Fifteen-minute therapy segments, 49
Financial resources, 170
First- and second-order principles, 539
First-order cybernetics, 85, 98
First-order learning, 69
Fluctuating therapies, 381–384
Fluid manuals
   collaborative learning, 66
   collaborative practice-based research, 64
   for feedback-informed systemic therapy, 70, 77
   FITS, 63, 65
   as a navigation tool in complex systems, 64–65
   social systems, 64
Focusing on strengths and positives, 287, 288, 291
"Forced assignment", 376, 377, 379
Friendships, 347
From silent and cautious to open and relaxed, 458
Functional Family Therapy (FFT), 191

G

Gender violence, 409
General Systems Therapy, 83, 95, 547
Generational boundaries, 383
Genogram, 91, 203, 209, 344, 471, 473–475, 560
   administration, 226
   classical structure, 225
   conventional symbols, 225
   as 'opening' tool, 225
   purpose, 226
   systemic psychology, 225
   use in practice, 225, 226
Giommi, Daniela Giommi, 471
Giommi, Eugenio Roberto, 471
Global analysis, 395
Gold standard' treatments, 124, 125
Google group, 329, 331
Greek health services, 557
Group supervision, 533, 537

H

Heraldic shield, 474
High-conflict family environment, 144
High-intensity psychological intervention, 126, 135
High level of reflexivity, 69, 76
Hikikomori, 381, 384, 385
Histograms, 333
Holistic intelligence, 475
Human Systems, 474
Human Systems Therapy (HST)
   biological level human systems, 85
   definition of the open system, 84
   effectiveness, 98
   epistemology, 84
   human intelligence
      aggression, 86
      control subsystem, 85
      increase of order and variety, 87
      interaction with the environment subsystem, 85
      modelling subsystem, 86
      paleologic thinking, 86
   method of systemic therapy, 97
   multilevel intervention, 98
   reality, 84
   steps of development, 82, 83
   steps of manualisation
      appropriate techniques, 92
      categorization, 90
      difficulties in therapy, 94
      genogram, 91
      goals of therapy, 89
      history of main steps, 87–88
      hypothesis, 90
      joining, 88–89
      monitoring, 93
      multilevel intervention (*see* Multilevel intervention, HST)
      over-positive description, 88, 89, 92
      presentation, 94
      therapeutic alchemy, 93

Index

therapeutic characteristics, 98
uses, 81
Hypothesis, 102
   conversational functions, 102
   "pillars of the hypothesis", 108
   PQCH, 111
   structural characteristics, 102
   systemic hypothesis, 106, 107
   therapist's, 102
   "truth"/"usefulness", 102
Hypothesizing process, 101

I

Identity narrative, CMs, 455
"Images and words in family therapy", 471
Images in therapy, 386
Implementation research, 191
Implicit mentalization, 304
Implicit Relational Knowing (IRK), 474
Improving Access to Psychological Therapies (IAPT), 126, 134, 135, 138
"Incurred cost", 152–154
Indirect communication, 420
Individual assessment, 303
Individual case assessment, 145
Individual functioning, 111, 119
Individual phenomenological, 111
Individual therapy, 146, 147, 152, 382, 384
Inductive thematic analysis, 458
Infant psychotherapy, 391, 392, 394
Infra-family, 409
Institute of Family and Systemic Psychotherapy, 527
Institute of Family Therapy London, 527
Institute of Relational Therapy (I.Te.R), 391
18 Instructions, 20–35
Integrative systemic three-column model
   exception formulation, 197
   interventions, 193, 198, 199 (*see also* Interventions, systemic therapy)
   problem formulation, 194–197
   therapy stages, 199
Interactional schemata, 86
Intercultural Exeter Model (IEM), 124, 134–136
Intergenerational couple therapy, 344, 347
Intergenerational reconciliation, 345
Intermingling movements, 543
International Association of Systemic Mediators, 468
International Family Therapy Association, 465
Internet newsletter, 470
Internet resources, 317, 328, 330, 334, 381, 623, 625

Interpersonal reconstructive therapy, 147
Interpretative Phenomenological Analysis (IPA), 583
Intersession tasks, 287, 288, 291, 292, 294
Intervention codification, 104, 115
"Intervention for change", 376, 377, 379
Intervention manuals, 460
Intervention methods, 381
Intervention models, 150
Interventions, 198, 199
   in schizophrenics, 83
   systemic therapy
      being courageous, Sue's challenge, 207
      building on exceptions, 206, 207
      building support, 209
      dilemmas to the therapists' experience, 210, 211
      disengagement, 209, 210
      externalizing the problem, 206
      interactional reframing, 206
      managing resistance, 207, 208
      parenting, 208, 209
      pinpointing strengths, 206
      relapse management, 210
      self-regulation, Tom's challenge, 207
Intimacy, 436, 437, 440, 441, 443
Intrapsychic intervention, 91
"Investigative function", 102
"Irreverence", 408
Isomorphic systems, 558
Isomorphism, 535, 543

J

Joining and engagement techniques, 287, 288, 291
Joint family drawing, 386, 388
Journal of Family Therapy (2014), 5
Journals, 468
Judge expert, 376, 378
Judiciary-legal system, 377

L

LACSM, *see* Leeds Attributional Coding System Manual (LACSM)
Language practices, 183
Latin X families, 523
Leadership designed to include everyone, 458
Learning activities, 496
Learning Assessment, 502
Learning-centered and outcome-based methods, 549

Learning hub, 162, 163
  assessment strategy, 165
  practice, 164
  supervision, 165, 167
  training students, 164, 165
  working relationships with professionals, 163
Learning Outcomes (LO), 483, 494–496, 499
Leeds Attributional Coding System Manual (LACSM), 40–43
Leeds Family Therapy & Research Centre (LFTRC), 263, 333, 469
  adherence protocol, 40, 41, 47, 54
  comprehensive systemic therapy, 46, 47
  family therapy, 44–46
  fifteen-minute therapy segments, 49
  LACSM, 40–43
  recognition of attachment processes, 43, 44
  research, 47–52
  SCORE Index of Family Functioning, 40, 41
  SFT manual development, reflections on, 54–56
  structure of manual, 50, 51
  systemic approaches, 57, 58
  systemic therapists, competences of, 56, 57
  in training, 53, 54
Leeds Systemic Family Therapy Manual (LSFTM), 171
Le fil rouge, 473
Legal dispute, 407
Legal system, 412, 413
"Legal truce", 418
Legislation, 470
LGBT relationships, 331
Liddle's development, 510
Lifebook, 272
Life cycle phase, 143, 148–150, 152–154
Likert scales, 333
Linkage Curriculum training, 522
Liquid Modernity, 469
Litigation-based approach, 416
Live supervision, 535
Living human systems (LHS), 557
Long-term therapy, 582, 583
Low level of reflexivity, 69, 75

M

Macrosystems, 377, 379, 412, 413, 416, 417
Maieutic questioning, 546
Malfunctions, 407
Manualization, *see* Manualisation (manualization)

Manualisation (manualization), 15, 263, 264, 317, 374, 425, 618
  AccEPT clinic, 128
  authoritarian, 624
  co-evolution, 626
  in cognitive behavioral therapy, 81
  competences, 622
  DAN model (*see* DAN (digital, analogical, narrative) model)
  developmental process, 620
  epistemological bases, 621
  evolution, 622
  Exeter Model, 124
  family functioning, 9
  family process, 9
  family systems therapy, 81
  family therapy sessions, 101
  fluctuating therapies, 382
  format of the manual, 619
  function, 621
  HST (*see* Human Systems Therapy (HST))
  integrative approach, 621
  at Iscra Institute, 216, 219
  Italian schools of psychotherapy, 466
  from LFTRC, 40, 41 (*see also* Leeds Family Therapy & Research Centre (LFTRC))
  Milan model, 381
  need of, 20
  procedures and processes, 8
  procedures towards process management, 9
  process-oriented research, 9
  in psychotherapy, 625
  purpose of therapy, 111
  research trials using HST, 95
    diploma in systems therapy, 96
    discharge of schizophrenics, 95
    elimination of hashish use, 96
    reduction of psychotic symptoms in schizophrenics, 96
    residential house, 95
    sessions of therapy, 97
    sessions on nonpsychotic psychiatric cases, 97
  root of, 20
  "scriptural", 624
  systemic approaches, 5, 81
  systemic hypothesis, 104
  in systemic perspective, 303
  systemic quadrilateral, 104
  systemic therapies, 191
  therapeutic process, 103, 104
  time spent in therapy, 82
  for training, 123

Index

validation, 6
viable, 622
"Manualisation of the procedure", 392
Manualised approach, 603
    anchor, 603
    delivering, 601
    disciplines, 598
    independent contracted work, 598
    MFT model, 603
    multidisciplinary mental health staff service, 595
    NVR, 598–600
    PPRR, 596
    practice, 597
    pressures, 600
    structure, 597
    systemic concepts, 601
    therapists, 598, 602
    training, 596
    treatment approaches, 596
Manualised intervention, 10
Manualised psychotherapy, 282
Manualised systemic family therapy, 63
    See also Systemic integrative family therapy (SIFT)
Manualised therapies, 541
Manualised training program, 479, 496
Manuals, 159, 177, 530, 531, 541
    approaches, 2
    in clinical teaching and training, 1
    and competence specifications, 622, 623
    cookery recipes, 2
    creation of manuals, 10
    criteria, 622
    evaluation of work, 1
    forms, 2
    good manuals, 2
    government business, 2
    instructions for assembling, 2
    manual development, 11
    manualisation, 620
    prospects for future development, 623
    purposes, 1
    repair manuals, 2
    research and training, 10
    research manuals, 619
    research-practice intersection, 2
    systemic manuals, 618
    systemic therapy clinic model, 167
        financial resources, 170
        professional relationships, 167–170
        progress report, 167
    training manuals, 11
    use in clinical practice, 11
    use in RCTs, 2

    YES manualisation, 620
Mariotti, Mauro, 473
Marte Meo (MM), 453, 454
Marte Meo and Coordination Meetings (MAC)
    comparison of SAU group, 458
    effectiveness, 457
    flowchart, 449
    goals, 448
    implementation, 459, 460
    overview, 448
    RCT, 458
    values, 460
Matching, 302
Maudsley family therapy
    clinical practice, 356
    early development, 350
    for eating disorders, 365
    manuals, 363, 365
    meal session, 355
    MFT-BN, 357
    phased nature of treatment, 351
    structural family therapy, 354
    treatment, adolescent AN, 350
    treatment model, 351
Maudsley originated FBT, 51
Meeting coordinator, 455
Meeting Parents, 163, 169
Meeting Professionals, 162
Meetings, 168
Mental health, 6, 39, 160, 177–179, 186, 282, 407, 486, 559, 566, 595
Mentalization, 304
    clinical process in psychotherapy, 305
    explicit, 304
    implicit, 304
    interpersonal component, 304
    pseudo, 304
    psychotherapeutic mechanisms, 305
    reflective functioning, 304
    reflective skills, 306
    RF, 304
    self-reflective component, 304
    systemic relational perspective, 306
Mentalization-Based Family Therapy (MBFT), 305
Mentalization Based Therapy (MBT), 305
Mentalizing, 304
Metacognition, 307, 308
Metacognitive Assessment Scale (MAS), 307
Metacompetences, 57
Meta-manual, 514
Metaphors, 386, 388, 389, 468, 579
Micro-level studies, 584
    progress of therapy, 584
Mikhail Bakhtin's theory, 547

Milan Approach, 373, 381
Mind-reading, 21
Minister of Education, University, and Research (MIUR), 466
Mirroring, 25, 391, 394–396
Model's systemic circularity, 129
Morphogenesis, 27, 217, 242
Morphostasis, 27, 217
Motivational Interviewing, 520
Movies, 468, 472, 475
Multidimensional Family Therapy, 191, 510
Multidirectional partiality, 455
Multi-disciplinary team (MDT), 352
Multi-epistemological systemic approach, 186, 187
Multi-family therapy (MFT), 598
   adherence research, 361
   clinical standards, 364
   conceptual developments, 360
   development of manuals, 359
   effect of adherence, 361
   formulation in manuals, 363–364
   FT-ED, 357
   intensive context, 357
   intensive day treatment programme, 358
   meta-analysis, 361
   training workshops, 359
   use of treatment manuals, 360
Multi-family therapy for anorexia nervosa (MFT-AN), 356, 357
Multi-family therapy for bulimia nervosa (MFT-BN), 357, 358
Multi-layered interdependence, 539
Multilevel assessment, 154
Multilevel intervention, HST
   family intervention, 92
   intervention in couples, 92
   intrapsychic intervention, 91
   relationships with core problem, 92
Multimodal intervention, 383
Multi-orientation clinical practices, 171
Multiproblematic families, 144
"Multipurpose" instruments, 270
Multisystemic therapy, 191
Mutual demonization, 410, 412
Mutual emotional regulation, 430

N
Narrative, 4, 6, 7, 218, 219, 224, 235–237
Narrative function, 102
Narrative perspective, 571
Narrative techniques, 292
Narrative theory, 544
National health system, 465

Negentropic effect, 101
Neural plasticity, 542
Neurosciences, 573
Neutrality, 455
"New images for family therapy training", 471
NICE (the National Institute of Health and Clinical Excellence), 124–130
NICE-recommended behavioural therapies, 127
Nonjudgmental approach, 385
Non-verbal channels, 474, 475
Non-violent resistance (NVR), 610
   components, 613
   manual, 611
   principles and practices, 611
   training, 612
   usefulness, 611
Not knowing stance, 549
Nuclear family, 412, 418, 419, 421

O
"Observational experience for research purposes", 393
"Observer assessment encoding" barrier, 153
Online, 163, 168, 317, 318, 321, 335, 522, 609
Online medical education platforms, 522
Open dialogue perspectives, 456
"Operational protocol", 391
Optimism, 227
Orientation, 550
Over-positive description, 88, 89, 92, 93

P
Paleologic, 81, 83, 87, 94, 98
Paleologic thinking, 86
Parallel stages, 575
Parental alienation, 412, 417, 419
Parental anxiety, 354–355
Parent–child attachment bonds, 265, 274
Parent Development Interview (PDI), 270, 271, 274, 275, 305
Parenting, 208, 209
Parents, 448, 451, 452, 454–459
Partial manual, 1
Patients' case formulation, 153
Patient-Therapist Adult Attachment Interview (PT-AAI), 303
PDM 2 (*Psychoanalytical Diagnostic Manual*), 6
Pedagogy of the Oppressed, 511
Personal and professional learning experiences, 538
Personal development, 531

Index

Personality disorders, 143–145, 149–151, 154
Personal therapy, 531
Person-of-the therapist training (POTT), 551
Pessimism, 227
Philosophical basis, 4
Photograph choice, 225, 229
Photographic genogram, 471, 474, 475
Physician-family relationship, 516, 519
Play Assistant Introduction Program, 163, 169
Political and philosophical narratives, 529
Positive connotation, 93
Postcommunist society, 545
Post-separation conflict, 407, 408, 412, 420, 424
    and intra-family/gender violence, 409
    obsessive ideation, 415
    separation, as an onset of trauma, 410
Practical forces, 69
Practical learning (PL)
    assessment, 498
    assessment criteria, 500, 501
    Bloom's taxonomy, 483
    demonstration phase, 484
    educational objective, 483
    first-person activities, 482
    intensive and dedicated program, 482
    manual, 482, 498
    steps, 484
    tasks vs. LO, 484
    taxonomy, 483
    theory, 497
    training process, 481
    and TT's, 487–494
Practice, 618–623
Practice-based evidence' approach, 123, 126
Practice Based Evidence Based Practice, 63, 64, 76–78, 624
Prevailing relational pattern (PRP), 113, 114
Prevention process, 224
Primary care physicians
    Bateson's epistemology, 513
    behavioral science curriculum, 510
        core beliefs, 516
        goal, 515
        number of hours of, 515
        objectives, 517
    community medicine residency, 509
    COVID-19 pandemic, 523, 524
    developing caring and trusting relationships, 517
    digital and analogic communication, 518
    dissemination of manualised curriculum, 522
    epistemology, 510, 511, 513, 514
    evolution of medicine in United States, 508
    family medicine, 509
    foster a reflective, engaged participation within the system, 517
    manualised training and therapy, 518, 519
    manualising, 514
    manuals, 511
        language in, 513
    pedagogy, 511
    physician-family relationship, 516
    program evaluation, 521, 522
    recurrent challenges
        desire to fix, 520, 521
        evidence-based treatments, 520
        reductionism, 519, 520
    UCSF SFGH family, 509
Problem-maintaining behaviour patterns, 193, 199
Problem-maintaining contextual factors, 199
Problem-solving, 286–288, 291, 292, 294
Problems-possibilities and resources-restraints (PPRR), 594
Process research, 166
Professional competencies, 469, 533
Professional relationships, 167–170
Progressive questions for the construction of the hypothesis (PQCH), 111
Progress of therapy
    assessed stories, 585
    coherence enhanced, 584
    narrative assessment tool, 585
    tools assess progress, 585
Proto-manual, 1
Provocation, 385, 388, 389
Pseudo-mentalization, 304, 308, 309
Psychiatric reform, 557
Psychoanalysis, 540
Psychoanalytic couple therapy, 343
Psychological therapies, 349
Psychopathological processes, 143, 152
Psychosomatic family, 349
Psychotherapeutic approach, 142
Psychotherapeutic intervention, 143
Psychotherapeutic process, 432
Psychotherapy, 3, 5, 276, 300, 465, 557, 560, 571, 574
    beneficial effects, 300
    childhood depression, 283
    effectiveness and manualisation, 299, 300, 302
    manual, 141, 142, 144, 145, 147, 150, 153
    research, 282
    theory, 568
    trainees, 480
Public education, 559
Public psychotherapy, 559, 566
Public sector, 559, 562

Q

Qualitative Criteria for Coherence in Narratives (QCCN) tool, 580
Qualitative study, 584
Questionnaire, 501

R

Racism, 508, 509, 516, 517, 523, 524
Radical constructivism, 529
Randomized clinical trial (RCT), 241
Randomized controlled trials (RCT), 299, 458
Reality-based collaboration, 301
Recognition Index, 249
Reconciliation, 442
Reductionistic evidence-based research, 8
Redundancies, 414
Reflective functioning (RF), 304, 305, 307
Reflective Functioning through the Parent Development Interview (RF/PDI), 307
Reflective function in the family (RFF)
  assessment, reflective skills, 306
  coding card, 309
  coding completed card, 310
  criteria for coding reflective statements, 307
  data table in Excel, 310
  vs. family sessions, 311
  family therapy of MAP, 306
  implicit mentalization, 309
  MAS, 307
  mentalization assessment, 306
  non-generic mental state, 307
  purpose, 306
  RF/PDI, 307
  systemic family treatment, 310–313
  use, 309
Reflective self (RS), 307
Reframing, 16, 30, 89, 93, 183, 205, 206, 288, 291, 292, 540
The "Regulation D.M. 11712 n.509", 465
Relational contextual lens, 533
Relational disorders, 144
Relational folder (RF), 104, 108–110
Relational generator, 111, 113
Relational hypotheses, 477
Relational phenomenological, 112
Relational psychotherapy, 141
Relational style profile (RSP), 215–217, 219, 220, 226–230, 245, 246
Relational style profile couple interview (RSPc), 216, 220, 221
Relational-Systemic model, 477
Relational therapy, 4, 514
Reliable Change Index (RCI), 458
Renunciation, 383
Research, 618–620
  DAN model (*see* DAN (digital, analogical, narrative) model)
  evidence-based research, 300, 302, 541
  fluid manuals, 63–66, 70, 77
  LFTRC (*see* Leeds Family Therapy & Research Centre (LFTRC))
  manuals, 362, 511, 619, 620, 625 (*see also* Manualisation (manualization))
  project, 128, 134, 141, 148, 161, 170, 178–179, 241, 333, 582, 619
  research-practice gap, 2
  research project BIOMED, 283–285
  triangular mirroring, 391, 394–403
Residency training, 509
Residential house, 83, 95
Resonance, 430
Resource-Based Family Therapy (RBFT), 497
Responsible, 528
Rigour and imagination, 594
Role-played family system, 532
Role playing, 387, 473, 474
Role reversal, 219, 220, 225, 229
Romanian trainers, 548
Rules of communication, 420

S

Sceno Test, 271
Schedule of Therapy Cataloguing (SCT), 119
Schismogenesis, 412
Schismogenetic couple, 411
Schismogenetic dynamic, 418, 419
Schismogenetic process, 411, 412
School-based intervention
  CMs, 454–456
  epistemic breakdown, teacher and the parents, 452
  epistemic trust, 451
  MM, 453, 454
  psychological interventions, 456
  psychosocial interventions, 456
  teachers and parents relationship, 455, 458
School-home system, 459
Scientific approach, 164
Scientific thinking, 164
SCL 90 scale, 117
SCORE AFT web, 321
SCORE Index of Family Functioning, 40, 41
SCORE outcome measure, 219–221, 225

Index   641

Second-order cybernetics, 18, 81, 85, 98, 103, 375, 544, 547, 549, 552
Second-order learning, 69
Secure base, 541
Seeing family subgroups, 287, 288, 294
Self, 383, 384
Self-correcting systems, 480
Self correction, 558
Self-healing, 375
Self-observation, 424
Self-organization, 558
Self-reflection, 534, 537
Self-reinforcing feedback, 64
Sequential intelligence, 475
Serotonin Selective Reuptake Inhibitors, 520
Services as usual (SAU), 457, 458
Sharing specialists' expertise, 470
Short-term Mentalization and Relational Therapy (SMART), 305
Signature themes, 551
Skill development and supervision, 534
Skype, 330
SLC 90 scale, 119
Slovenian values, 530
Social and cultural context, 529
Social constructionism, 48, 164, 178, 180, 186, 187, 539, 546, 547
Social constructionist approach, 55, 545, 546, 548, 549, 552
Social-constructionist knowledge-making theory, 546
Social constructivism, 123
Social learning, 146
Socratic debate, 546
Socratic thinking, 546
Softa-s version, 118, 119
Solidarity, 471
Solution-focused techniques, 287, 288, 294
Spatial metaphor, 547
"Standardised interactive sequence", 392
Step-by-step training, 496
Stern, Daniel, 474
Stimulated Recall, 519
Story Stem Assessment Profile, 271
Strategic therapy, 4
Structural family therapy, 4
Structured feedback protocols, 541
"Structured intervention", 391, 394
Supervised and unsupervised therapies, 537
Surprise-mild praise-doubts response, 29
Sutter-Eyberg Student Behaviour Inventory – Revised (SESBI-R), 458

Symptomatologic expressions, 415
Synthetic, systemic-experiential program, 560
   academic content, 562
   building process, 560
   contract question, 564
   developmental stages, 563
   education, 562
   educational program, 563
   genogram, 560, 564
   mental health professionals, 562
   personal genogram, 561
   principles, 562
   subgroups, 563
   supervisor-supervisee relationship, 561
   systemic thinking, 561
   therapy, 562
   treatment and management, 561
System family therapy, 303
Systemic approaches, 4, 5
Systemic assessment, 148
Systemic-behavioural central intervention, 124
Systemic circularity, 129, 131
Systemic Clinical Outcome and Routine Evaluation-15 (SCORE-15), 166
   administering measures to families, 321
   content and form at different stages/locations, 321
   couples version, 333
   data entry Excel files, 322
   Google Group materials, 329
   guide to, 322
   international applications, 324
   introduction and scoring, 322
   IT version, 333
   nomenclature, 319
   outcome measure, 319, 326, 329, 332
   outcome monitoring with couples and families, 322
   process, 319–321
   publications, 325, 326
   questions and answers, 329
   research projects, 333
   SCORE AFT web, 321
   scoring template, 322
   suggested changes to, 332
   therapist's scale, 117–119
   translation procedure, 322–324
   UK survey responses, 328, 329
   user feedback, 326–328
      email, 330
      Google groups, 330
      media, 331, 332

Systemic Clinical Outcome and Routine Evaluation (SCORE) Index of family functioning, 318
  See also Systemic Clinical Outcome and Routine Evaluation-15 (SCORE-15)
Systemic Condition of Family Alienation (SCFA), 412
Systemic couple (and family) therapy, 18
Systemic epistemology, 626
Systemic ERG, 127
Systemic Experiential Model, 480, 481
Systemic Family and Couples Therapy (SFCT), 329
Systemic family therapy (SyFT), 39, 51, 317, 320
  theory, 547–549, 553
  training, 528
Systemic house drawing
  analogical mode, 233
  goal, 234
  tridimensional genogram, 233
  use in practice, 233, 234
Systemic hypothesis, 102, 104, 106–108, 110, 114
Systemic ideas, 3, 4, 55, 179, 188, 601, 623
Systemic integrative family therapy (SIFT)
  family therapy issues, Athens team
    child's depression, 293
    circular interviewing, 294
    collaboration with external systems, 292
    dialogue, 292
    emotional atmosphere, 294
    family features, 290
    interventive techniques, 292
    post-session notes, 291–293
    preoccupation, 294
    supervision main issues, 290
    therapeutic process, 289–290
    transgenerational conflicts, 294
  manual, 286–288
  most frequently used SIFT techniques, 291
  therapeutic process, 287
  therapists reflections, 293, 294
  usefulness, SIFT manual, 295
Systemic interventions, 127, 193
  systemic-behavioural, 127
  systemic-empathic, 127, 128
Systemic manuals, 306, 448, 454, 455, 457, 618, 622, 623, 627
Systemic model, 263
"Systematic observation", 391
Systemic perspective, 576, 621

Systemic practices, 17, 18, 125, 127, 130, 529, 572
Systemic Practice Scale (SPS), 57
Systemic practitioner, 3
Systemic psychotherapy, 128, 529, 539, 548, 549, 552
Systemic quadrilateral, 104, 110, 111
Systemic racism, 523
Systemic-relational
  assessment, 148, 152
  interventions, 146
  model, 146
  therapist, 146
Systemic research, 9, 10
Systemic supervisors, 541
Systemic theory, 7, 379, 393, 394
Systemic therapeutic conversation, 221
Systemic therapy, 4, 7, 10, 103, 104, 113, 191, 216, 572, 574, 620, 627
  assessment contracting, 202
  and attachment theories, 343
  children in family therapy, 194
  competences, map of, 177, 178
    Axis 5, 178
    consists of, 188
    framework, 179, 180, 182–185
    limitations of research, 188, 189
    multi-epistemological systemic approach, 186, 187
    research, 178, 179
  DAN model, 217
  DAN tools, 217, 218 (*see also* DAN (digital, analogical, narrative) model)
  engagement, 194
  evidence-base, 194
  exception formulation, 204, 205
  formulation, 194
  giving directives, 194
  goal setting, 194
  indicators of change, 117
  interventions (*see* Interventions, systemic therapy)
  problem formulation, 202–204
  social worker for therapy, 202
  treatment contracting, 205
Systemic therapy clinic model, 159–161
  building, 161, 162
  learning hub, 162, 163
    assessment strategy, 165
    practice, 164
    supervision, 165, 167
    training students, 164, 165

Index 643

working relationships with
professionals, 163
manual, 167
financial resources, 170
professional relationships, 167–170
progress report, 167
Systemic thinking, 374
Systemic training, 531, 541, 568
Systemic treatments, 300

T
Taking Care of Adoption (TCA)
adoption, 269
and attachment theory, 266
development of a manual, 273
ecological framework, 271
goal of treatment, 267, 268
phases and duration, 273
systemic family therapy approach, 266
Tavistock-based Systemic Family Therapy
Research Centre (FTSRC), 333
Teacher, 451, 453–459
Teacher Satisfaction questionnaires, 504
Teacher's Report Form (TRF), 457
Teaching Systems Therapy, 83
Teamwork, 171
Tension regulation, 429, 430
Thematic analysis, 596
Theoretical concept/constructed
narratives, 540
Theoretical concepts, 529
Theoretical training (TT), 480, 482, 483, 486,
487, 494, 496–498
Therapeutic alchemy, 93
Therapeutic alliance, 118, 119, 351
Therapeutic applications, 318–320, 323, 326,
328, 332, 334
Therapeutic conversation, 275, 276
"Therapeutic couple", 417
Therapeutic effectiveness, 550, 551
Therapeutic encounter, 384
Therapeutic process, 216, 429
co-construction, systemic hypothesis, 108
coding and timing of interventions, 114
contact phase, 104
deconstruct and decode, 106
expansion, 106
family's trigenerational history, 109
intervention's efficacy, 115, 116
manualisation, 104
outcomes, 116–118
phases, 104, 105
purpose of manualising therapy, 111

"restructuring", 107
RF, 108, 109
Softa, 118
whole process, 104
Therapeutic relationships, 103, 373, 376, 384,
536, 540, 541
Therapeutic skills, 142, 534
Therapeutic style, 529
Therapeutic system, 540
Therapeutic teams, 530, 535
Therapist intervention, 145, 151, 153
Therapist role
guiding questions, 581
questions, 581
systemic model, 581
The Therapist's Map (*La Mappa del
Terapeuta*), 141, 142, 148, 155
Therapist's therapy, 566, 567
Therapy cataloging, 116, 119
Therapy effectiveness, 153
Therapy interventions, 147
Therapy process, 579
Therapy setting
emotional level, 575
initial contact, 575
members function, 575
personal growth, 574
Therapy team, 50, 55, 171, 281, 538
Third-order learning, 70
Third wave, 125
Three-column formulation, 197, 204, 211
Tom and Sue's exceptional episodes, 197
Tom and Sue's problematic episodes, 195
Three-column framework, 199
Three-column problem formulation, 194–195
Three-dimensional genogram, 219, 474
Three-generational subsystems, 392
Time and future, 471
Trainee-focused training (TFT)
definition, 548
dialogical relationships, 547
general specifications, 551, 552
in international context, 549–551
Mikhail Bakhtin's theory, 547
personal growth stages specifications, 553
present stage, 553, 554
in Romanian context, 548, 549
second-order cybernetics, 544
social constructivism, 546, 547
systemic family therapy theory, 547
theoretical training specifications, 553
Trainees epistemology changing
group supervision, 537, 538
therapeutic teams, 536

Trainees exploration, 532
Trainees report, 540
Training, 618–620
   approaches, 470
   clinic, 623
   codifying the training program, 511
   couple therapy training, 545
   development of manuals, 11
   evidence-based manualised training, 466
   family therapy training program, 44–46, 485, 486, 499
   in the Institute of Family Therapy of Florence, 477
   ISCRA training and DAN manualisation, 238
   LSFT manual, use, 53, 54
   manualised training program, 479, 496
   TFT (*see* Trainee-focused training (TFT))
   See also Training course
Training course, 527
   degrees and aims, 531, 532
   learning process, 533
   narrative, 541
   personal contexts, 532
   session guidance, 533, 534
   specifications, 531
   systemic psychotherapy, 529, 530
   therapeutic experience, 530, 531
   therapeutic teams formations, 530
Training Evaluation Form (TEF), 479, 480, 499, 502
Training Institutes Chamber (TIC), 470
Training manuals, 11, 44, 622, 625
Training programs, 511, 519, 622
   Family Therapy Unit (FTU), 284, 557–559, 566, 568
   manualised systemic family therapy, 479–504
Training therapy, 567
Translation, 53, 317, 318, 322–324
Transtheoretical model, 520
Treatment Plan Manual, 573, 574
Triangular mirroring, 391, 394, 395
   operational protocol, 402–403
   sessions in infant systemic psychotherapy, 396–401
Tridimensional genogram, 215, 217, 219, 220, 222, 471
Triggering generativity intervention, 415, 417
Triple P program, 169
Turkey, 159

U

Uncertainty, 540, 541
Unconscious collusion, 147
User manual, 408

V

Viable manual, 622
Videocollage, 474
Video Feedback Intervention to Promote Positive Parenting, 272
Videorecording, 395
Videotaped therapies, 276
Visualization technique, 385
Voices, 387

W

Websites, 317, 321, 325, 326, 333, 469, 612
Where Angels Fear, 510
Whodas 2.0 scale, 117, 119
Working alliance (WA), 301–303, 313
Working with children, 287, 288, 291
World Council for Psychotherapy, 465

Y

YES manualisation, 620

Z

Zeroth-order learning, 69
Zoom, 330